The Political Environment of Public Management

Second Edition

Peter Kobrak
Western Michigan University

Longman

New York • San Francisco • Boston
London • Toronto • Sydney • Tokyo • Singapore • Madrid
Mexico City • Munich • Paris • Cape Town • Hong Kong • Montreal

This Second Edition is dedicated
to our two delightful daughters-in-law,
Debbie and Marcy.

Vice President/Publisher: Priscilla McGeehon
Senior Acquisitions Editor: Eric Stano
Associate Editor: Anita Castro
Senior Marketing Manager: Megan Galvin-Fak
Production Manager: Denise Phillip
Project Coordination, Text Design, and Electronic Page Makeup:
  Thompson Steele, Inc.
Cover Design Manager: Wendy Fredricks
Cover Designer: Kay Petronio
Cover Photo: © PhotoDisc
Printer and Binder: The Maple-Vail Book Manufacturing Group
Cover Printer: Phoenix Color Corp.

For permission to use copyrighted material, grateful acknowledgment is made to the
copyright holders on pp. 431–432, which are hereby made part of this copyright page.

Library of Congress Cataloging-in-Publication Data

The political environment of public management / [compiled by] Peter Kobrak.--2nd ed.
      p. cm.
   Includes bibliographical references and index.
   ISBN 0-321-08901-4 (alk. paper)
     1. Public administration. 2. Bureacracy. I. Kobrak, Peter.

JF1351.P657 2001
351--dc21   2001033452

Please visit our website at http://www.ablongman.com

ISBN 0-321-08901-4

1 2 3 4 5 6 7 8 9 10—MA—04 03 02 01

Contents

Preface

Challenging Students to Be More Proactive Public Managers

A stimulating and growing literature on politics and administration provides an opportunity today to challenge our advanced undergraduate and graduate students to make the most of their present or future jobs—whether they be supervisors, middle managers, staffers, or part of a top-management team. This material can be understood and applied by upper-division, public administration and political science undergraduates, by MPA mid-career students and practitioners, and political science graduate students. It is also applicable to students concentrating on policy and administration issues in substantive fields related closely to the public sector such as criminal justice and corrections, social work, higher education, public health, and hospital administration.

The literature communicates loud and clear that there are opportunities in the public sector for pre-career and mid-career public managers to contribute at every level of government and in the nonprofit sector as well—even while it cautions that such contributions must be tempered by realism and by an understanding and appreciation of the need to act ethically and constitutionally.

About the Book

This reader is designed as a supplementary text for courses in the politics of bureaucracy, administrative theory, organizational behavior, the public administration proseminar, and the political environment of public managers. It can also be used with a series of case studies. The introductions to the selections are designed to provide a commentary that will relate the issues addressed by the authors here to the rest of the pertinent work (particularly where the selection is a chapter from a book). This will help students "get into" the articles and chapters and, where necessary, enable professors to exclude some readings without having students miss the basic argument. Particular attention is given to adding information needed sometimes by students of public administration, sometimes by students of political science, and usually by both to follow the argument in each selection more closely and to synthesize the material.

This book has several objectives:

1. To provide both new and experienced public managers with sound theories and concepts that will assist them in thinking about how to negotiate their internal and external political environment more effectively, more responsively, and with great ethical awareness.
2. To include material that reflects the increasingly high quality of the research now available on a wide range of topics pertaining to the politics of administration—selections by a number of leading scholars who have made a particular effort to make their work accessible to students.
3. To share with students and practitioners stimulating and readable works that address the why, what, and how of the political environment—theoretical works that also frequently integrate a rich assortment of case material drawn from differing administrative settings.
4. To include selections that are both sufficiently practical to attract the interest of our action-oriented students and practitioners and sufficiently theoretical to apply to a wide variety of administrative settings.
5. To draw on material that pertains to, and is written about, state, local, and nonprofit, as well as federal, agency issues.
6. To include selections which sometimes agree and sometimes disagree. The writers have differing viewpoints and emphasize different concerns, thereby compelling students to draw their own conclusions.

Thanks to these differing viewpoints and emphases, the works are representative of where the study of the politics of public administration appears to be at the moment. It is important that pre-career and mid-career students alike become more accustomed to reading such scholarly articles and chapters, and become more comfortable with the intellectual act of summarizing, synthesizing, and critiquing such material. Combining this reader with a course text, a series of case studies, or both should make for stimulating class sessions for both the professor and the student.

One reason for drawing on such material here is to provide ideas that are fresh and necessary for those who are tempted to muck around in the political environment. As David Gergen has observed, "not all readers lead, but all leaders read."[1] *These ideas would include the following:*

- "To accept a broader view of governance is to assert that government is not ultimately guided by a market model of competition and efficiency but by a citizenship model of governance. This broader view places businesslike management techniques in an instrumental position subordinate to the larger sphere of governance. It draws citizens, elected officials, and public service professionals together in the joint project of creating and implementing public policy."

- "The challenge then is not to prevent public managers from exercising leadership. The challenge is . . . to ensure that the other institutions of society . . . carefully channel this leadership in ways that promote the general welfare."

---

[1]Talk to the American Book Association on November 19, 2000 in Miami, Florida.

- "As middle managers and former middle managers, we are both perplexed and concerned that so little serious attention has been given to what middle managers actually do, especially within the public sector."

- "The responsibility of the city manager is to empower the governing body *and* citizens by helping to develop and use the tools of engagement. This is where the facilitative leadership roles enter . . ."

- Those organizations seeking real change do not merely patch or downsize. They know that "the way to get control of costs is not to start by reducing expenditures but to identify the activities that are productive, that should be strengthened, promoted, and expanded. Every agency, every policy, every program, every activity should be confronted with these questions: 'What is your mission? Is it still the right mission? Is it still worth doing? If we were not already doing this, would we now go into it?'"

- "The truth here comes, as truth usually does, in a small paradoxical package: The key to a genuinely *uncentralized* system is mutually agreed standards on whatever is *central* to the system and thus cannot be left to individual choices or market outcomes."

New Material in the Second Edition

Of the 25 articles included here, 14 are new. The article entitled "Why Public Relations Is Important Even to Public Administrators" was commissioned especially for this volume. Among the new topics addressed in this edition are bureaucrat bashing, diversity in the workplace, human resource development, information technology, privatization, and the role of leadership at different public agency levels. In addition to section, or part, introductions, there are now introductions to each article as well.

One problem confronting an editor on this topic is how to deal with the professor's need for both theoretical and case material. Trying to address both needs in the same reader results in a book that either is too long or fails to provide a sufficient body of theory as well as a satisfying range of cases. This book attempts to resolve this dilemma by focusing on a rich variety of articles, and providing here a case matrix guide for professors and students to three sources of case studies that deal with the political environment of public administration.

Case Study Options to Accompany This Reader

The case matrix in Table 1 identifies cases from Harvard's Kennedy School of Government, recent case studies from public administration and political science journals and books; and the classic case studies written by numerous outstanding scholars in the Interuniversity Case Program Series. In addition to this case matrix, several articles here include imbedded case studies on such topics as privatization, human resource development, dealing with the media, and stimulating public dialogue on administrative and policy issues.

Table 1   Cases Pertaining to *The Political Environment of Public Management*

Categories	JFK Kennedy School Harvard Case Studies	Historical Case Studies	Contemporary Case Studies
Politics and Administration	Ruckelshaus and Acid Rain	Defending "the Hill" Against Metal Houses	Voting for Smokey Bear: Accountability and the New Chief of the Forest Service
Management and Leadership	A Czar Among Bureaucrats: General McCaffrey Considers A Role in the War on Drugs	The New York City Health Centers	Accountability in the Public Sector: Lessons from the Challenger Tragedy
Civic Participation	Kansas City and the Ad Hoc Group Against Crime	Moses on the Green	Dumping $2.6 Million on Bakersfield (Or How Not to Build a Migratory Farm Workers' Clinic)
Exercising Power	The McCaffrey-Shalala Confrontation	The Transfer of the Children's Bureau	Mayor Brown and Mr. [City Manager] Bobb
Mission, Goals, Strategy, and Structure	Vision and Strategy: Paul H. O'Neill at the Office of Management and Budget (OMB) and Alcoa	The New York City Health Centers	Charity for Profit: How the New Social Entrepreneurs Are Creating Good by Creating Wealth
Mobilizing Political Support	HEW and Title IX: The Elimination of Sex Discrimination in Education	Cancellation of the Ration Stamps	Global Food Fight
Relations with the Media	Camp Edwards and the Press: Local Military-Media Relations, A–D	The Regional Director and the Press	Waco
Relations with the Legislature	Public Conversations and Legislative Deliberations: Oregon's Governor Barbara Roberts Takes on Fiscal Reform, case and Epilogue	The Cambridge City Manager	Commercial Free Speech
Budgeting	The Endicott Town Meeting	Seattle Seeks a Tax	What Do You Do When Your City Is Looking at a Million-Dollar Deficit in the Current F.Y.?
Personnel and HRD	Tailhook: The Navy Response, A and B and Epilogue	A City Manager Tries to Fire His Police Chief	A Twenty-First-Century Reception for Diversity in the Public Sector
Federalism, Regionalism, and IGR	Detroit Fiscal Crisis, A, B, B Sequel, and Statistical Profile of Detroit	The Battle of Blue Earth County	Dealing with "Disparate Impact" in Family Policy
Program Coordination and Public-Private Partnerships	Finding Black Parents: One Church, One Child, Epilogue and video	The Kings River Project	Mr. Rubin's Urban Crusade
Agenda Setting and Policy Formation	Gordon Chase and Methadone Maintenance, and commentary	The Reconversion Controversy	Entrepreneurship in Public Management: Wilbur Cohen and Robert Ball
Implementation and Privatization	Prison Fellowship Ministries, A, B, and Epilogues	The Trenton Milk Contract	Superfund: Red Ice and Purple Dogs
Accountability and Decision Making	Pendleton State School, and commentary	The Blast in Centralia No. 5: A Mine Disaster No One Stopped	Renewal in the Inner City: A Housing Fund for the Central Ward

continued

Table 1 *continued*

Categories	JFK Kennedy School Harvard Case Studies	Historical Case Studies	Contemporary Case Studies
Ethical Obligations and Dilemmas	Denver Income Mainte-nance Experiment, case and teaching note	The Glavis-Ballinger Dispute	A State Mental Health Commissioner and the Politics of Mental Illness
Globalization	Americanizing the Vietnam War, docu-ments and hypothetical	Indonesian Assignment	Dr. Helene Gayle: A Global Warrior in the Fight Against AIDS

SOURCES: The **Kennedy School** cases are drawn from the Case Program, John F. Kennedy School of Government, Harvard University *Case Catalogue,* 4th ed., and *Case Studies in Public Policy and Management* 4th ed. Catalog Updates 1–6. Mark H. Moore and Mark Ziering, "Gordon Chase and Methadone Maintenance," is in Mark H. Moore and Malcolm K. Sparrow, eds., *Ethics in Government: The Moral Challenge of Public Leadership,* eds. (Englewood Cliffs, NJ: Prentice-Hall, 1990), pp. 41–56. Colin S. Diver, "Pendleton State School," is in Robert B. Reich, ed., *Public Management in a Democratic Society* (Englewood Cliffs, NJ: Prentice-Hall, 1990), pp. 76–89.

The **historical cases** are from the following sources: Harold Stein, ed. *Public Administration and Policy Development: A Case Book* (New York: Harcourt, Brace, 1952) and Edwin A. Bock, ed. *State and Local Government: A Case Book* (Birmingham, AL: University of Alabama Press, 1963). John Bartlow Martin, "The Blast in Centralia No. 5: A Mine Disaster No One Stopped," is reprinted in Richard J. Stillman II, ed., *Public Administration* (Boston: Houghton Mifflin, 2000), pp. 30–45.

The **contemporary cases** in the order of their citation are: John M. Vandlik, "Voting for Smokey Bear: Political Accountability and the New Chief of the Forest Service, *Public Administration Review,* Vol. 55, No. 3, May/June 1995, pp. 284–292. Barbara S. Romzek and Melvin J. Dubnick, "Accountability in the Public Sector: Lessons from the Challenger Tragedy," *Public Administration Review,* Vol. 47, No. 3, May/June 1987, pp. 227–238. Michael Aron, "Dumping $2.6 Million on Bakersfield (Or How Not to Build a Migratory Farm Workers' Clinic), *Washington Monthly,* October 1972, pp. 23–32. Rob Gurwitt, "Mayor Brown and Mr. Bobb," *Governing,* January 2000, pp. 16–20. Carl M. Cannon, "Charity for Profit: How the New Social Entrepreneurs Are Creating Good by Creating Wealth," *National Journal,* June 17, 2000, pp. 1898–1904. Margaret Kriz, "Global Food Fight," *National Journal,* March 4, 2000, pp. 688–693; William J. Vizzard, *In the Cross Fire: A Political History of the Bureau of Alcohol, Tobacco and Firearms* (Boulder, CO: Lynne Rienner, 1997), pp. 155–188. "Commercial Free Speech?" is in Robert T. Golembiewski, Jerry G. Stevenson, and Michael White, eds., *Cases in Public Management,* 5th ed. (Itasca, IL: F.E. Peacock, 1997), pp. 32–34. Howard R. Balanoff and Charles W. Pinto, "What Do You Do When Your City Is Looking at a Million-Dollar Deficit in the Current Fiscal Year?" *Public Productivity and Management Review,* Vol. 23, No. 1, September 1999, pp. 83–88. Vidu Soni, "A Twenty-First-Century Reception for Diversity in the Public Sector: A Case Study," *Public Administration Review,* Vol. 60, No. 5, September/October 2000, pp. 395–407. Gerald Garvey, *Public Administration* (New York: St. Martin's Press, 1997), pp. 284–303. Christopher Swope, "Robert Rubin's Urban Crusade," *Governing,* August 2000, pp. 20–24. Theodore R. Marmor, "Entrepreneurship in Public Management: Wilbur Cohen and Robert Ball, " in Jameson W. Doig and Erwin C. Hargrove, eds., *Leadership and Innovation* (Baltimore: Johns Hopkins University Press, 1987), pp. 246–281. Donald F. Kettl, *Sharing Power* (Washington, D.C.: Brookings Institution, 1993), pp. 99–127. Gerald Garvey, *Public Administration,* pp. 148–165. Gary E. Miller and Ira Iscoe, "A State Mental Health Commissioner and the Politics of Mental Illness," in Erwin C. Hargrove and John C. Glidewell, eds., *Impossible Jobs in Public Management* (Lawrence, KS: University Press of Kansas, 1990), pp. 103–132. Norma M. Riccucci, *Unsung Heroes* (Washington, D.C.: Georgetown University Press, 1995), pp. 201–225.

Acknowledgments

No one writes a book alone. My colleagues at Western Michigan University's School of Public Affairs and Administration, R. Dee Woell and James Visser, pro-vided valuable suggestions after using the First Edition in their courses. Other col-leagues, Barbara Liggett and Robert Peters, supplied most useful suggestions on sources in their fields of specialty. Hardy Carroll and David Isaacson demon-strated once again why they are called reference librarians. Harry Kobrak greatly improved the graphics. Jackie Van't Zelfde rescued me on more than one occasion from our temperamental xerox machine. Barbara Kobrak proved an indefatigable proofreader.

Thanks also to my editor at Longman Publishers, Anita Castro, and particulary to Project Editor Nancy Freihofer, who provided gracious and skillful assistance on numerous occasions. Two reviewers, Jerry A. Gianakis, University of Central Florida, and Steven M. Neuse, University of Arkansas, used the First Edition to supply invaluable feedback for this work. I am in their debt.

Introduction

The political environment confronting public managers at every level of government today is somewhat akin to a three-ring circus. In the near ring, astride several stools stacked precariously one on top of another, stands the president, governor, or mayor—like a ringmaster, cracking a whip and screaming for "more, more, more." In the middle ring, there is apparent mass confusion as increasingly independent city council members, state legislators, and members of Congress struggle to do their jobs, assert themselves institutionally, and play to the crowd. In the far ring, presiding in a more inconspicuous, but no less strident, manner, sit the judges—seemingly more determined than ever that they will make their ring perform in practice the way that they have always said that it should work in theory. Meanwhile, observing this circus attentively, sit the media, stridently insisting on more "photo ops", and the customers, while they munch their popcorn, demanding both entertainment and, at the very least, their money's worth.

Where the public managers fit into the circus is not entirely clear. Are they the trained animals who the chief executives, legislators, and judges are controlling with the whip? Or are they the circus performers who have the public screaming? Whatever the case, they are certainly in an ambiguous position—the only ones at the circus who realize that they are not "the ringmasters," and yet also the only ones who can get the things done that will keep the show on the road.

The Challenge of a Turbulent Environment

This carnival-like atmosphere only serves to exacerbate the complex and rapidly changing environment that now characterizes the public sector. This environment includes both internal and external factors. Internal environmental factors, such as people and budgets within the organization, are presumed to be "controllable," at least in comparison to external stakeholders, forces, and trends. Strategic planners like to refer to these external forces and trends as "PESTs"—political, economic, social, and technological opportunities and threats.

The numerous PESTs in recent years have proven particularly stubborn for public managers because they have ushered in that least popular of all conditions—resource scarcity. To be sure, federal, state, and local government budgets are now balanced, but at every level, expectations exceed fiscal reality. Taxpayer demands to spend less are thus accompanied by citizen demands to do more, do it more efficiently, do it fairly, and, above all, do it right. Retrenchment, privatization, and program initiation have consequently come to coexist inevitably and uncomfortably at every level of government. These circumstances have compelled reluctant public managers to become more proactive, which has led them in turn further into the world of politics.

Growing Recognition of the Connection Between the Practice of Public Management and the Exercise of Power

Since the time of Woodrow Wilson, public administrators and political scientists have acknowledged the challenge that this world of politics poses for the achievement of effective administration.[1] It is only in the last two decades, however, that a literature has emerged which places greater emphasis on how public managers can and must exercise power and participate in the political process. To be sure, in 1949 Norton Long emphasized that "power is the lifeblood of administration," but with some notable exceptions,[2] few followed his lead. Discussions on this topic continued to say little about what political roles public leaders and managers should play, what strategies and tactics were involved in the exercise of administrative power, and what opportunities and constraints comprised the political environment of public administration.

Concern with the actual exercise of bureaucratic power, however, continued to grow in the public sector, and the resulting literature was well summarized and critiqued in the widely-read studies of Francis E. Rourke, Eugene Lewis, Douglas Yates, and James Q. Wilson.[3] Students of organizational behavior in the private sector elaborated on the exercise of administrative powers in the eighties with the publication of significant works by such writers as Jeffrey Pfeffer, John P. Kotter, and Rosabeth Moss Kanter.[4] Political scientists too were writing about judicial "guardians"[5] and "entrepreneurial" congressmen,[6] and sections on politics and policymaking expanded in public administration and "public management" texts. A few of these works, along with many more selections from the sophisticated literature that they spawned, together comprise this book.

---

[1] Woodrow Wilson, "The Study of Administration," in Jay M. Shafritz and Albert C. Hyde, eds., *Classics of Public Administration*, 2nd ed. (Chicago: Dorsey Press, 1987).

[2] Paul H. Appleby, *Policy and Administration* (Tuscaloosa, AL: University of Alabama Press, 1949); Philip Selznick, *TVA at the Grass Roots* (Berkeley: University of California Press, 1949); Arthur M. Schlesinger, *The Coming of the New Deal* (Boston: Houghton Mifflin Co., 1959).

[3] Frances E. Rourke, *Bureaucracy, Politics, and Public Policy*, 3rd ed. (Boston: Little, Brown & Co., 1984); Eugene Lewis, *American Politics in a Bureaucratic Age* (Cambridge, MA: Winthrop Publishers, 1977); Douglas Yates, *The Politics of Management* (San Francisco: Jossey- Bass Publishers, 1985); James Q. Wilson, *Bureaucracy: What Government Agencies Do and Why They Do It* (New York: Basic Books, 1989).

[4] Jeffrey Pfeffer, *Power in Organizations* (Boston: Pitman, 1981); John P. Kotter, *Power and Influence: Beyond Formal Authority* (New York: Free Press 1985); Rosabeth Moss Kanter, *The Change Masters: Innovation and Entrepreneurship in the American Corporation* (New York: Simon and Schuster, 1983).

[5] Donald L. Horowitz, "The Courts as Guardians of the Public Interest," *Public Administration Review* 37 (March/April 1977), pp. 148–154.

[6] Burdett Loomis, *The New American Politician: Ambition, Entrepreneurship, and the Changing Face of Political Life* (New York: Basic Books, 1988).

The Public Manager as "Entrepreneur"

One response to the demand that managers in government at all levels do more with less has been the rise of the "public entrepreneur." This theme of the public manager as a proactive, entrepreneurial type—rather than one who is willing to settle for "coping" and "muddling through" (important as these strategies frequently are)—runs through much of the material in this reader. These public entrepreneurs come in numerous shapes and sizes—some are agency directors, while others are middle managers, senior staffers, or street-level bureaucrats. More recently, still others have occasionally been nonprofit agencies working in partnership with government agencies to meet the needs of their mutual clients.

Definitions of entrepreneurship abound. Eugene Lewis' public entrepreneur is an agency or large-program director who "creates or profoundly elaborates a public organization so as to alter greatly the existing pattern of allocation of scarce public resources." Such a leader exploits the contradictory mix of values found within the organization, strives to minimize outside interference with technologies central to the organization, and seeks to enhance autonomy and flexibility in order to achieve the agency's mission.[7] Drawing on the works of Joseph A. Schumpeter and Alfred D. Chandler, among others, Doig and Hargrove emphasize that these leaders usually possess extraordinary motivation and knowledge of their substantive area, and are particularly acute in their understanding of the political environment.[8]

For her part, Rosabeth Moss Kanter writes of "quiet entrepreneurs" who "test limits and create new possibilities for organizational action by pushing and directing the innovation process."[9] She has christened these private sector middle managers and staffers (whose public sector counterparts are readily apparent) as "change masters." They may be systems builders, loss cutters, socially conscious pioneers, or sensitive readers of cues about the need for strategy shifts. These new entrepreneurs do not start businesses, but seek instead to improve them; they are good builders and users of teams. Finally, while differing in their motivation, they have something in common that distinguishes them from others who are bringing about change in their organizations, namely, "the need to exercise skills in obtaining and using power in order to accomplish innovation."[10]

David Osborne and Ted Gaebler, in stressing the importance of an entrepreneurial spirit in government at every level of the bureaucracy, draw on the work of French economist J. B. Say. He viewed the public entrepreneur as one who "uses resources in new ways to maximize productivity and effectiveness. By focusing on these two goals, public entrepreneurs can "reinvent government"

In summary, while these entrepreneurs differ in the nature and scope of their activities, they all share a commitment to undertaking what they regard as important changes that pertain to their jurisdiction, a willingness to work through the

---

[7] Lewis, *American Politics in a Bureaucratic Age*, p. 9.

[8] Jameson W. Doig and Erwin C. Hargrove, *Leadership and Innovation: A Biographical Perspective on Entrepreneurs in Government* (Baltimore: Johns Hopkins University, 1987).

[9] Kanter, *The Change Masters*, p. 210.

[10] Kanter, *The Change Masters*, pp. 209–212.

internal and external political processes relevant to achieving that task, and, last but not least, a readiness to accumulate and exercise the power necessary to get the job done.

"Getting the job done" is increasingly what public management is all about. Perhaps this is the case partly because retrenchment management and rapid change complicate even further the possibility of successfully implementing internally an organizational innovation or externally a public policy or administrative regulation. A proposed program must successfully run the policy gauntlet from formulation to implementation to evaluation and on to renewal or termination. A federal administrative regulation must negotiate the process beginning in Washington, D.C. and moving through a state administration and sometimes onto an administrative and possibly a judicial proceeding. No one sits in a position where he or she can control the progress of a major program or regulation. Small wonder that an entrepreneurial spirit is needed throughout the several stages of the policy-making process and that so much concern within the discipline of public administration now centers around successful implementation.

The theme of public entrepreneurship and the wide range of constraints that must be taken into account in "getting things done" pervade this reader. The danger is that the aspiring, proactive public manager will survey this literature, and simply recoil in horror. Such a reaction is particularly understandable because initially, it is far easier to identify problems and obstacles than to predict what will go right.

Even when proceeding, it is necessary to keep in mind what I call the three p's—perseverance, perspicacity, and patience. The literature here thus talks about skill and will (patience is apparently a lost art, but one that effective public managers need to cultivate). One can perhaps view the decision to act under such circumstances as akin to jumping into the ocean in those early days of summer. The water is seldom as cold as we anticipate. Hopefully, this book will assist those who want to plunge in and make a difference.

The Pluralistic World of the Public Manager

Along with public entrepreneurship, the second theme pervading this book is the need for the public entrepreneur to negotiate with a growing number of actors over whom she or he has little control. Democratic pluralism in America thus consists of heterogeneous institutions and organizations that represent diverse religious, economic, ethnic, and cultural interests and share in the exercise of power. They key assumption underlying our democracy is that elites representing these institutions and organizations "compete actively in the decision process for the allocation of values, and that new elites can gain access to power through the same political processes."[11] Pluralism has traditionally focused on the role of autonomous interest groups interacting with government.

---

[11]Jack C. Plano and Milton Greenberg, *The American Political Dictionary* (Fort Worth: Harcourt Brace Jovanovich College Publishers, 1993), p. 90.

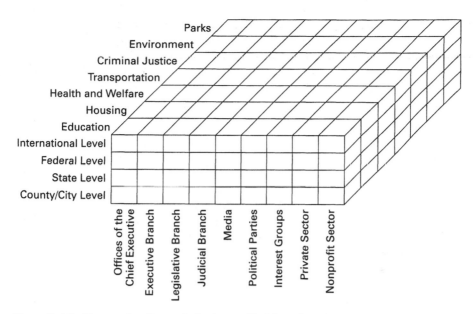

Figure 1   The Horizontal and Vertical Pluralist World of the Public Manager

Numerous other independent power centers today, however, have muscled their way into more prominent roles in the political fray. David M. Ricci's more all-inclusive definition of pluralism makes allowance for this larger cast of characters. He points to the contribution made by such writers as Morton Grodzins and William Kornhauser in emphasizing the importance for democracy of "maintaining pluralism—a host of competing power centers—in an open society."[12]

The variety of these competing power centers may be seen in Figure 1 which summarizes what I call the horizontal and vertical pluralistic world now confronting the public manager. Many of these institutions and organizations are semi-autonomous in that they depend on one another for their survival and growth, but none of the elites representing them are wholly subject to the will of any particular public agency and its managers. The scope of these actors extends vertically not only to the historical ties of local, state, and federal government and their actors, but now also to other countries and international regional arrangements such as the North American Free Trade Agreement (NAFTA) and the National Center for Disease Control's efforts to combat infectuous diseases globally. Similarly, control of the greenhouse effect depends on the U.S. Department of Energy's (DOE) success in working with a multinational coalition concerned with the size of global carbon dioxide emissions. Control here requires that this coalition control the top *per- capita* carbon emitters, consisting of such industrialized nations as Germany, Italy, France, and Spain, and the largest *total* emitting nations, including many developing countries such as China, Brazil, India, and Indonesia. Then there is the

---

[12] Ricci, *The Tragedy of Political Science* (New Haven: Yale University Press, 1984), p. 156.

United States which, largely thanks to its heavy reliance on burning coal for electricity, is the largest contributor of greenhouse gases both on an absolute and a per capita basis.[13]

Nor is such global activity limited to the federal government. Not only states, but also metropolitan areas—such as Phoenix, Seattle, Baltimore, Dallas, St. Paul, and Owensboro, Kentucky—now fund offices situated in other countries to foster closer economic ties. Neal R. Peirce characterizes these "citistates" within the United States as "critical actors, more on their own in the world economy than anyone would have dreamed since the birth of the nation-state in the 16th and 17th centuries." Sophisticated local changes are necessary to establish such transglobal connections and tap into the world population. These changes require nothing less than "a search for civic cohesion, a call for regional planning, genuine citizen involvement, and smart governance."[14] In addition, small as well as large urban areas have established cultural as well as economic ties with "sister cities" in Asia, Europe, and North and South America.

Public agencies must also forge horizontal ties not only with the legislative and judicial branches, but also with the office of their chief executive, be it the mayor, governor, or president. The interests of these elected officials and their staffs, formally described as the "chief executive" of their level of government, may, nonetheless, differ from the missions and goals of a particular bureaucracy. In addition, such informal groups as the media, political parties, and interest groups remain important stakeholders for the public entrepreneur. Thanks to the increased range and scope of government missions at every level, it is a rare public agency that is not engaged in contractual, regulatory, or other activities with the private and nonprofit sectors.

The third dimension of Figure 1 suggests that all of the actors listed in the horizontal and vertical dimensions of pluralism might be interested in a substantive area such as education, housing, or health. Clearly that is not the case, and one of the public entrepreneur's tasks is to identify which of these horizontal and vertical actors are actually interested in the task at hand. Much of this book's emphasis focuses on how to identify and work effectively with the varied cast of characters in the manager's particular substantive area.

Organization of the Book

The text is divided into nine parts. Part I addresses the roots of bureaucracy bashing. It is argued that most supposedly onerous and wasteful regulations are the work of the same elected public officials who decry "government regulation." New regulations are passed in response to rotten food, airline disasters, or other circumstances that require tight public control. Similarly, the demand to run government

---

[13]John A. Hird, "International Environmental Policy," in Hird, ed., *Controversies in American Public Policy* (New York: St. Martin's Press, 1995), pp. 340–341.

[14]Peirce, *How Urban America Can Prosper in a Competitive World* (Washington, D.C.: Seven Locks Press, 1993), pp. x–xi.

like a business—and resurrect the politics and administration dichotomy—ignores such other core values as citizen self-governance and the importance of having public managers act in accord with the public interest.

Part II argues that public managers can and must exercise leadership at several bureaucratic levels. The nature of American governance results in several types of political failure that upper-level public managers are in a unique position to correct if they exercise leadership. Under these circumstances, public managers have an obligation to lead. When professionals working with their agency clients decide what services to provide and how to provide them, these "street-level bureaucrats" represent their agencies. When taken together, these decisions add up to agency policy. In assuming responsibility for these actions, they too are exercising leadership. These policy-making roles of street-level bureaucrats result from the high degree of discretion and the relative autonomy from organizational authority that such professionals enjoy. Finally, middle managers play important roles for our democratic system by making government more responsive across organizational and jurisdictional boundaries, by promoting more efficient and effective services, and through ongoing contact with numerous community stakeholders.

Part III emphasizes the need, when possible, to engage the public in agency decision making. Public managers have an obligation to stimulate a public dialogue in order to explore jointly ideas about what is good for society. Such a dialogue raises the likelihood that the citizen and the agency can arrive at a mutual understanding of their problems and how to resolve them. Facilitating community and enabling democracy are roles that not only federal agency heads, but also city managers must play. These leaders are increasingly expected to facilitate participation and representation and to develop partnerships with the private and nonprofit sectors.

Part IV addresses the political role of the manager as a bureaucratic politician as reflected both in the multidimensional, sometimes unpleasant, exercise of administrative power and in the weaving of that "web of inclusion" frequently necessary to build a winning team. That team must include internal and external stakeholders, and it must focus on thinking harder about its mission, goals, and strategies if we are truly to "reinvent government."

Part V describes the political part of the public manager's job description, and how that person must identify the several sources of bureaucratic power and how to cultivate them. How to cultivate the media receives particular attention here. Part V also delves into the leadership role of the public entrepreneur in mobilizing and managing agency resources. Such management must recognize that budgetary decisions made in the 1930s and 1960s have now committed most federal funds for years to come, thereby compelling state and local as well as federal public managers to act more entrepreneurially in identifying funding sources. These managers must also now fully utilize information technology in their agencies.

Part VI focuses on that most stubborn of management tasks—fully utilizing the agency's human resources. Such human resource development must now move beyond simple affirmative action to dealing with the full and rich range of diversity available in the labor force. How best to accomplish this task is more subtle than the personnel literature suggests. This becomes apparent when examining the experience of a state that has striven to increase administrative flexibility through decentralization, and adopted many of the "reinventing government" personnel reforms, such as performance-based salary adjustments, group productivity incentives, and more frequent employee recognition.

Part VII addresses the inevitable involvement of at least some public managers in the public policy-making process. This involvement in policy formulation occurs through coalitions, subgovernments, and increasingly through network configurations. During the implementation stage, that involvement increasingly includes privatization. Even in the case of a public health laboratory, however, the task of deciding under what conditions to privatize, and how, requires considering a wide range of administrative concerns.

Part VIII underscores that public entrepreneurship is ethically acceptable only if it occurs within the democratic rules of the game. Public managers are not in business for themselves. This struggle is complicated by the "accountability battles" over who can and should control the bureaucrat. Nonetheless, the proactive public manager has a moral obligation both to contribute to a more rational political and policy discourse and to reconcile the twin needs at every level of government for more entrepreneurship and more democracy. This can be done, it is argued, by creating solutions to public problems that encourage the authentic involvement of as many citizens as would like to participate.

Part IX underscores what is perhaps the fundamental paradox of the 21st century. Thanks to new organizational and Internet technologies, public agencies in the future will have the capability to be more uncentralized. By agreeing on common norms and standards, future organizations can extend the already considerable realm of mutual adjustment unencumbered by fiat. And yet, the same globalization resulting in horizontal and vertical organizational restructuring has also led to an unprecedented concentration of corporate power at the global level. The same advanced nations that have inspired rising human expectations throughout the world—thanks to their demonstration that various forms of democratic capitalism can outcompete other political economies—may use their increased military and technological capability to dominate the world from both the earth and space. The challenges confronting public administrators toiling at every level of government are now global.

Politics, Administration, and Bureaucrat Bashing

Politics has become a dirty word. Calling a policy initiative or a person "political" is an insult. Yet, the importance and scope of politics extend far beyond the common meaning of the term. It encompasses more than cynical *partisan* (or elective) politics or *office* intrigues.

Politics

The art of politics lies in its ability to allocate values, or value preferences, that are often of critical importance to those who are competing for them. This competition may occur in the realm of the family, the church, the corporation, the public organization, or the political system. Should the family spend its discretionary income this year on a family vacation or the daughter's tuition? Should the 47 million Americans without health benefits be provided by the federal government with some form of minimum health care or should those funds be used to reduce the national debt?

Politics involving the institutions of government, however, differs from politics as practiced elsewhere in the society, since it entails an "*authoritative* allocation of values."[a] Government, frequently through the medium of the public

---

[a]David Easton, *The Political System* (New York: Alfred A. Knopf, 1960), p. 129.

manager, then has the last word in the debate, though the resolution may well reflect the influence of one or more other actors. Given the stature assigned in the eighties by so many Americans to the idea of a free and unfettered marketplace, it is significant how many critical decisions still are made by government institutions. The reason is perhaps best captured by one of Kenneth Dolbeare and Murray Edelman's definitions of the term: "politics is the activity by which people define themselves and their world and publicly seek their goals."[b]

Politics entails a social process, bargaining, that occurs when a decision is beyond the reach of the marketplace, outside of the actual hierarchy of a formal leader, and lacking in a clear electoral mandate. The bargainers may differ in power and concern about the issue at hand, but they must somehow resolve those differences. They must agree on whether to authorize, or not to authorize, and to fund, or not to fund, eagerly sought goods and services and controversial regulations inevitably competing for limited attention, support, and scarce resources. Politics thus is the decision-making forum of preference for a pluralist democracy—and for the public bureaucracies that operate within that political system. Politics is a viable, though sometimes disappointing, means of getting things done. It is also a challenge for public bureaucracies that share influence in this pluralistic system with the executive, legislative, and judicial branches, but also are constitutionally subordinate to these three branches of government. Reformers, political parties, and academicians have all at numerous times sought to determine just where politics ends and administration begins.

Administration

Early Twentieth Century Progressive reformers and public administration scholars were uncomfortable with the encroachment of partisan political considerations and boss rule on the ability of administrative agencies to operate in the most economic and efficient manner. They thus sought to define the role of public managers by drawing a sharp line between the tasks of the elected politician and the politically neutral, professional public manager. The "politics/administration dichotomy" distinguished between the politicians who represent the people and thus formulate policy in the name of the government and the administrators who implement those policies in a nonpartisan and impartial manner. The logic underlying this dichotomy is that there is no "Republican way to build a road" or to lay tarmac. Roadbuilding is dictated by the most efficient way to do the job.

But, as Nicholas Henry has written, "there is a Republican way to decide whether the road needed building, to choose the location for the road, to purchase the land, to displace the people living in the road's way, and most certainly a Republican way to let contracts for the road."[c] Democratic, Libertarian, or

[b]Kenneth M. Dolbeare and Murray J. Edelman, *American Politics* (Lexington, MA: D.C. Heath, 1985), p. 4.

[c]Nicholas Henry, *Public Adminstration and Public Affairs,* Eighth Edition, Upper Saddle River, NJ: Prentice Hall, 2001, p. 28.

other party politicians would surely make these allegedly "administrative" decisions differently. These political actors would not only take into account efficiency, but also would differ markedly in weighing such other value preferences as flexibility in meeting the concerns of numerous groups affected by the road, timeliness in expediting construction to reduce citizen inconvenience, and fair treatment to those displaced by the road.

These several value preferences, often expressed in controversial issues, are important to citizens, interest groups, and corporations. Furthermore, democracy entails not only *what* policies are formulated, but also *how* those policies are implemented. There are a number of these value preferences, as Figure 1 indicates, and their supporters may be found both inside and outside the bureaucracy. Each value carries with it a markedly different expectation of just what a public manager should be. Kenneth J. Meier contends that the initial four of these values fall under the rubric of responsiveness to public needs, while the remaining four pertain to competence in the performance of tasks.[d] These values often conflict. The tension, for example, between effectiveness and acting sensitively was neatly captured, intentionally or unintentionally, by the American colonel in Vietnam who explained that "it would have been necessary to destroy the village in order to save it." The ill-fated space shuttle, *Challenger*, was caught between its quest for cost-effectiveness and efficiency, on one hand, and the need to observe strict safety rules to insure effectiveness on the other.[e]

The attempt to build a firewall between politics and administration is understandable. After all, no one elected public administrators, and it is appealing to have such public managers strive for a "bottom line" of efficiency in the same purposeful manner that business executives seek the bottom line of profits. The separation of politics and administration holds out the hope that public managers can be held accountable for providing efficient government with the same rigor and discipline as corporate executives. Much of the private sector appeal lies in the conviction that these executives have been compelled to learn sound management practices by the competitive pressure of the marketplace. Stockholders brook no excuses from CEOs who fail to cut it, and "customers" have the right to expect comparable service in the public sector. Explanations of differing citizen expectations that result in higher costs are dismissed as excuses by incompetent public managers who could not cut it in the private sector.

The tensions between politics and administration can be reconciled where politicians and administrators share an understanding of their roles. This may be seen in council-manager government where, as James Svara has observed, many city managers consciously or unconsciously have adopted what he terms a new professional standard of complementarity. This standard emphasizes that the manager involved in policy formulation as well as implementation must maintain

[d]Kenneth J. Meier, *Politics and the Bureaucracy*, Fourth Edition (Fort Worth: Harcourt Publishers, 2000), p. 103.

[e]Barbara S. Romzek and Melvin J. Dubnick, "Accountability in the Public Sector: Lessons from the *Challenger* Tragedy," *Public Administration Review*, Vol 47, No. 3, May/June 1987, pp. 227–38.

a standard that "stresses interdependency along with distinct roles, compliance with independence, respect for political supremacy with a commitment to shape policy in ways that promote the public interest, deference to elected incumbents with adherence to the law and support for fair competition, and appreciation of politics with support for professional standards.[f] Provided that city managers acknowledge that they are ultimately accountable to their political superiors atop the administrative hierarchy, there is no reason why these managers cannot participate in all stages of the policy-making process.[g]

Table 1   The Value Preferences of the Internal and External Stakeholders Concerned with Public Bureaucracies

Value Preferences	What a Public Administrator Should Be	Where the Value Resides inside a Public Agency	Where the Value Resides Outside the Public Agency
1. Sensitivity to governmental institutions and the rule of law	Be responsible to those vested with the power to govern. Be a responsible sovereign.	Legal staff	The Executive, Legislative, and Judicial branches
2. Flexibility	Be open to criticism.	Representative employees	Clients
3. Observance of strict standards of administrative behavior	Be ethical.	Internal audit staff	Media and investigative reporters
4. Fairness and impartiality	Provide equal treatment and due process.	Human Resource Development unit	The courts
5. Effectiveness	Achieve the statutory goals.	Program managers	Congress and the President
6. Timeliness	Don't keep me waiting—time is money.	Street-level bureaucrats	Customers
7. Efficiency	Don't waste resources.	Management and budget staffs	Taxpayers
8. Reliability	Be consistent and predictable.	Top management	Citizens

SOURCE: The values are drawn from Kenneth J. Meier, *Politics and the Bureaucracy,* Fourth Edition (Fort Worth: Harcourt College Publishers), 2000.

---

[f]James H. Svara, "Complementarity of Politics and Administration as a Legitimate Alternative to the Dichotomy Model," *Administration & Society,* Vol 30, No. 6, January 1999, pp. 697–98.

[g]Robert S. Montjoy and Douglas J. Watson, "A Case for Reinterpreted Dichotomy of Politics and Administration as a Professional Standard in Council-Manager Government," *Public Administration Review,* May/June 1995, Vol. 55, No. 3, p. 238.

At the national level, however, dealing with the politics/administration dichotomy has taken a distinctly more hostile turn. Presidential and congressional leaders from both parties have attacked public bureaucracies without acknowledging that their political demands and those of citizens and interest groups often lead to some of the most frustrating bureaucratic actions. Democratic Presidents Jimmy Carter and Bill Clinton and Republican Presidents Gerald Ford and Ronald Reagan all took after big bureaucracy (interesting exceptions are Presidents George H. W. and George W. Bush).

It is one thing to argue that by 1992, there were an unacceptably large number of bureaucratic layers in federal agencies—as many as 32 levels in some cases, and 17 in at least half of the departments.[h] Or that large public bureaucracies, like their private counterparts, sometimes change too slowly thanks to their penchant for comfortable routines. It is quite another, however, to expect that analyzing an administrative response to a policy problem separately and distinctly from its political stimulus will provide meaningful answers.

Yet, that is precisely what the major attack on federal bureaucracies, the so-called reinventing government movement, did in the 1990s. Neither President Bill Clinton nor Vice President Al Gore, whom he appointed to lead this initiative, acknowledged that politics and administration represent a seamless web or that improvements in agency operations depend largely on changing the political system. Thomas Mann of the Brookings Institution raised this point at a 1993 "Reinventing Government Summit." He argued that part of the problem in managing the federal government might be the political system itself. Federal agencies and programs, he noted, are the creatures of a Congress driven by a public who, after scandals erupt, increasingly demand instant solutions to complex problems. Gore was having none of it: "I really disagree with that. It discounts the value of democracy."[i]

Furthermore, Clinton viewed administrative reform as lacking in political appeal. This was demonstrated, according to political insiders in the president's 1992 campaign, by the speech he never gave on "reinventing government" or "entrepreneurial government." While eager to discuss the subject, journalist Tom Shoop wrote that he held back for "fear of putting audiences to sleep with an arcane discussion of applying the ideas of management gurus like W. Edwards Deming to federal institutions."[j]

His subsequent reinventing government initiative, nonetheless, could serve political purposes. In August 1993, his pollster, Stanley Greenberg, told the president that three-fourths of Perot's followers were more likely to vote for a candidate who wanted to change government radically, and Clinton wanted to appease Democrats in Congress who viewed his delicately-balanced budget agreement as still short on spending cuts.[k] Reinventing government now became in part a

---

[h]Paul C. Light, *Thickening Government*, Washington, D.C.: Brookings Institution, 1995, p.7.

[i]Tom Shoop, "Goring the Bureaucracy," *Government Executive*, Vol. 25, October 1993, p. 16.

[j]Tom Shoop, "The Reinvention Rage," *Government Executive*, Vol. 25, March 1993, p. 10.

[k]Tom Shoop, "Goring the Bureaucracy," *Government Executive*, Vol. 25, October 1993, p. 12.

heavily promoted vehicle to reduce the size of government by 252,000 bureaucrats and to save $108 billion. The federal government would create "a government that works better and costs less."[l] Gore knew better. The previous spring he had told *Government Executive* that "I prefer not to focus on monetary savings, or the elimination of waste, fraud and abuse."[m]

Where political considerations clashed with administrative principles, however, it was no contest. The president pretended to win union support, Horner has written, by issuing an executive order hailing the formation of "labor-management partnerships." In actuality, this agreement instructed agencies for the first time to negotiate with unions over "numbers, types, and grades of employees." Because pay is attached to grade level, the order had the effect of allowing for negotiation over pay, a long-sought public service union goal. This reduced management flexibility to use pay as an incentive to strengthen performance, thereby undercutting a long-sought goal of administrative reformers.[n]

Bureaucracy and Bureaucrat Bashing

From such a posture of political opportunism and compromise, it was but a hop, a skip, and a jump from a serious public dialogue on administrative reform to politics as theater, with bureaucracy and its handlers cast as the villains. Inside the beltway, the Vice President's National Performance Review (NPR) published studies that focused on customer needs, abolished outmoded regulations, and decentralized agency functions, but outside the beltway, the public was treated to a series of photo ops and interviews that sounded such populist themes as eliminating waste, fraud, and abuse; cutting government spending; and reducing the number of bureaucrats. Clinton and Gore unveiled the NPR on the White House lawn with a backdrop of two forklifts piled high with thousands of pounds of regulations to illustrate the burden under which federal agencies operate. It was at this event that the President observed that programs passed by both political parties and the American people "are being undermined by an inefficient and outdated bureaucracy."[o]

The vice president then went on the road to sell the NPR by appearing on talk shows. The largest impact was achieved on the David Letterman show where, while wearing the appropriate goggles and wielding a hammer, he followed excessively detailed federal regulations designed to test an "ash receiver, tobacco (desk type)". The networks seized on the silliness of such overregulation and enabled Gore to declare on ABC's "Prime Time Live" that "whenever the

---

[l]Al Gore, *The Gore Report on Reinventing Government: From Red Tape to Results,* New York: Times Books, 1993.

[m]Tom Shoop, "Goring the Bureaucracy," p. 15.

[n]Constance Horner, "Deregulating the Federal Service: Is the Time Right?" in DiIulio, John J., ed., *Deregulating the Public Service,* Washington, D.C.: Brookings Institution, 1994, p. 97.

[o]Al Gore, *The Gore Report on Reinventing Government: From Red Tape to Results,* p. iv.

government buys something, it goes about it in a completely nonsensical way." (No one pointed out that 85 percent of the General Service Administration's purchases at the time were made on the basis of simplified, one-page product descriptions.)[p] While such actions and symbolic acts are alleged to have raised the President's popularity by 12 percent at the time of the announcement,[q] they were long forgotten by the 2000 election.

Public Choice Theory

More than political opportunism, however, was involved in this attack. It also reflected the endorsement by Clinton's pro-business Democratic Leadership Council wing of the Democratic Party as well as by conservative Republicans of public choice theory. The fundamental premise here is that not only business executives and consumers, but also politicians, bureaucrats, and citizens are motivated by rational self-interest. While the definition of rational self-interest differs somewhat in the hands of different writers, they agree that just as business executives are seeking to achieve maximum profits, so politicians focus on re-election and bureaucrats operate as "budget maximizers." Given the incentive structure in government bureaucracies, rational self-interest will lead these bureaucrats to act in ways that make big government even bigger. Actors making public choices differ from those in the private sector only in the constraints and opportunities offered by the political as opposed to the market environment.[r]

So the key becomes using economic analysis to structure appropriate incentives. While empirical studies have found that such budget-maximizing behavior only occurs under some conditions,[s] these "political economy" theorists have influenced the drive to reduce the size of government in numerous countries. The solution to these bureaucratic excesses lies in compelling public bureaucracies to compete in the marketplace much like their corporate counterparts. Management then becomes generic. The same management principles viewed as working well in business are applicable in the public sector too. The differing value preferences and public expectations of government are given short shrift here. Writing in the *Public Administration Review* in 1996, the former NPR Deputy Director was explicit: citizens are customers, and the notion of a public interest—separate and distinct from self-interest—is rejected. Public agencies should emulate such successful business practices as contracting out and competition in public service

---

[p]Tom Shoop, "Goring the Bureaucracy," p. 13.

[q]John J. DiIulio, "Works Better and Costs Less?" in DiIulio, John J., ed., *Deregulating the Public Service*, p. 2.

[r]James A. Caporaso and David P. Levine, *Theories of Political Economy,* Cambridge: Cambridge University Press, 1992, p. 135.

[s]Colin Campbell and Donald Naulls, "The Consequences of a Minimalist Paradigm for Governance: A Comparative Analysis," in Patricia W. Ingraham and Donald F. Kettl, eds., *Agenda for Excellence,* Chatham, NJ: Chatham House Publishers, 1992, pp. 66–93.

provision, developing cost-effective programs, a general preference for the use of monetary over nonmonetary incentives such as ethics, ethos, and status, and an emphasis on cost-cutting, efficiency, and cutback management.[t] The subsequent Bush administration too shares the longstanding Republican assumption that public agencies would benefit from greater emulation of the private sector, but seems less militant in pressing the issue.

---

[t]John M. Kamensky, "The Role of the 'Reinventing Government' Movement in Federal Management Reform," *Public Administration Review*, Vol. 56, No. 3, May/June 1996, pp. 250–52.

There is an old song that goes, "Be kind to your webfooted friends, for a duck may be somebody's mother." So it is with regulations. Someone wanted that regulation, and often that someone was the president or a member of Congress, acting on their own or at the behest of an interest group, citizen, or corporation. Furthermore, there is a reason that lies behind every such regulation, and many of those reasons may not become immediately evident when one applies the laws of logic or common sense. Instead, political negotiation and compromise are necessary to reduce obsolete regulations.

As the investigatory arm of the Congress, the General Accounting Office (GAO) is responsible for evaluating how effectively administrative agencies are implementing their missions, and this often involves assessing the soundness of regulatory policies and procedures. GAO executive Joseph A. Pegnato has thus occupied a front-row seat in watching the progress—and sometimes lack of progress—in the continuing struggle to eliminate, modify, or add government regulations as political, social, economic, and technological conditions change.

He reviews here a book that influenced both the conservative Republican wing that controlled the House in the mid-1990s under then-Speaker Newt Gingrich and the Clinton administration's reinventing government movement. Pegnato's argument is not that numerous regulations should not be abolished, but rather that eliminating regulations responsibly entails accurately understanding their purpose and impact. Pegnato emphasizes that regulations are not just designed to promote efficiency, but also to protect citizen rights and ensure equal treatment (as well as the other values identified in Figure 1). Even apparently similar value preferences may push public administrators in different directions. Taxpayers want efficiency in government, but they abhor waste and fraud. Pegnato observes that preventing waste and fraud may lead to additional regulatory safeguards that reduce efficiency. While corporations are often willing to accept the costs of fraud in order to run at a higher level of efficiency, taxpayers are not. Furthermore, even while numerous regulations are candidates for elimination, there may well be a need for additional regulations periodically, as when toxic hamburgers pose a health hazard or inadequate airline maintenance presents a safety hazard.

Pegnato's solution to regulatory problems also differs from that of Democratic and Republican critics. Since regulatory complaints often stem from the policies passed by elected officials, they and citizens favoring numerous regulations as well must work with the administrators in correcting such problems. Bashing bureaucrats for implementing such policies both confuses the real issues and unfairly places the blame on those responsible for implementing the policies passed by elected public officials. Furthermore, it is our democracy that ultimately determines the appropriate balance between regulation and deregulation.

The Death of Common Sense: How Law Is Suffocating America

Philip K. Howard
Reviewed by Joseph A. Pegnato

Most books on government regulation appeal to a very limited audience, generally lawyers inside the Washington, D.C., beltway. One striking exception is a book by Philip K. Howard called *The Death of Common Sense: How Law is Suffocating America,* published in 1995. Howard, in another article also published in 1995, argues that government regulations designed to prevent the squandering of public money achieve the exact opposite (Howard, 1995a). No doubt the book's popularity was due in part to publication timing. It was released during the halcyon days of the Republican Congress's attack on government regulation. One telling indication of its influence on government in 1995 can be seen from the title of the third report of the National Performance Review (NPR) issued that year: *Common Sense Government: Works Better and Costs Less* (Gore, 1995). This NPR report draws extensively on Howard's ideas; it calls for making "our government make sense again" (Gore, 1995, p. 19).

In early 1995, *The Washington Post* reported that Florida governor Lawton Chiles used his own money to purchase 200 copies of Howard's book to provide copies to his agency heads and every legislator in the state capital (Booth, 1995, p. A1). Chiles was proposing to repeal at least half of Florida's 28,750 rules so that they could be replaced by common-sense decision making. Obviously, this was another indication of Howard's influence.

Howard's Argument in Brief

According to Howard, in constructing America's modern legal system, "we seem to have achieved the worst of both worlds: a system of regulation that goes too far while it also does too little. . . . We have constructed a system of regulatory law that basically outlaws common sense" (p. 11). With humorous anecdote after anecdote, Howard portrays government bureaucrats as stupid, wasteful, mindlessly following the book, and only concerned with covering their rears: "Novocaine seems to have been injected into bureaucrats' brains" (p. 59).

In a counterintuitive way, precise rules instead create close loopholes, argues Howard (p. 43). The U.S. Constitution, a very short document, contains no loopholes; on the other hand, says Howard, 36,000 pages of tax code are almost all loopholes. Congress, in a 1992 attempt to protect consumers from high cable TV

Joseph A. Pegnato. *American Review of Public Administration,* Vol. 29, No. 4 (December 1999) pp. 411–423.
© 1999 Sage Publications, Inc.

prices, enacted detailed legislation. The result was the inverse: higher prices as cable companies exploited loopholes in the law (p. 44). Striving to create a system of rational rules for every eventuality is impossible and unwise, suggests Howard. Such a system would be doomed to failure, as was the Soviet system of rules and central planning. The federal system of regulation consists of more than 130,000 pages of rules in the *Code of Federal Regulations.*

Howard contends that government makes decisions at a snail's pace: "The lag in decision-making . . . is a national scandal" (p. 59). A New York state agency takes 5 months to hire someone. Government procurement procedures are legendary for their inefficiency. "Serving practicality. . . . is the last thing these procedures do," Howard writes (p. 65). The internal cost of processing a contract can approach the actual contract cost. Moreover, the government regularly buys the wrong thing because rigid procurement procedures prevent the normal give and take of commercial buying. According to Howard, the waste is easily billions (p. 74). Just as important, all of the red tape and paper-trail documentation seem to do nothing to stop fraud. Incidents of fraud lead to more layers of expensive review but no more insurance against fraud (p. 96). In a 1994 study, Coopers and Lybrand (1994, p. 47) concluded that the Department of Defense's procurement regulations added 18% to the cost of all goods and services.

William E. Kovacic (1992) argues that "the price tag for every airplane, missile, or tank that rolls out of an American factory today includes a significant cost increment attributable to the implementation of and compliance with procurement regulatory commands" (p. 34). Firms decline to do business with federal agencies when faced with the prospect of complying with onerous regulations, Kovacic says (p. 34).

Howard believes that whenever the rules are eased and American citizens are released from the shackles of red tape, quick results can be achieved. For example, when the governor suspended the rules, the Santa Monica Freeway was rebuilt in 66 days after the 1994 California earthquake instead of the 4 years it would normally take. According to Howard, "when the rule book got tossed, all that was left was responsibility" (p. 172).

To support his case for common-sense government, Howard quotes historian Arthur M. Schlesinger Jr.'s views on President Franklin D. Roosevelt's approach to governing: "It is common sense to take a method and try it, FDR said" (p. 184). Schlesinger goes on to say that if the method failed, FDR would admit it and try something else.

Implicit in Howard's call for common-sense government is the suggestion that regulations are an expensive burden on the American economy. What is the cost of regulation? A recent study cited by business journalist Robert J. Samuelson (1997, p. 39) lists $40 billion to $60 billion of savings due to deregulation of five industries: airlines, natural gas, railroads, telecommunications, and trucking. One estimate of the cumulative 1995 cost of all federal regulations was $607 billion (General Accounting Office [GAO], 1996a, p. 47). More recently, the Office of Management and Budget (OMB, 1997, p. 39364) estimated the total annual cost of regulation was $289 billion during 1997.

Is Common Sense a Useful Measure to Assess Regulation?

Howard's argument that many regulations lack common sense can be viewed as another call for government deregulation. He and many other critics of government regulation are convinced that these regulations retard economic growth and contribute to inflation. Martha Derthick and Paul J. Quirk (1985, pp. 238–253) suggest that deregulation is almost a natural phenomenon. They show that deregulation of the airline, trucking, and telecommunications industries occurred when political forces created the climate for deregulation. Some industries will be regulated, and some will be deregulated. In other words, deregulation will occur not because regulations lack common sense but because the American political system operates with common sense.

Howard makes effective use of examples to show how silly and nonsensical the regulatory system has become. He mentions the wastefulness of a full-time meat inspector from the U.S. Department of Agriculture (USDA) at the plant of a very small meat-packing firm of four employees (p. 30). Who could disagree that this arrangement lacks common sense? On the other hand, the public would probably object to reducing the number of meat inspectors given that in 1993, eating contaminated hamburger left hundreds of people sick and four children dead. Nancy Donley, whose 6-year-old and only child died during the July 1993 outbreak, said, "There seems to be a blanket statement that all regulation is bad. . . . But in some areas, regulation is good" (Weiss, 1996, p. A10). USDA reports that millions of people become ill and more than 4,000 people die every year from eating contaminated meat products (Evans, 1996, p. A27). In the summer of 1997, a Nebraska meat-packing plant recalled more than 25 million pounds of ground beef due to contamination from potentially deadly *E. coli* bacteria. The largest nationwide recall in U.S. history came after a recommendation by agriculture secretary Dan Glickman. Common sense seems to argue for more inspections, not less.

In the midst of this beef recall, the president of Burger King ran a full-page advertisement in *The Washington Post* declaring that the company's hamburgers are cooked "in accordance with the stringent standards of the Food and Drug Administration. . . . We buy from processors approved and inspected by the U.S. Department of Agriculture" (Clayton, 1997, p. A7). For Burger King, it is common sense to rely on the strict regulations of two federal agencies to provide assurance to its nervous customers about the safety of its product.

What meat overregulation is Howard complaining about? Is he complaining about meat safety rules, essentially unchanged for most of the past 90 years, that simply required looking at and smelling meat—also known as "poke and sniff"? Only after widespread illness in 1993 did the federal government propose to add scientific tests to the existing archaic inspection rules. With regard to the horror stories of regulatory mischief detailed by Howard, Richard Lacayo (1995), one of Howard's critics, says "some of them are memorable; some partial or misleading; some flatly wrong. . . . The problem with trial by anecdote is that it can play rough with the rules of evidence" (pp. 40–41).

Has deregulation of the airlines spilled over into deregulation of safety? For example, did cutthroat competition lead ValuJet to contract out most of its maintenance to reduce ticket prices? On May 11, 1996, a flaming nose-dive crash of ValuJet Flight 592 claimed 110 lives. The National Transportation Safety Board found a breakdown in the airline industry's self-checking, testing, and oversight systems. As a direct consequence of this crash, the Federal Aviation Administration (FAA) is implementing new regulations to require fire detection and suppression systems in aircraft cargo holds. The FAA will be adding more safety inspectors and adopting stronger rules for handling hazardous cargo (Phillips, 1997, p. A7). The air-safety-conscious public would probably say common sense calls for more regulation here, not less.

"We have a very serious problem that suggests government regulation of run-off from chicken farms and poultry operations likely will be needed to curb outbreaks of Pfiesteria," declared Parris Glendening, governor of Maryland (Babington & Shields, 1997, p. A1). This call for increased regulation was prompted by fears that outbreaks of Pfiesteria could threaten two lucrative Maryland industries, Chesapeake Bay seafood and Eastern Shore tourism. *Pfiesteria piscicida*, a toxic microorganism, has been blamed for large fish kills in several Maryland Eastern Shore rivers during the summer of 1997. It appears to make common sense, at least political common sense, for Glendening to ask the federal government to regulate Maryland's poultry industry to save its seafood industry. Contrary to Howard's arguments, common sense can easily lead to more rather than less regulation.

Howard (p. 172) argues that the Santa Monica Freeway could only be rebuilt quickly after the 1994 California earthquake because governmental rules had been suspended. This appears to be a clear example of efficiencies to be gained by rolling back inefficient barriers to quick action. Although this is true, it misses the point. Government structure and process were not designed to be efficient. Instead, the Founders were more concerned with designing a governmental structure that protected citizens' rights and ensured equal treatment. The designers sought to create a government that was not arbitrary or capricious in its use of power. Checks and balances were employed to avoid efficient tyranny. Although Howard seems to desire efficient government, efficiency does not seem to be the most important value of democratic governments. Ronald C. Moe and Robert S. Gilmour (1995) argue that "the value of accountability to politically chosen leaders outranks the premium placed on efficient, low-cost service" (p. 138).

Howard (p. 181) claims that the last thing that bureaucrats want is responsibility. Not only does that statement reveal Howard's antibureaucrat bias but it is also a cheap shot. It is understandable that bureaucrats would be timid about boldly taking risks given the fishbowl scrutiny provided by a battalion of second guessers. This oversight army, only a fraction of which populates private industry, includes auditors, inspectors general, the GAO, congressional oversight committees, the press, and others. The incentives driving overseers encourage pursuit and subsequent publicity of bureaucratic mistakes, not praise of bureaucratic success.

There is another reason why bashing bureaucrats may be misguided. The regulations bureaucrats write almost always implement political policies established by elected officials. To assume that bureaucrats write regulations and monitor compliance with regulations on their own initiative is to mistakenly assume they have more authority than they actually have. To blame bureaucrats for inefficient regulation is to not understand the American system of government.

Democratic government is messy and inefficient. It was not designed to be efficient and economical. By design, power is divided among branches and levels of government to protect and ensure the rights of citizens. The design does not facilitate efficient policy making and decision making. Many political scientists find beauty in this design; many business people do not.

Opponents of government regulation view such regulation as burdensome to the economy. Therefore, agencies' regulatory authority should be limited, and many regulations should be eliminated. Defenders of government regulation argue that such rules provide benefits to society, including, for example, cleaner air and water, safer transportation, greater workplace safety, and a disease-free food supply. Both opponents and defenders of federal regulation agree, however, that the federal regulatory process needs review.

On the question of whether common sense is a useful measure of the effectiveness of governmental regulation, the view here is that it is not. For every example of regulations lacking common sense cited by Howard, there are examples on the other side where common sense suggests more regulation to improve airline safety or meat inspection. Alternatively, many economists argue today that no regulation should be promulgated unless the benefits outweigh the costs. Cost-benefit analysis is a superior metric to soft common-sense analysis even with the huge difficulties associated with accurately measuring costs and benefits. On the other hand, many public health and safety issues involve public values that cannot be simply assessed with economic algorithms.

In a democracy, regulatory policies should be and are determined only by political negotiation and compromise. Whether it is common sense to deregulate or regulate is not reason enough to deregulate or regulate. The commonsense issues should be included in the political decision-making process. Likewise, regulatory cost-benefit analyses should not be sufficient reasons for decisions but should be factored into the decision process.

Federal Procurement: Common Sense Gone Awry Or?

Howard ridicules government procurement processes as requiring so much objectivity that "only a robot is truly adequate to the job" (p. 73). Unfortunately, government fishbowl environments are largely responsible for any obsession with objectivity. In this scrutinized fishbowl climate, it may actually make sense to be extremely concerned with objectivity. Business common-sense principles do not directly apply because of the high degree of scrutiny in government environments. "Government intensely watches itself in the mirror instead of focusing on how to get the job done," complains Howard (p. 75). But does one part of government watch itself to observe what the rest of its sometimes harsh critics (e.g., the press, Congress, public-interest groups) are observing to anticipate the inevitable criticism? Ironically, Howard makes this exact point in his report of a New York City budget director being forced to resign because of alleged procurement favoritism; the director was later cleared of these charges (p. 71).

A "culture of fear," to use Lisa Corbin's (1995, p. 40) term, describes the operating environment of the federal procurement community. Corbin suggests that federal contracting officers "generally avoid taking risks because of fears of penalties, protests, and—worst of all—prison" (p. 40). Evidently, an environment of constant second-guessing by auditors, lawyers, losing bidders, and Congress leads to a culture of fear. Moreover, the culture of fear may help to explain the obsession with objectivity described above.

"The problem with the current [procurement] system is that public officials cannot use common sense and good judgment," writes Steven Kelman (1990, p. 1), the former director of the Office of Federal Procurement Policy. He, like Howard, calls for significant deregulation of the procurement system. Kelman (1990) also calls for increasing the discretion of federal officials such as contracting officers. But where do these nonsensical inefficient regulations come from? James Q. Wilson (1989, p. 317) thinks that the regulations come from us. Every regulation derives from a legitimate demand. Procurement rules, for example, require time-consuming competition to respond to demands voiced by private industry that all contractors be given an equal chance to bid on every job. Small businesses have been successful in convincing Congress that they require preferential treatment in the award of federal contracts. Watchdog groups such as the GAO have been successful in having rules and procedures written that require government officials to take extraordinary steps to root out waste and fraud. The list goes on and on.

It is not surprising that government agencies are viewed as inefficient. These constraints were not designed to produce efficiency. To increase the efficiency of the procurement system, one must first make the difficult political decision of which competing constraint to eliminate or relax. For example, should equity be sacrificed for the sake of efficiency?

Wilson (1989) is surprised that the procurement system works as well as it does. He cites a 30-year study of procurement in which cost overruns, schedule slippages, and performance shortfalls have all decreased. There is evidence that the American system works as well or better than that in many European nations (Wilson, 1989, p. 325). At a Technology 2007 conference in September 1997, a member of the Russian Academy of Science, V. A. Fedorovich, indicated that the Russian government was patterning its procurement system after the U.S. procurement system (Breeden, 1997, p. 10). According to Fedorovich, Russia admires the business environment encouraged by the American procurement system in which business and government are equal partners.

If one were to ask any federal contracting officer if Howard were using common sense when he suggested that public employees might not have to be treated as crooks if "rudimentary precautions like audits" (p. 104) were employed more frequently, the answer would be a resounding no. Howard should be informed that all federal contracting activities are being audited and scrutinized to death by Inspectors General, the GAO, the Congress, press inquiries, Freedom of Information Act requests, and so forth. Increasing the number of audits, as he seems to suggest, will not lead to hoped-for reduction in regulation. Quite to the contrary, many view audits as part of the stifling regulatory control environment (e.g., "ABA Section Urges," 1994, p. 74; and Ink, 1993, p. 50).

The federal procurement system is often cited for being overregulated and inefficient. But as long as the nation's policies and laws call for giving every firm an opportunity to compete on every government procurement, federal contracts will be awarded inefficiently with regard to time and uneconomically with regard to administrative cost. On the other hand, the procurement process can be viewed as efficient in terms of making every contract opportunity available to every American business. Whether procurement regulations are perceived as inefficient or lacking common sense seems to depend on the frame of reference.

Moreover, whenever major emergencies occur, such as wars and natural disasters, the government tends to temporarily suspend protective regulation to respond to the emergency. For example, in every war in which America participated, the procurement rules have been eased so that troops could be supplied with weapons without delay. These rules, however, were reapplied after the emergency was concluded. This phenomenon has been thoroughly described in an unpublished doctoral dissertation (Pegnato, 1993, pp. 12–82).

Defense contracting programs in Europe face a regulatory environment far less burdensome than that faced here in the United States (Mayer, 1993, p. 297). Ironically, the U.S. defense acquisition programs produce better results than their European counterparts (Mayer, 1993, p. 297). In short, the federal procurement system may not deserve all the criticism it receives.

In 1996, after a long and mostly unsuccessful history of contracting for sophisticated air traffic control computer systems, Congress decided to liberate the FAA from the old, bureaucratic way of doing business. FAA's acquisition problems had been widely reported in the press. For example, the *Washington Times* reported that costs had tripled for the Advanced Aviation System, a key part of the FAA's modernization program (Larson, 1996). Costs on other major technology projects also rose dramatically; schedule delays averaged nearly 4 years. Using the freedom granted by Congress, the FAA quickly replaced a 10-foot stack of procurement rules with a 100-page document. The assumption here is that excessive procurement regulation must be the root cause of these problems. Is this not just another classic example of the death of common sense?

Not exactly. "FAA's organizational culture has been an underlying cause of the persistent cost overruns, schedule delays, and performance shortfalls in the agency's acquisitions of major air traffic control systems," reads a GAO (1996b, p. 22) report. In other words, FAA's flawed management culture is largely responsible for its procurement problems. This disease is just as likely to exist in the private sector as in the public sector. To focus on the rules misses the point, at least at the FAA. Focusing on the rules, a big fat target, ignores the larger problems of management competence and organizational culture. According to the GAO (1996b, p. 45), top officials at FAA agree that an agency-wide cultural change is necessary to correct its problems.

There is another way to look at whether procurement rules lack common sense and really are to blame for such government failures as $7,600 coffee pots, $748 pliers, and $435 hammers. According to the Federal Procurement Data Center, in fiscal year 1995 more than 18 million federal procurement transactions were completed (U.S. General Services Administration, 1996, p. 2). Common sense suggests that problems occurred on very few of those 18 million transactions. Even if newspapers covered a different $435 hammer procurement scandal every day, the total would be 365 out of 18 million, a very low percentage. From this perspective, the procurement rules seem to work pretty well.

Even if it is assumed that procurement rules lack common sense, as Howard argues, will the American public be in favor of eliminating this inefficient regulatory structure? It is important to keep in mind that $200 billion of taxpayer's money is spent every year by the federal government's procurement system. History shows that any support for regulatory flexibility and discretion evaporates the second that the press reports the existence of another $435 hammer. The public and their elected officials quickly switch from endorsing efficiency to demanding airtight controls. Under these conditions, any argument about how these controls are inefficient fails. The public seems to have zero tolerance for wasting one cent of taxes paid from hard-earned income. The logical, commonsensical business argument that it costs more to root out every penny of wasted government expenditure than it costs to tolerate a reasonable amount of waste is an ineffective argument in the public environment. By contrast, businesses thrive on these cost-effective trade-offs.

The benefits of procurement regulation, although not easily quantifiable into dollar terms, cannot be underestimated. These benefits include eliminating fraud and increasing taxpayer confidence in public expenditure of funds on federal procurement programs. The Russians want to copy the American system because they want to eliminate the corruption in their system.

Howard's recommendations (1995b, p. 17) to reform the procurement system include increasing the discretion of contracting officers, putting limits on competitive bidding, eliminating the protest system, and discarding most procurement regulations in favor of a system focused on oversight and accountability. Almost without exception, Howard's ideas, upon implementation, would drastically improve the efficiency of the procurement system. If Howard is so incisive and accurate about how to fix an inefficient administrative process, why are his prescriptions not immediately instituted? The answer is that government is not a business.

Efficiency is not the main imperative in government. Of equal importance are equity, due process, protection of individual rights, and accountability. Every measure to increase efficiency comes at a great cost to one of the other imperatives. For example, restricting competition means that some firms, probably the smaller ones, will have their opportunity to win federal contracts diminished. Eliminating the protest system means that a firm will no longer have the ability to challenge perceived unfair treatment by a government agency. The firm will have lost some of its rights.

The procurement system is being reformed in the general direction suggested by Howard. But the changes are on the margins. The public and its elected officials and interest groups (e.g., small-business lobby) will prevent anything but marginal changes. This seems to be the price of democracy and is often overlooked.

Why not just eliminate all constraints, including procurement regulations? Of course, this is part of the argument of those who call for a government based on entrepreneurial incentives. James Madison's (1961) views in *Federalist* No. 51 are relevant here (the credit for pointing out how relevant Madison's ideas are to this debate goes to Peters, 1991):

> If men were angels, no government would be necessary. If angels were to govern men, neither external nor internal controls on government would be necessary. In framing a government which is to be administered by men over men, the great difficulty lies in this: You must first enable the government to control the governed; and in the next place oblige it to control itself. (p. 322)

To repeat an earlier conclusion, common sense and efficiency are far too narrow measures to use to judge the overall worth to American society of procurement regulations—or any regulations for that matter.

Common Sense and Government

To fault government processes for lacking common sense and being inefficient is to fail to understand the complexities and challenges of governmental programs. How well government serves the people can only be assessed by checking to see if there is a healthy balance among all of the conflicting goals and values applicable to government programs. Are these programs run efficiently? Are they fulfilling legislative mandates? Are the officials running them being held accountable? Are individual and group rights protected? Are program outcomes as equitable and fair to all those affected as is practicable?

A big part of Howard's problem with regulations is that they are an expensive burden on the American economy. But the cost of regulation needs to be put in perspective. The OMB (1997, p. 39364) estimates the total annual costs of regulation to be $289 billion in 1997. The total annual benefits of regulation are estimated by OMB to be a slightly higher $298 billion. The breakdown of these costs and benefits in billions of dollars are in Table 1. The OMB data show no growth in the cost of regulation relative to the size of the economy in the last decade. The regulatory costs were about 4% of gross domestic product in 1988 and in 1997 (p. 39362). A GAO (1995, p. 2) report contains a similar conclusion. The costs of

Table 1   The Breakdown of the Costs and Benefits of Regulation as Estimated by the Office of Management and Budget (in billions of dollars)

Type of Regulation	Benefits	Costs
Environmental	162	144
Other social	136	54
Economic	0	91
Total	298	289

regulation as a percentage of gross domestic product were relatively flat from 1977 to 1994, decreasing from 4.6% in 1977 to 4.1% in 1994. If these data are accurate, regulations are less of a burden to the American economy than a benefit to the economy.

To argue that government regulation lacks common sense is to argue for deregulation. The call for deregulation is part of a political and economic strategy that includes downsizing, privatizing, and tax reduction. This fashionable conservative philosophy, to oversimplify, suggests that most of what government does is bad and most of what business does is good. This notion, albeit oversimplified, is seriously flawed. The vision sought is pure laissez faire capitalism. But market imperfections guarantee that government will always play a large role in American economic life. In fact, the American system is not pure capitalism; it is mixed capitalism. Robert Kuttner (1997, pp. 225–280) argues that regulation is a natural and inevitable consequence of market failures. For example, the Interstate Commerce Commission was created in 1877 because railroad bosses were using monopoly power to overcharge farmers (p. 230). In 1997, the governor of Maryland asked the federal government to regulate chicken farmers to reduce the toxic runoff into rivers and streams to eliminate huge fish kills and potential brain damage to fishermen.

Kuttner (1997, p. 300) admits that it is fair to ask whether particular regulations are efficient in addressing market failures, but he suggests that such a question builds in a bias against regulation. Even though society has limited economic resources, Kuttner describes the limits of cost-benefit analysis. For example, such analysis uses a narrow financial valuation of human life based on earning power (p. 300). More broadly, "cost-benefit analysis attempts to bring into the price-auction system things that most people think should not be for sale" (Kuttner, 1997, p. 300). A clear view of the Grand Canyon is one example. For society, the cost of an injury can be an average dollar amount. For the injured person, it is a profound personal loss. When most of the injuries and deaths from occupational hazards almost never affect executives, it is too easy to conclude that it is not worth half a million dollars to save another life (p. 301). Kuttner argues that cost-benefit analysis ignores distributive implications. Nevertheless, he is not suggesting that the cost of regulation should be ignored. Because cost-benefit analysis is flawed, it should not be the only tool used to assess the net worth of regulations (p. 303). Everything cannot be regulated or deregulated. The democratic political process will determine the right balance, as it should.

Government regulation is inefficient and messy. But so is democracy. That is the way it was purposefully designed. And that is the way it operates today, thankfully. In the end, the American people will not tolerate a government that efficiently fails to protect liberty and protect individual rights.

On the other hand, government program or administrative failures give voice to critics calling for deregulation and privatization. In *The Federalist* 70, Alexander Hamilton (1961) wrote, "A government ill executed whatever it might be in theory, must be in practice a poor government" (p. 423). Government critics will only be silenced when the American public's trust and confidence in government is restored.

References

ABA section urges that guiding principles for FAR rewrite address second guessing by auditors, uniformity, vendor trust. (1994, July 18). *Federal Contracts Report*, pp. 74, 75.

Babington, C., & Shields, T. (1997, September 12). Maryland poultry farmers may feel heat in war on Pfiesteria. *The Washington Post*, pp. A1, A22.

Booth, W. (1995, March 14). Florida seeks end to rule by the book. *The Washington Post*, p. A1.

Breeden, J., II. (1997, October 27). Russia is buying into U.S. procurement procedures. *Government Computer News*, p. 10.

Clayton, P. (1997, August 26). A letter to our customers about hamburgers, food safety and flame-broiling. *The Washington Post*, p. A7.

Coopers & Lybrand. (1994, December). *The DOD regulatory cost premium: A quantitative assessment.* Washington, DC: DOD.

Corbin, L. (1995). Culture of fear. *Government Executive, 27*(9), 40–45.

Derthick, M., & Quirk, P. J. (1985). *The politics of deregulation.* Washington DC: Brookings Institution.

Evans, E. (1996, July 4). Meat inspection rules near final approval. *The Washington Post*, p. A27.

General Accounting Office (GAO). (1995, June 15). *Costs of regulation* (PEMD-95-24R). Washington, DC: Author.

General Accounting Office (GAO). (1996a, November). *Regulatory burden: Measurement challenges and concerns raised by selected companies* (GGD-97-2). Washington, DC: Author.

General Accounting Office (GAO). (1996b, August). *Aviation acquisition: A comprehensive strategy is needed for cultural change at FAA* (RCED-96-159). Washington, DC: Author.

Gore, A. (1995, September 7). *Common sense government: Works better and costs less* (Report of the National Performance Review). Washington, DC: Office of the Vice President.

Hamilton, A. (1961). The Federalist, No. 70. In C. Rossiter (Ed.), *The Federalist Papers* (pp. 423–431). New York: New American Library.

Howard, P. K. (1995a, July 21). Cut the dead wood. *Wall Street Journal*, p. A10.

Howard, P. K. (1995b, September 18). Replace rules with responsibility and oversight. *Federal Computer Week*, p. 17.

Ink, D. (1993, October). Strengthen management and cut the second guessing. *Government Executive*, pp. 50–51.

Kelman, S. (1990). *Procurement and public management: The fear of discretion and the quality of government performance.* Washington, DC: AEI Press.

Kovacic, W. E. (1992). Regulatory controls as barriers to entry in government procurement. *Policy Sciences, 25*(1), 29–42.

Kuttner, R. (1997). *Everything for sale.* New York: Knopf.

Lacayo, R. (1995, April 20). Anecdotes not antidotes. *Time*, pp. 40, 41.

Larson, R. (1996, November 29). GAO blames FAA management for purchase problems. *The Washington Times*, p. A1.

Madison, J. (1961, Spring). The Federalist, No. 51. In C. Rossiter (Ed.). *The Federalist papers* (pp. 320–325). New York: New American Library.

Mayer, K. R. (1993). Policy disputes as a source of administrative controls: Congressional micromanagement of the Department of Defense. *Public Administration Review, 53*(4), pp. 135–146.

Moe, R. C., & Gilmour, R. S. (1995). Rediscovering principles of public administration: The neglected foundation of public law. *Public Administration Review, 55*(2).

Office of Management and Budget (OMB). (1997). Draft report to Congress on the costs and benefits of federal regulations. *Federal Register, 62*(140), 39352–39383.

Pegnato, J. A. (1993). *An assessment of the effects of organizational design on organizational performance.* Unpublished doctoral dissertation, George Mason University, Fairfax, VA.

Peters, T. (1991, Spring). Excellence in government. *The Bureaucrat*, p. 5.

Phillips, D. (1997, August 20). Oversights by FAA, SabreTech Contributed to ValuJet Crash, Safety Board Says. *The Washington Post*, p. A7.

Samuelson, R. J. (1997, February 3). The joy of deregulation. *Newsweek*, p. 39.

U.S. General Services Administration. (1996, January 29). *Federal procurement report: Fiscal year 1995 through fourth quarter.* Washington, DC: Federal Procurement Center.

Weiss, R. (1996, July 7). President orders overhaul of meat safety inspections. *The Washington Post*, p. A10.

Wilson, J. Q. (1989). *Bureaucracy: What government agencies do and why they do it.* New York: Basic Books.

Running government like a business sounds appealing, but Richard C. Box is concerned about what is lost through such an emphasis. Administration here is purely instrumental—appropriate means are determined by how government can most efficiently implement goals. The citizens, who formerly participated in such policy making, are now limited to a role as consumers of services. While some classical republican (with a small "r") writers and policy makers still exist who are concerned with engaging citizens actively in their government, market capitalism and classical liberalism focus on efficient government and individual rights. They pay little attention to how far economic inequality should extend or to what extent citizens should jointly, or collectively, use a dialogue within the community to make decisions on what is in the public interest.

Box explores what it is in our political culture that encourages such a heavy emphasis on the need for government agencies to emulate business practices. He argues that imitating private sector approaches has implications for the size and scope of government, the role of the public service practitioner, and the very meaning of citizenship and public service. The article's intent, however, is not to reject adoption of market pressures, but to find an appropriate balance between drawing on such management practices as privatization, downsizing, and enterprise operations even while preserving the ability of public agencies to operate democratically. It is not enough to pretend that there is a separation between politics and administration that permits public executives to pose simply as "neutral bureaucrats." Instead, these administrators must find a way to reconcile public service values with the business model (or dominant economic paradigm).

It is not surprising that the modern market economy is having a dramatic impact on democracy and public administration. In theory, it is possible to separate the spheres of capitalism and democracy, but in practice we have drifted away from the notion of citizens governing jointly, and replaced it with the capitalist emphasis on rewarding individual achievement and on protection from the power of government. In today's "post-modern" society, there can be "thick," or democratic, involvement of citizens at the local level, but national politics is characterized by "thin" limited involvement, since it is difficult to identify grand themes, shared beliefs, or common interests that unite large groups of citizens. Thanks to the difficulty of generating such large-scale communities with shared interests, Americans are more vulnerable to the argument that we are all merely self-interested "maximizers" willing, when able, to advance at the expense of others. Government then becomes merely another vehicle through which to acquire goods and services, and a less legitimate one at that, since the goodies were not earned through competition in the marketplace.

One such form of economic analysis often applied to the behavior of government or the bureaucrat is principal-agent theory. It analyzes the relationship between a principal, such as an elected public official, and an agent, in this case the public bureaucracy, responsible for implementing the principal's orders. The danger identified here is that the agent will shirk whenever possible and thus must be carefully monitored. Box argues that such economic analysis broke through the weak wall separating the values of the market and the values of public management during the Reagan administration. Such an economic rationale provided intellectual support for the antigovernmental ideology held by this ruling elite. The solution, according to this rationale, lay in smaller government and privatization to limit such waste and inefficiency.

Such economic terminology and assumptions now dominate much discussion over the appropriate size and role of government, as Box observes, but the application is less satisfying than the theory. A common distinction is between public and private goods, but the example of water shows that the distinction is not always a neat one. Certain goods are readily understandable as public—such as water in a town square—while others like bottled water are private goods where those unwilling to pay can be excluded and the good is consumed individually. But there are also toll goods like piped water which are distributed jointly but require some means of charging users individually, and common pool goods like an underground aquifer that are consumed individually but where it is virtually impossible to prevent free riders from tapping into the system.[a] Distinctions of this kind have been used not only to justify smaller government where service delivery can be handled through the private sector, but also in support of privatization where goods that must be provided by the public sector can at least be produced by the private sector.

There is, however, a tension between the values of the marketplace and the traditional values of public administration—particularly where the expert service provider (the public service professional) is separated from the customer (formerly the citizen). How does one strike a balance here between marketplace values and the values of traditional public administration? Box argues that we need a framework for discussing the relationship between the public and private sectors and the nature of public service. Rethinking the assumptions concerning these issues is subtle, because it involves thinking about what are often unique understandings about our public institutions, their history, organizational culture, and surrounding environment. But, Box concludes, a framework for an important dialogue about such matters can be established by thinking about four issues, namely, (1) services the public sector should provide, (2) services the public sector should produce, (3) democratic governance, and (4) the role of the public-service practitioner.

Running Government Like a Business: Implications for Public Administration Theory and Practice

Richard C. Box, University of Nebraska–Omaha

The public sector faces increasing demands to run government like a business, importing private-sector concepts such as entrepreneurism, privatization, treating the citizen like a "customer," and management techniques derived from the production process. The idea that government should mimic the market is not new in American public administration, but the current situation is particularly intense. The new public management seeks to emphasize efficient, instrumental implementation of policies, removing substantive policy questions from the administrative realm. This revival of the politics-administration dichotomy threatens core

Richard C. Box, *American Review of Public Administration*, Vol. 29, No. 1, March 1999, pp. 19–43. © 1999 Sage Publications, Inc.

[a]E. S. Savas, *Privatization and Public-Private Partnerships*, New York: Chatham House Publishers, 2000, pp. 41–53.

public-sector values of citizen self-governance and the administrator as servant of the public interest. The article examines the political culture that encourages expansion of market-like practices in the American public sector, explores the issues of the purpose and scope of government and the role of the public-service practitioner, and offers a framework for the study and practice of public administration based on citizenship and public service.

Increasingly, public administration practitioners and academicians are faced with demands from politicians and citizens that government should be operated like a business. By this, they mean that it should be cost efficient, as small as possible in relation to its tasks, competitive, entrepreneurial, and dedicated to "pleasing the customer." But, despite the considerable success of market-like reforms in increasing the efficiency of governmental bureaucracies, there remains a sense that something is wrong. For people who are concerned about the quality of public service and attention to issues of social injustice, fairness in governmental action, environmental protection, and so on, something about running government like a business does not feel right. It seems to degrade the commitment to public service, reducing it to technical-instrumental market functions not unlike the manufacture and marketing of a consumer product. Gone is the image of citizens determining public policy and its implementation to shape a better future because customers do not actively participate in governance but wait passively to respond to an "agenda set by others" (Schachter, 1997, p. 65).

The idea that the public sector should conduct its affairs in a businesslike way is not new in the United States. Though there are enduring classical republican elements in American political thought that emphasize citizens working together for the good of the community, the American public sector exists within a context of market capitalism and classical liberalism. The values of this context include limited and efficient government in combination with individual liberty and political competition. Relatively little attention is given to problems associated with the workings of the market, such as economic inequality or reduced opportunities for collective citizen decision making through discourse.

A strong governmental apparatus can operate to set the parameters of market activity and its impact on the lives of citizens, but in the United States big government must exert control without seeming to be like a centralized European-style state. Although they wanted a stronger government than that provided by the Articles of Confederation, the founders of the United States intended to avoid forming a state apparatus with a purpose and values of its own and a mandate to shape the broader society. This initial "statelessness" (Stillman, 1991) is manifest in contemporary public administration debates over the issue of legitimacy (*Public Administration Review*, 1993). The concept of statelessness can be overdrawn, as Americans built an extensive government to meet the challenges of the years 1877–1920, including "the emergence of a nationally based market" and "the growth of trusts and oligopolies with national orientations and national economic power" (Skowronek, 1982, p. 11). Because of this institution-building effort, contemporary American government has a significant interactive relationship with the private economy, but it retains from the founding era the cultural expectation of minimal interference in the private sector. This expectation forms a political-cultural context in which the values of the private sector are primary and the values of collective citizen deliberation and the public interest are secondary. Even in this setting, there historically has been recognition of a unique and different role for the public sector, however difficult to define. This was true in the founding era, in the era of Jacksonian democracy, in the reform era, and through several decades of the post–World War II era.

Today, even those elusive public-private differences are fading as the public sector is increasingly penetrated by the metaphor of the market, of "running government like a business." The expansion of such thinking in the public sector has important implications for theory and practice. This article examines the nature of the political culture that encourages market-based practices in the American public sector, explores the issues of the size and scope of government and the role of the public service practitioner, and offers a framework for the study and practice of public administration in this economistic environment that is based on citizenship and public service. The article is not about the specifics of any particular reform effort, and the intent is not to bemoan the condition of the public sector. Rather, the article suggests constructive ways that public-service practitioners and academicians can approach these issues in their work, seeking to preserve and enhance the essence of public service within the market context.

Public Administration's Response to Market Pressures

Expansion of market concepts in the public sector is taking place at the end of the 20th century thrust to build administrative systems that address the problems of a growing urban-industrial nation. That thrust produced a public sector that appears today to be large, cumbersome, wasteful, and beyond citizen control (King & Stivers, 1998b, p. 11), isolated from and out of touch with the rest of society (Peters & Pierre, 1998, pp. 228–229). Large government requires that a few elected people represent the wishes of the masses, and representative democracy has grown so remote from the everyday lives of people that it no longer bears a clear relationship to common experience (Hummel & Stivers, 1998). Many citizens are so alienated from the concept of self-governance that they think of government as something separate, not a reflection of their own will, though some others would like to participate directly in re-creating the machinery of government to allow for genuine self-governance. As a potential remedy, many politicians and citizens believe that government should be run more like businesses, becoming trim and lean, exhibiting competitive behaviors, and giving greater attention to the needs of "customers."

Evidence of the expansion of market concepts in the public sector may be found in the literature and practice of public administration in an emphasis on a constellation of cost-cutting and production management concepts taken from the private sector, currently drawn together as new public management. These concepts include, among others, privatization, downsizing, rightsizing, entrepreneurism, reinvention, enterprise operations, quality management, and customer service. New public management seeks to separate politics (in the sense of decision making by the people or their representatives) from administration, allowing (or making) managers to manage according to cost-benefit economic rationality, largely free from "day-to-day democratic oversight" (Cohn, 1997). Such a separation resembles the old politics-administration dichotomy and Herbert Simon's (1945/1997) description of administrative decisions that are largely "factual." In this reformed management setting, the public-private distinction is "essentially obsolete," and management is generic across sectors (Peters & Pierre, 1998, p. 229).

This desire to separate the activities of politics (deciding about public policies) and administration (implementing them) is part of a redefinition of the function of government based on "a new elite consensus on the role of the state in society. A substantial public sector is to be maintained, but its purposes and operating values are considerably different from that which was characteristic of the social welfare state. The goal is no longer to protect society from the market's demands but to protect the market from society's demands" (Cohn, 1997, p. 586). This is both an American and international phenomenon (Cheung, 1997; Cohn, 1997; Hood, 1996; Kettl, 1997; Lan & Rosenbloom, 1992), and it may be seen as evidence of a new equilibrium in relations between economic classes. We may no longer find useful the "stale discourse of class warfare" (Barber, 1998, p. 8), but expansion of economistic concepts in the public sector could reflect the reality that "big government has always been an ally of the little guy, and downsizing it has generally been a recipe for upgrading the power of private-sector monopolies. Schoolroom bullies are forever questioning the legitimacy of hallway monitors" (Barber, 1998, p. 5).

At the level of governmental operation, the question is the extent to which the functions of government should be modeled after the private sector. This gets to the heart of the matter for public-service practitioners, who want to know what is expected from public agencies, how they should relate to citizens (their customers, to use the language of the market), and what is the proper source of policy direction—professional interpretation of the public interest, decisions by elected officials, or the desires of citizens. For over a century, public administration practitioners and academicians have debated the normative role of practitioners, with opinions ranging from neutral implementers of policies determined by others to practitioners as active participants in the policy-making process (Kass & Catron, 1990; McSwite, 1997). Despite the intent of new public management, market concepts are not likely to remove the practitioner from policy making because government is so complex that citizens and elected representatives cannot govern alone.

Instead, running government like a business means that public managers increasingly regard the public as customers to be served rather than as citizens who govern themselves through collective discourse processes. They keep the public at a distance by conducting surveys and focus groups to identify existing opinions rather than engaging citizens face-to-face in exchanges of information, ideas, and values that result in informed governance. As elected officials withdraw from direct and frequent involvement in administration, the balance of control shifts toward professionals (Cope, 1997). With citizens excluded from collective governance and elected officials withdrawn from the daily world of policy implementation, the question becomes, "Who then is accountable?" (Peters & Pierre, 1998, p. 228).

An important task before public administration theorists is to describe the impact of governing and managing by market theory and practice on public service at all levels of government and to explore how theorists and practitioners can respond. Is a complete transformation of the public sector, mimicking the private sector, the answer in the face of pervasive public preference for use of market-like management practices and the apparent reduction of many processes and interactions to cost-benefit calculations? Is this really a problem, or are we approaching the old ideal of pure businesslike efficiency by walling off "unrelated" matters of politics and preferences from public management, squeezing out of professional practice substantive consideration of whether what we do efficiently, instrumentally, is the right thing to do?

Furthermore, in this market-like environment, is it possible to identify aspects of public service that are in some way fundamental to our notions of a good political culture, aspects that can coexist with market concepts of structure and function? At some point, theorists, and more so practitioners, may find it makes sense to worry less about the apparently unstoppable expansion of the market in the public sector and search for constructive ways to respond to it. For practitioners, one way to do this is to simply comply, mastering the expected economic techniques and carrying out policies as given without taking part in their formulation or questioning them. This response fits well with the traditional split between politics and administration, emulating the model of the neutral bureaucrat. For the academician, this approach means confining research to technical matters of management, such as pay-for-performance plans, budgeting systems, or information technology, thus avoiding critical analysis of the effects of market concepts on the public sphere.

A second way to respond to the expansion of market concepts in the public sector would be to protest vigorously in hopes that someone, someday, will listen, or at least that if the pendulum swings in the other direction in the future, we will be well positioned to say "we told you so." This could be a risky strategy for practitioners in the work world and it could position academicians as useful critics of current practice or place them so far outside the mainstream as to be ignored. A third path in responding to the current situation would be to hope for moderation of the impacts of market concepts in the future, but for today, to seek reasonable ways to adapt public service values to the dominant economic paradigm. This is the path outlined in the final section of the article.

The Social and Political Context

We can gain a broader perspective by considering the nature of the society that surrounds public administration, the society that creates, supports, and demands services from the public/governmental sector. A description of the nature of society may seem somewhat removed from daily administrative affairs, but of necessity public administration is a reflection of societal values. It is impractical, maybe irresponsible, to operate inside public organizations as if the demands of society do not matter. If we do, sooner or later the external environment will catch up to us, making painful demands for accountability and change that might have been foreseen and dealt with in less traumatic ways.

We have known for some time that the modern market economy would have serious impacts on society and in particular on democracy. In 1906, Max Weber asserted that

> it is utterly ridiculous to see any connection between the high capitalism of today—as it is now being imported into Russia and as it exists in America—with democracy or freedom in any sense of these words. . . . The question is: how are freedom and democracy in the long run at all possible under the domination of highly developed capitalism? (in Gerth & Mills, 1958, p. 71).

In 1931, John Dewey expressed concern for the future of democratic governance:

> The dominant issue is whether the people of the United States are to control our government, federal, state, and municipal, and to use it in behalf of the peace and welfare of society or whether control is to go on passing into the hands of small powerful economic groups who use all the machinery of administration and legislation to serve their own ends. (in Campbell, 1996, pp. 178–179).

Ramos (1981/1984) took for granted the "intrusion of the market system upon human existence," with its accompanying emphasis on instrumental rationality that advances the goals of the market, rather than substantive rationality that offers the individual an opportunity to achieve "truly self-gratifying interpersonal relationships" through reason, the activity of the human psyche (p. 23).

Scott and Hart (1979) documented the transition from a society based on the value of the individual in the pre-industrial era to one of organizational values in the 20th century. Now, in an age in which we are replaceable parts of large systems, we think with nostalgic fondness of a time when each person was an integral part of a local community. We spend part of our leisure time watching movies or television shows that glorify the heroic loner, but most of us in real life fulfill our destiny as small productive parts of larger systems.

In the United States, the nation's founders created a governmental structure that allowed limited popular participation in national political life while emphasizing order and stability. In so doing, they established a semi-democratic form in which "the 'people' was no longer being defined, like the Athenian demos, as an active citizen community but as a disaggregated collection of private individuals whose public aspect was represented by a distant central state" (Wood, 1996, p. 219). The focus was on individual rights and protection from the power of government, as contrasted with the classical republican ideal of citizen self-governance.

With the rise of capitalism in the 19th century, it became possible to combine democracy and capitalism by clearly separating the economic and political spheres. Thus, citizens maintained their formal public-sector liberal equality in relation to rights, voting, and the law, whereas private-sector inequalities of wealth and power generated by capitalism were largely off-limits to collective, public action. These were the conditions of creation of modern liberal democracy (Adams, Bowerman, Dolbeare, & Stivers, 1990; Wood, 1996, p. 234), a "Lockean accommodation" that "reconciled representative government with capitalism by disenfranchising the group most likely to contest the hegemony of wealth—the working class itself" (Bowles & Gintis, 1986, p. 42). It is semidemocratic in that the mass of people participate in a limited and marginal way in collective decision making. In the balance between the public and economic spheres, the public sector is allowed to trim off the rough edges of economic excess in relation to treatment of workers, consumers, and the physical environment, in exchange for keeping public-sector interference with the inequalities of the economic sector to a minimum. Thus, as the market has "insinuated itself into the domains of sentiment, life-style and psyche," it has "bound the state with subtle threads of economic dependency" (Bowles & Gintis, 1986, p. 34).

There do not at present seem to be any viable alternatives to this semidemocratic capitalist model (Dryzek, 1996). On a global level, there were competing models for much of the 20th century, but now those models have largely vanished. There are a few socialist enclaves remaining, and a number of relatively undeveloped countries with authoritarian regimes, now being pressured by the public and private institutions of developed nations to change their economic systems to conform with the semidemocratic capitalist model. Over time, it may be discovered that this model is not optimal for all nations, that it works best for mature, stable societies with institutions that can support it. It may not work well for a range of nations with cultural and political histories very different from those of developed Western societies, nations in which the semidemocratic capitalist model can lead to hardship and social unrest (Kaplan, 1997).

Today, even the possibility of alternative systems seems to be disappearing, and the market metaphor is dominant. We are apparently in the midst of postmodern conditions characterized by *thick* interpretations of reality at the micro, local level where people can interact directly and form coherent mutual interpretations of values and identity, and *thin* reality at the macro level of broad classes of people, regions, and nations. This results in a profusion of difference, an "assertion of the random nonpattern and the unassimilable anomaly" (Fox & Miller, 1995, p. 45) that shifts and changes constantly. In such an environment, postmodernists believe it is difficult if not impossible to identify grand themes of common belief or interest across large groups of people or geographic areas.

In the midst of this apparent fragmentation of meaning, the daily mechanics and values of the market permeate social, political, and economic life. Families are pressed by economic circumstances to alter their expectations about work, retirement, child rearing, and care of the elderly. Workers are forced to abandon the certainties of lifetime employment, instead constantly keeping an eye on the job market and the best opportunities to increase earning power. Private, public, and nonprofit organizations must constantly adapt to their rapidly changing environments. In the public sphere, it becomes harder and harder to generate large-scale communities of shared interest through direct discourse and personal action, even at a time when people yearn for a return to a sense of community and personal efficacy (Bellah, Madsen, Sullivan, Swidler, & Tipton, 1985; Box, 1998; Eberly, 1994). So, we live in postmodern times characterized by large-scale fragmentation of values and intensification of interest in local action, yet we are surrounded by the seemingly universal, global phenomenon of market mechanisms. Within this universal phenomenon, there appears to be general agreement that people are competitive self-maximizers out to lobby legislatures for their benefit at the expense of others, get the largest quantity of consumer goods their resources will command, climb over the backs of colleagues for career advancement, compete at the community level to draw the best companies to their town at the expense of other towns, and so on. Furthermore, this view seems to reflect not only a description of what we are but also a normative vision of what we should be, in a "celebration of wealth that now threatens to drown all competing values" (Lasch, 1996, p. 22). Times change, and if this competitive, consumerist life pattern affects the world's physical environment and social stratification in ways that clearly threaten individuals, the pendulum of public opinion and political action may shift, as it did during parts of the 1960s and 1970s. But for now, "more is more" instead of "less is more," and the market is our guide.

In such circumstances, it is hardly surprising that the language and methods of the market have made significant inroads into public-sector thought and practice over the past two decades. However, American public administration has not been a pure entity removed from the influence of the market during any period in its development. At all levels of government throughout the nation's history, there has been evidence of market-like behavior, such as 19th-century spoils politics that affected policy implementation at the national level and the local-level graft and machine politics that inspired urban reformers to take action. The progressive-era reaction to these perceived abuses was to separate politics and administration at least to the extent that administration would be more businesslike and scientific. Ironically, this meant that reformers wanted to use the management methods of the market to reduce the extent of market-like behavior in the public sector.

In the 20th century, with the rise of the administrative state, public professionals became more prominent in the formulation as well as implementation of public policy. As the overall scope of government expanded dramatically, the internal management of government retained an expectation of efficiency in the midst of a sense of broader public purpose. There were repeated examinations of management of the national government that advocated application of scientific, businesslike methods to improve efficiency (Arnold, 1995). At the local level, the council-manager plan was built on a corporate structural model with the expectation that it would produce efficiency and effectiveness.

Beginning in the 1950s, some economists turned their attention to the public sector, applying their assumptions about individual and collective behavior to the public sphere. By focusing on the individual as the unit of analysis, assuming that individuals seek to maximize their personal preferences in the "political market" as they do in the private sector, and treating the behavior of citizens, elected officials, political appointees, and public professionals as examples of self-seeking regard for their own interests, the public choice scholars discovered a public world very different from that of public administration scholars (Johnson, 1991). Where traditional theorists found people searching for a better society and the public interest, economic theorists found the public sector operating like an alternative form of market. In this view, traditional bureaucratic, hierarchical government is not a means to social betterment, but a mechanism that distorts private economic behavior, reduces individual freedom, and makes the economy less efficient. The way to reduce these negative effects, according to economists, is to decentralize government, make it smaller, and introduce market-like concepts such as fees and user charges, vouchers, and systems to monitor employee performance, such as merit pay plans (Jennings, 1991, pp. 115–116; Ostrom, 1973/1991).

At the conceptual level of the size and scope of government, the economic view is that, when it will be to their benefit, individuals, groups, politicians, and bureaucrats seek to maximize their gains in the public market by competing with others for the benefits offered by collective action (Downs, 1957; Niskanen, 1971; Olson, 1965). Corporations seek to make it harder for potential competitors to enter the market, associations seek tax breaks others cannot have, politicians fight for the power and money of office, and public-sector bureaucrats want their agencies to grow so that their status and freedom to act are increased. Governmental action coerces individuals in society into behaving in a manner consistent with majority will, whether or not they agree with it, and those who stand to benefit the most from governmental action will spend the time and resources to influence public policy decisions. A basic assumption of economics is that free and uncoerced individual choice should be maximized and that, where a clear need for collective action in the public interest is lacking, citizens should be allowed to act alone or in voluntary cooperation without governmental coercion (Schmidtz, 1991, chap. 7). But government grows larger and more powerful as people use it to gain advantage over one another. This rent-seeking behavior joins the economic inefficiency of government-as-monopoly-provider-of-services as an argument for smaller and more limited government.

At the conceptual level of public agencies and employees, economic rationality has had a significant impact on scholarly thinking about behavior in organizations. Niskanen's argument that public bureaucrats will seek to increase the size of their agency's budgets (1971; or as modified in 1991, the size of the discretionary budget) was an effort to reconceptualize the behavior of public employees, moving away from models of control by legislatures or a sense of duty to the public interest, to a model of the public professional as a self-interested maximizer of competitive position in the bureaucratic world. Niskanen's ultimate purpose was to shift attention from the attributes of bureaucrats to the characteristics of public agencies, especially the structural features that provide incentives for people to behave in certain ways (Niskanen, 1991, p. 28).

In the past few decades, economically oriented examination of public organizations has been a growth industry, adopting a variety of complex and interesting approaches. Summarizing this work in 1984 in an article on "The New Economics of Organization," Moe noted that it is "perhaps best characterized by three elements: a contractual perspective on organizational relationships, a focus on hierarchical control, and formal analysis via principal-agent models" (p. 739). Among approaches to organizations that fall within the new economics rubric, principal-agent theory is especially applicable in the public sector, where the relationships between citizens (principals) and politicians (their agents) and between politicians (principals in this case) and bureaucrats (their agents) are a constant source of fascination. Agency theory deals with questions that arise because "the desires or goals of the principal and agent conflict and it is difficult or expensive for the principal to verify what the agent is actually doing" (Eisenhardt, 1989, p. 58). It is assumed that agents will naturally do less work than principals want done or fail to do work in the way principals want it done. This is the problem of shirking, and principals meet it by seeking information on the activities of agents; this monitoring is time-consuming and costly. Thus, it behooves the principal (e.g., boss, superior, capitalist, or politician) to seek a wage rate that will motivate agents (employees, subordinates) and a level of monitoring that is not too costly but convinces agents that the risk of being caught shirking is substantial (Bowles & Gintis, 1986, pp. 77–78).

There are important implications of this line of thought for behavior in public organizations. The economics-based management tools being applied in the public sector are grounded in the economist's assumptions that employees will shirk and that monitoring is essential (though the assumption of economically rational behavior has been under attack for some time; see Anderson & Crawford, 1998). The focus is on explicitly specifying performance, through mechanisms such as clearly articulated contracts and/or pay-for-performance systems. In New Zealand, for example, many public agencies have been changed so that "top managers are hired by contract, rewarded according to their performance, and can be sacked if their work does not measure up" (Kettl, 1997, p. 448). Although this is more extreme than typical implementation of principal-agent concepts in the United States, such thinking can be found in the emphasis on various techniques to measure and reward performance and outcomes, as well as movement away from rigid civil-service systems. Although the elegantly simple structure of principal-agent theory is becoming more cumbersome and problematic with the accumulation of empirical data on its application (Waterman & Meier, 1998), it remains a powerful tool in the hands of contemporary governmental reformers.

It was in the 1980s, amid the antigovernment ideology of the Reagan administration and a wave of public sentiment for shrinking the public sector, that market-like concepts broke through the weak wall of separation between the values of the market and the values of public management. Trickle-down, supply-side economics and public choice economics pointed the way to prosperity through smaller government, and it was thought that bureaucratic waste could be eliminated through contracting out and becoming entrepreneurial, and soon the entire public sector would, supposedly, be as efficient as the private sector was assumed to be. The negative aspects of treating public purposes as if they were private became apparent through events such as the savings-and-loan crisis at the national level and reevaluation of the tenets of "reinvention" at the local level (Gurwitt, 1994), but the transformational impact of this period cannot be denied. This is reflected in the writing of a deputy project director for the Clinton administration's new-public-management-inspired National Performance Review. Although noting that "there is no single intellectual source for the reinventing government movement," he says that it "evolved during the past 10 to 15 years . . . based, in part, on the pioneering intellectual work of public choice theoreticians such as Mancur Olson, E. S. Savas, Gordon Tullock, and William Niskanen" (Kamensky, 1996, p. 248).

The Size and Scope of Government

As Weintraub (1997) has pointed out, there are several meanings, of the distinction between *public* and *private,* including the following: the liberal-economistic model, based on neoclassical economics, which regards the public-private distinction the same as that between state administration and the market economy; the civic perspective, which views the public realm as separate from both the market and the administrative state; and other perspectives, including feminism, that examine distinctions between public and private as involving the spheres of sociability and family and household (pp. 16–17). Here, we take a viewpoint looking outward from inside the administrative state to examine penetration of the market metaphor into public administration, so we are concerned with the liberal-economistic model that is "dominant in most 'public policy' analysis" (p. 16).

Given the development of the political environment described above, it is not surprising that Americans have always been searching for an acceptable balance between what is private and what is public. In the early to mid-19th century, there were debates over the national government's role in banking and funding internal improvements such as telegraph transmission and canals for water transportation. For the most part, the trend was toward resisting expansion of the national role amid prevailing public opinion hostile to action by the national government (White, 1954, pp. 437–481). Efforts to expand the role of government were more successful in the late 19th century and into the 20th century, as the regulatory and welfare state was built in response to the changing character of national economic life. Then, beginning with the Reagan administration in the 1980s, the growth of the national government was again brought into question. At the local level, the scope of governmental activity grew steadily, accelerating after World War II as the population expanded and suburbia was built.

Along with questioning the size and scope of government in the 1980s, there was a revival of interest in localism and limited government. If it seems to the individual that the national or state government is too distant, too big, and so dominated by entrenched interest groups that he or she cannot have much effect on public policy, it is natural to turn attention toward a locus of action small enough to offer the possibility of quick and satisfying results. As president, Ronald Reagan encouraged this sentiment as he sought to dismantle the welfare state and return its functions to states, localities, and private and nonprofit sector organizations. The communitarian movement emphasized nongovernmental action and citizen duties as well as rights. These ideas were given additional thrust by the withdrawal of the national government from many domestic initiatives and the phenomenon of tight resources at all levels of government.

In the midst of the 1980s milieu of negativity toward government, with its bureaucrat bashing and belief that government is the problem rather than the solution, economic thinking about the role of government in society blossomed and became part of the ordinary vocabulary of normative debate. By the 1990s, the idea that government needed to be smaller and more efficient had become accepted as common wisdom (though the reality was different at the state and local levels, as government continued to expand; see Walters, 1998). Of those people who spend time thinking about the size and scope of government and its role in society, many have come to hold the view that government at all levels is too big and it would be wise to spin off functions from the national government to the states and localities, or from government to the private and nonprofit sectors.

The economist's conceptual scheme for determining what is public and what is private has become standard fare for students of public affairs and underlies much of the public discourse about the role of government (Mikesell, 1995, pp. 1–6). Thus, we distinguish between public goods, such as national defense, and private goods, such as household appliances or a hamburger. Public goods would not ordinarily be offered by the private sector acting on the incentive of making a profit because people cannot be excluded from using it and so have no incentive to pay for it (the market failure to provide a good). If it is provided at all, it is available to everyone, and one person's use of a public good does not exhaust its usefulness to others (because I experience the benefits of being defended from foreign aggression does not mean that you cannot experience them, too). Because people could experience the benefits of public goods without paying for them (the free rider problem), government coercively forces members of the public to pay taxes or face financial penalties or imprisonment.

In the real world, things are not so simple, so there are modifications and exceptions to the concept of pure public goods and pure private goods. Toll goods are services that many people use but from which people may be excluded (such as swimming pools open for public use or expressways that charge fees), and common-pool resources are goods that can be exhausted as many people use them but for which exclusion is difficult (notably natural resources such as fisheries). The distinctions between types of goods are often fuzzy, and public-sector decision makers use criteria of public demand and political action to choose which services to offer rather than ideal conceptualizations of types of goods. Thus, government becomes involved in providing a variety of services that might appear to belong in the private or nonprofit sector. In addition, government regulates the activities of private actors as they work with toll, common-pool, or private goods, attempting to control negative effects (externalities) of private economic activity on people or the environment.

To add to the complexity, a distinction is made between the provision of public services and their production. Provision is the fundamental question of whether or not government will cause a service, or good, to be offered. It is a policy question to be decided by the people or their representatives. If the answer is negative ("No, we don't want to provide garbage pickup service"), then either private or nonprofit organizations will provide the service or no one will. If, using the example of garbage pickup, no one provides the service (a market failure), there will likely be a discussion of the public health implications and a revisiting of the negative provision decision. Production is a separate issue. If the provision decision is positive, then the question remains how to actually deliver the service, how to produce it. Osborne and Gaebler argued in their book *Reinventing Government* (1993) that government often does a better job of governance, or *steering* (making policy decisions) than of delivering services, or *rowing*. Osborne and Gaebler included in the steering-rowing distinction governmental decision making about contracting out services and a governmental role in serving as catalyst for private and nonprofit initiatives such as downtown renewal or building sports facilities.

In an appendix to their book, Osborne and Gaebler built on the work of Savas (1987) to offer decision-making criteria for choosing public, private, or nonprofit action, such as stability, regulation, and enforcement of equity (public-sector strong points), expertise and willingness to take risks (private-sector attributes), and compassion and promotion of community (nonprofit-sector attributes). Vincent Ostrom (1973/1991; 1977; 1991/1994) has written extensively about institutional structures, intergovernmental arrangements, and building institutional capacity that helps people to govern themselves. Using a combination of public choice theory and a historical analysis of American government, Ostrom emphasizes the benefits of a multifaceted, polycentric system of governmental organizations and their private and nonprofit partners, organized to fit the services they offer so that the result is the best possible blend of efficiency with responsiveness to the public (e.g., community police patrol may be more efficiently and effectively organized on a small local scale, whereas police communication systems, detention facilities, and crime laboratories may be handled better through large-scale organization [1977, pp. 1518–1520]). These ideas appear to be helpful, although the circumstances surrounding specific decisions are often complex and uncertain, making application of decision-making criteria difficult.

In the end, it appears that determinations about which goods are provided by the public sector are made according to the rule, "whatever people want and will pay for," and production arrangements are a matter of trial and error according to political preferences. At the national level, our attitudes about the scope and size of government change periodically as we face new challenges and social and economic conditions. In response to evidence of widespread poverty, hunger, and injustice, we mount a campaign to redistribute incomes, taxing the middle class and wealthy to help the poor. In good economic times, politicians find ways to give tax breaks and programmatic "goodies" to the middle class to secure their votes in the next election.

At the local level, the choices made about which services to offer vary significantly from community to community. Some places confine themselves to providing the basics of public safety, streets, and sewer and water. Others provide a wide variety of services, for example, public pools, bicycle trails, recreation programs, public hospitals, downtown redevelopment programs, public-private partnerships to encourage economic development, and so on. In a community in which the author of this article lived for 8 years, the city utilities department discussed offering repair of home appliances to residential customers to make the city more competitive when private-sector firms enter the deregulating market for electric service. As one might imagine, people in the appliance repair business were not pleased with this potential entrepreneurial endeavor, viewing it as public expansion into an area thought of by most as a private-sector activity.

The complexities of intergovernmental relations, deciding whether services should be offered by small local units of government, larger ones, or regional agencies, which services will be provided by government and which will be produced by government or by the nonprofit or private sectors, and so on, are matters often resolved incrementally. To some extent the theory of public goods may influence such decisions, but likely it serves in large part to describe and critique what has taken place after the fact. For some time, there has been disagreement in the public administration community about the size and scope of government and the application of market thinking, with its elements of maximum individual choice, decentralization, and privatization. These issues are unlikely to be resolved anytime soon, if ever (see, e.g., Golembiewski, 1997; Kettl, 1997; Lyons & Lowery, 1989; Phares, 1989; Ross & Levine, 1996, chap. 11; Stillman, 1991, pp. 176–185; Waldo, 1981, p. 97).

Market Values and the Nature of Public Service

Given the importation of private-sector management techniques into the public sector in the past two decades, many public administrators are expected to be entrepreneurial, offer great customer service, and practice the latest management techniques inside the agency (total quality management, pay for performance, and so on). On the surface, it appears that such techniques would make the public service much more efficient, with results that would please citizens (they get better service), elected officials (they get credit for public agency efficiency), and career public-service practitioners (they get more approval and respect from citizens and elected people). And indeed, anecdotal evidence as well as scholarly research indicates that market-based reforms have produced some desired changes in the way government operates in the United States, as well as significant changes in several other nations (Kettl, 1997).

There are, however, potential problems with making the public service more businesslike because there is a difference in the operating norms of private- and public-sector organizations. Terry (1993) described entrepreneurial values as including "autonomy, a personal vision of the future, secrecy, and risk-taking" (p. 393), along with "domination and coercion, a preference for revolutionary change (regardless of the circumstances), and a disrespect for tradition" (p. 394). According to Terry, these values are at odds with values of "democratic politics and administration," such as "accountability, citizen participation, open policy-making processes, and 'stewardship' behavior" (p. 393). In a response to Terry, Bellone and Goerl (1993) espoused "civic-regarding entrepreneurship," which offers a community-minded model of administration that is accountable to the public. Terry, however, is not sure entrepreneurship can easily be combined with public service. His overriding concern is that "public entrepreneurs of the neo-managerialist persuasion are oblivious to other values highly prized in the U.S. constitutional democracy. Values such as fairness, justice, representation, or participation are not on the radar screen" (Terry, 1998, p. 198).

The contemporary emphasis on entrepreneurship makes this debate appear new. However, it is to some extent a repackaging of the old politics-administration question that has been in play since the late 19th century and was highlighted by the Friedrich-Finer argument in the early 1940s over the role of the administrator as relatively independent, expert actor, or tightly constrained agent of political officials (for a description of this argument, see McSwite, 1997, pp. 29–52). The repackaging is occasioned by renewed pressure to manage like a business as economic concepts permeate the thinking of policy makers and implementers. Although administrators are pushed to use entrepreneurial and scientific techniques to please the "customer's" assumed desire for businesslike government, they paradoxically become less accountable to the public, whose members lose some control over administration. For example, administrators may use expenditure-control budgets, which allow flexibility to spend as the professional sees fit, and to save money to carry over for discretionary spending later to avoid direct budgetary control by politicians. The assumptions are that this flexibility will make for more nimble response to changing conditions, give managers an incentive to be frugal, and remove political motivations from what ought to be expert decisions. Using Bellone and Goerl's reasoning, the good public administrator will, in exercising this greater degree of discretionary space, take into account the wishes of citizens in making choices. This logic reopens the question of representative democracy and agency; that is, do public administrators answer to the public, or to their elected representatives (Box, 1998; Fox & Miller, 1995; Kelly, 1998)?

The argument against such flexibility in budgeting is that clear and detailed line-item budgets were created to avoid problems of financial abuse and to ensure that money is spent as citizens or their elected representatives decide it should be spent. Saving up money means that it has not been spent as intended by representatives but instead will be spent as nonelected administrators decide—thus, a question of accountability. Supposedly scientific techniques administered by experts, such as cost-benefit analysis, reengineering, and quality control, may lead to more precise and economically efficient service delivery, but they may also crowd out competing citizen preferences for public policy and service delivery, preferences that can be shown by experts to be inefficient or impractical. This sort of result is often seen in disputes over such relatively minor issues as whether to preserve a historic building or remove esthetically pleasing landscaped medians in major streets to make traffic flow smoothly.

In these and similar instances, there is a conflict between the idea of public management as efficient, businesslike, and scientific, and public management as responsive to these and to other public values as well. Jennings (1991) offered three approaches to public administration that capture the essence of this conflict. The bureaucratic approach "takes efficiency and equal treatment of citizens as its primary values," the pluralism approach "emphasizes responsiveness to multiple interests," and the market approach "takes efficiency as its prime value," differing from the bureaucratic approach in emphasizing diversity of product and maximum consumer choice (p. 122). It may be argued that public administration theorists have in the past tended to prefer one of the first two approaches. Those who favor greater status and discretion for public administrators lean toward the bureaucratic approach, and those who favor greater citizen discourse and self-governance lean toward the pluralist approach. But today, most agree that some measure of market-like matching of public services to consumer preferences, along with efficient and technically competent management, is inevitable if not desirable. The question is how much, in what ways, and whether there are aspects of public service that should not be governed or managed from a market perspective.

The problem in seeking a reasonable balance between approaches in the face of demands to run government like a business is that operating with private-sector entrepreneurial techniques in the public sphere can subvert values of openness, fairness, and public propriety. In such cases, the public-service practitioner may take on the appearance of an independent actor separated from the public, concerned less about the public interest (however defined) and more about making money and maximizing individual power and freedom to act without review. This decreased accountability carries the possibility of unexpected program outcomes, uneven treatment of citizens, and behaviors that have not generally been thought of as consistent with public service. Again, using the example of city utilities in a community in which the author lived, this time in relation to the question of openness, the utilities department attempted to deny public access to many of its documents on the premise that it must operate secretly to level the playing field with its private-sector counterparts. In relation to fairness and a sense of public propriety, the local publicly owned hospital in the same community is semiautonomous, competes aggressively and successfully for market share with the other hospital in town, advertises its high-tech services widely, makes a sizable surplus, and pays its top executive approximately $300,000 per year, including bonuses based on how much the hospital makes. To some people these may not seem like appropriate behaviors for the public sector.

Movement toward a market model thus may result in loss of citizen self-determination in the creation of public policy and the operation of public organizations. Today, most people recognize that a general return to the participatory democracy of an earlier time and simpler society is impossible. However, in this post-progressive era, many are working to rebuild citizen capacity for self-governance through discourse and active citizenship (Barber, 1984; Box, 1998; Eberly, 1994; King & Stivers, 1998a). Not everyone will take part in such efforts, but, as Fox and Miller (1995) put it, having "some-talk" is better than having "few-talk" (pp. 129–159). The goal is to move beyond the typical model of citizen participation that is "not designed primarily for citizens but for agencies" (Timney, 1998, p. 98), in which administrators use citizen involvement processes for "informing, consultation, and placation" (Timney, 1998, p. 97) rather than enabling people to govern themselves.

Market-driven new managerialism can run counter to self-governance, as it is structured around the idea of happy consumers rather than involved citizens. This is a problem because government is not a business from which customers can voluntarily decide whether to purchase a product. It is, rather, a collective effort that includes every person within a defined geographic area (city, county, district, state, nation), and membership is involuntary unless a resident moves out of the jurisdiction. Mandatory membership carries with it a sense of the right to be involved if one so wishes in the process of deliberating and deciding on creation and implementation of public policy. As Barrett and Greene (1998) wrote, "Governments that buy too heavily into the idea that customers are a higher form of life than citizens risk losing the participation of taxpayers as partners" (p. 62).

Customers, on the other hand, are people to be persuaded and sold an image, a product, or a service rather than people who deliberate and decide. Schachter (1997, pp. 57–58) pointed out that only some public agencies can have customers in the manner of private-sector organizations. Many public agencies cannot easily identify their customers because the public they deal with is divided into a variety of individuals and groups with conflicting goals. Many others are regulatory or stewardship agencies for which the immediate client may not be the true beneficiary of the service. An example of the former would be a school district, for which the customers could be students, parents, or all adults in the community. Examples of the latter could include a restaurant regulated by the local health department (Is the department's customer the restaurant owner or the people who eat at the restaurant?), or the forest service (Is the customer the wood products industry or current and future generations who would use the forests?). These examples illustrate the fundamental difference between the market and the citizenship models of governance. The model of management formed around the market metaphor may lead to channeling resources into creating an image through public relations, surveying citizen opinion, and responding to perceived individual service preferences, rather than bringing citizens together to make their own decisions. This requires keeping the public at arm's length while operating in an entrepreneurial manner behind a facade that gives the appearance of involving citizens and making decisions in the general public interest.

Conclusions: Practicing Public Service in the Market Environment

Few would argue that government should be inefficient on purpose or inattentive to the needs and desires of its clients. In this sense, reinvention, privatization, entrepreneurism, customer service, and other such techniques are good things, bringing a breath of fresh air, challenge, and constructive change to the public sector. But market-like techniques may become problematic when they overwhelm values traditionally associated with the public sector and with public service. The economic assumptions of individual self-maximization, the public interest as the aggregate of private interests, and the public sector as just another form of market are powerful, focused, elegantly simple tools of analysis. Like other powerful and narrow theoretical constructs, they draw appropriate attention to matters of importance, but they also insist on their way of knowing the world while excluding other valuable theoretical orientations.

James March (1992) argued that in the past few decades economic theorists have softened the pure application of their ideas to the public sector, moving from methodological individualism to recognition of the fabric of institutional and structural relationships that make up a community. They now take into account, along with their original assumptions, "a rich, behavioral interpretation attentive to limited rationality, conflict, ambiguity, history, institutions, and multiple equilibria" (p. 228). He also noted that this softer, more subtle application of economic concepts has not yet penetrated into the world of applied theory because "the news of the transformation of rational theory spreads rather slowly from the inner temples of microeconomics to the rationalizing missionaries in the rest of an economizing society and social science" (p. 229). As this news spreads, the current reforms will fade and reformers will move on to new ideas, but like earlier reforms, they are likely to leave a legacy. The legacy of economistic theory in the public sector may include greater attention to "performance-motivated administration" and the integration of economic concepts into the traditional intellectual matrix of public service (Lynn, 1998, p. 232).

Turning toward application of these ideas to the size and scope of government, the historical American attitude toward the public sector has been that it should not compete with the private sector but should provide services that the private sector will not. However, with time, the clarity of the public-private distinction has faded as people ask government to do more and citizens grow accustomed to things as they are. In the past two decades, this combination of a preference for limited governmental scope with incremental accumulation of services in violation of that preference has been complicated by expansion of economics-based theory and practice. The public-choice side of the running government like a business metaphor suggests shrinking government by contracting out services or returning them to the private sector on the premise that the private sector is more efficient (in the case of contracting) or the assertion that the public sector should simply be smaller (in the case of true privatization). Meanwhile, the entrepreneurial side of the metaphor suggests that government may retain its traditional services and operate them like a business, plus operating services ordinarily thought of as private in order to make money. One way government officials are able to accommodate these diverse demands without making government smaller is to make it appear to be morphing into a publicly owned business by charging user fees, contracting parts of its services, or adopting the language and practice of the private sector by, for example, calling certain services companies or businesses and using a variety of private-sector internal management techniques.

In the area of application of market concepts to the conduct of public service, the potential impacts are significant. The prevailing American attitude about the nature of public service has been to expect market-like efficiency and business-like operation but in combination with public service values such as accountability, fair and equal treatment, democratic self-governance, social justice, protection of the physical environment, and others. Schachter (1997) pointed out that progressive-era reformers, although striving for a more efficient government, also advocated informing citizens so they could be more active in governing. Today's expansion of economic thinking and the potential separation of expert service provider (public service professional) from customer (citizen) may be one of the most serious threats to public service values Americans have experienced.

This leaves contemporary academicians and practitioners with the task of defining preferred normative balances of public and private and of market-like management and public service. We can identify four broad areas in which economic thinking prompts reexamination of substantive assumptions about the public-private relationship and public service. As we do so, we recognize that these assumptions about public institutions are unique understandings that incorporate our history, institutional development, interpersonal interactions, and the surrounding political, social, and economic environment. They are unique because they vary and change by place, time, and human action; their "structural properties" exist as "practices and memory traces orienting the conduct of knowledgeable human agents" (Giddens, 1984, p. 17) rather than as fixed and fully understood phenomena. Taken together, the narrative of these four areas outlines a framework for discourse about the nature of the American public sector and public service. This framework cannot provide clear normative answers to the challenge of the economistic environment, but it can point toward ways of preserving a public-regarding essence of citizenship and public service while responding constructively to the contemporary economic-political environment.

Services the public sector should provide. In every community, region, state, and at the national level, there are at a given time services that a majority of citizens believe should be provided by the public. This belief may not be based on extensive knowledge and could change if people were to have more information (this is the problem of improving the quality of public judgment; see Yankelovich, 1991), but it is possible to identify attitudes about what services should be public. There are likely a range of reasons that people would give for wanting to have certain services provided by the public sector rather than by the private sector or not at all, but there may be a primary characteristic of public services that most Americans would agree forms a sound decision rule for determining what is public and what is private.

We may hypothesize that, asked to consider a particular service that they think should be publicly provided, people would generally agree that they want certainty that the public has the ability to maintain or change the service in keeping with what the majority thinks to be in the public interest (however defined; in this case, it can be assumed to be the long-term interests of the greatest number, when the public is provided adequate information to make a determination). The standard example of national defense is one on which strong majority agreement can be found and other examples would draw varying responses according to place, time, and the sampled population.

The decision rule of ability to maintain or change a service in accord with a majority view of the public interest is different from the market-driven service rule that uses individual preferences as the basis for governmental response. It focuses not only on efficiency or businesslike operation but also on citizen beliefs about the public interest, the good community, whatever it is that citizens think is best for themselves and others, acting collectively. How to inform and involve citizens in making such decisions may be unclear, but it is clear that this is a decision milieu driven by different values than those of the market. It is also a process that includes collective public deliberation and assistance from public-service professionals.

Services the public sector should produce. Within the category of services that people believe should be provided by the public, there are services involving discretion and accountability such that the public is uncomfortable with an arm's length contractual relationship and the possibility of the profit motive rather than public interest determining outcomes. Examples could include police patrol and crime investigation, protective services for children, land-use regulation, and some human resources functions.

These services can be contrasted with a range of things that do not involve the same level of discretion and accountability and are good candidates to be contracted out or fully privatized for reasons of cost efficiency, purchase of specialized expertise that would cost too much to maintain on staff, or greater flexibility in staffing levels. Examples could include operating a police impoundment facility for seized vehicles, conducting psychological evaluations of defendants awaiting trial, and constructing valid test instruments for jobs that draw large numbers of applicants.

Democratic governance. There are processes of governance that most Americans expect will be maintained as purely public, rather than being contracted, privatized, or operated by public employees in a closed, unilateral, market-like manner. Though people like good customer service when they need to pay their water bill or have a street repaired, they want to know that they have the option, whether exercised or not, to take part in determining policy and assessing implementation. This goes beyond Osborne and Gaebler's idea of steering rather than rowing, as the issue is not just what government does (steering, or making decisions, versus rowing, or carrying them out) but who has the right and ability to make policy and implementation decisions. This is at the heart of citizenship and self-governance.

Thus, although most would agree that government should use efficient business methods in technical, operational areas, this does not mean that business principles of efficiency, scientific management, or closed and centralized decision making should dominate the creation or evaluation of public policy, or exclude citizens from self-governance. To accept a broader view of governance is to assert that government is not ultimately guided by a market model of competition and efficiency but by a citizenship model of governance. This broader view places businesslike management techniques in an instrumental position subordinate to the larger sphere of governance. It draws citizens, elected officials, and public service professionals together in the joint project of creating and implementing public policy.

The role of the practitioner. It might be assumed, in the manner of the old politics-administration dichotomy or the current policy-management split of the market metaphor, that public-service practitioners should not play an active part in shaping issues, debates, and decisions on the questions of what is public or private or whether public policy and services should be approached using the market or the citizenship models. However, there is little doubt today that practitioners are an important part of policy formulation and implementation, providing information needed by citizens and elected officials to frame policy decisions and generating proposals that often form the basis for public action.

Thus, practitioners fill multiple roles in addition to the traditional bureaucratic role, serving as expert advisors and as facilitators of citizen discourse. The open question is how this is to be done in a society that expects nonelected public servants to maintain a position clearly subordinate to elected officials and citizens. This question involves issues of legitimacy and leadership. Is it possible to be an important actor in the creation and implementation of public policy without straying outside the legislative mandate or becoming dominating, self-serving, and causing restriction of public access and freedom to act?

Public practitioners are, because of proximity and knowledge, deeply involved in the broad issue of the extent to which the market metaphor should guide public governance. They exercise influence in discussions about what services should be public, how they should be operated, and whether the public practitioner serves customers or citizens. Though there will always be concern about the legitimacy of this role, many practitioners are in a position to shape the public sector by offering their knowledge to peers, citizens, and elected representatives trying to meet the challenge of governing in an economics-driven political culture. In doing so, they can serve the interests of public service and democratic will formation by keeping in mind the shifting and dynamic nature of the relationship of the market to the public sector and the importance of their actions in shaping the future.

References

Adams, G. B., Bowerman, P. V., Dolbeare, K. M., & Stivers, C. (1990). Joining purpose to practice: A democratic identity for the public service. In H. D. Kass & B. L. Catron (Eds.), *Images and identities in public administration* (pp. 219–240). Newbury Park, CA: Sage.

Anderson, T. T., & Crawford, R. G. (1998). Unsettling the metaphysics of neo-classical microeconomic and management thinking. *International Journal of Public Administration, 21,* 645–690.

Arnold, P. E. (1995). Reform's changing role. *Public Administration Review, 55,* 407–417.

Barber, B. R. (1984). *Strong democracy: Participatory politics for a new age.* Berkeley: University of California Press.

Barber, B. R. (1998). *A place for us: How to make society civil and democracy strong.* New York: Farrar, Straus, and Giroux.

Barrett, K., & Greene, R. (1998, March). Customer disorientation. *Governing, 11,* 62.

Bellah, R. N., Madsen, R., Sullivan, W. M., Swidler, A., & Tipton, S. M. (1985). *Habits of the heart: Individualism and commitment in American life.* New York: Harper & Row.

Bellone, C. J., & Goerl, G. F. (1993). In defense of civic-regarding entrepreneurship or helping wolves to promote good citizenship. *Public Administration Review, 53,* 396–398.

Bowles, S., & Gintis, H. (1986). *Democracy and capitalism: Property, community, and the contradictions of modern social thought.* New York: Basic Books.

Box, R. C. (1998). *Citizen governance: Leading American communities into the 21st century.* Thousand Oaks, CA: Sage.

Campbell, J. (1996). *Understanding John Dewey: Nature and cooperative intelligence.* Chicago: Open Court Publishing.

Cheung, A. B. L. (1997). The rise of privatization policies: Similar faces, diverse motives. *International Journal of Public Administration, 20,* 2213–2245.

Cohn, D. (1997). Creating crises and avoiding blame: The politics of public service reform and the new public management in Great Britain and the United States. *Administration and Society, 29,* 584–616.

Cope, G. H. (1997). Bureaucratic reform and issues of political responsiveness. *Journal of Public Administration Research and Theory, 7,* 461–471.

Downs, A. (1957). *An economic theory of democracy.* New York: Harper & Row.

Dryzek, J. S. (1996). *Democracy in capitalist times: Ideals, limits, and struggles.* Oxford, UK: Oxford University Press.

Eberly, D. E. (1994). *Building a community of citizens: Civil society in the 21st century.* New York: University Press of America.

Eisenhardt, K. M. (1989). Agency theory: An assessment and review. *Academy of Management Review, 14,* 57–74.

Fox, C. J., & Miller, H. T. (1995). *Postmodern public administration: Toward discourse.* Thousand Oaks, CA: Sage.

Gerth, H. H., & Mills, C. W. (1958). *From Max Weber: Essays in sociology.* New York: Oxford University Press.

Giddens, A. (1984). *The constitution of society: Outline of the theory of structuration.* Berkeley: University of California Press.

Golembiewski, R. T. (1977). A critique of "democratic administration" and its supporting ideation. *American Political Science Review, 71,* 1488–1507.

Hood, C. (1996). Beyond "progressivism": A new "global paradigm" in public management? *International Journal of Public Administration, 19,* 151–177.

Hummel, R., & Stivers, C. (1998). Government isn't us: The possibility of democratic knowledge in representative government. In C. K. King & C. Stivers (Eds.), *Government is us: Public administration in an anti-government era* (pp. 28–48). Thousand Oaks, CA: Sage.

Jennings, E. T., Jr. (1991). Public choice and the privatization of government: Implications for public administration. In J. S. Ott, A. C. Hyde, & J. M. Shafritz (Eds.), *Public management: The essential readings* (pp. 113–129). Chicago; Nelson-Hall.

Johnson, D. B. (1991). *Public choice: An introduction to the new political economy.* Mountain View, CA: Mayfield.

Kamensky, J. M. (1996). Role of the "reinventing government" movement in federal management reform. *Public Administration Review, 56,* 247–255.

Kaplan, R. D. (1997, December). Was democracy just a moment? *Atlantic Monthly, 280,* 55–80.

Kass, H. D., & Catron, B. L. (1990). *Images and identities in public administration.* Newbury Park, CA: Sage.

Kelly, R. M. (1998). An inclusive democratic polity, representative bureaucracies, and the new public management. *Public Administration Review, 58,* 201–208.

Kettl, D. F. (1997). The global revolution in public management: Driving themes, missing links. *Journal of Policy Analysis and Management, 16,* 446–462.

King, C. S., & Stivers, C. (1998a). *Government is us: Public administration in an anti-government era.* Thousand Oaks, CA: Sage.

King, C. S., & Stivers, C. (1998b). Introduction: The anti-government era. In C. S. King & C. Stivers (Eds.), *Government is us: Public administration in an anti-government era* (pp. 3–18). Thousand Oaks, CA: Sage.

Lan, Z., & Rosenbloom, D. H. (1992). Public administration in transition? *Public Administration Review, 52,* 535–537.

Lasch, C. (1996). *The revolt of the elites and the betrayal of democracy.* New York: Norton.

Lynn, L. E., Jr. (1998). The new public management: How to transform a theme into a legacy. *Public Administration Review, 58,* 231–237.

Lyons, W. E., & Lowery, D. (1989). Governmental fragmentation versus consolidation: Five public-choice myths about how to create informed, involved, and happy citizens. *Public Administration Review, 49,* 533–543.

March, J. G. (1992). The war is over, the victors have lost. *Journal of Public Administration Research and Theory, 2,* 225–231.

McSwite, O. C. (1997). *Legitimacy in public administration: A discourse analysis.* Thousand Oaks, CA: Sage.

Mikesell, J. A. (1995). *Fiscal administration: Analysis and applications for the public sector* (4th ed.). Belmont, CA: Wadsworth.

Moe, T.M. (1984). The new economics of organization. *American Journal of Political Science, 28,* 739–777.

Niskanen, W. A. (1971). *Bureaucracy and representative government.* Chicago: Aldine Atherton.

Niskanen, W. A. (1991). A reflection on bureaucracy and representative government. In A. Blais & S. Dion (Eds.), *The budget-maximizing bureaucrat: Appraisals and evidence* (pp. 13–31). Pittsburgh, PA: University of Pittsburgh Press.

Olson, M. (1965). *The logic of collective action.* Cambridge, MA: Harvard University Press.

Osborne, D., & Gaebler, T. (1993). *Reinventing government: How the entrepreneurial spirit is transforming the public sector.* New York: Penguin.

Ostrom, V. (1977). Some problems in doing political theory: A response to Golembiewski's "critique." *American Political Science Review, 71,* 1508–1525.

Ostrom, V. (1991). *The intellectual crisis in American public administration.* Tuscaloosa: University of Alabama Press. (Original work published 1973).

Ostrom, V. (1994). *The meaning of American federalism: Constituting a self-governing society.* San Francisco: ICS. (Original work published 1991).

Peters, B. G., & Pierre, J. (1998). Governance without government? Rethinking public administration. *Journal of Public Administration Research and Theory, 8,* 223–243.

Phares, D. (1989). Bigger is better, or is it smaller? *Urban Affairs Quarterly, 25,* 5–17.

Public Administration Review. (1993). Forum on public administration and the Constitution. *Public Administration Review, 53,* 237–267.

Ramos, A. G. (1984). *The new science of organizations: A reconceptualization of the wealth of nations.* Toronto, Canada: University of Toronto Press. (Original work published 1981).

Ross, B. H., & Levine, M. A. (1996). *Urban politics: Power in metropolitan America* (5th ed.). Itasca, IL: F. E. Peacock.

Savas, E. S. (1987). *Privatization: The key to better government.* Chatham, NJ: Chatham House.

Schachter, H. L. (1997). *Reinventing government or reinventing ourselves: The role of citizen owners in making a better government.* Albany: State University of New York Press.

Schmidtz, D. (1991). *The limits of government: An essay on the public goods argument.* Boulder, CO: Westview.

Scott, W. G., & Hart, D. K. (1979). *Organizational America.* Boston: Houghton Mifflin.

Simon, H. A. (1997). *Administrative behavior: A study of decision-making processes in administrative organizations* (4th ed.). New York: Free Press. (Original work published 1945).

Skowronek, S. (1982). *Building a new American state: The expansion of national administrative capacities, 1877–1920.* Cambridge, UK: Cambridge University Press.

Stillman, R. J. II (1991). *Preface to public administration: A search for themes and direction.* New York: St. Martin's.

Terry, L. D. (1993). Why we should abandon the misconceived quest to reconcile public entrepreneurship with democracy. *Public Administration Review, 53,* 393–395.

Terry, L. D. (1998). Administrative leadership, neo-managerialism, and the public management movement. *Public Administration Review, 58,* 194–200.

Timney, M. M. (1998). Overcoming administrative barriers to citizen participation: Citizens as partners, not adversaries. In C. S. King & C. Stivers (Eds.), *Government is us: Public administration in an anti-government era* (pp. 88–101). Thousand Oaks, CA: Sage.

Waldo, D. (1981). *The enterprise of public administration: A summary view.* Novato, CA: Chandler & Sharp.

Walters, J. (1998, February). Did somebody say downsizing? *Governing, 11,* 17–20.

Waterman, R. W., & Meier, K. J. (1998). Principal-agent models: An expansion? *Journal of Public Administration Research and Theory, 8,* 173–202.

Weintraub, J. (1997). Public/private: The limitations of a grand dichotomy. *Responsive Community, 7,* 13–24.

White, L. D. (1954). *The Jacksonians: A study in administrative history, 1829–1861.* New York: Macmillan.

Wood, E. M. (1996). *Democracy against capitalism: Renewing historical materialism.* Cambridge, UK: Cambridge University Press.

Yankelovich, D. (1991). *Coming to public judgment: Making democracy work in a complex world.* Syracuse, NY: Syracuse University Press.

II

The Public Manager as Leader

Until recently, the literature on leadership focused almost exclusively on the exploits of top management. It certainly remains true that decisions involving issues such as resource allocation, technological changes, reorganization and shifts in management philosophy, overall personnel recruitment, promotion, and termination policies are largely determined by an organization's leader or top management team. However, in addition, sooner or later the leadership often finds it advantageous to endorse proposed changes bubbling up from below on these and other matters without surrendering ultimate authority. After all, decentralization—which is often designed to enable middle managers and employees across-the-board to assume greater responsibility—remains an organizational strategy that top management can giveth and sometimes taketh away.

Centralization, Decentralization, and Leadership

Some of the best management consultants and researchers, nonetheless, point to the need today for enhanced flexibility, greater innovation, a faster response time, and more extensive reliance on specialized knowledge found throughout the organization.[a] As one distinguished public administrator has put it,

> A glance at the present world situation makes it clear that the modern state faces as never before the need for rapid and radical adaptation to changed conditions. Governments which cannot make the necessary evolutionary changes will not survive.

---

[a]Peter B. Vaill, *Managing as a Performing Act: New Ideas for a World of Chaotic Change* (San Francisco: Jossey-Bass, 1990). John M. Bryson, *Strategic Planning for Public and Nonprofit Organizations*, 2nd ed. (San Francisco: Jossey-Bass, 1995).

> It becomes necessary, therefore, in the structure of the organization to make more elaborate provision for those agencies of management which concern themselves with the processes of adaptation.[b]

Luther Gulick wrote those words in 1937, even while he also emphasized the need for sufficient coordination and control at the top that would enable public administrators to be responsive to elected democratic leaders.

Because decentralization involves fewer layers of organization and fewer middle managers between top management and those directly engaged in program activity, it has become more popular in both private and public organizations. Furthermore, computerization to some extent has enabled top management to have it both ways. Data can be collected in sufficient quantity (if not always quality) to enable decision makers to preserve more control and monitor progress even while gaining the advantages of decentralization by spreading responsibility throughout the organization.

The age-old dilemmas posed by the decision to centralize or decentralize, however, have not disappeared. As Harold Wilensky put it, "plans are manageable only if we delegate; plans are coordinated in relation to organizational goals only if we centralize."[c] Key decision makers, when opting for decentralization, still are trading off some access to expert information, now lodged further down in the hierarchy. In addition, they sacrifice the power to make more rapid decisions themselves in order to lead more through what Gulick called "coordination of ideas," and what we call today a pervasive sense of mission and core values widely understood within the organization. This strategy entails a willingness to accomplish "more by persuasion than by coercion and discipline."[d]

Centralization, though, will reappear when an IBM or General Electric finds itself compelled by technological change or market shifts to fundamentally alter its business. It will reappear too in the public sector when severe budgetary limitations or marked political shifts compel radical institutional change that extends to the organization's mission, core values, technology, and organizational culture. Middle managers and other employees aspiring to assume leadership responsibility must thus understand the changing nature of the environment (which will normally be translated through the medium of the political environment) and how it will impact on centralization and perhaps on hierarchy. While the degree of centralization may fluctuate over time, the intricacies of implementation will eventually compel the organization to return to its more decentralized form. The leaders further down in the organization can thus pursue their goals successfully if they comprehend the changes above, adapt accordingly, and persevere.

---

[b]Luther Gulick, "Notes on the Theory of Organization," in Luther Gulick and L. Urwick, eds., *Papers on the Science of Administration* (New York: Institute of Public Administration, 1937), pp. 3–45.

[c]Harold L. Wilensky, *Organizational Intelligence: Knowledge and Policy in Government and Industry* (New York: Basic Books, 1967) p. 58.

[d]Brian R. Fry, *Mastering Public Administration* (Chatham, NJ: Chatham House Publishers, 1989) p. 86.

The Manager as Entrepreneur

Until the 1980s, there was relatively little concern about how middle managers, senior staffers, street-level bureaucrats, and other concerned employees might play a leadership role in their organizations. Students of leadership focused on the activities of those at the top. In many respects, the increased interest in leadership at other organizational levels may, in and of itself, reflect the increased extent to which change is being initiated at numerous levels in public and private organizations alike.

Political scientist Eugene Lewis' public entrepreneur is an agency or large program director "who creates or profoundly elaborates a public organization so as to alter greatly the existing pattern of allocation of scarce public resources." Such a leader seeks to reconcile the invariably contradictory values found within the organization, strives to minimize outside interference with technologies (or skills) central to the organization, and seeks to enhance autonomy (or independence) and flexibility in order to achieve the agency's mission.[e] Such persons, Doig and Hargrove have noted, usually possess extraordinary motivation and knowledge of their substantive area, and are particularly sensitive to the political environment.[f] Both books compare and contrast the biographies of agency leaders well-known in the field of public administration.

In her work *The Change Masters*, Rosabeth Moss Kanter was one of the first writers to turn to those "quiet entrepreneurs" who "test limits and create new possibilities for organizational action by pushing and directing the innovation process."[g] She has christened these private sector middle managers and staffers (whose public sector counterparts, such as client-oriented, street-level bureaucrats, are readily apparent) as "change masters." They may be systems builders, loss cutters, socially conscious pioneers, or sensitive readers of cues about the need for strategy shifts. These new entrepreneurs do not start new businesses, but seek instead to improve the bureaucracies where they work. Unlike some entrepreneurs in the traditional sense of the word, they are good builders and users of teams. Finally, and most significantly, while differing in what they want to do, they have something in common in terms of how they must proceed that distinguishes them from others who are bringing about change in their organizations. This difference is "the need to exercise skills in obtaining and using power in order to accomplish innovation."[h] Having an idea for change is not enough. An integral part of gaining acceptance for the idea, quite apart from its substantive

[e]Eugene Lewis, *Public Entrepreneurship: Toward a Theory of Bureaucratic Political Power* (Bloomington: Indiana University Press, 1984), p. 9.

[f]Jameson W. Doig and Erwin C. Hargrove, eds., *Leadership and Innovation: A Biographical Perspective on Entrepreneurs in Government* (Baltimore: Johns Hopkins University Press, 1987).

[g]Rosabeth Moss Kanter, *The Change Masters: Innovation and Entrepreneurship in the American Corporation* (New York: Simon and Schuster, 1983) p. 210.

[h]Kanter, *The Change Masters*, pp. 209–212.

merits, lies in exercising power in order to alter the political environment sufficiently so that the change can be implemented.

The entrepreneurs in the private sector share in common this need to use
power with their counterparts in the public sector, such as Michael Lipsky's street-
level bureaucrats.[1] In short, while these public and private entrepreneurs differ
in the nature and scope of their responsibilities, they all share a commitment to
undertaking what they regard as important changes that pertain to their jurisdiction, a willingness to work through the internal and external political processes relevant to achieving that task, and a readiness to accumulate and exercise that power
necessary to get the job done.

"Getting the job done" is increasingly what public management is all about.
It is perhaps for this reason that quiet entrepreneurship now applies as much to
street-level bureaucrats and middle managers in the public as in the private sector.
Furthermore, in these days of scarce resources and complex tasks, the visible and
voluble CEO entrepreneurs may increasingly need these quiet entrepreneurs as
much as the latter in turn need nurture and support from above.

---

[1] Michael Lipsky, *Street-Level Bureaucracy: Dilemmas of the Individual in Public Services* (New York:
Russell Sage Foundation, 1980).

In recent years, numerous writers have viewed leadership by public managers with deep suspicion. In the eyes of public choice theorists, such managers are shirkers. For their part, those wishing to conserve the bureaucracy's institutional integrity fear that public entrepreneurs will undercut the established mission, institutional integrity, and principles that distinguish a public agency. Constitutionalists in turn caution that public managers must act strictly in accord with the law, and must obey political superiors above them in the hierarchy, Executive Branch, Congress, and the Judiciary.

Robert Behn takes a different tack. Surveying the political environment in the public sector, he concludes that the public manager, or entrepreneur, has an obligation to lead. This obligation follows from basic failures within the American political system. In theory, the system operates in a manner that should require little initiative by the public manager; in reality, our system of governance suffers from serious—not superficial or easily remedied—flaws. Take, for example, the branches of government. While the public manager must obey superiors in the Executive Branch, the case is less clearcut when the order is questionable or, more frequently, in those cases where the president is occupied elsewhere and thus neglecting the public agency. Then the "fallacy of executive comprehensiveness" may damage the agency if necessary actions are not undertaken. The "fallacy of legislative clarity," sometimes intentionally and sometimes unintentionally, leaves discretion in the hands of agency executives, while "the fallacy of judicial omnipotence" may threaten the agency as judges concerned with individual rights may raise other unexamined consequences for the action. Furthermore, these fallacies stem from normal presidential, congressional, and judicial branch actions; they do not speak to those cases where one branch or another abuses its power. Nor are the ultimate arbiters of the system immune. The "fallacy of civic engagement" means that poorly informed citizens may act inappropriately or ineffectively or, more frequently, may not act at all.

The other failures in the American system of governance identified by Behn refer to how the system functions. People in organizations do not function like robots, automatically obeying orders transmitted layer by layer down the hierarchy. Hence, leadership is necessary to combat "the fallacy of machines." Similarly it is the height of optimism to believe that a program's initial design will not require adjustment and sometimes termination—to think otherwise is to engage in the "fallacy of human prescience." Finally there is the danger of political failure, the danger that interest groups, unaccountable to any governmental overseer, will capture the agency.

Behn concludes that public managers confronted by one or more of these fallacies have little alternative but to lead. They are better informed about their agencies than others, have a greater incentive to fix the problems, and are in a unique position to interact with the political actors responsible for these actions. There may be times, however, when these fallacies are not posing a problem, and public managers can still make a contribution. After all, as Behn observes, "public managers know what goals their organizations can reasonably achieve and what policies their organizations will prove incapable of implementing." Such expertise should be included in a public policy dialogue. But public managers and their agencies may blunder too. There are then, Behn argues, numerous checks and balances to "catch them." In the meantime, public managers must lead.

What Right Do Public Managers Have to Lead?

Robert D. Behn

Leadership is not just a right of public managers.[1] It is an obligation. The American system of governance is certainly not perfect, and, by exercising leadership, public managers can help correct some of the imperfections.

Leadership from public managers is necessary because without leadership public organizations will never mobilize themselves to accomplish their mandated purposes, let alone figure out how best to do that. Leadership from public managers is necessary because the elected chief executive can provide that leadership for only a few of the many agencies and programs for which he or she is responsible. Leadership from public managers is necessary because the legislative branch of government gives public agencies missions that are vague and conflicting and often fails to provide enough resources to pursue seriously all of these missions. Leadership from public managers is necessary because a narrow interest can easily capture a public agency and redirect government programs for its own gain. Leadership from public managers is necessary because the citizenry often lacks the knowledge and information (or will) necessary to perform its responsibilities. Finally, leadership from public managers is necessary because the judiciary, which is charged with overseeing the constitutionality and legality of the activities of public agencies and public managers, often focuses on narrow issues of process rather than the broader concerns of achieving public purposes.

Neither the legislative, the judicial, nor the executive branches of government function perfectly. Nor will they ever do so. That is why the founders created a constitutional system with a network of checks and balances. Public managers can contribute to the working of that system by compensating for some of the failures of the legislature, the judiciary, and their elected chief executive. By leading, public managers can help to improve American governance.

Failures of Governance

Markets do not work perfectly. An economic system with theoretical markets (each possessing all the characteristics of a perfect market) functions wonderfully and produces all sorts of wonderful benefits. But actual markets, lacking one or

---

Robert D. Behn, *Public Administration Review*, Vol. 58, No. 3 (May/June 1998).

[1] For the purposes of this article, I will define a "public manager" in a conventional way: as anyone with managerial responsibility for some unit of government, from the top level political appointee who is a cabinet secretary or department head to the front-line supervisor who oversees half-a-dozen front-line workers. Thus, this public manager has the responsibility for getting his or her organization—and, thus, his or her people—to achieve some public purposes. For a different definition of a public manager, see Behn (1997).

several of these characteristics, function less well and generate fewer benefits for society. Only under unusual circumstances do real markets function exactly as predicted for a theoretical market or produce all the benefits as estimated for a theoretical market.

Moreover, there are many kinds of market failures. If all those participating in a market lack perfect knowledge of, for example, the relative quality of competing products, some sellers will be able to take advantage of buyers. If capital or labor cannot move freely to its most productive uses, producers will be unable to generate all their potential benefits. If one producer can monopolize the production or distribution of a product, it will be able to charge above-market prices denying some consumers the opportunity to purchase the product and shifting benefits from those consumers who do buy it to the producer. The list of potential market failures is long. In response, we, as a society, devise and experiment with a variety of mechanisms to correct such market failures and thus to capture more (if not all) of the benefits that can be obtained from a perfect market economy.

Similarly, governance systems do not work perfectly. Just as it is possible to describe a perfect market system, so it might be possible to conceive of a perfect governance system. When such a system is put into practice, however, the realities of human behavior and the limitations of human judgment will also create failures. For any system of governance to work as the Greeks, the founders, and political theorists suggest and to produce all of its predicted benefits, that system must possess a number of ideal characteristics: The citizenry needs to be informed about the important issues and actively engaged in the policy debate; the legislature needs to give clear instructions to the executive branch; the elected chief executive needs to be effectual in the oversight of all the agencies and programs created by the legislature. The list of such theoretical characteristics of an ideal system of governance is long—and, thus, so are the sources of potential failures of governance. Consequently, we, as a society, respond by devising and experimenting with a variety of mechanisms to correct such governance failures and thus to capture more of the benefits that can be obtained from an ideal system of governance.

Strangely—then, again, perhaps not so strangely, given our fear of bureaucracy (Kaufman, 1981a)—we have not looked to public managers to help correct some of these failures. Instead, we have looked at public managers—or at least the organizations that they manage—as one of the worst (and one of the most inevitable) sources of potential failure of any system of modern governance. Consequently, rather than asking whether and how public managers can help improve our system of governance, we worry only about controlling their ability to further exacerbate the failures.

Yet public managers can help to improve our American system of governance. Specifically, public managers can help correct seven failures of governance: organizational, analytical, executive, legislative, political, civic, and judicial failures. By exercising leadership, public managers can make government more democratic and more effective.

What Leaders Do and Why It Might Be Bad If Public Managers Did All That

Leaders exercise initiative.[2] This immediately raises a problem: Do we really want public managers to take any initiatives? Is not the job of the public manager to implement public policies—policies that our elected officials in the legislative and executive branches have already created? If public managers exercise initiative, are they not usurping the powers that we have—constitutionally—assigned to only those officials whom we elect?

Not really. (Or, at least, not completely.) Elected officials are not the only individuals authorized under our constitutional system to exercise initiative. We anticipate that business leaders, interest-group leaders, religious leaders, community leaders, educational leaders, intellectual leaders—even movie stars and professional athletes—will all exercise initiative, and do so not just within their own organizations but within society as a whole. The Constitution gives these leaders no explicit role, yet both the founders and we expect that these people will take initiatives. Indeed, we believe that they have an obligation to do so. Why should such an opportunity be denied to public managers? Indeed, why should we relieve them of such an obligation? Do not public managers have at least as much knowledge and wisdom as religious, corporate, or educational leaders about the nature of society's problems, the capabilities of governmental and nongovernmental organizations, the character of citizen concerns, and the nature of organizational capabilities? And public mangers certainly have as much concern as leaders from the private and nonprofit sectors for preserving the long-term political legitimacy of public institutions and our system of governance.

But public managers also have more power. We worry about them not because they lack knowledge or wisdom but because they possess it; they can easily convert their knowledge and wisdom into action with not only beneficial but also deleterious consequences. This is why we worry about the managers of the Internal Revenue Service. If these public managers exercise initiative (rather than simply implement the tax laws) they can harm individual citizens—lots of citizens—as well as the citizenry's respect for government as a whole.

As leaders, public managers do a lot of other things. They mobilize resources and motivate people. They make choices and explain decisions. They demonstrate agency competence and educate the citizens. But when we worry about public managers exercising leadership, we worry that they will take initiatives in directions that we—collectively or individually—do not desire.

Of course, there are checks and balances in the system. Indeed, the current system contains numerous mechanisms for balancing the power and checking the

---

[2]The usual concern is not that public managers will exercise initiative but that they will exercise discretion (Reich, 1998, 124–129). For example, Michael Spicer worries that "unchecked administrative discretion is a recipe for administrative tyranny" (1995, 97). I wish, however, to define the issue as more than administrative discretion, for exercising initiative is a more expansive activity than exercising discretion. To exercise discretion, a public manager need only wait for clear choices to present themselves and then act by consciously choosing. To exercise initiative, a public manager needs to go looking for (or even creating) circumstances that provide an opportunity to educate or motivate people, change administrative systems, correct mistakes, check excesses, or even launch new (though authorized) activities.

excesses of public agencies, their managers, and their employees. Within the executive branch, the elected chief executive provides supervision while auditors and inspectors generally provide independent surveillance. Both the legislative and judicial branches have constitutional responsibilities to provide oversight. And outside of government, organized interests, individual citizens, crusading journalists, independent analysts, and a conspiracy of lawyers examine and critique every government agency, pressuring them to change their policies, to improve their services, and to halt ineffective, unauthorized, illegal, or unconstitutional practices.[3]

None of these checks or balances is perfect. None is very efficient. But these checks and balances do work. Sometimes they take too long to work, permitting damage to accumulate before the check takes effect. Occasionally, these checks are wielded by self-interested people and institutions, thus only substituting one error for another. The American system of checks and balances does not eliminate all the failures of governance. Still, for controlling bureaucratic power—for deterring and correcting misguided initiatives by public managers and public agencies—the American system of checks and balances is quite effective.

Indeed, the remarkable effectiveness of the American system for controlling bureaucratic initiatives has created a backlash. The various incarnations of this backlash have been called the "new public management" (Hood, 1991), "civic-regarding entrepreneurship" (Bellone and Goerl, 1992), and the "post-bureaucratic paradigm" (Barzelay, 1992). The most obvious illustrations of the backlash are the book, *Reinventing Government,* by David Osborne and Ted Gaebler (1992) and the National Performance Review created by Vice President Albert Gore, Jr.

Predictably, this backlash has created a backlash of its own. For example, in a critique of "entrepreneurial government," Ronald C. Moe and Robert S. Gilmour (1995) note that "the framers of the Constitution consciously designed a government better suited to frustrate the concentration of political power than to govern effectively." As a result, they created the three branches of government along with the principle of separation of powers. "The purpose of such an unwieldy design was to prevent an over-concentration of power in any one branch," write Moe and Gilmour, "and, most critically, through the separation of governing institutions, to protect the people from the tyrannous exercise of governmental power." The "law-based principles of public administration," argue Moe and Gilmour, "protect the citizenry from an overbearing, arbitrary, and capricious use of government power" (1995, 136, 143).

But who or what uses government power overbearingly, arbitrarily, or capriciously? Any branch of government can. Almost any unit of government can. Almost any individual within government can. But we, as citizens, usually associate the overbearing, arbitrary, and capricious use of government power with executive-branch agencies—with government bureaucracies. Yet there is a difference between the excessive use of power by government bureaucrats and excessive initiative by public managers. Indeed, they may even be opposites. The easiest way for government bureaucracies to exercise power—which means the easiest way for a

---

[3] Herbert Kaufman devotes a quarter of his study of federal bureau chiefs to "The Confines of Leadership"—the various checks, balances, and other constraints that limit the ability of these public managers "to make things happen" (1981b, 91).

government bureaucrat to exercise power—is to simply follow the bureaucratic rules. By strictly obeying the rulebook, government bureaucrats can both exercise power and insulate themselves from legal retribution. They may be accused of being stupid or silly, arbitrary or narrow-minded, petty or perhaps even immoral, but they cannot be accused of acting illegally. The wonderful source of bureaucratic power lies in the bureaucrat's ability to refuse to exercise initiative, to hide cleverly behind some rule while, in fact, subtly exercising initiative by cleverly selecting a rule to achieve their own purposes (perhaps merely to protect their own power).

In contrast, as a leader, a public manager takes initiatives publicly. There is no hiding behind some law or regulation created by someone else. The initiatives of leadership are available for all to see—and for all to check and balance. While bureaucrats can exercise initiative by claiming they have no ability to exercise it, leaders exercise initiative by articulating and clarifying purposes; by setting and pursuing performance targets; by educating, persuading, and motivating people; by choosing among alternatives; and by experimenting with strategies and tactics. It is all very public. And it is all very personal. As a leader, a public manager (or a team of public managers) takes initiatives that are quite transparent. If citizens, stakeholders, journalists, legislators, or other public managers are unhappy with such initiatives, they will not only know about them; they will also have many opportunities to counter them. The American system of checks and balances offers those who oppose the specific leadership initiatives of specific public managers a variety of tools for frustrating these initiatives.

Do the failures of American governance warrant the drastic, unconventional, untraditional act of permitting—indeed, encouraging—public managers to be leaders? The seven failures may be unfortunate, even bad. But what about the remedy? Will authorizing public managers to take initiative produce more—rather than less—failure in governance? Does correcting these seven failures of American governance really require public managers to be leaders? Are there not some other ways to fix these problems? Perhaps. The answers require an analysis of the seven failures of American governance.

Organizational Failure

One of the most obvious failures in our system of governance lies in the behavior of large public agencies. These organizations do not function in the way that they are instructed to function nor do they produce the results they are expected to produce. Indeed, the implicit, operating assumption that public agencies can directly, simply, even mechanistically implement public policies contains a number of flaws.

The first flaw is found in the machine metaphor of human organizations. If organizations could, as suggested by Frederick Winslow Taylor and other advocates of scientific management, function as machines (with people as interchangeable parts), then public (and private) managers would not have to exercise internal leadership. But human organizations do not behave as machines. Without leadership, public agencies can quickly switch from seeking to achieve their authorized public purpose to pursuing organizational survival.

And even if an agency's top managers are exercising leadership, front-line workers—or, as Michael Lipsky called them, "street-level bureaucrats" (1980)— exercise a lot of discretion in carrying out their daily activities and their agency's mandate. Without leadership, the people in any public agency—indeed, in any organization—can quickly focus on preserving their institutional niche and maximizing their personal convenience.

These organizational failures reoccur throughout government at all levels[4] because we fail to recognize *the fallacy of organizational machines.* When we write authorizing legislation for public agencies, when we issue executive orders for agencies to implement, when we create personnel systems, indeed, whenever we tell agencies to do something or create administrative systems for them to use, we assume that these organizations will behave as machines. Then we are shocked, shocked to discover that the people in these human organizations behave not as machines but as people.

Thus, public managers have to lead. They need to articulate their organization's purpose and motivate people to achieve it. They have to keep their agency focused on pursuing its mission. They need to encourage people to develop new systems for pursuing that mission. Markets don't work perfectly. Neither do organizations. Without some kind of conscious, active intervention—without leadership—public agencies (like private and nonprofit organizations) will fail to achieve their purposes. The people best situated, best equipped to exercise this leadership are the managers of the agency.

John Kotter (1990) argues that in business there is a difference between management and leadership. Both involve three key activities: "(1) deciding what needs to be done, (2) creating networks of people and relationships that can accomplish an agenda, and (3) then trying to ensure that those people actually do the job." Yet, continues Kotter, managers and leaders accomplish "these three tasks in different ways" (1990, 4).

Managers, writes Kotter, carry out these tasks by (1) "planning and budgeting," (2) "organizing and staffing," and (3) "controlling and problem solving" (1990, 4). Kotter's memory is a little fuzzy. Somehow he inserted controlling and problem solving for directing, coordinating, and reporting.[5] Nevertheless, Kotter's description of what managers do is very much in the spirit of Luther Gulick's POSDCORB: planning, organizing, staffing, directing, coordinating, reporting, and budgeting (1937, 12).

In contrast, says Kotter, leaders perform these tasks by (1) "setting a direction," (2) "aligning people," and (3) "motivating and inspiring." Rather than produce detailed plans, leaders create a vision for their organization and strategies for achieving that vision. Rather than "create human systems that can implement plans as precisely and efficiently as possible," argues Kotter, leaders try "to get

---

[4]These organizational failures are not limited to government. They plague private and nonprofit organizations as well. This is why these organizations also need leadership.

[5]Actually, although the words "controlling and problem solving" are not the same as directing, coordinating and reporting, Kotter's point is. For by "controlling and problem solving," he means: "monitoring results versus the plan in some detail, both formally and informally, by means of reports, meetings, and other tools; identifying deviations; and then planning and organizing to solve the problems" (1990, 4)

people to comprehend a vision of an alternative future," which is "more of a communications challenge than a design problem." Lastly, Kotter contrasts the manager's "control mechanisms [that] compare system behavior with the plan and take action when a deviation is detected," with the leader's efforts "to generate highly energized behavior" (1990, 4, 5, 7).

Indeed, the leadership approach to Kotter's third task of "trying to ensure that those people actually do the job" best distinguishes leaders from managers. To leaders, the key is motivation and inspiration:

> Motivation and inspiration energize people, not by pushing them in the right direction as control mechanisms do but by satisfying basic human needs for achievement, a sense of belonging, recognition, self-esteem, a feeling of control over one's life, and the ability to live up to one's ideals (Kotter, 1990, 7).

To a manager or administrator, however, motivation is unnecessary and inspiration silly:

> For some of the same reasons that control is so central to management, highly motivated or inspired behavior is almost irrelevant. Managerial processes must be as close as possible to fail-safe and risk-free. That means they cannot be dependent on the unusual or hard to obtain. The whole purpose of systems and structures is to help normal people who behave in normal ways to complete routine jobs successfully, day after day (Kotter, 1990, 7).

The task of the manager is to make the human machine run smoothly and on time.

If human organizations are machines, they don't need motivation, and they don't need inspiration, and they don't need leadership. But if human organizations are composed of real humans—not a cloned collection of "normal" interchangeable people but diverse individuals with different competencies—then getting such people within these organizations to actually do their jobs requires motivation and inspiration.[6] It requires leadership.[7]

---

[6] Kaufman reports that one of the four basic activities of bureau chiefs in the federal government is "motivating their work forces" (1981b, 17).

[7] Noting that "the market paradigm [for public administration] assumes agencies and their management be responsive to the same types of incentives as the private sector," Moe goes on to argue that the public and private sectors are different and "federal activities do not lend themselves to the competitive market model" (1993, 48). Public and private organizations do possess some very important differences—particularly concerning the nature of their external environment and accountability mechanisms. Thus, the strategies employed for external management may need to be quite different.

Nevertheless, the people who work in government and the people who work in business are all people. Consequently, effective strategies for internal management may be quite similar in both sectors. Private-sector mangers, who often are able to deploy monetary incentives, nevertheless must, reports Kotter, motivate people "by satisfying basic human needs for achievement, a sense of belonging, recognition, self-esteem, a feeling of control over one's life, and the ability to live up to one's ideals" (1990, 7). Cannot public managers learn from this perspective? Ought not public-sector managers, who usually can offer no monetary incentives, also seek to motivate their employees with similar efforts to satisfy these basic human needs?

Woodrow Wilson (1887) argued that we ought "not to be frightened at the idea of looking into foreign systems of administration for instruction and suggestion." He emphasized that we could "study the administrative systems of France and Germany knowing that we are not in search of political principles." Indeed, Wilson was quite willing to adapt administrative practices from much less democratic nations:

> If I see a murderous fellow sharpening a knife cleverly, I can borrow his way of sharpening the knife without borrowing his probable intention to commit murder with it; and so, if I see a monarchist dyed in the wool managing a public bureau well, I can learn his business methods without changing one of my republican spots. (1887, 218, 220, italics in the original)

Certainly contemporary businesses have as much to teach us about the internal management of public agencies as European monarchies had to teach Wilson about "business methods."

Our system of governance frequently fails because we assume that organizations are machines—because we find it easy and convenient (even if we really know better) to base our design of programs and agencies on the fallacy of organizational machines. Yet no matter how much treating organizations as machines facilitates the task of crafting legislation, designing systems, and promulgating regulations, human organizations are not machines. If public agencies are to accomplish the purposes that they have been assigned—if the people who work within those agencies are to pursue those purposes with diligence, intelligence, and energy—they need leadership. By exercising leadership, by motivating and inspiring people, public managers can help to correct organizational failure in our system of governance.

Analytical Failure

It is often argued that if we could get people to pay attention to questions of organization and implementation from the beginning—when they first start to design a public program, organize a public agency, or create an administrative system—then, though the implementation problem might not disappear, it would certainly be mitigated (Cook, 1996, 162–166; Derthick, 1990, 215–216, 220–221, 224; Moe, 1993, 48, 60; Moe, 1994, 119; Moe and Gilmour, 1995, 143). If we would just take into account all that we know about human behavior in organizations, goes this argument, we would create policies that work—programs that can be easily implemented. But this suggestion is derived from the assumption that it is intellectually possible to design the ideal system—or, at least, a very good system—*de novo*.

Designing an effective implementation system from the beginning is difficult. It may be possible to get a good, general framework. But getting the details right is almost impossible. Even employing an innovation that has already proven effective elsewhere requires modification. As Paul Berman and Beryl Nelson (1997) argue, "no adaptation, no success." Berman and Nelson describe "the three-or-more-year period that it takes for a program to be adapted to the organization and for the organization to be adapted to the program" and argue that "to produce the desired outcomes, funders must allow replicators the flexibility to adapt the model during implementation" (1997, 320, 330). From a study of the Social Security Administration, Martha Derthick concludes: "Major policy change can never be expected to work smoothly from the start. Implementation must be to a considerable extent incremental, experimental, and adaptive" (1990, 211).

This adaptation requires what I have called "management by groping along" (Behn, 1988; Behn, 1991, ch. 7; Golden, 1990). The agency begins knowing what it wants to accomplish but not knowing exactly how it can get there. So, it gropes—though it gropes purposefully with a clear objective. It tries a variety of strategies and tactics, discovers what works and what does not, cancels its failures, and builds on its successes with new modifications. The strategy of groping along is derived from the observation that you can never get it right the first time. Thus, from the beginning, this strategy consciously builds in flexibility—the capacity to make modifications in structures and systems as the organization learns.

But this process of groping and adaptation is neither natural nor automatic. It requires people to accept that they are not brilliant—that they cannot predict perfectly how organizations will behave, how people will react to the incentives created by different systems, or even how citizens will respond. To undertake this process of groping and adaptation, people must recognize *the fallacy of human prescience*. Indeed, our inherent human, analytical inadequacies make it impossible to design a public program and its implementation system perfectly from the very beginning (Lindblom, 1959; Simon, 1957, ch. 5).

This process of groping and adaptation requires leadership. For unless the groping and adaptation are to be completely random (and thus any positive outcome purely fortuitous), they need conscious guidance. Someone or some team needs to orchestrate the experimentation, learning, and adaptation from which better organizational and institutional arrangements will evolve. Someone or some team needs to organize the process of encouraging experimentation, collecting data, analyzing results, creating forums to explain successes and failures, suggesting modifications, and keeping people focused on the real purpose behind the program and all the groping and adaptation. The people best situated to do all this—to exercise the necessary leadership—are the agency's managers.

Executive Failure

Okay. So public managers should be the internal leaders of their agencies. That just means that they should exercise a neutral competence that is intelligent rather than mindless. Frederick Winslow Taylor is dead; nobody really believes that human organizations are like machines. Nobody really thinks that once the boxes are drawn on the organization chart and the job descriptions written, the agency will run smoothly. Nobody thinks that you could just give orders; they don't even do that in the military anymore. Everyone accepts that to get an organization to accomplish any purpose, you have to motivate people. Everyone knows that different political environments and different organizational cultures require the adaptation of program specifics to the particularities of each situation. Still, when the elected chief executive gives an order, the public manager ought to salute. As Moe argues: "It is the constitutional responsibility of the President and his duly appointed and approved subordinates to see that these laws [enacted by Congress], wise and unwise, are implemented" (1994, 112).

Lord Vansittart summed up this ideal as it applied to the British civil service: "The soul of our service is the loyalty with which we execute ordained error" (Denhardt 1993, 252). Indeed, the British are famous for faithfully executing an obvious error. Alfred, Lord Tennyson's "Charge of the Light Brigade" was written to "honor" such behavior:

> Cannon to right of them,
> Cannon to left of them,
> Cannon in front of them,
> . . . .
> Into the jaws of death,
> Into the mouth of hell,
> Rode the six hundred.

And even though, as Tennyson confesses, "some one had blundered" and "the soldier knew," the job of the cavalry was clear:

> Theirs not to make reply,
> Theirs not to reason why,
> Theirs but to do and die.

Today, of course, the charge of the Light Brigade is viewed not as heroic but stupid—a perfect example of the British willingness to loyally execute ordained blunder.[8] Colin Powell would never have ordered the Light Brigade to charge: "600 cavalry? I need 6,000. No, 60,000." Hell, Colin Powell wouldn't have even fought the Crimean War: "1,500 miles away? Poor lines of supply? On their home turf? Against all those damn Cossacks? This isn't some schoolboy game on the playing fields of Eton. This isn't an opportunity to display our dashing heroism. It isn't how you play the game, but whether you win. A tie is worse than kissing your sister. We don't fight unless we know we can win!"[9] The American public servant is not enthusiastic about executing ordained error, even if it promises the opportunity to emerge a hero.

Of course, for the manager of a contemporary public agency, the challenge of execution is less ordained error than ordained ambiguity or ordained contradictions. On some issues, for some agencies, the elected chief executive will provide clear direction. If a major crisis emerges, or if a policy area is on the elected executive's personal agenda, then the chief is willing and able to issue specific directives. But most of the time for most public agencies, the elected chief executive practices benign neglect. At the biennial Seminar for New Governors, the senior governors tell their new colleagues: "Limit Your Agenda" (Beyle and Hueffner, 1983, 268; Behn, 1990, 15; Behn 1993, 36-37). And the best ones do: they focus on a few priorities and ignore the rest of state government. So unless a public manager heads an agency that is perpetually on the public's agenda, one that is subject to repeated crises, or one that is doing something in which the elected chief executive is personally interested, that public manager will receive few clear ordinations—either wise or unwise.

Indeed, most of the directives that public managers receive from their elected chief will be either ambiguous or contradictory. When Ellen Schall was sworn in as the head of New York City's Department of Juvenile Justice, Mayor Edward I. Koch gave her his instructions: "Don't let them out. Do as much for them as you can" (Varley, 1987, 4). That was it: just two sentences—simultaneously both ambiguous and contradictory. Never again in the seven years that Schall was the commissioner of the Department of Juvenile Justice did Koch give her explicit directions or even a policy suggestion. Schall had no choice; if her agency was to accomplish anything, she had to lead.

Moe and Gilmour (1995) advocate "the accountable executive model of organization" with "clear lines of authority and accountability." Indeed, they argue that "political accountability necessarily assumes legally based hierarchical reporting structures." For example, for the federal government, "the president is the chief executive officer of the executive branch and Commander-in-Chief of the armed forces and as such is responsible for the execution of the laws" (1995, 141, 140, 139).

---

[8] We should not be too tough on the English. After all, Pickett's charge wasn't that brilliant either.

[9] For a summary of the "Powell Doctrine," see Powell (1992/93).

But behind Moe and Gilmour's "hierarchical concept of the accountable executive" with its "vertical lines of accountability to the president" (1995, 137) lies the implicit assumption that the elected chief executive—be that the president, the governor, or the mayor—is actively engaged in the task of ensuring that *all* the laws are faithfully executed. Indeed, Moe summarizes several "organizational management studies" of the federal government as concluding: "For laws to be implemented, authority and accountability had to be centralized in the President" (1994, 112). This statement reveals *the fallacy of executive comprehensiveness.* We might all like to think that the chief elected executive is omnipresent and omnipotent—actively engaged in using the *full* authority of the executive to ensure the faithful execution of *all* the laws. Realistically, however, we know that no elected chief executive can.[10]

Indeed, even if elected executives possessed the human capacities necessary to actively oversee implementation of all the laws, political incentives encourage them to be focused rather than comprehensive. Maybe the elected chief executive should be responsible for the execution of all the laws. For the execution of most of the laws, however, most of the elected executives could hardly care.

With the possible exception of those agencies for which the elected chief executive has a personal concern for the implementation of the laws, the intelligent chief executive wants the agencies' managers to lead—to take initiative. If all the top public managers conclude that they need to check all decisions and initiatives with their elected chief, he or she will soon be inundated with memos, phone calls, and e-mails seeking approval or specific guidance. The elected executive needs to set the overall policy agenda that establishes the administration's macropurposes. But to accomplish these broad purposes, the elected chief executive needs public managers who will exercise real leadership.[11]

---

[10] Moe and Gilmour (1995) do note that "it is neither possible not desirable for the president to be involved in all executive actions taken in his name." Nevertheless, "it is possible," they continue, "to ensure that the president's institutional interests in an integrated executive branch are protected." Perhaps. But protecting the president's interests is not the same as ensuring that all the managers of all the federal agencies faithfully execute all the laws.

[11] Moe regrets that "recent presidents have chosen to shun their management responsibilities" (1994, 118), while he and Gilmour deplore "the long-term retreat of presidents from their organizational management responsibilities" (1995, 137). In particular, they are concerned about the president's responsibility for the "diligent execution of central management laws" concerning finances, personnel, procurement, and administrative procedures (1995, 139). And, they imply (or at least permit the reader to infer) that executing these "general management laws" that are designed to ensure governmental fairness is much more important than executing the substantive laws designed to achieve other public purposes such as to promote health or safety. Certainly there exists a tradeoff. An agency can implement the letter of the general management laws and, in the process, completely ignore the spirit of its authorizing legislation. Often, for public agencies, this is quite logical behavior. By violating a general management law, particularly by violating a general management law in such a way as to create the impression that it has also been unfair, a public agency exposes itself to public scrutiny and intense criticism.

Once there are two laws—once there are two public purposes to be achieved—there is always the potential for conflict. Someone must choose. The legislature has refused to do so. And public managers cannot go running to the judiciary or the elected chief executive every time they need to make such a tradeoff. So what options remain? The public manager can decide to favor the prescription of the general management law over the purpose of the substantive law. The public manager can turn this decision over to the agency's legal counsel (which would, inevitably, produce the same result). Or the public manager can lead.

I prefer leadership. I prefer the public manager who recognizes the inherent conflicts among the agency's formal mandate (as specified in its authorizing legislation) and its need to be fair (as outlined by the general management laws). I prefer a public manager who wrestles with such conflicts, educates others about the nature of these tradeoffs, seeks advice from multiple sources (from within the agency, from the legislature, from the elected chief, and from citizens and stakeholders, and occasionally an attorney) makes a judicious choice that balances multiple interests, explains that choice to anyone who will listen, and attempts to get it implemented through formal systems and effective persuasion.

Legislative Failure

In their critique of entrepreneurial government, Moe and Gilmour (1995) offer ten different "principles which have been historically fundamental to the administration of the federal government"—"axiomatic 'givens' in American public administration." Their first such principle is: "The purpose of agency management is to implement the laws passed by Congress as elected representatives of the people." This axiom would seem to obviate leadership by public managers. "The missions and priorities of agencies," emphasize Moe and Gilmour, "are determined by law, not by the president or by the department heads, either collectively or separately" (1995, 138).

Yet, just as elected chief executives rarely give clear instructions to their agency managers, so legislatures can also give directions that are ambiguous and contradictory—and often unrealistic too. Laws rarely determine clear missions or priorities for public agencies. Rather, an agency's authorizing legislation usually charges it with achieving multiple—and, often, conflicting—missions, while the agency's annual budget rarely provides the resources necessary to pursue more than a few of these purposes. This is *the fallacy of legislative clarity*. For example, in 1997, the United States Commission on Immigration Reform concluded that "Some of the agencies that implement the immigration laws, the I.N.S. [Immigration and Naturalization Service] in particular, have so many priorities that they have proved unable to manage all of them effectively" (Schmitt, 1997, A15). In fact, sometimes the legislature gives public managers instructions that are incoherent or bewildering. Supreme Court Justice Harry A. Blackmun once reported that a member of Congress told him "that legislators purposely insert 'unintelligible language' in statutes and let the court 'tell us what we mean'" (Barbash and Kamen, 1984, A42).

Morris Fiorina (1997) has argued that the members of Congress themselves benefit from writing ambiguous legislation that requires an agency to "translate a vague policy mandate into a functioning program." For when individual citizens or stakeholder organizations complain to a member about how this vague legislative mandate is being implemented, "the congressman lends a sympathetic ear, piously denounces the evils of bureaucracy, intervenes in the latter's decisions, and rides a grateful electorate to ever more impressive electoral showings." Thus, by enacting ambiguous laws, the members of Congress create a "bureaucracy [that] serves as a convenient lightning rod for public frustration and a convenient whipping boy for congressmen" (1977, 48–49).

Larry Terry reports that "the National Park Service is mandated to pursue two seemingly contradictory policy objectives: (a) to promote public use of the parks, and (b) to preserve the parks" (1995, 98). Indeed, many public agencies are charged with promoting or helping one interest while preserving or protecting another. This was Mayor Koch's charge to the Department of Juvenile Justice: to help the juveniles in its custody while protecting the general public.

In such circumstances, when either the legislature or the elected chief executive has charged the agency with multiple, conflicting missions, the managers of the agency are forced to exercise leadership. They have to develop a balanced strategy for pursuing these multiple purposes. They have to convey the subtlety of that strategy to those who work in the organization, to the various stakeholders (each of which may be concerned with only one purpose), and to the general public (which may not appreciate or recognize the conflict). And they have to make that subtle strategy work. When confronted with multiple, conflicting purposes set forth in legislation, the machine metaphor for public organizations breaks down completely.

What should the public manager do in the face of legislative ambiguity: ask for clarification or provide it? Asking for clarification from the legislature is not likely to produce it. Indeed, it is equally likely to create more ambiguity, more conflicting mandates, more unadministerable laws, and continued inadequate resources. This is why those in the executive branch try to avoid asking for clarifications in their existing mandate, or even for extensions of their mandate. They would rather cope with their current confusion, conflicts, and inadequacies—with which they are familiar and for which they have developed some adequate responses—than go back to the legislature. The most likely consequences of asking for legislative clarity are: (1) abuse for failing to sort out the existing contradictions to the personal satisfaction of this individual senator or that individual representative; and (2) greater confusion, additional conflicts, and more inadequacies.[12]

Moe and Gilmour (1995) argue that "the theoretical foundation" of public administration "is in public law," which is "founded on the body of the Constitution and the Bill of Rights and articulated by a truly enormous body of statutory, regulatory, and case law to ensure continuance of a republican form of government and to protect the rights and freedoms of citizens at the hands of an all-powerful state." To Moe and Gilmour, this "public law paradigm of federal government management" is key:

> Public law is the under-appreciated 'cement' that binds the separated powers of the administrative state, ensures political and legal accountability of its officials, and restrains abuses of administrative discretion and conflicts of interest.
>
> *The distinguishing characteristic of governmental management, contrasted to private management, is that the actions of governmental officials must have their basis in public law* (1995, 135, 142, 138, italics in original).

Similarly, Moe writes of "the public law basis of our polity and governmental management" (1994, 118) and argues that "the true purpose of government is to implement laws passed by politically accountable authorities" (1993, 47).

In contrast with "the market paradigm" of entrepreneurial government, Moe advocates "the legal paradigm" based on public law:

> The legal paradigm posits that the principal tool of federal management is public law, that a conceptually sound enabling statute supplemented by comprehensive, yet flexible, general management laws is a necessary basis for effective agency management (1993, 47).

And yet, Moe also recognizes the gap between the theory of this legal paradigm and its implementation: "Over time, legislation has suffered more and more from wishful thinking, sloppy drafting and woeful disregard for public-sector organiza-

---

[12]This is one of the foundations of what Richard P. Nathan called "the administrative presidency" that Richard M. Nixon sought to create: "using the discretion permitted in the implementation of existing laws rather than advancing these policy aims through the enactment of new legislation" (1983, 7).

tion." As a result, Moe observes, "few federal agencies and programs have clear, unambiguous missions under the law" (1993, 46, 48). "The principles of public law and administration," write Moe and Gilmour, "have been neglected, avoided for purposes of expedience and misapplied" (1995, 138).

Moe and others (Cook, 1996; Lowi, 1969) urge legislators to clean up their act. "Government agencies should be assigned functions that are administerable," recommends Moe (1994, 119). But two centuries of American history (or interviews with a few public managers) suggest that this is unlikely to happen soon. Legislators have little incentive—either individually or collectively—to correct legislative failure. So rather than wait for legislatures to begin enacting clear orders, we ought to seek other potential remedies. One such remedy is to permit—indeed, encourage—public managers to exercise leadership. Ideally, it might well be that the job of the public manager is strictly to implement the law. But this requires clear, implementable laws. Until the legislative branch begins to reform itself, those charged with managing public agencies and implementing the ambiguous laws need to compensate for this legislative failure. They can do so by exercising leadership. After all, it is difficult to mobilize the people in a public agency (or any organization) to accomplish something if you don't give them a specific something to accomplish.[13]

Still, what gives public managers the *right* to lead? They aren't elected by anybody. Since the beginning of the republic, the legislature has been the branch of government designed to reflect the will of the people. It is the legislature, not public managers, who should set purposes, policies, and priorities. After all, the citizens elect their legislators, not their public managers. And if the citizens are unhappy with their government's purposes, policies, and priorities, they have an easy remedy: replace their legislators during the next election with people who will establish more representative purposes, policies, and priorities.

Unfortunately, the practice of American government at all levels does not comport with this theory. Indeed, for a number of reasons, a legislature's directives to public managers may not, in fact, reflect the popular will. For one, there is the obvious problem created by the "paradox of voting": If society is attempting to choose from among three (or more) alternative policies, different voting mechanisms or rules will result in society making different choices (Nanson, 1882; Riker, 1958). (The same is true for choices among three or more candidates). Consequently, the processes and procedures that a legislature uses when deciding (by voting) on public policy influence the policy alternatives actually considered, the order in which they are compared, and the final choice. In legislatures (or elections), the rules for voting affect the choices that legislators (or citizens) collectively make[14] and thus the directives given to public managers.

---

[13] The first report of Vice President Gore's National Performance Review, argues Moe (1994), "is seeking to break the public law basis of an agency's mission and replace it with an 'outcomes' missions orientation as defined by the agency's political chief." And, continues Moe, "Congress is not likely to take kindly this obfuscation of its mission assignment process to agencies" (1994, 117, 118). Individually, legislators may well disagree with a public manager's choice of particular outcomes for operationalizing an agency's mission. Indeed, individual legislators may dispute the manager's prerogative to decide what specific outcomes to pursue. But until these legislators can collectively stop their own obfuscation of their mission-assignment process, someone must choose.

[14] For a more complete discussion of this problem of collective, social choice, see Arrow (1963).

There is also the difficulty of interpreting definitively any piece of legislation (Terry, 1995, 72–73), a problem that is compounded when the legislation is enacted before the development of some new technology. For example, how should the first amendment guarantee that "Congress shall make no law . . . abridging the freedom of speech, or of the press" be applied to the Internet? Or how should the section of the Pendleton Act that prohibits the solicitation of campaign funds in federal office buildings be applied to the use of the telephone given that the law was enacted in 1883—only seven years after the telephone was first patented?

Moreover, legislatures do not behave democratically. They are not what Madison called, in Federalist No. 10, "a pure democracy": "a society consisting of a small number of citizens, who assemble and administer the government in person" (1961a, 81). They certainly do not democratically conduct a series of mini-referendums on the various issues of the day. If they did, we might (ignoring the problem of the paradox of voting) argue that our representative's votes did, indeed, reflect the will of the people. But they don't. Legislators may be elected democratically, but legislatures do not function democratically. This is *the fallacy of legislative democracy.*

Legislatures are organizations. Even the smallest version—the five-member town council—has its own subunits (called committees), hierarchy, and rules. Rarely does a legislature collectively work on an issue and reach a final conclusion. Rather, it delegates different issues and different tasks to different legislators and different committees. And thus the result of any legislature's "deliberations" reflects not only the will of the populace (whatever that might be) but also how the legislature is organized (its structures and rules) as well as the effectiveness of various legislators in employing those structures and rules to enact (or reject) a piece of legislation (Oleszek, 1996; Sinclair, 1977). The result is hardly "democratic."

In the summer of 1997, for example, one individual prevented the United States Senate from exercising its constitutional prerogative to provide "the Advice and Consent" necessary for a presidential appointment. Single-handedly, Senator Jesse Helms of North Carolina prevented William F. Weld, President Clinton's nominee for the ambassador to Mexico, from even receiving a hearing, let alone a committee vote, or a vote by the full Senate. If the seven million citizens of North Carolina are unhappy with this policy, they can do something about it.[15] But the other 250 million-plus citizens of the nation have no recourse. Moreover, as Senator Helms pointed out, the case of Weld vs. Helms was hardly unique; over the previous decade, 154 presidential nominees were never granted a hearing by the Senate (Shribman, 1997). Not only do the legislative rules, processes, and procedures influence legislative outcomes, but so do the legislators who control the choices among these rules, processes, and procedures. Indeed, the rules of the United States Senate (as well as those of state senates and other legislatures) give an individual senator considerable power to frustrate the majority's will.[16]

---

[15] In contrast, the nine million hogs in North Carolina have no choice.

[16] Of course, these rules are designed not only to facilitate the organization of the legislature but also to inhibit too much democracy—to constrain the majority, as Madison wrote in Federalist No. 10, so that it will not "sacrifice to its ruling passion or interest both the public good and the rights of other citizens" (1961a, 80).

It isn't a question of legislative brilliance. There is nothing about our constitutional system that assumes that citizens will elect brilliant legislators.[17] And they don't.

Rather, it is a question of legislative incentives and of legislative structures and systems. Do legislators—individually and collectively—have the incentives to enact clear laws that public managers can easily implement? They don't. Do legislatures have the organizational structures, organizational systems, and organizational procedures to ensure that the laws they enact are a democratic reflection of their own views (if not necessarily of the citizenry's views)? They don't.

Just as bureaucracies have virtues and flaws, so do legislatures. And to correct their own flaws, they occasionally invent new systems or procedures.

For example, the federal base-closing procedure is designed to create a more balanced process for deciding the proper number (and distribution) of military facilities. If the Department of Defense proposes or decides to close one or more military installations, the natural workings of the legislative process can quickly check that decision. A representative from a district in which the base is to be closed is very concerned about this proposal and has a direct and obvious remedy: He or she can simply insert a provision into some authorizing or appropriations bill to prevent the closure. Other legislators care little about whether this particular base is open or closed and recognize that the total savings generated by closing this one base are trivial. Thus, they are quite willing to trade their vote to prevent the targeted base from being closed for some vote (to be named later) by the very concerned representative. And, of course, if the executive branch proposes to close many bases at once, it automatically creates a natural coalition (independent of party or ideology) that will work energetically to round up the rest of the votes.

Nevertheless, Congress recognized that the nation had too many military facilities. Thus, Congress itself designed a process to overcome its own failure. By giving the task of selecting which bases to close to a special commission, and by limiting its own discretion to a single up-or-down vote on the entire package, Congress forced itself to focus on the larger, national interest rather than a series of small, parochial interests. This base-closing process has worked so well that the National Commission on the State and Local Public Service recommended that state and local governments adapt it to overcome another case of legislative failure: the inability of legislatures to eliminate or consolidate "overlapping or underperforming" agencies (1993, 17–19). In this case too, the parochial interests of individual legislators can, through standard legislative procedures, frustrate what a majority believe to be in the broad, public interest.

Members of Congress have long recognized that their formal legislative procedures and informal norms of behavior do not always guarantee that the collective public will—or even the collective will of a majority of legislators—will be

---

[17] In Federalist No. 10, Madison suggested that republican government might "refine and enlarge the public views by passing them through the medium of a chosen body of citizens, whose wisdom may best discern the true interest of their country and whose patriotism and love of justice will be least likely to sacrifice it to temporary or partial considerations." Yet in the same paragraph, he also noted that the opposite might occur: "Men of factious tempers, of local prejudices, or of sinister designs, may, by intrigue, by corruption, or by other means, first obtain the suffrages, and then betray the interests of the people" (1961a, 82).

converted into law. Legislators know that there is such a thing as legislative failure (even if they don't call it that). And they occasionally search for ways to correct the most obvious or flagrant defects.

Clearly, the legislature needs to be checked and balanced. The judiciary does this when the legislature passes a law that violates the Constitution or when it enacts a vague or contradictory law that the courts must sort out. The elected chief executive does this for legislative failures that relate directly to his or her primary agenda or that create precedents that might affect his or her executive prerogatives. But the elected chief must choose his or her battles and will usually opt to ignore legislative failures with small consequences.

But legislative failures that generate small, adverse consequences for the elected chief executive may well create large, adverse consequences for an individual agency. Who then should check and balance the legislative branch? This is the public manager's responsibility. He or she needs to exercise leadership, to seek out remedies for the legislative failure. If the elected chief executive takes a pass, the public manager ought to respond. This is not optional; it is obligatory.

Political Failure

If the chief elected official does not have the time to exercise leadership over a public agency, and if the managers of that agency are either legally prevented or politically inhibited from leading, then who will take the initiative? The agency's stakeholders, of course. They face neither legal prohibitions nor political inhibitions. Moreover, they are quite prepared to fill any vacuum of leadership, so that they might direct the agency to employ its resources to the welfare of individual stakeholders, to the advantage of their formal organizations, and to the personal benefit of the leaders of these organizations.

In Federalist No. 10, Madison (1961a) addressed the "danger" of "factions": "that the public good is disregarded in the conflicts of rival parties, and that measures are too often decided, not according to the rules of justice and the rights of the minor party, but by the superior force of an interested and overbearing majority." Indeed, Madison was not really worried about minority factions: "If a faction consists of less than a majority, relief is supplied by the republican principle, which enables the majority to defeat its sinister view by regular vote." Instead, he focused on the dangers created by a majority faction: "When a majority is included in a faction, the form of popular government . . . enables it to sacrifice to its ruling passion or interest both the public good and the rights of other citizens." Madison's solution was a republican government, with "the delegation of the government . . . to a small number of citizens elected by the rest," combined with a large number of citizens electing these representatives, so that each delegate represented a wide variety of interests (1961a, 77, 78, 80, 82).

Madison worried about a *majority* faction that controlled the *legislature*. He—along with the other Federalist authors and the Constitution itself—ignored the problems created by a *minority* faction exerting undue influence on an *execu-*

tive-branch agency. Thus, Madison and the other designers of the constitutional system of checks and balances did not create any specific mechanism for preventing "factions"—now called "interest groups"—from capturing administrative agencies. Yet, two centuries later, this is a significant failure of our system of governance (Bernstein, 1955; Lowi, 1969).

One of Moe and Gilmour's ten principles of public administration is that "political accountability for the implementation of policy and law requires a clear line of authority from the president to the heads of the departments and agencies and from them to their subordinates" (1995, 139). This is *the fallacy of hierarchical accountability.* Our system of checks and balances creates not a hierarchy of accountability but a complex network of accountability with each element in that network checking on many of the others (Kaufman, 1981b, 166–169). Thus, a junior, unelected legislative aide can check the activities of a civil servant many levels down in the executive "hierarchy." Indeed, many lines of accountability go directly from a legislative committee or a district court to some executive-branch bureau.

This network of checks and balances does not merely consist of governmental units or employees. Private citizens and, more effectively, private organizations are engaged in the process as well. The lobbyist for an interest group can "educate" a legislative staffer about some (allegedly) nefarious practice of an executive agency, and a simple phone call from that staffer can check the practice. Journalists for both general-interest publications (such as daily newspapers) and special-interest periodicals (such as newsletters that cover one agency or one policy area) are constantly engaged in checking the powers of public officials—particularly those in executive-branch agencies—by publicizing specific practices, thus activating some existing but latent lines of informal accountability and even creating new ones. The American network of checks and balances consists of a hellava lot of official and quasi-official lines of accountability—and a hellava lot more dotted, faintly visible lines. Indeed, Moe and Gilmour note that "openness to congressional, judicial, and public scrutiny of department and agency decision-making processes is a hallmark of the governmental sector operating under public law" (1995, 139).

Within this network of accountability, however, some of the lines—particularly some of the informal, dotted lines—exercise more influence than others. Sure there exist lines from every individual citizen to every public agency. But these lines are rarely activated, and, when they are, they are usually not activated with much experience, much knowledge, or much clout. Far more effective are the lines that are in constant use, namely the lines to specific agencies from experienced and knowledgeable representatives of stakeholder organizations—people who have the time, resources, and motivation to know what they want done, know what they do not want done, and know who can make all that happen.

Who will check and balance these minority factions? Who will ensure that a stakeholder organization is not exercising undue influence on an agency? Who has the interest, resources, and time? The elected chief executive doesn't; except when the activities of an interest group directly threaten his or her own agenda or prerogatives, the elected executive will ignore both the group and its activities. The legislature collectively doesn't; it has delegated the task of overseeing each agency to a few committees, and, thus, the interest group has created a variety of dotted lines to every member of these committees plus all of its key staffers. The judiciary can't; unless the court is confronted with a specific case concerning a specific abuse of the agency's power or with a specific case concerning a specific failure of the agency to carry out a specific legislative instruction, it cannot act. Other interest groups don't; unless two interest groups both care deeply about the activities of any agency—and have conflicting stakes in these activities—the pressures from interest groups will not check or balance each other. A journalist may; if a journalist can uncover a particularly juicy example of excessive interest-group influence, he or she has a clear, professional interest in publicizing it, thus forcing others to check and balance interest-group pressures.

There is one other possibility: the managers of the agency themselves. If the managers of the agency accept that they have a responsibility to lead it—to set directions and accomplish purposes—and if their directions and purposes differ from those advocated by an interest group, then it is clearly in these managers' interest to attempt to check and balance the interest group's power. If they are effective leaders, they will create the time and mobilize the resources to do so.

The political failure of our system of governance created by the power of factions (and abetted by the fallacy of hierarchical accountability) has few real checks and balances. By preventing or inhibiting public managers from exercising leadership, we also suppress one of the few ways of combating this political failure of our system of governance.

Civic Failure

But aren't individual citizens—not interest groups—the core of our system of governance? Perhaps. Again, however, it is a question of interest, resources, and time. Usually, the stakes for individual citizens are so small compared with the time and resources necessary to make a difference that they conclude—from a simple, implicit benefit-cost analysis—that it makes little sense to try to even figure out how to affect something in which they have anything less than a major interest. This is *the fallacy of civic engagement.*

Two decades ago, George Bishop invented the "Public Affairs Act of 1975" and asked citizens whether it should be repealed. In 1995, *The Washington Post* conducted a poll that included this same question: "Some people say the 1975 Public Affairs Act should be repealed. Do you agree or disagree that it should be repealed?" Of the 501 people polled, 24 percent agreed and 19 percent disagreed, while 57 offered no opinion. The *Post's* pollsters found a way to get even more citizens to take a position on this fictitious legislation. Instead of starting the question with "Some people say . . ." they offered a more authoritative introduction: either "President Clinton says . . ." or "Republicans in Congress say . . ." Then, more than half of those polled offered a definitive opinion. Predictably, Democrats supported repeal when told the president did, while Republicans supported it when told their party's members in Congress did ("The 1975 Public Affairs Act," 1995). And yet, we continue to behave as if the public has well-thought-out ideas and beliefs about at least key policy issues.[18] How, you have to wonder, would citizens respond if asked: "Do you agree with President Dole's decision to help Czechoslovakia combat its smallpox epidemic?"

Public managers can help to correct this civic failure in our system of governance. But to do so, they need to lead. They need to educate. They need to explain to the public in general—not just to their own stakeholder organizations—what they are attempting to accomplish, why they are attempting to do so, what they have actually achieved in the past month, quarter, year, and decade. They need to clarify for the general public both their agency's broad purposes for the long-term future as well as the short-term performance targets that they are seeking to achieve. They need to explain what is realistic for their agency to accomplish; what is impossible; what might be possible; how additional resources, flexibility, or authority might convert something that is impossible into something that is possible; and what might transform something that is possible into something that is realistic.

This is, perhaps, the least objectionable form of public-manager leadership. Educating the public about the broad mission, specific goals, and latest accomplishments can only help to improve governance. It will not eliminate this civic failure. It will not convert couch potatoes into citizen activists. But it will help. It can move some people from indifference to civic engagement, and it will certainly give many more a better understanding of how the American system of governance really works.

Judicial Failure

Can the judicial branch fail too? Certainly, both local judges and Supreme Court justices can make a mistake interpreting the law or the Constitution. They're only human. All those five-to-four decisions can't be infallible. But do such mistakes really create failures in governance that require public managers to lead?

In the book *The Impossible Jobs in Public Management*, Gary Miller and Ira Iscoe (1990) describe the challenge of being a state mental health commissioner in this litigious age. To the traditional list of the capabilities required of a public manager, they add "a working knowledge of mental health law, litigation, and legal strategy." After all, they explain, "lawsuits are a fact of life for a state mental health commissioner:" in Texas, for example, the state mental health agency has "about fifty to sixty lawsuits pending at all times" (1990, 109, 121).

Miller and Iscoe are not too kind to "advocacy lawyers," their "ideological objectives," and the "litigation industry." For, as they note, "class-action suits are typically initiated and perpetuated by advocacy lawyers who recruit patients"—people who thereafter "play a relatively minor role in such litigation" (1990, 121, 122,124).

---

[18]The standard discussions of methods for aggregating individual preferences into social preferences assume that the preferences of all individuals are given and fixed. See, for example, Arrow (1963, 7–8,11).

Okay, so such lawsuits are more than a nuisance. They are a major waste of time and resources. But just because advocacy lawyers are a pain in the butt doesn't mean that this is a failure in the American system of governance, let alone a failure that can be or should be remedied (if only in part) by public managers who lead. Do all these lawyers really *require* the commissioner of mental health and the department's other top managers to exercise leadership?

For public managers, class-action lawsuits can create significant problems during litigation but even bigger problems after the court has rendered a judgment—or, at least, after the court has rendered its first judgment. For such a suit is not simply filed, litigated, and decided. Often, as one (initial) outcome of the lawsuit, the judge appoints a monitor or special master, someone to oversee the agency's compliance with either the judge's decision, some out-of-court settlement, or a consent decree. Yet, these court-appointed monitors usually do more than just monitor. Instead, write Miller and Iscoe, "they are in the business of managing the agency." Moreover, the litigation, it seems, is never over. Rather, observe Miller and Iscoe, consent decrees, which are "ordinarily considered devices for settling lawsuits, have instead allowed the litigation to grow to the point that it dominated virtually all policy- and decision-making" (1990, 123).

Moreover, continue Miller and Iscoe, this new, court-appointed public manager, "although lacking accountability to state government, is empowered by a federal district judge to exercise considerable authority over state government operations." In fact, "federal judges . . . and their monitors," they observe, "are free to play the same political game as other government officials, but without the attendant risks that provide moderation and balance—namely, the risk of not being reelected or reappointed to a position or of being fired" (1990, 122). This observation certainly suggests that the existing system of checks and balances is not working as well as designed.

For beleaguered mental health commissioners, Miller and Iscoe offer ways to cope with the micromanagement by the courts. But, they conclude, "there is no substitute for leadership skills":

> One of the most vital coping strategies for a commissioner is letting people in the agency and other interested parties know what the organization stands for and where it is going. Although . . . there is a price to pay for going in *any* direction, a commissioner who cannot motivate people and give them vision, a sense of direction, and a feeling of belonging to a greater enterprise may survive for a while but will probably accomplish very little (1990, 129, italics in original).

The judiciary influences the work of any public manager through a series of decisions and decrees prompted by a series of lawsuits filed by attorneys looking to establish a series of precedents. Yet, as Justice Oliver Wendell Holmes, Jr., noted, "great cases like hard cases make bad law" (1904). This reveals *the fallacy of judicial omnipotence.* There is nothing to guarantee that the result of a single lawsuit—or even a series of lawsuits—will improve the functioning of a public agency, let alone improve the public welfare. Although such lawsuits may be filed to protect the individual rights of one kind of citizen or another, the result can easily (if only indirectly) trample on the rights of others. In mental health, some lawsuits claim a "right" to treatment. Others claim a "right" to refuse treatment. Still others claim a "right" to be treated in the "least restrictive environment," i.e., not in an institution but in a community setting. Yet, as Miller and Iscoe point out:

> If a patient in a state hospital or special forensic hospital (for the 'criminally insane') no longer meets the legal standards for commitment, the mental health agency is not simply *allowed* to release the patient; it is *required* to release that patient—even if he or she has previously committed a violent act (1990, 122, 112, italics in original).

And, if the agency does acquiesce to "the release of dangerous patients from forensic hospitals, as the law often requires" (Miller and Iscoe, 1990, 112), and one of these individuals commits a crime, the agency is vulnerable to complaints for failing to protect the rights of these victims.

In the face of conflicting litigious pressures, a public manager has to exercise both internal and external leadership. He or she has to distinguish between micropurposes of the various individual litigants and the macropurpose assigned to the agency. And the manager has to explain this distinction externally—to journalists, legislators, judges, and the public—and also internally to the agency's staff. The manager needs to describe—to any audience that will pay attention—the individual consequences of each lawsuit and of the macro, aggregated consequence of all these micro actions.

The task of keeping a public agency focused on its real mission is always a challenge; it is particularly challenging when the agency is subjected to repeated litigation. For, explain Miller and Iscoe, "the most powerful effect of class-action lawsuits is psychological." Public employees are repeatedly portrayed in the lawsuits—and in the accompanying press coverage—as the "bad guys," while the lawyers wear the white hats. The impact on morale and productivity can be devastating (1990, 125). Under such circumstances, any public agency certainly needs leadership.

The judiciary is no more immune to failure than the other branches. All have power. All can abuse power. All can make mistakes that need to be checked and can engage in excesses that need to be balanced. Public managers should not believe that they are the only ones responsible for compensating for judicial failure. The legislature, the elected chief executive, journalists, citizens, and even a few other lawyers will all contribute. But public managers can contribute too. When faced with specious complaints from lawyers, disruptive decrees from judges, and declining morale from lawsuits, public managers need to keep their agency focused while drawing public attention to the deleterious consequences of such litigation. All these responsibilities require the public manager to exercise leadership.

Heroic or Conservatory Leadership?

So what kind of leadership exactly am I advocating? What kind of leaders should public managers be? What kind of initiative should public managers take to help correct these seven failures of American governance? What style of leadership can expose and help us cope with the various fallacies in our thinking about how different institutions of governance actually function?

Terry (1995) distinguishes between two models of leadership: (1) the traditional, "heroic conception of leadership"—all entrepreneurial and charismatic, antitraditional and innovative, aggressive and even reckless, powerful and perhaps coercive—and (2) his model of the leader as "conservator," who preserves the "institutional integrity" of the agency that he or she manages. Terry explains what he means by both institutional integrity and its preservation:

> To say that an institution has integrity is to suggest that it is faithful to the functions, values, and distinctive set of unifying principles that define its special competence and character . . . the preservation of institutional integrity involves protecting from injury, destruction, or decay those processes, values and unifying principles that determine an institution's distinctive competence (1995, 40, 44–45).

To Terry, institutional integrity is like money in the bank, and it is the manager's fiduciary responsibility to insure that the value of this institutional wealth is not eroded.

But between the reckless entrepreneur who bets other people's money on risky, untested ventures and the cautious banker who invests only in Triple-A bonds with a guaranteed return, there exists a broad spectrum of possibilities—a wide variety of investment strategies and a number of different conceptions of fiduciary obligations. Indeed, often the truly "safest" investment is a diversified portfolio that creates a variety of different opportunities not only to protect the total capital stock from eroding but also to help it grow.

To preserve your muscles, you have to use them. When ignored, muscle fibers wither. Judicious exercise not only maintains muscle mass but builds it. The same applies to the brain. When not used, neuron linkages wither. Whether you seek to maintain or to build your mental capacity, the prescription is the same: You better exercise your brain.

The same applies to the public manager's responsibility to preserve a public agency's institutional integrity. Public managers could view this task as requiring them to defend their agency against attacks, to follow the rules scrupulously to avoid any taint of organizational ineptitude, profligacy, corruptibility, or criminality, and to prevent the agency's resources and authority from being used for unconstitutional, illegal, prohibited, or unsanctioned purposes—or even for purposes for which authorization is not patently explicit. And yet, to truly preserve the agency's institutional integrity, its managers must do more than react defensively. To preserve any organizational characteristic, public managers have to exercise initiative.

To ensure that key organizational processes are preserved and, thus, available for future use, public managers have to employ them frequently—testing and verifying that the people who are responsible for making these processes work have the knowledge and capabilities to do so. Values and principles lose all meaning unless they are frequently applied to help resolve real problems. To preserve its "special competence and character," a public agency has to exercise its functions and processes, values and principles. Locking them up in a vault ensures that the agency's institutional integrity will wither.

Responsible public managers not only preserve their agency's institutional integrity. They also use it. They deploy it to accomplish their agency's mission. And, in the process, they add to it. Public managers who are also leaders recognize that to protect—and to enhance—their agency's processes, values, and principles, they have to ensure that the people in the agency use them frequently and, in the process, learn to use them more effectively.

I am certainly not advocating a model of agency management that constrains public managers to do only those things for which they have explicit, detailed instructions. That is a recipe for stalemate. At the same time, I am not advocating heroic leadership. I'll leave the superheroes to Marvel and DC Comics.

Neither am I advocating that public managers—or public agencies—should be viewed as a fourth branch of government—distinct not only from the judicial and legislative branches but also from the elected chief executive (Meier, 1993). Certainly, public managers do have a role in the system of checks and balances in coping with the failures of the legislative and judicial branches. But within the executive branch they do not so much check or balance the elected chief—though they do sometimes do this too—as exercise leadership about issues for which the elected chief lacks either the inclination or the time.

Public managers do not head up a collection of mini, fourth branches or government. But, within our constitutional system, they do have some important responsibilities and obligations. They can provide some useful checks and balances for the legislative and judicial branches and for elected chief executives—checks and balances that other individuals lack the knowledge, office, or incentive to provide.

Thus, I am advocating active, intelligent, enterprising leadership. I am advocating leadership that takes astute initiatives designed to help the agency not only to achieve its purposes today but also to create new capacity to achieve its objectives tomorrow. I am advocating a style of leadership that builds both an agency's and its government's reputation for accomplishment and thus competence. Such leadership requires public managers to exercise initiative within the framework provided by their legal mandate.

The Leadership Responsibilities of Public Managers

Is all this talk about the failures of American governance and fallacies in our thinking simply an apologia for the new public management—for public managers who usurp democratic prerogatives? Is this little more than another attempt at what Brian Cook calls "a long and arduous search for legitimating arguments to reconcile and thus artificially reattach administration to a regime predicated on popular sovereignty and individual rights" (1996, 137–138)? Maybe this is just one more effort to jerryrig some kind of fancy theoretical rhetoric about public-spirited public managers as leaders who contribute to the functioning of democracy to fit the unpleasant, practical reality of public managers as leaders who can and do take initiative.[19]

But even if citizens were capable of developing well-considered judgments about important public issues, even if legislators were capable of converting public views into representative public policies, even if humans possessed the analytical capacity to figure out from the beginning exactly how to implement such policies, even if elected chief executives gave clear directives to all agencies, even if public agencies were capable of implementing clear organizational directives, even if organized interests were incapable of capturing public agencies, and even if the judiciary were restrained from making multiple minute mutations in agency policies, practices, and priorities, we would still want public managers actively engaged as leaders in the democratic process. Public managers have a unique perspective that can contribute to democracy. Why would we assume that the manager of a business firm, the manager of a nonprofit social-service agency, the manager of a religious organization, or the manager of a political party would have something useful to contribute to the political process but a public manager would not? After all, public managers know what goals their organizations can reasonably achieve and what policies their organizations will prove incapable of implementing. Public managers have expertise, and we should not ask them to wait quietly and politely until they are formally asked for their judgments.

Rather, it should be an explicit part of the public manager's job to exercise leadership. Public managers should take initiative to correct the current failures of our system of governance—particularly those failures that impinge on the ability of the manager's agency to pursue its mission effectively.

The challenge then is not to prevent public managers from exercising leadership. The challenge is to accept that they will—and should—exercise leadership and, then, to ensure that the other institutions of society—from legislatures, to the press, to citizen organizations—carefully channel this leadership in ways that promote the general welfare.

Of course, as leaders, public managers can lead in pernicious as well as beneficial directions. By exercising leadership, public managers can subvert legislative intent or distort citizen desires. By exercising initiative, public managers can frustrate executive directives and destroy organizational competence. By exercising leadership, public managers can expedite agency capture by stakeholder organizations[20] and undermine judicial authority. Any form of initiative—whether by legis-

---

[19]Colin Diver (1982) has contrasted an "engineering model" of public management—"a process of supervising the execution of a previously defined governmental goal"—with an "entrepreneurial model," which "conjures up a kind of frontier image of the public manager alone in the political wilds, surrounded by concealed pitfalls and drawn by undiscovered wealth." These two models, observes Diver, create a dilemma: "The entrepreneurial model seems, to many at least, the more faithful image of reality, yet it is morally unacceptable. The engineering model is ethically preferable, but unrealistic." To resolve this dilemma, Diver proposes two possible approaches: "make the engineering model more realizable or rehabilitate the ethical status of entrepreneurship." He then notes that "the largest amount of attention has been lavished on the first of these two options," but this effort is "severely limited by some rather intractable realities." Consequently, Diver concludes that the only way to resolve this dilemma "is to elevate the ethical status of the entrepreneurial strategy." Yet, he writes, "I must confess that I'm not sure how," Diver does suggest, however, a two-part effort: a philosophical approach that seeks "to elaborate a principle of legitimacy with which public managerial entrepreneurship can be made compatible," and an empirical strategy to "explore the social consequences of entrepreneurial behavior" (1982, 402–406).

[20]If the public manager was previously a member or an employee of a stakeholder organization, his or her leadership might be more likely to abet such capture.

lators, elected executives, judges, justices, stakeholders, citizens, or public managers—can be deployed to foster or corrupt democratic governance.

It "is certain" under "the entrepreneurial management paradigm," argue Moe and Gilmour, "that political accountability for government programs, whether assigned to federal agencies or to third and fourth parties, is being weakened" (1995, 142). Maybe this is happening. Maybe this will happen. But it is not "certain." It is possible that if public managers exercise leadership intelligently—particularly if they are explicit about the results they and their agencies plan to produce in both the short and long run—they will enhance political accountability. It is possible that, if public managers take seriously their responsibilities for civic education, they will improve political accountability.

Angels and Public Managers

Public managers are not angels. We ought not to expect them to be. We certainly ought not to design a system of governance that depends upon public managers acting as angels. Similarly, we ought not to design a system of governance that depends upon legislators, judges, elected chief executives, interest groups, or private citizens to be angels. After all, as James Madison wrote in *Federalist* No. 51, "If men were angels, no government would be necessary" (1961b, 322). Or, as Finley Peter Dunne's Mr. Dooley put it a century later:

> A man that'd expict to thrain lobsters to fly in a year is called a loonytic; but a man that thinks men can be turned into angels be an iliction is called a rayformer an' remains at large (1900, 261).

We don't believe that public managers are angels. That is why we have created a variety of checks and balances, so that when they succumb to temptation, other people and other institutions are available to catch them.

But we should also not pretend that elected chief executives, legislators, or judges and justices are angels either. They are subject to the same temptations; indeed, because of their larger powers and influence, they are subject to even greater temptations than public managers. Certainly, in any democratic system, the ideas, decisions, and actions of elected executives and legislators have greater legitimacy than those of appointed public managers. But this legitimacy is not absolute. It does need to be checked. And public managers do offer one more, useful check.

Sir Winston Churchill once observed: "No one pretends that democracy is perfect or all-wise. Indeed, it has been said that democracy is the worst form of government except for all those other forms that have been tried from time to time" (1947). There are obvious imperfections in democracy—not only because of the theory but also because of our practice. But we need not ignore such practical problems. We can try to correct them. We will not always be successful, of course, and some of our corrections will create other problems. Nevertheless, it makes sense to fix the current problems, while trying to do it in such a way as to avoid creating many more. In attempting to do so, in attempting to correct the failures of our American system of governance, public managers who exercise leadership can help.

References

Arrow, Kenneth J. (1963). *Social Choice and Individual Values*. 2nd ed., New Haven, CT: Yale University Press.

Barbash, Fred, and Al Kamen (1984). "Blackmun Says 'Weary' Court Is Shifting Right." *The Washington Post*, 20 September, A1, A42.

Barzelay, Michael (1992). *Breaking through Bureaucracy: A New Vision for Managing in Government*. Berkeley, CA: University of California Press.

Behn, Robert D. (1988). "Management by Groping Along." *Journal of Policy Analysis and Management* 7:643–663.

——— (1990). *The many Roles of the Governor's Chief of Staff*. Washington, DC: National Governor's Association.

——— (1991). *Leadership Counts: Lessons for Public Managers*. Cambridge, MA: Harvard University Press.

——— (1993). *Being There: More Candid Views on Governing 1992*. Washington, DC: National Governor's Association.

——— (1997). "Branch Rickey as a Public Manager: Fulfilling the Eight Responsibilities of Public Management." *Journal of Public Administration Research and Theory* 7:1–33.

Bellone, Carl J. and George Frederick Goerl (1992). "Reconciling Entrepreneurship and Democracy." *Public Administration Review* 52(2): 130–134.

Berman, Paul and Beryl Nelson (1997). "Replication: Adapt or Fail." In Alan A. Altshuler and Robert D. Behn, eds., *Innovation in American Government: Challenges, Opportunities, and Dilemmas*. Washington, DC: The Brookings Institution, 319–331.

Bernstein, Marver (1955). *Regulating Business by Independent Commission*. Princeton, NJ: Princeton University Press.

Beyle, Thad L. and Robert Hueffner (1983). "Quips and Quotes from Old Governors to New." *Public Administration Review* 43(3):268–270.

Churchill, Sir Winston (1947). *Speech in the House of Commons*. Hansard, 11 November, col. 206.

Cook, Brian J. (1996). *Bureaucracy and Self-Government: Reconsidering the Role of Public Administration in American Politics*. Baltimore: Johns Hopkins University Press.

Denhardt, Robert B. (1993). *The Pursuit of Significance: Strategies for Managerial Success in Public Organizations*. Belmont, CA: Wadsworth.

Derthick, Martha (1990). *Agency Under Stress: The Social Security Administration in American Government*. Washington, DC: Brookings Institution.

Diver, Colin S. (1982). "Engineers and Entrepreneurs: The Dilemma of Public Management." *Journal of Policy Analysis and Management* 1:402–406.

Dunne, Finley Peter (1900). *Mr. Dooley's Philosophy*. New York: R. H. Russell.

Fiorina, Morris P. (1977). *Congress: Keystone of the Washington Establishment*. New Haven, CT: Yale University Press.

Golden, Olivia (1990). "Innovation in Public Sector Human Services Programs: The Implications of Innovation by 'Groping Along.'" *Journal of Policy Analysis and Management* 9:219–248.

Gulick, Luther (1937). "Notes on a Theory of Organization." In Luther Gulick and Lyndall Urwick, eds., *Papers on the Science of Administration*. New York: Institute of Public Administration, 3–13.

Holmes, Oliver Wendell, Jr. (1904). *Northern Securities Co. v. United States*. 192 U.S. 197.

Hood, Christopher (1991). "A Public Management for All Seasons." *Public Administration* 69:3–19.

Kaufman, Herbert (1981a). "Fear of Bureaucracy: A Raging Pandemic." *Public Administration Review* 41(1):1–9.

——— (1981b). *The Administrative Behavior of Federal Bureau Chiefs*. Washington, DC: Brookings Institution.

Kotter, John P. (1990). "What Leaders Really Do." *Harvard Business Review* 68: 103–116.

Lindblom, Charles E. (1959). "The Science of 'Muddling Through.'" *Public Administration Review* 19(1):79–88.

Lipsky, Michael (1980). *Street Level Bureaucracy*. New York: Russell Sage Foundation.

Lowi, Theodore J. (1969). *The End of Liberalism*. New York: W. W. Norton.

Madison, James (1961a). "Federalist No. 10." in Clinton Rossiter, ed., *The Federalist Papers*. New York: New American Library, 77–84.

——— (1961b). "Federalist No. 51." In Clinton Rossiter, ed., *The Federalist Papers*. New York: New American Library, 320–325.

Meier, Kenneth J. (1993). *Politics and the Bureaucracy: Policymaking in the Fourth Branch of Government*. 3rd ed. Pacific Grove, CA: Brooks/Cole.

Miller, Gary E. and Ira Iscoe (1990). "A State Mental Health Commissioner and the Politics of Mental Illness." In Erwin C. Hargrove and John C. Glidewell, eds., *Impossible Jobs in Public Management*. Lawrence, KS: University Press of Kansas.

Moe, Ronald C. (1993). "Let's Rediscover Government, not Reinvent It." *Government Executive*. 25 (June):46–48, 60.

———— (1994). "The 'Reinventing Government' Exercise-Misinterpreting the Problem, Misjudging the Consequences." *Public Administration Review* 54(2):111–122.

Moe, Ronald C. and Robert S. Gilmour (1995). "Rediscovering Principles of Public Administration: The Neglected Foundation of Public Law." *Public Administration Review* 55(2):135–146.

Nanson, E. J. (1882). "Methods of Election." *Transactions and Proceedings of the Royal Society of Victoria* 19:197–240.

Nathan, Richard P. (1983). *The Administrative Presidency*. New York: John Wiley and Sons.

National Commission on the State and Local Public Service (1993). *Hard Truths/Tough Choices: An Agenda for State and Local Reform*. Albany, NY: Nelson A. Rockefeller Institute of Government.

Oleszek, Walter J. (1996). *Congressional Procedures and the Policy Process*, 4th ed. Washington, DC: CQ Press.

Osborne, David and Ted Gaebler (1992). *Reinventing Government: How the Entrepreneurial Spirit Is Transforming the Public Sector*. Reading, MA: Addison.

Powell, Colin (1992/93). "U.S. Forces: Challenges Ahead." *Foreign Affairs* 72:32–45.

Reich, Robert B. (1988). "Policy Making in a Democracy." In Robert B. Reich, ed., *The Power of Public Ideas*. Cambridge, MA: Harvard University Press, 123–156.

Riker, William H. (1958). "The Paradox of Voting and Congressional Rules for Voting on Amendments." *American Political Science Review* 52:349–366.

Schmitt, Eric (1997). "U.S. Study Panel Recommends Plan to Break Up I.N.S." *The New York Times*, 5 August, A1, A15.

Shribman, David M. (1997). "Helms Orchestrates a Sharp Lesson in Senate's True Heritage." *The Boston Globe*, 13 September, A7.

Simon, Herbert A. (1957). *Administrative Behavior: A Study of Decision-Making Processes in Administrative Organization*, 2nd ed. New York: Free Press.

Sinclair, Barbara (1977). *Unorthodox Lawmaking: New Legislative Processes in the U.S. Congress*. Washington, DC: CQ Press.

Spicer, Michael W. (1995). *The Founders, The Constitution, and Public Administration: A Conflict of World Views*. Washington, DC: Georgetown University Press.

Terry, Larry D. (1995). *Leadership of Public Bureaucracies: The Administrator as Conservator*. Thousand Oaks, CA: Sage.

"The 1975 Public Affairs Act: Never Was—But Not Forgotten" (1995). *The Washington Post*, 26 February.

Varley, Pamela (1987). "Ellen Schall and the Department of Juvenile Justice." Case C16-87-793.0. Cambridge, MA: Harvard University, John F. Kennedy School of Government.

Wilson, Woodrow (1887). "The Study of Administration." *Political Science Quarterly* 2:197–222.

―――――

The task of delivering social services effectively, fairly, and flexibly is no mean feat. Such leadership falls largely to those serving as "street-level bureaucrats." These teachers, social workers, police officers, and other public service workers interact directly with citizens, and, in making decisions critical to their lives, rely heavily on their discretion. What can and should their students learn? Who is eligible for welfare services under the agency's guidelines? Are the suspect's actions sufficient to justify making an arrest? Clients in these situations are vulnerable to "the system." These relationships are particularly significant for the poor, since they occur in institutions where decisions sometimes literally determine the fate of these individuals and their families. Drawing on the work of Frances Fox Piven and Richard Cloward, Lipsky points out that such decisions are made all the more difficult, because these institutions, and the street-level bureaucrats who represent them, are also expected to socialize their clients in such a way as to prevent riots and other behavior disruptive for the larger society.[a]

Much of the public debate over these controversial services, Lipsky has found, revolves around the actions of these officials. To the extent, then, that there is a debate over the conflict and scope of public services, it is often a debate over just what these street-level bureaucrats should—and should not—be doing. Clients want to be treated personally and sympathetically, but it is taxpayer funds that are "redistributed" to these clients, and the taxpayers too have expectations as to what constitutes appropriate treatment under these circumstances. Street-level bureaucrats must also be concerned about client reactions to their actions, whether it be to promote a positive self-concept in a school child or to "keep the lid on" in a high-crime neighborhood. Just as in the sixties when Lipsky gathered the data for his classic book, so today, heated community conflicts continue over the conduct of schools and police departments. Enlightened policies may exist in such departments, but the significance of those policies lies in the actions of these street-level bureaucrats. Clients, neighbors, and concerned citizens do not read "the regs;" for them, as Lipsky observes, street-level bureaucrat demands, expectations, and actions *are* the department.

The Critical Role of Street-Level Bureaucrats

Michael Lipsky

Public service workers currently occupy a critical position in American society. Although they are normally regarded as low-level employees, the actions of most public service workers actually constitute the services "delivered" by government. Moreover, when taken together the individual decisions of these workers become, or add up to, agency policy. Whether government policy is to deliver "goods"—such as welfare or public housing—or to confer status—such as "criminal" or "mentally ill"—the discretionary actions of public employees are the benefits and sanctions of government programs or determine access to government rights and benefits.

Most citizens encounter government (if they encounter it at all) not through letters to congressmen or by attendance at school board meetings but through their teachers and their children's teachers and through the policeman on the corner or in the patrol car. Each encounter of this kind represents an instance of policy delivery.

Public service workers who interact directly with citizens in the course of their jobs, and who have substantial discretion in the execution of their work are called *street-level bureaucrats* in this study. Public service agencies that employ a significant number of street-level bureaucrats in proportion to their work force are called *street-level bureaucracies.* Typical street-level bureaucrats are teachers, police officers and other law enforcement personnel, social workers, judges, public

---

[a]Frances Fox Piven and Richard A. Cloward, *Regulating the Poor* (New York: Pantheon Books, 1971).

Lipsky, Michael. *Street-Level Bureaucracy: Dilemmas of the Individual in Public Services,* New York: Russell Sage Foundation. 1980. Chapter 1.

lawyers and other court officers, health workers, and many other public employees who grant access to government programs and provide services within them. People who work in these jobs tend to have much in common because they experience analytically similar work conditions.[1]

The ways in which street-level bureaucrats deliver benefits and sanctions structure and delimit people's lives and opportunities. These ways orient and provide the social (and political) contexts in which people act. Thus every extension of service benefits is accompanied by an extension of state influence and control. As providers of public benefits and keepers of public order, street-level bureaucrats are the focus of political controversy. They are constantly torn by the demands of service recipients to improve effectiveness and responsiveness and by the demands of citizen groups to improve the efficacy and efficiency of government services. Since the salaries of street-level bureaucrats comprise a significant proportion of nondefense governmental expenditures, any doubts about the size of government budgets quickly translate into concerns for the scope and content of these public services. Moreover, public service workers have expanded and increasingly consolidated their collective strength so that in disputes over the scope of public services they have become a substantial independent force in the resolution of controversy affecting their status and position.

Street-level bureaucrats dominate political controversies over public services for two general reasons. First, debates about the proper scope and focus of governmental services are essentially debates over the scope and function of these public employees. Second, street-level bureaucrats have considerable impact on people's lives. This impact may be of several kinds. They socialize citizens to expectations of government services and a place in the political community. They determine the eligibility of citizens for government benefits and sanctions. They oversee the treatment (the service) citizens receive in those programs. Thus, in a sense street-level bureaucrats implicitly mediate aspects of the constitutional relationship of citizens to the state. In short, they hold the keys to a dimension of citizenship.

Conflict Over the Scope and Substance of Public Services

In the world of experience we perceive teachers, welfare workers, and police officers as members of separately organized and motivated public agencies. And so they are from many points of view. But if we divide public employees according to whether they interact with citizens directly and have discretion over significant aspects of citizens' lives, we see that a high proportion and enormous number of

---

[1] These definitions are analytical. They focus not on nominal occupational roles but on the characteristics of the particular work situations. Thus not every street-level bureaucrat works for a street-level bureaucracy [for example, a relocation specialist (a type of street-level bureaucrat) may work for an urban renewal agency whose employees are mostly planners, builders, and other technicians]. Conversely, not all employees of street-level bureaucracies are street-level bureaucrats (for example, file clerks in a welfare department or police officers on routine clerical assignments).

The conception of street-level bureaucracy was originally proposed in a paper prepared for the Annual Meeting of the American Political Science Association in 1969, "Toward a Theory of Street-Level Bureaucracy." It was later revised and published in Willis Hawley and Michael Lipsky, eds., Theoretical Perspectives on Urban Politics (Englewood Cliffs, N.J.: Prentice-Hall, 1977), pp. 196–213.

public workers share these job characteristics. They comprise a great portion of all public employees working in domestic affairs. State and local governments employ approximately 3.7 million people in local schools, more than 500,000 people in police operations, and over 300,000 people in public welfare. Public school employees represent more than half of all workers employed in local governments. Instructional jobs represent about two-thirds of the educational personnel, and many of the rest are former teachers engaged in administration, or social workers, psychologists, and librarians who provide direct services in the schools. Of the 3.2 million local government public employees not engaged in education, approximately 14 percent work as police officers. One of every sixteen jobs in state and local government outside of education is held by a public welfare worker.[2] In this and other areas the majority of jobs are held by people with responsibility for involvement with citizens.

Other street-level bureaucrats comprise an important part of the remainder of local government personnel rolls. Although the U.S. Census Bureau does not provide breakdowns of other job classifications suitable for our purposes, we can assume that many of the 1.1 million health workers,[3] most of the 5,000 public service lawyers,[4] many of the employees of the various court systems, and other public employees also perform as street-level bureaucrats. Some of the nation's larger cities employ a staggering number of street-level bureaucrats. For example, the 26,680 school teachers in Chicago are more numerous than the populations of many of the Chicago suburbs.[5]

Another measure of the significance of street-level bureaucrats in public sector employment is the amount of public funds allocated to pay them. Of all local government salaries, more than half went to public education in 1973. Almost 80 percent of these monies was used to pay instructional personnel. Police salaries comprised approximately one-sixth of local public salaries not assigned to education.[6]

Much of the growth in public employment in the past 25 years has occurred in the ranks of street-level bureaucrats. From 1955 to 1975 government employment more than doubled, largely because the baby boom of the postwar years and the growing number of elderly, dependent citizens increased state and local activity in education, health, and public welfare.[7]

---

[2] U.S. Bureau of the Census, Public Employment in 1973, Series GE 73 No. 1 (Washington, D.C.: Government Printing Office, 1974), p. 9. Presented in Alan Baker and Barbara Grouby, "Employment and Payrolls of State and Local Governments, By Function: October 1973," Municipal Year Book, 1975 (Washington, D.C.: International City Managers Association, 1975), pp. 109–112, table 4/3. Also, Marianne Stein Kah, "City Employment and Payrolls: 1975," Municipal Year Book, 1977 (Washington, D.C.: International City Managers Association, 1977), pp. 173–179. These figures have been adjusted to represent full-time equivalents. For purposes of assessing public commitments to providing services, full-time equivalents are more appropriate statistics than total employment figures, which count many part-time employees.

[3] Jeffry H. Galper, The Politics of Social Services (Englewood Cliffs, N.J.: Prentice-Hall, 1975), p. 56.

[4] Lois Forer, Death of the Law (New York: McKay, 1975), p. 191.

[5] New York Times, April 4, 1976, p. 22.

[6] Baker and Grouby, "Employment and Payrolls of State and Local Governments."

[7] New York Times, July 10, 1977, p. F13.

Street-level bureaucracies are labor-intensive in the extreme. Their business is providing service through people, and the operating costs of such agencies reflect their dependence upon salaried workers. Thus most of whatever is spent by government on education, police, or other social services (aside, of course, from income maintenance, or in the case of jails and prisons, inmate upkeep) goes directly to pay street-level bureaucrats. For example, in large cities over 90 percent of police expenditures is used to pay for salaries.[8]

Not only do the salaries of street-level bureaucrats constitute a major portion of the cost of public services, but also the scope of public services employing street-level burcaucrats has increased over time. Charity was once the responsibility of private agencies. The federal government now provides for the income needs of the poor. The public sector has absorbed responsibilities previously discharged by private organizations in such diverse and critical areas as policing, education, and health. Moreover, in all these fields government not only has supplanted private organizations but also has expanded the scope of responsibility of public ones. This is evident in increased public expectations for security and public safety, the extension of responsibilities in the schools to concerns with infant as well as post-adolescent development, and public demands for affordable health care services.[9]

Public safety, public health, and public education *may* still be elusive social objectives, but in the past century they have been transformed into areas for which there is active governmental responsibility. The transformation of public responsibility in the area of social welfare has led some to recognize that what people "have" in modern American society often may consist primarily of their claims on government "largess," and that claims to this "new property" should be protected as a right of citizens.[10] Street-level bureaucrats play a critical role in these citizen entitlements. Either they directly provide public benefits through services, or they mediate between citizens and their new but by no means secure estates.

---

[8] Of four cities with populations over one million responding to a *Municipal Year Book* survey, the proportion of personnel expenditures to total expenditures in police departments averaged 94 percent and did not go below 86 percent. Cities with smaller populations showed similar tendencies. These observations are derived from David Lewin, "Expenditure, Compensation, and Employment Data in Police, Fire, and Refuse Collection and Disposal Departments," *Municipal Year Book*, 1975 pp. 39–98, table 1/21. However, the variation was much greater in the less populous cities because of smaller base figures and the fact that when cities with smaller bases make capital investments, the ratio of personnel to total expenditures changes more precipitously.

That public expenditures for street-level bureaucracies go to individuals primarily as salaries may also be demonstrated in the case of education. For example, more than 73 percent of all noncapital education expenditures inside Standard Metropolitan Statistical Areas goes toward personal services (i.e., salaries). See Government Finances, Number 1, Finances of School Districts, 1972 U.S. Census of Government (Bureau of the Census, Social and Economic Statistics Administration, U.S. Department of Commerce), table 4.

[9] Many analysts have discussed the increasing role of services in the economy. See Daniel Bell, *The Coming of the Post-Industrial Society: A Venture in Social Forecasting* (New York: Basic Books, 1973); Alan Gartner and Frank Reissman. *The Service Society and the Consumer Vanguard* (New York: Harper & Row, 1974); Victor Fuchs, *The Service Economy* (New York: Columbia University Press, 1968). On transformations in public welfare, see Gilbert Steiner, *Social Insecurity* (Chicago: Rand McNally, 1966), chap. 1; on public safety, see Allan Silver, "The Demand for Order in Civil Society," in David Bordua, ed., *The Police: Six Sociological Essays* (New York: John Wiley, 1967), pp. 1–24.

[10] Charles Reich, "The New Property," *Yale Law Journal*, vol. 72 (April, 1964): 733–787.

The poorer people are, the greater the influence street-level bureaucrats tend to have over them. Indeed, these public workers are so situated that they may well be taken to be part of the problem of being poor. Consider the welfare recipient who lives in public housing and seeks the assistance of a legal services lawyer in order to reinstate her son in school. He has been suspended because of frequent encounters with the police. She is caught in a net of street-level bureaucrats with conflicting orientations toward her, all acting in what they call her "interest" and "the public interest."[11]

People who are not able to purchase services in the private sector must seek them from government if they are to receive them at all. Indeed, it is taken as a sign of social progress that poor people are granted access to services if they are too poor to pay for them.

Thus, when social reformers seek to ameliorate the problems of the poor, they often end up discussing the status of street-level bureaucrats. Welfare reformers move to separate service provision from decisions about support payments, or they design a negative income tax system that would eliminate social workers in allocating welfare. Problems of backlog in the courts are met with proposals to increase the number of judges. Recognition that early-childhood development largely establishes the potential for later achievement results in the development of new programs (such as Head Start) in and out of established institutions, to provide enriched early-childhood experiences.

In the 1960s and early 1970s the modal governmental response to social problems was to commission a corps of street-level bureaucrats to attend to them. Are poor people deprived of equal access to the courts? Provide them with lawyers. Equal access to health care? Establish neighborhood clinics. Educational opportunity? Develop preschool enrichment programs. It is far easier and less disruptive to develop employment for street-level bureaucrats than to reduce income inequalities.

In recent years public employees have benefitted considerably from the growth of public spending on street-level bureaucracies.[12] Salaries have increased from inadequate to respectable and even desirable. Meanwhile, pubic employees, with street-level bureaucrats in the lead, have secured unprecedented control over their work environments through the development of unions and union-like associations.[13] For example, teachers and other instructional personnel have often been able to maintain their positions and even increase in number, although schools are more frequently under attack for their cost to taxpayers. The ratio of instructional personnel in schools has continued to rise despite the decline in the

[11] Carl Hosticka, "Legal Services Lawyers Encounter Clients: A Study in Street-Level Bureaucracy" (Ph.D. diss., Massachusetts Institute of Technology, 1976), pp. 11–13.

[12] See Frances Piven's convincing essay in which she argues that social service workers were the major beneficiaries of federal programs concerned with cities and poor people in the 1960s. Piven, "The Urban Crisis: Who Got What and Why," in Richard Cloward and Frances Piven, The Politics of Turmoil (New York: Vintage Books, 1972) pp. 314–351.

[13] J. Joseph Loewenberg and Michael H. Moskow, eds., Collective Bargaining in Government (Englewood Cliffs, N.J.: Prentice-Hall, 1972). A. Laurence Chickering, ed., Public Employee Unions (Lexington, Mass.: Lexington Books, 1976); and Margaret Levi, Bureaucratic Insurgency (Lexington, Mass.: Lexington Books, 1977).

number of school-age children[14] This development supplements general public support for the view that some street-level bureaucrats, such as teachers and police officers, are necessary for a healthy society.[15]

The fiscal crisis that has affected many cities, notably New York and more recently Cleveland and Newark, has provided an opportunity to assess the capacity of public service workers to hold onto their jobs in the face of enormous pressures. Since so much of municipal budgets consists of inflexible, mandated costs—for debt service, pension plans and other personnel benefits, contractually obligated salary increases, capital expenditure commitments, energy purchases, and so on— the place to find "fat" to eliminate from municipal budgets is in the service sector, where most expenditures tend to be for salaries. While many public employees have been fired during this crisis period, it is significant that public service workers often have been able to lobby, bargain, and cajole to minimize this attrition.[16] They are supported in their claims by a public fearful of a reduced police force on the street and resentful of dirtier streets resulting from fewer garbage pickups. They are supported by families whose children will receive less instruction from fewer specialists than in the past if teachers are fired. And it does not hurt their arguments that many public employees and their relatives vote in the city considering force reductions.[17]

The growth of the service sector represents the furthest reaches of the welfare state. The service sector penetrates every area of human needs as they are recognized and defined, and it grows within each recognized area. This is not to say that the need is met, but only that the service state breaches the barriers between public responsibility and private affairs.

The fiscal crisis of the cities focuses on the service sector, fundamentally challenging the priorities of the service state under current perceptions of scarcity. Liberals have now joined fiscal conservatives in challenging service provision. They do not do so directly, by questioning whether public services and responsibilities developed in this century are appropriate. Instead, they do it backhandedly, arguing that the accretion of public employees and their apparently irreversible demands upon revenues threaten the autonomy, flexibility, and prosperity of the political order. Debates over the proper scope of services face the threat of being overwhelmed by challenges to the entire social service structure as seen from the perspective of unbalanced public budgets.

---

[14]The decline is a function of the lower birthrate and periodicity in the size of the school-age population originally resulting from the birth explosion following World War II. See Baker and Grouby, *Municipal Year Book, 1975,* pp. 109ff., on serviceability ratios.

[15]This perspective remains applicable in the current period. However, in reaction to this tendency, programs that would eliminate service mediators and service providers, such as negative income taxation and housing allowances, have gained support. Fiscal scarcity has brought to public attention questions concerning the marginal utility of some of these service areas.

[16]Consider the New York City policeman who, in October 1976, agreed to work overtime without pay so that a crop of rookie patrolmen would not be eliminated. *New York Times,* October 24, 1976, p. 24.

[17]There can be no better illustration of the strength of the organized service workers and their support by relevant interests than the New York State Assembly's overriding of Gov. Hugh Carey's veto of the so-called, Stavisky bill. This legislation, written in a period of massive concern for cutting the New York City budget, required the city to spend no less on education in the three years following the fiscal collapse than in the three years before the crisis, thus tying the hands of the city's financial managers even more. *New York Times,* April 4, 1976, p. E6; April 18, 1976, p. E6.

Conflict Over Interactions With Citizens

I have argued that street-level bureaucrats engender controversy because they must be dealt with if policy is to change. A second reason street-level bureaucrats tend to be the focus of public controversy is the immediacy of their interactions with citizens and their impact on peoples' lives. The policy delivered by street-level bureaucrats is most often immediate and personal. They usually make decisions on the spot (although sometimes they try not to) and their determinations are focused entirely on the individual. In contrast, an urban renewal program might destroy a neighborhood and replace and substitute new housing and different people, but the policy was prolonged, had many different stages, and was usually played out in arenas far removed from the daily life of neighborhood residents.

The decisions of street-level bureaucrats tend to be redistributive as well as allocative. By determining eligibility for benefits they enhance the claims of some citizens to governmental goods and services at the expense of general taxpayers and those whose claims are denied. By increasing or decreasing benefits availability to low-income recipient populations they implicitly regulate the degree of redistribution that will be paid for by more affluent sectors.

In another sense, in delivering policy street-level bureaucrats make decisions about people that affect their life chances. To designate or treat someone as a welfare recipient, a juvenile delinquent, or a high achiever affects the relationships of others to that person and also affects the person's self-evaluation. Thus begins (or continues) the social process that we infer accounts for so many self-fulfilling prophecies. The child judged to be a juvenile delinquent develops such a self-image and is grouped with other "delinquents," increasing the chances that he or she will adopt the behavior thought to have been incipient in the first place. Children thought by their teacher to be richly endowed in learning ability learn more than peers of equal intelligence who were not thought to be superior.[18] Welfare recipients find or accept housing inferior to those with equal disposable incomes who are not recipients.[19]

A defining facet of the working environment of street-level bureaucrats is that they must deal with clients' personal reactions to their decisions, however they cope with their implications. To say that people's self-evaluation is affected by the actions of street-level bureaucrats is to say that people are reactive to the policy. This is not exclusively confined to subconscious processes. Clients of street-level bureaucracies respond angrily to real or perceived injustices, develop strategies to ingratiate themselves with workers, act grateful and elated or sullen and passive in reaction to street-level bureaucrats' decisions. It is one thing to be treated neglectfully and routinely by the telephone company, the motor vehicle bureau, or other government agencies whose agents know nothing of the personal circumstances surrounding a claim or request. It is quite another thing to be shuffled, categorized, and treated "bureaucratically," (in the pejorative sense), by someone to

---

[18]The seminal work here is Robert Rosenthal and Lenore Jacobson, *Pygmalion in the Classroom* (New York: Holt, Rinehart and Winston, 1968).

[19]Martin Rein, "Welfare and Housing," Joint Center Working Papers Series, no. 4 (Cambridge, Mass: Joint Center for Urban Studies, Spring, 1971, rev. Feb. 1972).

whom one is directly talking and from whom one expects at least an open and sympathetic hearing. In short, the reality of the work of street-level bureaucrats could hardly be farther from the bureaucratic ideal of impersonal detachment in decision making.[20] On the contrary, in street-level bureaucracies the objects of critical decisions—*people*—actually change as a result of the decisions.

Street-level bureaucrats are also the focus of citizen reactions because their discretion opens up the possibility that they will respond favorably on behalf of people. Their general and diffuse obligation to the "public interest" permits hope to flourish that the individual worker will adopt a benign or favorable orientation toward the client. Thus, in a world of large and impersonal agencies that apparently hold the keys to important benefits, sanctions, and opportunities, the ambiguity of work definitions sustains hope for a friend in court.

This discussion helps explain continued controversy over street-level bureaucracies at the level of individual service provision. At the same time, the peculiar nature of government service delivery through street-level bureaucrats helps explain why street-level bureaucracies are apparently the primary focus of community conflict in the current period, and why they are likely to remain the focus of such conflict in the foreseeable future. It is no accident that the most heated community conflicts since 1964 have focused on schools and police departments, and on the responsiveness of health and welfare agencies and institutions.[21] These are the sites of the provision of public benefits and sanctions. They are the locus of individual decisions about and treatment of citizens, and thus are primary targets of protest. As Frances Fox Piven and Richard Cloward explain:

> . . . people experience deprivation and oppression within a concrete setting, not as the end product of large and abstract processes, and it is the concrete experience that molds their discontent into specific grievances against specific targets. . . . People on relief [for example] experience the shabby waiting rooms, the overseer or the caseworker, and the dole. They do not experience American social welfare policy. . . . In other words, it is the daily experience of people that shapes their grievances, establishes the measure of their demands, and points out the targets of their anger.[22]

While people may experience these bureaucracies as individuals, schools, precinct houses, or neighborhood clinics are places where policy about individuals is organized collectively. These administrative arrangements suggest to citizens the possibility that controlling, or at least affecting, their structures will influence the quality of individual treatment. Thus we have two preconditions for successful community organization efforts: the hope and plausibility that individual benefits may accrue to those taking part in group action and a visible, accessible, and blamable collective target.[23]

---

[20] On the alleged importance of bureaucratic detachment in processing clients see Peter Blau, *Exchange and Power in Social Life* (New York: John Wiley, 1964), p. 66.

[21] See National Advisory Commission on Civil Disorders, *Report* (New York: Bantam, 1968); Peter Rossi et al., *Roots of Urban Discontent* (New York: John Wiley, 1974).

[22] Frances Fox Piven and Richard Cloward, *Poor People's Movements* (New York: Pantheon, 1977), pp. 20–21.

[23] Michael Lipsky and Margaret Levi, "Community Organization as a Political Resource," in Harlan Hahn, ed., *People and Places in Urban Society* (Urban Affairs Annual Review, vol. 6) (Beverly Hills, Calif.: Sage Publications, 1972), pp. 175–199.

Community action focused on street-level bureaucracies is also apparently motivated by concerns for community character. The dominant institutions in communities help shape community identity. They may be responsive to the dominant community group (this has been the traditional role of high schools in Boston) or they may be unresponsive and opposed to conceptions of community and identity favored by residents, as in the case of schools that neglect the Spanish heritage of a significant minority. Whether people are motivated by specific grievances or more diffuse concerns that become directed at community institutions, their focus in protesting the actions of street-level bureaucracies may be attributed to the familiarity of the agency, its critical role in community welfare, and a perception at some level that these institutions are not sufficiently accountable to the people they serve.

Finally, street-level bureaucrats play a critical role in regulating the degree of contemporary conflict by virtue of their role as agents of social control. Citizens who receive public benefits interact with public agents who require certain behaviors of them. They must anticipate the requirements of these public agents and claimants must tailor their actions and develop "suitable" attitudes both toward the services they receive and toward the street-level bureaucrats themselves. Teachers convey and enforce expectations of proper attitudes toward schooling, self, and efficacy in other interactions. Policemen convey expectations about public behavior and authority. Social workers convey expectations about public benefits and the status of recipients.

The social control function of street-level bureaucrats requires comment in a discussion of the places of public service workers in the larger society. The public service sector plays a critical part in softening the impact of the economic system on those who are not its primary beneficiaries and inducing people to accept the neglect or inadequacy of primary economic and social institutions. Police, courts, and prisons obviously play such a role in processing the junkies, petty thieves, muggers, and others whose behavior toward society is associated with their economic position. It is a role equally played by schools in socializing the population to the economic order and the likely opportunities for different strata of the population. Public support and employment programs expand to ameliorate the impact of unemployment or reduce the incidence of discontent; they contract when employment opportunities improve. Moreover, they are designed and implemented to convey the message that welfare status is to be avoided and that work, however poorly rewarded, is preferable to public assistance. One can also see the two edges of public policy in the "war on poverty" where the public benefits of social service and community action invested neighborhood institutions with benefits for which potential dissidents could compete and ordinary citizens could develop dependency.[24]

---

[24] See James O'Connor's discussion of "legitimation" and his general thesis concerning the role of the state service sector, in O'Connor, *The Fiscal Crisis of the State* (New York: St. Martin's, 1973). On social control functions in particular policy sectors see Samuel Bowles and Herbert Gintis, *Schooling in Capitalist America* (New York: Basic Books, 1976); Frances Fox Piven and Richard Cloward, *Regulating the Poor* (New York: Pantheon, 1971); Jeffry Galper, *The Politics of Social Services;* Richard Quinney, *Criminology* (Boston: Little, Brown, 1975); Ira Katznelson, "Urban Counterrevolution," in Robert P. Wolff, ed., *1984 Revisited* (New York: Alfred Knopf, 1973), pp. 139–164.

What to some are the highest reaches of the welfare state are to others the furthest extension of social control. Street-level bureaucrats are partly the focus of controversy because they play this dual role. Welfare reform founders on disagreements over whether to eliminate close scrutiny of welfare applications in order to reduce administrative costs and harassment of recipients, or to increase the scrutiny in the name of controlling abuses and preventing welfare recipients from taking advantage. Juvenile corrections and mental health policy founder on disputes over the desirability of dismantling large institutions in the name of cost effectiveness and rehabilitation, or retaining close supervision in an effort to avoid the costs of letting unreconstructed "deviants" loose. In short, street-level bureaucrats are also at the center of controversy because a divided public perceives that social control in the name of public order and acceptance of the status quo are social objectives with which proposals to reduce the role of street-level bureaucrats (eliminating welfare checkups, reducing parole personnel, decriminalizing marijuana) would interfere.

Public controversy also focuses on the proper kind of social control. Current debates in corrections policy, concerning automatic sentencing and a "hard-nosed" view of punishment or more rehabilitative orientations, reflect conflict over the degree of harshness in managing prison populations. In educational practice the public is also divided as to the advisability of liberal disciplinary policies and more flexible instruction or punitive discipline and more rigid, traditional approaches. The "medicalization" of deviance, in which disruptive behavior is presumed cause for intervention by a doctor rather than a disciplinarian, is another area in which there is controversy over the appropriate kind of social control.

From the citizen's viewpoint, the roles of street-level bureaucrats are as extensive as the functions of government and intensively experienced as daily routines require them to interact with the street ministers of education, dispute settlement, and health services. Collectively, street-level bureaucrats absorb a high share of public resources and become the focus of society's hopes for a healthy balance between provision of public services and a reasonable burden of public expenditures. As individuals, street-level bureaucrats represent the hopes of citizens for fair and effective treatment by government even as they are positioned to see clearly the limitations on effective intervention and the constraints on responsiveness engendered by mass processing.

The power of street-level bureaucrats to make policy lies in their wide exercise of discretion and their autonomy, or independence, from their agency's authority. Even enlightened actions by these officials may put them in conflict with middle managers who must also be concerned about other bureaucratic values. A struggle periodically erupts between these workers and their public managers who are seeking to extend agency control over policy implementation, limit resource expenditures, and maintain some uniformity of treatment. The tension between these professionals working at the grassroots level and their managers pertains to the professionals' inevitable attempt to increase their autonomy for personal as well as professional reasons, and the power that these workers possess due to the critical nature of their interactions with the clients.

The street-level bureaucrats, despite the standards and canons of their professions, are thus caught between societal demands, usually from taxpayers, and their clients. On the one hand, societal demands require close monitoring and other efficiency mechanisms employed by all bureaucracies striving to coordinate and control large programs. Hence, the street-level bureaucrats must cope personally by finding ways to process large case loads at a sufficiently rapid rate to maintain an acceptable work environment from their own perspective. On the other hand, these street-level bureaucrats must create a more flexible, humane approach designed to best meet the client's needs, and, consequently, their professional goals.

The street-level bureaucrats, Lipsky shows, in many cases have other personal reasons for preserving their discretion by resisting authority, and public service unions assist them in that pursuit. Their personal goals may sometimes be met at the client's expense. It is the addition of their professional goals, however, that enables street-level bureaucrats (and many other professionals in government) to exercise more power in resisting hierarchical controls than one would expect from perusing the organization chart of a command-control bureaucracy.

Street-level bureaucrats can thus combine the need for discretion to accomplish the complex nature of their job at the "grass roots" level with a claim to the specialized knowledge, or expertise, of the professional. Under these circumstances, Lipsky maintains, the power relationship between the street-level bureaucrat and middle managers becomes reciprocal, and frequently involves conflict.

In the concluding chapter of his book (not included here), Lipsky argues that if their needs are to be met, the clients too must possess something of a balance of power with the street-level bureaucrats. When the professional is in a controlling position, the burden of proof lies on the client in raising issues related to service delivery. In most cases, their knowledge of the "welfare system" or "education system" is confined to their own level, but client autonomy and influence could result if closer attention were paid to their individual views on the quality of service delivery. The views of client activists representing their communities should also be encouraged "to insure that clients contribute to the way street-level bureaucrats define their roles."[a]

Lipsky argues, however, that street-level bureaucrats must take on, as a professional obligation, the development of "techniques to educate clients toward making better judgements of service provision."[b] While at first glance, it might seem that bringing such pressure down upon themselves would reduce their discretion, creation of a client reference group would enable the street-level bureaucrats to point authentically to client pressure in seeking to justify decisions also regarded as professionally sound. Indeed, Lipsky contends that the street-level bureaucrats must, in addition, work on a team basis to encourage more professional, and less arbitrary, decision making on individual cases. Having designed such a power configuration, constructed both around greater client and more effective professional participation, they can then "survive in a context in which people are dedicated to public service and receive support from client groups, fellow workers, and the community."[c] Under these conditions, clients would have a greater likelihood of being empowered even while receiving the services that many still desperately need.

---

[a]Michael Lipsky, *Street-Level Bureaucracy: Dilemmas of the Individual in Public Services*, p. 196.

[b]Michael Lipsky, *Street-Level Bureaucracy: Dilemmas of the Individual in Public Services*, p. 208.

[c]Michael Lipsky, *Street-Level Bureaucracy: Dilemmas of the Individual in Public Services*, p. 209.

Street-Level Bureaucrats as Policy Makers

Michael Lipsky

Street-level bureaucrats make policy in two related respects. They exercise wide discretion in decisions about citizens with whom they interact. Then, when taken in concert, their individual actions add up to agency behavior. The task . . . is to demonstrate that the position of street-level bureaucrats regularly permits them to make policy with respect to significant aspects of their interactions with citizens.

The policy-making roles of street-level bureaucrats are built upon two inter-related facets of their positions: relatively high degrees of discretion and relative autonomy from organizational authority.

Discretion

Unlike lower-level workers in most organizations, street-level bureaucrats have considerable discretion in determining the nature, amount, and quality of benefits and sanctions provided by their agencies.[1] Policemen decide who to arrest and whose behavior to overlook. Judges decide who shall receive a suspended sentence and who shall receive maximum punishment. Teachers decide who will be suspended and who will remain in school, and they make subtle determinations of who is teachable. Perhaps the most highly refined example of street-level bureaucratic discretion comes from the field of corrections. Prison guards conventionally file injurious reports on inmates whom they judge to be guilty of "silent insolence." Clearly what does or does not constitute a dirty look is a matter of some subjectivity.[2]

This is not to say that street-level workers are unrestrained by rules, regulations, and directives from above, or by the norms and practices of their occupational group. On the contrary, the major dimensions of public policy—levels of benefits, categories of eligibility, nature of rules, regulations and services—are shaped by policy elites and political and administrative officials. Administrators and occupational and community norms also structure policy choices of street-level bureaucrats. These influences establish the major dimensions of street-level policy and account for the degree of standardization that exists in public programs from place to place as well as in local programs.

To the extent that street-level bureaucrats are professionals, the assertion that they exercise considerable discretion is fairly obvious. Professionals are expected to exercise discretionary judgment in their field. They are regularly deferred to in their specialized areas of work and are relatively free from supervision by superiors

Michael Lipsky. *Street-Level Bureaucracy: Dilemmas of the Individual in Public Services,* New York: Russell Sage Foundation. 1980. Chapter 2.

[1] See Chris Argyris, *Integrating the Individual and the Organization* (New York: John Wiley, 1964), pp. 35–41.

[2] Frank L. Morris, Sr., "The Advantages and Disadvantages of Black Political Group Activity in Two Northern Maximum Security State Prisons" (Ph.D. diss., Massachusetts Institute of Technology, 1976), p. 40.

or scrutiny by clients.[3] Yet even public employees who do not have claims to professional status exercise considerable discretion. Clerks in welfare and pubic housing agencies, for example, may exercise discretion in determining client access to benefits, even though their discretion is formally circumscribed by rules and relatively close supervision.

Rules may actually be an impediment to supervision. They may be so voluminous and contradictory that they can only be enforced or invoked selectively. In most public welfare departments, regulations are encyclopedic, yet at the same time, they are constantly being changed. With such rules adherence to anything but the most basic and fundamental precepts of eligibility cannot be expected. Police behavior is so highly specified by statutes and regulations that policemen are expected to invoke the law selectively. They could not possibly make arrests for all the infractions they observe during their working day.[4] (Like doctors and clergymen in many jurisdictions, they are required to be on-duty and ready to intervene even during their off-duty hours.) Similarly, federal civil-rights compliance officers have so many mandated responsibilities in comparison to their resources that they have been free to determine their own priorities.[5] It would seem that the proliferation of rules and responsibilities is only problematically related to the degree of discretion street-level bureaucrats enjoy.[6]

Although the case for the pervasive existence of discretion in street-level work is fairly easy to make it is important to remember that in public services some interactions take place with citizens that involve relatively little bureaucratic discretion. Patrolmen assigned to traffic duty or gun permit applications, for example, may interact with the public but exercise little discretion in performing these tasks. Discretion is a relative concept. It follows that the greater the degree of discretion the more salient this analysis in understanding the character of workers' behavior.

Since many of the problems discussed here would theoretically disappear if workers' discretion were eliminated, one may wonder why discretion remains characteristic of their jobs. The answer is that certain characteristics of the jobs of street-level bureaucrats make it difficult, if not impossible, to severely reduce

[3] For some analysts the defining characteristic of professionalism is simply the discretion to make decisions about clients. In this view street-level bureaucrats would unquestionably be professionals. See Albert Reiss, *The Police and the Public* (New Haven: Yale University Press, 1971), p. 122.

[4] On rules and the police, see James Q. Wilson, *Varieties of Police Behavior* (Cambridge: Harvard University Press, 1968), p. 31; David Perry, *Police in the Metropolis* (Columbus, Ohio: Charles Merrill, 1975), p. 168. See also Gresham Sykes' discussion of the dilemma of prison guards in being formally required to intervene in all cases of observed infractions, in Sykes, *The Society of Captives* (Princeton, N.J.: Princeton University Press, 1958).

[5] For example, the Office of Civil Rights of the Department of Health, Education, and Welfare has responsibility to monitor potential violations as follows: a racial discrimination under Title VI of the Civil Rights Act of 1964 in 16,000 public school districts, 2,800 institutions of higher education, and 30,000 institutions of health and social services; in the same areas, discrimination against handicapped people under Section 504 of the Vocational Rehabilitation Act of 1973; sex discrimination under Section 799A of the Public Health Service Act in 1,500 health education institutions, and under Section 745, sex discrimination in nursing schools; sex discrimination under Title IX, Education Amendments of 1972, in 16,000 public school districts; discrimination by federal contractors under Executive Order 11246, innumerable contractors at 863 higher-education campuses, and more than 3,500 additional locations. Virginia Balderama, "The Office of Civil Rights as a Street-Level Bureaucracy," unpublished seminar paper, University of Washington, March, 1976.

[6] David Perry and Paula Sornoff report that welfare workers' behavior with clients in California is ruled by 115 pounds of regulations; that the average police officer is obliged to enforce approximately 30,000 federal, state, and local laws. Perry and Sornoff, "Street-Level Administration and the Law: The Problem of Police Community Relations," *Criminal Law Bulletin*, vol. 8, no. 1 (January–February, 1972), p. 46.

discretion. They involve complex tasks for which elaboration of rules, guidelines, or instructions cannot circumscribe the alternatives. This may be the case for one of at least two reasons.

First, street-level bureaucrats often work in situations too complicated to reduce to programmatic formats. Policemen cannot carry around instructions on how to intervene with citizens, particularly in potentially hostile encounters. Indeed, they would probably not go out on the street if such instructions were promulgated, or they would refuse to intervene in potentially dangerous situations.[7] Similarly, contemporary views of education mitigate against detailed instructions to teachers on how and what to teach, since the philosophy prevails that to a point every child requires a response appropriate to the specific learning context.

Second, street-level bureaucrats work in situations that often require responses to the human dimensions of situations. They have discretion because the accepted definitions of their tasks call for sensitive observation and judgment, which are not reducible to programmed formats. It may be that uniform sentencing would reduce inequities in the criminal justice system. But we also want the law to be responsive to the unique circumstances of individual transgressions.[8] We want teachers to perceive the unique potential of children. In short, to a degree the society seeks not only impartiality from its public agencies but also compassion for special circumstances and flexibility in dealing with them.[9]

A third reason discretion is not likely to be eliminated bears more on the function of lower-level workers who interact with citizens than with the nature of the tasks. Street-level discretion promotes workers' self-regard and encourages clients to believe that workers hold the key to their well-being. For both workers and clients, maintenance of discretion contributes to the legitimacy of the welfare-service state, although street-level bureaucrats by no means establish the boundaries of state intervention.

The search for the correct balance between compassion and flexibility on the one hand, and impartiality and rigid rule-application on the other hand presents a dialectic of public service reform. Reformers attempt to limit worker discretion at one time, and increase it at another. In order to make ambulance dispatch by untrained personnel more efficient, health planners work to rationalize emergency dispatch procedures by developing a programmed format to aid in identifying health emergencies.[10] Meanwhile, other health planners seek to replace untrained admission clerks with health professionals in order to insure greater sensitivity to the health problems of prospective patients.[11] Programmed learning materials are introduced to release teachers for more intensive work with some students, while

---

[7]Consider police assertions that they would be less willing to risk intervention if civilian review boards could penalize them for errors of judgment made under hectic and confusing circumstances which civilians might not appreciate.

[8]For a discussion of attempts to introduce uniform sentencing for juvenile offenders, see the report of the findings of the Juvenile Justice Standards Project, *New York Times*, November 30, 1975, p. 1; for adult offenders, New York Times, October 16, 1977, p. 1.

[9]See James Q. Wilson, "The Bureaucracy Problem," *The Public Interest* (Winter, 1967). pp. 3–9.

[10]Keith Stevenson and Thomas Willemain, "Analyzing the Process of Screening Calls for Emergency Service" (Cambridge, Mass.: Operations Research Center, Massachusetts Institute of Technology, September, 1974), Technical Report TR-08-74.

[11]Interviews with administrative personnel, Veterans Administration Hospital, Bedford, Mass., August, 1974.

all students benefit from these motivational and self-paced features. Later this innovation is found wanting because it eliminated teachers' feedback to students and encouraged regimentation rather than individualized learning.[12] To the extent that tasks remain complex and human intervention is considered necessary for effective service, discretion will remain characteristic of many public service jobs.

Relative Autonomy From Organizational Authority

Most analysts take for granted that the work of lower-level participants will more or less conform to what is expected of them. Organizational theorists recognize that there will always be some slippage between orders and the carrying out of orders, but this slippage is usually attributed to poor communication or workers' residual, and not terribly important, disagreement with organizational goals. In any event, such difficulties are usually considered unimportant enough that organizations can overcome them.

This observation is partly derived from the recognition that lower level workers' behavior in organizations, including public agencies, appears to be cooperative. Workers for the most part accept the legitimacy of the formal structure of authority, and they are not in a position to dissent successfully.

But what if workers do not share the objectives of their superiors? Lower-level participants in organizations often do not share the perspectives and preferences of their superiors and hence in some respects cannot be thought to be working toward stated agency goals. At least this is the case when workers are not recruited with an affinity for the organization's goals; workers do not consider orders from "above" legitimate; or the incentives available to supervisors are matched by countermeasures available to lower-level participants. One can expect a distinct degree of noncompliance if lower-level workers' *interests* differ from the interests of those at higher levels, and the incentives and sanctions available to higher levels are not sufficient to prevail.[13]

Sometimes different levels of organizations are more appropriately conceived as intrinsically in conflict with each other rather than mutually responsive and supportive.[14] At times it is more useful to view lower-level workers as having distinctly different interests and the resources to pursue those interests. Here discrepancies between policy declarations and actual policy would be expected and predictable. And explanations for the discrepancies would be searched for not in the break-

---

[12] Fred Hechinger, "Where Have All the Innovations Gone?" *New York Times,* November 16, 1975, p. ED30.

[13] The emphasis here is on structural explanations. Lower-level participants may also personally disagree with policy objectives. See Donald Van Meter and Carl Van Horn, "The Policy Implementation Process: A Conceptual Framework," *Administration and Society,* vol. 6, no. 4 (1975), pp. 482–483.

[14] For this analysis I have drawn on Dahrendorf's observation that assuming ubiquitous conflict among social units helps in understanding some political events better than assuming inclinations toward stability, integration, and interdependence. For Dahrendorf, conflict relations are inevitable since authority relations, which are present in all social units, are necessarily relations of subordination and superordination. However, Dahrendorf for general purposes is unable to choose between the two models of social dynamics—the integration or the "coercion" model—although for an analysis of class formation and development he favors the coercion perspective. Similarly, the model stressing conflict outlined here may be applicable under the circumstances outlined here, while the systems-integration model may be appropriate for other aspects of policy analysis. Generally see Ralf Dahrendorf, *Class and Class Conflict in Industrial Society* (Stanford, Calif.: Stanford University Press, 1959), chap. 5.

down or inadequacy of the compliance system but in the structure of the work situation from which workers' "antagonistic" interests arise.

In such organizations policy may be carried out consistent with the interests of higher levels, but this should be understood as resulting from the mutual adjustment of antagonistic perspectives as well as the result of shared interests. In such cases the latent conflict in the interests of different levels is suppressed or is a matter of indifference to one or both parties. This approach takes as problematic the mutuality of interests, and it searches instead for the mechanisms by which essentially antagonistic or divergent interests are adjusted.[15]

Some of the ways lower-level workers can withhold cooperation within their organizations include such personal strategies as not working (excessive absenteeism, quitting), aggression toward the organization (stealing, cheating, deliberate wasting), and negative attitudes with implications for work (alienation, apathy).[16] Workers may take advantage of collective resources to act noncooperatively by forming trade unions or by exercising rights under collective bargaining agreements or civil service regulations. These collective strategies for noncooperation contribute to workers' willingness to display lack of motivation and to perform at only minimal levels.[17]

These forms of noncooperation injure organizations' abilities to achieve their objectives because workers perform at less than full capacity. The management challenge perceived to be at the heart of the problem is how to make workers' needs for personal, material, or psychological gratification mesh with the organization's needs. Thus the management problem regarding worker absenteeism becomes how to improve job satisfaction while retaining productivity.

However, there is another class of conflicts between lower-level workers and the organizations that arise not from the personal needs of the workers alone but also from their positions within their organizations. The role of street-level bureaucrats, like other roles, may be conceived as a set of expected interests[18] as well as expected behaviors. Street-level bureaucrats may be shown to have distinctly different interests from the interests of others in the agencies for which they work. Moreover, certain features of their role make it possible for them to make these differences manifest. Differences in interests, and the possibility of surfacing the differences, permit analysis of the structural position of street-level bureaucrats from a conflict perspective.[19]

---

[15] The perspective developed in these paragraphs is elaborated in Michael Lipsky, "Standing the Study of Public Policy Implementation on Its Head," in W. Dean Burnham and Martha Wagner Weinberg, eds., *American Politics and Public Policy* (Cambridge, Mass.: Massachusetts Institute of Technology Press, 1978), pp. 391–402.

[16] Argyris, *Integrating the Individual and the Organization*, pp. 59–67.

[17] On low motivation of public service workers, see Eric Nordlinger, *Decentralizing the City* (Cambridge, Mass.: Massachusetts Institute of Technology Press, 1972), chap. 3; and E. S. Savas and Sigmund Ginsburg, "The Civil Service—A Meritless System?" *The Public Interest*, no. 32 (Summer, 1973), pp. 70–85.

The problem of maintaining worker participation in organizations is a classic issue of organizational theory. For a significant early analysis, see James March and Herbert Simon, *Organizations* (New York: John Wiley, 1958).

[18] Dahrendorf, *Class and Class Conflict in Industrial Society*, p. 178.

[19] Donald Van Meter and Carl Van Horn point out that the "disposition of implementors" is critical to policy implementation success. The following discussion elaborates two of the conditions under which, they assert, policy implementors will resist implementation: when the policies to be implemented offend their sense of self-interest, and when the policies threaten features of the organization and procedures they desire to maintain. Van Meter and Van Horn, "The Policy Implementation Process: A Conceptual Framework," pp. 482–483.

In the following brief discussion, the nature of the conflict between the objectives and orientations of street-level bureaucrats and those in higher authority roles is considered first. Then the capacity of street-level bureaucrats' ability to resist organizational directives is treated.[20]

Differences Between Street-Level Bureaucrats and Managers

In general lower-level workers have different job priorities than managers. At the very least, workers have an interest in minimizing the danger and discomforts of the job and maximizing income and personal gratification. These priorities are of interest to management for the most part only as they relate to productivity and effectiveness. In street-level bureaucracies lower-level workers are likely to have considerably more than minimal differences with management. Earlier it was suggested that worker compliance is affected by the extent to which managers' orders are considered legitimate. Street-level bureaucrats may consider legitimate the right of managers to provide directives, but they may consider their managers' policy objectives illegitimate. Teachers asked to participate in compensatory education programs in which they do not believe, or policemen no longer able to arrest derelicts for alcoholism, may resist these policy objectives in various ways.

One way in which the interests of street-level bureaucrats depart from those of managers is their need to process workloads expeditiously, free from real and psychological threats. The fact that street-level bureaucrats must exercise discretion in processing large amounts of work with inadequate resources means that they must develop shortcuts and simplifications to cope with the press of responsibilities. The coping mechanisms street-level bureaucrats develop often are unsanctioned by managers of their agencies.

Managers are interested in achieving results consistent with agency objectives. Street-level bureaucrats are interested in processing work consistent with their own preferences and only those agency policies so salient as to be backed up by significant sanctions. Theses sanctions must be limited. If everything receives priority, nothing does. Work-processing devices are part of the informal agency structure that may be necessary to maintain the organization, even though the procedures may be contrary to agency policy.[21]

This is a neat paradox. Lower-level participants develop coping mechanisms contrary to an agency's policy but actually basic to its survival. For example,

---

[20] The discussion is necessarily schematic to a degree. For example, it is an oversimplification to treat street-level bureaucracies as comprised of lower-level workers and managers. In this discussion the term "manager" refers to someone in an immediate supervisory position vis-á-vis street-level bureaucrats (for example, a supervisor in a public welfare agency, a police captain in charge of a precinct sector, or a principal in a nondepartmentalized public school). "Objectives" refers to the goals that the supervisor is charged with realizing. It is necessary to put it this way because the role of supervisor is itself subordinate to other roles in a complex bureaucracy. The focus on the divergence of objectives between the organization and the lowest-level workers could with some modifications be applied to the relations between the lowest-level supervisor and the roles to which this position is subordinate.

[21] Argyris, *Integrating the Individual and the Organization*, p. 36.

brutality is contrary to police policy, but a certain degree of looking-the-other-way on the part of supervisors may be considered necessary to persuade officers to risk assault. Street-level bureaucrats have a role interest in securing the requirements of completing the job. Managers, on the other hand, are properly result-oriented. They are concerned with performance, the cost of securing performance, and only those aspects of process that expose them to critical scrutiny.

Another aspect of street-level bureaucrats' role interests is their desire to maintain and expand their autonomy. Managers try to restrict workers' discretion in order to secure certain results, but street-level bureaucrats often regard such efforts as illegitimate and to some degree resist them successfully. Indeed, to the extent that street-level bureaucrats (and this would include police, teachers, social workers, and nurses, as well as doctors and lawyers) expect themselves to make critical discretionary decisions, many of managers' efforts to dictate service norms are regarded as illegitimate. To the extent that this is the case we have uncovered a condition for noncompliance of lower-level workers. This does not mean that efforts to constrain street-level bureaucrats are in fact illegitimate. Street-level bureaucrats have some claims to professional status, but they also have a bureaucratic status that requires compliance with superiors' directives. It does mean, however, that street-level bureaucrats will perceive their interests as separate from managers' interests, and they will seek to secure these interests.[22]

Street-level bureaucrats conspicuously create capacities to act with discretion and hang on to discretionary capacities they have enjoyed in the past. The maintenance and enhancement of discretion is so important that some detailed illustrations may be useful.

Lower-court judges have recently encouraged the development of a great many alternatives to incarceration, in essence turning the courts into social work referral services. In Massachusetts and elsewhere lower-court judges can refer presumptive offenders to many social programs, the successful completion of which will result in obviating their sentences. These include programs to provide first offenders with counseling, job training, and placement assistance, and alcoholics, reckless drivers, and drug offenders with appropriate counseling. In addition, judges have the services of psychiatrists, social workers, probation officers, and others who might be able to provide treatment as an alternative to imprisonment. These developments have been conceived by humanitarian reformers who believe, along with many judges, that prisons create more criminals than they deter by exposing people to experienced crooks, and by pragmatists, who recognize that the courts have become revolving doors of repeat appearances without deterrent effect.

It is conspicuous to court observers that these programs take a heavy burden off the judge. The judge is now able to make what appears to be a constructive decision rather than simply to choose between the unattractive alternatives of sending a person to jail or releasing the putative offender without penalty. Indirect evidence that these programs fill critical institutional needs is suggested by the

---

[22] For an extended treatment of the sources of street-level bureaucrats' influence, see Jeffrey Prottas, *People-Processing: The Street-Level Bureaucrat in Public Service Bureaucracies* (Lexington, Mass.: Lexington Books, 1979).

Boston pretrial diversion programs. These programs were utilized beyond their capacity by judges, sometimes without regard for the extremely important initial interview or the relatively stringent eligibility requirements the programs sought to impose in order to maximize effectiveness. Dependent upon judges for referrals and, indeed, for their programs' existence, administrators found it difficult to refuse judges who referred too many clients, or inappropriate clients, to them.[23]

The Veterans Administration hospital system is a fascinating bureaucracy because it employs doctors, the preeminent professionals, in highly rule-bound organizations. The country's system of socialized medicine for the indigent veteran has developed an extremely complex series of rules because of simultaneous congressional concern to provide veterans with hospital services, maintain strict cost accounting, and (particularly in the past) not compete with private medical practice. In large part because the VA system was to provide hospital care, leaving to private physicians the business of office consultations, the VA hospitals were prohibited from treating patients on an outpatient basis. This conflicted with the doctors' prerogative to prescribe a level of treatment appropriate to the problem presented. There are many patients who need treatment, but not hospitalization, and to hospitalize such people would be to deny others the hospital space.

However, there was an allowable exception to the rule limiting services to hospitalized veterans. Under the "Pre-Bedcare" category (PBC) veterans who required health services prior to their anticipated admission (for example, blood tests prior to surgery) could be treated. Despite various requirements intended to limit PBC treatment to those whose admission was clearly expected, actual admission to the hospitals from PBC lists was traditionally very low. It seems that doctors, chafing under the restriction that they could not treat patients according to their best estimate of need, were treating patients as outpatients under the fiction that they were expected to be admitted. This supposition is supported by observing what happened when the VA introduced an Ambulatory Health Care (AHC) policy, permitting outpatient treatment for the first time. PBC admissions plummeted, while AHC admissions rose steadily. In one hospital AHC received 148 patients in the first five months of the program, while PBC dropped from 122 to 73 patients during that period. Fifty-one of these patients transferred directly to the AHC program.[24] In retrospect it seems that doctors were able to utilize existing bureaucratic structures to impose their views of proper treatment on the organization, despite organizational efforts to circumscribe their discretion.

Street-level bureaucrats will also use existing regulations and administrative provision to circumvent reforms which limit their discretion. In December 1968, in response to pressure from the Department of Housing and Urban Development, the Boston Housing Authority (BHA) adopted new tenant-selection guidelines designed to insure housing project racial integration. The plan utilized what was known as the "1-2-3 rule." To eliminate personnel discretion in assignments the

[23] This paragraph is based upon personal observations, conversations with court personnel, and sustained discussions with workers in the Boston Court Resources Project.

[24] See Jeffrey Prottas, *People-Processing*, chapter 3.

1-2-3 rule provided that prospective tenants would be offered places only in the housing projects with the three highest vacancy ratios. If these offers were refused, the application would be returned to the bottom of the waiting list.

The BHA integration plan did not work. Many housing authority employees objected to assigning people to projects in which they did not want to live. They were particularly concerned for their traditionally favored clientele, the elderly, poor whites who populated the "better" BHA projects. Among the reasons the reform did not work were that housing authority personnel were so inundated with work that proper administrative controls were not feasible, and in the chaos of processing applications, those who wished to favor some prospective tenants over others were able to do so. Housing officials took advantage of provisions for exceptions to the 1-2-3 rule, interpreting reasonable provisions for flexibility in extremely liberal ways when they wanted to. They volunteered information to favored prospective tenants concerning how to have their applications treated as emergencies or other high-priority categories, while routinely processing the applications of others. Applications were frequently lost or misplaced so that workers could favor tenants simply by locating their files and acting on them, while other files remained unavailable for processing. Meanwhile, public housing managers contributed to the sustained biases of the agency by failing to report vacancies to the central office when they occurred, not informing prospective tenants when units were available, or showing tenants they wished to discourage only unattractive or unsafe units, although others in the project were available. Thus the press of work combined with workers' desires to continue to serve particular clients restored the discretionary powers the new rules were designed to eliminate.[25]

The power of street-level bureaucrats to thwart reforms by manipulating legal loopholes is suggested in a strategy paper prepared by New York City officials to reduce welfare rolls. It indicates managerial awareness of the limits of agency reform without worker cooperation. The paper rejects the possibility of shortening intake hours too drastically, in part because of the chance that "welfare workers would go out of the centers and take applications from people at home, on the street, etc., since application may be made [under existing Federal law] at agency office, in own home, by telephone, by mail, or in any suitable place."[26]

A dramatic example of the instinct to retain discretionary options is provided by the response to the New York State laws sponsored by then Governor Nelson Rockefeller to impose mandatory, severe jail sentences for drug dealers, while providing relatively minor penalties for those caught with small amounts of drugs. The rationale for the law was to provide a strong deterrent to the drug trafficker. Predictably, some people arrested were not the rapacious drug dealers whom the law was designed to deter. This was the case, for example, with drug addicts on

---

[25] See Jon Pynoos, "Breaking the Rules: The Failure to Select and Assign Public Housing Tenants Equitably," (Ph.D. diss., Harvard University, 1974).

[26] Internal memo, "Budget Bureau Recommendations for Saving in the Welfare Budget," March 24, 1969, p. IV–6 (author's files).

methadone who occasionally sold a dosage. The law presented a dilemma for court personnel, who believed that the mandatory, minimum sentence (life imprisonment for the methadone hustlers) was too severe for the offense. In these cases New York District Attorney Richard Kuh began to charge the alleged offenders not with the crimes which they had committed, but rather with crimes for which the punishments were compatible with what he conceived to be the severity of the offense. In this way, the district attorney attempted to provide the discretion demanded by a just court system in the face of legislation designed precisely to eliminate this discretion.[27]

Still another source of sustained differences in the interests of street-level bureaucrats and managers is their continuous interaction with clients and the varying degrees of complexity in this interaction. Modern bureaucracies gain legitimacy by (often rhetorical) commitments to standards of fairness and equity. But street-level bureaucrats are constantly confronted with the apparent unfairness of treating people alike (just as they recognize the obvious inequities of unequal treatment). Since individuals are so much more than their bureaucratically relevant characteristics—age, sex, place of residence, income level, etc.—a failure to recognize these differences sometimes seems unfair in itself. The public housing manager believes that there are degrees of need for public housing not circumscribed by the categories of eligibility. The teacher recognizes that all children deserve her or his attention but thinks some require more attention than others.

Not only are the standards of fairness insufficient to dictate levels of concern, but also street-level bureaucrats, like everyone else, have personal standards of whether or not someone is deserving. The public housing manager may be more sympathetic to the elderly than to other eligibles. Housing inspectors may be sympathetic to the plight of the landlord although nothing in the formal structure of the agency encourages such a bias.[28]

Under some circumstances it may be appropriate to apply standards of service with respect to personal characteristics. Street-level bureaucrats enjoy considerable discretion in part because society does not want computerized public service and rigid application of standards at the expense of responsiveness to the individual situation. The New York district attorney was praised editorially for contriving to circumvent the mandatory sentencing requirement. The VA doctors were acting on behalf of patients and in opposition to limitations on practice when they assigned pre-bedcare status to patients who did not require hospitalization. Clearly discretion provides opportunity to intervene on behalf of clients as well as to discriminate among them. Yet at best bureaucracies are highly ambivalent about personalistic service delivery. At the least it is an enduring source of conflict between the objectives of managers and workers.

---

[27] Kuh said he acted under a general provision of the law permitting prosecutors to use discretion to assure humane and rational dispositions. See *New York Times,* June 19, 1974, p. 1. At this date 87 methadone "sellers" were affected by his decision.

[28] Pietro Nivola, "Municipal Agency: A Study of the Housing Inspectional Service in Boston," (Ph.D. diss., Harvard University, 1976, chap. 7).

Resources for Resistance

In general, lower-level workers always possess minimal resources with which they can resist managers' orientations or achieve a modicum of response from managers in exchange for compliance. If nothing else, since the costs of recruiting and training a worker are rarely trivial, there is always a degree of noncompliance that can be threatened or realized by workers. If it were otherwise, there would be no problem of management.

Public service workers currently enjoy the benefits of collective resources that strengthen their position considerably. Civil service provisions greatly reduce managers' capacity to manipulate benefits and sanctions to induce performance. Civil service provisions for advancement, introduced originally to eliminate biases in promotion, tend to be irrelevant for the skills they purport to test, thus eliminating incentives for meritorious performance. The costs of firing or demoting workers tend to be so great under civil service regulations that managers often prefer to retain workers than to endure a prolonged period of arbitration while the post in dispute remains unfilled, or worse, remains filled by the accused incompetent. This practice results in a mediocre standard of public service performance. Public employee unions in some cases have increased worker protection by building additional safeguards to capricious management decisions into the collective bargaining process.

This does not mean that managers have no control over workers. Formal sanctions, although costly for managers to invoke, are also costly to workers, who thus try to avoid receiving them. Managers also can manipulate discretionary perquisites they control, such as recommendations for advancement or transfer, or shift and work assignments. They also can facilitate or retard individual workers' efforts, granting a day off here, speeding the processing of work there, and generally making a job more or less desirable.

Lower-level workers under some conditions enjoy additional resources stemming from their critical positions in the organization. Sociologist David Mechanic has suggested that under the right circumstances several factors affect the power of lower-level workers. These factors include qualities and characteristics such as expertise, willingness to become interested and to expend effort, and personal attractiveness. They also include structural considerations such as location within the organization, which affects command of information and access and command over organizational tools.[29] These resources enhance the power of lower-status workers to the extent that higher-ranked organizational participants become more dependent on them.[30] It is the situational characteristics which are of greatest interest to us, since the effectiveness of the personal characteristics depend in large part on the worker's organizational location.

Street-level bureaucrats command a degree of expertise, and indeed, of deference, in some policy areas. (And they more or less display the personal characteristics that enhance their influence.) But it is the discretionary role of street-level bureaucrats and their position as de facto policy makers that critically affect

---

[29] David Mechanic, "Sources of Power of Lower Participants in Complex Organizations," *Administrative Science Quarterly*, vol. 7, no. 2 (December, 1962), pp. 349–364.

[30] Mechanic, *Administrative Science Quarterly*, p. 352.

managers' dependence upon their subordinates. The sanctioned discretion they exercise means that to demonstrate their own ability and competence, managers are highly dependent upon subordinates without being able to intervene extensively in the way work is performed.

Workers can punish supervisors who do not behave properly toward them, either by refusing to perform work of certain kinds, by doing only minimal work, or by doing work rigidly so as to discredit supervisors. Police officers, for example, can refuse to make vice arrests for a captain they dislike, can refuse to take shortcuts through department regulations in order to achieve results, or can rigidly and comprehensively enforce traffic or parking regulations to the fury of an outraged public and the eventual embarrassment of police officials.[31] Lower-level participants may also refuse to make decisions that their superiors are formally obliged to make, at some costs to superiors. Doctors who informally delegate dosage decisions to ward attendants,[32] or judges who informally allocate sentencing decisions to probation officers, are dependent on their hierarchical subordinates for the smooth functioning of their jobs.

The relationship I have described between street-level bureaucrats and managers has two primary characteristics. First, it is a relationship best conceived in large part as intrinsically conflictual. The role of the street-level bureaucrat is associated with client-processing goals and orientations directed toward maximizing autonomy. Managers' roles in this context are associated with worker-management goals directed toward aggregate achievement of the work unit and orientations directed toward minimizing autonomy. Second, it is a relationship of mutual dependence. Thus managers typically attempt to honor workers' preferences if they are rewarded by reciprocity in job performance. To a degree reciprocity will characterize all working relations: in street-level bureaucracies, however, the resources of lower-level workers are greater than those often possessed by subordinates in other work contexts. Hence, the potential for reciprocity is greater.

This picture of workers and managers in street-level bureaucracies is substantially different from the one usually used to analyze problems of policy making and implementation. Compliance with agency objectives may still be the managerial problem, but it is complicated by the capacity of street-level bureaucrats to resist organizational pressures with their own resources. Some of these resources are common to public service workers generally and some are inherent in their position as policy deliverers with broad discretion.

When relationships between policy deliverers and managers are conflictual and reciprocal, policy implementation analysis must question assumptions that influence flows with authority from higher to lower levels, and that there is an intrinsic shared interest in achieving agency objectives. This situation requires analysis that starts from an understanding of the working conditions and priorities of those who deliver policy and the limits on circumscribing those jobs by recombining conventional sanctions and incentives.

---

[31]See Jonathan Rubinstein, *City Police* (New York: Farrar, Strauss, Giroux, 1973), chap. 2.

[32]Thomas Scheff, "Control over Policy by Attendants in a Mental Hospital," *Journal of Health and Human Behavior,* vol. 2 (1961), p. 97, cited in Mechanic, "Sources of Power," p. 363.

Arguing that agency executives or street-level bureaucrats under certain conditions should act as public entrepreneurs sounds reasonable, but making such a case for middle managers in this day and age sounds little short of radical. After all, middle managers are widely viewed as the bureaucratic deadbeats who shuffle paper and increase the number of bureaucratic layers, while doing calculations better performed by computers as we progress toward the paperless society. The elimination of these layers decentralizes the organization, and brings the decision makers (the "strategic apex") closer to those actually doing the work (the "operating core"). Given the limited funding available to do the job, what better way to simultaneously become more efficient and improve productivity than to downsize by eliminating middle managers? Contracting out former middle management tasks makes particularly good sense, so the argument goes, because the public sector should focus on steering the ship of state (deciding what to do), and leave the rowing (actually doing the job) to the more efficient private sector. Furthermore, the time is propitious for such privatization, given the inferiority complex—or "administrative self-doubt"—currently infesting the public sector.

The argument is even more controversial because Douglas Morgan and his colleagues do not justify their plea for middle management on behalf of efficiency. Furthermore, they agree that rewarding managers on the basis of the number of employees reporting to them has led to much organizational game playing and to some middle management layers that can be eliminated with impunity.

Rather, the importance of middle managers lies in their performance of four leadership tasks and the two uniquely public values promoted by those tasks. First, middle managers interpret and represent their work unit's interests with citizens, the media, and to other units working in their organization and others when concerns overlap. Second, they lend their expertise to interorganizational teams and task forces designed to bring the skills of multiple professions and agencies to bear on a complex problem. Third, it is middle managers who come to know those in other organizations with whom new initiatives can be developed. Fourth, by representing the organization in various government settings, they leverage (or preserve) the limited time of top management.

In performing these tasks, they play distinctive roles as the "keepers of two functions" critical to the health and effectiveness of democracy within a political jurisdiction, namely, helping to define "acceptable service" and making their units publicly accountable to citizens for the delivery of that service. Good service may mean something quite different to the client than to citizens in a jurisdiction. There is a tension between clients who want help as individuals (and the street-level bureaucrats who want to help them) and citizens who want reasonably objective evidence that the organization is providing service inputs and actually improving client circumstances and thereby having a positive impact on their lives.

But there is often limited agreement on how to achieve such goals, and the challenge for middle managers is to define good service in a manner that meets expectations at the top and bottom of the organization. The middle manager facilitates reaching agreement as to what constitutes a successful outcome with other organizations often involved with the same client, and in doing so reads the community culture in finding an appropriate balance between the need for efficiency and concern with effectiveness and other standards.

The middle managers similarly work with these other organizations as "boundary spanners" seeking to insure the accountability of their agency when its jurisdiction overlaps with that of other organizations. Here they are going beyond the formal evaluation of client impacts and seeking to help make sense of the multiple sources of authority—executive, legislative, and judicial—which govern their agency. Middle managers play an important role in divining what these several sources of agency legitimacy and power really want. They gain legitimate authority for the agency to act, as Morgan and his colleagues emphasize, by satisfying the board policies, strategic plans, purchasing rules, and other specific requirements imposed by these sources. They also develop solutions to complex problems by cutting across organizational or jurisdictional boundaries while making themselves accountable to the public for these agreements, and representing their organizations with constituency groups.

Such discussions and negotiations extend beyond mere public relations. They extend to the most critical tradeoff in a democracy, that between insuring equality and maintaining efficiency. This tradeoff is subtle in that it occurs even while trying to balance community needs. It is difficult to tell, for example, when the streets are safer, but we can see to it that all citizens receive a comparable police response. A middle manager in the police force is thus both seeking to reduce crime and dispense justice. Both are important community values, but they may lead that middle manager in quite different directions. As more and more activities are shifted downward from the federal and state levels, these middle managers will increasingly play a stewardship role, that is, the critical role of safeguarding such local government values, the authors conclude. If a substantive task, such as law enforcement, is privatized, the corporation may meet contract crime reduction specifications, but may do so in a manner that violates a concern for justice or overlooks other community needs, thereby undercutting the health of our democratic polity (or society) and underscoring the significance of the public manager's stewardship role.

What Middle Managers Do In Local Government: Stewardship of the Public Trust and the Limits of Reinventing Government

Douglas Morgan, Kelly G. Bacon, Ron Bunch, Charles D. Cameron, and Robert Deis

The most serious resistance to teamwork and participatory management often comes from middle managers, not unions. If employees are making decisions and solving problems, middle managers become superfluous. Too often they stand in the way of actions, because their instinct, to justify their existence, is to intervene (Osborne & Gaebler, 1992; 265).

Middle management in most organizations really has little role beyond "make work" activities, such as stopping ideas coming down and stopping ideas going up. Middle managers . . . are a sponge (former United Airlines President, Ed Carlson, quoted in Peters & Waterman, 1983; 313).

Douglas Morgan, Kelly G. Bacon, Ron Bunch, Charles D. Cameron, and Robert Deis, *Public Administration Review*, Vol. 56, No. 4 (July/August 1996).

Eliminating layers of middle management through contracting out for services and flattening organizations has become accepted catechisms of the modern management faith. It is a faith that is constantly being kindled in the public sector by recurring waves of administrative self-doubt. Some of this self-doubt results from financial pressures to save money by getting rid of costly layers of the organization. Other sources of self-doubt include various organizational and human resource management theories, such as TQM, theory Z, and project team management, which argue that employee ownership, satisfaction, and productivity will be increased if those who produce the service/product have more direct responsibility for managing the conditions of their success (Peters & Waterman, 1983; Cohen & Brand, 1993; Scherkenbach, 1990). More recently, administrative self-doubt in the public sector has been fostered by the call to reinvent government. One of the underlying assumptions of the reinvention movement is that the need for middle managers as well as direct service providers will be less as government abandons its role of rowing in favor of steering (Osborne & Gaebler, 1992; 265 ff.). Like most successful catechisms, these external sources of administrative self-doubt have served to reify the assertions about the useless, costly, and even dysfunctional role middle managers are seen to play in modern organizational life.

As middle managers and former middle managers, we are both perplexed and concerned that so little serious attention has been given to what middle managers actually do, especially within the public sector. On the basis of our 80 years of combined experience in the public sector, representing more than a dozen different local government organizations, we do not believe that it is accurate to characterize middle managers as "superfluous," "hour-glass" bottlenecks, or "make work" featherbedders.[1] In defending the role of middle managers in this article, we do

---

[1] Some comments on methodology are in order. This article began as a focus group study undertaken by Douglas Morgan, director and professor of public administration at Lewis and Clark College. It is part of a larger focus group study of the changing role and function of career administrators in the public sector (D. Morgan & H. D. Kass, 1993, especially p. 187). However, unlike previous focus groups conducted by the author, the middle-manager topic under exploration touched an especially visceral cord among participating members of the focus group, and they increasingly became active agents of authorship by offering numerous considerations and written case examples. Thus, the focus group has produced the article! The practitioners have written all of the case examples, while the lead author has provided the larger theory of democratic governance that helps to explain and provide a normative basis for the kind of discretionary role played by local government middle managers discussed in this article.

Because this study departs from traditional focus group techniques, it raises some difficult methodological problems, the most important of which is the line between empirical evidence and generational theory. How much of our findings are a result of the theory we share at the outset, and how much of our theoretical speculations in the conclusion of our article are genuinely informed and guided by the empirical evidence surfaced in the focus group meetings? While focus group research is subject to this criticism more than other methodological approaches, we recognize that our study is especially vulnerable to this criticism. We have sought to temper the urge "to find what you are looking for" by (1) confining the observations of the participants to personal experience that can be documented; (2) cross-checking the immediate experience of the participants against other jurisdictional, organizational, and geographic experiences found within the focus group; and (3) cross-checking the experience of the participants against current research and writing on the topic of concern.

A final concern raised by our approach is that it draws conclusions primarily from the perspective of those who currently supervise middle managers. While the focus group participants viewed themselves as still performing middle-management functions, their conclusions may not, in fact, accurately capture what many middle managers do on a daily basis in most public organizations. Our study emphasizes the importance of capturing this kind of information before undertaking extensive reorganization of the middle-management layers of public organizations. We need to know by whom and where the middle-management functions identified in our study will be performed when public organizations are flattened, reorganized, contracted out, and undergo other changes that are variations on the reinvention theme.

not wish to quarrel with the obvious need to eliminate unnecessary layers of an organization or the need to increase organizational efficiency and effectiveness through more employee involvement and team management. Middle managers in some organizations have received some bad publicity for some very good reasons. We agree that the traditional corporate hierarchy has tended to reward employees based on the number of individuals they supervise, thus creating excessive competition and expansion at the middle management levels of public as well as private organizations. However, we do not believe that the solution to the problem is to be found in a wholesale attack on the middle-management structure of public organizations. We focus our attention in this article on the role of middle managers in local governmental organizations. While our case observations are drawn from our experience at the local government level, we also believe these functions are performed by public managers in large-scale bureaucratic organizations at both the state and federal levels of government.

We first summarize what we believe are the essential generic functions middle managers perform in local levels of government. Contrary to much of the current thinking, we argue that the work is generic to the success of almost all organizations. In the next two sections, we discuss the two peculiarly important functions middle managers perform in public sector organizations at the local level. The second section addresses the role of middle managers in defining what counts for "good" service. The third section focuses on the role of middle managers in holding local public organizations accountable to multiple and sometimes conflicting public standards. Taken together, these sections argue that middle managers in local public organizations perform the uniquely democratic tasks of facilitating a definition of "good" service and of making certain the delivery of public services is carried out in a manner that meets all of the "accountability" standards that have been put into place. Finally, we offer a theory of democratic governance which not only captures the descriptive role we have depicted for local government middle managers, but also provides a normative framework for assessing contracting out, privatizing, reinventing government, and other mechanisms to reshape the role and function of democratic governance.

What Middle Managers Do in Local Government

Over the last several decades, we have acquired considerable empirical information on the kind of work managers do. Largely through the integrative efforts of Henry Mintzberg, many of the conventional myths about managers have been dispelled. Contrary to popular folklore, managers are not systematic planners who rely on the assemblage of "hard information" to make decisions in a scientific fashion. Instead, they "dislike reflective activities" and rely on "soft information" to make intuitive decisions that do not conform to a scientific model (Mintzberg, 1975, 1989). These findings have had a significant impact on our thinking about managerial structures, training, and education over the past two decades.

While we now know a great deal more about how managers in general go about their work, we know very little about how managerial functions vary at different levels of public organizations and between different types of public organizations. Although distinctions are readily made between operators and managers (Wilson, 1989; Kanter, 1977), very little attention has been given to the specific functions performed by middle managers. For purposes of this article, we will use Mintzberg's definition of middle managers (Mintzberg, 1989; 98–99): Middle managers are those who occupy positions between the strategic apex and the operating core of an organization. Managers at the strategic apex have responsibility for establishing the mission of the organization, ordering priorities, and engaging in strategic-planning decisions. Those at the operating core perform the basic work of producing the products and rendering the services. Most often, middle managers occupy the hierarchical space between first-line supervisors and department heads in local government. However, we prefer to define middle managers functionally rather than hierarchically because, in smaller jurisdictions, department heads and first-line supervisors may well perform the functions of middle managers that we identify below.

Based on our experience, middle managers in local government perform four tasks that are central to the effective functioning of their organizations: (1) interpret and represent their work unit's interest; (2) lend or secure assistance; (3) develop organizational relationships; and (4) leverage other's time.

Interpreting and Representing Their Work Unit's Interests

In most instances, mid-management work routinely requires meeting with others over the potential and actual distribution of resources. Any time budgets, grants, and other financial resources are at stake, you will find representatives from various groups and organizations planning, organizing, debating, and thinking about the appropriate use and allocation of those resources. Although their decisions may be far from final or authoritative, these kinds of meetings are at the core of the daily routine of a mid-manager in local government.

The development of public policy responses to issues of the day is another major component of a middle-manager's work. Questions regarding the demographics of the organization, its strengths, its weakness, and its interests are often conveyed and delivered by a mid-manager to others not associated with the unit or organization.

Other examples that rely upon the manager's familiarity with the interests of the parent work unit are intra- and inter-organizational activities that affect the distribution of duties, responsibilities, or tasks. Specifically, community or neighborhood projects, task forces, any attempt at defining performance roles and standards, and bids to change or alter the manner in which tasks are performed and delivered are magnets which will quickly attract a multitude of middle managers. For example, the introduction and evolution of community policing within law enforcement organizations requires countless get-togethers involving community groups, police professionals, elected policy makers, and others with various kinds of expertise. The effort of these meetings is directed at moderating, changing, and influencing the manner in which police work has been historically delivered. The sergeants and above who attend are classical middle managers.

Lending or Securing Assistance

Another major task of middle managers in local government is marketing and delivering the work group's expertise to group's efforts. Prosecutors meeting with police officials and members from the Federal Bureau of Investigation (FBI), Immigration and Naturalization Service (INS), and local community groups to plan anti-drug strategies within an area involve people who have been entrusted by the prosecutor's office to represent and project the interests of the organization beyond its own walls. Similar organizational trust is placed in a fire battalion captain's effort in working on an enhanced 911 system or a precinct captain's development of a policy that allows business owners to directly prepare police reports regarding shoplifters. In short, much of a middle manager's time is spent finding areas in which the organization can be helpful and not be hurt in these interorganizational negotiations.

Developing Organizational Relationships

The middle manager develops and relies upon organizational relationships with others outside of the work unit in order to get things accomplished that are beyond the ability of the organization unit itself. A successful and seasoned middle manager, new to an organization, will quickly take steps to identify and associate with contemporaries in other allied organizations, knowing that familiarity and personal relationships go far in getting things done. Successful middle managers are also aware and take advantage of the ongoing nature of established relationships.

Leveraging Other's Time

Middle managers are also called upon to attend meetings and perform tasks where the purpose of the task or meeting is vague, ill defined, or even ill conceived. In many instances, this is because a superior wants to use his or her time on other matters. A middle manager's task is not simply to be physically present and occupy space. Middle managers are expected to be able to represent a collection of interests and be incisive enough to determine that the issues discussed have a bearing on the capacities, concerns, and interests of their own organizational unit. Sometimes, it is simply a "flag flying exercise" to maintain visibility and recognition that the organization or the unit has a sphere of interest and a stake in the topic under discussion.

In summary, almost all local governments need middle managers to represent the core group's interests, to secure or lend assistance, to develop professional relationships, and to leverage other people's time (especially their superior's). In performing these functions, middle managers serve as essential communication links between the organization's senior-level managers and the line personnel. To be successful, they must interpret and synthesize a variety of powerful influences on the work of the organization, including the demands of various internal and external leaders, the interests of consumers/clients, the perception of the general public, the need of line personnel, the expectations of the organization's CEOs, and the goals of board members/elected officials. The middle managers' ability to successfully carry out this role plays a critical part in transforming public organizations into what Philip Selznick (1993) calls "thick institutions." In contrast to bureaucratic organizations, "thick institutions" create a distinctive and more-or-less integrated sense of community (pp. 231–264). This is increasingly important for local governmental organizations where a shared sense of community has become both a major need and a fierce challenge.

Our observations raise some obvious and important questions for various efforts to reinvent government. Who will perform the functions described above when public organizations rely on the private and nonprofit sectors for the delivery of services and when organizations are flattened and middle layers of the organization are eliminated? How can organizational change be carried out in ways that preserve the institutional stewardship roles performed by middle managers?

There may be answers to these questions and some lessons to be learned from isolated pockets within the private sector where some sober second thoughts have been raised about the wholesale assault on the middle-management function of organizational life. Many are taking notice of the Chrysler Corporation's remarkable success in using a team of mid-level managers to reverse declining automobile sales. Chrysler sent a team of middle managers to Japan to examine its competition at Toyota. The team combined the knowledge from this examination with its "thick understanding" of Chrysler to design the Neon. Their efforts were singularly responsible for Chrysler Corporation's dramatic economic turnaround in a very competitive market (Ingrassi & White, 1994).

Although middle managers in the public sector carry out functions that are similar to those of their counterparts in the private and, to a lesser extent, the nonprofit sectors, there are two important differences. First, a common dollar denominator is lacking for measuring "good" service in the public sector. Second, public sector managers need to coordinate activities across multiple boundaries of authority. Because of these two differences, middle managers in the public sector have service and accountability responsibilities that are not faced by their counterparts in the private sector.

The Uniqueness of Middle Managers in the Public Sector: Interpreting What Good Service Means

What Is Good Service?

Because government has more difficulty than the private sector in measuring its outputs and products, it ends up having to define what good service means both up and down in the organization and outwardly to clients and other interested parties. Those who are responsible for delivering the service at the counter or in the field need to be provided with performance standards. Given the frequent absence of objective criteria, especially for the quality dimensions of the delivery of public services, middle managers are needed to negotiate the meaning of "good service," both in general terms and in particular cases where the person being served disputes either the amount or quality of service being provided.

As the issue of good service moves upward in the organization, middle managers are needed to negotiate the tension between those at the bottom of the organization, who are inclined to use particular standards to define good service (i.e., the ability to meet the needs of each individual served), and those at the top, who are inclined to use more general formulaic standards (i.e., average clients serviced, the greatest cost/benefit ratio, the total number of tasks performed/clients served, etc.). In addition to the problems posed by the tendency to define good service somewhat differently at the bottom and top of public organizations, there is the additional problem of dealing with the ambiguity of what good service means externally to various clientele groups and interested parties. Both the organization and external clientele groups may tend to define good service differently than the individual client being served.

How Middle Managers Play a Decisive Role in Defining Good Service

The service-definition problems outlined above are equally present in both the public and private sectors. However, the private sector possesses two major advantages in addressing them. First, in a market economy, dissatisfied customers frequently can find more readily accessible alternatives than consumers of a public service who may need to move to another jurisdiction to have their needs satisfied. Second, in the private sector, it is easier to resolve disputes over service by falling back on a quantitative dollar standard. When these alternatives and standards are not available in the public sector, middle managers are frequently required to negotiate and mediate conflicting views of service. There are three distinctive ways that middle managers participate in this critical task.

Reconciling Service Differences. One of the more difficult tasks of the middle manager, especially during an era of constrained resources, is to make the best use of the money available to meet the service expectations of various constituent groups. This has become an increasingly difficult task as demands have expanded for shrinking general fund dollars. The following case example illustrates the kind of role middle managers are increasingly likely to play in the future.

The county parks manager is responsible for the county park and another small neighborhood park. His span of control is rather small during the winter and grows during the peak summer season with temporary help. The County 2000 Plan mandates that the county will not be in the park-expansion and development business. The plan limits the county's future commitment to just two park sites. Pressures against this hold-the-line strategy include a large influx of population, a park advisory board, and an enthusiastic group of fans who actively maintain the pressure for park expansion and improvements.

What does the parks manager tell his rangers, his overworked seasonal workers, and the parks advisory board? How does the board policy affect day-today service to the park area? Is the County 2000 Plan a vote of nonsupport for parks? If so, does the staff have license to give the citizens of the county what they pay for, that is, poor services?

Under these circumstances, the parks manager is responsible for taking the County 2000 policy and communicating to employees and other stakeholders that the county is not in the park-expansion business. The manager should be able to represent the reasons behind this position. Yet, at the same time, the manager should not let this be an obstacle to providing quality services. But what does quality mean, especially when governing boards cannot provide any specific policy guidance? Does it mean providing the most service to the greatest number of people within available resources? Or does it mean providing service to those who have the fewest recreational alternatives? Or does it mean trying to avoid such hard choices by identifying alternative sources of revenue and ways of meeting the service expectations of park clientele? In the case described, the manager collaborated on timber thinning on county land and used these revenues to acquire federal matching funds without increasing the claim on general fund revenues. This opportunity for creativity is a direct result of the middle-manager's proximity to both the philosophical policies of the organization and the realities of constituent and line-employee needs.

This type of middle manager role is replicated throughout public organizations on a daily basis. The transportation planners and engineering project managers take a jurisdiction's road priority policy, such as limiting the expenditures to only major arterial roads and emergency repairs, and convert this into a completed list of roads that get repaved each year. They do this with the goal of providing the biggest societal benefit to the intra- and inter-jurisdictional transportation system. The project managers then ensure that each project gets completed with the appropriate qualitative and quantitative standards in order to protect and enhance the jurisdiction's road system investment. Without middle managers, this complicated process of translating guidelines and constraints into good service is not likely to get done.

Facilitating Interorganizational Service Standards. Middle managers are the chief agents in facilitating interorganizational standards of service. For instance, a sheriff's deputy who believes that a child-abuse multidisciplinary team is a useful enterprise has to market the idea to other organizations. In addition, the deputy has to take leadership in finding the necessary resources to accomplish the task. It will be middle managers who develop answers to such questions as who interprets the appropriate level of commitment, the length of time the commitment can last, how much effort to expend, and whose role and responsibility it is to accomplish those tasks.

Reading the Community Culture. The concept of good service is dependent on the type and size of the community and organization and the role one plays within the organization. Thus, good service within the public sector is very much a cultural value. It is important for the public manager to be in touch with, and sympathetic to, the values and culture of the constituent community and the organization.

One of the complaints often heard by public land-use planning professionals is that, "Most of the planners live somewhere else and commute to this town to work! How can these bureaucrats understand or much less represent my interests or that of the community, if they do not live here?" The middle-level manager must tap deep into the community's culture and sometimes put aside standardized and prescribed ways of doing things.

For example, in many local jurisdictions, the efficiency and effectiveness of transportation plans are being challenged by local residents who oppose projects on the simple ground that they conflict with "quality of life considerations." Middle managers play a key role with local neighborhoods in negotiating how much transportation efficiency will be compromised to serve community values through the use of street closures, speed bumps, curb pushouts, and similar devices to slow or divert traffic. Local land-use planners also frequently find themselves in a similar negotiating role with local residents. For example, market forces in many wealthy local jurisdictions result in housing densities considerably lower than those required under state mandated land-use goals and the professional norms of planners who have been schooled in certain notions of "adequate housing choices" for those with moderate incomes. Faced with this conflict between community standards and those of the state and profession, the middle manager is required to craft a course of action that develops consensus and produces legally acceptable solutions through neighborhood planning processes. In short, the standard of good service must be informed and guided by the deeply held beliefs of residents within the community.

The Uniqueness of Middle Managers in the Public Sector: Insuring Accountability

One of the chief differences between middle managers in the public and private sectors is the role the former play in dealing with a variety of accountability problems arising from our constitutional system of governance.

Making Sense Out of Multiple Sources of Authority

Middle managers play a critical role in ensuring a constancy of purpose in public organizations in the midst of multiple sources of authority. Unlike private and most nonprofit organizations, public organizations have multiple sources of authority that need to be reconciled and translated into a plan of action. Starting with annual budgets, each organizational work unit is explicitly, or at least implicitly, committed to certain service levels. In addition, there are a variety of state and federal laws, multitudinous boards governing policies, and department-level guidelines that must be complied with. In the most negative case, there may be only vague philosophical direction. What does all of this jumble mean to the employees on the street or the front line? What does this ambiguous and general direction mean to the juvenile counselor, the deputy sheriff, the transportation engineer, and the people responsible for the delivery of each service?

The middle managers play a key role in answering these questions. As the guardians of public accountability, they use their knowledge of the more general guidelines, direction, and parameters of the organization to reconcile tensions between service levels and service quality. In short, they perform the interpretative role necessary to transform policies, laws, and so forth into tangible services to the citizenry.

Acquiring the Legitimate Authority to Act

Public organizations have to conduct their entire business in an open setting where all of the decisions they make and almost every document they produce can be scrutinized and second guessed by any citizen within the jurisdiction. Operating within this fishbowl, public organizations must be sensitive to local political pressures from organized citizens groups who may have conflicting or unformed opinions. They must satisfy board policies, detailed strategic plans, purchasing rules, civil service guidelines, public hearings' requirements, and a multitude of other similar public constraints.

The success of an organization in balancing these multiple sources of authority is critical to acquiring the legitimacy to take any given action. Frequently, it is the middle manager who bears this primary responsibility for weaving together these multiple threads of authority into a fabric of public legitimacy. Take, for example, the steps necessary to complete a local road improvement project. The middle manager must try to reconcile the interests of local residents in noise control, safety, access, and landscaping with the needs of the community at large in building effective and cost-efficient road projects. These middle managers do not have stockholders, profit-sharing schemes, the profit-and-loss statement, or competition to tell them exactly how they are doing. They must intuit how they are doing by being in tune with myriad patterns of community influence and concern.

Accountability in the Management of Interorganizational Boundaries

Middle managers in local governments spend considerable time and energy crafting and implementing solutions to problems that cut across organizational boundaries within their own jurisdictions. An example of this complex process of defining interorganizational accountability is found in one local county's quest to preserve affordable housing in a high-growth housing market.

As the county continued to expand its major arterial street system, it aggressively acquired privately held parcels needed for widening and realignment projects. During and after construction, the county was left with surplus parcels of land. Traditionally, these surplus properties had been offered to the highest bidder in a public auction. This process insured the taxpaying public the highest rate of return and provided the street fund with the greatest amount of revenue.

Faced with a growing demand for low-cost housing, the new housing director approached other county managers to generate some organization-wide support in helping the jurisdiction expand its stock of low-income housing. The transportation director arrived at an obvious conclusion: move surplus houses to surplus land and turn the units over to the housing authority. However, this simple solution was difficult to implement. The transportation staff was known throughout the jurisdiction for its commitment to excellence, for its desire to preserve the integrity of transportation programs, and for its ability to stretch scarce transportation dollars to meet the county's growth needs. To succeed, the director was required to broaden the source of staff accountability away from departmental loyalties to encompass a larger accountability for the overall socioeconomic well-being of the community. After several months of discussion this was accomplished.

The managers in this case clearly operated within the confines of middle management. They had the technical knowledge to develop the program, the credibility and proximity to the line personnel to share a broadening of perspective beyond their provincial loyalties, the time to work out the details, and the proximity to executive decision makers to sell the program.

Accountability in the Management of Interjurisdictional Boundaries

The middle-level manager in most local jurisdictions is engaged in an almost continuous dialogue with other governmental entities. The objective of this dialogue is to make our system of fragmented governance work more efficiently and effectively. Within a typical metropolitan region, cooperation and information sharing is essential to the success of local governments and their elected officials. Common examples include regional transportation, metropolitan area land-use planning, open-space acquisition, law enforcement, sewer and water service coordination, and taxation issues. This level of cooperation and information sharing is not present within the private sector where competition for profit is the dominant paradigm. While some jurisdictions still function to a certain extent on the competitive model, scarce public resources inspire new levels of cooperation. When this occurs, middle managers are the ones who translate general cooperative agreements into workable plans of action that meet the test of public accountability. The following case example illustrates our point.

In one local jurisdiction, the board of commissioners also serves as the governing board of a special sewer district. The special district is treated under state law as an entirely separate local government. A recent performance audit of the sewer district's operations recommended that its fleet maintenance activities could be performed better by consolidating them into the county's operation. This recommendation presented a dilemma for both jurisdictional entities. First, serious customer service problems could arise if the consolidation occurred with the grudging reluctance of the staff. Second, the audit indicated that the savings from the consolidation would exclusively accrue to the special district. In short, the county staff had little to gain and, possibly, much to lose as a result of the consolidation. Without staff support on both sides, the consolidation was not likely to occur.

A critical role was played by the middle managers in both organizations in laying the groundwork for successful consolidation. They redefined the issues governing consolidation from narrow organizational efficiency and effectiveness questions to issues of accountability. The managers successfully argued with their respective staff members that while they were accountable to their fleet operations and needed to protect these operations from being undermined by customer service problems, they had a greater accountability to the public taxpayers as a whole.

Accountability Through Representing the Organization to Constituency Groups

Considerable time is spent by middle managers in representing their organization to various constituency groups in the community. One of the interesting dilemmas in flattening the organization and reducing the number of middle managers is figuring out who performs the representational role in settings where the public, or some other constituency, expects authoritative participation, either in the form of making binding commitments or demonstrating attention and care. No matter how enthusiastic city councils may be about dispensing with middle management, it is unlikely they will embrace with equal enthusiasm the notion of a decentralized, empowered line employee speaking for department X. The loss of middle managers will in turn create additional demands on top managers to be available to deal with representational contacts, even if this leaves less time for engaging in other tasks. In short, one of the ironies of reducing middle management layers of our public organizations is that top managers will assume greater responsibility for maintaining internal accountability at the very same time that demands on their time from external constituencies is growing.

Balancing the Tradeoff between Equality and Efficiency

In the public sector, middle-level managers play a critical role in the great tradeoff between equality and efficiency. By tradeoff, we simply mean striking a balance between following procedural rules in the interest of promoting the equal treatment of agency members or clients, on the one hand, and, on the other, making an exception to the rules in order to promote greater efficiency or effectiveness. Because of the difficulty of judging efficiency, in most public organizations equality is more important than efficiency. As James Q. Wilson points out, "[w]e cannot easily say whether the pupils were educated, the streets made safer, or some diseases prevented; but we can say whether every pupil got the same textbook, every citizen got the same police response, and every patient got the same vaccine" (Wilson, 1989; 132). As a consequence of this bias toward equality and rule following, the burden of providing legitimating authority for making exceptions falls on the middle managers, as the following examples illustrate.

What should a local planner do when faced with a request by a low-income family whose house has burned to be allowed a camper trailer on their property until a new structure is built? Or what does a code enforcement officer do when he or she discovers 156 persons occupying disabled recreational vehicles, old buses, campers, and so forth in mobile home parks? In both cases, the decision to strictly enforce the letter of the law and enlarge the homeless population or to allow continued occupancy by seeking amendments to the city code is primarily the responsibility of the middle manager.

Accountability in Balancing Community Needs

The rush to contract out services at the local level has placed middle managers in a critical role in shaping the way many human service needs of the population are met. Once a decision has been made by the governing body to contract out a given range of services, the middle manager is left free to negotiate the contracts with only *pro forma* approval by the governing body. While there are numerous guidelines provided by accountants and lawyers, the middle manager has considerable discretion to establish performance standards that not only impact the mix of services and clientele groups but the types of nonprofit organizations that will be eligible to bid on the contract and the kind of citizen participation that will be required. Needless to say, through the exercise of this discretion, middle managers have an important influence in shaping the civic fabric of their local community.

Recognizing this potential, one local jurisdiction reevaluated the decision it had made in the 1970s to privatize the provision of mental health services. The jurisdiction decided in the 1980s to reclaim all planning responsibilities and to perform all activities requiring interorganizational and interjurisdictional negotiations. The county reclaimed these two functions because it recognized that the delivery of mental health services within the community were complex and crossed various socioeconomic, demographic, and organizational lines. Furthermore, it recognized that solutions required cooperation among various stakeholders in both the government and the nonprofit community. In short, identifying problems and crafting new approaches for the delivery of mental health services required leadership by middle managers who understood and empathized with the county's values, philosophy, and mission and who could easily develop coalitions among county organizational stakeholders. While direct service could be contracted out, these planning and coordinating functions could not be contracted out without seriously impairing overall governance responsibility for the community.

Local Government Middle Managers and Democratic Theory

Over the past decade, we have witnessed a growing recognition of the important role that career public servants play in preserving the health of the democratic polity. However, most of this attention has focused on the discretionary role of senior-level administrators (Nalbandian, 1991; Rohr, 1986, 1989; Kass and Catron, 1990; Morgan and Kass, 1993; Terry, 1995). Our findings suggest that middle managers have discretionary responsibility that is every bit as critical to the successful functioning of our system of democratic governance as those career administrators occupying leadership positions at the top of our public organizations. In fact, our description of these responsibilities embodies nearly all of Nalbandian's (1991) tenets of contemporary professionalism which sometimes, and perhaps carelessly, are associated with what professional chief executive officers do. The middle management responsibilities we have described here are precisely those which Jane Jacobs (1993) has argued constitute the moral basis for public life and which set the world of politics off from the world of commerce.

Current efforts to reinvent government by contracting out services, moving from categorical to block-grant funding, flattening organizations, and decentralizing service, and regulatory responsibilities should serve as a wake-up call to pay more attention to the role of those occupying the middle positions in our public agencies. This is especially the case at local levels of government.

For the following reasons we believe middle managers in local government will play an even more critical role than they have played in the past: Local governments will be pressed to develop mechanisms that improve interactions between government and its citizens; local governments will have an opportunity to push reinvention more quickly and further than most state and federal levels of government; the issues of accountability, openness, and citizen/employee interaction will be of greater concern at local levels of government than at the state and federal levels (Gibbs, 1994; 105; Chrislip, 1993; 235); issues of responsiveness and accountability will be pushed down to lower levels of the administrative structure in local government than will be the case at the federal and state levels of government; and, finally, local governments are likely to be the beneficiaries of political efforts at both the national and state levels to increase local control and stimulate experimentation. All of these developments will increase the responsibilities of the middle management levels of our local public organizations.

In summary, our experience suggests that local government middle managers perform a growing stewardship role in maintaining and furthering the health of our democratic polity in three major ways. First, they help make government more responsive by facilitating interorganizational and interjurisdictional cooperation, by translating the community's values to lower levels of the organization, by representing the organization to constituency groups, and by increasing the organization's capacity to deliver good service. Second, middle managers make government more efficient and effective by facilitating common ground across fragmented structures of local authority, by stimulating intraorganizational cooperation, and by developing cooperative relationships with important community stakeholders. Finally, middle managers are strategically positioned to make government more sensitive to the unmet needs of the community through their ongoing contact with the community and through their oversight of key planning and contracting activities. By making government more responsive, by enhancing efficiency and effectiveness, and by keeping a watchful eye on the unmet needs of the citizens, middle managers play a decisive role in legitimating the exercise of public authority. Even more important, they play a key role in maintaining a balanced system of constitutional governance. Our experience suggests that the future health of our democratic polity depends on us taking the role of these middle managers much more seriously than we have in the past.

References

Chrislip, David D., 1993. "The Failure of Traditional Politics." *National Civic Review.* (Summer), 235–240.

Cohen, Steven and Ronald Brand, 1993. *Total Quality Management in Government.* San Francisco: Jossey-Bass Publishers.

Gibbs, Christine, 1994. "Reinventing Government: A Mini-Forum." *Public Administration Review,* vol. 54 (1).

Ingrassi, Paul and Joseph B. White, 1994. *The Comeback: The Fall and Rise of the American Automobile Industry.* New York: Simon & Schuster.

Jacobs, Jane, 1993. *Systems of Survival: A Dialogue on the Moral Foundations of Commerce and Politics.* New York: Random House.

Kanter, Rosabeth Moss, 1983. *The Change Masters: Innovation and Entrepreneurship in the American Corporation.* New York: Simon and Schuster.

Kass, Henry D. and Bayard Catron, 1990. *Images and Identities in Public Administration.* Newbury Park, CA: Sage Publications, Inc.

Mintzberg, Henry, 1975. "The Manager's Job: Folklore and Fact." *Harvard Business Review,* vol. 53 (July/August). The President and Fellows of Harvard College.

———, 1989. *Mintzberg on Management.* New York: Free Press.

Morgan, D. and H. D. Kass, 1993. "The American Odyssey of the Career Public Service: The Ethical Crisis of Role Reversal." In H. George Frederickson, ed., *Ethics and Public Administration.* Armonk, NY: M.E. Sharpe.

Nalbandian, John, 1991. *Professionalism in Local Government: Transformations in the Role Responsibilities and Values of City Mangers.* San Francisco, CA: Jossey-Bass.

Osborne, David and Ted Gaebler, 1992. *Reinventing Government: How the Entrepreneurial Spirit is Transforming the Public Sector.* Reading, MA: Addison-Wesley Publishing Company.

Peters, Thomas and Robert H. Waterman, 1983. *In Search of Excellence: Lessons from America's Best-Run Companies.* New York: Harper & Row Publishers.

Rohr, John A., 1986. *To Run a Constitution: The Legitimacy of the Administrative State.* Lawrence, KS: University of Kansas Press.

———, 1989. *Ethics for Bureaucrats: An Essay on Law and Values,* 2nd ed. New York: Marcel Dekker.

Scherkenbach, W. H., 1990. *The Deming Route to Quality and Productivity.* Washington, DC: CEEPress Books.

Selznick, Philip, 1993. *The Moral Commonwealth: Social Theory and the Promise of Community.* Los Angeles, CA: University of California Press.

Terry, Larry, 1995. *The Administrator as Conservator: The Leadership of Public Bureaucracies.* Los Angeles: Sage.

Wilson, James Q., 1989. *Bureaucracy.* New York: Basic Books.

PART

III

Engaging the Public in Agency Decision Making

Loss of Political Trust

While opinions vary markedly on just why it has happened, there is considerable agreement that since the sixties the link between many Americans and their government has grown more tenuous at every level. Seemingly every month, another study emerges purporting to explain this "disconnect." In one sense, suspicion and distrust of government are nothing new; these attitudes are deeply lodged in our history and culture. We have inherited them from the founding fathers, much as we have inherited other parts of the American creed such as the Protestant ethic, freedom, equality, and a commitment to capitalism. But there is a difference between healthy skepticism and destructive cynicism, and a disturbing number of Americans are crossing that line.

The steep decline in political trust from 1960 through 1997 is well documented by several prestigious public opinion surveys. From 1958 through 1997, the American Enterprise Institute/Roper Center reported that the percentage of Americans believing that you "can trust the government in Washington to do what is right" sank from 77 percent to 22 percent.[a] The Pew Research Center similarly found in 1964 that 78 percent felt that "the government in Washington

---

[a]American Enterprise Institute/Roper Center chart included in Charles Murray, "Americans Remain Wary of Washington," *Wall Street Journal*, December 23, 1997, p. A14.

can be trusted to do the right thing usually or just about always," while only 38 percent agreed in 1997.[b] These findings have alarmed social critics across the political spectrum.[c]

Local Civic Participation

There is, however, considerable disagreement about just why this disconnect between citizen and government exists. Not surprisingly, then, opinions also differ on what to do about it. Social scientists and public administrators have tackled the problem differently at the local and national levels. At the local level, discussion has focused on how citizens can more effectively participate in decision making; at the national level, where such direct contact is more difficult, some commentators have stressed the need to expand a "politics of ideas" that engages citizens, public managers, and elected officials.

The Politics of Ideas

Promotion of a more widespread competition of ideas by engaging the public is not something that public managers have traditionally welcomed. As Robert Reich has observed, it is difficult enough now to interpret legislative intent, comandeer the necessary resources, overcome bureaucratic inertia, and develop the systems necessary for the effective implemention of services and of regulations. Nonetheless, he argues that sometimes, "higher-level public managers have an obligation to stimulate public debate about what they do." Such debate can "clarify ambiguous mandates," and, more importantly, "help the public discover latent contradictions and commonalities in what it wants to achieve." The public manager's job is thus partly "to participate in a system of democratic governance in which public values are continuously rearticulated and recreated."[d]

Steven Kelman also stresses the importance of a competition of ideas. He views this value clarification process as a critical democratic alternative and a healthy antidote to the exclusive emphasis of public choice scholars on maximizing one's self-interest. In the political realm, for example, this "self-interest axiom" is expressed through the medium of single-purpose interest groups seeking to "maximize" the pressure they can bring to achieve their particular solution to the one problem that concerns their membership—regardless of the impact on others in the society.

There is little question that many political decisions "have been crucially determined by participants furthering quite narrow selfish interests." Pork-barrel

---

[b]Pew Research Center, *Deconstructing Distrust: How Americans View Government*, www.people-press.org/trustpt.htm, p. 3.

[c]See, for example, the works of conservatives Charles Murray and Gerald Seib and liberals Theda Skocpol and Ruy Teixeira.

[d]Robert B. Reich, "Policy Making in a Democracy," in Robert B. Reich, ed., *The Power of Ideas* (Cambridge, MA: Ballinger, 1988), pp. 123–24.

legislation, tax expenditures, private bills, and their ilk litter the Congressional landscape. However, Kelman emphasizes that "the more important a policy is, the less important self-interest is in determining the policies we get."[e] Kelman has a point. How does self-interest account for the increases in spending for the poor in the 1960s and early 1970s? Or the environmental movement or civil rights movement? The Tax Reform Act of 1986? The Freedom to Farm Bill of 1996?

Paul Quirk makes a parallel case for the politics of ideas by focusing on deregulation. He asks how it can be explained that the more powerful business interests involved in these airline, telecommunications and trucking regulatory battles were on the losing side in every case. After all, if political economists are correct in arguing that politicians and administrators act in their own self-interest and will trade off their power in exchange for votes and resources, then the regulatory agencies should have been "captured" by their politically stronger adversaries. Politicians focusing on re-election—in exchange for campaign funds—should similarly have joined with these large corporations seeking to protect their quasi monopolies. Instead, "procompetitive deregulation" carried the day.[f]

But it is not enough simply to pursue a politics of ideas in conjunction with those interest groups already in the political fray, and here too, public administrators historically have entered the process. As Rhynhart reminds us, to be truly democratic, city managers must participate too; they must "act as trustees for the vulnerable, dependent, and politically inarticulate."[g] Numerous state and federal administrative agencies have traditionally felt a similar obligation to equalize the differences between organized and unorganized interests. The administrator feeling an obligation to promote some degree of social equity, Meier points out, can either "advocate the interests of the disadvantaged or discount the interests of the better represented."[h]

The noted behaviorist B.F. Skinner has observed that five such populations have historically remained classic examples of mistreatment: "They are the care of the very young, of the aged, of prisoners, of psychotics, and of the retarded." These populations are vulnerable, because "the young and the aged are too weak to protest, prisoners are controlled by police power, and psychotics and retardates cannot organize or act successfully."[i] While some of these populations, such as the aged and the young, may be better treated in some cultures than this analysis suggests, in the American pluralistic society, which places such a premium on the power of organized groups, the inability of these populations to organize historically has left them open to abuse.

---

[e]Steven Kelman, "'Public Choice' and Public Spirit," *The Public Interest*, vol. 87, p. 86.

[f]Paul Quirk, "Deregulation and the Politics of Ideas in Congress," in Jane J. Mansbridge, ed., *Beyond Self-Interest* (Chicago: University of Chicago Press, 1990), pp. 183–99.

[g]Frederick W. Rhynhart, "The City Manager: Public Trust Overrides Entrepreneurship," *P.A. Times*, October 1, 1993, p. 8.

[h]Kenneth J. Meier, *Politics and the Bureaucracy: Policymaking in the Fourth Branch of Government*, 3rd ed., (Pacific Grove, CA: Brooks/Cole, 1993), p. 202.

[i]B.F. Skinner, *About Behaviorism* (New York: Alfred A. Knopf, 1974), p. 191.

Robert Reich begins here by contrasting the assumptions of the "prevailing view" of public administration with the "revised theory" that he advocates. The prevailing public choice view assumes, among other things, that personal preferences are not significantly altered by politics, social norms, or previous policy decisions. The "public interest" consists of the sum total of everyone's personal preferences. "Social improvement" occurs when some people's individual preferences can be satisfied without making other people worse off. Public preferences can only be justified if they can make such improvements more efficiently than the market can.

Reich agrees that these assumptions have proven useful in helping to take into account the multiplicity of values and viewpoints in our heterogeneous, pluralist society, and to recognize that, consequently, interests will collide and political trade-offs are inevitable. Such assumptions also lead one to ask the critical, political questions necessary to consider in relation to any important public policy issue. Who wins and who loses? Who gets what, when, and how? The model further stresses compromise and bargaining.

Reich's view of public policy making does not ignore democratic pluralism—hence the term, "*revised* view." But Reich wants this revised view to include also the role of ideas about what is good for society and to stress the merit of a debate laying out alternatives on these issues. Furthermore, the prevailing view "tends to overlook the ways such normative visions (or value preferences) shape what people want and expect from their government, their fellow citizens, and themselves."[a] Answers to these questions must raise normative, as well as objective, questions. Objective models can shed little light on questions essentially dealing with what should be.

It is, furthermore, these normative issues that often motivate citizens to participate in policy deliberations and to focus on substantive issue areas of particular concern to them. Policy makers play a critical leadership role in raising these issues for consideration in the policy-making process. Reich thus is

> struck by how much the initial definition of problems and choices influences the subsequent design and execution of public policies. The act of raising the salient public question . . . is often the key step, because it subsumes the value judgements that declare something to be a problem, focuses public attention on the issue, and frames the ensuing public debate.

Indeed, policy makers in taking such positions "find themselves espousing substantive conceptions of the public good." The subsequent debate over the substance of a particular issue, such as welfare, environmental preservation, or economic development, compels everyone involved to rethink how they truly feel on the issue. Out of the crucible of the debate comes, Reich argues, an informed public which can then either endorse the initial view of the issue (with its implicit conception of the public good or public interest) or revise it through interaction with other concerned citizens and policy makers. This emphasis on the entrepreneurial role of the public manager and the enhanced participation of citizens in their government through public deliberation entails, Reich contends, a dramatically different view of the relationship between policy making and democracy.

Reich observes that stimulating such public debate is hardly the traditional view of what a bureaucracy should be doing while implementing policy. This is particularly true in the implementation stage after the policy has been "made." He suggests, however, that higher-level public managers have an ethical obligation to enter into

---

[a]Robert B. Reich, "Introduction," in Robert B. Reich, ed., *The Power of Ideas* (Cambridge, MA: Ballinger, 1988), p. 3.

such a dialogue, partly because they must "participate in a system of democratic governance in which public values are continuously rearticulated and recreated."

This obligation emerges from the public manager's power to exercise administrative discretion. But how can administrative performance under these circumstances be reconciled with democracy? Reconciling administrative performance and democracy is particularly challenging, because when exercising discretion, policy ends are even more difficult to separate from the means through which they are implemented.

The discipline of public administration has offered little guidance on how to link the public manager's actions to a democratic form of government. Reich sees "two procedural visions of how public managers should decide what to do" as having caused part of the problem. In the first of these two paradigms (or models of reality), "interest group mediation," the public manager serves as little more than a referee accommodating well-organized interest groups as they clash on the basis of their acknowledged self-interest in the issue area. The public interest lies in the ability of the public manager to appease as many of these claimants as possible.

The second paradigm, "net benefit maximization," emphasizes instead the need for issue analysis, and places its faith accordingly in policy analysts. These analysts, using microeconomic decision-making techniques, focus on allocating resources as efficiently as possible. They are guided in making these decisions essentially by how people would have acted in the marketplace. In weighing policy alternatives, the analyst is guided by which alternative provides the most satisfactory ratio of benefits to costs—or net benefit maximization.

Reich's ultimate quarrel with the two paradigms, and their hybrid versions when they become intertwined, lies in their "profound failure to reflect an authentic governmental character—that is, to inspire confidence among citizens that the decisions of public managers are genuinely in the 'public interest.'" In both paradigms, communication is one-way—from powerful interest groups or individuals to government. These preferences "are assumed to exist apart from any process designed to discover and respond to them—outside any social experience with democratic governance." This failure is critical, since the nature of the process for a democracy is at least as important as the final decision. Reich also contends that in their view of public management in a democracy, the two paradigms suffer from two other difficulties—empirically, they only describe part of reality and normatively, they promote a questionable set of value preferences for a community.

A preferable paradigm for Reich is one constructed around "the power of ideas." He argues that only through "public deliberation" and debate can citizens really become part of policy making in a democracy. This debate occurs through "social learning" and "civic discovery." Social learning can only occur through the policy debate itself, as each side listens, and learns, from the other. The debate also contributes to democratic governance through a series of "civic discovery" tasks that the engaged citizens, elected officials, and public managers perform, such as stimulating voluntary action, legitimating preferences, enabling initial, individual preferences to be influenced by considerations of what is good for society, and providing the opportunity to discover deeper conflicts.

These normative debates pose moral and democratic challenges for the public manager who, in relating to the public here, must avoid being manipulative or passive. In such a "deliberative relationship," the manager articulates certain values and ideas in a dialogue with the citizenry even while seeking their guidance. The three case studies that conclude the essay reveal that such an open forum can occasionally backfire, but more often, it offers possibilities. Groups with little previous understanding of each other's problems through such dialogue and social learning can arrive at a satisfactory solution previously not even contemplated.

Policy Making in a Democracy

Robert B. Reich

The ideas in this chapter are derived from the argument that citizens are motivated to act according to ideas about what is good for society; that such ideas determine how public problems are defined and understood; that government depends on such ideas for mobilizing public action; that, in consequence, policy makers find themselves espousing substantive conceptions of the public good (although the expression is often implicit); and that this role, in turn, raises questions about the place of policy making in a democratic society. If conceptions about what is good for society are different from mere aggregations of selfish wants, where should policy makers look for guidance about what they should do? What is the relationship between policy making and democracy? Here I offer tentative responses to these questions, grounded in the idea of public deliberation.

For the typical public manager who heads a bureaucracy charged with implementing the law, public debate is not something to be invited. It is difficult enough to divine what the legislature had in mind when it enacted the law, how the governor or president wants it to be interpreted and administered and what course is consistent with sound public policy. It is harder still to commandeer the resources necessary to implement the program, to overcome bureaucratic inertia and institutional rigidity, and to ensure that a system for producing the desired result is actually in place and working. In the midst of these challenges, public controversy is not particularly welcome. The tacit operating rule holds that the best public is a quiescent one; the manager should work quietly, get the job done without disturbing the peace, and reassure everyone "out there" that there is no reason to be concerned or involved.

But sometimes, I believe, higher-level public managers have an obligation to stimulate public debate about what they do. Public deliberation can help the manager clarify ambiguous mandates. More importantly, it can help the public discover latent contradictions and commonalities in what it wants to achieve. Thus the public manager's job is not only, or simply, to make policy choices and implement them. It is also to participate in a system of democratic governance in which public values are continuously rearticulated and recreated.

The first part of this chapter considers the problem of administrative discretion in its historical context. The next section examines the two techniques of constraining administrative discretion that have come to dominate our thinking about responsive government. In the third section I will show why these two dominant forms have failed to solve the problem of administrative discretion in a democracy. The fourth section suggests why public deliberation may, at least on occasion, offer a desirable alternative to the dominant forms. The final sections will examine some applications of this errant concept and the lessons they reveal about the possibilities and limits of public deliberation.

Robert B. Reich, ed. *The Power of Public Ideas*, Cambridge: Ballinger Publishing Company, 1988.

The Problem of Administrative Discretion

Nonelected public managers at the higher reaches of administration—commissioners, secretaries, agency heads, division chiefs, bureau directors—rarely can rely on unambiguous legislative mandates. The statutes that authorize them to take action are often written in vague language, unhelpful for difficult cases of a sort the legislative drafters never contemplated or did not wish to highlight for fear that explication might jeopardize a delicate compromise. The legislators may have had conflicting ideas about how the law should be implemented and decided to leave the task to those who would be closer to the facts and circumstances of particular applications. Or they may simply have wanted an administrator to take the political heat for doing something too unpopular to be codified explicitly in legislation. Or the legislators may have felt that the issue was not sufficiently important to merit their time and resources.

As a result, higher-level public managers are likely to have significant discretion over many of the problems they pursue, solutions they devise, and strategies they choose for implementing such solutions. To be sure, they will need to keep in touch with key legislators and elected officials within the executive branch who have an interest in the policy area—periodically informing them of plans, seeking their approval of broad purposes and strategies, and reporting on important problems and accomplishments. But despite these informal ties, public managers will have considerable running room. There are typically too many decisions to be made, over too wide a range of issues, for even informal ties to bind. Administrative discretion is endemic.

Given this range of discretion, it may seem curious that so little thought has been given to the relationship between administrative performance and democratic values. It is particularly curious in light of the extraordinary attention devoted to the parallel problem facing the judiciary—the other domain of nonelected discretion in government. A seemingly endless stream of critical commentary has sought to reconcile judge-made law with democratic values. Although the *Federalist* described the judiciary as the "least dangerous branch" of government, having no direct influence over "the sword or the purse,"[1] generations of scholars and commentators have fretted over where judges should find their substantive conception of the public interest—whether from some transcendent notion of natural law, principles deducible from the common law, historical inquiries into what the framers of the Constitution (or the drafters of various statutes) "really" had in mind, or some set of "neutral principles" that reconcile and give consistent meaning to various constitutional and common law provisions.[2]

At the very least, the public has come to expect that judges will justify their decisions by reference to general principles lying beyond the particular situation

---

[1]Alexander Hamilton et al., *The Federalist*, No. 78, B. Wright, ed. (Cambridge, MA: Harvard University Press, 1961), pp. 103–10.

[2]Jurisprudential schools have risen and fallen with some regularity. Some have confined their concerns to constitutional norms, while others have taken on the whole corpus of judicial activity, including statutory construction and common law adjudication. But regardless of their precise field of vision, most have somehow addressed themselves to the fundamental question of how judicial discretion can be reconciled with democratic values.

confronting them, reflecting some intelligible and coherent normative ideas—or that they will refrain from deciding at all. Judges are in the business of articulating public values, within a form of argumentation and logic fundamentally concerned with how such values can and should be found. Judicial opinions are attempts at stating public ideas—trying them out first on other judges, who are either persuaded by them or compelled to say why they are not. This ongoing conversation among judges, as they grapple with public ideas in differing contexts, is a form of public deliberation. Judicial opinions are arguments for public legitimacy. The ultimate test of such an articulation is how persuasive the public finds the argument.

History may explain the different treatments accorded judges and administrators. Judicial discretion has been long understood as a potential threat to democratic values. Not so administrative discretion. In the half-century before World War II, the standard American attitude toward administrative discretion vacillated between efforts to improve its exercise and to deny its existence. Initially, the two coexisted quite peacefully. Administrative action was seen less as an act of discretion than as an application of expertise—the discovery of the best means of executing preordained public goals. No less a Progressive reformer than Woodrow Wilson saw public administration as a "detailed and systematic execution of public law" in which discretion was confined to the expert choice of means for carrying out policies decided on by elected officials.[3] Fellow political scientists Frank Goodnow and Charles Beard called for a science of administration through which public administrators could use their knowledge of administration and the tools of social science to serve the public interest.[4] By 1914 several American universities were offering one-year master's degrees in public administration, and by 1924 the first semi-independent school for training public officials was founded at Syracuse University.

As these Progressive era ideals found expression in independent administrative agencies, some members of the legal community grew concerned about the extraordinary delegation of legislative-like responsibilities these schemes implied. Legal scholars like Ernst Freund warned that broad grants of administrative discretion to set rates and standards would reduce public accountability and cause democratic institutions to atrophy.[5] With increasing enthusiasm—culminating in the Supreme Court's determination that Title I of the National Recovery Act of 1933 represented an unconstitutional delegation of congressional authority—the federal courts struck down statutes that contained broad delegations of administrative responsibility.[6]

This conceptual tension between the benefits of administrative expertise and the evils of administrative discretion continued into the 1930s. New Dealers like

---

[3] Woodrow Wilson, "The Study of Administration," *Political Science Quarterly* 2 (June 1887): pp. 197–217.

[4] Progressives were no less confident about the capacity of managers in the private sector to discover the "single best way" of making and delivering goods and services. See, for example, Frederick Winslow Taylor, *The Principles of Scientific Management* (New York: Harper and Brothers, 1911), pp. 20–28. For a general discussion, see Robert B. Reich, *The Next American Frontier* (New York: Times Books, 1983), chapter 4.

[5] See, for example, Ernst Freund, *Legislative Regulation* (New York: Commonwealth Fund; 1932).

[6] See, for example, *Panama Refining Co. v. Ryan*, 293 U.S. 388 (1935); *Schechter Poultry v. United States*, 295 U.S. 495 (1935).

Felix Frankfurter and James Landis, among others, saw in the development of administrative agencies a capacity to solve social and economic problems quickly and efficiently, applying systematic knowledge to public issues. These New Deal theorists of public administration perceived no conflict between their vision and democratic ideas: elected representatives would define the broad goals and problems to be addressed; the agencies would solve them. Others, however, particularly those sitting on the federal courts, took a dimmer view.

By the middle of the decade, under pressure from Franklin D. Roosevelt, the courts relented. Most broad delegations of authority would thereafter be declared constitutional. But it was not just Roosevelt's threat to pack the Supreme Court that tipped the scales at the time. Public opinion was solidly behind the ideal of administrative expertise. From the depths of the Depression the public goals seemed self-evident—to get the economy moving again and ameliorate some of the worst suffering. The challenge was to discover and implement solutions. And this was manifestly a job for expert judgment. If not delegated to expert agencies, that job could only be handled by the courts, through case-by-case adjudication of specific applications of broad statutes. But the courts lacked the expertise, they could not be counted on to act quickly, and they had no capacity to solve the inevitable problems of implementation.[7] The logic of the reformers seemed irrefutable.

In reality, of course, no sharp line could be drawn between ends and means, between making policy and implementing it. During the Depression decade of the 1930s and the subsequent war years, there was a broad consensus about the problems that needed to be solved. This left considerable room for administrative discretion that *looked* like implementation. After peace and prosperity had been substantially attained, the next set of goals—having more to do with the quality of the life Americans would lead thereafter—was less clear-cut. Accordingly, administrative discretion began looking more like policy making. This shift in public perceptions, in turn, brought into sharper focus the problem of reconciling discretion with democratic values.

There was another reason why the American public became more sensitive to administrative discretion after 1945. The fresh experience of fascism, Soviet totalitarianism, and then McCarthyism at home caused many to view with alarm any scheme of governance that permitted moral absolutism or smacked of social engineering. To Americans who had emerged from the shadow of demagoguery, the virtue of American democracy appeared to lie in political pluralism and ethical relativism.[8] Political scientists of the era slipped gingerly from description to prescription: American politics was pluralist, composed of shifting and overlapping groups whose leaders bargained with one another; the vast majority of Americans were members of one or more of these groups, even if they remained mostly uninvolved. These features helped to explain why democracy had survived so well in the United States, by contrast to many other nations; these features were thus

---

[7]These arguments were advanced by Felix Frankfurter in *The Public and Its Government* (New Haven: Yale University Press, 1930), and James Landis, in *The Administrative Process* (New Haven: Yale University Press, 1938). See also James W. Fesler et al., *The Elements of Public Administration* (New York: Prentice-Hall, 1946), pp. 7–9.

[8]For a thoughtful treatment of this issue, see Edward Purcell, Jr., *The Crisis of Democratic Theory: Scientific Naturalism and the Problem of Value* (Lexington: University of Kentucky Press, 1973).

desirable prerequisites for democracy.[9] Economists began to entertain a similar vision of democracy as a contest among leaders to represent the interests of competing groups.[10]

Broad grants of administrative discretion to the "experts" seemed dangerously inconsistent with these newly discovered democratic virtues. Accordingly, the postwar intellectual and political agenda turned toward *reducing* administrative discretion rather than justifying and enlarging on it. But this proved no mean task. Given the complexities of modern government, legislatures could not simply reclaim responsibilities of the sort they had been delegating to administrators. At the same time, given the premises of pluralism and relativism, it was quite impossible to construct a set of substantive standards to guide administrators in discovering the public interest. For there was no longer assumed to be any unified "public interest" capable of discovery. What passed for the public interest at any moment was now thought to be the product of an ongoing competition among groups for power and influence.

One needed some means of reconciling the practical necessity of administrative discretion with this emerging pluralist norm—a way to retain the broadly delegated authority of administrators to make choices in the public interest, while radically limiting their substantive discretion over where the "public interest" might lie. The solution was found in the idea of administrative process. Henceforth, public administrators were to be managers of neutral processes designed to discover the best ("optimal") public policies. Their substantive expertise about a particular set of public problems was to be transformed into procedural expertise about a set of techniques applicable to all sorts of public problems. At the same time, new emphasis was given to the details of making administrative decisions. Public managers would have to follow certain preordained steps for gathering evidence and arriving at conclusions. The Administrative Procedure Act of 1946 and its subsequent amendments codified the prevailing expectations. The burgeoning field of administrative law thereafter concerned itself primarily with the procedural steps judges should demand of public administrators, rather than with the substance of what administrators ought to do. The effect was to treat administrative law as the consequence of judicial review rather than as a set of substantive standards of public administration.

Even the words used to describe the responsibilities of administrators subtly changed. Instead of finding the "common good" or the "public interest," the new language of public management saw the task in pluralist terms—making "trade-offs," "balancing" interests, engaging in "policy choices," and weighing the costs and benefits. Graduate schools of public administration henceforth would pay less attention to the purposes and methods of governance than to the techniques of making and implementing public policy. Courses in "analysis" and "implementation" would frame the core curricula.[11]

---

[9] See, for example, Robert A. Dahl, *A Preface to Democratic Theory* (Chicago: University of Chicago Press, 1956); David Truman, *The Governmental Process: Political Interests and Public Opinion* (New York: Knopf, 1951).

[10] Joseph Schumpeter, *Capitalism, Socialism, and Democracy* (New York: Harper, 1942); Anthony Downs, *An Economic Theory of Democracy* (New York: Harper, 1957).

[11] See Fesler et al., *The Elements of Public Administration*, pp. 37–41; *The John F. Kennedy School of Government: The First Fifty Years* (Cambridge, MA: Ballinger, 1986), pp. 25–48.

The Two Paradigms

The postwar transformation of public administration centered on two related but conceptually distinct procedural visions of how public managers should decide what to do. The first entailed *intermediating among interest groups;* the second, *maximizing net benefits.* Intermediation was the direct intellectual descendant of pluralist theory. Maximization was a stepchild, claiming equal descent from decision theory and microeconomics. Together the two procedural visions embodied the postwar shift from a description of how democratic institutions work to a powerful set of norms for how public decision making should be organized.

Interest Group Intermediation

Interest group intermediation took as its starting point the prevailing pluralist understanding of American politics, along with its prescriptive tilt. The job of the public manager, according to this vision, was to accommodate—to the extent possible—the varying demands placed on government by competing groups. The public manager was a referee, an intermediary, a skillful practitioner of negotiation and compromise. He was to be accessible to all organized interests while making no independent judgment of the merits of their claims. Since, in this view, the "public interest" was simply an amalgamation and reconciliation of these claims, the manager succeeded to the extent that the competing groups were placated.

In time, as the rather self-congratulatory pluralist theories of the 1950s and early 1960s gave way to a deepening critique of the American "administrative state" for its insensitivity to less organized interests and its corresponding tendency to be captured by dominant interests, the job of the manager-as-intermediator was refined. The central challenge came to be understood as ensuring that *all* those who might be affected by agency action were represented in decision-making deliberations—including interests dispersed so widely and thinly over the population that they might otherwise go unexpressed.

The federal courts took an early, active role in this refinement. As early as 1966 the Court of Appeals for the District of Columbia Circuit ruled that, within a license renewal proceeding, the Federal Communications Commission was obliged to permit the intervention of spokesmen for significant segments of the listening public. The basis for the ruling was that, since consideration of such viewpoints was necessary to ensure a decision responsive to public needs, failure to allow intervention rendered decisions arbitrary and capricious. The court noted that in "recent years, the concept that public participation in decisions which involve the public interest is not only valuable but indispensable has gained increasing support."[12] Subsequent court decisions required that the agency seek out representatives of opposing views, that it affirmatively consider all such views, and that it also consider alternate policy choices in light of their impact on all

---

[12] *Office of Communication of the United Church of Christ v. Federal Communications Commission,* 359 F. 2d 994, 1000–06 (C.A. D.C. 1966).

affected interests.[13] State courts imposed similar requirements on state agencies. Public participation was further aided by several statutes that provided funding for interest groups to be represented in agency proceedings. The Federal Trade Commission Improvement Act of 1975, for example, authorized the FTC to pay attorneys' fees and costs of rule-making participation to any group representing an interest that "would not otherwise be represented in such a proceeding" and whose representation "is necessary for a fair determination of the rule-making proceeding."[14]

As opportunities for participation grew, the task of interest group intermediation became more open to public scrutiny—or rather to the scrutiny of organized groups with the resources to ferret out information from the government. Courts required, for example, that all relevant information from agency files or consultants' reports be disclosed to all participants for comment, that agency announcements of proposed rule making give the agency's view of the issues, and that agency decision makers generally refrain from communicating in secret with participants.[15] Moreover, in the 1976 Government in the Sunshine Act, Congress declared it "the policy of the United States that the public is entitled to the fullest practicable information regarding the decision-making processes of the Federal Government." The act required that, with limited exceptions, agencies make their decisions in public.[16]

These developments tended to formalize the administrative process, making it resemble a trial court proceeding. But their more consequential effect was to impose ever more severe penalties on a public manager who failed to reach a workable compromise with groups that had the resources to challenge his decision in the courts, on some procedural ground. The penalty they could threaten was delay; litigation could drag on for years. Procedural formality thereby upped the ante, making accommodation all the more important.

Accommodation was possible largely because participation was conditioned on specific, concrete, and self-serving claims, rather than on general views about what policies were in the "public interest." To be sure, these self-interested claims typically were encased within arguments appealing to general principles of law or public interest that tended to favor the claimants' position. But it was well understood that the purpose of the inquiry was not to discover the public interest directly, only to find it indirectly by identifying programs or solutions that accommodated most groups. The courts would not guarantee groups espousing so-called ideological interests—who had no selfish stake in the outcome—a right to participate in the proceedings. Participation was conditioned on a showing that the proposed agency might cause some material "injury in fact" to a member of the group, or that the group's interest was specifically protected by the statute in question.

---

[13] See, for example, *Scenic Hudson Preservation Conf. v. Federal Power Commission*, 354 F. 2d 608 (C.A. 2, 1965), cert. denied, 384 U.S. 941 (1966); *Friends of the Earth v. Atomic Energy Commission*, 485 F. 2d 1031, 1033 (C.A. D.C. 1973); and other cases cited in Richard Stewart, "The Reformation of American Administrative Law," *Harvard Law Review* 88 (1975): p. 1667.

[14] 15 U.S.C. 57a(h) (1976).

[15] For a summary of these and related reforms, see generally Stewart, "Reformation," and Colin Diver, "Policymaking Paradigms in Administrative Law," *Harvard Law Review* 95 (1981): p. 393.

[16] 5 U.S.C. 552b (1976).

This condition aided accommodation in two ways. First and most obviously, it limited participation. If the proceedings were open to anyone who claimed to know what was best for the public, there might be no efficient way of reaching agreement among so large a crowd. Even more importantly, the requirement that participants have experienced a concrete injury ensured that grievances could be remedied and compromises devised. There would be no efficient way to bargain with parties espousing purely "ideological" views about what was good for the community or the nation, because there would be no obvious means of compensating them for their potential loss. Their injuries would involve values rather than palpable harms. Such values are often impossible to measure or rank, and they have an all-or-nothing quality that makes them stubbornly resistant to tradeoff. They cannot be compromised easily without losing their inherent moral character.[17]

Net Benefit Maximization

Net benefit maximization proceeded along a different route. This paradigm took as its starting point the decision-making tools that had been successfully applied in World War II for allocating resources and planning strategy, and added to them microeconomic theory, which supplied the idea of allocative efficiency. But the shift from description to prescription was as complete as in the preceding vision. How people acted in the market to satisfy their desires was taken as a model for how public managers should decide what to do. In this view government intervention was justified primarily when it would result in an allocation of goods and services better matched to what people want than the outcome generated by market forces alone (as under conditions of natural monopoly or other forms of "market failure"). Even when allocative efficiency was not the goal of a given intervention, consideration of economic effects presumably would lead to a more efficient intervention—that is, one that achieved its goal at minimal cost.

Here the public manager was less a referee than an analyst. His responsibilities were, first, to determine that the market had somehow failed and that intervention might improve overall efficiency; second, to structure the decision-making process so as to make explicit the public problem at issue, alternative means of remedying it, and the consequences and tradeoffs associated with each solution; and third, to choose the policy option yielding the highest net benefits—where there was the greatest social utility. Along the way he (or his staff) might employ a range of analytic tools: probability theory, to deal with uncertainty; econometric, queuing, diffusion, and demographic models, to help predict the remote consequences of particular actions; linear programming, to perform complex resource

---

[17] In *Sierra Club v. Morton*, 405 U.S. 727 (1972), the Supreme Court denied standing to the Sierra Club to contest an Interior Department ruling, on the ground that the club's asserted interest in the broad principle that wilderness areas should be preserved did not place the club or any of its members in jeopardy of a material injury by the department's proposed actions. The club's assertion in a subsequent proceeding that the rule would deny certain of its members the enjoyment of the wilderness area in question was deemed by the court to be sufficient to confer standing. Some commentators have criticized these seemingly inconsistent decisions as examples of legal legerdemain; they argue that almost any ideological group can contrive some material injury to one of its members sufficient to gain standing. But this critique misses the important difference between the two instances in these cases. A view about what constitutes a good society does not readily lend itself to hard bargaining; by contrast, a specific and identifiable injury, as to particular individuals' enjoyment of particular wilderness areas, lends itself to negotiation and perhaps compensation. In the latter case, the public manager-as-intermediator can do his job.

allocation computations; discounting, to measure future outcomes in terms of present values; and other variations on game theory, statistics, and mathematics. Social science data derived from empirical experiments and field studies might be applicable to these analytic processes, of course, particularly to anticipate the consequences of various alternatives. But unlike his prewar predecessors who wielded substantive expertise, the public manager who sought to maximize net benefits relied primarily on procedural expertise. His focus was on how to organize the process of discovering the optimal policy.

Net benefit maximization became a cornerstone of regulatory reform efforts. Between 1965 and 1980, Congress passed approximately forty new laws—on health, education, transportation, housing, the environment, and agriculture— that required evaluations of the economic impact of regulations proposed under them. Six of these laws specifically authorized funding of, or required that a fixed percentage of the agency program budget be set aside for, such evaluations.[18] In addition, the Ford, Carter, and Reagan administrations actively pursued economic impact analysis. Executive orders required that agencies subject major regulations to a "regulatory analysis" that contained a succinct statement of the problem requiring federal action, the major ways of dealing with it, analysis of the economic effects of the proposed regulation and of alternative approaches considered, and a justification of the approach selected. These analyses were to be reviewed by groups within the Office of Management and Budget, or affiliated with the Council of Economic Advisors, to ensure that major regulations were justifiable in terms of costs and benefits.[19] Similar efforts cropped up among the states. At the same time, and with increasing boldness, the courts also embraced net benefit maximization. They deemed evidence "insufficient" or the process of decision making "arbitrary and capricious" when an agency disregarded important economic effects of its actions, artificially narrowed options, failed to set forth its theories, or employed faulty analysis and a weak chain of analytic reasoning.[20]

Net benefit maximization shared with interest group intermediation the central premise that the "public interest" could—and should—be defined only by reference to the disparate, selfish preferences of individuals. But rather than uncritically accept the preferences articulated by and through group leaders, net benefit maximizers sought to measure preferences directly by observing how people behaved. If people were simply asked what they wanted, their responses would not necessarily reflect tradeoffs implied in the choice. A preferable course was to observe how people expressed their priorities within the numerous market transactions of their daily lives. If the policy at issue concerned something that was not traded on the market, like clean air, the net benefit maximizer would seek a surrogate measure of

---

[18] For example, the Consumer Product Safety Commission's product safety rules must "express in the rule itself the risk of injury which the standard is designed to eliminate or reduce" (15 U.S.C. 2058(b), 1976).

[19] The Reagan order forbad any regulatory action, whether major or minor, by executive agencies unless "the potential benefits to society . . . outweigh the potential costs to society" and the alternative chosen to achieve the goal maximizes the aggregate net benefit to society. Executive Order No. 12,291, 46 Fed. Reg. at 13,193 (1981).

[20] *Pilai v.* CAB, 485 F. 2d 1018 (C.A. D.C. 1973); *Portland Cement v. Ruckelshaus*, 486 F. 2d 375 (C.A. D.C. 1973), cert. denied 417 U.S. 921 (1974); *Aqua Slide N' Dive v. Consumer Products Safety Commission*, 569 F. 2d 831 (C.A. 5, 1978).

citizens' willingness to pay for such a good, like the price of homes in a nonpolluted area of town relative to housing prices in a polluted section nearby.

Policies that would make one group of people worse off and another group better off posed a special problem. Interest group intermediators attempted to solve it by pitting the groups against one another, presumably until an accommodation occurred through which the gainers shared some of their benefits with the losers. This approach still left open the possibility that certain groups might have more organizational strength than others and thus could impose substantial (although perhaps widely dispersed) costs on the others for the sake of relatively small gains for themselves. Net benefit maximizers sought to solve the problem through cost-benefit analysis; policies would be chosen that conferred larger benefits on some than losses for others. Because there is no theoretically defensible means of determining that the wants of one group of people are either stronger or more worthy than those of another, net benefit maximizers felt more confident about these decisions if the two groups—the gainers and the losers—started in roughly equivalent circumstances or, if not, the resulting redistribution at least moved them closer together.[21] But such judgments ultimately rested on a pluralist vision as well—one that perceived individuals as members of groups, the members as possessing certain common characteristics, and the groups existing in some specific and identifiable relationship to one another. These perceptions, in turn, could be drawn reliably only from the ways in which the groups actually organized themselves—what criteria defined their memberships, how they described their central purposes, and how they characterized themselves.

The Two Paradigms in Practice

These two approaches to policy making—interest group intermediation and net benefit maximization—have coexisted uneasily. Both have rested on the same pluralist vision and understood the "public interest" as nothing more (or other) than the disparate sentiments of diverse groups of people about what they want for themselves, combined with procedural norms for weighing and balancing such interests. And from a strictly theoretical perspective (ignoring agency and transaction problems) there is no difference in outcome between the two methods. After all, any "solution" whose benefits exceed its costs would enable those who gain from it to compensate those who lose (or who receive none of the direct benefits) and still come out ahead. Since actual compensation would cause losers and nongainers to acquiesce to the change, the mere fact of unanimous agreement to a compromise would signal that it is efficient.

As a practical matter, however, the two approaches have diverged in several ways. The first involves the objectives to be sought by government intervention. Interest group intermediators have assumed that the objective will emerge only from the interactions of divergent participants and cannot be fully defined in advance. This lack of definition enables each of the participating groups to believe

---

[21]See Edith Stokey and Richard Zeckhauser, *A Primer for Policy Analysis* (New York: W. W. Norton, 1978), p. 281.

(or at least its leader to claim to his clients and constituents) that the intervention served the group's purposes. As a result, the public goal of the government action is established after the fact, if at all. But net benefit maximizers have required that the objective be articulated as specifically and narrowly as possible in advance, so that alternative (and less costly) means of attaining it can be considered.

A second divergence has to do with evidence. Interest group intermediators have assumed that the facts at issue are the articulated preferences of parties likely to be affected by the rule. Relevant evidence therefore properly includes a substantial amount of testimony by group representatives about what the group wants and needs. On the other hand, net benefit maximizers have not concerned themselves with articulated preferences. The facts at issue are the potential overall costs and benefits of the proposed action and its alternatives. Articulated preferences offer a poor means of measuring these values.

A final divergence concerns the criteria for a good decision. Interest group intermediators have believed the best decision is the one most acceptable (or least objectionable) to the groups affected—that outcome to which the greatest number of participants ultimately subscribe most enthusiastically. But net benefit maximizers have believed the best decision is the most efficient one—that which maximizes benefits for a given cost or minimizes costs for a given benefit. Negotiation and compromise have nothing to do with it; an efficient solution might be unpopular with many participants.

To get a concrete sense of these differences, imagine a town in a river valley periodically subject to flooding. The public manager has a broad statutory mandate to "manage the environment" or "manage water resources"; or perhaps he is a city manager charged with overseeing the local government. If he views his role as interest group intermediator, he would listen to the complaints of various group representatives who came to his office—business and civic associations representing downstream merchants and householders who want a dam constructed. He also would listen to residents of the less populous area upstream, who would lose their businesses and homes if a dam turned the upstream area into a reservoir. The intermediator's objective is neither to stop the downstream flooding nor to save upstream homes, but only to reach an accommodation that basically satisfies the various groups. Our manager-as-intermediator also might solicit the participation of other, less organized groups, such as lower-income people who now rent houses on the flood plain (whose rents would substantially increase if the land values were to rise). The resulting decision would reflect a great deal of negotiation. The dam may be built; but if so, upstream owners will be paid for their land and their moving expenses, and perhaps given an additional "sweetener," and some of the poorer renters downstream will be allocated parcels of the new land made habitable as a result of the project.

A manager who viewed his role as net benefit maximizer would proceed quite differently. He would be open to the possibility of a dam project, since the market cannot be expected on its own to generate a "public good" like a dam. But he would carefully examine the costs and benefits of building it or taking any other measure to reduce downstream flooding. He might gather evidence of the market values of property on the flood plain, above it, and upstream—thereby discovering how much money people in principle would be willing to spend to avoid flooding, on the one hand, or to live in the rural area upstream that would be permanently flooded by construction of a dam. In the end, let us suppose, the administrator decides that the benefits of the dam far outweigh the costs. The dam will be built. But upstream landowners will not necessarily be paid anything (beyond the "just compensation" required by the Fifth Amendment to the Constitution) since actual compensation need not be paid to make the outcome efficient, and there is no particular income difference between upstream and downstream owners that might justify such a payment. Poorer renters downstream will receive a cash transfer instead of an allocation of the newly habitable public lands; such a transfer will represent a more efficient redistribution than a donation of the land, since the poor can then choose how they wish to spend it.

It is hardly surprising that these two different approaches have, in practice, resulted in something of a hybrid. While the formal language of policy making increasingly has borrowed forms of argument and analysis from net benefit maximization, the actual process of coming to a decision has rested ever more firmly on interest group intermediation. Each participating group typically submits its own data and analysis tending to support a definition of the problem and a proposed solution that best serves its wants. To return to our example, upstream homeowners could be expected to submit data and analyses suggesting that the periodic costs of downstream flooding are really quite minor, while the costs of damming the river and flooding upstream would be high, and that, in any event, the problem could be alleviated simply by building a drainage canal. Downstream owners, on the other hand, would submit data and analyses tending to show that the costs of failing to remedy the problem are higher than those of building the dam, and that there are no less costly alternatives. Typically the public manager would compromise among these competing estimates, choosing a set of valuations approximately halfway between those offered by the competing camps (thereby practicing interest group intermediation while applying the form of net benefit maximization).[22]

Ironically, the hybrid of the two procedural visions occasionally has thwarted both. The strategic use of the *form* of net benefit maximization in the *process* of intermediation has tended to exacerbate a central problem of intermediation: the underrepresentation of poor and diffused interests. The very insistence on analytic argument has altered the rules of the game; proffered "views" are no longer assertions of preference for certain outcomes, but estimates of costs and benefits, and predictions about future consequences. Wealthy and well-organized groups have been able to offer sophisticated analyses and rebut alternative (often less sophisticated) analyses supplied by less well-endowed groups. The very complexity of the analysis has tended to discourage the involvement of a wider range of participants, who feel that they have nothing legitimate to add to this form of public debate.

---

[22] In one real-world example, the Civil Aeronautics Board (CAB) was presented with two conflicting estimates of the changes in air traffic that would result from a fare increase then under consideration. The CAB staff offered estimates based on an analysis of air traffic and prices over the previous twenty years. The industry, using an analysis that omitted certain years considered to be unrepresentative, offered a very different estimate. The CAB ultimately accepted neither estimate completely, but found it could "form the basis for a reasonable judgment on the issue." Its "reasonable judgment," not surprisingly, fell between the two estimates. See *Domestic Passenger Fare Investigation, Phase 7,* Part 9, 1971.

At the same time, the commingling of the two approaches has aggravated a central problem of net benefit maximization, which is the interpersonal comparisons of utilities implied when some people gain and others lose from a policy deemed to maximize net social benefits. The analytic form of argument has obscured the actual patterns of group organization and membership lying behind it. This in turn has made it more difficult to judge whether groups of gainers and losers are in roughly equivalent circumstances to begin with, or whether the resulting redistribution brings them closer together.

The net result of these conceptual impasses has been to undermine further the legitimacy of administrative decision making and subject it to repeated criticism both for failing to respond adequately to affected interests *and* for failing to yield efficient solutions. Proposals for reform have cycled back and forth between interest group intermediation and net benefit maximization as the inadequacies of first one, then the other vision are exposed. Not surprisingly, the resulting policy decisions have often lacked broad and sustained public support.

The Problem of Neutrality

The muddle into which both types of policy making have fallen is due, I believe, to difficulties lying deeper than the problems of reconciling them or the technical challenges of accommodating diffused interests and comparing the utilities of different groups. These are symptoms of a more profound failure to reflect an authentic governmental character—that is, to inspire confidence among citizens that the decisions of public managers are genuinely in the "public interest."

Both procedural devices are premised on the view that democracy is simply (or largely) a matter of putting public authority to the service of what individual people want. These individual preferences in turn are assumed to exist apart from any process designed to discover and respond to them—outside any social experience with democratic governance. Both interest group intermediation and net benefit maximization share a view of democracy in which relevant communications all flow in one direction: from individuals' preferences to public officials, whose job it is to accommodate or aggregate them. The formal democratic process of electing representatives is only the most traditional manifestation of this communications system. Since elected representatives cannot or will not fully instruct public managers in what to do, the formal process has needed to be enlarged and supplemented by a separate system that links individual preferences more directly to administrative decision making: hence interest group intermediation and net benefit maximization.[23]

This view of the place of public management in a democracy suffers from two related difficulties. First, it is inaccurate. Individual preferences do not arise outside and apart from their social context, but are influenced by both the process and

---

[23] It has been suggested that certain of these devices are applicable even in absence of formal democratic institutions. See, for example, Stokey and Zeckhauser, *Primer:* "Most of the materials in this book [concerning the techniques of policy analysis] are equally applicable to a socialist, capitalist, or mixed-enterprise society, to a democracy or a dictatorship, indeed wherever hard policy choices must be made" (p. 4).

the substance of policy making. Communications move in both directions, from citizen to policy maker and from policy maker to citizen, and then horizontally among citizens. The acts of seeking to discover what people want and then responding to such findings inevitably shape people's subsequent desires. Occasionally these effects are so profound that neither interest group intermediation nor net benefit maximization can do its job, even in the limited terms of linking public authority to selfish wants. In addition, this view of policy making is normatively suspect. It leaves out some of the most important aspects of democratic governance, which involve public deliberation over public issues and the ensuing discovery of public ideas. As we will see, these two shortcomings are connected. For it is only through public deliberation that the shared understandings that animate public policy can be examined and the tacit assumptions about what is wanted can be revised.

Consider, first, the possible effects of interest group intermediation on the way a citizenry understands what is important to its collective life, what problems it must address, what is at stake in such decisions, and its capacities to deal with such problems in the future. Returning to our earlier example, suppose the intermediator has sought out the views of citizen groups on construction of a dam. He has been willing to listen to spokesmen of any established organization, and he has actively encouraged the leaders of other, less prominent groups to proffer their views as well. He has listened to the president of the local Chamber of Commerce, the head of the Downtown Merchant's Association, the chairman of the Board of Realtors, the leader of the Upper Valley Homeowners Association, and a variety of other groups representing homeowners and merchants, living upstream and downstream from the proposed dam. Each group leader has presented formal testimony; some have filed reports, analyses, and extensive commentary. The local media have duly reported their views. Editorialists, commentators, and political leaders have begun to take sides in the emerging controversy. It is soon understood as a contest between upstreamers and downstreamers.

But note that the controversy itself has been shaped largely by how representatives of the various groups have expressed their views about what their constituents want for themselves. These spokespeople have identified the key issues and arguments, defined the relevant constituencies, and structured the emerging debate. The public might have developed a very different understanding about what was at stake had a different set of representatives and groups participated—for example, downstream tenants or those who loved to fish and hike in the upstream woodlands. Rather than a contest between upstreamers and downstreamers, the controversy might have been understood as one between economic growth and environmental conservation, or between land speculators and poor renters, or all of these and more—a decision rich with implications, potentially creating all sorts of gainers and losers. Each of these frames would have caused a different set of issues to be explored in the media and in various public forums, a different set of arguments and questions to be considered by the public, and a different set of connections to be made to other issues and values lying at the perimeter.

The implicit selection of certain groups and leaders to participate has subtly altered the configuration of influence and political authority in the community.

These groups and those who have spoken on their behalf are now seen as having access to power, and this perception feeds on itself. Earlier there were probably many *incipient* groupings in the community, since at any point in time there is a variety of ways in which citizens might join together to express different constellations of concerns. Many of these fledgling organizations and leaders were presumably weak—disorganized, lacking a clear focus, as yet incapable of generating strong support and a dedicated following. Those that become recognized as participants in the decision making process, however, find their roles legitimized and strengthened. The groups and leaders that were encouraged to participate have now become semiofficial channels through which community views are expressed; accordingly, their focus and support are both enhanced. As issues arise in the future, these groups and their leaders will be among the first to be consulted. Incipient groups and leaders that were not selected or encouraged to participate, on the other hand, suffer a corresponding decline in influence and status. Citizens have less reason to involve themselves in such groups or support such leaders next time because they are perceived to lack standing to articulate public views.

Finally, the act of participation has rendered the articulated concerns appropriate subjects of public debate and, by implication, public action. Their very expression has legitimized them. The concerns of downstream merchants now have a clear place on the public agenda; the periodic flooding to which they are exposed has been transformed from an act of nature causing private loss into a public problem to public remedy. To the extent possible, these concerns must now be accommodated in the eventual decision. For under interest group intermediation, the primary criterion of a good decision is that it addresses such articulated concerns. There are no principled limits to, or goals for, public involvement apart from this. Once they become legitimate subjects of public debate and action, such concerns will remain on the public agenda, to be accommodated in future decisions as well. The welfare of downstream merchants has now become a *public goal.*

In all these ways, the interest group intermediator is an active participant in the political development of the community. By recognizing "established" groups and leaders, and subtly encouraging others to participate, the intermediator effectively shapes public understandings of what is at stake, perceptions of who has power in the community, and assumptions about what subjects merit public concern. In this way he alters the political future. To view him merely as a neutral intermediator dramatically understates his true role.

Net benefit maximization is no less influential. But here it is the initial selection of objectives to be achieved and options to be weighed, rather than the groups and leaders to participate, that shapes public perceptions about what is at stake; and it is the choice of proxy for "willingness to pay" that affects how the public values these stakes.

Let us return to our example, but this time with our public manager as a net benefit maximizer. To analyze the problem and measure public preferences for different solutions, he first must simplify it. Asking himself how the costs of downstream flooding can most efficiently be reduced, he estimates the costs and benefits of three alternatives: a dam, a drainage canal, and a dike along the edge of the river. The cost of the dam will include the loss of upstream wilderness that will be flooded. The manager estimates this loss by adding to the market value of the land its recreational value, calculated by estimating how many people visit the wilderness area in a given time period, how much money they spend to get there, and how much more they would have to spend to travel to alternative wilderness areas. Assume that after estimating the costs and benefits of each alternative he concludes that the dam will generate the greatest net benefits, and the dam is constructed.

The issue is not the "correctness" of his conclusion about the social utility of a dam relative to the other alternatives, although that will be how opponents of the dam will approach the subject. Any formal analysis necessarily entails a somewhat simplified characterization of reality and a host of choices about how and what to simplify. Of more enduring consequence is the effect of such choices on the social utility function itself. Like the intermediator's implicit choices of whom to encourage to participate, these net benefit maximizing choices reverberate through the community because they have public authority behind them. They influence the way people in the community come to think about the problem, its possible solutions, and the values at stake in the decision.

To state the objective as reducing the costs of downstream flooding, for example, constitutes an important public act. That technical objective is transformed into a public goal to which the community attaches its collective aspirations and around which citizens mobilize. Just as mere participation serves a legitimizing function in interest group intermediation, such a statement of objective legitimates a whole class of similar problems as appropriate subjects for public action—for example, acts of nature (rock slides, dust storms, tornadoes) that periodically imperil the area or hardships that periodically befall those who live downstream. It simultaneously makes other ways of thinking about the issue less legitimate—for example, the thought that periodic flooding is not really a public problem at all, since downstream owners have always coped with it.

The identification of alternative solutions also sends powerful social messages that will influence the way people think about, and act on, similar problems in the future. One such message is that appropriate solutions are to be found in complex engineering projects, rather than in social endeavors like organizing a voluntary brigade to clean up after each flood. Another, related message is that the identification of alternative solutions is primarily a technical task for which the average person has no particular competence or relevant knowledge. Together these messages may tend to discourage social responses that draw inspiration and energy from citizens' sense of their shared responsibility for community problems and their competence in devising solutions.

Finally, the methods used by the net benefit maximizer to evaluate the alternatives affect the way citizens come to view certain attributes of their lives. The official act of placing a monetary value on the upstream wilderness, for example, constitutes a powerful public statement that feelings toward such wilderness *can* be expressed in monetary terms. It thereby transforms wilderness areas into consumer goods whose worth depends on how well they satisfy us, rather than entities with their own constitutive values, whose worth to us is bound up in the belief that a monetary value cannot be placed on them. The further assumption that "willingness to pay" to travel to such a wilderness area is the proper measure of how we value it, moreover, dismisses as irrelevant any positive feelings people have simply because the wilderness area exists there upstream. It suggests that the only grounds for complaint or despair, should the area disappear, derive from the direct and personal loss of access to it. Together, such ideas—that wilderness areas should be valued in terms of how well they satisfy people, and then only on the basis of people's direct and personal experience with them—are powerful social norms that may influence how citizens think about their environment in the future.[24]

The *substantive* decisions that emerge from both types of policy making, or some hybrid of the two, also influence future preferences. These decisions alter the world that people experience. To return to our example, the experience of future generations in the community will be quite different if the dam is constructed. People will then grow to adulthood without enjoying relatively easy access to the upstream wilderness. Not knowing what experiences they have missed, they will never learn to place the same high value on accessible wilderness as earlier generations did. Because their relationship with the environment is likely to be more attenuated, they will probably be more willing to make subsequent decisions that sacrifice the environment to other values. If the dam is not built, the experience of future generations will not change in this way. Over time, the divergence between the two paths of decisions (and the preferences on which they are based) would grow larger. Several generations hence, the descendants of the dam builders are likely to live in a profoundly different setting and to have different norms, espouse different causes, dream different dreams. The decision to build the dam, then, does not just reflect the values of the present generation; it sets a trajectory of future values.

Even the choice of a policy instrument can generate powerful social signals that shape future norms. As we have seen, for example, the net benefit maximizer typically prefers to give the poor cash rather than a scarce commodity—like a portion of the downstream lands rendered habitable by construction of the dam—on the rationale that it is more efficient to let individuals decide how to spend the cash than to give them something that might not exactly meet their needs. But this view ignores the quite different public perceptions attached to the two transfers. The transfer of newly habitable land has a clear social meaning. The land is indelibly "public"; it was created through public action aimed at improving the habitability of the entire downstream area. This particular parcel could have been used for a park or a school, but the public has chosen instead to give it to those in need. It is thus a particular gift, reflecting a particular sort of public generosity, linked to particular public purposes. The homes that the poor can now build in this area will continually remind the community of these purposes and thus shape the

---

[24] See Steven Kelman, *What Price Incentives?* (Cambridge, MA: Arbor House, 1981). It should also be noted that market prices and expressions of willingness to pay depend on the current distribution of wealth and income. If the current distribution is deemed to be unfair, then a different set of prices and expressions of willingness to pay might be more appropriate.

way the public thinks about future projects of a similar sort. A simple transfer of cash would be devoid of these social meanings—so devoid, in fact, that it might not summon sufficient political support to be authorized in the first place.[25]

In sum, both the process and the substance of policy decisions generate social learning about public values and set the stage for future public choices. They give rise to new understandings and expectations; they shape policy debates in other, related policy areas; they reconfigure social ideals. It is therefore misleading to view the job of public managers simply as responding to pre-existing preferences, expressed either through group leaders or market transactions. Their responsibility is much broader and more subtle.

Civic Discovery

Within the context of either interest group intermediation or net benefit maximization, disagreements among people are assumed to derive from incompatible preferences—conflicts among selfish desires. The challenge to the public manager under these circumstances is thought to be a technical one: either to intermediate among groups until an accommodation is reached or to measure people's willingness to pay for certain things (and avoid other things) and then maximize their combined welfare. As we have seen, neither of these techniques is entirely neutral; both can alter how the initial problems are perceived and solutions understood. In addition, neither creates an opportunity for the public to deliberate about what is good for society. Yet it is through such deliberation that opinions can be revised, premises altered, and common interests discovered.

To return once again to our example, imagine now that the public manager eschews both types of conventional policy making. Instead of assuming that he must decide whether the dam should be build, he sees the occasion as an opportunity for the public to deliberate over what it wants. Accordingly, he announces that various people living and working downstream are complaining about periodic flooding of the river. He then encourages and instigates the convening of various forums—in community centers, schools, churches, and workplaces—where citizens are to discuss whether there is a problem and, if so, what it is and what should be done about it. The public manager does not specifically define the problem or set an objective at the start. He merely discloses the complaints. Nor does he take formal control of the discussions or determine who should speak for whom. At this stage he views his job as generating debate, even controversy. He wants to bring into the open the fact that certain members of the community are disgruntled and create possibilities for the public to understand in various ways what is at stake. He wants to make the community conscious of tensions within it, and responsible for dealing with them. In short, he wants the community to use this as an occasion to debate its future. Several different kinds of civic discovery may ensue.

---

[25] See M. Landy, "Policy Analysis as a Vocation," *World Politics* (April 1981): 469; Steven Kelman, "A Case for In-Kind Transfers," *Economics and Philosophy* 2 (1986): pp. 55–73.

The Problem and Its Solutions May Be Redefined. During the course of such deliberations, people may discover that their initial assumptions about the nature of the problem and its alternative solutions are wrong or inappropriate. Through sharing information about what concerns them and seeking common solutions to those concerns, they come to see that the issue should not be defined as whether to build the dam, but how best to relocate people off the flood plain. Viewed this way, a potentially sharp conflict within the community is transformed into a project that almost everyone can support (even though it may be no one's most preferred outcome). Had the public manager sought to make the decision on the basis of the interest groups through which people express their wants, or through measurements of their willingness to pay, this possibility for redefining the issue and garnering widespread support would have been overlooked.

Voluntary Action May Be Generated. Their consideration of the plight of the downstream residents and businesses may lead others to volunteer time and money to the effort—erecting dikes, digging drainage canals, or relocating people and businesses. This willingness to volunteer stems from the discovery that others are also willing to lend a hand. Had there been no such deliberation, individuals might not have recognized how they could voluntarily help remedy the situation. Those who were inclined to help might have assumed that their charitable impulses were not widely shared, so that it would have been futile to act on them. The discovery empowers people, together, to take voluntary action.

Preferences May Be Legitimized. Some people may discover that there are many others like them who have not visited the upstream wilderness, but who nevertheless share a deep feeling for it and wish it to be preserved. Had there been no such deliberation, each might have continued to assume that his feelings were somehow illegitimate since they were not based on direct experience—and for this reason were not measurable on a willingness-to-pay scale and did not fit within an established interest group. Indeed, people might have denied having such feelings, regarding them as invalid or immature. But the discovery emboldens these people to admit and express such views, and seek to persuade others of their validity.

Individual Preferences May Be Influenced by Considerations of What Is Good For Society. Some people may discover a conflict between their personal, pecuniary interests in the problem and their hopes for their community. A downstream property owner who realizes that the dam would increase property values downstream, enhancing his personal wealth, may nevertheless believe it would be bad for the community. The dam would continue to be a divisive issue for years to come; future generations would no longer have access to the unspoiled wilderness areas upstream; and too many people would move to the downstream area, eventually overloading the roads, schools, and sewage lines. The citizen may still choose to favor his own pecuniary interest. Public deliberation does not guarantee that people will become more altruistic. But the deliberation at least creates the opportunity for such weighing and balancing. Had there been no such deliberation, the downstream owner might never have considered the future of the community.

Deeper Conflicts May Be Discovered. People may discover that their disagreements run much deeper than previously imagined. Those who want to preserve the upstream wilderness also want to minimize downstream development and preserve parks and open spaces within and around the city; downstream owners who want the dam also favor extensive development. The discovery of this more fundamental conflict might have been avoided (or delayed, or denied) had the public manager decided whether to build the dam on the basis of interest group demands or willingness to pay.

In these ways, public deliberation provides an opportunity for people to discover shared values about what is good for the community, and deeper conflicts among those understandings. Deliberation does not automatically generate these public ideas, of course; it simply allows them to arise. Policy making based on interest group intermediation or net benefit maximization, by contrast, offers no such opportunity. The self-interested preferences of individuals as expressed through their market transactions do not reflect potential public ideas. Interest groups, for their part, are instrumental devices for fulfilling the individual desires of their members, not bodies for deliberating what is good for society; their leaders are paid to be advocates and conduits, not statesmen.

The failure of conventional techniques of policy making to permit civic discovery may suggest that there are no shared values to be discovered in the first place. And this message—that the "public interest" is no more than an accommodation or aggregation of individual interests—may have a corrosive effect on civic life. It may invalidate whatever potential exists for the creation of shared commitments and in so doing may stunt the discovery of public ideas. Such a failure may in turn call into question the inherent legitimacy of the policy decisions that result. For such policies are then supported only by debatable facts, inferences, and tradeoffs. They lack any authentic governmental character beyond accommodation or aggregation. Those who disagree with the procedures or conclusions on which the policies are based have every reason to disregard them whenever the opportunity arises. Under these circumstances disobedience is not a social act reflecting on one's membership in a community, but merely another expression of preference.

Real-World Applications

Can public managers realistically hope to enhance public deliberation and social learning about what is good for society? Some real-world illustrations will suggest both the possibilities and limitations of such a role.

Ruckelshaus and Tacoma

Under the Clean Air Act Amendments of 1970, the Environmental Protection Agency (EPA) is required to issue national emissions standards for hazardous air pollutants, so as to provide an "ample margin of safety" to protect the public health.[26] Congress gave EPA no guidance for deciding how much safety is "ample," however. Even a small exposure to certain hazardous pollutants can pose substantial health risks. But to ban any air pollutant that caused even a small risk to health would substantially impair the national economy.

The problem received national attention in 1983 when the agency was trying to decide what, if anything, should be done about inorganic arsenic, a cancer-causing pollutant produced when arsenic-content ore is smelted into copper. The issue was dramatized especially in the area around Tacoma, Washington, where the American Smelting and Refining Company (Asarco) operated a copper smelter. The EPA had concluded that if Asarco's emissions were not controlled, approximately four new cases of lung cancer would be contracted each year in the area; even the best available pollution control equipment would still emit enough inorganic arsenic into the air to cause one cancer death a year. But the cost of such equipment would render the plant uneconomical, forcing the company to close it. The closing would have a devastating effect on the local economy: Asarco employed 570 workers with an annual payroll of about $23 million, and the company purchased $12 million of goods from local suppliers.

William Ruckelshaus, then administrator of the EPA, decided that the citizens of the Tacoma area ought to wrestle with the problem in a series of public meetings held during the summer of 1983. EPA officials began each meeting by explaining how the agency had estimated the health risks; they then divided the audience into three groups for more informal discussion with agency officials and staff. Some of the ensuing discussion concerned technical questions of measurement and emissions control, but many of the citizens' questions concerned the possible effects of the emissions on their gardens, animals, and overall quality of life. As the dean of the University of Washington School of Public Health observed, "the personal nature of the complaints and questions made a striking counterpoint to the presentations of meteorological models and health effects extrapolations."

These meetings, together with the national attention that Ruckelshaus had deliberately drawn to them, generated considerable and often unfavorable press coverage. In one editorial entitled "Mr. Ruckelshaus a Caesar," the *New York Times* argued that it was "inexcusable . . . for him to impose such an impossible choice on Tacomans." The *Los Angeles Times* pointed out the difficulties in "taking a community's pulse. . . . [Should he] poll the community . . . [or] count the pros and cons at the massive hearing?" Ruckelshaus was not surprised by the controversy. "Listen, I know people don't like these kinds of decisions," he said. "Welcome to the world of regulation. People have demanded to be involved and now I have involved them, and they say 'don't ask that question.' What's the alternative? Don't involve them? Then you are accused of doing something nefarious."

By 1985, the EPA still had not promulgated regulations for arsenic emissions, but declining world copper prices in the interim had forced the closure of the Asarco smelter. What then did Ruckelshaus accomplish? For one thing, the

---

[26]This illustration is based primarily on Henry Lee, "Managing Environmental Risk: The Case of Asarco," John F. Kennedy School of Government Case Program, Harvard University, 1985.

problem was redefined. Instead of focusing on how best to control hazardous air pollutants, citizens began to ask how they could diversify a local economy and attract industry that would not generate such substantial hazards. Attendance at the meetings, along with massive media exposure, had personalized the controversy in ways that induced people to look at it differently. As area residents heard a tearful woman, diagnosed as ultrasensitive to arsenic, describe how she and her husband had to sell their farm at a severe loss and leave the area, or saw copper workers in danger of losing their jobs, energies shifted from "winning" to changing the way the problem was understood and finding workable solutions. As Ruckelshaus described it, "Even the residents of Vashon Island, who were directly exposed to the pollution and yet had no employment or financial stake in the smelter, began to ask whether there was a means of keeping the smelter going while reducing pollution levels. They saw the workers from the smelter—encountered them in flesh and blood—and began incorporating the workers' perspective into their own solutions."

Several participants attacked the fundamental perception of "the environment versus jobs issue," arguing that discussion should focus instead on the development of new pollution control technologies that could control arsenic emissions and allow the plant to stay open. Others argued that Tacoma would do better to diversify its employment base and that the real problem was the local economy's dependence on a few industries like copper. Gradually, for many participants, the goal came to be understood as finding new jobs for the Asarco workers and new industry for the region, by attracting and developing nonpolluting businesses.[27] This view gained substantial support. By 1985, when the Asarco smelter closed down, Tacoma already had begun the task of diversifying its economy.

For Ruckelshaus, the value of the Tacoma experiment also included social learning about the health risks of pollution and the enormous costs of eliminating them altogether, not only in Tacoma but also in other communities that saw what occurred there. The deliberation in Tacoma thus helped launch a national debate over environmental policy, giving the public a deeper understanding about what would have to be sacrificed to reduce risks to health. Looking back more than a year later, after he had left the EPA, Ruckelshaus assessed the Tacoma experiment:

> Perhaps I underestimated how difficult it would be to get people to take responsibility, to educate themselves and one another about such a difficult issue. Probably not more than a relatively few citizens of Tacoma learned that for issues like this there is no "right" answer. . . . They would have to decide what they wanted for their community. They would have to determine their own future. But even if a handful learned this lesson, then you have a basis for others learning it. You have the beginnings of a tradition of public deliberation about hard issues. And you also have all the other people in the country who watched what happened there in Tacoma, and indirectly learned the same lesson from it.[28]

---

[27]*Seattle Times,* June 30, 1984, p. A10, col. 3.

[28]William Ruckelshaus, interview with author, February 27, 1985.

Pertschuk and Children's Advertising

In 1914 Congress created the Federal Trade Commission (FTC) as an indepen-dent agency to ferret out "unfair and deceptive acts and practices in commerce," but it left to the agency the task of defining these vague terms.[29] In 1977, Senator Warren Magnuson, chairman of the Senate Commerce Committee, which oversaw the FTC, suggested that the agency, under the direction of its new chairman, Michael Pertschuk, should look into the issue of advertising directed at children as a possible "unfair act." Magnuson knew very little about the subject and had only the vaguest of concerns. "Now, we've all been interested here in chil-dren's advertising," he said when Pertschuk first came to the Commission. "It's a difficult, complex subject. . . . I would hope that you would take a good, long look. . . . I hate to narrow this down, but the abuses seem to be in children's advertising, advertising directed to children."

Pertschuk saw in the issue a perfect means of raising consciousness about public susceptibility to advertising in general and in particular the vulnerability of young children to commercial inducements to buy sugary cereals and candy. Accordingly the Commission launched a preliminary investigation, and by April 1978 was considering several possible remedies: a ban on the number of advertise-ments for sugared products that could be directed at children during a certain period of time, or on a particular medium; controls on the kinds of advertising techniques that could be used; a requirement that nutritional information be dis-closed in such advertisements; a ban on advertisements for sugar-coated products; and a ban on all children's advertising. The proposals drew significant media atten-tion. Pertschuk received even more when he gave strongly worded speeches and provocative interviews about the dangers of advertising directed at children.

The proposals and Pertschuk's speeches and interviews set off a firestorm of criticism from industry groups. Broadcasters, advertisers, cereal manufacturers, grocery manufacturers, and sugar producers all felt threatened and counterat-tacked through the press and their lobbyists in Congress. The *Washington Post* editorialized that the FTC was aiming to be the "national nanny" and that it had no business interfering in an area of parental responsibility. One lobbyist felt that the Commission's confrontational strategy had contributed to the tumult. "We could have gotten some of the more enlightened companies to say, let's go in and bargain a little bit, and get half a loaf," he observed. "But they got everyone 100 percent against them, willing to commit war chests and time, the personal time of chief executive officers, saying, we cannot allow this to happen. They basically accused well-known businessmen of deliberately trying to foreshorten the lives of kids."

In the end, Congress reined in the FTC. Indeed the Commission's powers to issue all rules were curtailed; the agency's appropriations were reduced and its credibility severely crippled. What then did the campaign accomplish? Looking back several years later, Michael Pertschuk regretted the tactics, but not the goals.

---

[29] This illustration is based primarily on Arthur Applebaum, "Mike Pertschuk and the Federal Trade Commission," John F. Kennedy School of Government Case Program, Harvard University, 1981.

I suppose we made some mistakes. We came on too strong. If the goal was to preserve and develop the FTC's powers over the long haul, then Kidvid was a disaster. . . . But I'm not sure that was or should be the goal. After all, the FTC is merely a shell. It changes its color with every new administration. Why should I worry about its powers over the long term? The real goal was to get issues like children's advertising out there in front of the public. . . . I wanted to stir up a debate, get people thinking. You know, that's one of the most important things we can do, get the public to grapple with hard issues. And they did. The public had a chance to understand children's advertising, the press played it up. . . . We probably should have gone easier with it, given the issue more time to boil. But even so, you look around now in the stores, you see a lot less sugary cereal. You watch cartoons on Saturday morning, you see a lot fewer advertisements for sugary cereals and candy. Was consciousness raised about advertising directed toward children? Yes, and I think we contributed.[30]

Bennett and Educational Reform

Our final illustration concerns William Bennett, who became secretary of education in 1985.[31] The Department of Education administers a wide variety of programs, but they are tightly connected to individual congressional committees and to state and local programs. Most educational policy in the United States is determined at the state and local levels, where the bulk of the money is raised and spent. Accordingly a secretary of education has quite limited scope to affect change directly. Bennett, however, was determined to raise issues about American education that might affect change indirectly, through public debate. He began boldly, perhaps too boldly. At his first news conference, when announcing tighter standards for student loans, Bennett opined that students should help meet tuition by "stereo divestiture, automobile divestiture, three weeks at the beach divestiture." The speech infuriated many middle-class parents who relied on the student loan program and angered several members of Congress who had long supported it. By the end of Bennett's first month in office, the *Washington Post* ran an article entitled "Another Watt?" referring to the former secretary of interior's tendency to offend.

In subsequent months, however, Bennett's pronouncements were accompanied by detailed position papers and proposals for changes in various department regulations. Among other things, he advocated improved teacher training, higher standards for promoting students to the next grades, a return to "basics" in the classroom, educational vouchers as a means of generating competition among schools and giving students a choice of where to attend, a reconsideration of the place of religion in public education, and a rethinking of the tenets of bilingual education. Amid much press attention, Bennett traveled around the country, sitting and teaching in public classrooms and continuing to raise issues about educational policy. As his credibility increased, many of his ideas gained begrudging

---

[30] Michael Pertschuk, interview with author, March 7, 1986.

[31] This illustration is based primarily on Glenn Tobin, "Creating Discussion in Modern America," unpub. ms. Kennedy School of Government, Harvard University, 1986.

respect, even from groups that opposed him, like the National Educational Association and the American Federation of Teachers. Prominent politicians were picking up some of his themes. By March 1986, *Newsweek* remarked that Bennett's style was "guaranteed to win some enemies . . . but even critics recognize its usefulness. As Diane Ravitch, a professor at Teachers College of Columbia, says: 'The main role of the Secretary of Education is to keep the attention of the country focused on education.' By that standard, Bennett has been a resounding success. He has turned his office into a bully pulpit . . . He has barnstormed the country." One of Bennett's assistants explained the overall strategy:

> Bennett sees himself as in the business of raising the level of debate, focusing the public's attention where it hasn't been focused before. We've had to be sufficiently controversial to get the attention, but solid enough to gain the public's respect. It's a delicate balance. . . . It's okay to get the front-page story the next day, but you really want the feature stories that follow a few days or weeks later, that set out the arguments on both sides, and the editorials. The subject gradually becomes a respectable topic of debate. Politicians pick up the ideas. University presidents talk about them. . . . You know, most people think of speeches and position papers and all that stuff as being in the service of specific regulations or legislation. Around here it's the other way around. The specific policies are in the service of raising issues.[32]

Lessons

In each of the situations described above, a public manager sought to stimulate public deliberation over what was good for society rather than to decide specific policy. Each felt that public learning was at least as important a part of his job as policy making, because the public had to understand and decide for itself what value it was to place on certain issues lying within the manager's domain. Deliberation was worthwhile both in itself and because it could clarify ambiguous mandates and perhaps even move Congress to a different course of action. Rather than view debate and controversy as managerial failures that made policy making and implementation more difficult, these managers saw them as natural and desirable aspects of the formation of public values, contributing to society's self-understanding.

Were they successful? The answer depends on what is meant by success. Each succeeded in stimulating debate and focusing attention. There is some evidence— scattered, impressionistic—that each succeeded in altering the terms of public debate, engendering some sorts of civic discovery. Each insisted that such public deliberation was crucial to his mission. Ruckelshaus made the point explicitly: "My view is that these are the kinds of tough, balancing questions that we're involved in here in this country in trying to regulate all kinds of hazardous substances . . . [T]he societal issue is what risks are we willing to take and for what benefits? . . . For me to sit here in Washington and tell the people of Tacoma what is an acceptable risk would be at best arrogant and at worst inexcusable."[33]

---

[32] Interview with author, June 4, 1986. The assistant's name is withheld at his request.

[33] *Los Angeles Times*, August 13, 1983, p. 20, col. 3.

But there were costs. Ruckelshaus's Tacoma experiment reduced his credibility with environmentalists, whose support he vitally needed on other EPA projects. Pertschuk almost destroyed the Federal Trade Commission. Bennett spent so much time and energy in instigating debate that he had none left for legislative battles. All three managers faced a hostile press.

The cases also suggest that public deliberation is not easy to manage well. Public managers and the public at large often tend to equate administrative effectiveness with active decision making and successful implementation. These are concrete achievements that can be measured and on which reputations can be built. The nurturing of social learning about public values, on the other hand, is an elusive undertaking. A manager who tentatively advances several proposals and stirs controversy about them may appear indecisive or indifferent at best, as did Ruckelshaus, or he may be cast as a villain, as was Pertschuk. Moreover the public will wish to avoid facing difficult issues and examining the values bound up in them. Many people will resent the tensions and ambiguities inherent in such deliberation. They would prefer that the public manager take responsibility for making such decisions, as did many Tacomans, or that unsettling problems and questions not be raised at all.

There will also be procedural obstacles. To instigate public discourse the manager will have to make speeches, stage events, and use the press artfully. But in doing so he may deflect public attention from the issue to himself. It is far easier to attract the public's curiosity to a personality than to a substantive problem. Ruckelshaus, Pertschuk, and Bennett all became the focus of the media. Ruckelshaus managed to refocus on the issues; Pertschuk never quite pulled it off; Bennett, at this writing, is still struggling with the problem. The manager must also contend with well-established interest groups, whose strong advocacy can drown out any semblance of public thought. Their easy dominance of the media and of legislatures can push issues back off the table or reconfigure them into older debates. Ruckelshaus avoided this by staging his event in Tacoma, far from the center of organized group activity on the Potomac. Much of Pertschuk's message was jammed by the trade associations and major corporations that waged war against the FTC. Bennett took his show on the road, where established groups could not override his message, but teacher's lobbies and textbook manufacturers continually sought to define the issues he raised in ways they could control.

Public deliberation will take up inordinate time and resources (all three of our managers were almost consumed by it), and it can easily cycle out of control. There is no guarantee that the resulting social learning will yield a clear consensus at the end. Instead the process may exacerbate divisions within the community and make it more difficult to achieve consensus in the future. The FTC debacle made it more difficult for the Carter administration as a whole to gain the cooperation of the business community later on issues for which its support was needed.

The experience of public deliberation is not likely to be enjoyable for either politicians or agency employees. Politicians will resent a process that is beyond their control, often involving issues they would rather not have to deal with (that is why those issues were handed over to the public manager in the first place). All three of our public managers met with hostility from important congressional committees. Agency employees, for their part, are unlikely to understand the importance of fostering public discourse rather than getting on with the job of making policy. Their jobs and reputations depend on getting something done (or undone), and they will have little role in instigating or managing the debate. Furthermore, they will have to live with the results, often long after the top manager has left. Pertschuk's employees did not appreciate his willingness to sacrifice the agency's powers to the more immediate goal of raising the public's consciousness.

Lastly, there are lingering doubts about the propriety of nonelected bureaucrats' taking on this sort of responsibility. The line between ideological chest-thumping and the instigation of public debate can be a narrow one, easily missed even by managers who sincerely believe they are letting the public decide. Ruckelshaus stayed well to one side, but Pertschuk and Bennett both approached the line. James Watt, Reagan's errant secretary of the interior, seemed to have crossed it. Although there is no clear guide for where the line should be drawn, the cases examined here suggest a rule of thumb. The public manager may be in a better position than a legislator or senior elected official to foster a national debate over certain value-laden issues when the manager deals with specific applications of general principles. It is through detailed and vivid applications that the public comes to understand the principles and the tradeoffs and stakes they imply. Tacoma dramatically illustrated the principle that the cost of achieving zero health risk is prohibitive. Advertising directed at children was a less specific application, and Congress could have instigated a similar public deliberation. Similarly with many of the issues that Bennett sought to dramatize.

For all these reasons, prudence is advised. The public manager should not completely abandon interest group intermediation and net benefit maximization in favor of public deliberations. Each of the more traditional techniques has its place, especially for the vast majority of comparatively routine decisions, which are not fundamentally bound up with public values and are unlikely to have important effects on future choices.

But public managers must be willing to venture occasionally into the third sphere, in which public deliberation takes prominence. As we have seen, they have little choice in the matter. Enabling statutes are often vague, as was Congress's requirement that the EPA ensure an "ample margin of safety" for hazardous emissions or that the FTC ban "unfair" advertising. In certain areas of policy making, any decision is likely to have profound effects on how people understand and value the objects of policy. Instigating deliberation on controversial issues may sometimes be the only way for a public manager to effect change. In these circumstances, it is wise to allow, or even invite, some public discourse rather than to aim single-mindedly at making a decision. Public managers must understand that public debate and controversy over a domain within their control are not necessarily to be avoided. Although heated discourse may make their jobs somewhat less comfortable, it comes with the territory.

City managers are not political theorists. When they gather at conferences, the talk often turns to labor problems, fire truck deals, and other such nitty-gritty issues. They pride themselves on their pragmatism, and on running efficient governments that deliver services effectively. It is, therefore, significant when John Nalbandian, a scholar closely affiliated with the city management profession, writes that "facilitating community" and "enabling democracy" are emerging as new roles for local government managers. Granted, he is hardly working with a random sample of city managers, thanks to a healthy sprinkling of city managers who had written "state of the profession" articles for a leading journal in the field, *Public Management*, and winners of the prestigious Mark E. Keane Award for Excellence in Local Government. But it is precisely because these managers are exemplars in the field that their views and actions are likely to constitute a preview of coming attractions.

Furthermore, these city managers have come to this realization not as a philosophical choice, but out of necessity. It is political, economic, social, and technological trends that form and reform the local, state, or national environment of a society. These city managers are finding that, as a result of this changing environment, they are now increasingly held responsible by their constitutents for community building, and they are expected to facilitate the participation and representation that will help make this happen. In light of the concern over the growing distance between citizens and their government, there is greater emphasis on the themes of building community, civil society, and civic infrastructure. Community is difficult to define, but Nalbandian finds a desire for a *sense of community*—a sense of working together to solve problems of mutual concern to those living within a certain jurisdiction.

City managers are traditionally concerned with efficiency, and so it is significant that these exemplars are now placing more emphasis on process—on *how* decisions are reached and implemented as well as *what* should be done. They are thus trading off some expertise as to what in the eyes of their profession are the best practices in return for gaining greater citizen involvement in government. It is such activities that build "social capital," a term that, according to Robert Putnam, calls "attention to the ways in which our lives are made more productive by social ties."[a] Such social ties can promote individual goals, as in the case of networking, or may be directed at group goals. Such groups may be predominantly social, as in the case of a bowling league, or more inclusive, as in the civil rights movement. Putnam and others emphasize, however, that these kinds of social capital are interrelated. To the extent that people trust one another and are engaged in many kinds of social activity, the community is rich in social capital (though dysfunctional groups may engage in socially destructive behavior).

City managers are hardly in a position to reverse the decline in the number of bowling leagues, but they can, as Nalbandian says, engage in community building by building political capacity: "the capacity to make collective decisions amidst diverse and conflicting interests. A crucial component of this capacity is developing a sense of responsibility among citizens to participate in and obligate themselves to collective decisions." This civic engagement in turn leads citizens to understand that collective and public action are necessary to solve certain problems (the best government is not necessarily the smallest government), and encourages a greater

---

[a]Robert Putnam, *Bowling Alone* (New York: Simon & Schuster, 2000), pp. 18–26.

sensitivity among government managers and employees to the values of representation, individual rights, and some degree of social equity. The role of the individual as a customer in the marketplace is important, but so is the role as a citizen engaged in meeting joint responsibilities for the good of the entire community.

Under these circumstances, diversity is not an exercise in political correctness; it is an ingredient necessary for facilitating community and enabling democracy. Citizens as well as elected officials and public managers are involved in making the tradeoffs between technical standards and other values important at least to some in the community. Partnerships are another expression of participation and community engagement. In the view of Nalbandian's city managers, such partnerships are formed not only with the private sector, but also with school districts, counties, non-profits, community-based organizations, and neighorhood associations.

There is a tendency to view concerns such as facilitating community and enabling democracy as "warm and fuzzy." Not in the view of these city managers, who emphasize that tough and honest collective problem solving can be painful, since it involves developing consensus among diverse interests. Like attracting religious followers, building governance capacity and credibility these days often involves reaching out to suspicious and reluctant converts. Such activity is time consuming, and requires a thick skin. It seems likely that more and more communities in the future will be seeking and rewarding leaders who possess both technical and capacity-building skills.

Facilitating Community, Enabling Democracy: New Roles for Local Government Managers

John Nalbandian

Dennis Hays, administrator of the Unified Government of Wyandotte County/ Kansas City, Kansas, found himself in an unfamiliar role. In the presence of the governor, the mayor, and other dignitaries, Hays was asked to take the lead in a press conference announcing that the International Speedway Corporation had begun negotiating with the Unified Government as a partner in the construction of a NASCAR racetrack. His highly visible role in the project was being recognized and future expectations were being cast.

Kansas City, Kansas, once a manufacturing stronghold in northeast Kansas, is a city searching for lost pride. Hays, analytical and compassionate, and educated to believe that the role of the manager is to work backstage, found himself leading a project that would have significant effect on the sense of community in this city and on his own definition of professionalism.

This research, based on data gathered from open-ended survey questions, correspondence, and in-depth panel discussions, also utilizes earlier findings for a "then and now" examination of the contemporary roles, responsibilities, and values of city managers. City managers are seen as community builders and enablers of

John Nalbandian. *Public Administration Review*, Vol. 59, No 3 (May/June 1999).

democracy. With those goals, they have become skilled at facilitative leadership and at building partnerships and consensus.

Also, they have become more aware that legitimacy of the city manager role demands more than a legal foundation in council-manager government, the manager's adherence to the value of efficiency, and making recommendations based on "the greatest good for the greatest number over the long run." In today's political environment of diverse and conflicting interests, managers must anticipate and attend to claims for equity, representation, and individual rights if they are to succeed as partner to the elected officials and citizens they serve and as leader of the professional staff they supervise.

The Past

In my earlier review of professionalism in local government I concluded that city management had transformed itself over several decades in three fundamental ways. It had "moved from an orthodox view of a dichotomy between politics and administration to the sharing of functions between elected and appointed officials; from political neutrality and formal accountability to political sensitivity and responsiveness to community values themselves; and from efficiency as the core value to efficiency, representation, individual rights, and social equity as a complex array of values anchoring professionalism" (Nalbandian, 1991, 103). The first change represented an evolution of roles, the second a broader statement of professional responsibility, and the third set out to capture the contemporary value base of city management.

Those familiar with professionalism in local government will see that to a large extent many recent changes have reinforced these transformations. During the ten years, the following changes stand out:

- Community building has become part of the city management professional's responsibility.
- Managers are expected to facilitate participation and representation and to develop partnerships.
- There is less adherence to council manager government as the "one best form."
- The manager's internal administrative role has become more process oriented.

What's New

Community Building

Historical reviews of city management reveal a continuing search for the meaning of professionalism (Stillman, 1974). As social, economic, political, and technological trends create new contexts, the roles, responsibilities, and values of practicing professionals change. In my earlier project, I tried to define professionalism in local government as grounded in a broader array of community values than had been posited traditionally. But what I failed to articulate was the search for a

---

Methodology

Ten years ago Raymond G. Davis and I set out to explore the meaning of professionalism in local government through a series of interviews with city and county managers. Around the same time, George Frederickson invited a group of city management professionals to Lawrence to discuss "ideal and practice" in council-manager government. Each project resulted in publications commenting on the meaning of professionalism in local government (Frederickson, 1989; Nalbandian 1989; 1990; 1991).

In order to make a ten-year comparison, I contacted the professionals who had participated in the original projects and who were still connected with local government, asking them to review their ten-year old interview or essay. To that number I added city managers who had written "state of the profession" articles in *Public Management* over the past five years. In addition, I contacted ICMA winners of the Mark E. Keane Award for Excellence in Local Government and I invited participation of a few more local government professionals who, over the years, I have found particularly drawn to this topic.

I asked these 26 professionals to answer the following three questions in writing:

- What are the most significant changes that have occurred in local government in the last ten years?
- What changes have occurred in relationships between the governing body and chief administrative officer and in the politics of local government?
- What parts of the manager's job have remained the most stable over the last ten years? Which parts have changed the most?

I collected the responses and convened two panel discussions at the 1997 annual ICMA meeting in Vancouver with six of the participants. I added their transcribed remarks to the original comments, then reviewed everything I had received along with the few articles that appeared in *Public Management* magazine. I selected passages exemplifying what appeared to me as emergent themes and conveyed those remarks to all of the participating managers, asking for additional comments. With those in hand, I settled on the themes that best describe the meaning of professionalism in local government at it has evolved over the past ten years. Seeking additional feedback, I sent a draft of the resulting manuscript to the managers who had provided comments I quoted. Where possible, I have used the words of local government professionals extensively to illustrate the changes that have occurred, as experienced by these public servants.

---

sense of community as a way to conceptualize a context for contemporary professional work.

Since the original research in the late 1980s, many voices have spoken to the themes of building community, civil society, and civic infrastructure as partial solutions to the growing distance between citizens and governing institutions. In his study of Italian regional governments Putnam (1993) found that the presence of social capital, identified with the concepts of a rich network of local associations, active engagement in community affairs, egalitarian patterns of politics, and trust and lawfulness, positively affected economic development and the performance of governing institutions. Rice and Sumberg's (1997) research, focusing on the United States, reinforces Putnam's conclusions. In another academic vein, many have argued that reconnecting citizens to government requires government oriented toward citizen involvement rather than control by professional elites (Box, 1998; Lappe and DuBois, 1994; Mathews, 1994). Frederickson poses a complementary challenge, asserting that local government professionals are in a unique position to enhance civil society and help build social capital if "the community paradigm were to become part of the bureaucrat's understanding of how the city ought to be" (1997, 31).

None of the city managers in this study actually used the term *community building* to describe his or her work. But the term seems apropos to how they describe what they do, especially when considered in the following theoretical way. From a public official's perspective, community building essentially involves building political capacity—the capacity to make collective decisions amidst diverse and conflicting interests. A crucial component of this capacity is developing a sense of responsibility among citizens to participate in and obligate themselves to collective decisions. The obligation stems: (1) from an understanding that certain tasks require collective and public action rather than private, individual decisions, and (2) from an expectation that the agents of governing institutions will respect the values of representation, individual rights, and social equity so that individual citizens do not suffer from capricious or arbitrary collective decisions (Tussman, 1960). In short, getting problems solved collectively while respecting the values of representation, individual rights, and social equity builds a sense of obligation to the collective good and constitutes one way of looking at community building.

With renewed interest nationwide in the paradigm of community, one can argue that in the future the legitimacy of professional administrators in local government will be grounded in the tasks of community building and enabling democracy—in getting things done collectively, while building a sense of inclusion. Contemporary comments by Karma Ruder, director of the Neighborhood Planning Office in Seattle, and Eric Anderson, city manager in Des Moines, illustrate this point.

Describing the professional's role in local government, Ruder (August 12, 1997) writes, "Who is doing the work that makes people respect their government and become committed to making life in their communities better? The crucial issue is how local governments stay legitimate in the eyes of those they serve."

Anderson (August 26, 1997) writes:

> I am increasingly convinced that we are accountable for more than the quality of our management. We are also accountable for how well we have performed in the governance of our communities. Our jobs are to assure a fundamentally productive combination of the two [politics and administration] in the daily life of local governments. We need to be more specific about the responsibility we carry for governance as well as service delivery.

He (Anderson, September 17, 1997) develops this notion further with these thoughts:

> We have a strong responsibility to make sure that we provide not only information to our governing bodies, but to support the processes of governance that support the representative nature of the city council. I'm not talking about getting involved in electoral politics, but in things like public hearings, discussion, and deliberation; training

people in the organization to anticipate and foster participation; and building structures of participation that will be seen as legitimate. I don't think we have done a very good job on the governance side of our responsibilities.

In a panel discussion at the ICMA conference in Vancouver, British Columbia, Norm King (September 16, 1997), executive director of San Bernardino Associated Governments in southern California, and former ICMA president, said, "There is a remarkable degree of value consistency in what we all represent. And I heard it today, especially in terms of the focus on the engagement of citizens in creating a more just society."

He went on to talk about how he would advance that goal. "The primary goal of government, and especially local government, is to create conditions that insure, foster, or encourage responsibility. This means creating responsibility in the people who work for us; in our customers; and in our citizens."

Community building is a theme that expresses our understanding of how the city management profession is evolving, but this work does not come without a challenge. On the one hand, community building as a context for grounding professional practice seems a clarion call from many voices (Etzioni, 1995; Glendon, 1991; Mathews, 1994; Selznick, 1992). In Howard Gardner's (1995) terms, *it is a good story,* it conveys a noble message Americans today want to hear even as they strive to enhance the quality of their private lives. The concept of community building is attractive as a base for the practice of city management, because with it comes an understanding that both politics and administration are crucial, often inseparable, and must work in the kind of partnership that most local government professionals value rather than the adversarial relationship with their governing body in which they occasionally find themselves.

The challenges to the call for community building are the long-term social, political, and economic trends that have fragmented society and insufficient transferable knowledge of how exactly to build and maintain a sense of community. In addition, for city managers, as issues become broadly regional or narrowly oriented around neighborhoods, municipal boundaries become less relevant demarcations of community (Church, November 27, 1997; O'Neill, Jr., October 29, 1997). But perhaps the most formidable challenge to the community paradigm is a compelling counterstory. This is the respected and enduring tale of self-reliance and self-interest, adherence to market-based values, and skepticism regarding the value of government (Fowler, 1991). As local government professionals come to realize that their work connects them to the processes of governing through community building, they also come to acknowledge that those advocating market values pose a vigorous challenge.

Local government professionals regard this challenge in contrasting ways. For some, it appears simply as another political change to be accommodated. Examples include comments from William Buchanan (October 17, 1997), manager in urban Sedgwick County, Kansas, which includes Wichita. "Today, I believe elected officials are clearly more diverse and have a higher sense of public service than witnessed recently. They certainly come to the task from a much more 'Reaganesque' approach than ten years ago. Government is to be used only as a last resort, power is to be shared, and partners are to be used to solve problems. This kind of reluctant use of power requires a different style of leadership [for the manager]."

David Watkins (July 21, 1997), city administrator in Lenexa, Kansas, a conservative suburb of Kansas City, writes, "I think the movement toward customer service as a value has helped our image. In Lenexa, we work hard trying to create an image that we are tough but fair problem solvers who value the benefits of business and residents in the community and who want to work with you, not against you."

Jan Perkins (July 13, 1997), city manager in Fremont, California, adds, "The city manager needs to lead the organization in changing and adapting to community expectations—becoming entrepreneurial, customer focused, citizen involved—in order for the city council to have faith and confidence in the direction the city manager is taking the organization."

Buchanan, Watkins, and Perkins help us understand that local government professionals must ground their practices in the political context of their work. In contemporary America, they are working in various partnerships to build a sense of community in places where "community" and "individual" compete vigorously in determining public purposes and the role of government.

Facilitative Role of the Manager

Participation and Representation. Local government professionals from California to Virginia comment that the greatest change they have seen over the past ten years is the amount and character of participation expected in public policymaking and problem solving. The theme is not new; it has been emphasized in city management literature since the 1960s, and it is completely consistent with the community building/enabling democracy theme (Rutter, 1980). What seems different now is its pervasiveness and its transforming quality. Bill Buchanan (October 17, 1997) writes, "We are required to share power. How we manage special needs and the fragmentation of centralized power seem to me to be the parts that have changed the most. How we define and then use and manage democracy to provide service will control the styles and types of skills municipal managers will need to be successful." And Charles Church (November 27, 1997), city manager in Lynchburg, Virginia, writes, "Reform should allow citizens to be fully engaged in the processes of local governance. I anticipate that neighborhood councils will increasingly take over many of the responsibilities of city councils and administrators for setting priorities and evaluating service delivery." The participation and representation theme is seen in working with diverse council members; through community problem-solving processes; and in a variety of partnerships.

Diversity. The diversity on councils is seen with more representation of race and gender, with more special interest candidates, and with more antigovernment council members. Potentially, each represents a different way of viewing the role of government, the council's work, and relationships with citizens and professional staff (Bledsoe, 1993). The differences would seem to be greater than those seen in the past, at least from a local government professional's perspective.

These differences produce contrasting consequences. On the one hand, when effectively blended they increase the problem-solving capacity of the governing body. On the other hand, the differences can easily consume a council and render it ineffective (Mahtesian, 1997). The diversity on councils can be more extensive than the differences confronted in familiar daily work groups. In the absence of hierarchy, task specialization, systematic and credible feedback, and specific task definition, it is no wonder that councils flounder and the local government professionals seeking leadership and policy guidance from them become frustrated.

When effectively managed, this diversity seems to make a positive difference in communities. David Mora (December 5, 1997), city manager in Salinas, California, writes:

> The local government manager is responsible for advocating comprehensive participation and representation in governance issues. Part of the frustration today is the diversity and overwhelming nature of service demands from parts of the community that in the past either were not represented or were taken for granted by both elected and appointed local government officials. The new generation of local elected officials, representing a significantly diverse variety of interests, is demanding legitimate and comprehensive responses from management.

He continues by suggesting that the way to deal with diversity on the council is by reflecting that diversity among staff. He says that he himself had to learn to be more inclusive, to accept the diversity of the community. He and Eric Anderson argue that as city managers trying to relate to councils more representative of the community, it is easier to work with a staff that reflects an array of values and anticipates the council's expectations because then staff can tacitly understand them.

The connection between diversity and problem solving marks a significant departure from diversity as affirmative action. What was seen in the past, sometimes cynically as diversity for the sake of political correctness or, more positively, as moral virtue, is now seen as diversity for the sake of problem solving. What was once seen as the "right thing to do" is now seen as a prudent way to staff an organization for problem solving, especially in environments in which problem solving among diverse interests and political legitimacy go hand in hand.

Problem Solving. The relationship between politics, participation, problem solving, and legitimacy marks a departure from previous conceptions of the connection between citizens and local government officials. John Thomas (1986) notes that local governments began a few decades ago to invite a relationship based on the negotiation of interests. He contrasted this to the historic relationship based on "petition" or "redress." Current comments from local government professionals suggest that this association may be moving again, this time from "adversarial negotiations" toward "interest-based policy-making."

Karma Ruder (December 15, 1997) states, "Citizens more and more want to be part of establishing the framework for standards and for balancing the trade-offs between technical standards and perception of services or different values regarding what services are more important." The director of the Neighborhood Planning Office in Seattle characterizes her task as "figuring out how we make people shift from being fighters against city hall to having lots of different perspectives getting together to solve problems" (September 16, 1997).

Partnerships. Another expression of participation and community engagement is the number of partnerships that local governments are involved in both externally and internally. The external partnerships are evident in joint undertakings with school districts, counties, nonprofits, community-based organizations, neighborhood associations, and private sector organizations. The importance of the partnerships appears to have affected the manager's role significantly. Perkins (July 13, 1997) writes, "[the prevalence of partnerships] requires the city manager to lead by example and foster relationships within the community to help pave the way for those organizational partnerships to be formed."

In Mora's (September 16, 1997) experience, the trend has had a similar impact on staff, especially regarding the partnerships with neighborhood groups. He notes that when hiring department heads, he specifically considers the ability to develop "partnerships, and work with community goals, and elected officials. The partnership element and involvement of neighborhoods and elected officials as well as the connections within and between departments is crucial."

Having been a city manager and now serving as executive director of a civic group of business leaders in Kansas City, Missouri, Jewel Scott (July 25, 1997) observes that there has been a significant shift toward community involvement and ownership of programs and service delivery.

> If I were a manager today, I would focus on finding ways to work creatively with the not-for-profit community to provide services and to evaluate and design service delivery systems. Also, I would be more open to building community ownership of issues and projects and to seeking the assistance of others in the community to do so. Finally, I would think very differently about what is important to a community's well-being. I would work harder to move decisions out into the community.

This discussion of community building and facilitative leadership points the profession of city management in a particular direction—away from professional elitism and toward a community paradigm. It appears that local government administrators must be able to move in this direction if they are to maintain their effectiveness and influence. There is a tacit understanding here that council-manager government itself no longer provides a comfortable, protective cover for the city manager's legitimacy.

Form of Government and the Added Value of City Managers

Frederickson (1996) has shown how adaptations to both council-manager and strong mayor forms of government have moderated the distinctions between the two. It is hard to imagine that to the average citizen the remaining differences really do make a difference. Whether they are important remains a point of contention among city management professionals. Tom Downs (November 24, 1997), former chairman of AMTRAK and a former city manager, argues that they do.

He observes, "The institutions we create are more important [than he formerly thought], enduring, and effective over the long term." He suggests that the collapse of local government in the nation's capital should teach us something about unfulfilled faith in charismatic leadership. Also, it should reinforce our belief that there is long-term value in governmental institutions that sustain and protect continuity, stability, expertise, and the value of public service—like those fostered by council-manager government.

In contrast, Mora (December 5, 1997) observes that council-manager government in its traditional definition is not always the best or most appropriate for a community. He writes, "Our emphasis as professionals must be on providing expert local government management, regardless of the form of government. This 'ideal' of service can and should be a core value of the profession without dependence on the form of government." Ruder (August 12, 1997)—who formerly worked in Phoenix and Billings, both council-manager cities, and now works in Seattle, a strong mayor city—adds: "Distinctions about form of government seem much less critical to me than whether people are engaged as problem solvers in their own neighborhoods."

Anderson (August 26, 1997) suggests that the success of council-manager government in eliminating corruption has actually diminished its contemporary attractiveness. Its success has eliminated its original raison d'être. While the reform story is diminishing in attractiveness, strong mayor cities have come to rely more on professionally trained staff and accepted business practices, thus increasing their administrative effectiveness step by step.

As a corollary, Anderson observes, "Mayors have somehow emerged in this decade as the political 'reformers,' with mayors in Indianapolis, Philadelphia, New York, Chicago, and Los Angeles getting excellent press and praise as the standard bearers for progressive municipal government." Jan Perkins (July 13, 1997) concurs by suggesting that the perceived responsiveness of high-profile mayors easily leads to the notion that "we" [professional managers and advocates of council manager government] may be seen as the institution that needs reforming.

The popularity of the charismatic mayor elicited many comments from participants in this research. In many ways the discussion about form of government and concern over the present emergence of the strong mayor as a "reformer" is crucial to the meaning of local government professionalism. It calls into question the value city managers add to municipal government, and thus aims at the heart of professional legitimacy.

For years, the value of city managers has been embedded in the form of government itself. Council manager government without a city manager is inconceivable, by definition. And as long as the form of government retained its prominence as "good government," the value and credibility of the city manager was, in large measure, unquestioned. Robert O'Neill, Jr. (October 29, 1997), county executive in Fairfax County, Virginia, observes that among the greatest changes in the relationship between elected and appointed officials is the increasing skepticism that elected officials have regarding the value of senior management. As the contemporary reform story unfolds with the "mayor taking on the bureaucracy," council-manager government becomes an old story, and the value of the city manager is exposed. This calls for a new definition of the local government professional's roles, responsibilities, and values. Norm King (December 10, 1997) says it best: "The primary issue is not the council-manager plan. The issue is better articulating the added value of professional management. And in doing so, we must distinguish a well run city from a poorly run city *in a way which is understood by the citizenry* [emphasis added]."

In sum, as prominent mayors become seen as the new reformers, council-manager government becomes an old story. The search for legitimacy is really a search for identifying what value the city manager adds to a community. This is where the community-building, facilitative leadership paradigm holds promise.

Process-Oriented Management

Some of the changes identified by the local government administrators in this research focused on managing their internal, organizational role. Technological, demographic, and market-based pressures on governing institutions bring about the changes (Klingner and Nalbandian, 1998, Chs. 1 and 8). Technological advances are noteworthy for two reasons—the amount of knowledge that is generated and the rapidity of change. Increasing knowledge often requires occupational special-ization. More specialization means that teamwork is even more necessary to link diverse specialists. Interdepartmental differences in perspective are greater than in the past and are articulated more clearly and forcefully by better-educated, techni-cally trained staff. The rapidity of technological change suggests that the occupa-tional specializations themselves can become obsolete more quickly than in previous generations. This means that many teams have to exist as temporary orga-nizational fixtures, and employees must become accustomed to working in more than one setting.

Demographic changes are reflected both in the diversity of people who con-stitute the workforce and in the tremendous demands for flexible work arrange-ments to accommodate family needs of today's single parents and dual income families. The challenge of workforce diversity manifests itself in different expecta-tions that employees have of one another. In addition, men and women often approach problem solving and managing people differently. Accommodations to family needs include newer benefits such as child care, long-term care, and elder care; and work arrangements include flex-time, flex-place, job sharing, and a greater desire for part-time, yet permanent work.

George Caravalho (October 20, 1997), city manager in Santa Clarita, California, says, "The most significant change that has occurred in our profession is the impact that women have had in the workplace. Women seem less concerned with hierarchy and structure, tending to be more facilitative in their style. They look for areas of commonality; and they often have a calming approach to problem solving and conflict." Sandra Tripp-Jones (December 30, 1997), city administrator in Santa Barbara, California, adds, "Women have provided more behaviors not stereotypically male, so that both men and women have more freedom to use styles and skills that suit them individually. Among firefighters, for example, women have added and made it acceptable for men also to demonstrate compassion, empathy and sensitivity to people in traumatic situations. In addition, the offices of women managers often seem safe places for others to talk/vent/try out ideas in a less competitive setting."

And last, competitiveness in the marketplace puts a premium on responsiveness, quality, and speed. As David Watkins (December 10, 1997) says, "I understand that the role of government does not lend itself entirely to the service model of the private sector, but certain values such as fairness, timeliness, and unified decision making are transferable. Lenexa is moving toward a system where applicants will be viewed in a positive manner and staff will serve as problem solvers."

Gene Denton (June 25, 1997), county manager in suburban Johnson County, Kansas, indicates the kinds of internal changes that have come about in response to these types of external pressures:

> The structure of government has flattened. We have retrained most of our workers to be more self-reliant and departments to be interdependent. Creativity and innovation have replaced the more sterile values of efficiency and economy. Leadership has leaped ahead of management. Coaches have replaced supervisors. Connectedness, communication, and cooperation have outclassed competition. Quality is more valued than speed. The respected leader is one who is more concerned about how workers are progressing and what they *should be,* rather than what they *should do.*

The flattening of hierarchy is prudent when seeking rapid response by technically trained staff. City managers today cannot mandate changes because, more than before, they do not command the technical knowledge to fully understand what they are asking for. A city manager cannot tell a public works director that the council favors a proposed development that requires hooking up to a particular sewer line because it is more economical for the applicant, when the public works director says the downstream capacity won't handle the added load of wastewater. In addition, as city staff begin to incorporate facilitative management practices into their own work, city managers who exercise hierarchical control over them put at risk the often fragile agreements staff has negotiated among contending parties. For example, on a controversial development project involving landowners, regulatory bodies, financial institutions, and neighbors, planning staff may have negotiated an agreement that incorporates provisions regarding annexation, payment for infrastructure, and land use. City managers who would exercise hierarchical control over planning staff could jeopardize this agreement. Professional norms and the confidence that comes with the mastery of technical knowledge *and process skills* permit and sometimes encourage technical workers to question hierarchy. Because managers cannot dictate to staff, Denton's statement about being concerned with what workers *should be* rather than what they *should do* seems on target.

Denton observes that as managers are forced to reduce reliance on hierarchy, the personal attributes of workers become more crucial to performance. In fact, in the personnel field, it is not uncommon in the private sector to incorporate "personal attributes" into discussions about merit and competence (Borman and Motowidlo, 1993). This flies in the face of traditional personnel practices in which personal attributes are excluded from considerations of knowledge, skills, and abilities.

King's (September 16, 1997) comments capture the overarching thrust of the city manager's administrative role when he says, "I think the most important responsibility of any manager is to manage the values of the organization and to instill a sense of responsibility in employees for them." This is exactly what David Mora was referring to when he commented that the values of staff were crucial to him in his dealings with a diverse council, thus the hiring process must attend to more than just technical competence.

Furthermore, King says that while the vast majority of a city's work can be handled through traditional departments, the most important problems fall outside traditional departmental boundaries. In Denton's words hierarchy is of little use in handling those problems that require "independence, creativity and innovation, connectedness, communication, and cooperation." This is precisely what Donald Schon predicted in 1974 when he wrote *Beyond the Stable State* and suggested that amidst continual change, values provide stability.

Complicating internal, administrative transitions, according to several managers, is the increasing tendency of councils to become involved in the "how to " rather than the "what" part of governance. Svara's (1995; 1998) work shows how the politics/administration dichotomy is more fruitfully viewed in terms of relative involvement of the city manager and city council members in the city's mission, policy, administration, and management functions. Using his terminology, elected officials have become more involved in administration and management, according to the participants in this research.

Buchanan (October 17, 1997) sums up the involvement of elected officials in this way:

> In an evaluation not too long ago, one of the Commissioners suggested that she would be more comfortable if I brought to her the projects as I was working on them rather than when they were completed. She used the analogy of a baby. She said she was part of the family and she wanted to see the baby. She wanted not only to see the clean baby with a shiny ribbon in her hair, but she wanted to see the baby, messy diaper and all.

Commenting on Buchanan's metaphor, Sandra Tripp-Jones (December 30, 1997) writes:

> They [the governing body] like being able to 'dress the baby,' to plan how to promote the idea. I need to be comfortable brainstorming with them as opposed to 'providing the best and only answer.' This is a change from even five years ago. Like the facilitation skills needed to foster more public participation without controlling it, the professional manager needs the self-confidence to brainstorm with council and be wrong, and to not need to have all the answers. This also means developing staff who can do the same.

The increasing interest elected officials show in "how to" is understandable if one recognizes that how decisions are reached conveys as much about representation, individual rights, and equity—*essential values in community building*—as the substance of the decision itself. If professional staff fails to acknowledge this council interest, it distances itself from the council and plants the seeds of council skepticism and distrust.

Discussion and Conclusions

Several years ago I described the changes that had occurred in the meaning of professionalism in local government as three transformations in roles, responsibilities, and values of city managers. I conclude by returning to those three transformations, relating them to the primary conclusions in this present research.

As long as the council-manager plan symbolized reform government, the city manager's roles, responsibilities, and values were protected—even if they were not easily articulated or understood. The legitimacy of the city manager rested in the form of government and the story it promised—non-political, efficient, and responsive government. But as the memory of patronage and widespread corruption has faded, the most persuasive rationale for council-manager government is lost not only for citizens, but for governing body members themselves. In this environment, city managers are vulnerable to elected officials and citizens skeptical of the expertise of any government employee, even questioning the value of government itself.

Burdened with maintaining their legitimacy, some managers seek from their peers and ICMA a renewed and vigorous defense of council-manager government. My impression is that the value of professionalism in local government must be established independent of government form, and I think the comments of several managers in this study point in that direction. In searching for the connection between political leadership and administrative capacity, the concepts of community building and facilitative leadership are recurring themes. These themes provide clues to the present and future roles, responsibilities, and values of city managers as models for local government professionals in general.

Roles

Many aspects of the manager's job remain the same; keeping the council informed, providing continuity and stability, telling the council what it does not necessarily want to hear, and balancing short-run interests against a long-run, "greater good" perspective. The difference between now and ten years ago is in the emphasis on the facilitative role of the manager. Some 20 years ago, the International City Management Association's Future Horizons Committee (Rutter, 1980, 2) characterized its dialogue with the sentence: "Welcome, I am Jennifer Stene, the city coordinator." After examining the comments I received for this study, it appears that the future is now! Frederickson's (1997, Ch. 3) review of literature on governance includes numerous references to academic studies emphasizing partnerships, networking, coordinating, and connecting as the essence of the "new public management."

Throughout the discussion of building community, the internal and external facilitative roles of the manager have been emphasized. These roles grow from the emphasis on partnerships, responsiveness and customer service, quality management, and coordinating divergent departmental perspectives. In short, "how" a city government conducts its business, whether with its own employees or with the governing body or citizens, has become as important as "what" is done.

In this environment, supporting the council's work—a long-standing role expectation of the chief administrative officer and staff—requires a facilitative orientation as part of the definition of professionalism in local government. There is a growing understanding that facilitative work is not designed to "make people feel better." It is designed to help promote a problem-solving orientation and to develop consensus among diverse interests. Eric Anderson (September 17, 1997) says, "This is not warm and fuzzy stuff; it is hard work. I have found it to be the toughest work we do. You've got to be incredibly patient and thick-skinned, and you have to have some sense that there truly is value in these processes because they are tremendously time consuming and occasionally abusive."

The connection he makes between facilitative staff work, support for the governing body, and building governance capacity and credibility places the facilitative role into a more important theoretical perspective than local government professionals commonly understand. Developing facilitative staff work requires more than just skill building. It takes us back to the values argument that King and Mora made earlier. Managing the values of the organization means connecting the overarching organizational sense of what is good/right with the work of the governing body *and* the community.

Responsibilities

The second tenet discussed in 1991 asserted that managers were responsive to their governing body but responsible to values expressed in the community more broadly. That responsibility is given more form when linked to community building.

The partnership between staff and governing body achieved through facilitative leadership is targeted toward community building. The concept of community building, as elusive as it might be to define, nevertheless provides more guidance than the vague, simplistic counsel that staff and the governing body are partners in governance with the governing body establishing priorities and staff carrying out policy. The community-building concept provides a legitimate anchor because it establishes a concrete purpose of government that citizens can readily understand and endorse. It is not the only one, but it can provide a fruitful point of departure for real governing bodies and real managers seeking an effective relationship and a way to engage citizens. It provides a way to make democracy work.

The responsibility of the city manager is to empower the governing body *and* citizens by helping to develop and use the tools of engagement. This is where the facilitative leadership roles enter—framing issues and processes to deal with diverse interests, to focus on interests rather than positions when problem solving, and to develop collaborative partnerships in policymaking and service delivery.

Values

As a third tenet, in 1991, I argued that representation, individual rights, and social equity combined with efficiency to form a value base for professionalism in city management. The concept of community building organizes those values. It suggests that building a sense of community requires a foundation of rights, fairness, and representation along with evidence that collectively a community can accomplish some tasks more efficiently and effectively than its members could do on their own—streets and sewer maintenance, storm water management, land-use planning, and so on. Giving up some freedom on behalf of the collective good is made more palatable when right, equity, and representation of interest are guaranteed (Tussman, 1960).

In addition to providing a connection among these values, the community-building concept can help us see the future of facilitative leadership within an internal organizational community as well as within external political communities. Increasing levels of diversity within organizations place a premium on facilitative leadership aimed at building commitment to collective organizational purposes. The same can be said when hierarchy is replaced by collegiality and teamwork.

In asserting that the contemporary meaning of professionalism incorporates facilitative leadership and community building, I have chosen to downplay "the enduring commitment to public service" (Frederickson, 1997) as a central feature. I do not doubt this sense of obligation to the public good as a defining element for those who choose to become city managers. I have serious reservations, however, whether those outside of academic and professional circles find that commitment believable enough to grant city managers legitimacy. Those who come to our governing institutions seeking satisfaction of their private interests always find ways to mask those interests as the public good. We have become so facile at manipulating data to suit these hollow portrayals that claims of advancing, nurturing, or living by the public interest have become suspect by dispassionate citizens and governing body members alike. Brint (1994) has shown that professional status is more likely to be conferred upon those who can demonstrate skills employed in ways average citizens value rather than in the virtue of self-proclaimed motives. That is why skill in community building rather than a calling to public service is more persuasive to me as an anchor for contemporary professionalism.

Finally, the success at postulating facilitative leadership and community building as the anchors for contemporary professionalism in local government will depend upon two factors. The first is whether city managers are willing to acknowledge that the value they add to governing processes can be found in facilitative leadership and community building rather than associated principally in the issue of form of government. A second, and more challenging, task is whether the profession can formulate these two concepts into a "new story" that will connect and build on the reform heritage in a way that appeals to citizens.

Acknowledgement

I would like to thank George Frederickson, Barbara Romzek, and Joe Freeman for helpful comments on a draft of this article.

References

Anderson, Eric (1997). Correspondence with John Nalbandian, 26 August.

———— (1997). Panel discussion at ICMA conference in Vancouver, British Columbia, 17 September.

Bledsoe, Timothy (1993). *Careers in City Politics: The Case for Urban Democracy.* Pittsburgh: University of Pittsburgh Press.

Borman, W. C. and S. J. Motowidlo (1993). "Expanding the Criterion Domain to Include Elements of Contextual Performance." In F. L. Schmitt, W. C. Borman, and Associates, eds. *Personnel Selection in Organizations.* San Francisco: Jossey-Bass.

Box, Richard C. (1998). *Citizen Governance: Leading American Communities into the 21st Century.* Thousand Oaks, CA: Sage.

Brint, Steven (1994). *In an Age of Experts.* Princeton, NJ: Princeton University Press.

Buchanan, William (1997). Correspondence with John Nalbandian, 17 October.

Caravalho, George (1997). Correspondence with John Nalbandian, 20 October.

Church, Charles (1997). Correspondence with John Nalbandian, 27 November.

Denton, Eugene (1997). Correspondence with John Nalbandian, 25 June.

Downs, Thomas (1997). Correspondence with John Nalbandian, 24 November.

Etzioni, Amitai, ed. (1995). *New Communitarian Thinking.* Charlottesville: University Press of Virginia.

Fowler, Robert Booth (1991). *A Dance with Community: The Contemporary Debate in American Political Thought.* Lawrence, KS: University Press of Kansas.

Frederickson, H. George (1997). "Facing the Community." *Kettering Review* (December): 28–37.

————, ed. (1989). *Ideal and Practice in Council-Manager Government.* Washington, DC: International City Management Association.

———— (1997). *The Spirit of Public Administration.* San Francisco: Jossey Bass.

———— (1996). "Type III Cities." Unpublished manuscript. Department of Public Administration, University of Kansas.

Gardner, Howard (1995). *Leading Minds.* New York: Basic Books.

Glendon, M. A. (1991). *Rights Talk: The Impoverishment of Political Discourse.* New York: Free Press.

King, Norm (1997). Correspondence with John Nalbandian, 10 December.

———— (1997). Panel discussion at ICMA conference in Vancouver, British Columbia, 16 September.

Klingner, Donald E., and John Nalbandian (1998). *Public Personnel Management: Contexts and Strategies,* 4th ed. Upper Saddle River, NJ: Prentice Hall.

Lappe, Frances Moore, and Paul Martin DuBois (1994). *The Quickening of America: Rebuilding our Nation, Remaking Our Lives.* San Francisco: Jossey-Bass.

Mahtesian, Charles (1997). "The Politics of Ugliness." *Governing Magazine* 10: 18–22.

Mathews, David (1994). *Politics for People: Finding a Responsible Public Voice.* Urbana, IL: University of Illinois Press.

Mora, David (1997). Correspondence with John Nalbandian, 5 December.

———— (1997). Panel discussion at ICMA conference in Vancouver, British Columbia, 16 September.

Nalbandian, John (1989). "The Contemporary Role in City Managers." *American Review of Public Administration* 19: 261–278.

———— (1991). *Professionalism in Local Government: Roles, Responsibilities, and Values of City Managers.* San Francisco: Jossey-Bass.

———— (1990). "Tenets of Contemporary Professionalism in Local Government." *Public Administration Review* 50: 654–663.

O'Neill, Robert, Jr. (1997). Correspondence with John Nalbandian, 29 October.

Perkins, Jan (1997). Correspondence with John Nalbandian, 13 July.

———— (1997). Correspondence with John Nalbandian, 21 July.

Putnam, Robert D. (1993). *Making Democracy Work: Civic Traditions in Modern Italy.* Princeton, NJ: Princeton University Press.

Rice, Tom W. and Alexander F. Sumberg (1997). "Civic Culture and Government Performance in the American State." *Publius* 27: 99–114.

Ruder, Karma (1997). Correspondence with John Nalbandian, 12 August.

———— (1997). Correspondence with John Nalbandian, 15 December.

———— (1997). Panel discussion at ICMA conference in Vancouver, British Columbia, 16 September.

Rutter, Lawrence (1980). *The Essential Community.* Washington, DC: International City Management Association.

Schon, Donald (1974). *Beyond the Stable State.* New York: Norton.

Scott, Jewel (1997). Correspondence with John Nalbandian, 25 July.

Selznick, Philip (1992). *The Moral Commonwealth: Social Theory and the Promise of Community.* Berkeley, CA: University of California Press.

Stillman, II., R. J. (1974). *The Rise of the City Manager.* Albuquerque: University of New Mexico Press.

Svara, James H. (1985). "Dichotomy and Duality: Reconceptualizing the Relationship Between Politics and Administration in Council-Manager Cities." *Public Administration Review* 45: 221–232.

——— (1998). "The Politics-Administration Dichotomy Model as Aberration." *Public Administration Review* 58(1): 51–58.

Thomas, John C. (1986). *Between Citizen and City.* Lawrence, KS: University Press of Kansas.

Tripp-Jones, Sandra (1997). Correspondence with John Nalbandian, 30 December.

Tussman, Joseph (1960). *Obligation and the Body Politic.* New York: Oxford University Press.

Watkins, David (1997). Correspondence with John Nalbandian, 21 July.

——— (1997). Correspondence with John Nalbandian, 10 December.

P A R T

IV

The Manager
as Bureaucratic
Politician

It has been said that public and private management are "fundamentally alike
in all unimportant respects."[a] There is, however, one important respect where
public, private, and nonprofit management have much in common, namely,
bureaucratic politics. While the rules of the game differ in these types of organizations, the quest for power is universal, unavoidable, and a prerequisite for the
success of even the noblest goals. In this sense, these three types of management
are generic.

Power—The Currency of Politics

Practitioners of public administration may not always be able to define power
elegantly, but they have an instinctive feeling for what it is. Almost always, when
asked, they can complete the following analogy: Capital is for the businessman
what power is for the politician or public manager. As Norton Long observed in
a passage as close to poetry as public administration ever gets: "There is no more
forlorn spectacle in the administrative world than an agency and a program possessed of statutory life, armed with executive orders, sustained in the courts, yet

[a]This aphorism is attributed to Professor Wallace Sayre in Graham T. Allison, "Public and Private
Management: Are They Fundamentally Alike in All Unimportant Respects?" in Jay M. Shafritz
and Albert C. Hyde, eds., *Classics of Public Administration*, 2nd ed. (Chicago: Dorsey Press, 1987,
pp. 510–529.

stricken with paralysis and deprived of power. An object of contempt to its enemies and of despair to its friends."[b]

More than four decades have passed since Long emphasized the unavoidable connection between mastering the means of using power and achieving important administrative ends. During these years too, political strength has had much to do with the fate of numerous programs and regulations. The realization has grown that if public managers are to achieve their institutional and personal goals, they must both acquire skill in their program or professional area, and learn how to influence the internal and external political environment of their administrative agencies.

---

[b]Norton Long, "Power and Administration," in Francis E. Rourke, ed., *Bureaucratic Power in National Policy Making*, 4th ed. (Boston: Little, Brown, 1986), pp. 7–16.

John Kotter argues that the manager must understand that four different types of power are at his or her disposal, and that conditions will largely determine when and where they can be effectively used. While Kotter's formulation of these "face-to-face methods of power" seems to cast him in the role of a Machiavelli for managers, they emerge from his realization that "formal authority" does not guarantee a certain amount of power, and is merely one resource, among many, that a manager must use to create sufficient power to do the job. The fundamental irony for those climbing the rungs of the organizational ladder is that the higher they go, the less they can control—or, as Kotter puts it, "the more dependent they are on others." The methods come across as manipulative—and, indeed, in a sense they are—but Kotter is aware of this danger. Hence, his caution that managers must be "sensitive to what others consider to be legitimate behavior in acquiring and using power."

The creation of obligations on the employee also creates obligations on the manager. If the manager, for example, attends the funeral of a subordinate's relative (one of Kotter's examples), the person must possess some concern for the individual, or the probable exposure of such phoniness eventually will cause far more problems for the manager than it alleviates. There is then ambiguity in the exercise of power—personal and institutional goals are intertwined. Each manager must rely primarily on those sources of power which are consistent with his or her own predilections and style as well as those of the individual one wants to influence. But there is no escaping that "being a bit ornery," whether we like to admit it or not, evokes respect.

Kotter found these types of power both in the public and private organizations that he studied. It is, however, no accident that he draws his examples of those power sources that are less hierarchical and coercive in nature from the public sector, where bargaining is the prevalent social process. The "use of persuasion" thus relies largely on the work of political scientists Richard E. Neustadt (talking about the American presidency) and Edward Banfield (talking about Chicago politics in the good old days). Neustadt's definition is also what public managers must often use to influence their political environment:

> the essence of a President's persuasive task, with congressmen and with everybody else, is to induce them to believe that what he wants of them is what their own appraisal of their own responsibilities requires them to do in their interest, not his. Because men may differ in their views on public policy, because differences in outlook stem from differences in duty—duty to one's office, one's constituents, oneself—that task is bound to be more like collective bargaining than like a reasoned argument among philosopher kings.[a]

Then, once formal authority, power, and other resources are assembled, what Banfield called these "bits of influence" are reinvested to acquire more power.[b] The first Mayor Richard J. Daley of Chicago was a master at creating obligations in this manner through "tacit" as well as "explicit" bargains. Recipients of power resources knew, without necessarily having been in contact with the Mayor, that they in turn would be expected to deliver at some future time. Acceptance of such resources is what at least in politics passes for a contract.

The strength of that contract, however, varies with the power of the politician, or manager, tomorrow as well as today. Neustadt thus underscores that the chief

---

[a] Richard E. Neustadt, *Presidential Power and the Modern Presidents* (New York: Free Press, 1990) p. 40.

[b] Edward Banfield, *Political Influence* (New York: Free Press, 1961) pp. 241–242.

executive must continually protect both his or her *professional reputation* within what is now called the "Washington beltline" and *public prestige* which lies beyond the purview of the internal organization. Just as one's amount of money fluctuates as the stock market moves up and down, so "political capital" fluctuates as well. Small wonder that Kotter endorses Neustadt's caution that the use of persuasion can be time-consuming and requires that the other person listen.

There is, however, a limit to how much one can rely on face-to-face methods of exercising power other than persuasion. As Kotter points out, when used, they may fall outside the subordinate's zone, or perception, of legitimate behavior, conflict with how one identifies with the manager, or eventually invite retaliation. Even when this article was written in the seventies, there was thus already a need to draw more extensively on persuasion as a source of power. But in large organizations, managers must also use "indirect methods" of influence. A strength of Kotter's article lies in his discussion of what each face-to-face and indirect method can influence and his recognition that each method has its own advantages and drawbacks. His conclusions on "generating and using power successfully" are worth more than the tips in any three self-help books on "how to succeed in business or government without even trying."

Power, Dependence, and Effective Management

John P. Kotter

Americans, as a rule, are not very comfortable with power or with its dynamics. We often distrust and question the motives of people who we think actively seek power. We have a certain fear of being manipulated. Even those people who think the dynamics of power are inevitable and needed often feel somewhat guilty when they themselves mobilize and use power. Simply put, the overall attitude and feeling toward power, which can easily be traced to the nation's very birth, is negative. In his enormously popular *Greening of America,* Charles Reich reflects the views of many when he writes, "It is not the misuse of power that is evil; the very existence of power is evil."[1]

One of the many consequences of this attitude is that power as a topic for rational study and dialogue has not received much attention, even in managerial circles. If the reader doubts this, all he or she need do is flip through some textbooks, journals, or advanced management course descriptions. The word *power* rarely appears.

This lack of attention to the subject of power merely adds to the already enormous confusion and misunderstanding surrounding the topic of power and

John P. Kotter. *Harvard Business Review*, Vol. 55, No. 4 (July-August, 1977), pp. 125–136.

Author's note: This article is based on data from a clinical study of a highly diverse group of 26 organizations including large and small, public and private; manufacturing and service organizations. The study was funded by the Division of Research at the Harvard Business School. As part of the study process, the author interviewed about 250 managers.

[1] Charles A. Reich, *The Greening of America: How the Youth Revolution is Trying to Make America Liveable* (New York: Random House, 1970).

management. And this misunderstanding is becoming increasingly burdensome because in today's large and complex organizations the effective performance of most managerial jobs requires one to be skilled at the acquisition and use of power.

From my own observations, I suspect that a large number of managers—especially the young, well-educated ones—perform significantly below their potential because they do not understand the dynamics of power and because they have not nurtured and developed the instincts needed to effectively acquire and use power.

In this article I hope to clear up some of the confusion regarding power and managerial work by providing tentative answers to three questions:

1. Why are the dynamics of power necessarily an important part of managerial processes?
2. How do effective managers acquire power?
3. How and for what purposes do effective managers use power?

I will not address questions related to the misuse of power, but not because I think they are unimportant. The fact that some managers, some of the time, acquire and use power mostly for their own aggrandizement is obviously a very important issue that deserves attention and careful study. But that is a complex topic unto itself and one that has already received more attention than the subject of this article.

Recognizing Dependence in the Manager's Job

One of the distinguishing characteristics of a typical manager is how dependent he is on the activities of a variety of other people to perform his job effectively.[2] Unlike doctors and mathematicians, whose performance is more directly dependent on their own talents and efforts, a manager can be dependent in varying degrees on superiors, subordinates, peers in other parts of the organization, the subordinates of peers, outside suppliers, customers, competitors, unions, regulating agencies, and many others.

These dependency relationships are an inherent part of managerial jobs because of two organizational facts of life: division of labor and limited resources. Because the work in organizations is divided into specialized divisions, departments, and jobs, managers are made directly or indirectly dependent on many others for information, staff services, and cooperation in general. Because of their organization's limited resources, managers are also dependent on their external environments for support. Without some minimal cooperation from suppliers, competitors, unions, regulatory agencies, and customers, managers cannot help their organizations survive and achieve their objectives.

Dealing with these dependencies and the manager's subsequent vulnerability is an important and difficult part of a manager's job because, while it is theoretically

---

[2] See Leonard R. Sayles, *Managerial Behavior: Administration in Complex Organization* (New York: McGraw-Hill, 1964) as well as Rosemary Stewart, *Managers and Their Jobs* (London: Macmillan, 1967) and *Contrasts in Management* (London: McGraw-Hill, 1976).

possible that all of these people and organizations would automatically act in just the manner that a manager wants and needs, such is almost never the case in reality. All the people on whom a manager is dependent have limited time, energy, and talent, for which there are competing demands.

Some people may be uncooperative because they are too busy elsewhere, and some because they are not really capable of helping. Others may well have goals, values, and beliefs that are quite different and in conflict with the manager's and may therefore have no desire whatsoever to help or cooperate. This is obviously true of a competing company and sometimes of a union, but it can also apply to a boss who is feeling threatened by a manager's career progress or to a peer whose objectives clash with the manager's.

Indeed, managers often find themselves dependent on many people (and things) whom they do not directly control and who are not "cooperating." This is the key to one of the biggest frustrations managers feel in their jobs, even in the top ones, which the following example illustrates:

- After nearly a year of rumors, it was finally announced in May 1974 that the president of ABC Corporation had been elected chairman of the board and that Jim Franklin, the vice president of finance, would replace him as president. While everyone at ABC was aware that a shift would take place soon, it was not at all clear before the announcement who would be the next president. Most people had guessed it would be Phil Cook, the marketing vice president.

Nine months into his job as chief executive officer, Franklin found that Phil Cook (still the marketing vice president) seemed to be fighting him in small and subtle ways. There was never anything blatant, but Cook just did not cooperate with Franklin as the other vice presidents did. Shortly after being elected, Franklin had tried to bypass what he saw as a potential conflict with Cook by telling him that he would understand if Cook would prefer to move somewhere else where he could be a CEO also. Franklin said that it would be a big loss to the company but that he would be willing to help Cook in a number of ways if he wanted to look for a presidential opportunity elsewhere. Cook had thanked him but had said that family and community commitments would prevent him from relocating and all CEO opportunities were bound to be in a different city.

Since the situation did not improve after the tenth and eleventh months, Franklin seriously considered forcing Cook out. When he thought about the consequences of such a move, Franklin became more and more aware of just how dependent he was on Cook. Marketing and sales were generally the keys to success in their industry, and the company's sales force was one of the best, if not the best, in the industry. Cook had been with the company for 25 years. He had built a strong personal relationship with many of the people in the sales force and was universally popular. A mass exodus just might occur if Cook were fired. The loss of a large number of salesmen, or even a lot of turmoil in the department, could have a serious effect on the company's performance.

After one year as chief executive officer, Franklin found that the situation between Cook and himself had not improved and had become a constant source of frustration.

As a person gains more formal authority in an organization, the areas in which he or she is vulnerable increase and become more complex rather than the reverse. As the previous example suggests, it is not at all unusual for the president of an organization to be in a highly dependent position, a fact often not apparent to either the outsider or to the lower level manager who covets the president's job.

A considerable amount of the behavior of highly successful managers that seems inexplicable in light of what management texts usually tell us managers to do becomes understandable when one considers a manager's need for, and efforts at, managing his or her relationships with others.[3] To be able to plan, organize, budget, staff, control, and evaluate, managers need some control over the many people on whom they are dependent. Trying to control others solely by directing them and on the basis of the power associated with one's position simply will not work—first, because managers are always dependent on some people over whom they have no formal authority, and second, because virtually no one in modern organizations will passively accept and completely obey a constant stream of orders from someone just because he or she is the "boss."

Trying to influence others by means of persuasion alone will not work either. Although it is very powerful and possibly the single most important method of influence, persuasion has some serious drawbacks too. To make it work requires time (often lots of it), skill, and information on the part of the persuader. And persuasion can fail simply because the other person chooses not to listen or does not listen carefully.

This is not to say that directing people on the basis of the formal power of one's position and persuasion are not important means by which successful managers cope. They obviously are. But, even taken together, they are not usually enough.

Successful managers cope with their dependence on others by being sensitive to it, by eliminating or avoiding unnecessary dependence, and by establishing power over those others. Good managers then use that power to help them plan, organize, staff, budget, evaluate, and so on. *In other words, it is primarily because of the dependence inherent in managerial jobs that the dynamics of power necessarily form an important part of a manager's processes.*

An argument that took place during a middle management training seminar I participated in a few years ago helps illustrate further this important relationship between a manager's need for power and the degree of his or her dependence on others:

- Two participants, both managers in their thirties, got into a heated disagreement regarding the acquisition and use of power by managers. One took the position that power was absolutely central to managerial work, while the other argued that it was virtually irrelevant. In support of their positions, each described a very "successful" manager with whom he worked. In one of these examples, the manager seemed to be constantly developing and using power,

---

[3] I am talking about the type of inexplicable differences that Henry Mintzberg has found; see his article "The Manager's Job: Folklore and Fact," HBR July-August 1975, p. 49.

while in the other, such behavior was rare. Subsequently, both seminar participants were asked to describe their successful manager's jobs in terms of the dependence *inherent* in those jobs.

The young manager who felt power was unimportant described a staff vice president in a small company who was dependent only on his immediate subordinates, his peers, and his boss. This person, Joe Phillips, had to depend on his subordinates to do their jobs appropriately, but, if necessary, he could fill in for any of them or secure replacement for them rather easily. He also had considerable formal authority over them; that is, he could give them raises and new assignments, recommend promotions, and fire them. He was moderately dependent on the other four vice presidents in the company for information and cooperation. They were likewise dependent on him. The president had considerable formal authority over Phillips but was also moderately dependent on him for help, expert advice, the service his staff performed, other information, and general cooperation.

The second young manager—the one who felt power was very important—described a service department manager, Sam Weller, in a large, complex, and growing company who was in quite a different position. Weller was dependent not only on his boss for rewards and information, but also on 30 other individuals who made up the divisional and corporate top management. And while his boss, like Phillips's was moderately dependent on him too, most of the top managers were not. Because Weller's subordinates, unlike Phillips's, had people reporting to them, Weller was dependent not only on his subordinates but also on his subordinates' subordinates. Because he could not himself easily replace or do most of their technical jobs, unlike Phillips, he was very dependent on all these people.

In addition, for critical supplies, Weller was dependent on two other department managers in the division. Without their timely help, it was impossible for his department to do its job. These departments, however, did not have similar needs for Weller's help and cooperation. Weller was also dependent on local labor union officials and on a federal agency that regulated the division's industry. Both could shut his division down if they wanted.

Finally, Weller was dependent on two outside suppliers of key materials. Because of the volume of his department's purchases relative to the size of these two companies, he had little power over them.

Under these circumstances, it is hardly surprising that Sam Weller had to spend considerable time and effort acquiring and using power to manage his many dependencies, while Joe Phillips did not.

As this example also illustrates, not all management jobs require an incumbent to be able to provide the same amount of successful power-oriented behavior. But most management jobs today are more like Weller's than Phillips's. And perhaps more important, the trend over the past two or three decades is away from jobs like Phillips's and toward jobs like Weller's. So long as our technologies continue to become more complex, the average organization continues to grow larger, and the average industry continues to become more competitive and regulated, that trend will continue; as it does so, the effective acquisition and use of power by managers will become even more important.

Establishing Power in Relationships

To help cope with the dependency relationships inherent in their jobs, effective managers create, increase, or maintain four different types of power over others.[4] Having power based in these areas puts the manager in a position both to influence those people on whom he or she is dependent when necessary and to avoid being hurt by any of them.

Sense of Obligation

One of the ways that successful managers generate power in their relationships with others is to create a sense of obligation in those others. When the manager is successful, the others feel that they should—rightly—allow the manager to influence them within certain limits.

Successful managers often go out of their way to do favors for people who they expect will feel an obligation to return those favors. As can be see in the following description of a manager by one of his subordinates, some people are very skilled at identifying opportunities for doing favors that cost them very little but that others appreciate very much:

- "Most of the people here would walk over hot coals in their bare feet if my boss asked them to. He has an incredible capacity to do little things that mean a lot to people. Today, for example, in his junk mail he came across an advertisement for something that one of my subordinates had in passing once mentioned that he was shopping for. So my boss routed it to him. That probably took 15 seconds of his time, and yet my subordinate really appreciated it. To give you another example, two weeks ago he somehow learned that the purchasing manager's mother had died. On his way home that night, he stopped off at the funeral parlor. Our purchasing manager was, of course, there at the time. I bet he'll remember that brief visit for quite a while."

Recognizing that most people believe that friendship carries with it certain obligations ("A friend in need. . . . "), successful managers often try to develop true friendships with those on whom they are dependent. They will also make formal and informal deals in which they give something up in exchange for certain future obligations.

Belief in a Manager's Expertise

A second way successful managers gain power is by building reputations as "experts" in certain matters. Believing in the manager's expertise, others will often defer to the manager on those matters. Managers usually establish this type of

---

[4] These categories closely resemble the five developed by John R. P. French and Bertram Raven; see "The Base of Social Power" in *Group Dynamics: Research and Theory*, Dorwin Cartwright and Alvin Zandler, eds. (New York: Harper & Row, 1968), Chapter 20. Three of the categories are similar to the types of "authority"-based power described by Max Weber in *The Theory of Social and Economic Organization* (New York: Free Press, 1947).

power through visible achievement. The larger the achievement and the more visible it is, the more power the manager tends to develop.

One of the reasons that managers display concern about their "professional reputations" and their "track records" is that they have an impact on others' beliefs about their expertise. These factors become particularly important in large settings, where most people have only secondhand information about most other people's professional competence, as the following shows:

- Herb Randley and Bert Kline were both 35-year-old vice presidents in a large research and development organization. According to their closest associates, they were equally bright and competent in their technical fields and as managers. Yet Randley had a much stronger professional reputation in most parts of the company, and his ideas generally carried much more weight. Close friends and associates claim the reason that Randley is so much more powerful is related to a number of tactics that he has used more than Kline has.

Randley has published more scientific papers and managerial articles than Kline. Randley has been more selective in the assignments he has worked on, choosing those that are visible and that require his strong suits. He has given more speeches and presentations on projects that are his own achievements. And in meetings in general, he is allegedly forceful in areas where he has expertise and silent in those where he does not.

Identification With a Manager

A third method by which managers gain power is by fostering others' unconscious identification with them or with ideas they "stand for." Sigmund Freud was the first to describe this phenomenon, which is most clearly seen in the way people look up to "charismatic" leaders. Generally, the more a person finds a manager both consciously and (more important) unconsciously an ideal person, the more he or she will defer to that manager.

Managers develop power based on others' idealized views of them in a number of ways. They try to look and behave in ways that others respect. They go out of their way to be visible to their employees and to give speeches about their organizational goals, values, and ideals. They even consider, while making hiring and promotion decisions, whether they will be able to develop this type of power over the candidates:

- One vice president of sales in a moderate-size manufacturing company was reputed to be so much in control of his sales force that he could get them to respond to new and different marketing programs in a third of the time taken by the company's best competitors. His power over his employees was based primarily on their strong identification with him and what he stood for. Emigrating to the United States at age 17, this person worked his way up "from nothing." When made a sales manager in 1965, he began recruiting other young immigrants and sons of immigrants from his former country. When made vice president of sales in 1970, he continued to do so. In 1975, 85% of his sales force was made up of people whom he hired directly or who were hired by others he brought in.

Perceived Dependence on a Manager

The final way that an effective manager often gains power is by feeding others' beliefs that they are dependent on the manager either for help or for not being hurt. The more they perceive they are dependent, the more most people will be inclined to cooperate with such a manager.

There are two methods that successful managers often use to create perceived dependence.

Finding and Acquiring Resources. In the first, the manager identifies and secures (if necessary) resources that another person requires to perform his job, that he does not possess, and that are not readily available elsewhere. These resources include such things as authority to make certain decisions; control of money, equipment, and office space; access to important people; information and control of information channels; and subordinates. Then the manager takes action so that the other person correctly perceives that the manager has such resources and is willing and ready to use them to help (or hinder) the other person. Consider the following extreme—but true—example.

When young Tim Babcock was put in charge of a division of a large manufacturing company and told to "turn it around," he spent the first few weeks studying it from afar. He decided that the division was in disastrous shape and that he would need to take many large steps quickly to save it. To be able to do that, he realized he needed to develop considerable power fast over most of the division's management and staff. He did the following:

- He gave the division's management two hours' notice of his arrival.
- He arrived in a limousine with six assistants.
- He immediately called a meeting of the 40 top managers.
- He outlined briefly his assessment of the situation, his commitment to turn things around, and the basic direction he wanted things to move in.
- He then fired the four top managers in the room and told them that they had to be out of the building in two hours.
- He then said he would personally dedicate himself to sabotaging the career of anyone who tried to block his efforts to save the division.
- He ended the 60-minute meeting by announcing that his assistants would set up appointments for him with each of them starting at 7:00 A.M. the next morning.

Throughout the critical six-month period that followed, those who remained at the division generally cooperated energetically with Mr. Babcock.

Affecting Perceptions of Resources. A second way effective managers gain these types of power is by influencing other persons' perceptions of the manager's resources.[5] In settings where many people are involved and where the manager does not interact continuously with those he or she is dependent on, those people will seldom possess "hard facts" regarding what relevant resources the manager commands directly or indirectly (through others), what resources he will command in the future, or how prepared he is to use those resources to help or hinder them. They will be forced to make their own judgments.

Insofar as a manager can influence people's judgments, he can generate much more power than one would generally ascribe to him in light of the reality of his resources.

In trying to influence people's judgments, managers pay considerable attention to the "trappings" of power and to their own reputations and images. Among other actions, they sometimes carefully select, decorate, and arrange their offices in ways that give signs of power. They associate with people or organizations that are known to be powerful or that others perceive as powerful. Managers selectively foster rumors concerning their own power. Indeed, those who are particularly skilled at creating power in this way tend to be very sensitive to the impressions that all their actions might have on others.

Formal Authority

Before discussing how managers use their power to influence others, it is useful to see how formal authority relates to power. By *formal authority,* I mean those elements that automatically come with a managerial job—perhaps a title, an office, a budget, the right to make certain decisions, a set of subordinates, a reporting relationship, and so on.

Effective managers use the elements of formal authority as resources to help them develop any or all of the four types of power previously discussed, just as they use other resources (such as their education). Two managers with the same formal authority can have very different amounts of power entirely because of the way they have used that authority. For example:

- By sitting down with employees who are new or with people who are starting new projects and clearly specifying who has the formal authority to do what, one manager creates a strong sense of obligation in others to defer to his authority later.
- By selectively withholding or giving the high-quality service his department can provide other departments, one manager makes other managers clearly perceive that they are dependent on him.

On its own, then, formal authority does not guarantee a certain amount of power; it is only a resource that managers can use to generate power in their relationships.

---

[5] For an excellent discussion of this method, see Richard E. Neustadt, *Presidential Power* (New York: John Wiley, 1960).

Exercising Power to Influence Others

Successful managers use the power they develop in their relationships, along with persuasion, to influence people on whom they are dependent to behave in ways that make it possible for the managers to get their jobs done effectively. They use their power to influence others directly, face to face, and in more indirect ways.

Face-To-Face Influence

The chief advantage of influencing others directly by exercising any of the types of power is speed. If the power exists and the manager correctly understands the nature and strength of it, he can influence the other person with nothing more than a brief request or command:

- Jones thinks Smith feels obliged to him for past favors. Furthermore, Jones thinks that his request to speed up a project by two days probably falls within a zone that Smith would consider legitimate in light of his own definition of this obligation to Jones. So Jones simply calls Smith and makes his request. Smith pauses for only a second and says yes, he'll do it.
- Manager Johnson has some power based on perceived dependence over manager Baker. When Johnson tells Baker that he wants a report done in 24 hours, Baker grudgingly considers the costs of compliance, of noncompliance, and of complaining to higher authorities. He decides that doing the report is the least costly action and tells Johnson he will do it.
- Young Porter identifies strongly with Marquette, an older manager who is not his boss. Porter thinks Marquette is the epitome of a great manager and tries to model himself after him. When Marquette asks Porter to work on a special project "that could be very valuable in improving the company's ability to meet new competitive products," Porter agrees without hesitation and works 15 hours per week above and beyond his normal hours to get the project done and done well.

When used to influence others, each of the four types of power has different advantages and drawbacks. For example, power based on perceived expertise or on identification with a manager can often be used to influence attitudes as well as someone's immediate behavior and thus can have a lasting impact. It is very difficult to influence attitudes by using power based on perceived dependence, but if it can be done, it usually has the advantage of being able to influence a much broader range of behavior than the other methods do. When exercising power based on perceived expertise, for example, one can only influence attitudes and behavior within that narrow zone defined by the "expertise."

The drawbacks associated with the use of power based on perceived dependence are particularly important to recognize. A person who feels dependent on a manager for rewards (or lack of punishments) might quickly agree to a request from the manager but then not follow through—especially if the manager cannot easily find out if the person has obeyed or not. Repeated influence attempts based on perceived dependence also seem to encourage the other person to try to gain

Exhibit   Methods of Influence

Face-to-face methods	What they can influence	Advantages	Drawbacks
Exercise obligation-based power.	Behavior within zone that the other perceives as legitimate in light of the obligation.	Quick. Requires no outlay of tangible resources.	If the request is outside the acceptable zone, it will fail; if it is too far outside, others might see it as illegitimate.
Exercise power based on perceived expertise.	Attitudes and behavior within the zone of perceived expertise.	Quick. Requires no outlay of tangible resources.	If the request is outside the acceptable zone, it will fail; if it is too far outside, others might see it at illegitimate.
Exercise power based on identification with a manager.	Attitudes and behavior that are not in conflict with the ideals that underlie the identification.	Quick. Requires no expenditure of limited resources.	Restricted to influence attempts that are not in conflict with the ideals that underlie the identification.
Exercise power based on perceived dependence.	Wide range of behavior that can be monitored.	Quick. Can often succeed when other methods fail.	Repeated influence attempts encourage the other to gain power over the influencer.
Coercively exercise power based on perceived dependence.	Wide range of behavior that can be easily monitored.	Quick. Can often succeed when other methods fail.	Invites retaliation. Very risky.
Use persuasion.	Very wide range of attitudes and behavior.	Can produce internalized motivation that does not require monitoring. Requires no power or outlay of scarce material resources.	Can be very time-consuming. Requires other person to listen.
Combine these methods.	Depends on the exact combination.	Can be more potent and less risky than using a single method.	More costly than using a single method.

Indirect methods	What they can influence	Advantages	Drawbacks
Manipulate the other's environment by using any or all of the face-to-face methods.	Wide range of behavior and attitudes.	Can succeed when face-to-face methods fail.	Can be time-consuming. Is complex to implement. Is very risky, especially if used frequently.
Change the forces that continuously act on the individual: Formal organizational arrangements. Informal social arrangements. Technology. Resources available. Statement of organizational goals.	Wide range of behavior and attitudes on a continuous basis.	Has continuous influence, not just a one-shot effect. Can have a very powerful impact.	Often requires a considerable power outlay to achieve.

some power to balance the manager's. And perhaps most important, using power based on perceived dependence in a coercive way is very risky. Coercion invites retaliation.

For instance, in the example in which Tim Babcock took such extreme steps to save the division he was assigned to "turn around," his development and use of power based on perceived dependence could have led to mass resignation and the collapse of the division. Babcock fully recognized this risk, however, and behaved as he did because he felt there was simply *no other way* that he could gain the very large amount of quick cooperation needed to save the division.

Effective managers will often draw on more than one form of power to influence someone, or they will combine power with persuasion. In general, they do so because a combination can be more potent and less risky than any single method, as the following description shows:

- "One of the best managers we have in the company has lots of power based on one thing or another over most people. But he seldom if ever just tells or asks someone to do something. He almost always takes a few minutes to try to persuade them. The power he has over people generally induces them to listen carefully and certainly disposes them to be influenced. That, of course, makes the persuasion process go quickly and easily. And he never risks getting the other person mad or upset by making what that person thinks is an unfair request or command."

It is also common for managers not to coercively exercise power based on perceived dependence by itself, but to combine it with other methods to reduce the risk of retaliation. In this way, managers are able to have a large impact without leaving the bitter aftertaste of punishment alone.

Indirect Influence Methods

Effective managers also rely on two types of less direct methods to influence those on whom they are dependent. In the first way, they use any or all of the face-to-face methods to influence other people, who in turn have some specific impact on a desired person.

Product manager Stein needed plant manager Billings to "sign off" on a new product idea (Product X) which Billings thought was terrible. Stein decided that there was no way he could logically persuade Billings because Billings just would not listen to him. With time, Stein felt, he could have broken through that barrier. But he did not have that time. Stein also realized that Billings would never, just because of some deal or favor, sign off on a product he did not believe in. Stein also felt it not worth the risk of trying to force Billings to sign off, so here is what he did:

- On Monday, Stein got Reynolds, a person Billings respected, to send Billings two market research studies that were very favorable to Product X, with a note attached saying, "Have you seen this? I found them rather surprising. I am not sure if I entirely believe them, but still. . . ."
- On Tuesday, Stein got a representative of one of the company's biggest customers to mention casually to Billings on the phone that he had heard a rumor

about Product X being introduced soon and was "glad to see you guys are on your toes as usual."

- On Wednesday, Stein had two industrial engineers stand about three feet away from Billings as they were waiting for a meeting to begin and talk about the favorable test results on Product X.

- On Thursday, Stein set up a meeting to talk about Product X with Billings and invited only people whom Billings liked or respected and who also felt favorably about Product X.

- On Friday, Stein went to see Billings and asked him if he was willing to sign off on Product X. He was.

This type of manipulation of the environments of others can influence both behavior and attitudes and can often succeed when other influence methods fail. But it has a number of serious drawbacks. It takes considerable time and energy, and it is quite risky. Many people think it is wrong to try to influence others in this way, even people who, without consciously recognizing it, use this technique themselves. If they think someone is trying, or has tried, to manipulate them, they may retaliate. Furthermore, people who gain the reputation of being manipulators seriously undermine their own capacities for developing power and for influencing others. Almost no one, for example, will want to identify with a manipulator. And virtually no one accepts, at face value, a manipulator's sincere attempts at persuasion. In extreme cases, a reputation as a manipulator can completely ruin a manager's career.

A second way in which managers indirectly influence others is by making permanent changes in an individual's or a group's environment. They change job descriptions, the formal systems that measure performance, the extrinsic incentives available, the tools, people, and other resources that the people or groups work with, the architecture, the norms or values of work groups, and so on. If the manager is successful in making the changes, and the changes have the desired effect on the individual or group, that effect will be sustained over time.

Effective managers recognize that changes in the forces that surround a person can have great impact on that person's behavior. Unlike many of the other influence methods, this one doesn't require a large expenditure of limited resources or effort on the part of the manager on an ongoing basis. Once such a change has been successfully made, it works independently of the manager.

This method of influence is used by all managers to some degree. Many, however, use it sparingly simply because they do not have the power to change the forces acting on the person they wish to influence. In many organizations, only the top managers have the power to change the formal measurement systems, the extrinsic incentives available, the architecture, and so on.

Generating and Using Power Successfully

Managers who are successful at acquiring considerable power and using it to manage their dependence on others tend to share a number of common characteristics:

1. They are sensitive to what others consider to be legitimate behavior in acquiring and using power. They recognize that the four types of power carry with them certain "obligations" regarding their acquisition and use. A person who gains a considerable amount of power based on his perceived expertise is generally expected to be an expert in certain areas. If it ever becomes publicly known that the person is clearly not an expert in those areas, such a person will probably be labeled a "fraud" and will not only lose his power but will suffer other reprimands too.

   A person with whom a number of people identify is expected to act like an ideal leader. If he clearly lets people down, he will not only lose that power, he will also suffer the righteous anger of his ex-followers. Many managers who have created or used power based on perceived dependence in ways that their employees have felt unfair, such as in requesting overtime work, have ended up with unions.

2. They have good intuitive understanding of the various types of power and methods of influence. They are sensitive to what types of power are easiest to develop with different types of people. They recognize, for example, that professionals tend to be more influenced by perceived expertise than by other forms of power. They also have a grasp of all the various methods of influence and what each can accomplish, at what costs, and with what risks. (See the *Exhibit.*) They are good at recognizing the specific conditions in any situation and then at selecting an influence method that is compatible with those conditions.

3. They tend to develop all the types of power, to some degree, and they use all the influence methods mentioned in the exhibit. Unlike managers who are not very good at influencing people, effective managers usually do not think that only some of the methods are useful or that only some of the methods are moral. They recognize that any of the methods, used under the right circumstances, can help contribute to organizational effectiveness with few dysfunctional consequences. At the same time, they generally try to avoid those methods that are more risky than others and those that may have dysfunctional consequences. For example, they manipulate the environment of others only when absolutely necessary.

4. They establish career goals and seek out managerial positions that allow them to successfully develop and use power. They look for jobs, for example, that use their backgrounds and skills to control or manage some critically important problem or environmental contingency that an organization faces. They recognize that success in that type of job makes others dependent on them and increases their own perceived expertise. They also seek jobs that do not demand a type or a volume of power that is inconsistent with their own skills.

5. They use all of their resources, formal authority, and power to develop still more power. To borrow Edward Banfield's metaphor, they actually look for ways to "invest" their power where they might secure a high positive return.[6]

---

[6] See Edward C. Banfield, *Political Influence* (New York: Free Press, 1965), Chapter II.

For example, by asking a person to do him two important favors, a manager might be able to finish his construction program one day ahead of schedule. That request may cost him most of the obligation-based power he has over that person, but in return he may significantly increase his perceived expertise as a manager of construction projects in the eyes of everyone in his organization.

Just as in investing money, there is always some risk involved in using power this way; it is possible to get a zero return for a sizable investment, even for the most powerful manager. Effective managers do not try to avoid risks. Instead, they look for prudent risks, just as they do when investing capital.

6. Effective managers engage in power-oriented behavior in ways that are tempered by maturity and self-control.[7] They seldom, if ever, develop and use power in impulsive ways or for their own aggrandizement.

7. Finally, they also recognize and accept as legitimate that, in using these methods, they clearly influence other people's behavior and lives. Unlike many less effective managers, they are reasonably comfortable in using power to influence people. They recognize, often only intuitively, what this article is all about—that their attempts to establish power and use it are an absolutely necessary part of the successful fulfillment of their difficult managerial role.

―――――――――

By the time that Sally Helgesen wrote *The Female Advantage* in 1990, the exercise of bureaucratic power had somewhat changed in emphasis. Helgesen views such change as occurring partly because "pressed by global competition and a fast-changing technology characterized by flexibility and innovation, companies are casting aside old-culture values, trimming the pyramid, and rooting out cumbersome and bureaucratic structures."[a] It was also partly because women were gradually moving into management positions.

In order to examine how women use power, Helgesen drew on the methodology of Henry Mintzberg. In 1968, Mintzberg followed five white male managers and informally charted what they actually did with their time through extensive interviews and carefully constructed "diary studies." Helgesen knew that during the years since Mintzberg's work, female managers had risen in the ranks or, in a significant number of cases, founded their own companies. But did these successful women manage differently from their male counterparts, and, if so, what could be learned from their experience? To answer that question, Helgesen too relied on "diary studies" of outstanding female executives.

Before turning to these differences, it is important to stress one similarity—the road to becoming the CEO was a tough one, and these women too learned how to play the corporate power game. "In this little office," reported one female CEO,

[7]See David C. McClelland and David H. Burnham, "Power Is the Great Motivator," HBR March-April 1976, p. 100.

[a]Sally Helgesen, *The Female Advantage: Women's Ways of Leadership* (New York: Doubleday Currency, 1990), pp. xviii–xix.

"I wear my general manager's hat. I'm less important when I'm in here. In my big office, I can be more corporate."[b] Another of the CEOs

also took joyous relish in playing different parts with clients, bankers, and employees—whatever was called for at the moment. With some, she was the strict but concerned mother; with others, the savvy deal maker; with yet others, the wise and experienced leader. The process was very conscious. 'It's not as if I'm different people. I'm just playing up different parts of who I am'.[c]

Helgesen observes that these women may have become particularly sensitive to human relations skills partly because a fierce weeding out process takes place among female executives; in contemplating the winners and losers, a Center for Values Research study found that women lacking human relations skills encountered more hostile and negative resistance than men in seeking positions of authority and influence.[d] Helgesen is emphatic that these women reserve the final decisions to themselves. Nonetheless, their leadership style emphasizing a "web of inclusion" is far different in emphasis and in its assumption of where wisdom is most likely to be found.

Helgesen selected four women—two entrepreneurs, a Ford Company executive, and one CEO of a private nonprofit organization. She recognized that the (white) males would presumably act somewhat differently today, but felt that "other discrepancies are so striking (and so reflective of the differences in male and female psychology noted by researchers like Carol Gilligan and Jean Baker Miller) that they do seem to indicate a basic dissimilarity of approach."[e] The similarities and differences between Mintzberg's male and Helgesen's female executives are clear from the comparisons in her selection.

Helgesen's female executives are consciously and systematically engaged, both internally and externally, in their political environment. She skillfully identifies a series of metaphors that bring the nature of this interpersonal and political involvement to life—metaphors such as the significance of being located at the heart versus the head of the organization, of the ecology (with its stress on the interrelatedness of all things), and, most importantly, of the "web of inclusion."

The Web of Inclusion

Sally Helgesen

Far into the night, while the other creatures slept, Charlotte worked on her web. First she ripped out a few of the orb lines near the center. She left the radial lines alone, as they were needed for support. As she worked, her eight legs were a great help to her. So were her teeth. She loved to weave, and she was an expert at it.

—*Charlotte's Web*
E. B. White

Sally Helgesen. *The Female Advantage.* New York: Doubleday Currency, 1990.

[b]Helgesen, *The Female Advantage: Women's Ways of Leadership*, pp. 26–27.

[c]Helgesen, *The Female Advantage: Women's Ways of Leadership*, p. 27.

[d]Helgesen, *The Female Advantage: Women's Ways of Leadership*, p. 31.

[e]Helgesen, *The Female Advantage: Women's Ways of Leadership*, p. 19.

It is lunchtime in the pink-and-green garden dining room of the Cosmopolitan Club in upper Manhattan, the all-women's club started by Abigail Rockefeller when the Union, her husband's club, refused to serve her. The atmosphere is genteel, with stone planters trailing petunias and women mostly over fifty, some even wearing hats with veils.

It seems an unlikely place in which to be discussing modern leadership and management techniques, but I am with Frances Hesselbein, chief executive of the Girl Scouts, a woman who bridges the paradox with ease. With her low, well-disciplined voice, Hermès scarf and bag, and grooming so perfect you expect that, like the Duchess of Windsor, she must polish the soles of her shoes, Frances Hesselbein clearly belongs to the world represented by the Cosmopolitan Club. Yet she is also the woman who brought modern management to her organization with such success that Peter Drucker called her "perhaps the best professional manager in America."

I am attempting to interview her, despite the club's rather archaic ban on "visible paper"; apparently ladies are not to engage in business over lunch. So I am balancing my notebook on my knees under a napkin and scribbling without looking while an elderly waitress serves Parker House rolls with silver tongs. Frances Hesselbein is describing the management structure she devised for the Girl Scouts, a replacement for the old hierarchical pyramid.

The new system is circular, she explains; positions are represented as circles, which are then arranged in an expanding series of orbits. "I use circles," she says, "because symbolically they are important. The circle is an organic image. We speak of the *family* circle. The circle is *inclusive,* but it allows for flow and movement; the circle doesn't box you in! I've always conceived of management as a circular process. When I was head of my regional organization, I devised a structure similar to the one I'm using now. It wasn't something I'd read I should do, it was just something I felt. These days, there are all these theories about the circular management model, but with me it was intuitive—this attraction I've always had to the circle."

Suddenly, Frances Hesselbein seizes a wooden pepper mill and sets it in the middle of our table. "This is me," she says, "in the center of the organization." She moves a glass of iced tea and several packets of sugar to form a circle around the pepper mill. "And this is my management team, the first circle." Using cups and saucers, Frances Hesselbein constructs a second circle around the first. "These are the people who report to the first team. And beyond this outer circle, there's another, and another beyond that. And they're all interrelated." She picks up knives and forks and begins fashioning radials to link up the orb lines. "As the circles extend outward, there are more and more connections. So the galaxy gets more *interwoven* as it gets bigger!"

The table at the Cosmopolitan Club is a mess, but I am fascinated. Frances Hesselbein has created the perfect image of a spider's web. And the image of the web has been haunting me lately, for I have been thinking about structure. More specifically, about how women structure things differently from men—companies, office spaces, human relationships, even their own presumed place in the universe.

The Web As Structure

While doing the diary studies, I became aware that the women, when describing their roles in their organizations, usually referred to themselves as being in the middle of things. Not at the top, but in the center; not reaching down, but reaching out. The expressions were spontaneous, part of the women's language, indicating unconscious notions about what was desirable and good. Inseparable from their sense of themselves as being in the middle was the women's notion of being connected to those around them, bound as if by invisible strands or threads. This image of an interrelated structure, built around a strong central point and constructed of radials and orbs, quite naturally made me think of a spider's web—that delicate tracery, compounded of the need for survival and the impulse of art, whose purpose is to draw other creatures to it.

The image of the web not only imbued the language of the women in the diary studies; it also evident in the management structures they devised, and in the way they structured their meetings. Frances Hesselbein's "circular management chart," drawn with cutlery and sugar packets, was the most obvious example, and perhaps the most fully articulated. Jokingly called the Girl Scouts' "Wheel of Fortune" by Peter Drucker, the wheel actually *spins;* most management jobs are rotated every two or three years. Frances Hesselbein explains that job rotation used in conjunction with the circular chart is ideal for team-building. Teams can be formed to address needs as they arise—for example, the devising of an eighteen-month plan—then disbanded once the task has been accomplished. People serve both on different teams and in different positions, which offers staff people wide experience in the organization. In addition, being rotated into different jobs instills a feeling of common enterprise, cuts down on the tendency to form cliques and fiefdoms, and helps managers understand firsthand both the difficulties that face and the priorities that drive their fellows. "But the reason we have such team-building freedom is because of our circular chart," says Frances Hesselbein. "When someone gets shifted, he or she is simply moved around or across—it doesn't feel like a demotion because there is no up or down. There's no onus attached to being moved."

Nancy Badore's entire career has been built on the notion that management is best done by interrelating teams; she helped to develop the model for training Ford's top executives in this style on the factory floor, and then brought it, to the chagrin of some, to the executive suite. She runs the Executive Development Center along participatory lines; the management chart shows her in the center, with team members (who head the various programs for executives) branching out like the arms of a tree, rather than in a wheel configuration. Her monthly team meetings, at which the program managers make their progress reports, are not, she explains, "about them reporting to *me.* They're about *them* getting exposure to one another's projects and ideas." Thus she appears not so much to be chairing the meeting, but acting as facilitator, extracting and directing information. This is very much like Dorothy Brunson's view of her role as "a transmitter," absorbing information, then beaming it out "to wherever it needs to go."

Similarly, when Barbara Grogan chairs a meeting of the governor of Colorado's Small Business Advisory Council (which she had founded), she focuses attention on encouraging the participants to exchange ideas with one another, and forge new alliances among themselves. She describes the process of using her central position to promote interchange as "encouraging the flow," echoing Frances Hesselbein's language.

Implicit in such structurings is the notion of group affiliation rather than individual achievement as having the highest value. This emphasis was obvious in the ways the women described their notions of success. "I never wanted success if it meant clawing my way over other bodies," said Barbara Grogan. "I always knew that would make it pretty lonely once I got there." Frances Hesselbein expressed a similar notion. "I don't have the pressure on me that people have who think of themselves as being out there alone. I think of myself as part of a long continuum. That continuum includes my family, but also all of the fifty-six million women who have ever been in the Girl Scouts—a long green line going back in time and giving me support. Thinking of yourself as part of something larger frees you. You don't feel this sense of individual burden. It's been the source of so much of my energy."

The web of concern may be very large, as Nancy Badore notes. "The Executive Development Center trains Ford executives all over the world, so I try to think in global terms. I don't just see Ford as this company, an entity unto itself; it's a piece of the world, interrelated by politics, history, and economics. And I'm part of that. So while I'm asking myself what role the company can play, I'm also asking what role I can play, particularly as a woman. I'm asking it in terms of the world: where can I make my best contribution? The question really gets down to *why was I born?*"

Thus thinking in terms of the larger group is an important component of the "ecological" focus that I found among the women in the diary studies. This enlarged consciousness derives in part from the women's awareness of themselves as women, in the vanguard of a movement that is changing history. Thus a kind of hidden agenda informs their actions and decisions, manifesting itself as a mission both to improve the status of women and change the world.

This sense of having a larger concern—a concern for the group or whole—is of course implicit in the imagery of the web. The orb and radial lines bind the whole together; every point of contact is also a point of connection. The principle, as Frances Hesselbein observed about the circle, is *inclusion*. You can't break a web into single lines or individual components without tearing the fabric, injuring the whole.

From Hierarchy to Web

Carol Gilligan, in *A Different Voice*, consistently opposes the image of the hierarchy to that of the "web of connection" in describing the difference between what women and men view as valuable in this world. She writes, "The images of hierarchy and web, drawn from the texts of men's and women's fantasies and thoughts, convey different ways of structuring relationships, and are associated with different views of morality and self."[1] She notes that these images are in their way mirror opposites, because *the most desirable place in the one is the most feared spot in the other.* "As the *top* of the hierarchy becomes the *edge* of the web, and as the *center* of the network of connection become the *middle* of the hierarchical progression, each image marks as dangerous the place which the other defines as safe."[2] In the hierarchical scheme of things, "reaching the top"—where others cannot get close—is the ultimate goal; in the web, the top is too far from the center. The ideal center spot in the web is perceived in the hierarchical view as "being stuck" in the middle—going nowhere.

The contrasting models also reveal different notions of what constitutes effective communications. Hierarchy, emphasizing appropriate channels and the chain of command, discourages diffuse or random communication; information is filtered, gathered, and sorted as it makes its way to the top. By contrast, the web facilitates direct communication, free-flowing and loosely structured, by providing points of contact and direct tangents along which to connect.

The women in the diary studies, eager to be "in the center of things" and chilled by the notion of being "alone at the top," echo the values, principles, and presumptions that Carol Gilligan found to be characteristic of women in general, that indeed she believed to be structured into the female psyche. These values have long been restricted to the private sphere, but that is dramatically changing; the women in the diary studies, having attained positions of authority and influence in the public realm, are able to structure their principles into the way they do business. Thus, using the model of the web to design management charts and apportion office space, to construct meetings and evolve more direct means of communication, they are participating in an *institutionalizing of the web.*

In *Re-inventing the Corporation,* Naisbitt and Aburdene propose the lattice or grid as the structural model for the new corporate economy.[3] It is interesting to note that these structures, with their interconnecting points and intersecting lines, are quite similar to the web—except that they are bound by boxlike shapes rather than circles. Thus the structure of the reinvented corporation is far closer to the female perception of what is desirable, though it retains an essential "male" angularity. The grid of interlocking pieces facilitates direct communication, can shift to meet changing demands, and hastens the flow of information. The image recalls that of the microchip—making quick connections, breaking information into bits, processing, rearranging the units: energy moving in pulses rather than being forced to run up and down in channels.

Such a model is obviously more suited to the information age than the hierarchical structure, which found its most widespread application in the industrial era.[4] Yet hierarchical concepts have continued to influence institutional structures because they represent a particular manifestation of male psychology, meeting

---

[1] Carol Gilligan, *A Different Voice.* Cambridge: Harvard University Press, 1982, p. 62.

[2] Gilligan, *A Different Voice,* p. 61 ff.

[3] John Naisbitt & Patricia Aburdene, *Reinventing the Corporation.* New York: Warner Books, 1986, pp. 43–44.

[4] Naisbitt and Aburdene, *Reinventing the Corporation.* pp. 57–59.

male needs for limits and boundaries on relationships in the workplace, and satisfying the male value for ends over means. But as women continue to assume positions of influence in the public sphere, they are countering the values of the hierarchy with those of the web, which affirms relationships, seeks ways to strengthen human bonds, simplifies communications, and gives means an equal value with ends.

The Point of Authority in the Web

When organizations are structured in a top-to-bottom chain of command, lines of authority are extremely clear. The old "if it moves, salute it" mentality prevails. But how does authority manifest itself when the head of an organization sees herself as being at its center? How does a manager in her various roles as information gatherer, decision maker, planner, figurehead, and information disseminator exert authority from the fixed point at the center of the web?

First, it must be noted that, although lines of authority in a web structure may appear diffuse, even tangled, the women in the diary studies are very much the leaders in their organizations, the ones upon whom final responsibility rests. All could be characterized as strong leaders: they have vivid personalities, are direct, and, most important, have specific visions of where they wish to lead and the methods they must use to achieve their goals. Nor are their organizations run as participatory democracies, with everyone contributing in a haphazard way. The women are authorities as much as if they sat at the very top of a hierarchical ladder, but that authority has more subtle ways of manifesting itself.

A prime example is in information-gathering. In a top-down management, information flows upward through channels; authority is established by having access to this progressively filtered information. The chain of command is broken, however, if the authority bypasses established channels in order to ask direct questions down the ladder. By contrast, being at the center, connected to every point in the whole, makes it possible to gather information directly from all sources. Frances Hesselbein made it a practice to receive and answer herself any suggestions made by any member of the 500-person paid staff, whether an accountant or mailroom employee. The most important aspect of this direct contact was that there was no filter, no supervisory layer through whom "lower-downs" were expected to go.

In regard to decision-making, the manager operating from the center of the web can use this direct access to information not only to widen input, but to test reception to decisions in advance. Both these benefits give the decision maker more data when making a decision, but do not dilute the necessity for the *leader* to make it; diffuse lines do not mean fuzzy decisions. Dorothy Brunson, meeting with her young disc jockeys to get their input on a decision, could also solicit their views of how her decision would impact their listeners and the way in which they programmed their shows, and get their reactions on different options she was considering. She described the process: "I never make hasty decisions. The main thing is to cast a wide net, look in many directions, seek a lot of information. Then I maybe take a walk in the evening, let the information jell. And when I make my decision, that's *it.*"

In terms of planning for the future, the process of leading from the center of the web is very subtle, and derives its strength from nourishing and fortifying the bonds between intersecting points. In Frances Hesselbein's management team meeting, when conflict arose over issues relating to future plans, she asked the antagonists to work out a plan between themselves and then bring it to her for discussion—which of course implies that the final judgment would be hers. But handling the conflict in this way assured her that the plan the team members devised would meet the requirements of both their departments, while also helping them forge tighter bonds to strengthen the fabric of the organization as a whole. Further, because her circular management chart eliminates ups and downs as well as layers, Frances Hesselbein was able to invite the antagonists to work things out among themselves without regard to who was above or below whom in rank.

Figurehead authority derives in top-down management from being literally the head; it manifests itself as power to set an organization's vision, to represent it in the world. In a web construction, the figurehead is the *heart* rather than the head, and so does not need layers and ranks below to reinforce status. Authority comes from connection *to* the people around rather than distance *from* those below; this in itself helps to foster a team approach. In acting as a figurehead, the leader with a web conception need not insist on rank, authority, and importance in order to convincingly represent the organization. This can be an effective disarming technique, as when Barbara Grogan, at the Governor's Small Business Advisory Council meeting, was able in effect to trumpet her company's latest success and at the same time underplay it by including others in her success: "Can you imagine, our little consulting branch is actually real! Now we're all on our way!"

As a disseminator of information, the leader who operates from the center of the web has the same advantages as when in an information-gathering role. She has direct access to anyone within the organization without having to resort to channels, and thus avoids the attendant risks of dilution and distortion. Further, because releasing information does not lessen authority in the web (as happens in the top-down structure whenever information flows *down*), that information can function as a tool to draw people together.

As mentioned, Nancy Badore made a point of structuring her monthly meetings with the managers who devised programs for the EDC "*not* in order for them to report to me, but so that they can have a chance to share what they're doing, feed off one another's ideas, know exactly what is going on." Again, the concept of strengthening ties is most important; the leader at the center derives strength from building up connections rather than from compartmentalizing, dividing in order to conquer. There is nothing to be gained by restricting the flow of information to the top—hoarding it, as Mintzberg noted his men were wont to do.

There is an aspect of teaching that accompanies authority as it flows from the center of the web. The process of gathering and routing information, of guiding relationships and coaxing forth connections, strikes an educational note. Frances

Hesselbein telling two team members to work things out between them, Nancy Badore devising a meeting "for them, not for me," —both these women have something of the air of good teachers taking pains to help others learn, and knowing when to let students use what they have learned. But this teacher-like quality exhibited by the women in the diary studies does not seem unusual, since the teacher is most people's first model of female authority in the public realm. As such, it informs ideas and assumptions about how women use power influence and create structures in order to lead.

The Strategy of the Web

As we have seen, books such as *The Managerial Woman* attributed some measure of men's success in the workplace to what the authors saw as the male focus on "winning; on achieving a goal or reaching an objective." These goals or objectives were conceived of in very specific terms: bring in six new customers next month, make vice president within three years. By contrast, women were supposed to be hampered by a more diffuse, less goal-oriented notion of their careers: by tending to see their work "as personal growth, as self-fulfillment, as satisfaction, as making a contribution to others, as doing *what one wants to do.*"[5] The difference, then, came down to a question of *strategy:* men had a definite, objective plan for getting to where they wanted, while women, as a general rule, lacked such a plan.

And yet, when we consider the contrasting images of hierarchy and web, the question falls into a different focus. For what the authors of *The Managerial Woman* define as strategy is in fact the strategy of the hierarchy. It is preoccupied with targeting position, climbing the ladder, knocking out the competition, playing factions against each other, achieving an objective by manipulating the chain of command. Both its goals and methods assume the existence of a hierarchical structure.

This is surely how strategy is generally perceived, but it need not be the only way. The strategy of the web employs different methods in order to achieve different goals. Since the most desirable spot in the web is the center, the strategy of the web concentrates on drawing closer to that center by drawing others closer, and by strengthening the lines and orbs that knit the fabric together. Emphasizing interrelationships, working to tighten them, building up strength, knitting loose ends into the fabric, it is a strategy that honors the feminine principles of inclusion, connection, and what Carol Gilligan calls "being responsible in the world." And by emphasizing the continual drawing closer and strengthening of parts, it betrays the female's essential orientation toward *process,* her concern with the means used to achieve her ends.

The strategy of the web is less direct, less focused on specific goals, and so less driven by pure will than the strategy of the hierarchy. Thus it is appropriate to the diffuse and growth-centered notions of success that women have been criticized for holding. Proceeding by means of strengthening the fabric as well as defining a series of objectives, it works in a less linear fashion than hierarchical strategies.

---

[5] Margaret Hennig & Anne Jardim. *The Managerial Woman.* New York: Pocket Books, 1976, p. 33.

British Prime Minister Margaret Thatcher, so often thought of as a woman who exemplifies male values, nevertheless gave perfect expression to this female sense of strategy when asked how she had attained her success. She replied that she had never spelled out specific goals for herself or aspired to a particular position, but had rather seized opportunities as they came and made the best of them.[6] Nancy Badore cited Thatcher's remarks when asked what her career objectives had been, and how she conceived her goals for the future. And Barbara Grogan echoed this theme: "I can't say where I'll be in five years; five years ago, I could never have foreseen where I am now. I don't draft five-year plans—I just do the best job I can, and trust that it will lead me to where I'm supposed to be next. I know that sounds sort of squishy, but it works."

Where I'm supposed to be next: clearly an element of trust is at work here; also a sense of fate, a conviction of destiny that is anything but passive. The strategy of the web is guided by opportunity, proceeds by the use of intuition, and is characterized by a patience that comes of waiting to see what comes next. It is the strategy used by the spider Charlotte in E. B. White's *Charlotte's Web.* When Charlotte is confronted by the need to save Wilbur, the barnyard pig facing slaughter, she does not devise a list of objectives in order to decide how to proceed. Instead of being "like men, who rush, rush, rush every minute," she relies on intuition and patience. "Charlotte knew from experience that if she waited long enough, a fly would come into her web; she felt sure that if she thought long enough about Wilbur's problem, an idea would come into her mind."[7] And the solution, when it came, required her to weave a web; after all, Charlotte "loved to weave, and she was an expert at it."

The image of weaving is one of the most ancient associated with the female domain; the archaic word for woman, *distaff,* also refers to a skein of flax, and to the staff on the loom that holds the unspun wool. In mythologies all over the world, female deities are depicted at the loom, knitting together the fabric of human life, spinning out the thread that links the events of the past with the potentialities—the unborn people and events—of the future. Thus the strategy of the web, of weaving, acknowledges the importance of what Frances Hesselbein called "the continuum," that sense that one is a part of what has gone before, and of what will follow.

For this reason, the spinning goddesses of Germanic and Greek myth were also the goddesses of fate. Their recognition and acceptance of destiny as the interweave of past and future, of chance and work, is the ultimate expression of the strategy of the web. And at the most profound level, this is what Barbara Grogan and Nancy Badore (and Margaret Thatcher) echo when they describe themselves as trusting that the opportunities which come their way will unlock their futures. Like the ancient female goddesses, they understand that the future cannot be reduced to a simple matter of objectives, nor achieved by the mere application of will.

---

[6] Interview in *Mirabella,* September 1989.

[7] E. B. White, *Charlotte's Web.* New York: Harper & Row, 1952, p. 67.

he executives in Helgesen's study demonstrate an acute awareness of the external environment and its significance for their organizations. Myron Fottler and his colleagues pursue the task of helping hospital CEOs to identify key stakeholders in that environment, and in doing so demonstrate how managers in any organization can monitor their political environment. These key stakeholders "have a vested interest in the hospital." In some cases, they are internal to the organization or work for the organization in the role of "interfacing" with critical external stakeholders. Others, however, are completely outside the boundaries of the formal organization. Regardless, all three kinds of stakeholders have in common that they are "individuals, groups, and organizations who have a stake in the decisions and actions of hospitals and may attempt to influence those decisions and actions."

The means of identifying these organizational stakeholders is through asking what are essentially the classic questions of political analysis. Who are the stakeholders, or key actors, in the organization? Who benefits and who loses as a result of agency decisions? Who is able to influence whom during the decision-making process? Which issues (with their different core values) are critically important to which stakeholders? Fottler and his colleagues choose to seek out the answers through a formal survey process. Where the resources for such an elaborate study are unavailable, a public manager, instead, can examine those cases involving serious conflicts in his or her organization where stakeholders were compelled to emerge and compete or cooperate in pursuit of their goals.

Fottler and his associates provide excellent advice in their conclusion where they caution that stakeholders vary in different hospitals as well as nonhospital health care settings, and they also vary over time. Such stakeholders, or actors, must, therefore, be constantly monitored by public managers in terms of their identity and their changing critical concerns.

Assessing Key Stakeholders: Who Matters to Hospitals and Why?

Myron D. Fottler

Summary

A key stakeholder perspective, informed by illustrative quantitative and qualitative data, is developed for hospital administrators. These data provide answers to the questions, Who matters to hospitals? and Why do they matter? A tool kit for assessing stakeholders also is presented to help hospital executives identify their institutions' key stakeholders, determine the power of these stakeholders and their core values, and define who within their institutions should be responsible for the routine management of different stakeholders. These tools facilitate the management of each key stakeholder, ensuring that each strategic decision is examined in

Myron D. Fottler. *Hospital & Health Services Administration*, Vol. 34, No 4 (Winter 1989).

terms of the likely reaction of key stakeholders and is supplemented with plans for gaining stakeholder acceptance. Managers should recognize that the answers to Who matters? and Why? will vary by type of hospital and by the specific issue being addressed.

Hospitals are experiencing fundamental, turbulent, and in some cases, revolutionary change.[1] One source of change has occurred because health care executives must respond to an increasing number of active and powerful stakeholders. As a result, stakeholders now exert influence on issues ranging from hospital governance to financial reimbursement to patient services. As the realities of hospital management change, different perspectives for developing alternative models and approaches to management are also needed.

Stakeholder management is becoming an important approach to conceptualizing and performing the management role in all organizations.[2] The organizational stakeholder concept is also becoming increasingly significant to the analysis of the forces affecting health care organizations and their managers.[3] Hospital stakeholders have a vested interest in the hospital. More specifically, they are the individuals, groups, and organizations who have a stake in the decisions and actions of hospitals and who may attempt to influence those decisions and actions.[4]

Stakeholder management integrates in a systematic way what managers often deal with separately—strategic management, marketing, human resource management, public relations, organizational politics, and social responsibility. It focuses attention on managing stakeholders, both internal and external to the hospital. To illustrate, a hospital might manage patient-physician relationships to increase utilization or collaborate with competing hospitals to minimize costly technology duplication. In essence, the stakeholder management approach extends the traditional management paradigm to include external stakeholders; this approach is especially significant when stakeholders are active and hospital-stakeholder interdependence is high. Under these circumstances, the ability to manage relationships with key stakeholders particularly affects hospital performance.

The stakeholder management paradigm is still in the formulation and theory development stage, and its application to health care organizations is growing. Nonetheless, until recently, middle-range theorizing has been missing. Such theories of the "middle range" permit both the researcher and the health care executive to go from the interesting yet broad and abstract notion that stakeholders are

[1] E. Johnson and R. Johnson, *Hospitals Under Fire: Strategies for Survival* (Rockville, MD: Aspen, 1986). H. Smith and R. Reid, *Competitive Hospitals* (Rockville, MD: Aspen, 1986). D. Coddington and K. Moore, *Market-Driven Strategies in Health Care* (San Francisco, CA: Jossey-Bass, 1987).

[2] R. O. Mason and I. I. Mitroff, *Challenging Strategic Planning Assumptions* (New York: John Wiley & Sons, 1981). R. E. Freeman, *Strategic Management: A Stakeholder Approach* (Marshfield, MA: Pitman Publishing, 1984).

[3] M. D. Fottler, "Health Care Organizational Performance: Present and Future Research," in *1987 Yearly Review of Management of the Journal of Management,* J. D. Blair and J. G. Hunt, ed., 13:2 (1987) 179–203. R. L. Keele, K. Buckner, and S. Bushnell, "Identifying Health Care Stakeholders: A Key to Strategic Implementation," *Health Care Strategic Management* 5 (September 1987) 4–10. J. D. Blair and C. Whitehead, "Too Many on the Seesaw: Stakeholder Diagnosis and Management for Hospitals," *Hospital Health and Services Administration* 33 (Summer 1988) 153–166. J. D. Blair, G. T. Savage, and C. Whitehead, "A Strategic Approach for Negotiating with Hospital Stakeholders," *Health Care Management Review* 14 (Winter 1989) 13–23.

[4] Fottler, "Health Care Organizational Performance: Present and Future Research," 1987. Blair and Whitehead, "Too Many on the Seesaw: Stakeholder Diagnosis and Management for Hospitals," 1988.

important to the hospital to a conceptually informed and organized way of under-standing and managing hospital stakeholders.[5] For example, Fottler describes how stakeholders influence the effectiveness of health care organizations.[6] Blair and Whitehead specify the important diagnostic dimensions that can be applied to stakeholders and suggest the most appropriate strategies to manage different types of stakeholders.[7] Blair, Savage, and Whitehead show how to integrate the strategies of business, stakeholder management, and negotiation.[8] However, the process of assessing stakeholders and determining the most important or key stakeholders has not been well developed. In this article, those middle-range con-cepts of hospital stakeholder management are extended to include the notion of stakeholder assessment.

Different types of hospital stakeholders are described, and then the article shows why stakeholders and stakeholder management are becoming more impor-tant to hospitals, describes the research approach we used to develop the stake-holder assessment concept, analyzes the power and the values of those stakeholders who *typically* are most important to hospitals, prescribes a tool kit for assessing those stakeholders and issues of importance to a *specific* hospital, and links stake-holder assessment to the overall stakeholder management process.

Types of Hospital Stakeholders

Hospital stakeholders can be categorized into three groups—internal, interface, and external. *Internal stakeholders* are those who operate entirely within the bounds of the organization and typically include management, professional, and nonprofessional staff. Management attempts to manage these internal stake-holders by providing sufficient inducements to gain their continued contributions.

Interface stakeholders are those who function both internally and externally to the organization—that is, those who are on the interface between the organization and its environment. The major categories of interface stakeholders include the medical staff, the hospital board of trustees, the corporate office of the parent company, and stockholders, taxpayers, or other contributors. These tend to be among the most powerful stakeholders in health care organizations. As in the case of internal stakeholders, the organization must offer each interface stakeholder sufficient inducements to continue to make appropriate contributions. Whereas the internal and interface stakeholders are at least partly supportive of the hos-pital, many of the external stakeholders are neutral, nonsupportive, or hostile.

External stakeholders fall into three categories in their relationship to the health care organization. Some provide inputs into the organization, some com-pete with it, and others have a special interest in how the organization functions.

---

[5]R. Merton, *Social Theory and Social Structure* rev. ed. (New York: Free Press, 1957).

[6]Fottler, "Health Care Organizational Performance: Present and Future Research," 1987, 179–203.

[7]Blair and Whitehead, "Too Many on the Seesaw: Stakeholder Diagnosis and Management for Hospitals," 1988, 153–166.

[8]Blair, Savage, and Whitehead, "A Strategic Approach for Negotiating with Hospital Stakeholders," 1989, 13–23.

Suppliers, patients, third party payers, and the financial community are among those providing input. The relationship between the organization and these external stakeholders is a symbiotic one because the organization depends on these stakeholders for its survival. In turn, these stakeholders depend on the organization to take their outputs. The degree of the hospital's dependence on these stakeholders (and vice versa) depends on the number and relative attractiveness of alternate providers of similar services. Mutual interdependence characterizes these relationships.

Competitors, the second category of external stakeholders, seek to attract the focal organization's dependents. These stakeholders may directly compete for patients (i.e., other hospitals) or for skilled personnel (i.e., related health organizations). Competitors do not need one another to survive. While cooperation between hospitals and their competitors has increased in recent years, so too has competition, which is more characteristic of the current relationship.[9]

Special-interest groups, the third category of external stakeholders, are concerned with the impact of the hospital's operations relative to their specific interests. The major special-interest groups affecting hospitals are government regulatory agencies, private accrediting associations, professional associations, labor unions, the media, the local community, and various political-action groups such as the American Association of Retired Persons (AARP) and right-to-life groups. Because of the special interest, conflict most often defines the nature of this relationship; compromise rather than collaboration is most often the solution to the conflict.

The Increasing Significance of Stakeholders to Hospitals

Figures 1 and 2 illustrate vividly how extensively hospital stakeholder complexity has increased between the late 1950s (Figure 1) and the late 1980s (Figure 2). These figures reflect our best judgment of hospital-stakeholder relationships in these two time periods and are based on our qualitative synthesis of the health care policy and management literatures. In the late 1950s, competition was low and sometimes nonexistent, Medicare and Medicaid had not yet been passed, most hospitals were freestanding, regulation at all levels was low, health maintenance organizations (HMOs) and preferred provider organizations (PPOs) were virtually nonexistent, physicians were the dominant stakeholder, nonprofit health institutions were self-funding, patient support was taken for granted, labor unions represented few employees, horizontal and vertical integration were rare, employers were unconcerned about employee health costs, boards were passive, philanthropy and direct private-pay patients were the norm, and third-party reimbursement was not very important. Relationships between the hospital and its stakeholders were generally positive, as indicated by the plus signs in Figure 1.

Contrast that situation with the nature of the health care industry in the late 1980s. Now many hospitals are part of corporate chains that are both horizontally

---

[9]Coddington and Moore, *Market-Driven Strategies in Health Care*, 1987.

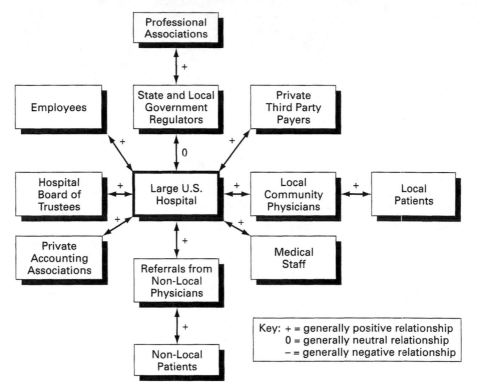

Figure 1   A Simplified Map for a Large U.S. Hospital in the Late 1950s.

and vertically integrated. The corporation as a whole, as well as each component, has separate boards of trustees. Competition on the basis of price, quality, and access is intense in most product lines. Product segmentation and marketing of services are necessary for survival. The role of government at all levels has expanded in terms of both regulation and reimbursement. The general public, patients, and special interest groups are more sophisticated and have higher expectations concerning health services. Pressure from professional associations and labor unions is increasing. Financial pressures are greater since cost-based reimbursement is being phased out. Capital requirements as well as the importance of the financial community have increased. Indigent care threatens the survival of some institutions. Medicare and Medicaid often fail to cover the direct costs of care, but cost shifting to private insurance has become more difficult. Most relationships between the hospital and its stakeholders are either neutral or negative, as indicated by the zeros and minus signs in Figure 2.

In summary, the number and diversity of stakeholder groups and their power vis-à-vis the health care organizations have increased, but the level of their supportiveness has decreased. Consequently, the pressures on hospital executives to identify key stakeholders and to develop appropriate strategies for managing them has increased.

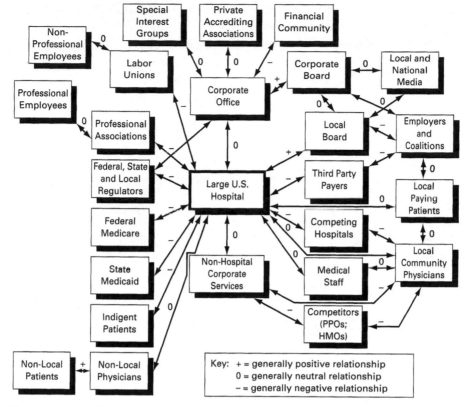

Figure 2   A Simplified Stakeholder Map for a Large U.S. Hospital in the Late 1980s.

Research Approach

Our research approach, the "Stakeholder Management in Action Study," incorporates both qualitative and quantitative data gathered in a systematic but exploratory fashion. These complementary techniques facilitated developing and extending comprehension of the stakeholder management approach for health care systems in general and for hospitals in particular. This method of data collection was designed to enhance the development of stakeholder management concepts and was not intended to be a complete description of all hospital stakeholders. Thus, stakeholder management theory is informed by these data rather than tested by them. In other words, this article presents both a conceptual *and* a limited empirical exploration of hospital-stakeholder relationships, including the identification of *key* hospital stakeholders, their power bases, and their stakes in various hospital management issues.

As part of the research, a survey instrument was administered to 16 hospital administrators at a symposium sponsored by a major university's department of health services administration in August 1987. The respondents to the exploratory survey part of this research included ten chief executive officers (CEOs), five assistant administrators, and one department head. The hospitals they represented were quite diverse in terms of control, type of hospital, bed size, system affiliation, and resource availability:

- Control—5 investor owned, 5 not for profit, 6 public
- Type of hospital—3 university medical centers, 1 specialty hospital, and 12 general hospitals
- Number of beds—3 with 1–99, 3 with 100–199, 4 with 200–299, and 6 with 300 or more
- System affiliation—8 free standing and 8 system members
- Resource availability—10 stable or increasing and 6 decreasing.

In addition to this pilot survey, qualitative in-depth interviews of 14 selected executives were also conducted in different regions of the country and in several types of health care organizations. These interviews averaged one and one-half hours each and were conducted primarily with hospital executives but also included representatives of health care vendors and insurance companies. These respondents included one or more of each of the following: CEOs, chief operating officers (COOs), vice presidents for marketing, as well as one or more directors of public relations or corporate services (e.g., services involving for-profit ventures and hospital-physician outpatient joint ventures).

Typical Key Hospital Stakeholders

While there is a wide range of possible stakeholders for hospitals, as previously stated, it would be unwieldy and unnecessary to consider all of these stakeholders. Some stakeholders are generally influential and powerful, others are only influential and powerful regarding certain issues, and still others lack influence and power. Hospital executives do not have time to consider all possible stakeholders so it is important for them to focus on the most important ones. Stakeholder influence can constrain management and limit strategic choices. Knowing the players is an important first step to understanding why health care managers behave in particular ways and how they can better manage their key stakeholders.

Assessing the Extent of Stakeholder Power

Table 1 shows the key stakeholders identified in response to an open-ended question in the survey. In addition to cataloging all of the stakeholders identified by the respondents, the first column shows the percentage of respondents listing each particular stakeholder. Power is an important issue for hospitals as well as for other organizations.[10] The second column indicates the total power score for each stake-

---

[10] W. B. Carper and R. J. Litschert, "Strategic Power Relationships in Contemporary and Nonprofit Hospitals," *Academy of Management Journal* 26:2 (1983) 311–320. H. Mintzberg, *Power In and Around Organizations* (Englewood Cliffs, N.J.: Prentice-Hall, 1983).

holder, defined as the number of mentions multiplied by the perceived degree of power. For example, if a particular stakeholder were mentioned four times and the degree of power (on a 10-point scale) were 8 in two cases and 6 in two others, the total power score is $(2 \times 8) + (2 \times 6) = 28$. The third column indicates the percentage of respondents—among those mentioned by at least 25 percent of respondents—who mentioned a particular stakeholder was increasing in power vis-à-vis the hospital. As to whether stakeholder or hospital power was increasing, the following responses were gathered: 63 percent said stakeholder power was increasing, 31 percent said hospital power was increasing, and 6 percent said there was no change. Clearly, most executives view stakeholders as increasing their power and influence.

While the survey data presented on this issue and the other issues should not be viewed as definitive in any sense, they probably *suggest* the identity of most of the key stakeholders and their relative influence. In addition, the findings are

Table 1 Key Hospital Stakeholders and Their Power as Identified By Hospital Executives (N = 16)

Key stakeholders identified	Respondents identifying stakeholder (percent)	Total power score	Respondents indicating stakeholder increasing power (percent)
1. Medical staff (IF)	94	124	40
2. Patients (E)	81	83	77
3. Hospital management (I)	50	65	62
4. Nonphysician professional staff (I)	56	58	67
5. Board of trustees (IF)	44	56	43
6. Federal government (E)	37	55	67
7. Corporate office (IF)	44	48	50
8. Nonprofessional staff (I)	44	38	27
9. Third party payers (E)	31	33	100
10. Elected public officials (E)	25	26	50
11. Political pressure groups (E)	19	15	—
12. Local business/industry (E)	19	14	—
13. Accreditation (licensing agencies) (E)	12	13	—
14. Medical school officials (IF)	12	12	—
15. Other hospitals (E)	12	10	—
16. State government (E)	6	9	—
17. Health maintenance organizations (E)	19	6	—
18. Media (E)	6	5	—
19. Labor unions (E)	6	2	—

*E = external stakeholder, IF = interface stakeholder, I = internal stakeholder.
— = less than 25 percent of respondents identified a stakeholder as increasing power.

consistent with the in-depth, qualitative interviews conducted with senior health care executives. The interviews also revealed one stakeholder not listed in the survey—the church organization (e.g., synod or diocese) or religious order—that clearly influences religious hospitals. This omission was due to the lack of religious hospital respondents in the survey sample.

The ordering of the various stakeholders in terms of their degree of influence should vary depending on the nature of the hospital. For example, the corporate office is only of moderate importance for the sample as a whole; however, only 50 percent of the sample hospitals were part of a multi-institutional system. For these latter hospitals, the corporate office was one of the two or three most important stakeholders. For the others, it was of no importance whatsoever.

As shown in Table 1, the medical staff and patients were the two most important stakeholders. Other key stakeholders included hospital management, non-physician professional staff, board of trustees, federal government, corporate office, nonprofessional staff, third party payers, and elected public officials. The majority of respondents felt that patients, hospital management, the professional staff, and third party payers were increasing their power. The implication is that hospitals will need to pay increasing attention to managing these stakeholders in the future.

This listing provides averages for all hospitals represented by the respondents and, therefore, does not represent any one particular hospital. Consequently, any one of the stakeholders identified by less than 20 percent of the respondents could be a key stakeholder for a given hospital at a specific time. For example, the media could become a significant stakeholder if a particular hospital experienced very high death rates in particular diagnosis-related group (DRG) categories while such data were being reported to the media by the U.S. Health Care Financing Administration.[11] The resulting negative publicity could adversely affect the hospital's image and its ability to market services in the local community.

Clearly, the process of developing a list treats stakeholders as distinct and cohesive entities. However, not all stakeholders can be so clearly identified. For example, the medical staff is actually a loose coalition of physicians that may split into several cohesive but competing coalitions on any particular issue. As Blair, Savage, and Whitehead have noted, factors that must be considered in assessing and interacting with stakeholders include both the potential for one stakeholder to form a coalition with another stakeholder and the ability of the representative to unify the members of the stakeholder group.[12]

Assessing the Sources of Stakeholder Power and Core Values

A discussion of the sources of power and the core values of the top ten key stakeholders identified in Table 1, derived both from the questionnaires and the in-depth interviews, is presented. Seventy-five percent of the respondents felt the

[11] M. D. Fottler, D. Slovensky, and S. J. Rogers, "Public Release of Hospital-Specific Death Rates: Proactive Responses for Health Care Executives," *Hospital and Health Services Administration* 32 (August 1987) 343–356.

[12] Blair, Savage, and Whitehead, "A Strategic Approach for Negotiating with Hospital Stakeholders," 1989, 13–23.

values of key stakeholders are at least partly incompatible with the values held by most hospitals.

The medical staff admits patients, controls the patient care process (including the use of resources), and provides the major services of the institution. The high degree of dependence of the hospital on these physician inputs makes the medical staff the single most important hospital stakeholder. In most larger communities, physicians are affiliated with several hospitals and may shift patients from one to another if their needs are not being met. However, the physician surplus in urban communities, which is predicted to increase over the next decade, has reduced the power of physicians. Now more physicians are competing for a stable number of medical staff openings. Hence, the physician-hospital relationship is best characterized as mutually dependent; hospitals are dependent on physicians for patients and patient care, and physicians need hospitals to practice their craft.

The core values of the medical staff as regards the hospital include high clinical quality (sometimes identified as the latest in high technology), convenient access for patients, medical training programs, adequate support services, and physician autonomy. The medical staff is not generally concerned with the requirements of external regulators nor supportive of internal administrative mechanisms to contain costs or enhance profitability.

The sources of power for patients include their ability to choose providers (physicians, hospitals, and ambulatory facilities) and their ability to influence other potential patients regarding these choices. Like the physician, they are concerned with clinical quality and patient access. Unlike the physicians, patients are also concerned with service quality (i.e., amenities) and low cost to them. Specifically, they are very concerned with containing those costs that directly affect them but are less concerned about costs absorbed by others.

Hospital management controls operations and influences or controls budgets. Values include cost containment, profitability, and institutional leadership. The latter value can cover a wide range of activities that may be compatible or incompatible with the values of other key stakeholders. Management's emphasis on cost containment and profitability often creates an "uneasy truce" among it, the medical staff, and the professional staff.

The professional staff possesses critical skills necessary to health service delivery. Different professional occupations are more or less critical in a given institution. Moreover, supply and demand in the labor market can also influence how much power a given professional group exerts in a hospital. For example, in the late 1980s, the shortage of nurses has enhanced the power of the nursing staff to obtain concessions from hospitals. Professional staff members are concerned with clinical quality, personal independence and influence, and an environment that is consistent with their professional ethics. They want to be treated as professionals.

The board of trustees is a key stakeholder due to its authority. The board alone possesses formal authority and control, may veto administrative proposals or decisions, and may discharge the CEO. The board usually represents a broad spectrum of influential citizens in the community and, therefore, is concerned with community needs identified by these board members. The board is also interested in increasing or maintaining the hospital's image, profitability, and overall effectiveness as judged by other influential individuals and groups.

The federal government is powerful because it regulates and controls reimbursement under the Medicare program and influences reimbursement under the Medicaid program. Major federal concerns are the hospital's consistency with federal regulations, cost containment, and patient access—particularly for uninsured, indigent patients.

The corporate office controls resources and may disapprove of individual hospital decisions that are not compatible with corporate goals or strategies. It is concerned with cost containment, profitability, and market share in the profitable markets. A high market share in an unprofitable market such as indigent care would not be viewed favorably.

The nonprofessional staff provides necessary services and influences patient's perceptions of the hospital on the basis of how well such services are delivered. Concerns of the nonprofessional staff include adequate salaries, job security, and job satisfaction. The nonprofessional staff is less powerful than the professional staff because nonprofessionals do not possess unique skills and are easy to recruit and replace. However, they could become more powerful if they become unionized, engage in strikes, or initiate work slowdowns.

Third party payers negotiate and enforce the rules regarding reimbursement for their insured patients. The power to deny payment and to reduce the income of hospitals is their source of power. Third party payers are concerned that reimbursements are based on an insured service that actually has been delivered. They are also concerned with expanding their own market. They usually accomplish the latter by meeting the needs of employers and employees for health insurance packages that cover desired services with a cost-competitive premium.

Finally, elected public officials exert influence in areas that affect them or their constituents. Since all hospitals receive some public funding, the threat to cut the budget of programs that provide such funding is a concern for hospitals. The funding threat is obviously greater in the case of public hospitals. Elected public officials are concerned with hospital service to their constituents, cost containment, and a positive community image.

A Suggested Stakeholder Assessment Tool Kit

Typical hospital stakeholders having been described, a managerial tool kit to facilitate the assessment in a specific hospital is presented with examples of three assessment approaches that can help administrators: identifying and clarifying key stakeholder relationships, analyzing the likely significance of certain issues for each key stakeholder, and ascertaining management responsibility for key stakeholders. The first method involves mapping a particular institution's key stakeholders, the second uses a matrix to link stakeholders with critical issues, and the third ensures that managerial responsibility for stakeholder management is clearly delineated. Taken together, these approaches permit hospital executives to be more proactive in assessing and managing their stakeholders.

Key Stakeholder Maps: Two Examples

While the key stakeholders identified by administrators in a variety of hospitals have been discussed, this did not describe stakeholders in any one particular type of hospital. Nor were key stakeholders in other types of health care organizations described. Space limitations preclude a depiction of all the possible permutations and combinations. However, the following two illustrations indicate how a stakeholder map for two specific types of hospital might look. These hypothetical figures, moreover, reflect both our data and the extant literature about these different types of hospitals. Mapping such key stakeholder relationships for a particular hospital helps management identify its most important stakeholders and the nature of their interdependencies.

Figure 3 illustrates some of the key stakeholders in a medical center that is supported partly by state funding. Key business strategies for such institutions often involve differentiation based on quality of care, physician bonding, and centers of excellence.[13] The state legislature provides some funding and approves appointments to the university's board of trustees. The medical center hospital is under the medical school administration, and the medical staff is composed mostly or entirely of medical school faculty members. In addition to state funding, the medical center receives funding from medical research funding agencies and from patients who are referred by hospitals and primary care physicians in the region.

On a particular issue facing medical center managers, coalitions among stakeholders may form because of their similar values or interests. In Figure 3, a coalition between the medical staff and the board of trustees is shown; it is a coalition that is likely to be powerful. The communication between these two stakeholder groups effectively bypasses the bureaucratic chain of command by "back channeling" issue-relevant information and, thus, activating this latent coalition. To display this likely coalition, the map has been modified by placing the stakeholders in rounded boxes and linking them with a wider arrow to show stronger ties than those connecting other stakeholders on this issue.

Figure 4 provides a key stakeholder map for a multiunit religious hospital. Key business strategies for this type of institution often include diversification, aggressive marketing, downsizing some units, and developing centers of excellence.[14] The church or religious order affects the hospital through its ability to approve trustees to the system board and the hospital board. In some cases, the church also provides some funding and becomes more directly involved in policy decisions. Since it is a multiunit system, the corporate office is a major stakeholder for each individual hospital. The corporate office approves budgets, strategic plans, and key executive appointments. It holds individual hospitals accountable for achieving particular corporate goals and objectives. Of course, the hospital also receives certain system services and functional directives, such as personnel policies and procedures.

---

[13] Coddington and Moore, *Market-Driven Strategies in Health Care*, 1987.

[14] Coddington and Moore, *Market-Driven Strategies in Health Care*, 1987.

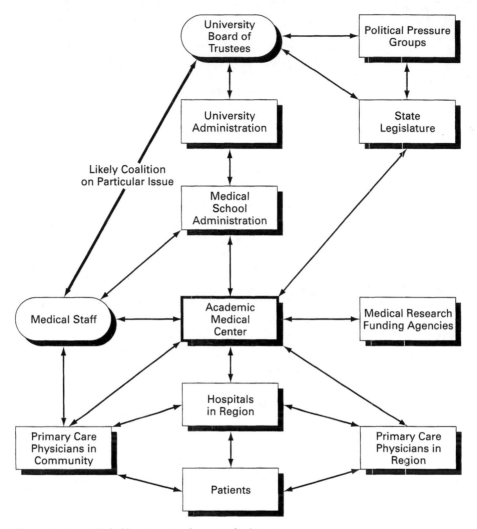

Figure 3 Key Stakeholders in an Academic Medical Center.

Patients are referred to the individual hospital through both community physicians and HMOs and PPOs. The individual hospital cooperates with other system hospitals through mechanisms such as joint purchasing agreements. They also interact with competitive, nonsystem hospitals both by competing for the same markets and by sometimes forming joint ventures. Joint ventures with members of the medical staff are also becoming more common.[15]

[15]J. D. Blair, C. R. Slaton, and G. T. Savage, "Hospital-Physician Joint Ventures: Two Dimensions of Success," *Hospital & Health Services Administration* in press. S. M. Shortell, T. M. Wickizer, and J. R. Wheeler, *Hospital-Physician Joint Ventures: Results and Lessons from a National Demonstration in Primary Care* (Ann Arbor, MI: Health Administration Press, 1984). I. Snook, Jr. and E. Kaye, *A Guide to Health Care Joint Ventures* (Rockville, MD: Aspen, 1987).

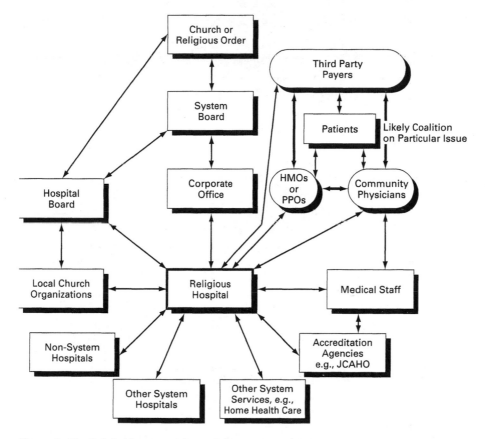

Figure 4 Key Stakeholders in a Multiunit Religious Hospital System.

Additionally, as in Figure 3, we have identified another likely issue-specific coalition using the same mapping technique previously described. Figure 4 shows that third party payers, such as employers, may seek to manage their health benefits costs by collaborating with local or national HMOs or by cooperating with insurance companies offering PPO arrangements. These managed care organizations may have, or may be seeking, contracts with community physicians that are key stakeholders for the hospital. However, the types of physicians included in HMOs and PPOs can affect hospital admissions either positively or negatively. As Greer has pointed out, physicians who are community specialists are much more likely to admit patients to one preferred hospital than are community generalists or referral specialists.[16] Thus, on an issue such as whether to contract with a given HMO or PPO, the hospital needs to examine both the membership of the potential stakeholder coalition as well as its power.

[16]A. L. Greer, "Medical Conservatism and Technical Acquisitions: The Paradox of Hospital Technology Adoptions," in *Research in the Sociology of Health Care IV* J. Roth and S. Ruzak, eds. (Greenwich, CT: JAI Press, 1986) 185–235. A. L. Greer, "Medical Technology and Professional Dominance Theory," *Social Science and Medicine* 18:10 (1984) 809–817.

Stakeholder Issues Matrices: An Example

Table 2 provides a stakeholder issues matrix for a hypothetical health care organization. In this hypothetical matrix, the ten key stakeholders discussed previously are listed with local business and industry, the media, and competitors. The degree of concern with issues ranging from offering a new service to the amount of financial return the organization receives would vary widely among these 13 stakeholders. None of the key stakeholders would be equally concerned with all issues, and executives need to keep this in mind when formulating and implementing strategies. Health care executives should identify the key stakeholders who would be most concerned with each particular issue, anticipate their concerns, take steps to alleviate those concerns, and manage the process of implementing changes with these stakeholders in mind. By using a stakeholder issues matrix, health care managers can be more proactive in anticipating and dealing with likely stakeholder reactions as well as likely coalitions of stakeholders with similar high levels of concern.

Health care executives need to be concerned with identifying and managing *all* of their key stakeholders who might have an interest in any of the issues faced by the institution. Blair and Whitehead have examined several factors, such as power, that affect stakeholders' potential for threat or cooperation.[17] This article has been concerned with identifying the sources of stakeholder power, their values, and the importance of different issues to various key stakeholders.

Table 2   Stakeholder Issues Matrix for a Hypothetical Hospital

	Issues						
Stakeholder	New Services	Truth in advertising	Patient death rates	Price policy	Clinical quality	Service quality	Financial return
Medical staff	2	4	2	4	1	3	5
Patients	2	1	1	3	1	1	5
Hospital management	1	4	2	2	3	2	1
Professional staff	2	2	2	4	2	3	4
Board of trustees	2	3	2	3	2	3	2
Federal government	5	2	1	1	2	4	4
Corporate office	2	4	3	3	3	4	1
Nonprofessional staff	4	5	4	5	3	3	4
Third party payers	4	4	3	1	2	3	2
Elected public Officials	2	2	2	2	3	2	3
Local business/industry	2	1	2	1	2	3	2
Media	4	2	1	3	3	3	3
Competitors	1	1	3	2	3	2	5

1 = critically important to stakeholder, 3 = somewhat important to stakeholder, 5 = not at all important to stakeholder.

---

[17] Blair and Whitehead, "Too Many on the Seesaw: Stakeholder Diagnosis and Management for Hospitals," 1988, 153–166.

Identifying Managerial Responsibility for Different Stakeholders

While the previous sections have shown the variety of stakeholders who have an interest in today's hospital, it would be a mistake to assume that the CEO or any other single individual manages all of these diverse stakeholders. Instead, the evolution of some of these organizations has seen the development of management specialists whose major purpose is to manage particular stakeholders. For example, in some organizations a medical staff director has the major responsibility for managing the medical staff. Nonetheless, others, including CEOs, are also available to help handle problems that are not routine.

Table 3 also reflects qualitative and quantitative data and provides examples of management personnel who might have *primary* responsibility for managing particular stakeholders. These are examples of health executive titles that may vary widely from organization to organization. Not only do titles vary, but the particular functional areas and the managers who are primarily responsible for particular stakeholders also vary. Thus, Table 3 furnishes some common titles for those managers who are often responsible for particular stakeholders.

Table 3   Hospital Executives Responsible for Particular Key Stakeholders

Key Stakeholders	Responsible Managers
Medical staff	CEO, COO, associate administrator, medical staff director
Patients	director of marketing, director of guest relations
Hospital department managers	COO, associate administrator, assistant administrator, product or service line manager
Professional staff	CEO, COO, associate administrator, human resources director
Board of trustees	CEO, COO, associate administrator
Federal government	depends on issue
Corporate office	CEO, COO
Nonprofessional staff	human resources director
Third party payers	VP for finance, reimbursement manager
Elected public officials	CEO, director of government relations, director of public relations
Political pressure groups	CEO, director of government relations, director of public relations, director of community relations
Local business/industry	CEO
Accrediting/licensing agencies	VP for risk management, director of quality assurance, appropriate department head
Other hospitals	CEO, COO
Media	director of public relations, director of marketing
Labor unions	director of human resources

Conclusions and Implications

Stakeholder management represents a new way of thinking for hospital executives. Given the importance of the key stakeholders for a hospital's overall business strategy, successful implementation of the stakeholder management concept should provide a hospital with a competitive advantage. Our research indicates a definite need for emphasis on stakeholder management by hospital executives. While most hospitals (75 percent) in our questionnaire study claimed to have an explicit stakeholder management strategy, the examples provided by the respondents indicated that most were ignoring the majority of their stakeholders and focusing on only one to three who they deemed of critical importance. The most common stakeholders mentioned in terms of explicit management strategies included the corporate office, the medical staff, and the board of trustees. At best, hospital executives' stakeholder management perspectives are incomplete, and their approaches to stakeholder assessment are underdeveloped and haphazard. At worst, they display a total lack of explicit awareness of, and involvement in, a systematic and effective stakeholder management approach.

The focus here has been on further developing systematic stakeholder assessment approaches. As indicated throughout, such an assessment is only one part of the overall stakeholder management process. In fact, stakeholder management cannot be effective without integrating it into still broader strategic management. In Figure 5, stakeholder assessment in this broader perspective is presented, including stakeholder's potential for threat and cooperation with a specific hospital. As noted previously by Blair and Whitehead, administrators need to diagnose key hospital stakeholders in terms of their potential to threaten or to cooperate with the hospital.[18] The current existing degrees of threat and cooperation for each key stakeholder provide the context for stakeholder identification in Figure 5. This identification includes the values and power of each stakeholder. The feedback loops show that this process should be constantly updated in the dynamic world facing hospitals today.

Stakeholder assessment both provides input into the hospital's business strategy and is affected by that strategy. Some stakeholders may represent either major opportunities for, or significant threats to, the success of the business strategy. Similarly, the hospital's strategies for managing its key stakeholders are influenced by its business strategy. The tool kit of key stakeholder maps, issues matrices, and managerial responsibility are all part of the stakeholder assessment process. Collectively, these activities should influence the implementation of the hospital's stakeholder management strategies and affect its subsequent efforts to increase the cooperation and lower the threat of the hospital's key stakeholders. If all goes well, when the administrator has gone through the entire process of stakeholder assessment and management illustrated in Figure 5, the subsequent threat to the institution from some of its key stakeholders will have been reduced and the subsequent cooperation on the part of other key stakeholders will have been enhanced.

---

[18] Blair and Whitehead, "Too Many on the Seesaw: Stakeholder Diagnosis and Management for Hospitals," 1988, 153–166.

Potential for Threat and Cooperation of Hospital Stakeholders

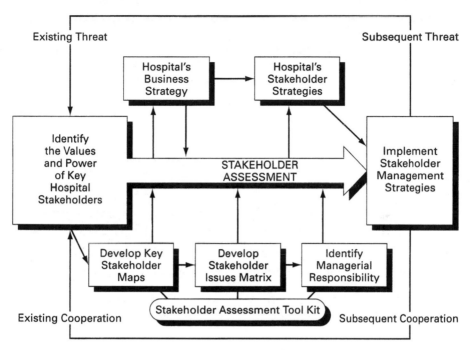

Figure 5   Stakeholder Assessment's Role in Overall Stakeholder Management.

The key stakeholder approach we developed, informed by the illustrative data presented, has some important managerial implications for hospitals and their managers. Clearly, all health care organizations should assess explicitly their key stakeholders as well as the major issues of concern for these stakeholders. Moreover, as indicated previously, managers must recognize that stakeholders are seldom either a monolithic entity or isolated from other stakeholders. Rather, hospital executives should be aware that many stakeholders are actually loose coalitions of individuals, groups, and organizations. Additionally, depending on the issue, disparate stakeholders may form powerful coalitions and make the assessment and management of such stakeholders a difficult matter.[19] For example, the formation of coalitions among groups of trustees and physicians is often a major determinant of many of the activities within hospitals.

Therefore, the stakeholder assessment process should be integrated fully into the process of formulating and implementing the organization's strategy. Each strategic decision should be examined in terms of the likely reaction of key stakeholders and should involve plans for gaining stakeholder acceptance. The management of a hospital's key stakeholders is ultimately the responsibility of the CEO.

---

[19] Blair and Whitehead, "Too Many on the Seesaw: Stakeholder Diagnosis and Management for Hospitals," 1988, 153–166. Blair, Savage, and Whitehead, "A Strategic Approach for Negotiating with Hospital Stakeholders," 1989, 13–23.

However, the day-to-day management of each key stakeholder should be the responsibility of a manager in the appropriate functional specialty.

The success in managing key stakeholders should be evaluated continuously, and adjustments in organizational structure or personnel made when appropriate. Managers should recognize that Who matters? and Why do they matter? varies in different types of hospitals as well as in different nonhospital health care settings. Equally important, the answer to these questions also depends on the specific issue being addressed by hospital managers.

––––––––––––

Peter Drucker has written extensively on private and nonprofit strategic management issues. He criticizes the Republican downsizers and Democratic reinventers here for focusing on changes that effective corporations make through an ongoing organizational commitment to "continuous improvement" and by "benchmarking." These changes, Drucker argues, are sufficiently routine so that they are handled corporately at the regional and local levels as part of a continuing quest for greater effectiveness and profitability (though he acknowledges that political baggage in the federal government accompanies some of these programs and complicates good management).

Rethinking Government

The most effective corporations succeed, Drucker emphasizes, by taking a giant step and periodically *rethinking* what they do, as conditions change, and as they expand. For example, while originally a capital goods provider, General Electric (GE) made a conscious decision to shift its focus from the production of capital goods to devoting an increasing amount of its attention to financial and medical services and to servicing the airplane engines it produces. In order to remain effective, large-scale organizations must simultaneously redefine *what* they do and *how* they do it—the two are integrally related. Organizations that merely continue to expand incrementally without re-examining their policies, goals, structures, and rules become outmoded. Attempts to change the rules and procedures without thinking about the mission, goals, and structure may make some marginal improvements—as the Reinventing Government movement did—but the effort, Drucker feels, amounts to little more than patchworking. As for the Republican emphasis on downsizing, he terms it "amputation before diagnosis."

Federal administrative agency *rethinking* must begin not with costcutting but with examining what the organization does well. Drucker asks: "Is this still the right mission?" "Is it still worth doing?" The worst cases, he observes, are those "programs and activities that are unproductive or counterproductive without our quite knowing what is wrong, let alone how to straighten it out." One of his examples is the welfare program. The favorite solution for dealing with such a malfunctioning program is to reform it, "but to reform something that malfunctions—let alone something that does harm—without knowing why it does not work can only make things worse. The best thing to do with such programs is to abolish them."

When programs are rethought in this manner, the main product of such an approach is "a tremendous increase in performance, in quality, and in service." Costcutting then emerges as a welcome by-product. There are exceptions such as the war on drugs, Drucker argues, which citizens view as a "moral imperative;" termination of such a program would be condemned as "immoral." Fortunately, such moral crusades in his view constitute only about 10 percent of federal domestic program activity.

Wrong Problems and Unachievable Goals

Drucker's insistence on simultaneously thinking about goals, mission, structure, and programs enables us to avoid what Frederickson has termed "the wrong-problems-problem," where difficult political and policy issues are redefined into management issues.[a] This policy failure is particularly tempting, since it allows politicians to avoid tough substantive choices, substitute optimistic promises for highly-touted efficiency innovations, and then bash the bureaucracy when the promises remain unfulfilled.

In numerous substantive areas, the public service is now bedeviled by failure at the federal level to set achievable goals. Goodsell describes the four-step process through which politicians pandering to the public establish such goals and then set up the bureaucracy for failure in such areas as stamping out drugs, eliminating AIDS, or ending the trade deficit. "Elected officials, political activists, and intellectual gurus," he writes, "delineate the 'progress to be made'." Then, after expectations have been raised, it becomes the bureaucrat's task to actually get us there. Consequently, "we (1) assume 'progress' is inevitable; (2) assign responsibility for progress to government; (3) expect insoluble problems to be solved; and (4) hand over the job of solving them to the bureaucrats."[b]

The fundamental difficulty in extending Drucker's strategic prescription from the private to the public sector lies precisely in the area of these seemingly insoluble problems confronting government at all levels. Drucker sensibly argues that goals cannot effectively be posed when we do not understand the nature of the problems an organization is expected to solve. GE can follow its corporate creed of abandoning those businesses where it fails to overcome its competitive problems sufficiently to become the number one or number two-ranked company in the industry. In the public sector, however, the public *expects* government to deal with the problems it identifies—not write them off.

Hargrove and Glidewell capture the resulting frustration in their discussion of the "impossible jobs" found today in the field of corrections, criminal justice, mental health, and welfare."[c] These substantive areas are particularly significant, since they are large and highly visible at various levels of government. They extend well beyond the 10 percent of federal programming that Drucker consigns to "moral imperatives." Criminal justice frequently constitutes half of the budget at the local level; corrections and mental health are two of the largest five budgetary items in most states; and welfare and related safety net programs for the poor are among the most hotly debated programs at the federal level despite their comparatively small

[a]H. George Frederickson, "George and the Case of the Reinventers," *P.A. Times*, Vol. 17, No. 1, January 1, 1994, p. 9.

[b]Charles T. Goodsell, *The Case for Bureaucracy*, 3rd ed. (Chatham, NJ: Chatham House Publishers, 1994), p. 77.

[c]Erwin C. Hargrove and John C. Glidewell, "Dimensions of Impossibility," in Erwin C. Hargrove and John C. Glidewell, eds., *Impossible Jobs in Public Management* (Lawrence, KS: University Press of Kansas, 1990), pp. 10–26.

size. A number of welfare critics would join Drucker in condemning what have in some cases been the program's deleterious effects on its clientele. Few, though, would endorse his recommendation to abandon the program, and thus in effect write off the single mothers and young children served by the program.

Missions, Goals, and Strategy

The public sector cannot afford the luxury of making its investments on the basis of where it can gain its best return, but it can benefit from Drucker's advice that the government *rethink* its goals more vigorously and more often in light of our changing knowledge about these problems. When he was governor of Wisconsin, Tommy Thompson rethought welfare, and made a national reputation largely on the strength of his successful model. It is unclear how adversely a recession would affect the new safety net, but that is an argument for rethinking again if and when that becomes necessary.

Strategic planning for the public and nonprofit sectors has gained a growing following even in the face of wicked problems. Where government's key decision makers have blended substantive and political rationality in their decision making, as Bryson has shown, state and local governments in particular have achieved marked success in utilizing a ten-step strategy change cycle.[d] Indeed, where strategic planning engages the public, the process can encourage realistic public expectations and thus more achievable goals. Policy makers in the state of Oregon, for example, now use a strategic planning process that includes university faculty and students to introduce new ideas into the public debate, analyzes benchmarks and other information to address outdated beliefs, involves a bottom-up approach that increases public awareness of the complexity and interrelatedness of the region's issues, and insists that every major research finding be linked to a recommendation and benchmarks that would help determine if the state is moving in the right direction.[e]

Experience with realistic strategic planning thus supports Drucker's argument for more strategic thinking—particularly at the federal level. He is on solid ground in arguing that not all programs are indispensable. Even Jacob Weisberg, who has written in defense of government, concedes that "in a healthy government, programs would not accumulate like junk in the attic. They would be sorted out in an annual spring cleaning."[f] Emphasis on continuous improvement and benchmarking is also to the point, particularly where government is compelled to deal with intransigent problems. Benchmarking is important, because, as Moran and Riesenberger have written, it "helps companies gain the knowledge of their relative strengths and weaknesses in essential business processes and core competencies."[g] Public agencies can learn such best practices from each other as well as the private sector. When criticizing OSHA for its approach to safety, Drucker himself thus pointed to the nuclear submarine program as an appropriate benchmark.

[d] John M. Bryson, *Strategic Planning for Public and Nonprofit Organizations*, rev. ed. (San Francisco: Jossey-Bass Publishers, 1995).

[e] Gerald R. Kissler, Karmen N. Fore, Willow S. Jacobson, William P. Kittredge, and Scott L. Stewart, "State Strategic Planning: Suggestions from the Oregon Experience," *Public Administration Review*, July/August 1998, Vol. 58, No. 4, pp. 353–58.

[f] Jacob Weisberg, *In Defense of Government* (New York: Scribner, 1996), p. 169.

[g] Robert T. Moran and John R. Riesenberger, *The Global Challenge: Building the New Worldwide Enterprise* (London: McGraw Hill, 1994) p. 94.

Really Reinventing Government

Peter F. Drucker

Vice President Al Gore's promise to "reinvent government," proclaimed with great fanfare in the first year of the Clinton Administration, produced only a nationwide yawn. (The similar promise made in the Republicans' "Contract With America," last year, initially met with no better response.) There has been no lack of publicity about the Gore initiative since. Press release after press release has announced the reinvention of yet another agency or program; big conferences, one chaired by the President himself, have been convened, and any number of TV appearances made. Of all the domestic programs of the Clinton Administration, this is one of the few in which there actually have been results and not just speeches. Yet neither the public not the media have shown much interest. And last November's elections were hardly a vote of confidence in the Administration's performance at reinventing government.

There are good reasons for this. In any institution other than the federal government, the changes being trumpeted as reinventions would not even be announced, except perhaps on the bulletin board in the hallway. They are the kinds of things that a hospital expects floor nurses to do on their own; that a bank expects branch managers to do on their own; that even a poorly run manufacturer expects supervisors to do on their own—without getting much praise, let alone any extra rewards.

Here are some examples—sadly, fairly typical ones:

- In Atlanta, Georgia, six separate welfare programs, each traditionally with its own office and staff, have consolidated their application process to give "one-stop service." The reinvented program is actually getting phone calls answered, and on the first try.
- In Ogden, Utah, and Oakland, California, among other places, the Internal Revenue Service is also experimenting with treating the taxpayers as customers and with one-stop service, in which each clerk, instead of shuffling taxpayers from one office to another, has the information to answer their questions.
- The Export-Import Bank has been reinvented. It is now expected to do what it was set up to do all of sixty years ago: help small businesses get export financing.
- The U.S. Geological Survey office in Denver is supposed to sell maps of the United States to the public. But it is almost impossible to find out what maps to order and how and where to order them, since the catalogue is carefully hidden. And the very fact that a map is in demand by the public all but guarantees that it will be unobtainable. It cannot be reprinted simply because the public wants to buy it; another government agency must order it for internal use. If the map sells well, it therefore immediately goes out of print. What's more, the warehouse is so poorly lit that when an order for a map in print comes in, the clerks cannot find it. The task force that the Geological Survey

Peter F. Drucker. *Atlantic Monthly*, Vol. 275, No. 2 (Feb. 1995) pp. 49–61.

created seven months ago to reinvent all this has succeeded so far in putting more lights in the warehouse and making a few other minor improvements. For the future, however, more-ambitious things are promised:

- The Department of Agriculture proposes to trim its agencies from forty-two to thirty, to close more than 1,000 field offices, and to eliminate 11,000 jobs, for savings of about $3.6 billion over five years.
- Of the 384 recommendations of ways to reinvent government identified by the Vice President in 1993, about half are being proposed in the budget for fiscal year 1995. If all these recommendations are accepted by Congress, they should result in savings of about $12.5 billion over two years.

But neither the trimming of the Department of Agriculture nor the Vice President's 384 recommendations are new. We have long known that a great many agricultural field offices are in cities and suburbs where few if any farmers are left. Closing them was first proposed in the Eisenhower years. And a good many, perhaps the majority, of Gore's 384 recommendations were made ten years ago, in the Grace Report, under President Ronald Reagan.

Nor is it by any means sure that all of these proposals and recommendations will become law. Mike Espy unveiled large cuts in the bloated USDA on December 6. But he had announced in October that he would be resigning effective December 31, and there is no guarantee that there will be someone at the top of the department committed to presiding over these changes.

Even if all of these proposals were to be enacted, the results would be trivial. The proposed Agriculture Department saving of $3.6 billion over five years works out to about $720 million a year—or around one percent of the annual department budget of almost $70 billion. A saving of $12.5 billion looks like a lot of money. But over two years the federal government spends $3 trillion. An annual saving of $6 billion—and this is many times more than Congress is likely to accept—would thus be a cut of no more than two tenths of one percent of the budget. Surely the only way to describe the results of Gore's efforts so far is with the old Latin tag "The mountains convulsed in labor only to give birth to a ridiculous, teensy-weensy Mouse."

Restructuring

The reason most often given for this embarrassment of nonresults is "resistance by the bureaucracy." Of course, no one likes to be reinvented by fiat from above. But actually, one positive result of Gore's program has been the enthusiastic support it has received from a great many people in the government's employ—especially the low-level people who are in daily contact with the public and are thus constantly frustrated by red tape and by such inane rules as the one that prevents their selling the beautiful Geological Survey maps, of which they are justly proud.

Nor is lack of effort the explanation. Some of the most dedicated people in Washington meet week after week to produce these embarrassing nonresults. They include the deputy secretaries of the major government departments. Vice

President Gore—an unusually energetic man—pushes and pushes. And the driving force behind the whole endeavor is the most knowledgeable of all Washington insiders, Alice Rivlin, formerly the director of the Congressional Budget Office, and now the director of the Office of Management and Budget.

These able people are getting nowhere fast because their basic approach is wrong. They are trying to patch and to spot-weld, here, there, and yonder—and that never accomplishes anything. There will be no results unless there is a radical change in the way the federal government and its agencies are managed and paid. The habit of continuous improvement has to be built into all government agencies, and has to be made self-sustaining.

Continuous improvement is considered a recent Japanese invention—the Japanese call it *kaizen.* But in fact it was used almost eighty years ago, and in the United States. From the First World War until the early eighties, when it was dissolved, the Bell Telephone System applied "continuous improvement" to every one of its activities and processes, whether that was installing a telephone in a home or manufacturing switch gear. For every one of these activities Bell defined results, performance, quality, and cost. And for every one it set an annual improvement goal. Bell managers weren't rewarded for reaching these goals, but those who did not reach them were out of the running and rarely given a second chance.

What is equally needed—and is also an old Bell Telephone invention—is "benchmarking": every year comparing the performance of an operation or an agency with the performances of all others, with the best becoming the standard to be met by all the following year.

Continuous improvement and benchmarking are largely unknown in civilian agencies of the U.S. government. They would require radical changes in policies and practices which the bureaucracy, the federal employees' unions, and Congress would all fiercely resist. They would require every agency—and every bureau within it—to define its performance objective, its quality objective, and its cost objective. They would require defining the results that the agency is supposed to produce. However, continuous improvement and benchmarking need different incentives. An agency that did not improve its performance by a preset minimum would have its budget cut. And a manager whose unit consistently fell below the benchmark set by the best performers would be penalized in terms of compensation or—more effective—in terms of eligibility for promotion. Nonperformers would ultimately be demoted or fired.

But not even such changes, though they would be considered radical by almost anybody in Congress or the federal bureaucracy, would warrant being called a reinvention of government. Things that should not be done at all are always mishandled the worst —and thus here we see the greatest improvements when attempts are made to do better what is already being done.

Any organization, whether biological or social, needs to change its basic structure if it significantly changes its size. Any organization that doubles or triples in size needs to be *restructured.* Similarly, any organization, whether a business, a nonprofit, or a government agency, needs to rethink itself once it is more than forty or fifty years old. It has outgrown its policies and its rules of behavior. If it continues in its old ways, it becomes ungovernable, unmanageable, uncontrollable.

The civilian part of the U.S. government has outgrown its size and outlived its policies. It is now far larger than it was during the Eisenhower Administration. Its structure, its policies, and its rules for doing government business and for managing people go back even further than that. They were first developed under William McKinley after 1896, and were pretty much completed under Herbert Hoover from 1929 to 1933.

In fact there is no point in blaming this or that President for the total disarray of our government today. It is the fault neither of the Democrats nor of the Republicans. Government has outgrown the structure, the policies, and the rules designed for it and still in use.

Rethinking

The first reaction in a situation of disarray is always to do what Vice President Gore and his associates are now doing—patching. It always fails. The next step is to rush into downsizing. Management picks up a meat-ax and lays about itself indiscriminately. This is what the Republicans and (as of last December) President Clinton now promise. In the past fifteen years one big American company after another has done this—among them IBM, Sears, and GM. Each first announced that laying off 10,000 or 20,000 or even 50,000 people would lead to an immediate turnaround. A year later there had, of course, been no turnaround, and the company laid off another 10,000 or 20,000 or 50,000—again without results. In many if not most cases, downsizing has turned out to be something that surgeons for centuries have warned against: "amputation before diagnosis." The result is always a casualty.

But there have been a few organizations—some large companies (GE, for instance) and a few large hospitals (Beth Israel in Boston, for instance)—that, without fanfare, did turn themselves around, by *rethinking* themselves. They did not start out by downsizing. In fact, they knew that the way to get control of costs is not to start by reducing expenditures but to identify the activities that are productive, that should be strengthened, promoted, and expanded. Every agency, every policy, every program, every activity, should be confronted with these questions: "What is your mission?" "Is it still the right mission?" "Is it still worth doing?" "If we were not already doing this, would we now go into it?" This questioning has been done often enough in all kinds of organizations—businesses, hospitals, churches, and even local governments—that we know it works.

The overall answer is almost never "This is fine as it stands: let's keep on." But in some—indeed, a good many—areas the answer to the last question is "Yes, we would go into this again, but with some changes. We have learned a few things."

An example might be the Occupational Safety and Health Administration, created in 1970. Safety in the workplace is surely the right mission for OSHA. But safety in the American workplace has not improved greatly in the past twenty-five years. There may be slightly fewer disabling injuries now than there were in 1960 or 1970, and to be sure, the work force has increased tremendously over those years. But considering the steady shift of the labor force from highly unsafe to fairly safe work (for example, from deep-level coal mining to the safer surface strip mining, and especially the shift from inherently dangerous manufacturing jobs to inherently safe office and service jobs), safety in the American workplace may actually have deteriorated since 1970. Such a result may mean that we have been going about the task in the wrong way. In OSHA's case we actually understand the problem. OSHA runs on the assumption that an unsafe environment is the primary cause of accidents, and it therefore tries to do the impossible: create a risk-free universe. Of course eliminating safety hazards is the right thing to do. But it is only one part of safety, and probably the lesser part. In fact, by itself it achieves next to nothing. The most effective way to produce safety is to eliminate unsafe behavior. OSHA's definition of an accident—"when someone gets hurt"—is inadequate. To cut down on accidents the definition has to be a "violation of the rules of safe behavior, whether anyone gets hurt or not." This is the definition under which the United States has been running its nuclear submarines. Anyone in a nuclear sub, whether the commanding officer or the most junior seaman, is punished for the slightest violation of the rules of safe behavior, even if no one gets hurt. As a result, the nuclear submarine has a safety record unmatched by any industrial plant or military installation in the world; and yet a more unsafe environment than a crowded nuclear sub can hardly be imagined.

OSHA's program should, of course, be maintained, and perhaps even expanded. But it needs to be refocused.

This analysis will consider a number of agencies whose mission is no longer viable, if it ever was—agencies that we would definitely not start now if we had the choice.

The mission may have been accomplished, for instance. An example is that most sacred of cows, the Veterans Administration's 171 hospitals and 130 nursing homes. When they first became accredited hospitals, around 1930, competent hospitals were scarce in the rural areas and small towns where many veterans lived. Today a competent hospital is easily accessible to a veteran almost anywhere. Medically, most VA hospitals are at best mediocre; financially, they are costly to the government. Worst, they are not neighborhood facilities, and thus veterans—especially elderly, chronically ill ones—sometimes have to travel far from their communities and their families just when they most need community and family support. The VA hospitals and nursing homes long ago accomplished what they were set up to do. They should be closed and the job contracted out to local hospitals and HMOs.

Or there may be no mission left. For example, would we now establish a separate Department of Agriculture? A good many Americans would answer with a loud no. Now that farmers are no more than three percent of the population, and productive farmers are half that (and "agribusinesses" to boot), a bureau at Commerce or Labor is probably all we need.

Some perfectly respectable activities belong elsewhere. Why, for instance, should a scientific agency like the Geological Survey run a retail business? Surely there are enough businesses around, map stores or book chains, to sell its maps. Or they could be offered in the catalogues of firms that sell outdoor gear.

Continuing with activities that we would not now choose to begin is wasteful. They should be abandoned. One cannot even guess how many government activities would be found to be worth preserving. But my experience with many organizations suggests that the public would vote against continuing something like two fifths, if not half, of all civilian agencies and programs. And almost none of them would win a vote—that is, be deemed to be properly organized and operating well—by a large margin.

Abandoning

Together the qualified yea votes and nays are likely to be awarded in any organization to some three fifths or two thirds of programs and activities. The thorny cases are the programs and activities that are unproductive or counterproductive without our quite knowing what is wrong, let alone how to straighten it out.

Two major and highly cherished U.S. government programs belong in this category. The welfare program is one highly visible example. When it was designed, in the late 1930s, it worked beautifully. But the needs it then tackled were different from those it is supposed to serve today: the needs of unwed mothers and fatherless children, of people without education, skills, or work experience. Whether it actually does harm is hotly debated. But few claim that it works or that it even alleviates the social ills it is supposed to cure.

And then there is that mainstay of U.S. foreign policy during the Cold War years: military aid. If it is given to an ally who is actually engaged in fighting, military aid can be highly productive: consider Lend-Lease to Great Britain in 1940–1941, and military aid to an embattled Israel. But military aid is counterproductive if it is given in peacetime to *create* an ally—a principle that Plutarch and Suetonius accepted as proved. Surely our worst recent foreign-policy messes—Panama, Iran, Iraq, and Somalia are prime examples—were caused by our giving military aid to create an ally. Little, if any, military aid since the beginning of the Cold War has actually produced an ally. Indeed, it usually produced an enemy—as did Soviet military aid to Afghanistan.

The favorite prescription for such programs or activities is to reform them. President Clinton's welfare reform is one example, as is the welfare reform proposed by the new Republican majority. Both are quackery. To reform something that malfunctions—let alone something that does harm—without knowing why it does not work can only make things worse. The best thing to do with such programs is to abolish them.

Maybe we should run a few—a very few—controlled experiments. In welfare, for instance, we might try, in some carefully chosen places across the country, to privatize retraining and placing long-term welfare recipients. Indianapolis Mayor Stephen Goldsmith has achieved promising results in this area. In health care we might try several different approaches in different states: for example, managed competition in California, home of the strong and experienced health-care wholesaler Kaiser Permanente; single-player health care on the Canadian model in New Jersey, where there has been support for it; and in Oregon rationing on the basis of medical expectations, which is now being tried for the care of indigents.

But in areas where there are no successes to be tested—for example, military aid—we should not even experiment. There are no hypotheses to test. We should abandon.

Rethinking will result in a list, with activities and programs that should be strengthened at the top, ones that should be abolished at the bottom, and between them activities that need to be refocused or in which a few hypotheses might be tested. Some activities and programs should, despite an absence of results, be given a grace period of a few years before they are put out of their misery. Welfare may be the prime example.

Rethinking is not primarily concerned with cutting expenses. It leads above all to a tremendous increase in performance, in quality, in service. But substantial cost savings—sometimes as much as 40 percent of the total—always emerge as a by-product. The main result, however, would be a change in basic approach. For where conventional policymaking ranks programs and activities according to their good intentions, rethinking ranks them according to results.

An Exception for Crusades

Anyone who has read this far will exclaim, "Impossible. Surely no group of people will ever agree on what belongs at the top of the list and what at the bottom." But, amazingly enough, wherever rethinking has been done, there has been substantial agreement about the list, whatever the backgrounds or the beliefs of the people involved. The disagreements are rarely over what should be kept or strengthened and what should be abandoned. They are usually over whether a program or activity should be axed right away or put on probation for two or three years. The programs that people do not agree on are the ones concerned not with results but with "moral imperatives."

The best American example is the war on drugs. After many years it has had little effect on substance abuse and addiction, and much of the effect it has had is deleterious. But it underlies the destruction of our cities in that addicts are prostituting themselves, mugging, robbing, or killing to earn enough for the fix that the war on drugs has made prohibitively expensive. All the war on drugs is actually doing, in other words, is enriching drug dealers and penalizing and terrorizing nonusers, especially in the inner city. But the war on drugs is a crusade. What lies behind it is not logic but outrage. Stopping it, no matter how beneficial, would be "immoral." The smart thing to do is to exclude such crusades from the rational analysis involved in rethinking. Fortunately, there are never a lot of them. As for the rest—more than 90 percent of all programs and activities—rethinking will in all probability produce substantial agreement.

Effective Government

Surely, it will be argued, even total agreement among highly respected people will be futile. Congress will not accept anything like this. Neither will the bureaucracy. And lobbyists and special interests of all persuasions will be united in opposition to anything so subversive.

Perfectly true: action on rethinking is impossible today. But will it be impossible tomorrow? In the last presidential election almost one fifth of the electorate voted for Ross Perot, the man who promised to get rid of the deficit by slashing government expenditures. A substantial number—perhaps another fifth—agreed with his aims even though they could not bring themselves to vote for him. Just now the federal deficit is declining. But even without health-care reform or welfare reform the deficit will again grow explosively. And then the demand for cutting the deficit may become irresistible and overwhelm Congress, the bureaucracy, and the lobbyists. If no rational rethinking of government performance has yet occurred, we will in all likelihood do what so many large companies have done—apply the meat-ax and downsize. We will then destroy performance. In fact, it is predictable that the wrong things will then be cut—the things that perform and should be strengthened.

But if we have a plan that shows how and where the government needs to be rethought, we have a chance. In a crisis one turns to people who have thought through in advance what needs to be done. Of course, no plan, no matter how well thought through, will ever be carried out as written. Even a dictator has to make compromises. But such a plan would serve as the ideal against which the compromises were measured. It might save us from sacrificing things that should be strengthened in order to maintain the obsolete and the unproductive. It would not guarantee that all—or even most—of the unproductive things would be cut, but it might maintain the productive ones. Within a few years we are likely to face such a crisis, as the federal budget and the federal deficit resume explosive growth while taxpayers grow ever more resistant to tax increases and ever more contemptuous of government and its promises.

In fact, we may already be very close to having to reinvent government. The theory on which all governments in the developed world have operated at least since the Great Depression (Harry Hopkins, Franklin Delano Roosevelt's adviser, called it "Tax and Tax, Spend and Spend") no longer delivers results. It no longer even delivers votes. The "nanny state"—a lovely English term—is a total failure. Government everywhere—in the United States, the United Kingdom, Germany, the former Soviet Union—has been proved unable to run community and society. And everywhere voters revolt against the nanny state's futility, bureaucracy, and burdens. The landslide in which California's voters last November enacted Proposition 187, abolishing health care and even free public education for illegal immigrants, is but one example. But the countertheory that preaches a return to pre-First World War government has also not proved out—the theory that was first formulated in 1944 in Friedrich Hayek's *The Road to Serfdom,* and that culminated in neo-conservatism. Despite its ascendancy in the 1980s, despite Ronald Reagan and Margaret Thatcher, the nanny state has not shrunk. On the contrary, it is growing ever faster. As the new Republican majority is soon going to find out, neither maintaining nor curtailing the nanny state is acceptable to the public.

Instead we will have to find out what government programs and activities in community and society do serve a purpose. What results should be expected of each? What can governments—federal, state, local—*do* effectively? And what nongovernmental ways are there to do worthwhile things that governments do not and cannot do effectively?

At the same time, as President Clinton learned in his first two years, government cannot opt out of the wider world and become domestic only, as he so very much wanted it to be. Foreign brush fires—in Bosnia, in Rwanda, in the former Soviet Union—have to be attended to, because they have a nasty habit of spreading. And the growing threat of international terrorism, especially if used as a weapon by outlaw governments, will surely require more government involvement in foreign affairs, including military matters, and more international cooperation.

By now it has become clear that a developed country can neither extend big government, as the (so-called) liberals want, nor abolish it and go back to nineteenth-century innocence, as the (so-called) conservatives want. The government we need will have to transcend both groups. The megastate that this century built is bankrupt, morally as well as financially. It has not delivered. But its successor cannot be "small government." There are far too many tasks, domestically and internationally. We need *effective* government—and that is what the voters in all developed countries are actually clamoring for.

For this, however, we need something we do not have: a theory of what government can do. No major political thinker—at least not since Machiavelli, almost 500 years ago—has addressed this question. All political theory, from Locke on through *The Federalist Papers* and down to the articles published by today's liberals and conservatives, deals with the process of government: with constitutions, with power and its limitations, with methods and organizations. None deals with the substance. None asks what the proper functions of government might be and could be. None asks what results government should be held accountable for.

Rethinking government, its programs, its agencies, its activities, would not by itself give us this new political theory. But it would give us the factual information for it. And so much is already clear: the new political theory we badly need will have to rest on an analysis of what does work rather than on good intentions and promises of what should work because we would like it to. Rethinking will not give us the answers, but it might force us to ask the right questions.

Now is the time to start, when polls show that less than a fifth of the American public trusts government to do anything right. Vice President Gore's "reinventing government" is an empty slogan so far. Yet what the slogan implies is what free government needs—and desperately.

P A R T

V

Managing the Resources of Public Agency Power

If public managers are compelled to exercise power and play a proactive, entrepreneurial role in meeting their organizational responsibilities, they must develop skill in drawing on bureaucratic resources. There are both external and internal sources available for exercising such power. Externally the public manager must develop skill in mobilizing the several kinds of political support and in utilizing the media. The time-honored internal source of power remains the budget, while the new kid on the block is information technology (IT). Contrary to popular stereotype, the primary challenge confronting the manager is not mastering the intricacies of computer software, but rather managing IT.

While striving to exercise power and bring about effective change within their own organizations, public managers must also develop strong relations with the individuals, groups, and institutions that constitute their external environment. It is the identification, development, and cultivation of relations with these critical stakeholders that constitute much, though not all, of the political part of the public manager's job description. Public organizations depend largely on these sources of support that are accessible only through the political environment. How do public managers proceed to find sources of support? And how do they proceed once the sources are identified?

Francis E. Rourke argues that an administrative agency may draw power from four sources: symbolic power, bureaucratic expertise, administrative statecraft, and mobilizing public support. Symbolic power stems from "organizational esprit" where enthusiasm for its mission (such as the Peace Corps during its early years) enables an administrative agency to "generate (support) for its functions from both those who worked for it and the community at large."[a]

Sometimes an agency's major claim to fame lies in its "bureaucratic expertise." For example, the military knowledge resulting in the Desert Storm victory resides largely within the Pentagon. Professional knowledge even on military matters, however, is now more widely disseminated within our highly literate society, Rourke points out in his seminal work, and the public's confidence in professionalism has declined in recent years. Nonetheless, an agency can still benefit significantly where it can put together the combination of "a highly technical body of knowledge that the layperson cannot readily master" and "the capacity to produce tangible achievements that the average citizen can easily recognize."[b] A number of agencies pursue this avenue because, contrary to popular stereotype, proportionally more highly qualified professionals reside in the public than in the private sector.[c]

Rourke acknowledges the role of leadership skills through a nice turn of phrase, "administrative statecraft." He sees leadership as of principal value in two areas of an executive's responsibility: first, "externally, in ensuring a favorable response to the agency from the outside groups and organizations that control resources upon which it depends," and second, "internally, in maintaining the morale of the agency's employees and their commitment to its goals."[d]

He argues that externally it is necessary to "mobilize political support" from attentive publics and the public at large, from the legislature, and from other administrative agencies and staff units in the executive branch. The Rourke selection included here deals with the extraordinary variety of relationships that agencies must establish, sometimes for better and sometimes for worse, with their more immediate publics and with the public as a whole. While the *examples* are drawn largely from literature on the federal government, the *generalizations* apply with few exceptions to the state and local levels and to nonprofit agencies.

The critical external relationship under normal circumstances is between the administrative agency and one or more of its key attentive publics (or constituencies). The attentive public receives goods and services from the agency, while the agency in turn gains greater legitimacy by meeting the constituency's needs. The relationship between the agency and constituency gains strength over time, and each becomes identified with the interests of the other. The relationship, however, is a dynamic one; it may function smoothly or go awry, depending on the political success of its stakeholders. Success also depends on the public manager's astuteness (or administrative statecraft) in selecting effective allies and in avoiding cooptation, capture, and some of the other dangers that Rourke identifies. He also describes the rise of the "PIG's" (or public interest groups), which are significant for the public manager, since they become an alternative, or additional, attentive public. They must be used with care, since they often lack the power of other "attentive public"

[a]Francis E. Rourke, *Bureaucracy, Politics, and Public Policy*, 3rd ed. (Boston: Little, Brown, 1984), p. 104.

[b]Francis E. Rourke, *Bureaucracy, Politics, and Public Policy*, p. 94.

[c]Frederick C. Mosher, *Democracy and the Public Service*, 2nd ed. (New York: Oxford University Press, 1982).

[d]Francis E. Rourke, *Bureaucracy, Politics, and Public Policy*, pp. 110–111.

competitors. For public managers who want to pursue significance, however, they provide another arrow in the quiver.

Rourke points out that the public manager's task is made more complicated by the existence not only of attentive publics and the public at large, but also of a "potential" public which may surface if, for example, a serious event occurs, a citizens' movement arises, or an issue within the agency's jurisdiction unexpectedly becomes salient for the general public. Under these circumstances, the public manager cannot anticipate the problem—the test lies in how that person reacts to such circumstances which may present opportunities, threats, or both.

Mobilizing Political Support

Francis E. Rourke

Although . . . expertise is a vital source of power for all bureaucracies, it is equally important, especially in democratic societies, for an administrative agency to command strong political support. In the United States, it is fair to say, strength in a constituency is no less an asset for an administrator than it is for a politician, and some agencies have succeeded in building outside support as formidable as that of any political organization. The lack of such support severely circumscribes the ability of an agency to achieve its goals, and may even threaten its survival as an organization. Norton Long writes: "The bureaucracy under the American political system has a large share of responsibility for the public promotion of policy and even more in organizing the political basis for its survival and growth."[1]

This entanglement with politics has been a prominent characteristic of American administration since the days of President Andrew Jackson, though it certainly existed before that time. The intrusions of politics came first from the political parties, eager to use administrative jobs as building blocks in constructing party organizations. After the Pendleton Act in 1883 established the Civil Service Commission, however, the ability of political parties to exploit administrative agencies in this way was increasingly subject to legal restriction. Slowly but surely, the principle came to be accepted that appointments to career positions in the public service should go to those who are technically qualified without regard to their party affiliation.[2] The parties were reluctant to accept this change, because they viewed access to the positions and preferments of bureaucracy as indispensable incentives for party workers and as necessary for the health of party organizations.

But even with this development, politics was by no means banished from American administration. American political parties did not always function effec-

Francis E. Rourke. *Bureaucracy, Politics, and Public Policy*, 3d ed. (Boston: Little Brown, 1984).

[1] Norton Long, *The Polity* (Chicago: Rand McNally, 1962). p. 53. The best study of the origins, structure, and operation of the oustide groups with which executive agencies deal is James Q. Wilson, *Political Organizations* (New York: Basic Books, 1973).

[2] For a careful analysis of this development over the course of American history, see Herbert Kaufman, "The Growth of the Federal Personnel System," in Wallace Sayre, ed., *The Federal Government Service* (Englewood Cliffs, N.J.: Prentice-Hall, 1965), pp. 7–69. For a more recent view, see Michael Nelson, "A Short, Ironic History of American National Bureaucracy," *Journal of Politics* 44 (August 1982), especially pp. 764–767.

tively as organizations for developing and supporting policy objectives, so that administrative agencies were forced to develop their own basis of political support, negotiating alliances in and out of government with a variety of groups that could be used to advance bureaucratic objectives or to assist an agency in fending off attack. The political neutralization of bureaucracy is impossible in a country in which the political parties are incapable of performing the functions expected of them in the governmental structure of which they are a part. When the parties do not provide for program development and mobilization of political support, executive agencies must perform these tasks for themselves, seeking support from outside groups that will help advance their policy objectives. It is noteworthy that legislation like the Pendleton Act excluded political parties from intervening in the affairs of executive agencies but left other political organizations such as interest groups free to become involved in agency decision making.

From the point of view of an administrative agency, political support may be drawn from three vital centers: the outside community, the legislature, and the executive branch itself. All these sources of political strength may be cultivated simultaneously, and usually are; or one may be nursed virtually to the exclusion of the others. The possibility of choice often calls for exercise of administrative statecraft of a high order to balance one source of strength against another, in this way building an enclave of political independence. Sometimes, however, no choice is possible. A state treasurer directly elected by the legislature cannot easily look elsewhere for political support. An executive budget office is, in most circumstances, politically captive to the chief executive it serves. If the executive does not choose to give it political standing, then it has none. These and other possibilities are examined in the pages that follow, as each of the various ways in which administrative agencies build political support is examined in turn.

Bureaucracy and Its Publics

Basic to any agency's political standing in the American system of government is the support of public opinion. If it has that, an agency can ordinarily expect to be strong in the legislative and the executive branch as well. Because public opinion is ultimately the only legitimate sovereign in a democratic society, an agency that seeks first a high standing with the public can reasonably expect to have all other things added to it in the way of legislative and executive support. Power gives power, in administration as elsewhere, and once an agency has established a secure base with the public, it cannot easily be trifled with by political officials in either the legislative or the executive branch.

Attentive and Mass Publics

Public support may be cultivated essentially in two ways. The first is by creating a favorable attitude toward the agency in the public at large. The second is by building strength with "attentive" publics—groups that have a salient interest in the agency—usually because it has either the capacity to provide them with some significant benefit, or the power to exercise regulatory authority in ways that may have a critical effect on the groups.

These methods are not mutually exclusive. An agency can seek to create general public support while assiduously building alliances with interest groups that have a special stake in its work. This is in fact the strategy most agencies follow, to the extent that is available to them. Actually, comparatively few agencies carry on functions that have high visibility for the general public. An agency like the FBI, which has been performing a dramatic role in American life for several decades, does command a broad pattern of public support that stretches through all strata of society. Part of this public standing may be said to spring from skillful use of publicity—agencies like the FBI exploit every opportunity to catch the public eye with their achievements. But the power of publicity is not boundless, even in America where good public relations are an obsession with every large organization, and an agency whose activities do not match the FBI's in intrinsic dramatic appeal will not equal it in public esteem no matter how assiduously it carries on public relations activity.[3]

There may be occasions, of course, when any agency may find itself basking temporarily in the limelight. The Food and Drug Administration may languish out of sight of the general public until suddenly the injurious effects of a new drug arouse public concern, as in the 1960s with thalidomide, a tranquilizer whose use by pregnant women brought about delivery of a large number of infants with birth deformities. Immediately, the agency and its pronouncements became a matter of front-page interest. For a brief period at least, it was an organization with a very extensive public indeed. Or a state air pollution commission, conducting its affairs in almost total obscurity, may suddenly find itself projected to the forefront of public attention by severe atmospheric smog. Or consider the Nuclear Regulatory Commission—on the front pages of every newspaper in the country after a nuclear accident at Three Mile Island in Pennsylvania in 1979. In the Reagan administration the EPA suddenly found itself the object of unwelcome publicity as the dangers posed by toxic waste became a critical problem in various parts of the country. An administration that had sought to downplay the importance of environmental issues quickly found that those issues were high priority concerns for large segments of the public. In situations of this kind agency heads may find that they have become celebrities overnight, with television reporters camped on their doorstep, and their every word recorded for posterity.

These illustrations suggest that many agencies have a potential public that far exceeds the size of their normal clientele. That it has such a potential public means that an agency carries on activities that affect the interests of a far larger group than the public that consistently identifies itself with its program. Both the food and drug and air pollution agencies are in the public health field, where agencies perform functions that are vital to a general public that may not even be aware of their existence. If events arouse the attention of a latent public, however, as the

---

[3] For analysis of the power of government publicity, see Francis E. Rourke, *Secrecy and Publicity: Dilemmas of Democracy* (Baltimore: Johns Hopkins Press, 1961); Delmer D. Dunn, *Public Officials and the Press* (Reading, Mass.: Addison-Wesley, 1969); Leon V. Sigal, *Reporters and Officials: The Organization and Politics of Newsmaking* (Lexington, Mass.: Lexington Books, 1973).

environmental and energy crises have done in recent years, an agency's image in the community and the legislature may suddenly swell in importance. To the extent that it is affected by shifts in the general climate of public opinion, administrative power may thus be extremely volatile, shifting, like a politician's, with changing tides of public sentiment, which Anthony Downs calls the "issue-attention cycle."[4]

Any sudden expansion in the public that takes an interest in its activities may be a threat rather than an opportunity for an executive agency. Its new following may include groups of organizations that are extremely suspicious of the way in which the agency has been carrying on its activities. The agency may thus come under a critical scrutiny it had never experienced, and it may soon find itself under strong pressure to change the thrust of its decisions. E. E. Schattschneider emphasizes that the outcome of the policy deliberations in which governmental actors engage can be altered by shifts in the size and character of the audience before which these deliberations take place.[5] A forestry agency may find that decisions on the use of public lands in harvesting timber that were quite acceptable to the lumber industry with which it has long worked are highly repugnant to environmentalists who move into the agency's constituency.

A study by Charles Jones of the national air pollution agency shows the kind of danger that a sudden and substantial expansion in its constituency can represent for an agency.[6] Between 1965 and 1970 the number of people who cared about air pollution jumped markedly, and these new constituents expected the national agency to do much more to solve the problem of pollution than it was capable of doing. Great expectations can thus be as threatening to an agency as public indifference. If these expectations are disappointed, they can quickly be converted into hostility.

Hence, it is essential to every agency's power position to have the support of attentive groups whose attachment is built on an enduring tie. The groups to which an agency provides tangible benefits are the most natural basis of such political support, and it is with these interest groups that agencies ordinarily establish the firmest alliances. Such groups have often been responsible for establishment of the agency in the first place. Thereafter, the agency and the group are bound by deeply rooted ties that may be economic, political, or social. From an economic perspective, the agency usually carries on activities that advance the material welfare of members of the group. The group in turn may supply private employment opportunities for employees of the agency.

Moreover, in return for the political representation with which the agency provides the group in the executive apparatus, the group ordinarily supports the agency's efforts to achieve a variety of its own political objectives, including its requests for financial support, its attempts to secure passage of legislation expanding its powers, or its need to defend itself against legislative proposals that threaten its administrative status. Finally, frequent social contact between the

[4]Anthony Downs, "Up and Down with Ecology—the 'Issue Attention Cycle,'" *The Public Interest* 28 (Summer 1972), pp. 38–50.

[5]E. E. Schattschneider, *The Semisovereign People* (New York: Holt, Rinehart and Winston, 1960).

[6]Charles O. Jones, "The Limits of Public Support: Air Pollution Agency Development," *Public Administration Review* 32 (September/October 1972), pp. 502–508. Cf. also his *Clean Air: The Policies and Politics of Pollution* (Pittsburgh, Penn.: University of Pittsburgh Press, 1975).

agency and the group breeds familiarity and friendship that help seal the alliance. The Smithsonian Institution through its Associates program and in other ways has been very adept at using social ties to build support for the agency. In its most highly developed form the relationship between an interest group and an administrative agency is so close that it is difficult to know where the group leaves off and the agency begins.

This identity between an interest group and an executive agency is strongly reinforced by the practice, especially common at the state level, of having occupational or professional qualifications as a requirement for appointment to administrative office. Under law, the members of a state real estate commission may have to be licensed real estate brokers, and similar requirements often prevail with other administrative boards having the power of occupational licensing in the states. In fields such as law or medicine, the state may virtually turn over a licensing agency to its professional constituency—to be used at the group's discretion for its own purposes.

Such arrangements merely give formal legal blessing to the common political practice of allowing interest groups to have a major voice in, if not veto power over, appointments to agencies that administer functions in which they have a vital stake. Legal support for interest group involvement in the affairs of administrative agencies may also come from statutes requiring group representation on agency advisory committees, or stipulating, as is common in agricultural administration, that the agency secure the consent of interest group members before exercising certain regulatory powers. There are also cases—administration of grazing on public lands in the West, for example—where individuals representing interest groups are given the power to enforce administration regulations at their point of application.[7]

Organizing a Clientele

Agencies that are not in a position to dispense important benefits or favors of substantial value to any segment of the community are in a disadvantageous position with respect to their ability to attract organized group support. The State Department is commonly regarded as having no "natural constituency" in the sense of clientele groups for which the department is able to do tangible and significant favors. Even though the fate of the entire population may depend on the effective conduct of foreign affairs, no strongly organized group structure in the outside community regards the department as "its department," and stands ready to defend and assist it in attaining its goals.

Even the State Department, however, has been able to identify a large number of groups with which it maintains close liaison on foreign policy matters.[8] And some of these groups can play a significant role in the conduct of foreign affairs. The International Longshoreman's Association has periodically refused to load commodities like wheat on ships destined for the Soviet Union and other Communist countries. For many of these outside organizations, however, the work

[7] See Phillip O. Foss, *Politics and Grass* (Seattle: University of Washington Press, 1960).

[8] See William O. Chittick, *State Department, Press, and Pressure Groups* (New York: John Wiley, 1970), esp. chap. 8.

of the department is of secondary rather than primary importance. Except for ethnic groups that have an intense attachment to their homeland, their interest in foreign affairs is something less than a persistent preoccupation.

Hence, in order to secure public backing on matters of major interest to it, the department itself has often had to resort to organizing outside group support. If the mountain will not come to Mahomet, Mahomet will go to the mountain. The organization by the department of a blue-ribbon committee of distinguished citizens to lead a campaign in behalf of the Marshall Plan in 1947 illustrates the department's success in establishing its own public support,[9] and this kind of stratagem has since been used by the State Department to accomplish a variety of other foreign policy objectives. A committee of prominent citizens was organized to support President Johnson's policies during the Vietnam War and was given the resounding title of Citizens Committee for Peace with Freedom in Vietnam.

The truth of the matter is that agencies in the field of national security affairs give a good deal of lip service to the idea of consulting with the public, but in practice this consultation commonly consists of getting groups of citizens together so that they can be indoctrinated with the official point of view. These national security agencies are much better at transmitting than they are at receiving messages from the public. Viewing themselves as having the best information available on the issues with which they deal, they communicate with the public not to obtain feedback that will be useful in shaping policy, but to structure public opinion so as to make it more supportive of their policies, or to prevent opposition from developing.

Executive agencies like the State Department can also be extremely adroit in organizing pressures upon themselves to which they seem to be responding, but which they are in fact initiating. The organization of such apparent pressure group activity thus provides a means by which these agencies can conceal their own central role in the policy process. The initiative appears to be with outside organizations, but the activities of these external groups are actually instigated by the agency itself. Of course, one risk an agency runs in following this strategy is that the mass opinion it is helping to create may eventually be a constraint upon it if it decides to change the policies for which it is currently seeking public support.

Critics of the State Department would argue that although the agency has been weak in traditional kinds of interest group support, it has been locked into or even captured by a peculiar community of its own—sometimes referred to as the "Eastern establishment"—an amorphous title that seems to embrace Ivy League schools, Wall Street lawyers, and international bankers. The members of this group have a journal, *Foreign Affairs*, through which their views are reflected, and an organization, the Council on Foreign Relations, that brings them together at meetings that generate solidarity in outlook. From this perspective the State Department is linked not so much to one set of interest groups as to a social class, whose consensus on foreign policy issues is mirrored in the department's decisions.[10]

---

[9] See Richard E. Neustadt, *Presidential Power: The Politics of Leadership from FDR to Carter* (New York: John Wiley 1980, pp. 38–39.

[10] Compare also the description of the American Establishment in Arthur M. Schlesinger, *A Thousand Days: John F. Kennedy in the White House* (Boston: Houghton Mifflin, 1965), p. 128.

Whatever may happen in foreign affairs, domestic agencies have always been quite adept at organizing an infrastructure of interest group support. The Department of Agriculture played a principal role in the organization and development of the American Farm Bureau Federation, the largest and most powerful of the agricultural interest group organizations.[11] And very early in its history the Department of Labor became convinced that the only way in which it could reach the wage-earning clientele it was obligated to serve was by encouraging the development of trade unions. Labor organizations provided an avenue for disseminating the informational material that was, in the beginning, the department's chief contribution to improving the welfare of its wage-earner clientele. The department had to communicate with its constituency, and, as it was to point out itself. "Freely as conferences with unorganized wage earners are welcome, official intercourse with individuals as such has practical limits which organization alone can remove."

Not only did the department thus defend its close liaison with trade union organizations; it also came, not illogically in view of the need to facilitate communication with its clientele, to support extension of trade union organization among wage earners. The reason the department gave for this support was that the growth of labor union membership would facilitate collective bargaining and promote industrial peace. "The absence of organization," the department stated, "means the absence of a medium through which the workers en masse can discuss their problems with employers. The denial of this organization is the denial of the only means of peaceable settlement they have." Of course, pragmatic considerations were also involved in the department's support of expanded trade unionism, including the fact that the strengthening of wage-earner organizations would increase the department's effective clientele and the weight of its political support.[12]

Perhaps the worst hazard an agency faces, when it deliberately sets out to establish an infrastructure of interest group support, is the possibility that, once established, these groups may break away from agency control, or even become a focus of opposition to it. The parent-teacher associations set up in conjunction with school systems at the local level generally are useful in providing citizen support for the education officials. But if these PTA organizations are captured by opponents of the educational system, as they have been in some areas in the United States, they provide a formidable vehicle for mobilizing opposition to school administrators—more effective, because of their organizational capability and the legitimacy that flows from their semi-official status, than any other resource at the disposal of critics of the educational establishment.

One major advantage that the support of interest groups has for an executive department is that such groups can often do for a department things that it cannot easily do for itself. In national politics, interest groups can take a position on policy questions that department officials secretly hold but cannot publicly advocate because it may put them in disfavor with the president. The outside groups that support each of the various branches of the armed forces in the Department of

[11] See David B. Truman, *The Governmental Process* (New York: Alfred A. Knopf, 1951), pp. 90–92.

[12] Francis E. Rourke, "The Department of Labor and the Trade Unions," *Western Political Quarterly* 7 (December 1954), pp. 661–662.

Defense have often given military officials assistance in precisely this way. Samuel P. Huntington writes:

> The allies and supporters of a service are at times more royalist than the king. They do not necessarily identify more intensely with service interests than do the members of the service, but they do have a greater freedom to articulate those interests and to promote them through a wider variety of political means.[13]

Although deference to their commander in chief may not permit military officials to disagree openly with the president when he cuts their appropriation or gives another service jurisdiction over a weapons system they believe to be rightfully theirs, no such restrictions prevent defense industries with which they have contractual relations from springing to their defense, or keep a backstop association, such as the Navy League and the Air Force Association, from vociferous protest against efforts to trim the appropriations or the jurisdiction of a military agency.

Outside organizations thus have a valuable role in enabling administrative agencies to oppose directives from the chief executive. They are also useful in helping these agencies evade legislative controls. Congress has enacted statutes designed to prevent administrative agencies from propagandizing the public in their own behalf, or lobbying in the legislature to secure passage of bills they favor. These laws are difficult to enforce, because administrative agencies are also charged with keeping the public informed of what they are doing, and the line between unlawful propaganda and legitimate public information activity is as fine as any distinction in the American political system. But agencies can always escape these restrictions by having outside organizations carry on such public relations or lobbying activity for them. Senator Barry Goldwater of Arizona observed that "the aircraft industry has probably done more to promote the Air Force than the Air Force has done itself."[14] This kind of claim could be made for a great variety of interest groups that identify and associate themselves with the fortunes of an executive agency.

There are other intermediaries that bureaucratic organizations can use in their efforts to shape public opinion. Agencies will often give information they want disclosed to sympathetic members of Congress and rely on them to perform the task of disseminating it to the public at large. Transmitting information in this way is a profitable exchange for both parties. Members of Congress attract public attention to themselves and enhance their own careers by generating news. The executive organization gets its message across to the public and in doing so ties congressional supporters even more firmly to its own cause, because they have benefited from their role as intermediary for the organization. Members of the Armed Services Committee in both the House and the Senate have often served their own and the Pentagon's purposes in precisely this fashion.

A friendly representative of the news media can perform the same function. An agency can "leak" information to reporters or allow them to identify it as coming

---

[13] Samuel P. Huntington, *The Common Defense: Strategic Programs in National Politics* (New York: Columbia University Press, 1961), p. 397.

[14] Huntington, *The Common Defense: Strategic Programs in National Politics*, p. 400.

from "anonymous" or "highly placed" sources in the agency. Again the transaction serves the interests of both the giver and the receiver of information. The agency succeeds in getting information disseminated to the public and the reporter or columnist obtains a highly prized exclusive story. Such relationships between secretive agencies like the CIA and friendly newspaper columnists are not uncommon in the United States.[15] An agency with secrecy as a distinguishing characteristic is in an advantageous position to give a reporter preferred access to a story.

The Captive Agency

The help an administrative agency receives from interest groups is not without its perils, however. The agency may come to lean so heavily on the political support of an outside group that the group in time acquires veto power over many of the agency's major decisions. In extreme cases, the agency becomes in effect a "captive" organization, unable to move in any direction except those permitted it by the group upon which it is politically dependent.

Administrative units that are especially vulnerable to domination of this sort are clientele agencies—public organizations established to provide comprehensive services to a special segment of the population. On the national scene such clientele agencies include the Veterans Administration, the Department of Agriculture, and the Department of Labor. Each has a long history of close association with and subordination to outside organizations representing its clientele.

We have seen that the Department of Labor was from its very beginning closely identified with the trade union movement. When it was first set up in 1913, the department was, as Samuel Gompers put it, intended to be "Labor's Voice in the Cabinet." Although this relationship was helpful in many ways, it also tended to narrow the scope of the department's authority. For one thing, the trade unions were allowed to exercise a great deal of influence over major department decisions, including selection of assistant secretaries of labor. This association with the union movement also made the department suspect in the eyes of other groups— employers, for example—and for a long time its jurisdiction over labor activities was limited by the reluctance of business and agricultural groups to allow the department to administer functions where its bias in favor of the trade unions might be disadvantageous to their interests. An agency makes enemies as well as friends when it identifies itself with a population group, because it inherits hostilities directed at the group with which it has entered into an alliance.

The submissive posture of a clientele agency toward its constituency is not, of course, a permanent genuflection. During the Eisenhower administration the assistant secretaries of labor were not chosen by the trade unions. Compared with other periods in its history, the Veterans Administration displayed a great deal of independence from the veterans' groups with which it is allied when it was headed by General Omar Bradley, a career officer with a distinguished record in World War II.

---

[15] For an analysis of the role of leaks in the relationship between executive agencies and the media, see Sigal, *Reporters and Officials*, pp. 143–148, and Morton B. Halperin, *Bureaucratic Politics and Foreign Policy* (Washington, D.C.: Brookings Institution, 1974), pp. 173–195.

Leadership by a vigorous personality may thus uncover latitude for independent action by an executive agency that previously had not been thought possible.

The tendency of clientele agencies to fall under the control of the groups they serve has often been used as an argument against organizing the executive branch upon the clientele principle. The contention is that executive agencies can be prevented from becoming the tools of political groups only if administrative tasks are divided on some other principle of organizational design. But in fact it is difficult to identify a principle of organization that will not engender a very close relationship between an administrative agency and the groups that benefit from the activities it carries on. In classical organization theory, the principal alternatives to clientele as a basis for allocating tasks among administrative agencies are the criteria of function to be performed, process or skill to be carried on by agency personnel, or geographical area to be served. Agencies organized by function, however, such as highway, welfare, or education departments, are also susceptible to domination by outside groups, as are agencies organized on the process or skill criterion—the Corps of Engineers, for example.

On organization by area, Philip Selznick's classic study of the interaction between a public agency and its environment—*TVA and the Grass Roots*[16]— clearly revealed a pervasive pattern of outside control over the foremost agency of the national government organized on the basis of geographical area, the Tennessee Valley Authority. In return for the support it received from important groups in the Valley area, the TVA proceeded to modify many of the original objectives of its agricultural program that were offensive to this constituency.

Of course, in its own defense, the agency could point out that the goals it modified were not vital to it, that its real concern was with its public power program in the Tennessee Valley, and if support for this activity could be obtained only by "selling out," so to speak, on agricultural goals, then this was an exchange well worth making. Selznick himself later conceded the validity of such a strategy:

> . . . the TVA purchased a considerable advantage with these concessions. It gained the support of important local interests and of a powerful national lobby. These defended not only the agricultural program but TVA as a whole. In this way, by modifying its agricultural program and certain broad social policies, the Authority was able to ward off threatened dismemberment and to gain time for the successful development of its key activity—the expansion of electric power facilities.[17]

Any public agency may thus find it necessary to yield control over a segment of its program to a significant interest group in order to buy the support of that group for more important policy goals. A state university may tailor its program of agricultural education to the needs of important farm groups, so as to obtain the support, or at least neutralize the opposition of rural groups to other educational

---

[16]Philip Selznick, *TVA and the Grass Roots* (Berkeley: University of California Press, 1949). For more recent studies of the TVA, see Martha Derthick, *Between State and Nation: Regional Organizations of the United States* (Washington, D.C.: Brookings Institution, 1974), pp. 18–45; Marguerite Owen, *The Tennessee Valley Authority* (New York: Praeger, 1973); and North Callahan, *TVA: Bridge over Troubled Waters* (South Brunswick, N.J.: A. S. Barnes, 1980).

[17]Philip Selznick, *Leadership in Administration* (Evanston, Ill.: Row, Peterson, 1957), p. 44.

activities in which the university may wish to engage. Some of an agency's activities may thus serve as "loss leaders"—activities which represent a loss or at least small profit from the point of view of an agency's major goals, but which simultaneously widen the basis of political support for objectives that are more significant to it. For a state university, its intercollegiate football program may represent just such a "loss leader." The support engendered by the achievements of its football team may quicken the allegiance of alumni and other citizen groups to the university in areas of science and culture far from the gridiron.

There is always the possibility that this kind of support will be purchased at the price of great damage to major institutional goals. Activities that are initially designed to be merely supportive may in time grow so large as to have wide-ranging and debilitating effects upon an institution's capacity to achieve its major goals. For the state university an agricultural school may dominate the image a university radiates to the outside world, and this reputation as a "cow college" may badly handicap its ability to attract faculty and students for nonagricultural programs. Or a football program established to win support for academic activities may eventually lead to some dilution in educational quality as standards are lowered in order to recruit athletic talent.

Goal distortion of a serious kind is thus always a possible price of constituency support. The worst instances have occurred in regulatory administration. At both the state and national level of government, agencies established to regulate particular kinds of economic activity have exhibited an extraordinary penchant for falling under the control of the groups placed under their jurisdiction. The regulatory agency thus becomes in effect the pawn of the regulated industry. This kind of relationship is a radical inversion of organizational goals, for the agency enters into collusion with the very group whose behavior it is supposed to control.[18] However, recent studies have tended to question whether regulatory agencies are really captured by the groups they regulate. In many cases, such as the FCC, regulatory agencies were set up at the behest of such groups.[19]

Although it is easy to censure this kind of collusion, a close relationship between a regulatory agency and the groups under its jurisdiction is often essential to an agency's achievement of its goals. The effectiveness of an air pollution commission may be enormously enhanced by including in its membership representatives of some of the principal industries responsible for discharging waste materials into the atmosphere. These representatives can help secure compliance by their firms with air pollution regulations—a consideration that is especially important when an agency has very little coercive authority and must rely mostly on voluntary compliance to achieve its regulatory goals. In its inception, at least, cooperation with the groups it is trying to control may thus be functional for a regulatory

---

[18] For an analysis of this tendency in regulatory agencies, see Marver H. Bernstein, *Regulating Business by Independent Commission* (Princeton: Princeton University Press, 1955), pp. 74–102. Bernstein argues that all regulatory agencies go through a "life cycle" in which capture by the regulated groups is a culminating phase.

[19] See Erwin G. Krasnow, Lawrence D. Longley, and Herbert A. Terry, *The Politics of Broadcasting Regulation*, 3rd ed. (New York: St. Martin's Press, 1982). For a more general critique of the "capture" model, see Paul Sabatier, "Social Movements and Regulatory Agencies: Toward a More Adequate—and Less Pessimistic—Theory of Clientele Capture," *Policy Sciences* 6 (September 1975), pp. 301–342.

agency. It becomes dysfunctional only when, further along in the relationship, an agency modifies or even abandons its goals in order to retain group support.

Generally speaking, in clientele, regulatory, and other administrative agencies, the tendency for capture by an outside group is greatest when an agency deals with a single-interest constituency. Here an agency has nowhere else to turn if the group upon which it depends threatens to withdraw its support. Diversification of support is as desirable for a government agency as product diversification is for a private business firm eager to minimize the impact that shifts in consumer taste will have if it sells only a single product. Consider the case of grazing administration:

> The Grazing Service suffered because of its rather complete dependence on stockmen and those who spoke for them in Congress. By merging the Service into an expanded Bureau of Land Management, an act accomplished with the aid of interests adversely affected under the previous arrangement, the new organization has reduced its dependence by being able to appeal to a broader constituency.[20]

Of course, if diversification brings into an agency's constituency groups that are weak or unpopular, then its net effect may be harmful. The Social Security Administration was certainly not strengthened when it was given jurisdiction over the Supplemental Security Insurance program and impoverished groups were added to its clientele.

In any case, the heterogeneity of an administrative agency's group support thus seems to be more important in determining its freedom of action than the question of whether it is organized on the basis of clientele, purpose, process, or area to be served. The design of its political system, rather than its organizational structure, is the critical consideration.

For all agencies it is highly important to keep abreast of changes in the structure of interests affected by the activities they carry on. Huntington traces the administrative decline of the Interstate Commerce Commission to the failure of the agency to develop support among the new transportation interests that grew in the twentieth century out of technological change—the truckers, the water carriers, and the airlines. Instead, the agency tied itself to the railroads—a declining industry whose excesses it had been originally created to curb in the nineteenth century but which it now spent more and more of its time trying to resuscitate. "The ICC," Huntington says, "has not responded to the demands of the new forces in transportation. . . . Consequently, it is losing its leadership to those agencies that are more responsive to the needs and demands of the times.[21] The establishment of the Department of Transportation in the 1960s as the major transportation agency of the national government provided striking confirmation of this argument.[22]

---

[20]Aaron Wildavsky, *The Politics of the Budgetary Process*, 3rd ed. (Boston: Little, Brown, 1979), p. 172.

[21]Samuel P. Huntington, "The Marasmus of the I.C.C.: The Commission, The Railroads, and the Public Interest," *Yale Law Journal* 61 (April 1952), pp. 472–473.

[22]For an analysis of this development, see Emmette S. Redford and Marlan Blissett, *Organizing the Executive Branch: The Johnson Presidency* (Chicago: University of Chicago Press, 1981), pp. 46–76.

Public Interest Groups

The relationships described here between executive agencies and their constituencies have long presented American democracy with some of its most perplexing problems. At its best this interaction enhances the representative character of government. Agencies serve as advocates for major community groups and in this way ensure that the interests of these groups are not neglected when governmental decisions are being made. Although legislators represent citizens grouped in geographic localities, administrative agencies usually represent them in their productive role in society—in a variety of professions and occupations and in innumerable subcategories of activity in the broad fields of business, agriculture, and labor.

Viewed in this way, the executive branch provides a system of representation based on economic and social role, supplementing the territorial representation furnished by Congress and other legislative bodies.[23] This system might be criticized as redundant on the grounds that the executive is performing a task that the legislature already carries on. But it is doing so in a different way—representing people by what they do rather than where they live. At the least, this is a useful sort of redundancy, because it sensitizes and more finely tunes the governmental apparatus to the intensity and variety of citizen concerns and needs.[24] Matthew Holden argues that it is in the interest of agencies to seek out groups that are not presently part of any executive constituency, because these new groups can add to an agency's administrative strength and security.[25] In this way the selfish interest of agencies in expanding their constituency coincides with the public interest in having the government be as inclusive as possible in performing its representational role.

But there is a dark side also to the intimacy between agencies and their publics, and it has been starkly drawn.[26] At its worst—in the captive-agency phenomenon already discussed—the relationship degenerates into the transfer of public authority to private groups that use it to advance their own interests at the expense of the general public. An executive agency then becomes simply the governmental outpost of an enclave of private power—able to exercise its public authority only at the sufferance of private groups. A result may be total neglect of the public interest in administrative decision making, and underrepresentation of groups in society that are too weak to compel an executive agency to heed their complaints.

One of the most important developments in American politics has been the rise to power in recent years of public interest organizations—groups like Common Cause and the cluster of reform organizations sponsored if not actually managed by

[23] For an interesting discussion of the executive role in representation, see Roger H. Davidson, "Congress and the Executive: The Race for Representation," in Alfred DeGrazia, coord., *Twelve Studies of the Organization of Congress* (Washington, D.C.: American Enterprise Institute, 1966).

[24] For a compelling argument on behalf of redundancy in the design and operation of governmental institutions, see Martin Landau, "Redundancy, Rationality, and the Problem of Duplication and Overlap," *Public Administration Review* 29 (July/August 1969), pp. 346–358.

[25] Matthew Holden, "'Imperialism' in Bureaucracy," *American Political Science Review* 60 (December 1966), pp. 943–951.

[26] The disadvantageous aspects of this relationship are clearly spelled out in Grant McConnell, *Private Power and American Democracy* (New York: Alfred A. Knopf, 1966), and Theodore J. Lowi, *The End of Liberalism*, rev. ed. (New York: W. W. Norton, 1979).

Ralph Nader. Although much of their activity has been directed at the legislature, they have also been extremely important in monitoring the activities of executive agencies. Spokesmen for public interest groups have criticized the preferential treatment agencies often give to powerful private groups, and pressured them to expand their conception of their clientele to include the public at large and disadvantaged groups whose needs have been previously neglected in administrative decision making.

One major development in modern American society to which the rise of public interest groups testifies is the increasing ability of citizens affected by the exercise of administrative power to mobilize in their own defense. Recent decades have seen the multiplication of citizen groups designed to offset the power of bureaucratic organizations. Most of the new citizen associations aim to speak for interests not previously represented or grossly underrepresented in political decision making. A variety of new environmental groups have sprung up, older citizens are now represented by their own lobbying organizations, and the women's movement has acquired a new power and effectiveness. The roster of new citizen organizations and of established citizen groups "reborn" in some sense is a long one. A study of public interest groups in modern American society shows that 63 percent have been established since 1960.[27]

The influence that such citizen or public interest organizations have been able to exert over executive agencies stems in no small measure from their ability to arouse the indignation and rally the support of their followers through the media of mass communication. The news media have been tremendously important in the ascending power of public interest organizations.[28] They provide an avenue through which an alleged misuse of administrative power can be quickly and widely publicized. Moreover, investigative reporters often work together with public interest organizations to expose misconduct in office, whether by an agency like the FTC that is felt to be insufficiently vigilant in enforcing consumer protection legislation,[29] or a water resource agency like the Corps of Engineers that is charged by conservationists with neglecting environmental interests in constructing dams, dredging harbors, and other activities.[30]

In assessing these efforts to push executive agencies toward responsiveness to a broader public we must realize that the administration of a good many governmental functions demands a narrowness in perspective on the part of an executive agency. A public agency charged with administering a program of assistance for

[27] Jeffrey M. Berry, *Lobbying for the People: The Political Behavior of Public Interest Groups* (Princeton: Princeton University Press, 1977), p. 34. Jack L. Walker presents a comprehensive survey of the birth of interest groups in the United States in "The Origins and Maintenance of Interest Groups in America," *American Political Science Review* 77 (June 1983), pp. 390–406.

[28] However, these groups seemed much less influential in the early years of the Reagan administration than had earlier been the case. See, in this regard Hugh Heclo, "One Executive Branch or Many?" in Anthony King, ed., *Both Ends of the Avenue: The Presidency, the Executive Branch, and Congress in the 1980s* (Washington, D.C.: American Enterprise Institute, 1983), pp. 26–58.

[29] Edward Cox, Robert Fellmeth, and John Schulz, *The Nader Report on the Federal Trade Commission* (New York: Grove Press, 1970). There are a great many task force reports by Nader study groups on other executive agencies, including the National Institute of Mental Health, the U.S. Forest Service, and the Interstate Commerce Commission.

[30] See Walter A. Rosenbaum, *The Politics of Environmental Concern* (New York: Praeger, 1973), esp. pp. 172–189.

the handicapped will be expected to give priority and preference to the needs of its special clientele. Such specialization in viewpoint would not ordinarily be regarded as inconsistent with the pursuit of the public interest. Moreover, it can be argued that competition within the executive branch from a variety of agencies advocating support for special groups is a necessary part of the entire process through which the public interest can ultimately be determined.

Perhaps the most important function that public interest groups perform is to provide the reform impulse with a continuing presence in the governmental process. In a celebrated analysis of political "quiescence," Murray Edelman argues that reformers have traditionally tended to be satisfied with merely symbolic rewards for their political efforts.[31] They tend to lose interest in politics once they have succeeded in establishing a regulatory agency, because this achievement gives them a false sense that the public is now being protected against exploitation. A typical result of this dissipation of reform energy is that the agency's decisions become more and more sympathetic to the regulated groups with which it is dealing continuously. With the rise of public interest groups, however, the reform spirit may be said to have become permanently institutionalized. Under the watchful eye of these groups, the day-to-day decisions of regulatory agencies can be made to correspond much more closely with the public interest, and reformers may begin to obtain more than a merely symbolic return on their investment in political activity.

In at least one important respect the perspective of many public interest organizations differs sharply from that of traditional interest groups. In their attitudes toward the work of administrative agencies, many public interest groups like Common Cause tend to be "process-oriented"—to have a high-minded interest in the procedures agencies follow rather than the policies they carry out. Thus, these public interest groups lobbied strongly and successfully for freedom of information laws designed to open up the proceedings of administrative agencies to public scrutiny. Traditional interest groups are much less interested in the character of the procedures agencies follow than they are in whether agency decisions, however arrived at, benefit or contribute to their own needs and welfare. Hence, they may work harder at influencing an agency's day-to-day decisions on policy, while the attention of public interest groups is focused on the agency's procedures.

Kelly Rossman-McKinney and R. Dee Woell are skilled practitioners in linking public agencies to the media. While their observations are based on their experience in Michigan, public managers in other jurisdictions will have little difficulty recognizing comparable examples in their own jurisdictions. In an essay written especially for this volume, the authors make a persuasive case that effective public relations is as important for public as for corporate managers.

---

[31]Murray Edelman, *The Symbolic Uses of Politics* (Urbana: University of Illinois Press, 1964).

It is thus a myth, Rossman-McKinney and Woell contend, that public managers do not need a public relations (PR) plan. Furthermore, much of what constitutes good PR is good public administration. Particularly at the local and state levels, administrative agencies are often engaged in delivering services. The political appointee heading such an agency and planning to run for higher office knows that it is vital to "deliver the goods" both literally and figuratively, and that voters will hold him or her accountable for how well the agency performs.

Rossman-McKinney and Woell's description of the PR plan designed to alter the performance of Michigan's Department of Motor Vehicles (DMV) demonstrates that such a strategy must sometimes delve deep into an agency's organizational culture. The novel approach of strengthening DMV by keeping the customer out of the branch office and doing business as much as possible through fax, mail, and the Internet is nothing less than a new strategic plan for the agency. Such dramatic changes are not always necessary, but, whatever it takes, the authors show that effective PR is fundamentally an exercise in good public management. When an agency such as the DMV is in serious trouble, the necessary PR corrective steps are an integral part of what Peter Drucker called strategic *rethinking*.

Image Management

Once an agency has a clear sense of what it is doing and why, the question becomes when and how best to communicate that message to the public. As Rossman-McKinney and Woell show, that task is more challenging because "the public sector is different from the private sector in one critical regard, and that is the political environment in which everyone in the public sector operates. Whether working in the legislative, executive or judicial branch, politics lies at the very core of every agency and every job." Small wonder that the authors argue that it is a myth to think that any fool can do PR.

Image management thus becomes important, and specialists in any large public agency now confer and work with public managers on a continuing basis in communicating critical issues to the public. Rossman-McKinney and Woell contrast advertising—conveying a specific message to a specific audience at a specific time—with public relations and its focus on "the long-term image and how to build, strengthen and maintain that image." Such image building is closely tied to what they call "the eight C's of communication."[a] The body of the article consists of the whys and wherefores of the messenger's credibility, message content, message context, consistency and continuity, communication channels, audience capability, customer benefits, and the all-important call to action.

Almost every public manager whose job involves media contact can relate some horror story about having been misquoted or having had an idea distorted in a media story. The natural reaction after such a negative experience is to pull back—to become what Phyllis Kaniss calls a "paranoid media-avoider."[b] The mistakes are inevitable, since busy print and television reporters have deadlines to meet, and little time—and sometimes little inclination—to massage their stories. Rarely, however, does a mistake in coverage of an individual story make much of an impact. Rossman-McKinney and Woell emphasize that the bottom line is the pattern of

---

[a]Seven of these eight C's are drawn from Scott M. Cutlip, Allen H. Center, and Glen M. Broom, *Effective Public Managers*, 6th ed. (Englewood Cliffs, NJ: Prentice-Hall, 1985), pp. 283–285.

[b]Phyllis Kaniss, *Making Local News* (Chicago: University of Chicago Press, 1991), pp. 170–171.

media coverage over time—the long-term image—established by the public manager that is potentially of critical importance for the leader, for the programs and regulations at issue, and for the administrative agency's image as a whole. To insure that the message in a particular PR campaign is working, the authors emphasize the importance of measuring first through focus groups and then through surveys. The more rigorous such measurements, the better. Gone are the days when the advertising guru made seat-of-the-pants judgements on such critical questions. Emphasis on accurate assessment is in part what the authors mean by the science of the PR profession.

The art lies largely in what is perhaps the most challenging part of communicating an effective agency or program image, namely, becoming skilled in the use of symbols. This is a talent useful in politics and administration generally, but it is most visible in relation to the media. Deborah Stone, a noted political scientist, observes that we talk about policy problems in words, but those "words are used to represent things." A symbol then is

> anything that stands for something else. Its meaning depends on how people interpret it, use it, or respond to it. It can be an object, a person, a place, a word, a song, an event, even a logo on a T-shirt. The meaning of a symbol is not intrinsic to it, but is invested in it by the people who use it. In that sense sense, symbols are collectively created.[c]

Meeting the media need for good backdrops, usable sound bites, and "sexy stories" often entails skillful symbol manipulation by the public manager, usually with the advice and consent of the PR advisor.

Media coverage is important for public managers both as a means of communicating with their stakeholders and with the public at large. Their relationship with the media is much like their symbiotic relationship with other key stakeholders. Not every administrative agency enters into the relationship with the same potential for media success—any public manager would prefer to announce the award of a highway beautification grant rather than the location of a toxic waste site. The media will sometimes be an opportunity and other times an impediment. The assertion of leadership by public managers may well determine which it will be.

Why Public Relations Is Important Even to Public Administrators

Kelly Rossman-McKinney, A.P.R. and R. Dee Woell, D.P.A.

Introduction

The First Myth—*Why Bother?*

There are two great public relations (PR) myths in the public sector. The first is that public managers do not need a PR plan. After all, when you operate a monopoly like governmental services, good communication is irrelevant. Where else can someone obtain a driver license, except through the Department of Motor Vehicles?

---

[c]Deborah A. Stone, *Policy Paradox and Political Reason* (Glenview, IL: Scott, Foresman, 1988), p. 108.

The horror stories abound. There are whole lists of agencies that have, in the past, succumbed to their own bad publicity to the point where the term "going postal" has entered the common lexicon. The Department of Natural Resources which issues hunting licenses, the Department of Transportation which handles road repair, the Social Security Administration which handles your money, all have the customer at their mercy—or so it seems.

Recently, there has been some softening of this position. The threat of privatization and competition have led to a "kinder, gentler" postal service. The requirement that the U.S. Postal Service operate at a profit has raised stamp prices while at the same time raising awareness among management that they are not the only service out there.

Even the Internal Revenue Service is working to humanize its image. Did you read the letter from the IRS Commissioner in the inside of your federal tax booklet? Neither did we, but we understand that it was intended to persuade us that the IRS is serious about improving customer satisfaction. The reason? The IRS has something it wants to sell us. It wants more people to file electronically, or at least use electronic software. Electronic filing involves considerably less work for the IRS and decreases the number of simple filing errors.

This change in the old "you do it our way, or else" mentality is occurring for several reasons. One is that more and more agencies are headed by bureaucrats and elected officials who come from the private sector. More are finding that a business plan, evaluation and good public relations pay off for their organization's bottom line. And, yes, there is a bottom line. Public funds are less and less available; increased technological services, increased customer demands, and increasingly knowledgeable, organized and vocal constituency groups all require astute business management.

Secondly, public officials are being held more accountable for performance. Elected officials need votes to survive. Customer satisfaction with government services translates directly into votes.

A simple example of how times are changing. The Michigan Secretary of State collects almost a billion and a half dollars in revenue a year. After two former Secretaries of State had been in office a combined total of 44 years, a new Secretary was elected. She found that within the almost 200 branch offices that issued all of the driver licenses, I.D. cards, and vehicle registrations for millions of Michigan residents each year, none had a copier or fax machine. Branch managers had to go to local copy services. If a customer forgot his or her proof of insurance, the person had to leave, obtain a copy and return to stand in line again.

Most branch offices were understaffed, and limited in space and equipment. Staff were required to stand at counters all day. You tend to get grumpy when your feet hurt. Almost all transactions had to occur at a branch office. Transaction quotas were a mainstay. Some, like voter registrations or changes of address, generate no revenue and so did not count in the daily totals—another great incentive for being grumpy if a customer is "wasting your time."

Yet, the branch office is the face of the Department of State—the first and perhaps only contact millions of Michiganians have with the Department each year.

The answer was a novel approach. The initiative is to keep the customer out of the branch office by allowing business through fax, mail and the Internet. At the same time, even as the number of customers is expected to drop, branch office services are enhanced. That means updated computer equipment, taxes, copiers, more staff, stools for staff to sit on, a take-a-number system, quick lines for simple transactions, and even a "get back in line free" card. A PIN pre-approves insurance. Or, if there is no PIN and the customer forgets the proof of insurance, the insurance company can fax a copy or electronically transmit it while the customer waits. Staff even received customer service training—what a novel approach!

Other initiatives were as simple as placing VCRs in branch offices. Old-time managers worried that the noise level would be raised significantly, or that staff would watch football games or cartoons. An open-captioned tape about departmental services easily resolved both concerns. When the video was playing, surveys found that customers thought they had been waiting less time than they actually had been. When there was no video, customers thought they had been waiting longer than they actually had. Of course, the video also serves as a good sales tool, especially when the majority of customers are oriented toward, and get their information from, television.

The scary part is that many public agencies still believe they do not need a public relations plan. Good business practices will suffice. Some may have emergency plans that tend to involve disasters—fire, earthquake or flood. But, what if a police officer is killed, or a road construction worker? What if an employee takes all of the charitable contributions and goes to Aruba? It is hard to think about the worse case scenario, but it does not have to be an earth-shattering disaster to have significant consequences. A reporter who grabs an issue such as "record privacy" can lay the guts of an agency wide open to public scrutiny.

On the other hand, great opportunities to promote new initiatives have been lost because of a lack of appreciation of the value of promoting good programs—or worse, a lack of knowledge regarding how to do so properly.

Before we move on to offer some examples of positive public relations and address how to get out of the mess created by bad PR or none at all, we would like to briefly mention the second great myth.

The Second Myth—*Any Fool Can Do It*

Although this perspective is also changing, there has always been the belief that there are two types of people who provide information from public agencies to the media. The first is the PR flack. This is an agency person through and through, generally an administrator who has been with the agency forever and who is perceived as part of the problem, willing to do whatever it takes to hide the truth and support the administration at all costs. Such flacks are defensive and remember when whatever the suggestion is was tried a decade ago and did not work. They run, dodge and spin until they are dizzy, all in the name of covering up whatever roiling waters may be prepared to boil in the agency. Such a mouthpiece comes across like a used car salesman. The credibility problem is compounded if the person has no credentials and is unfamiliar to the local media.

The other type of person providing public information is the professional within the agency. If the psychiatric hospital has a problem with its neighbors, it would make sense for the reporter to ask the Medical Director to comment. Or, if a restaurant is closed because of cockroaches, the chief food inspector from the Department of Agriculture is called upon to speak. Unfortunately, these professionals, while highly skilled in their own areas of expertise, may not have a good television presence, may be unprepared, or may mumble, stumble and generally sound inarticulate. They are clearly uncomfortable in the spotlight and with that sheen of sweat on their brow, look like they are lying no matter what they say.

There is an art and a science to good public relations. It requires someone who knows what they are doing, in good times and in bad. Here are some hints gleaned from people who really know how to be proactive, and when disaster strikes, respond professionally, courteously and do the right thing—no matter how painful.

The Do's and Don'ts of PR in the Public Sector

We begin with the acknowledgment that the public sector is different from the private sector in one critical regard, and that is the political environment in which everyone in the public sector operates. Whether working in the legislative, executive or judicial branch, politics lies at the very core of every agency and every job. Even the clerk in the bowels of a state department doing little more than responding to Freedom of Information requests is affected daily by inherently political behaviors dictated from higher up.

Not that the private sector is devoid of politics. But those are internal politics as opposed to external, taxpayer, voter-driven politics. In any organization the general rule is survival of the fittest. In the public sector, however, only the politically astute survive.

It should be a wake-up call to anyone in the public sector that because we are in a politically-driven environment, supported by taxpayer dollars, we are far more accountable to the public and far more on display to the public on any given day than any private organization. So, the public sector must be even more savvy than the private sector when it comes to public relations.

The public sector mantra has traditionally been, "We're from the government. We'll do what we do and your place is not to ask questions." Because public service programs can be legislatively or judicially mandated, there is a feeling of ownership and entitlement in their management—sometimes at the expense of the recipient's understanding or involvement. It is only recently that governmental officials have become more astute in recognizing the truism that "he who tells the story first, tells it best." Public administrators are becoming more sophisticated in terms of positioning issues and policy. As a result, what used to be an almost nonexistent area of public relations called *issue management* has blossomed, especially in state capital cities around the country. Every state department in Michigan, for example, has a public information officer. At one time they simply responded to media inquiries. Now, they are much more engaged in marketing and public relations. Their job is to identify the message, shape the message, and figure out how best to deliver the message.

Ten years ago, we waited until a reporter called and just answered the question. Now, we want to know who the reporter is before the person even knows where city hall is. We want to be building a solid, mutually respectful relationship before the first story is ever written.

In *issue management* our mantra is "maximize public support, minimize public opposition," regardless of what the issue may be. The job is to figure out ways in which we, as a unit of government, can shape the issue and our message to garner the most public support. Governmental officials have as many communication tools at their fingertips as those in the private sector. However, they are more accountable for how they invest in those tools. They have to tell the taxpayers where their money goes. That is why every Michigan government document lists how much it costs per piece to print. We have to be cognizant of the fact that people are going to look askance at a full color brochure produced with taxpayer dollars.

About 12 years ago, Lansing Mayor Terry McKane was getting ready to run for reelection. The mayor met with us and asked, "what do you think my image is?" He did not have an image. City government did not have an image, except perhaps a negative one. So our first priority was to publicly define who he was and what he was accomplishing, driven by his need to be reelected. We became proactive, even aggressive, in increasing the mayor's visibility. We began issuing news releases from the mayor's office instead of letting those concerns appear in city council meetings as agenda items. The mayor went out into the neighborhoods and held news conferences. If the city council resolved to develop blockades against prostitution on high traffic streets, we held a news conference followed by the mayor and chief of police hauling out the first barricade. Prior to our involvement, there had been no realization that increasing the visibility of government action was either appropriate or necessary. The prevailing thought was, "the media will find out soon enough" and the longer the inevitable could be delayed, the better.

Don't you think that now, especially in politics, **everyone** *is looking for the opportunity to get their name or picture in the media?* It is almost embarrassing to what extent some communities are holding news conferences and creating photo opportunities. It is equally embarrassing that the media continues to cover events that are not necessarily newsworthy.

Is that bad for the communities? Any time information is disseminated about government, it is a good thing. Even an orchestrated event is preferable to operating in the dark or avoiding the public eye. The only way to project a message with sufficient depth and breadth so that ultimately it will be embraced by residents is to put it out there as frequently and consistently as possible. Mayor David Hollister's message is, "Lansing is a 'can do' city. We're aggressive, we're doing this, we're doing that, we're a success, we're a success, we're a success." He averages one news conference, news event or photo opportunity a day. Five years ago it would have been verboten to initiate contact with the media as often as once a week.

As a result, today people know a lot more about what is going on in the city, simply based on what they are hearing, reading and seeing in the media. Some of the more traditional grassroots neighborhood organizations have developed their own PR machines, partly because they were used to having the inside track on all the information, and now everybody has the inside track. They are thus forced to take the next step in order to stay out in front of an issue.

How do you distinguish a PR machine from a political machine? There is not always a distinction. In the public sector there is, at the core of every issue, a politician who either wants to get reelected or wants to assure that his or her successor is elected. In some ways it is impossible to separate public relations and politics in the public sector because public sector leadership is always driven by a need to get reelected. That is not necessarily bad from a PR standpoint, as it generates a desire to provide information to constituents. The challenge is—and this is the challenge for the media and for anyone else who disagrees with leadership—to judge how balanced the information is. Are you just dealing with a spin machine?

More and more public agencies at every level of government are recognizing the need for an in-house public information officer—someone who is politically savvy, but whose primary responsibility is to communicate with the residents. Some of these staffers are political appointees; some are civil servants. But most good public information officers have survived changes in administrations because what they bring foremost to the job is institutional knowledge and a rich network of relationships.

The City of Lansing has a public relations firm that handles all of the city's communication needs and answers directly to the mayor. As a result, public information is driven very much by the mayor's agenda, whether or not that differs from the city council's agenda. This model generally does not work well in the long run. It is also much more expensive to have an outside consulting firm handling ongoing PR.

If you do not have a public information office in place, it is appropriate to "borrow" one for the short term. But in the long run you need a public information office that is responsible and responsive to both the city council and the mayor, has an insider's knowledge of what is happening, and recognizes the different roles of the city departments. An insider has much better insight into what is going on behind the scenes, especially since you generally will not tell an outside firm your internal problems. In fact, you may not even be aware of them. A good public information officer may have to step up and say to the boss, "I think we need to reconsider this photo op. There might be some repercussions that we haven't addressed." A PR firm may not feel comfortable being so blunt and thereby jeopardizing a lucrative contract.

The best arrangement may be some combination of an in-house public information officer and an agency which can bring in the strategic expertise and resources an individual would not possess. However, there will not be a smooth handoff if the organization constantly switches PR firms. No firm willingly gives away its secrets, or wants to make its successor look good, especially if they are in direct competition. Furthermore, the program will lose continuity.

What distinguishes a PR firm from an advertising agency? An advertising agency is focused on selling through a paid delivery of a message. It might be a paid ad in a newspaper, on television or radio. It might be a billboard. But the focus is on developing a paid advertising campaign to reach a specific audience with a specific message, without taking into consideration the long-term underpinnings of relationships. Conversely, public relations is all about the long-term image and how to build, strengthen and maintain that image. How are you learning about your weaknesses and addressing them? How are you bringing along others so that they buy into your philosophy?

The Eight C's of Communication

Content of Message

In the public sector, good communication is no longer just news releases and responding to specific media questions. Government has gone from being almost exclusively reactive to a recognition that if the press has a story and we are just responding to it, we have little or no control over the message. If you are the first person talking to a reporter about an issue, you set the stage. It is as if someone said, "paint me a picture" and you choose the canvas, paints and medium. If you merely react to reporters, then you are turpentine. Someone else painted the picture. You merely rinse off the brushes. You can never really erase the picture that is already out there, you only create a muddy smear.

Here is an example. City of Lansing officials overlooked an opportunity when it came to the infamous "rain tax" issue. First, they themselves inadvertently dubbed a combined sewer overflow assessment a "rain tax." The term stuck. Words have great symbolic value. "Rain tax" makes us think, as citizens, that every time it rains, we are being taxed for it. That is like being taxed for an act of nature. The city never made a strong, concerted effort to change that phrase early enough and thereby redefine the issue. We are really talking about a sewer overflow assessment. Does that roll off your tongue like rain tax? No, but it pretty much says what it is.

Polls showed that if people were told that the city was in danger of having its sewers overflow into the rivers any time there was a heavy rain, and, as a result, the city would be fined $25,000 per day per overflow by the federal government, and that it would actually cost less in taxes to be proactive, people would have embraced the issue as an environmentally sound approach. Conveying that information early and often would have helped immensely.

At the most basic level, the city should have issued news releases indicating how many sewer overflows resulted from a rain because the sewer system had not been upgraded. Or it could have provided a chart showing how much bacteria had entered the water system. Appeal to people's conscience.

People are willing to sacrifice if they understand what the greater good is and how they can help reach it. That requires finding a word or a phrase that crystallizes an issue in the public eye so intensely and so well that the phrase immediately brings to mind the philosophy the government wants people to embrace.

Consistency and Continuity

An example in state government is former Michigan Governor James Blanchard's constant use of the phrase, "jobs, jobs, jobs." He said that for two years in every speech. Every department director said it everywhere. Every minion who was out and about said "jobs, jobs, jobs." And then there was the secondary message, "a place to live, work and raise a family"—whether it was a safe place, a fun place, a healthy place, or whatever. Those phrases were used two years before reporters started picking up on them. We said them constantly, never missing an opportunity to repeat them. That is a good example of frequency of message and why it is so important to grab on to a key message and then repeat it as often as possible so that it begins to take hold in the public mind.

The phrase we use with BioPort, a small bioengineering company that provides anthrax vaccine for the military, is: "We make a safe, pure and effective vaccine." There is not an interview or an opportunity where we do not use that phrase at least twice, to the point where reporters will repeat it with us, "yeah, yeah, yeah . . . it's safe, pure, effective." But, they still run the quote. If it is part of your quote and you are consistent about it, the message gets disseminated. It is heard and eventually becomes internalized.

"Frequency of message" is actually an advertising term, but harkens back to the understanding that an agency cannot convey its message in a single venue to a single group through a single person and expect the public to recall, embrace, or act on it. The agency must convey the message until it becomes part of the public lexicon. The agency must be prepared to take a complex issue and boil it down to something as simple as "jobs, jobs, jobs." This serves as a reminder to everyone, including your internal audience and your own staff, about what your message and goal is.

That is why the Michigan gas tax finally passed several years ago, after ten years of beating the drums about how bad the roads were. That gas tax only passed when we could show legislators that the roads were becoming so bad that they were a political liability. There was a groundswell of support over time through a variety of associations like the County Road Commission and the Michigan Road Builders Association. We honed in on one key message—"just fix the roads." We did not say, "just raise taxes." We said "do whatever it takes to fix the roads."

Context of Message and Customer Benefits

We wrote news releases about how bad the potholes were. We were constantly taking the pulse of public opinion to determine at what point we could safely move to the next step, which was to call for a tax increase. We needed the demand to be fueled by the taxpayer. Governor John Engler then announced a stopgap measure by initiating "Build Michigan," which was offered as a stepping stone leading to the next solution. He then combined the "Build Michigan" news conference with an announcement of his support for a gas tax increase to help fund "Build Michigan."

But weren't you sending out a negative message? We needed to increase the appreciation and awareness of how bad the roads were so that people would recognize there was a problem that required additional money to fix. We could not call for a tax without public recognition that there was a serious problem. So in that case, we conceded that government was doing a lousy job because we had lousy resources. We were providing a negative message because we were laying the groundwork for our solution and for public acceptance of that solution.

As long as the agency can clearly say, "this problem is out of our hands" and offer a call to action, this approach can be effective. We certainly would not want to raise a concern without offering a solution. But neither the legislature nor the administration was delivering that negative message. It was the Michigan Road Builder's Association which was beating the drum with a wink and a nod from the administration.

The prior administration did not spend enough time setting the stage for an income tax increase, temporary though it was. As a result, it experienced a painful recall and lost the Senate majority. Administrators failed to recognize that the public did not know how bad the deficit was. They merely said, "Look, the books are all screwed up. We need a tax increase," instead of systematically pushing the story out over time.

Timing is critical. The message will be heard only when the issue is important to people. There is no point in talking about snow removal service in July. People do not think about an issue until it is ready to confront them. The road message became increasingly easy to relay and quicker to embrace when we took advantage of events like the annual spring breakup when highways start falling apart because of the freeze-thaw cycle. The roads are heaving and contracting again, and all of a sudden it is like walking on the moon.

In Lansing, city officials planned to completely close I-496, the main east-west route across town. The Tuesday, June 13, 2000 front page headline and subhead in the *Lansing State Journal* article, written by Todd Schulz, read: "Spring repairs to close I-496. But motorists can expect seven months of grief, not two years." The initial paragraphs reported:

> The first major overhaul of Interstate 496 will take seven months in 2001 instead of the two years originally proposed, state officials said Monday. But 65,000 motorists who travel the artery each day must suffer if the state is to meet the tighter deadline . . . "It's like going to the dentist—let's get it done," Lansing Mayor David Hollister said. "People will put up with the inconvenience for seven months rather than two years."[1]

So, people were told about the closing a year in advance. Officials were laying the groundwork so that they could begin to build awareness. But notice that they were not going into much detail yet and would not become specific until closer to the actual closure date. First comes what is called the *ramping up* of message. We wanted to begin building awareness so that people did not suddenly wake up one morning and find that the city's major travel artery was closed. At the same time, we did not want to give residents too much information too early because they could not act on it anyway. That only increases anxiety unnecessarily.

Our experience on most public issues is that the greatest hue and cry in terms of opposition is from people who did not know something was going to happen to

---

[1] Todd Schultz, "Spring repairs to close I-496. But motorists can expect seven months of grief, not two years," *Lansing State Journal*, June 13, 2000, Sec. A, p. 1.

them and did not feel that they had any input or recourse. So small articles started appearing in the newspaper as early as a year ahead of the I-496 closure process. City leaders started holding neighborhood and public meetings. They began building awareness with key groups and opinion leaders. They identified tiers of stakeholders or "influencers" and those area people who had the most stake in the I-496 issue. Perhaps they were the most vocal individuals and groups, but not necessarily. Small groups started to organize around this issue. City leaders reached out early to those who had a stake in this problem, although the communication was still subtle and subliminal for most citizens at this stage.

Developing a communication strategy. Faced with such a challenge, the agency must first determine its desired outcome. *What* do you want to accomplish? *Who* do you need on board to accomplish that and *what* do you need them to do? You also have to determine how much information is out there. How much do people know and is it accurate? Some of these decision points exist on parallel tracks.

In public relations terms, begin by identifying the target audience. Figure out who needs to be persuaded to do something so that the agency can reach its goal. If you do not identify the audience for your issue, you cannot answer the question of *who* you are trying to reach. Nor will you have any idea of *what* message must be developed to reach them. You could spend a lot of time and money on expensive campaigns and never accomplish much. You need to be *very* specific about who constitutes your target audience. For example, taxpayers, as a category, is far too broad.

Having identified the target audiences, you then need to determine how ready they are to do what you want them to do. Only at that point can you determine what the existing base of support and opposition is. What are, pardon the pun, the roadblocks in your way?

Take, for example, the need to minimize opposition and maximize support for completely closing I-496 for a significant period of time in order to fix it. The primary target audience would be people who drive I-496 daily. Certainly there are subgroups like student commuters to Michigan State University and government workers or state employees commuting downtown. The more you can narrow down exactly who you want to reach, the more effective your message will be.

The next question concerns the existing level of awareness of the problem. Within each key target audience, is there an unaided awareness about the issue? Are they already aware of the deteriorated condition of the highway and the need for extensive repair? Do they even know that there is a need to fix I-496? Probably not.

Then you have to figure out how best to reach this target audience with the closure message. There are some intuitive ideas, like billboards or outdoor advertising. But research needs to be more systematic. At this stage, a public opinion survey of anywhere from 400 to 800 people would provide a reliable sample from which to make decisions. The larger the sample group, the more accurate the results. The more you spend, the more you know. The more you spend in research, the more detailed, the more specific, the more valuable the resulting information. The more you know about whom you are trying to reach, the better you will be able to target them with a communication tool that will really grab their attention.

So, it may be that you find out initially in your quantitative research that nobody thinks there is a problem with I-496. The next step is to test various bits of information to determine which might serve as the most effective message with specific target audiences. For instance, you might ask, "If I told you that most interstate highways had a life span of 20 to 30 years and I-496 is 28 years old, would you be more or less supportive of closing the highway completely for major repairs?"

The aggregate results will help determine what information is most effective in changing opinion about the closure. Is it the age of the road, the potential reduction in the number of accidents, the ability to put in new signs that will be easier to read, or the elimination of a long-term minor inconvenience through the use of a short-term major inconvenience?

At this stage you may want to convene some initial focus groups, because they will help shape the questions and the response mode. A focus group is a small group of people who do not constitute a random sample, but are representatives drawn from the target audience. If 100 percent of the people in the focus group feel one way, that does not mean that 100 percent, plus or minus some margin of error, of your entire sample will feel that way. A focus group allows the researcher to probe the issue in greater depth. It can help establish how people feel and what they feel, as well as why they feel that way. You can explore issues of importance to your target audience, some of which you may never have considered.

Focus groups can also help provide the foundation for a formal survey if it is unclear what will motivate people to support your issue. During a public opinion survey, you may list eight or ten priorities and ask people to identify their top five. You will have developed the list of priorities based on the most common responses made in a focus group. Focus groups help provide some parameters and give a sense of what kinds of questions matter to your target audience. A quantitative survey gives empirical, replicable results that you can really trust. And you can make wise decisions based on those survey results.

Can I handle surveys by myself? We recommend that only trained people develop the survey instrument and handle the actual survey. To obtain good results, you need experienced market researchers. Good results mean that the instrument measures reliably what it says it measures.

Can I handle focus group research myself? We would not recommend that anyone with a stake in the outcome facilitate their own focus group. Indeed, you should not even be there. Your tendency will be to explain or defend, and that is not the group's purpose. The best facilitator is one who asks questions and never answers a single one other than where the bathroom is.

Let us use I-496 again as an example. That survey instrument should be administered to a representative sample of the 65,000 motorists who travel this highway every day. It should include a series of questions that ultimately provides the information needed to determine who the strongest block of supporters are and what messages influence people to change their minds or embrace the issue because they now have additional information.

Officials have already decided to take the dramatic approach of shutting down the expressway. As a public information officer, you need to find out what messages are going to resonate with people so that they recognize, appreciate, and even reluctantly support closing the expressway because it will eventually be more time- and cost-efficient. What messages do people really care about? Suggestions for alternative routes might be one such message.

The city started pulling together focus groups on a regular basis at this point. One served as an advisory committee. Three or four standing focus groups were called in on a regular basis and asked "What do you think?" "How are we doing?" They served almost in an advisory capacity, which took them out of the research mode to a certain extent. But they were still the eyes and ears in the community. They were hearing comments and paying attention to things in a way that officials could not.

Channels of Communication and Capability of Audience

The research should ideally provide a road map to build your communication strategy. It may be that you need to develop a variety of strategies based on the different target audiences you need to reach. For example, you may have one series of communication messages and tools that are specific to commuters at Michigan State University, and a different set for state government commuters. Perhaps you develop a completely different series of communications targeted to the occasional driver or the traveler from out of town. Each subset of your target audience may have a message that resonates most and best with them. These strategies are developed based on what the survey identifies as your issue's strengths and weaknesses. The survey will also identify those messages that influenced the most people.

Can I develop the campaign strategy myself? If you can be truly objective and not defensive about the survey results, and can remember what your goal is and who your target audiences are, you should be able to develop a strategic plan.

In that plan you have to identify the target audiences, the tools that will have the most credibility with those target audiences, and the messengers and messages that have the most credibility. However, you should never develop a strategy in a vacuum, i.e., develop the strategy all by yourself. Work with people, both inside and outside your organization, who are expert in communication and have an appreciation for the need to get ahead of an issue. A politician might call this group his or her kitchen cabinet.

You must make sure that the communication tools are credible and within the capability of your audience. Be sure the audience can receive and understand the message. If you are trying to reach a senior audience, for example, do not use a busy, high color design with lots of neon. Anybody who wears reading glasses has trouble with black ink on any kind of color.

The umbrella message may be the same for every subset of your target audience. However, you should also develop messages particular to smaller target audiences which resonate with them, but do not necessarily affect or even reach other target audiences.

The campaign does not need to be expensive to be good. Nor does it have to be expensive to be credible. It has to be strategic. It has to be thoughtful. You should include a mix of communication tools to improve frequency of message, which means people are seeing and hearing your message over time in a variety of ways. A new car campaign is a good example. You hear an ad on the radio. You see it on a billboard. You read about it in a magazine and newspapers. You receive a direct mail piece. You are seeing and hearing a variety of messages over a period of time, and each one reinforces the others.

On issues, in general, our first and most precious communication tool is *earned media* because it has extraordinary credibility. Earned media is whatever you do to generate news or editorial coverage without paying for it. It might not be anything more newsworthy than a photo opportunity. A week before the close of I-496, a great photo op might be when the detour signs go up. It may generate a story, but all you really need is the detour sign and a caption that says, "Remember—I-496 closes in a week. Your map enclosed."

Earned media in an issue campaign generally has the most credibility and is the least expensive. It is the public sector's vehicle of choice. It is also the messenger you can least control. You cannot approve the photo before it runs in the newspaper. You cannot review the story before it airs. The reporter may have found a detractor who is going to trash you. We hope not, of course, but it happens.

If you have trouble attracting earned media, look at other communication tools to which your target audience will respond. Do you need to do some advertising? You may decide to send out a direct mail piece. You may organize a speaker's bureau. You may develop a video. You may establish an Internet campaign. The I-496 closure program had a strong Internet component. However, as with any medium, remember that whenever you are communicating on the Internet, you are reaching a small, differentiated subgroup.

Credibility of Messenger

The communication tool through which you deliver your key message must be as credible as possible for your target audience. The credibility of a message on MTV is not nearly as strong as it would be if you saw it on *60 Minutes* or read it in *Newsweek*. So the message vehicle does matter, based on what your particular audience perceives to be credible. That is why there is more and more focus on *peer communication*, especially in issue management. Peer-to-peer information has the strongest credibility. It is seen as more truthful, reliable and trustworthy. If you hear something about a program for state employees that is supposed to be wonderful, you are much more likely to believe it from a fellow state employee or a state employee union rep than from your own boss—or a politician.

Here is a good example of peer comunication on the front page of the September 18, 2000 *State News*, Michigan State University's student newspaper. The headline by Vincent Estes reads, "Gore's daughter to rally at 'U'." Jeanne Raven, president of the College Democrats and a social relations senior, said about Karenna Gore Schiff, "She's been through it, and she's not that far off from the rest of us." Later in the article, Curtis Hertel, Jr., former president of the MSU College Democrats, is quoted as saying, "I think having someone their own age will encourage voters, even more than the candidates themselves."[2]

---

[2]Vincent Estes, "Gore's daughter to rally at 'U'," *State News*, September 18, 2000, p. 1.

The public sector often uses peer communication. That is why task forces are assembled. A legislator wanting to address school issues may assemble a parental task force because parents have credibility with other parents. There was an I-496 public involvement team responsible for formulating the strategy and monitoring its effectiveness.

Evaluating Your Plan

Call to Action

Part of the communication plan must include ongoing ways to evaluate how well the PR campaign is going. Evaluation might involve public opinion surveys every three months, monitoring a hotline, or checking letters to the editor. No matter how you choose to monitor the campaign's progress and evaluate its effectiveness, it must be done in a timely enough manner so you are able to react quickly, especially if public response proves slow or poor.

Do I have to evaluate? It is just too hard and expensive to evaluate. It is not hard to evaluate progress, and it can become much more expensive if you are spending money for communications that are off target or in the wrong medium. You have to evaluate all the time. Let us say there is only one year to communicate the program. If you do not start evaluating until nine months into the campaign—and you suddenly find out that everything you have done for the first nine months has been totally ineffective—you only have three months to make a course correction. If you are continually evaluating progress and find out that outdoor advertising is the single most effective way to communicate with drivers, you can invest more resources in outdoor advertising and less in television time. Perhaps more money needs to be spent for ads in the local shoppers' guide newspaper, because people are gleaning all of their detour tips from a little newspaper column it started. Your evaluation, the ongoing monitoring, highlights the PR campaign's strengths and weaknesses and where adjustments are needed.

Let us say, for example, a hotline was provided. It turns out there is a huge problem that no one anticipated until people started calling the hotline. We have a mechanism for people to tell us what they think. But that is only as good as our ability to monitor and respond. You cannot afford to have people calling and complaining who subsequently never hear from you.

How do we measure success? It may be that for I-496, there is a tiered goal starting with "public recognition of and support for the need to close I-496 for a complete rebuild." We are going to measure effectiveness based on how many problems were encountered on the first day of the closing, determined by how many negative media stories occurred that day, as well as how many accidents there were, how many people were late to work, and how many calls were made to the hotline. We anticipated a thousand hotline calls a day for the first month, and then we anticipated usage tapering off. Did we have more or fewer calls? Regardless of the number of calls, did they decrease in number? Did those calls help identify problems that could be easily addressed and corrected?

You will also want to monitor letters to the editor. Try to initiate positive letters so that you can build support. You might, for example, set up an *editorial board.* If somebody calls the hotline with a positive message, you might say, "Hey, would you mind sending a letter to the editor? And, by the way, we have a sample if you want one."

Most organizations are not comfortable with that approach. There are companies in Washington, D.C. whose sole purpose is to do what is called *astro turf* or skim the surface out in the grass roots—identifying and generating letters in particular communities for particular legislators on a particular issue. The key is to generate a real letter from a real person. It must be an authentic letter with a real signature, not a form letter with a machine signature. Most politicians will tell you that five individual letters from constituents trump anything else in dictating how much attention they will pay to an issue. Such letters beat volumes of petitions. They beat volumes of phone calls. They beat volumes of e-mails. They beat any association or lobbyist knocking on the door. Five real letters from five real people. Now, if the decision maker knows those letters were generated by an outside firm, they have far less credibility. You can actually diminish your credibility if you send a form letter—especially if it has a typo. A complaining constituent who lives next door to a legislator conveys a message far more powerful than 100 form letters.

Aren't we spending a lot of money on public relations that could be better used to fill in potholes? If you do not have public support, you are not going to have the resources to fill potholes. You will not have a public that believes in its policy makers, and frankly, you are not going to have legislators who ultimately believe policy—good policy—is the right thing to do because they are seeing bad outcomes. For example, if you just closed I-496 and did not tell anybody, what legislator would not be bombarded with complaints? You are much better off spending the money up front than on damage control. Damage control is always expensive, rarely effective, and often does serious harm to somebody's reputation. By definition, damage has occurred. Most repairs are simply patches that look exactly like what they are—attempts to fix a problem that should not have occurred in the first place.

Summary and Conclusions

Good public relations will not save a bad program. Unfortunately, the reverse is not true. Good programs can be destroyed by the failure to pay attention to public relations or by inexpert handling and disclosure of core program issues. At its most basic, public relations is two-way communication with constituents. It is listening to what people are worried about and sharing with them what the agency is doing and why. Inattention, insularity, arrogance and ignorance by public officials is no longer tolerated in this media age. At the very least, public officials must learn to be proactive. At the very best, they can encourage participation in the public debate to make programs stronger and thereby better serve their constituents.

Like Vitamin C, the eight C's of communication can often help, and will never harm you or your agency. In fact, we strongly recommend a daily dosage.

The Eight C's of Communication

Content of message	Is the message catchy? Is it meaningful? Does it mean what you think it means? Is it going to resonate with your target audience? Does it crystallize your campaign into a memorable sound bite? Is it simple and compelling? As a simple rule of thumb, your message should be seven words or less. Semper Fi.
Consistency and continuity	Your message has to be the same regardless of how it is delivered or by whom. Without consistency and continuity, message dissonance will occur, which means messages are conflicting. As a result, credibility will drop.
Context of message	Is the message being delivered at a time when the audience is likely to pay attention? What is happening in your target audience's community that will make them care about the message?
Customer benefits	In public relations we call it WIFM, "What's in it for me?" The target audience, the customer, always wants to know how she will benefit. "I know why it is good for you. Why is it good for me?" Make sure you are communicating the benefit to your target audience. One example was the recent 2000 national census. It was easy to see why big government would want the information, but what was in it for the resident? Why do you need to know how many bathrooms I have? Census takers were asking questions that people found quite personal. But, the Detroit census committee was good at explaining the economic benefits to the Detroit community. It demonstrated that the population had been severely undercounted in past censuses and therefore lost school and other public funding. It was also important to recognize that illegal aliens, squatters and other nonresidents needed to be targeted with messages and included in the count. So, part of the message was "No INS, No IRS, No FBI." The key message was, "Stand Up and Be Counted." That is a great action-oriented message, and another "C".
Channels of communication	These are your communication tools. You must select those tools that are most effective for your particular audience. You would not send a brochure on the importance of learning to read to an illiterate audience. Nor should you use a country western radio station to urge teenagers to vote. Inner city churches and their pastors, for example, can serve as a powerful channel of communication for many public issues.
Capability of audience	You need to make sure your audience is capable of receiving the message. If you want to reach a Mexican-American or Chaldean population with a message about organ and tissue donation, materials should be in Spanish or Aramaic. You have to ask yourself the question, "Is my audience capable of receiving this message?" Am I delivering it in a way that they can accept? Today, most people draw the majority of their information from television in short sound bites. However, if you want to reach long-distance truck drivers, you will not want to spend too much money on television spots. Is your message packaged properly to reach your target audience?
Credibility of messenger	Whoever delivers the message must have strong credibility with the target audience. If you want to convince kids not to drink and drive, provide an impact panel of speakers including a teenager who killed a child while driving drunk. On that same panel might be the child's mother. The credibility of the messenger is of tremendous importance. This is difficult for elected officials to accept because they like to think they are the most credible messenger. They are also looking for *face time*, the greatest number of minutes of television exposure or lines of newspaper copy possible.
Call to Action	Tell people what you want them to do. The call to action can be as easy as, "Let us know what you think" and then give people a way to respond. Make sure there is a way for people to act. However, you do not want people simply to call and complain. You want to give your audience something positive to do that represents authentic action. The call to action regarding the I-496 closure? It might be, "get ready." It might be, "know your route." It might be, "give us tips on the hotline or via the Internet." The easier that action step, the better the response. An organ and tissue donation registry form is mailed with every new Michigan driver license or state I.D. The person's name and address are already printed on the postage-paid card. All a person has to do is sign the card, tear it off the form, and put it in a mail box. This simple campaign has generated a tremendous response because the call to action is so easy.

In 1964, Aaron Wildavsky argued in *The Politics of the Budgetary Process* that "if politics is regarded in part as conflict over whose preferences shall prevail in the determination of national policy, then the budget records the outcomes of this struggle." Budgets are "political things" that answer the question: "Who gets what the government has to give?" Politics is in one sense a process, or series of stages, by which the government "mobilizes resources to meet pressing problems (and) the budget is a focus of these efforts."[a]

In light of the need for public managers to understand the budget and be able to use it effectively, one would, therefore, normally include a selection here from a book such as Irene Rubin's *The Politics of Public Budgeting*.[b] After all, the manager who makes program mistakes is more likely to survive than the one who fouls up the finances, so he or she has to learn both how to read, write, and understand a budget as well as the politics of the budgetary process. But these are not normal times for the federal budget, and so managers must also understand the coming federal budgetary changes and what they portend for every level of government.

For much of the post-World War II period, the federal budget has been the best friend of public managers working at every level. While state and local governments collect significant amounts of taxes, federal government expenditures in recent years have approximated one-quarter of the country's gross domestic product (the sum of all goods and services produced in the U.S.). Funding for new state and local government initiatives often comes from the federal level, and a number of state and local agencies receive federal funds in exchange for implementing national programs and regulations.

But how can Eric Patashnik expect such a limited future role for the federal government when both the Congressional Budget Office (CBO) and the White House's Office of Management and Budget (OMB) are projecting surpluses as far as the eye can see? Part of the answer lies in the difficulty of making predictions for any extended time period. After all, few economists or policy analysts during the recession in the early nineties predicted the New Economy with the unprecedented prosperity that it provided for most of the decade.

So the eye can see only about ten years at best, which means that predictions now are rosy. OMB in 2001 projected that budgetary receipts would increase from $2,025 trillion, what they actually were in 2000, to $3,434 trillion in 2011, while budgetary outlays would grow from $1,789 to $2,623 trillion. The difference between these receipts and expenditures is the "unified surplus"—a combination of monies collected mostly for future dissemination to social security and medicare recipients. The remaining "on-budget" surplus consists of what is left. This on-budget surplus is not expected to reach $99 billion until 2005 (when it would represent three-tenths of one percent of the projected $2,525 billion in budget receipts). In the subsequent "outyears," it then climbs more rapidly to $410 billion in 2011.[c]

---

[a]Aaron Wildavsky, *The Politics of the Budgetary Process*, 4th ed. (Boston: Little, Brown, 1964) p. 4.

[b]Irene S. Rubin, *The Politics of Public Budgeting: Getting and Spending, Borrowing and Balancing*, 3rd ed. (Chatham, NJ: Chatham House Publishers, 1997).

[c]Office of Management and Budget, *2002 Economic Outlook* (Washington, D.C.: Government Printing Office, 2001), p. 7

The Changing Composition of the Federal Budget

The cause for Patashnik's concern lies in those years beyond what the eye can see. There is justification for caution in predicting entire budgets for future decades; however, demographic projections are different. We know the nation's population and age distribution and so, barring nuclear war or pestilence, can predict how long people will live, and what that means for the growth of the two largest "entitlement" programs—social security and medicare payments. Even between 2000 and 2011, defense spending is expected to decline from 15 percent to 12 percent of the total budget, and the nondefense discretionary budget category will probably shrink from 16 percent to 14 percent of the federal budget. The latter includes funding for the Education Department, Federal Communication Commission, and other domestic departments and agencies that comprise "government" as we know it for most Americans. Such changes may not sound dramatic, but by 2011, one percent of the budget would be $34 billion. Meanwhile, social security, medicare and medicaid, means-tested entitlements, and other mandatory (or statutorily required) payments to individuals are expected to grow from 47 percent to 53 percent of the budget. All other things being equal, the unified surplus would then be $810 billion, though much of this money would be committed to paying future entitlement obligations.

In light of these figures, it is easier to see why Patashnik believes that we will be "budgeting more and deciding less." He begins with the sixties when budget deficits were negligible, programs were growing incrementally, and there was ideological consensus between the political parties on many spending and taxing issues. Under these circumstances, the conflicts were manageable, and took place among a relatively small number of concerned congressional, White House, and large interest group actors. By the 1980's, all of these conditions had changed. Deficits were mounting, and moderates in both parties were replaced by Democrats further to the left and Republicans further to the right. Congressional budgetary reforms had ushered in procedures that required the two parties to reach agreement on, among other things, an appropriate size for the total budget, an acceptable level of taxation, and a suitable deficit level— issues that had caused little stir in a period of comparatively stable, incremental growth. Now tighter budgets in stringent economic times inflamed partisan passions that heightened "dissensus" (or strong disagreement) over the budget. Congress also now had its own Congressional Budget Office that enabled it to compete on more equal terms with the president in setting the budget.

In addition, Patashnik observes that it was during the seventies and early eighties when the government largely abandoned its reliance on Keynesian fiscal policy, that is, on higher government spending, lower taxes, and transfer payments to individuals hard-hit during a recession to stimulate economic demand. Some important "automatic stabilizers" remain, such as unemployment insurance, food stamps, and welfare programs, which respond quickly without the need for government action to assist the needy and thereby increase demand for goods and services. Keynes, however, did not anticipate, explain, or provide a solution for dealing with "stagflation"—the new set of economic conditions characterized by high inflation *and* high unemployment. Fiscal policy faced a dilemma here. If it increased government spending to combat the stagnation, already high inflation rates would rise further, and if it decreased government spending to reduce inflation, the result would be even higher unemployment.

Monetary policy—with its emphasis on control of the money supply by the Federal Reserve Bank—now came to the fore. By injecting into or withdrawing money from the banking system, the "Fed" can affect how much money a bank can

loan and at what rate of interest. These changes work their way through the economic system comparatively quickly, and are made by this relatively autonomous
regulatory commission. The Fed compelled banks to raise their interest rates to hith-
erto unprecedented rates, and thus eventually broke the back of the inflation after
putting the country through its worst economic time since the Depression. Monetary
policy also triumphed over fiscal policy because it did not require the federal government to assume additional debt during recessions.

Furthermore, Patashnik observes, by the 1980s the federal government was
"involved in numerous policy sectors, programs were mature, and many spending
items were deeply entrenched." But there are still the questions of where best to
allocate funds and how to perform critical government functions. These questions
could result in budgetary shifts. However, Patashnik points also to the erosion of
budgetary flexibility—the shift whereby a decreasing proportion of funds are allocated today at the discretion of the president and Congress annually, while the proportion of entitlement funds and monies allotted through cost-of-living adjustments
and through the tax code has increased. These trends are unlikely to change unless,
as Patashnik concludes, we return to a more activist economic policy, political support for major entitlement programs erodes, or "strong demands emerge for major
new federal programs or sweeping tax cuts." In the meantime, unlike the old days,
public entrepreneurs will have to do more than simply look to the federal government to fund exciting new ideas and programs.

Budgeting More, Deciding Less

Eric M. Patashnik

"Budgeting is governing," declares Pete V. Domenici, chairman of the Senate
Budget Committee. Few would challenge this statement. Budgeting has always
been at the heart of policy making. Since the early 1980s, however, the budget has
been the major issue of American politics. As Norman Ornstein observes, elected
officials, businessmen, and journalists alike have been "obsessed with the budget
process, endlessly analyzing and arguing over it." Though people might disagree
about how well (or poorly) the budget process is working, few doubt that the
budget matters more than it once did.

But while budget issues undeniably acquired a new prominence in the 1980s
and 1990s because of the struggle to control the deficit, the budget-making
process has in fact declined in importance as a framework for governing the
economy and setting national priorities. I certainly do not want to be understood
as saying that the annual budget process is unimportant. The national budget
mobilizes resources and maintains the bureaucracy. Politicians continue to make
budget decisions that materially affect the lives and prospects of constituents. And
while the federal pork barrel is smaller than it once was, plenty of benefits remain
for lawmakers to ladle out.

Eric M. Patashnik. *The Public Interest*, no. 138 (Winter 2000), pp. 65–78. A longer version of this article will appear
in *Durability and Change: Policymaking in the 1990s*, edited by Marc Landy, Martin Levin, and Martin Shapiro.
Some passages are drawn from an essay published in the journal, *Governance*.

Still, I contend that budgeting has become a less important setting for deciding public policy—even as it has become a more significant arena for political debate. This seemingly paradoxical state of affairs is the product of dramatic changes in economic ideas, political institutions, and the composition of the federal budget itself. The budget has moved to the center of political life in the United States because budget politics is a major battleground for partisan and ideological struggles over the future of activist government. Yet while the budget involves high political stakes, the policy importance of budget-making has declined over time. In the 1950s and 1960s, the Keynesian revolution elevated the importance of the national budget because effective fiscal policy was viewed as the key to economic prosperity. But now most policy makers place their economic faith in monetary policy and the Federal Reserve. Meanwhile, the budget has become a less powerful instrument for directing spending priorities because more and more of the budget goes for entrenched long-term programs like Social Security. Politicians may be fighting over budget issues more—but they are deciding less. And as I explain below, the recent emergence of budget surpluses has not fundamentally changed these dynamics. The budget story is a case study of the contradictions of the modern American polity.

Budgeting Then and Now

Since the early 1980s, the budget has been the dominant issue of American national politics, overshadowing all other policy concerns. A good indicator is media coverage. According to David W. Brady and Craig Volden, the attention paid to the budget by the media has increased dramatically. During the 1970s, the *New York Times* ran an average of about 200 stories per year on the budget; during the 1980s, it averaged 1,800 stories a year. This trend has continued into the 1990s. When reporters cover Congress, their stories are frequently budget related.

The reason journalists emphasize budget issues today is not because they are deeply interested in the substance of public policy (though some reporters no doubt are), but because reporters instinctively love a good political fight—and the budget process is where some of the biggest recent clashes have occurred. Think of the Clinton-Gingrich budget battle of 1995. Or the squabble between House Republicans and President Bush over the abandonment of his "no new taxes" pledge at the 1990 budget summit at Andrews Air Force Base. The arcane federal budget process is now the stuff of high politics.

This is a relatively new development in American government. Traditionally, budgeting attracted little political attention. Standard accounts of federal budgeting during the 1950s and 1960s—such as the late Aaron Wildavsky's classic 1964 book *The Politics of the Budgetary Process*—described budgeting as a vital, but sedate, process of incremental bargaining between Congress and bureau chiefs. Budgeting was considered so technical and dull when the book was first published that Wildavsky felt compelled to reassure his readers on the book's first page that the topic was actually of some political interest.

Budgeting in the 1950s and 1960s lacked obvious drama for three main reasons: First, budget deficits were generally small as a percent of GDP. While programs were growing, spending was considered to be under control. Second, there was a rough ideological consensus among politicians over many taxing and spending issues. To be sure, liberals and conservatives during this era had their budget fights. But the scope of conflict over the budget was muted by the backdrop of the Cold War, the distributive nature of many spending programs—the pork barrel was still growing—and the existence of large numbers of political moderates in Congress. Finally, the rules of congressional budgeting created an artificial, yet meaningful, distinction between money decisions and policy decisions—and thus between high politics and mundane public administration.

Prior to 1974, Congress did not even consider the budget as a whole. When people spoke of the "budget," they meant the president's budget, which was then (as now) submitted to Congress each year, right after the president's State of the Union address. But the president's budget is only a set of executive proposals. Significantly, Congress did not debate these proposals as a package in the 1950s and 1960s. Rather, the president's budget proposals were taken up piecemeal by the 13 appropriations subcommittees in each chamber. Congress as a whole did not debate and vote on the total size and content of each year's budget. The effect was to cordon off funding skirmishes from broader political battles.

The New Budget Regime

By the 1980s, all this had changed. First, the economic and budgetary situation had worsened. Budget deficits began rising after the mid 1970s and exploded after 1981. Second, as Sarah Binder of the Brookings Institution has documented, the number of political moderates on Capitol Hill declined. The Democratic congressional caucus became more liberal, the Republican conference more conservative. Finally, the rules of federal budgeting were transformed. Provoked by President Nixon's blatant abuse of his impoundment authority, and by concern about increasing budget deficits, Congress adopted a landmark reform, the Budget Act of 1974. The measure curbed impoundments, created the Congressional Budget Office, and established new budget committees in each chamber. The House and Senate budget committees were given the job of formulating overall budget packages ("budget resolutions") for lawmakers to debate and decide upon.

These three factors—rising budget deficits, the disappearance of the political center, and congressional budget reform—combined to create a wholly new and different budget regime. Because the deficit was large, lawmakers faced tough budget choices. Because Republicans and Democrats were more ideologically distant from one another, partisan conflict over budget matters increased. And because Congress now had to vote on total spending, taxing, and deficit levels—which is to say, on the total direction of national public policy—the conflicts between the parties took on heightened meaning, especially because top party leaders like the Speaker came to play an active role in appointing members of the key budget committees and crafting omnibus budget legislation.

The budget deficit was not just another policy issue during the 1980s and the 1990s. It was the master issue, subsuming all the others. Policy experts began speaking of "the fiscalization of the policy debate." By this phrase, they meant the new tendency for politicians and policy makers to debate programs not according to their particular merits but according to their impact on the government's overall fiscal condition. "The measure of all arguments became dollars," observes former Congressional Budget Office (CBO) director Robert D. Reischauer. The key question became: "What would the policy do to the deficit?" The obsession with the budget deficit transformed the political debate. As Paul Pierson of Harvard argues, the preoccupation with budget constraints displaced pragmatic disagreements over operational details with "broader, more abstract arguments about the appropriate role of government."

There is nothing inherent in budget deficits that must produce ideological and partisan conflict. Given the context of American national politics in the 1980s and the 1990s, however, fundamental disagreement over the budget was virtually guaranteed. The underlying policy differences between the two parties were large. Moreover, the new budget process forced these differences out into the open. Some 40 percent of congressional roll calls on budget resolutions between 1976 and 1990 found 75 percent or more of Republicans opposing 75 percent or more of Democrats. On 10 percent of the roll calls, 90 percent or more of one party opposed 90 percent or more of the other. Even though the gap between Democrats and Republicans was hard to bridge, party leaders pushed their agendas in the context of the budget process because budget measures enjoyed special procedural advantages not available to other legislation. Thus Republicans in 1995 tried to use the budget process not only to lower deficits but to cut taxes, kill programs, reform welfare, restructure Medicare and Medicaid, and send power back to the states. Of course, many of these proposals failed. The important point is that the budget process became the leading legislative game in town.

Under the rules of the game, every measure must conform to budget enforcement provisions. The leading keeper of the rules is the CBO. Because the CBO's scorekeeping decisions can have a decisive impact on policy outcomes, politicians complain vigorously when rulings don't go their way—as in House Republicans' ongoing complaint that the CBO fails to recognize the "dynamic" impact of tax cuts in its statistical models. As political sociologist Theda Skocpol notes, during the Progressive era and the New Deal, drafters of legislation spent a lot of time trying to guess what the Supreme Court would accept as constitutional. Today, lawmakers live in fear that the CBO will "reject their proposals as not 'costed out.'"

Keynesianism's Rise and Fall

In sum, everything is now a budget issue and the congressional budget process has become more centralized, complex, and politically adversarial. Meanwhile, the power of professional budget forecasters has greatly increased. What makes these developments all the more interesting is that they have occurred during an era when the annual budget process has been of declining importance. The budget can be used to steer the economy and direct government priorities—two functions that it performs to a much lesser extent than it once did.

With the triumph of Keynesian economics—or at least the applied version of it—in the 1950s and 1960s, the budget became the supposed key to governing the American economy. Before World War II, policy makers' lack of scientific knowledge about how the economy worked prevented them from using the budget to promote economic growth with low inflation. Politicians were also constrained by the belief that the budget must be balanced every year. As James Savage of the University of Virginia has shown, since the nation's founding, a balanced federal budget has carried a symbolic importance far beyond its objective economic meaning, signaling democratic control, social harmony, and the preservation of republican government. By contrast, budget deficits have stood for inefficiency and corruption. Even Franklin D. Roosevelt, whose New Deal programs resulted in a string of massive peacetime deficits, never really abandoned the view that government, except in times of crisis, had a moral obligation to balance its books.

By the late 1950s, however, leading economists increasingly saw the balanced-budget dogma as the main obstacle to rational economic policy making. With the triumph of Keynesian doctrine in the early 1960s, that obstacle was temporarily removed. President Kennedy's economic advisers believed in fiscal activism—that is, in deliberately pursuing the precise level of aggregate taxing and spending most appropriate given the current state of the economy. If economic conditions were disappointing, fiscal adjustments should be made. Budget deficits were no longer considered evil in themselves; what mattered was their impact on aggregate output and consumer demand. "The federal budget can help achieve the overall economic goals of a high level of employment and reasonable price stability," confidently asserted two Brookings economists in 1971. "To serve this purpose, the amount of stimulus or restraint coming from the budget must be responsive to the needs of the economy at any particular time." Although monetary policy was not entirely discounted, most Keynesians during this era believed that fiscal policy would be more effective.

The national budget thus came to be seen as the key to economic prosperity. Keynesianism's greatest triumph came with the large tax cut enacted by Congress in 1964. Whether the Kennedy-Johnson tax cut actually achieved its stated goal of spurring economic growth remains a matter of dispute among professional economists. But clearly elected officials believed that it had worked. To deny the essential correctness of Keynesian prescriptions was to declare oneself a know-nothing.

The Triumph of Folk Wisdom

The Keynesian intellectual revolution did not convert everyone, however. Public-opinion surveys indicate that ordinary Americans never really abandoned the traditional belief that budget deficits are intrinsically decadent and immoral. What James Q. Wilson calls the "elite abandonment" of fiscal orthodoxy in the 1960s thus opened a normative gap between leaders and average citizens on budget politics.

But in the United States the values of ordinary citizens are not easily brushed aside. Many Keynesian experts took the position that budget balancing was no more than an accounting fetish. Yet few politicians were willing to tell the public it was foolish. Keynesian presidential advisers therefore developed a hybrid concept, the "full employment" budget. Instead of strict balance, the idea was that the government would adopt fiscal policies that would cause the budget to be in balance at full employment. The Kennedy-Johnson tax cut was explicitly sold to the public on these grounds. According to the late Herbert Stein, "Keynesian economists were willing to make use of the vulgar prejudice in favor of a balanced budget, even if they did not share it."

The power of Keynesian thought was substantially tied to its standing among professional economists. But economic theories can be discredited if the world doesn't work as predicted. When the economy experienced "stagflation" in the mid 1970s, Keynesians were bewildered and lost confidence. The dominant economic goal shifted from stimulating consumer demand to controlling inflation and boosting productivity. Economists continued to accept the idea of protecting family income through the use of "automatic stabilizers" such as food stamps and unemployment insurance. But they increasingly argued that politicians were incapable of "fine tuning" fiscal policy to the business cycle. Primary responsibility for the nation's economic performance, they said, was better left to unelected experts at the Federal Reserve.

As the decade of the 1970s came to a close, the idea of a "full employment" budget was heard less and less. In the 1984 presidential campaign, every major Democratic candidate condemned deficit spending. Over the remainder of the decade, the balanced-budget idea became increasingly powerful, and politicians increasingly catered to the traditional fiscal orthodoxy of average citizens. As columnist Robert Samuelson observes, the recovery of the balanced-budget concept can be seen as a "reassertion of folk wisdom over professional economics."[1]

Budget Meltdown

By the mid 1980s, very few politicians or mainstream economists believed anymore in using the budget to manage the economy. We were all monetarists now. This was enormously frustrating to those few remaining activist liberals in the executive branch who felt that the government should use spending increases to boost economic performance. "In case you hadn't noticed, America's domestic policy is now being run by Alan Greenspan and the Federal Reserve Board," lamented former Labor Secretary Robert Reich. "Their decisions about interest rates are determining how many of us have jobs and how many of us get a raise.

---

[1] To be sure, Reagan's supply-side advisers—very much like the Keynesians before them—renewed the familiar argument that a balanced budget is of little intrinsic economic importance. But the brief supply-side episode hardly revised fiscal activism. Supply siders were not interested in using the budget to govern the economy. They wanted to get the government out of the way. What really mattered, they argued, were the incentives for individuals and corporations to save, produce, and invest. Private entrepreneurship, not public budgeting, was their watchword.

Congress is out of this loop." President Clinton did emphasize the need for government "investment" early in his first term. But the administration proposed only a very modest economic stimulus plan, which Congress ultimately scaled back under deficit pressures and the new economic consensus.

As the Federal Reserve was acting with dispatch to control inflation in the 1980s and 1990s, the congressional budget process was coming apart at the seams. Politicians talked endlessly about the urgency of getting the nation's fiscal house in order. Yet appropriations bills were constantly late. Between 1981 and 1985, the federal government shut down six times. Three more government shutdowns occurred between 1986 and 1990, and two more during the historic budget battles of 1995-96. These funding interruptions were not inconsequential. "Nonessential" federal workers were furloughed. Tourists hoping to see the pandas found the National Zoo closed. Americans planning to travel abroad were temporarily unable to obtain passports. But the most sensitive parts of the budget—the massive income transfer programs—were largely unaffected. For most Americans, the functioning of the federal budget process—the topic of endless news coverage—simply wasn't that relevant.

Of course, even as the federal budget became less central to economic management, budgeting could still have remained a vital process for setting national spending priorities. Certainly, it is difficult to imagine a time when budgeting will not matter for resource allocation. Policy makers will always confront questions about how to divvy up scarce taxpayer dollars. Nonetheless, the scope for priority-setting in the U.S. budget has long been narrower than many believe. As Wildavsky explained in 1964, the budget is never actively reviewed as a whole every year. To save energy and time, politicians generally accept the prior year's budget as the starting point for the current one, confining their attention to changes at the margins. But—and this point is crucial—there is even less room for shaping government priorities through the budget today than there was in the 1950s and 1960s. There are two main reasons for this. First, the federal government's era of program building is all but over. Second, a greater share of spending goes for long-term commitments like Social Security.

It is easy to forget just how much program building took place over the post-war period. Reischauer provides a useful reminder:

> In the mid-1950s, numerous government agencies did not exist. A partial list includes the Departments of Transportation, Education, Energy, and Housing and Urban Development and agencies such as NASA, EPA, the Nuclear Regulatory Commission, the National Endowments for the Arts and Humanities, the Federal Emergency Management Agency, and the Legal Services Corporation.

Such program building gave Congress the opportunity to make important funding decisions during the 1950s, 1960s, and early 1970s.

By the 1980s, however, the federal government was involved in numerous policy sectors, programs were mature, and many spending items were deeply entrenched. The very permanence of big government further narrowed the scope for active decision making and increased the overall stability of budget results.

According to an important recent study in the *American Journal of Political Science,* year-to-year changes in domestic spending priorities were actually more volatile during the post-war decades than during the 1980s and early 1990s, even though the modern budget process is so much more rancorous and conflictual.

The Expansion of Long-Term Commitments

The increased stability of budget outcomes is not merely the product of the maturation of big government. It also reflects an erosion of budgetary flexibility. Since the 1950s, annual appropriations paid out of general tax revenues—the accounts over which politicians possess the most discretion—have declined from more than two-thirds to less than one-third of the budget. This development reflects the growth of entitlement spending (mainly for Social Security and Medicare), the expansion of trust funds dedicated to specific purposes, and the adoption of automatic cost-of-living adjustments for social benefits and the tax code. More and more of the budget is on automatic pilot. As Eugene Steuerle argues, "Never before in our history has the law pre-ordained so much of our future spending patterns. Never before have dead and retired policy makers so dominated officials elected today."

Because so much of future budgets is already spoken for, the CBO is further encouraged to make long-term budget forecasts. Yet, because future budgets are so sensitive to changes in economic conditions, these forecasts often turn out to be quite wrong. For example, no one foresaw the disappearance of the budget deficit in 1998. One effect of our long-term public commitments has thus been simultaneously to reduce uncertainty for program beneficiaries and increase uncertainty for budget projections.

Entitlements, in particular, have stabilized budget outcomes but destabilized the budget process. In the 1950s and early 1960s—before the big increase in entitlement spending—the budget process was relatively insulated. Budget officials had cordial relations with one another and seemingly bargained in good faith. Interest groups could testify at appropriations hearings and seek to influence key legislators and bureaucrats. They could form coalitions. But clientele groups— and the media—were generally shut out from the meetings where the crucial deals were made. As Wildavsky wrote of budgeting during this era, "Secrecy is maintained."

The implicit rationale for this closed-door policy was that the U.S. budget was fundamentally the government's business—not the public's. Most federal spending during this era financed goods and services, especially defense. But most entitlements are income transfers. The expansion of entitlement commitments thus made ordinary Americans increasingly dependent on the government for their personal well-being. As budget expert Allen Schick notes, entitlements gave a host of clientele groups—the elderly, coal miners, and others—a direct, "open-ended draw on the Treasury." These budget claimants "brought demands, rights, and intense conflict to what once had been a sedate process." In the era of entitlements, a closed, secretive budget process could no longer be sustained.

Struggle and Consensus

The budget deficit grew between the mid 1970s and mid 1990s chiefly because spending on long-term entitlement programs outpaced economic growth. To be sure, the Reagan administration in 1981 won the enactment of a major budget package featuring a significant tax cut, reduction in domestic discretionary spending, and defense buildup. After the mid 1980s, however, the impact of current political decisions on budget outcomes was relatively modest.

Virtually every influential politician, Democrats and Republicans alike, agreed on the need for courageous action on the budget after 1981. Yet for all the political emphasis on deficit reduction, the actual level of legislative progress made in easing the deficit was comparatively modest. In 1985, Congress enacted the Gramm-Rudman-Hollings legislation, which required a balanced budget in six years. But when the Gramm-Rudman deficit-reduction targets started to bite, they were postponed and then essentially scrapped. A number of beneficiaries (especially Medicare providers, upper-income taxpayers, and the defense sector) suffered genuine losses, and deficit-reduction bills during the 1980s and 1990s definitely caused some pain. Yet strong political support for the federal government's long-term spending promises severely circumscribed the range of feasible cutbacks.

Efforts to make deep reductions in the deficit were also thwarted by ideological conflict in Congress. Both liberals and conservatives developed coherent deficit reduction plans. But neither had the votes to go it alone, making compromise necessary. Despite the resort to bipartisan summits over the 1980s and 1990s, conflict, stalemate, and delay were the rule. During the intense, highly partisan battle over the 1996 budget, 13 separate stopgap measures had to be enacted.

In sum, the deficit wars did not make budget outcomes nearly as volatile as one might expect. While budget reforms like Gramm-Rudman and the Budget Enforcement Act of 1990 probably did help restrain spending on existing programs to some extent, their most important effect was to discourage Congress from creating expensive new budget promises. This implied that deficits would eventually recede as economic growth caught up with the rate of entitlement growth. And that is basically what occurred. The legislative changes made in the Balanced Budget Act of 1997 were not expected to bring about a balanced budget until 2002. Congress achieved a balanced budget in 1998, four years ahead of schedule, primarily because medical inflation slowed and economic performance greatly surpassed expectations.

Future Prospects

In sum, during the 1980s and 1990s, the budget became a major issue in American politics. At the same time, the use of the budget as a framework for governing the economy came to an end and spending priorities became increasingly entrenched.

This is ironic to say the least. Before 1974, Congress had no organizational capacity to effect fiscal policy even though Keynesianism was the dominant economic theory. After the establishment of a top-down congressional budget process in 1974, legislators had the budgetary tools for economic management. By then, however, the idea of using the budget to drive the economy had lost legitimacy.

An even deeper irony is the gap between the tremendous attention paid to current budget battles and the narrow maneuvering room of the contestants. The most important decisions affecting today's allocation of budget resources were made by politicians no longer in office. When settled long-term commitments crowd out the freedom to choose, the budget comes to reflect policy priorities more than set them.

It remains to be seen whether mounting budget surpluses will influence political struggles between the two parties. To be sure, the surpluses create some new policy options. But it seems unlikely that they will usher in a new era of political consensus. In the first place, the budget surpluses are temporary. Large deficits will re-emerge early in the next century, once the Baby Boomers begin to retire. About two-thirds of the total budget surpluses forecast over the next decade reflect surpluses generated by Social Security—a situation that creates nasty dilemmas for both parties. The remaining one-third of the projected surpluses assumes large reductions in discretionary domestic spending. Congress has shown little stomach for such cuts in the past. Finally, a growing share of the budget will go for retirement and health programs for the elderly.

If and when the policy significance of budgeting increases, it will be because of one of the following three things: Politicians embrace new economic theories that emphasize the advantages and feasibility of fiscal activism; political support for the government's long-term commitments, especially the major entitlements, seriously erodes; or strong demands emerge for major new federal programs or sweeping tax cuts. At the moment, all three possibilities seem remote. As a result, elected officials in the years and decades ahead are likely to continue to budget more and decide less.

Information technology—the use of computers, the Internet, and their offshoots—has dramatically altered how public, private, and nonprofit organizations operate, and how managers manage. Opinions differ on the effectiveness of information technology in particular administrative agencies, but everyone agrees that such technology has already changed organizational behavior dramatically, and will continue to do so. The computer-illiterate manager is becoming an endangered species.

Thanks to their extraordinary complexity and because they touch so many citizens, computers in such agencies as the Internal Revenue Service and the Social Security Administration are most visible in the federal government. However, state and local governments together spend more than the federal government on computers. If the eighties was the decade when computers swept across the organizational landscape, the nineties was the decade when more sophisticated computer software became available and widely used. As Nicholas Henry has said, "the workers of the world have now united" not through Karl Marx doctrine but "through the emergence of *groupware*, or computer networks that interactively link, via cable or phone line, many people at the same time. Electronic mail—e-mail—and electronic bulletin boards are early examples."[a]

The Promise of Well-Managed Information Technology

There are two basic types of information systems. One is the *management information system* (MIS) that accumulates, stores, and retrieves data on such items as services, employees, salaries, and facilities, and converts that data into a form that managers can use in making decisions. A *decision-support system* (DSS) moves beyond organizing data. It not only integrates data, but also assists managers in thinking through decisions. A series of "what if" questions, drawn from formal decision-making models, prompt managers concerned with solving a particular problem. Such software thus makes sophisticated decision-making techniques accessible to managers not schooled in the modeling of "nonroutine" decisions.

Geographic information systems (GIS) is one such decision-support system that combines data and maps in creative and useful ways. For example, Kandell and Craig provide an excellent case study of an innovative GIS-based approach by the Bureau of Land Management that not only combined mapped information of numerous kinds but also promoted public participation in the planning process. When President Clinton proclaimed nearly 1.9 million acres in Southern Utah as the Grand Staircase–Escalante National Monument, he assigned the task of planning and implementing the land management to BLM. Environmentalists had long since nicknamed BLM the "Bureau of Livestock and Mining," and were deeply suspicious. To involve as many stakeholders as possible, BLM utilized GIS to share the planning data widely. BLM, therefore, had to convert its old GIS system, with more than 30 "data layers," and integrate it with data layers from other federal and state agencies.

But the GIS data would have been irrelevant without the 13 public meetings involving more than 1,000 people, without the distribution of 2,500 hard copies and 700 CD-ROM's to interested individuals and without posting the plan on the Internet. The public was invited to download copies and build that material into their comments. The BLM received 6,800 comments on its draft plan, including 30 percent by e-mail. The final management plan was changed considerably as a result of these comments—about 210 miles of road were added and 235 miles were removed.[b]

While increasingly sophisticated information technology offers exciting possibilities, Sharon Dawes and her Center for Technology in Government (CTG) colleagues emphasize that IT innovation ultimately depends on harnessing IT to agency goals, measuring whether an IT innovation is meeting its goal, addressing numerous stakeholder needs and program complexity when implementing the program, and drawing on tenacious and committed professionals to help overcome those challenges.

The failure of some dot.com businesses to heed such advice led many to crash and burn their investors' money in the process. The power of the software makes it almost irresistible to expand too rapidly rather than growing at a measured pace that allows for incremental adjustments. The dangers of headlong expansion are

---

[a]Nicholas Henry, *Public Administration and Public Affairs*, 8th ed. (Upper Saddle River, NJ: Prentice Hall, 2001), p. 152.

[b]William J. Craig and Stephen J. Kandell, "Monumental Steps: GIS and the Planning Process for Grand," *Geo Info Systems*, February 2000, pp. 22–30.

particularly high in the public sector where a program may involve more than one level of government, nonprofits or corporations, and numerous stakeholders with different goals.

Even a seemingly obvious term may have more than one valid meaning. For example, at the Union Pacific Railroad, there is little agreement on what a "train" is. "Is it," asks Davenport, "a locomotive, all cars actually pulled from an origin to a destination, or an abstract scheduling entity?" Answering this question requires a number of productive face-to-face meetings, and it will need to be resolved in a manner that allows for one "global" meaning and the use of a number of "particular" meanings in particular contexts.[c]

Extensive organizational changes will also result, Evans and Wurster suggest, from the so-called net technologies: "the *Internet*, which connects everyone; *extranets*, which connect companies to one another; and *intranets*, which connect individuals within companies."[d] The emergence of such universal, open standards for exchanging information will enhance pressure in the public sector to work vertically along local-state-federal lines and horizontally across more than one department and within more than one departmental unit. IT will thus flatten organizational hierarchies and put pressure on an agency's culture. Individuals and units will continue to hoard information—a time-honored source of power—but IT will increase tension among internal and external stakeholders as to who should get what information, when, and how. Small wonder that Cats-Baril and Thompson, after examining IT projects in Vermont, advised, among other things, that the agency "first, reengineer, then automate."[e]

Successful IT efforts thus require attention to the same management concerns as other program initiatives. Once the technology, organizational goals, and culture are in sync, the public agency will be able to meet the expectation of citizens with access to computers and e-mail who, as CTG puts it, "want a government that is organized around their needs and available 24 hours a day."

Four Realities of IT Innovation in Government

Sharon S. Dawes, Peter A. Bloniarz, David R. Connelly, Kristine L. Kelly, and Theresa A. Pardo

The Center for Technology in Government (CTG) at the University at Albany/SUNY celebrates its fifth anniversary this year. Since 1993, CTG has worked with more than 100 New York state and local government agencies on projects

Sharon S. Dawes, Peter A. Bloniarz, David R. Connelly, Kristine L. Kelly, and Theresa A. Pardo. *The Public Manager*, Vol. 28, No. 1 (Spring 1999), pp. 27–31.

[c]Thomas H. Davenport, "Saving IT's Soul: Human-Centered Information Management," *Harvard Business Review*, March-April 1994, p. 122.

[d]Philip B. Evans and Thomas S. Wurster, "Strategy and the New Economics of Information," *Harvard Business Review*, September-October 1997, p. 74.

[e]William Cats-Baril and Ronald Thompson, "Managing Information Technology Projects in the Public Sector," *Public Administration Review*, Vol. 55, No. 6, November/December 1995, p. 565.

designed to increase their understanding of how information technology (IT) can be used effectively to transform public services. The projects have ranged from economic development to mental health to intergovernmental relations and have involved technologies ranging from decision support to geographic information systems to advanced data integration and analysis tools.

In these projects, we've seen first-hand what it takes to turn a promising technical idea into a productive system. We've seen how difficult this is to do—to identify opportunities in a fast-moving technological environment and apply them within the deliberate and slower pace of governmental processes. We've seen how government decision making, with separation of powers and multiple points of review, can create frustrating roadblocks to rapid innovation. At the same time, we've also seen how governments can make it work—how agencies and individuals with vision and commitment can use technology to make substantial improvements in the quality of government services, often at a reduced cost. We've seen how people working within the complexities of government can build the coalitions and master the technical details to create effective and innovative government services supported by technology.

This article discusses some of the general lessons we have learned from five years of project experience. In these projects, government agencies work in partnership with the private sector and the academic community in the pursuit of new ways to use computing and communications technologies to solve practical service delivery and administrative problems. Over the years, we have been involved in a variety of projects. Most were initiated by the programmatic needs of agencies, while others focused on issues associated with a class of emerging technologies. Our initial projects tended to focus on a program need of a single agency, while more recent projects have tackled strategic cross-agency issues such as interorganizational information systems and data sharing. Our goal is to help project participants develop sufficient understanding of the interplay among policy, management, and technology issues to inform their IT initiatives, and to make materials and advice available to others facing a similar situation.

The IT Environment in Which We Work

The government information technology environment is one of opportunity and risk. The world has changed because of information technology, and so have the public's expectations of government. With ready access to personal computers and electronic information in the business community, people expect a comparable level of service from the public sector. They want a government that is organized around their needs and available 24 hours a day.

Government managers are working hard to incorporate innovative technologies into the way government works. They see value in using data mining tools to evaluate their services. They see how electronic commerce can improve responsiveness and reduce costs. They see the Internet as a way to exchange data between stovepipe applications to streamline services. These and other technologies offer enormous opportunity, and have been used very effectively in government.

At the same time, government agencies are grappling with a number of complexities: significant public policy shifts, budgetary constraints, and the unique decision-making environment that is the result of our democratic system of government. Within this context, IT managers are trying to maintain currency with emerging technologies, and deal with the shortage of IT-skilled workers and aging technical infrastructures. As a result, IT innovation in the public sector bears a special element of risk—a risk highlighted by the press every time a significant public information system goes over budget or fails to meet a deadline.

What We've Learned in Our Projects

Four broad themes or "realities" have emerged from our first five years of project work. In our experience, these realities can make or break a project.

Program needs must drive IT innovation. While this may sound like a cliché, government program goals must be the driver. Far too often, it is the technology proponents that initiate a project. This usually causes problems in the long run.

Use a learning model in developing a system—prototype it, evolve it, measure it. Program goals should drive the development of the entire system, and should define the expectations of the system. Starting with those expectations, it's best to start small and allow for evolution based on working experience. By paying attention to the goal from the start, you're in a position to measure your results against your objectives and improve your system in incremental steps.

Government is complex—deal with it. It's hard to develop government IT systems for many reasons—systems involve more than one level of government, systems involve the not-for-profit and business communities, government development takes place in a fishbowl, and many people have a stake in most projects. Never underestimate the complexity of what may look like a simple problem. This complexity cannot be wished away; it needs to be faced squarely and managed accordingly.

Professionalism and personal commitment make a real difference. A very important factor in ensuring project success is the commitment and professional dedication of the IT and program staff who design and develop the system. They set the tone, establish a culture of innovation, and take the calculated risks that are necessary to effect real change. It is critical that these individuals envision IT solutions in the context of programmatic objectives, and that agencies empower them to lead and act.

The manner and degree to which these themes or "realities" are addressed influence the success of IT projects in government. While the first two are similar to standard business-school maxims, the latter two may be uniquely governmental. We describe these "realities" more fully below.

Reality # 1: Program Goals Are the Driver, Technology Is the Vehicle

In an age when technology seems to promise everything, a public manager is often asked to simply solve problems with the "latest, greatest" technology. Going to a trade show with a dazzling array of technologies attractively presented only compounds the situation. As one public manager described it, "our commissioner sees a new technology and without understanding the implications of the change, decides we should 'go out and get some.' However, when it comes time to deal with the training needs, policy implications, and staffing requirements associated with this decision, the high-level support may diminish or disappear."

If Your Goal Is Better Service, Consider the Outcomes First

The drive to use the Internet as a new mechanism for service delivery is a good example. As the Internet took off, government agencies, many under directives from upper management, rushed to establish world wide web pages. Many local governments were among the first to develop Web sites. However, in the rush to "get something up" few stopped to consider the management and policy implications associated with this new mechanism of information and service delivery. Who would answer e-mail requests? Who would update the Web site? What information was needed on the Web site? What about security and issues of confidentiality? What about maintaining access to this information over time?

The list of issues could go on for pages. Inevitably, many of those managers who went forward found that doing business "on-line" is just as complex as doing it the old-fashioned way and in many instances much more so. Technology offers alternatives that can allow services to be delivered better, cheaper, and faster but, just like the old system, people, processes, and policies must be in place and managed well if the technology is to truly "change the way we do business."

Technology Is a Powerful Agent and Enabler of Change

While technology cannot and should not be in the driver's seat, it can play a significant role in changing the way government does business. Seeing examples of IT applied to important goals in the public or private sector can stimulate creative thinking that can lead to ideas for improved services and more efficient operations.

One example is New York State's Geographic Information Systems (GIS) Clearinghouse. The clearinghouse allows both public and private organizations that have spatial data sets to describe and share them with others who could benefit from their use. By doing this, the significant costs and benefits of developing digital spatial data sets can be spread among a number of users. The world wide web provided a good vehicle to support the sharing of information, so CTG worked with a range of private and public organizations to create a prototype system to support the sharing of existing data resources. By demonstrating that a system like this could work to the benefit of many different users, a host of management and policy issues were identified and people began to see that the benefits of sharing make the effort to resolve the issues worthwhile. Today, the clearinghouse is a valuable statewide information resource maintained on-line by the New York State Library and supported by a formal GIS coordination program.

Reality # 2: Government IT Innovation Should Be Approached from a Learning Perspective—Prototype It, Evolve It, Measure It

We have found that IT innovation is more than anything else a learning process—from broad consideration of program needs, and stakeholders and their goals, to a review of others' practices and experiences, to prototyping and evaluating solutions. We use and advocate an evolutionary approach to system definition and development and urge our partners to be explicit about how they will incorporate and measure the factors that define success.

Start Small and Grow

Whenever possible, it's best to take an evolutionary approach to designing and building information systems. When starting with a technology that is new, it is particularly difficult to anticipate every need that the technology can address—or every problem it can create. Thinking in the abstract about how a technology can be used usually doesn't lead to the best ideas. Therefore, we recommend that projects begin by trying out the technology in an experimental environment before pilots or full implementations are attempted.

There are many advantages in doing this. By testing a technology outside of a production environment, the pressures of doing it right the first time are alleviated. By exploring the technical resources needed to construct the prototype, the exercise can help point out what will be needed to support the ultimate system. If the prototype shows users how the system will look and behave, it will not only help fine-tune the requirements of the full system, it will also help in devising implementation plans and building organizational support for the full system. This better understanding makes it more likely that when a system is ultimately built or procured, it will meet the real needs of the organization.

Starting small also helps deal with occasional executive directives to "get me some of that." Developing a prototype will demonstrate quickly how well an idea might work; it can save money and possibly prevent an embarrassing failure. Growing a system allows you to take advantage of improved technology. A phased or evolutionary approach will also allow for early results—something tangible and useful that will grab people's attention and let them see how the system might be of use to them.

A key to using a phased approach is to build systems that maximize flexibility. Avoid locking into nonstandard tools and technologies that will close the door for future changes. Identify system options that will demonstrate the direct value of the system to users and decision makers so that they will see its value and support subsequent phases of activity. And revisit the program or business objectives early and often as new phases are planned.

Measure It

Despite the declining costs of many information technology components, most Government IT projects are expensive. How do you know if the benefits of an information system will exceed the costs? You measure them.

Identifying the costs of a system implementation is often the easy part. The key is to be comprehensive, and include ongoing or annual as well as development costs. The costs of data preparation may exceed those for hardware and software, so it's important to include them as well. Training costs and ongoing maintenance must be identified. Hiding or ignoring these ancillary costs is not an appropriate strategy—it doesn't do any good to see a system wither and die because funds to maintain it were not allocated.

Estimating benefits is usually much harder. Many of the expected benefits may be intangible or difficult to quantify. Often, new benefits of a system are only identified after the system has been developed because it allows you to do new things. You may not be able to put a dollar figure on some of the most important benefits, but describe them anyway. Mixing quantitative and qualitative descriptions of benefits is okay, just be as explicit as possible.

In identifying potential system benefits, look for and estimate cost savings associated with system implementation, reductions in the time it will take to serve customers, and improvements in the quality of service or decision making that may result. Estimating, these "cheaper, faster, better" benefits is difficult—often painful—but it is very important.

This kind of analysis can go a long way in making a business case, justifying a budget request, and promoting a common understanding of why a project should be supported. Done early, such an analysis can help identify the main phases of a project so that key stakeholders see benefits early and continue to support the project through subsequent phases.

Reality # 3: Government Is Complex—Deal with It

Many of the most critical public policy issues or problems addressed by government cross program areas, and span levels of government, agency boundaries. and economic sectors. As of 1992, there were 85,006 governmental units in the United States. In New York State alone, there are 3,299 units of government. None of these government organizations is autonomous, but they do different things and exercise different forms of authority. Their relationships are not simple. Depending on the circumstances, they work cooperatively with each other, they give one another mandates or apply regulations, and they exchange information and other resources. In doing this, they interact to form what citizens expect to be a cohesive "government." In fact, the cohesiveness comes with a multiplicity of differences—differences of responsibility, viewpoint, authority, tradition, and approach. Adding the private and nonprofit sectors to the environment only makes it more complicated. Into this environment go complex social objectives: public education, social welfare, public safety, and economic development. Stakeholder views are many and diverse. The effective design and implementation of government information systems must recognize and take into account all of this complexity and diversity.

Stakeholder and Program Complexity—the Dissension Is in the Details

A major step in dealing with complexity is to create a common understanding of goals across stakeholder groups. Project or program participants often come to the table believing that they have a common understanding of a problem and how IT can help solve it. However, we have discovered that methods such as process mapping often uncover very different perceptions of what the *real* problem is that a group is trying to solve. When pressed further, the supposed common understanding of problems and solutions is often only skin deep. There is agreement around the abstract. The dissension—and the answer—is often in the details.

Dealing with this reality is a time-consuming, painstaking, and worthwhile task. Successful Government IT projects may require buy-in from a multitude of actors, modifications to laws or policies, or redefinitions of regulatory relationships. Key stakeholders should be brought into the planning process at an early stage. Such tools as stakeholder analysis, process mapping, and cost-performance analysis can help uncover significant disagreements about problems and potential solutions. Visual representations of problems such as formal models of an environment can help create a common picture of a problem and potential solutions.

Reality # 4: Professionalism and Personal Commitment

In reviewing our projects for this article, we were struck with the levels of personal commitment and professionalism that motivate public managers to effect positive change. Without dedicated professionals who made personal investments, many projects would have failed. Professional integrity, demonstrated in difficult decisions and steadfast commitment to long-range goals, was also very evident in successful projects. This occurred over and over despite the fact that these actions were seldom individually recognized or rewarded.

Personal Investments Often Augment Agency Investments

Government managers are drawn to projects at CTG by their interest in improving services through effective applications of technology. However, they are also drawn by their interest in learning about new technologies and management trends, by the opportunity to participate in a high profile project and by the chance to act on their personal commitment to their jobs. Personal commitment to projects was evidenced in many ways. Staff members spent their own time training, themselves to understand new technologies and management issues. They bought books and used their home computers to search for reference materials on the web. In extreme cases, people used their own money to buy hardware components and software to test whether they might work in their agencies.

Professionalism Helps Resist the Allure of Technology

New technologies receive a lot of attention in the popular and business press. Often IT initiatives are launched in reaction to unchallenged assumptions about what a technology can do. Top level executives are sometimes unaware or ill-informed about the specific impact a particular technology might have on agency performance. Project teams are often left to establish a purpose and focus for their efforts. Individual professionalism was a significant factor in efforts to resist the temptations of using technology for its own sake. In our experience, high levels of professionalism allowed project teams to find the right "match" between the technology and program needs by insisting that technology be addressed within a framework of program requirements.

It Takes Real Commitment to Prototype, Evolve, Measure, and Learn from Experience

In government, program evaluations are used to guide program refinement, policy development, and resource allocation decisions. However, in government (and elsewhere), we seldom evaluate the effectiveness of our information systems. The steps are not as clear, the models not as robust. However, it is possible. Our government partners have developed conceptual frameworks and skills necessary to carefully test or prototype technologies, to start small and learn from experience, to apply that learning to the next stage of evolution, and to measure the effects of their efforts on customers and agency alike. Government managers that we have worked with have been willing to back out of a particular path if experience tells them that the desired benefits are not there. They've demonstrated that it's a good management decision, not a bad one, to pull out of a project that you've determined won't meet your needs at an affordable price.

Skill and Willingness to Work with, Not Against, the Complexity of Government

Working within the complex government environment is a challenging task and not one for the faint of heart. In our experience, committed, professional government managers are well informed and tenacious in dealing with the environment. They focus on the outcome while dealing with all the internal and external influences that can stall a project. They resist the simple answer and reject an "us vs. them" mentality. Instead, they are inclusive, good listeners and communicators, resourceful, and respectful of the viewpoints of others. Projects have been successful thanks to the willingness of our government partners to address the complexities of government head-on and to manage them actively from outset to conclusion.

Conclusion

None of the first three realities makes it easy to develop effective information systems in government—and the fourth alone cannot entirely overcome these hurdles. Often, the easiest way to deal with a directive to "just do it" is to just do it, sometimes with disastrous consequences. Going with a well-advertised solution may be easier than defining your goals and measuring whether you have achieved them. Working behind agency walls may be easier than opening the doors to wide participation in program and system development. The projects at CTG have shown that resisting the temptations of technology for technology's sake requires a commitment to purpose, and may require a willingness to stand firm against a tide of uninformed enthusiasm.

In order to promote and reward more effective approaches to IT development, it is necessary to develop a culture in government that encourages innovation, fosters experimentation, and values thoughtful analysis. IT is a powerful means of effecting change, but it is up to public managers and the people they serve to define the changes they want and the ways they want to achieve them.

P A R T

VI

The Politics of Managing Human Resources

Its human resources (HR) represent an administrative agency's most important and challenging asset. The management of these resources has undergone significant change over the last two decades. Evan Berman and his colleagues have observed that traditional *personnel administration* was concerned primarily with internal processes—recruitment, compensation, and discipline—and the application of the rules and procedures of the civil service system. The management of people, however, has now evolved into public *human resource management*. This term "embraces a broader, more 'people-focused' definition of the management of human resources with an eye to the kind of workforce needed in government (i.e., employee and organizational development, organizational design, performance appraisal and management, reward systems and benefits, productivity management, staffing, employee-employer relations, and health and safety)."[a]

Human Resource Management and the Civil Service System

While striving to become the very model of a modern public manager, it is also necessary to cope with a civil service system—constructed more than a century ago—that is designed not only to enhance program effectiveness, but also numerous other goals. These include, as Frederick Mosher ticked them off

---

[a]Evan M. Berman, James S. Bowman, Jonathan P. West, and Montgomery Van Wart, *Human Resource Management in Public Service* (Thousand Oaks, CA: Sage Publications, 2001), p. 7.

back in 1965, the prevention of political interference with career civil servants, representation of all constituencies affected in the policy process by the actions of a particular agency, political responsiveness to the public's will, and equal treatment regardless of race, ethnic background, gender, or age.[b]

The challenge then is simultaneously to facilitate the development of a system that will provide sufficient autonomy for managers to pursue agency goals and somehow achieve an appropriate balance with these other values that remain deeply embedded in the personnel process. Too often historically, the system has tilted in the direction of one or another of these competing values that can, on occasion, become an impediment to getting things done. Even when between fads, the civil service system poses numerous problems for the proactive manager striving to recruit the best person for the job at the entry level, to classify positions in a manner that allows for the promotion of talented people, to appraise performance in such a way that credit is given where credit is due, and to reward outstanding performance with higher pay.

Frustration with the federal civil service system is hardly new, but in recent years it has increased. One scholar, Robert Maranto, even wrote a polemic advocating that it be abolished.[c] Abolition of tenure and allowing a president to make more appointments would empower political leaders to accomplish more and public managers to better lead their organizations. Furthermore, he argued, there are more than enough media and institutional watchdogs to allow for increasing effectiveness, representation, and legitimacy without necessarily increasing corruption. The present era of increased privatization combined with historically unprecedented corporate campaign contributions, though, hardly seems a propitious time for a deliberate return to the spoils system.

Few have advocated quite such a draconian solution at the federal, state, or local level, but strong support has grown for moving toward diversity management and toward a leaner, more flexible and competitive civil service system more closely in accord with the principles of human resource management. Mosher would have felt at home with the reformers' core values. They too are seeking responsiveness, representativeness, and the other values sought by the system. The significant differences lie in *how* reformers want to achieve these goals.

---

[b]Frederick C. Mosher, "Features and Problems of the Federal Civil Service," in Wallace S. Sayre, ed., *The Federal Government Service* (Englewood Cliffs, NJ: Prentice-Hall, 1965), pp. 164–172.

[c]Robert Maranto, "Thinking the Unthinkable in Public Administration: A Case for Spoils in the Federal Bureaucracy," *Administration & Society*, Vol. 29, No. 6, January 1998, pp. 623–642.

S everal trends have increased the number of advocates for greater diversity in the workplace. First, affirmative action, for better or worse, has largely run its course politically. While it is unlikely to disappear entirely, developments in the late nineties have eroded the support for race-conscious programs. Ewoh and Elliott argue that the damage has been done by the increasingly conservative makeup of the U.S. Supreme Court and lower courts and the "strict scrutiny" they are applying to affirmative action cases, by the Republican control of the House and sometimes the Senate, and by Proposition 209 in California. In this relatively liberal state, the voters, by a 54-46 percent margin, adopted this initiative that called for the state "not to discriminate for or against any group in state employment or benefits."[a] Second, a number of forward-thinking companies feel the need for a sufficiently diverse labor force to reach out to new markets, while some public agencies similarly are hiring persons with diverse economic and social backgrounds in order to deal more effectively with the changing demographics of the populations they serve. Confronted by the backlash against affirmative action, these organizations are quietly supporting diversity as a more politically and socially acceptable alternative.[b] Finally, there emerged a number of professionals who view diversity as an integral part of human resource management in the 21st Century. James Slack falls into that category.

Full Spectrum Diversity

Part of diversity's appeal is that it does not leave anyone out. While still primarily concerned with blacks, Hispanics, women, and the physically disabled, Slack emphasizes that diversity must reach out to all parts of our population—even white males. The emphasis is on the need for a "representative bureaucracy"—an administrative agency must represent all of the various population segments that it serves. A representative bureaucracy reflects the value of social equity, since it is based on the belief that in a democracy, public service should reflect the racial, ethnic, and gender composition of an agency's constituency, so that responsive public policy can be made.[c] While the evidence does not always support the assumption that the person representing a minority in an agency will act in accord with the minority's interest,[d] the preponderance of evidence suggests that diversity inside an organization is important in changing its attitudes toward the minorities whom it wishes to serve. IBM's global workforce diversity theme, for example, is: "None of us is as strong as all of us." It has established eight task forces consisting respectively of women, Asians, African-Americans, Hispanics, Native Americans, Gays and Lesbians, white males, and people with disabilities. The objectives of these task forces are "to determine, 1) What is required for the group to feel welcome and valued at IBM, 2) What IBM and the group can do to maximize their productivity, and

[a] Andrew I. E. Ewoh and Euel Elliott, "End of an Era? Affirmative Action and Reaction in the 1990s," *Review of Public Personnel Administration*, Fall 1997, p. 46.

[b] Norma M. Riccucci, "The Legal Status of Affirmative Action," *Review of Public Personnel Administration*, Fall 1997, p. 34.

[c] Ralph C. Chandler and Jack C. Plano, *The Public Administration Dictionary*, 2nd ed. (Santa Barbara, CA: ABC-CLIO, 1988), p. 236.

[d] Kenneth J. Meier, *Politics and Bureaucracy*, 4th ed. (Fort Worth: Harcourt College Publishers, 2000), pp. 177–181.

3) What IBM can do to maximize the pursuit of market share from the constituency's community."[e]

Slack vigorously argues that diversity must recognize that many immigrant groups do not want to "melt" into the population. Diversity must thus involve not only a representative bureaucracy, but one that also respects the individuality of those from all groups. One need not be like us to work with us. He echoes other diversity proponents in arguing that we must move from "reactive" affirmative action efforts to "redress" past discrimination, and focus instead on *full spectrum diversity*, that is, designing work settings that "reflect proactively the gender, cultural and ethnic complexity of each local community as well as the American society."

Full spectrum diversity is necessary now because affirmative action, he argues, is a product of externally-driven forces. One cannot expect an organization to develop the necessary internally-driven forces when it is under a court order or federal agency fiat to change. Furthermore, the organization will only change to the extent necessary to comply, and thus ignore a number of groups that may be suffering from discrimination within the organization. Regulatory responses also tend to be relatively superficial, which in the case of affirmative action results in stereotyping and oversimplification. Such regulations, he observes, inevitably result in contradictions and resentment. We must be "color- and gender-blind" but also "color- and gender-conscious," and the manager must both hire affirmatively and in accord with the merit principle.

The way to combat these dilemmas and regulatory problems is to design a new organizational paradigm where the organization assumes responsibility for meeting the full spectrum of its diversity opportunities. It proactively builds diversity into its thinking about its strategic planning and organizational culture. Managers can thus think of diversity in terms of what is best for the organization and building a truly representative bureaucracy. He develops a five-stage hiring procedure that builds merit into the job description and job pool analysis stages, even while reaching out proactively through wider advertising, exploring diversity during the interview stage, and, once the merit of the finalists has been established, considering the contribution that they would make to organizational diversity as well. This new hiring process is hardly foolproof—and may require reconsideration if diversity does not result—but by considering the needs and concerns of all groups, there is more basis for mutual trust and progress and for taking into account the "new" and the "old" America.

But Slack is no wooly optimist. While acknowledging the irony of the suggestion, he concludes that "a new set of external factors might be required to encourage the leadership of an organization to accept and implement an internally-based paradigm." In addition to citizen re-education, "external preferences and politics" may have to change. Other scholars too are nervous about loosening the federal requirements. Riccucci fears that "the commitment to diversity may be ephemeral," and if it is, public and private sector organizations will then "have the power to promote diversity in their workplaces when it suits them, but completely disregard it when it doesn't."[f] Vidu Soni's survey in 2000 of diversity in a U.S. Environmental Protection Agency Regional Office identified such persisting problems as uneven understanding of the meaning of diversity, a different perception of their work environment on the part of women and minorities and white males, differences in perception of discrimination in treatment, and agreement on the part of

---

[e]John M. Ivancevich and Jacqueline A. Gilbert, "Diversity Management: Time for a New Approach," *Public Personnel Management*, Vol. 29, No. 1, Spring 2000, p. 80.

[f]Norma M. Riccucci, "The Legal Status of Affirmative Action," p. 34.

60 percent of all groups except white males that there is a need for improvement in communications among persons of different racial and ethnic backgrounds.[g]

Consequently, a number of authors emphasize the need for diversity management with strong support from top management. R. Roosevelt Thomas introduced the term "managing diversity" in his 1991 book, *Beyond Race and Gender.*[h] Ivancevich and Gilbert draw on Thomas' work in defining *diversity management* as "the commitment on the part of organizations to recruit, retain, reward, and promote a heterogeneous mix of productive, motivated, and committed workers including people of color, whites, females, and the physically challenged."[i]

From Affirmative Action to Full Spectrum Diversity in the American Workplace: Shifting the Organizational Paradigm

James D. Slack

More so than any other cultural attribute, diversity is the cornerstone of the American experience. There are currently over 50 distinctive ethnic groups in the U. S., ranging in population from nearly 60 million German-Americans to fewer than 260,000 Yugoslavian-Americans. (See Table 1) All strive to acquire economic and political power. Linguistic diversity also seems more pronounced today than at any other time this century. Over 32 million Americans—nearly 15 percent of the population—speak one of 25 languages other than English at home. (See Table 2) Among the non-English speaking Americans are 17 million Hispanics, almost seven million Europeans, and just over 100,000 Asian Indians who speak Gujarathi as their first language.

Perhaps because it is so central to our common experience, diversity has also been the focal point of some of our most perplexing challenges over the past two centuries. The crux of the matter is really two-fold. On the one hand, certain groups have never been accepted fully due to the antecedents of prejudice and ignorance. And consequently, while all groups have had to struggle to be included within the political mainstream of American life, some groups have had to wage more costly battles than others. Sadly, some battles remain unwon. The same is true within the economic sphere, where certain groups have had greater difficulty than others in receiving and enjoying the benefits incumbent with being within the American mainstream.

On the other hand, there remains a cultural desire to regard everyone as "Americans," despite the persistence of ignorance and prejudice. But the fact that

James D. Slack. *Rev. of Public Personnel Administration,* Fall 1997, pp. 75–87.

[g]Vidu Soni, "A Twenty-First-Century Reception for Diversity in the Public Sector: A Case Study," *Public Administration Review,* Vol. 60, No. 5, September/October 2000, pp. 395–408.

[h]R. Roosevelt Thomas, *Beyond Race and Gender: Unleashing the Power of Your Total Workforce by Managing Diversity* (New York: American Management Association, 1991).

[i]John M. Ivancevich and Jacqueline A. Gilbert, "Diversity Management: Time for a New Approach," p. 77.

diversity ultimately means a recognition of distinctiveness can easily convert the hope of commonality into a feeling of unease among many people within the mainstream. Not surprisingly, the uneasiness felt about diversity seems to transcend racial, ethnic and gender differences among those who are already in the mainstream. For some, there is a tendency to resent those who rebuff the invitation to "be like us." For others, there is a likelihood to suspect people who press to maintain a distinct and separate ethnic, linguistic, religious or lifestyle identity. Moreover, philosophical tensions always exist between the American demand for its *raison d'etre,* individualism, and the American need for the concomitant value of equality that is fundamental to ensuring individual rights.

The quandary over diversity has led government to take many and often contradictory actions, including conducting armed conflict during the 1860s and imposing Jim Crow laws and implementing "separate but equal" doctrines in the decades that followed. In perhaps more rational times we have experimented with a wide array of employment strategies, ranging from patronage practices to equal employment opportunity policies, designed with the dual hope of opening further the doors of opportunity to members of additional, underutilized groups while ensuring the right of every individual, regardless of group identification, to walk through those same doors. During the last part of the twentieth century, we have relied heavily on affirmative action principles in our efforts to accomplish this twofold objective.

This article addresses the need to enhance both group diversity and individualism in the workplace by shifting attention away from affirmative action principles and strategies, as they are commonly implemented, and focusing more on securing a comprehensive, or full spectrum version of diversity in the workplace. To do so, an accompanying shift in organizational paradigm must also occur. By affirmative action, I mean the development and implementation of reactive workplace practices designed to redress the adverse ramifications of past discrimination against people holding protected-class status: women, African Americans, Hispanic Americans, Asian Americans, Native Americans, and Pacific Islanders. By full spectrum diversity, I mean having work settings reflect proactively the gender, cultural and ethnic complexity of each local community as well as the American society.

The first section examines some of the limitations which current affirmative action practices tend to place on the realization of full spectrum diversity. The second section focuses on the need for a shift in organizational paradigm, from one externally-driven to one that uses internally-based incentives to accomplish full spectrum diversity. A workplace strategy is then constructed which attempts to: (1) eliminate the weaknesses found currently in affirmative action practices; and, (2) maintain and enhance the asset of diversity in the American workplace.

Affirmative Action and Constraints on Diversity

Despite much evidence about the political (Riccucci, 1997) and employment (Hale, 1996; Naff, 1997) limitations of affirmative action, it remains true that members of protected groups have benefited from such policies over the past several decades. In comparison to just a generation ago, there are more minorities (Murray & Terry, 1994; Page, 1994) and women (Guy, 1993; Kelly, Guy & Bayes, 1991) in government now, although still too few are at the upper echelons of management. Some agencies are less successful than others in accomplishing affirmative action outcomes (Kellough, 1989) but there is a growing number of public sector organizations which excel in the processes of including more members of protected groups in the work force (Chambers & Riccucci, 1997). Certainly American society, and its workplace, has benefited greatly from the implementation of affirmative action strategies in the public and private sectors.

Yet the outcome of current affirmative action policies is a product of externally-driven forces. For many workplace managers, the primary incentives to develop and implement affirmative action plans are three-fold: compliance with federal laws, fear of adverse court rulings in response to non-compliant practices, and concern over potential political consequences within the outside community or the larger organizational structure for either defiant non-compliance or zealous over-compliance with the law. The philosophical rationale behind affirmative action, that it is a means to realize a truly representative bureaucracy, as well as the organizational rationale, that a representative bureaucracy is good for the health and effectiveness of the organization, all become lost to the intergovernmental, legal and political dimensions of the process. Therefore, current affirmative action practices offer workplace managers few internally-based, organizational incentives to pursue work force diversity actively and aggressively.

Three consequences tend to follow from this situation. First, exclusively focusing on some groups which historically have experienced workplace discrimination, current affirmative action strategies limit the utilization of the vast, full spectrum of American diversity. In terms of the workplace diversity equation, therefore, externally-driven factors designate some groups as irrelevant, while earmarking others as being obstructive. The vast majority of cultural and ethnic groups in America (see Table 1 and Table 2) do not enjoy protected-class status and, therefore, are excluded from diversity calculations. One side-effect is that people in these groups can fall prey to subtle and unchecked discrimination in employment decisions. Gay Americans also remain unprotected by federal affirmative action guidelines. They, too, are deemed irrelevant to diversity considerations and can be discriminated against legally in many work settings.

Moreover, current affirmative action policies prevent European Americans and Canadian Americans from contributing in a positive way to the workplace diversity equation. The same is true of men who, in comparison to women, are not regarded as meaningful weights in that equation. As a result of externally-driven forces, current affirmative action programs also deem religious and linguistic diversity as being irrelevant to the American workplace composition.

Second, current affirmative action policies also have a tendency to involve a substantial degree of stereotyping, or oversimplification, of the many attributes of diversity. Consequently, externally-driven factors not only prevent a recognition of the full spectrum of diversity in society, but they also lend credence to ignoring the complete diversity within individuals who are members of protected groups. Complex cultural and ethnic considerations are melted down and poured into denotative boxes on pre-employment documents. Complex individual identities are easily assigned to these oversimplified categories in the minds of employers and coworkers alike. One is "thought of" as being primarily African American, overriding perhaps more important personal experiences, religious beliefs and family attributes. One is "viewed" simply as being Latino, regardless of national and cultural origin, or as Native American without thought to tribal ancestry or geographical identity.

Third, there is the omnipresent possibility that, throughout the hiring and promotion processes within each workplace, an artificial tension will be created

Table 1   U. S. Population, by Selected Ancestry Group, 1990

Region/Nation	Population	Region/Nation	Population
Asian:		*European (cont.):*	
Asian Indian	520,000	Greek	1,110,000
Chinese	1,505,000	Hungarian	1,582,000
Filipino	451,000	Irish	38,736,000
Japanese	1,005,000	Italian	14,665,000
Korean	937,000	Lithuanian	812,000
Vietnamese	536,000	Norwegian	3,869,000
Cent. & So. American & Spain:		Polish	9,366,000
Cuban	860,000	Portuguese	1,153,000
Dominican	506,000	Russian	2,953,000
Hispanic	1,113,000	Scandinavian	679,000
Mexican	11,587,000	Scotch-Irish	5,618,000
Puerto Rican	1,955,000	Scottish	5,394,000
Salvadoran	499,000	Slovak	1,883,000
Spanish	2,007,000	Swedish	4,681,000
West Indian/Jamaican	435,000	Swiss	1,045,000
		Ukrainian	741,000
European:		Welsh	2,034,000
Austrian	865,000	Yugoslavian	258,000
British	1,119,000		
Croatian	544,000	*North American:*	
Czech	1,296,000	Acadian/Cajun	668,000
Danish	1,635,000	African-American	23,777,000
Dutch	6,227,000	American Indian	8,708,000
English	32,652,000	American	12,396,000
European	467,000	Canadian	550,000
Finnish	659,000	French Canadian	2,167,000
French	10,321,000	United States	644,000
German	57,947,000	White	1,800,000

Note. From *Statistical Abstract of the United Sates,* 1995, 56, p. 53, by U.S. Department of Commerce/ Bureau of the Census, Washington, DC.

Table 2   **Persons Five Years Old and Over Speaking a Language other than English at Home, by Language: 1990**

Language	Population	Language	Population
Spanish	17,339,000	Hindi (Urdu)	331,000
French	1,702,000	Russian	242,000
German	1,547,000	Yiddish	213,000
Italian	1,309,000	Tai (Laotian)	206,000
Chinese	1,249,000	Persian	202,000
Tagalog	843,000	French Creole	188,000
Polish	723,000	Armenian	150,000
Korean	626,000	Navaho	149,000
Vietnamese	507,000	Hungarian	148,000
Portuguese	430,000	Hebrew	144,000
Japanese	428,000	Dutch	143,000
Greek	388,000	Mon-Khmer (Cambodian)	127,000
Arabic	355,000	Gujarathi	102,000

Note. From *Statistical Abstract of the United States,* 1995, 57, p. 53. U.S. Department of Commerce/ Bureau of the Census, Washington, DC.

between the value of merit and the value of diversity. The artificial tension tends to send misleading and confusing signals to well-intentioned workplace managers. This phenomenon, too, is the result of externally-driven forces because it is the seemingly contradictory nature of federal guidelines and court decisions which permits the tension to emerge in the first place. On the one hand, equal employment opportunity (EEO) guidelines require employers to remain color- and gender-blind in making hiring and promotion decisions. Managers are supposed to take into consideration only the issues of merit and performance. Yet current affirmative action guidelines call for color- and gender-consciousness. Employers are required to take into consideration the oversimplified categories of human characteristics, or ethnic and cultural stereotypes, as discussed above. The dilemma is that workplace managers must comply simultaneously with both sets of guidelines, representing two distinct sets of values.

In this quagmire, managers can conclude mistakenly that they must either be "blind but to merit" or be "conscious only of color and gender." For some workplace managers, implementation of affirmative action strategies can become the overriding goal in the hiring and promotion processes rather than simply one of several important objectives in the workplace equation. For other managers, the fact that it is far too easy to pit unnecessarily the value of merit against the value of diversity is welcome ammunition. They use it to underscore "tokenism" in the selection and promotion processes. For the vast majority of well-intentioned managers, perceived or real pressures to give priority to the value of affirmative action can leave a foul taste in the mouth of merit. Yet this group of professionals also tends to want to distance itself from bigot-driven arguments about tokenism.

Unfortunately, this conflict can also lead to a vastly diminished self-view for some members of protected-groups, even though the overwhelming majority are hired and promoted under the principle of merit.

Toward Full Spectrum Diversity

Certainly the solution to the dilemma of enhancing workplace diversity does not lie in dismantling affirmative action results; it may not even lie in the dismantling of affirmative action programs. The original intent of affirmative action, that of establishing a truly representative bureaucracy, must remain a sacred principle to the public service regardless of what workplace strategies are adopted.

It is for this one common mission, the realization of a representative bureaucracy, that the concept of affirmative action becomes the antecedent to the concept of full spectrum diversity. The objective of full spectrum diversity, however, is more than a singular focus on protecting members of selected groups which have a long and painful history of being victims of workplace discrimination. In addition, a focus on full spectrum diversity ensures that contributions of members of all groups, however they define themselves, are viewed as having important value in the human resource equation.

A shift in organizational paradigm is required to accomplish the transition from affirmative action to full spectrum diversity. We must move from a focus that reacts primarily to externally-driven factors to one that is more proactive and inward-looking about shaping the future of the organization.

Managers who think primarily in terms of externally-driven factors—compliance with federal guidelines, avoidance of court mandates, and accommodation to local political pressures—fall prey to ignoring other diversity considerations and stereotyping members of protected groups. In far too many instances, they also find themselves pitting the value of merit against the value of diversity.

In order to accomplish full spectrum diversity in the workplace, and to avoid the pitfalls of current affirmative action practices, managers need to think selfishly about what is best for their organizations and even their own careers. They need to consider an internally-based rationale for taking proactive measures to enhance the mix of human resources. From this perspective, diversity means bringing qualified professionals to the organization's "table" because these people not only possess prerequisite technical knowledge and work-related expertise, but they also have unique backgrounds and intangible insights which are quintessential to addressing organizational needs and solving public problems.

The greater the number of diverse people with technical merit at this table, the more likely the organization will be successful in accomplishing its mission and be effective in responding to the citizenry. Consequently, there is a greater chance that the manager will be successful in her own career. Rather than being responsive to externalities, therefore, the manager has internally-based incentives to seek out independently and aggressively a work force characterized by full spectrum diversity. The side-effects of doing so can also be enormously beneficial to the health and well-being of all employees. Not only will pursuing such a strategy actually accomplish the goals of current federal affirmative action regulations, the participation of non-protected group members will also become truly meaningful in the workplace diversity equation. The presence of European American males at the organization's table, for instance, will be just as important as the presence of Pacific Islander females. The presence of people who speak English or Yiddish in their homes will be just as significant as having individuals who speak Spanish or Tagalog as first languages. The presence of Jews, Muslims, and atheists will be as important as the presence of Methodists, Catholics, and other Christians. As both active and passive representation (Mosher, 1982) is embraced by the organization, the self-worth of every group—and every individual—in society is reaffirmed.

In summary, the concepts of affirmative action and full spectrum diversity are similar in that both share the goal of building a representative bureaucracy. As outlined in Figure 1, however, there are several substantive and procedural differences between the practice of affirmative action in many organizations and an effort to realize full spectrum of diversity in any workplace. Affirmative action strategies represent a historically reactive process that is designed to correct the consequences of past discrimination. Full spectrum diversity, on the other hand, entails a more proactive outlook. It attempts to gauge and assess the nature and composition of the current work force with a constant eye toward changes which might occur in the community.

Only specific groups are protected in the case of affirmative action, whereas full spectrum diversity considers all groups to be important in the workplace equation. While affirmative action tends to result in the stereotyping of individuals, a concern for full spectrum diversity encourages the realization that each individual is a complex, diverse entity who cannot be placed into over-simplified categories. Whereas a concern for affirmative action sometimes results in an artificial conflict between the values of diversity and merit, a concern for full spectrum diversity facilitates a better understanding about the non-competitive nature of the relationship between these two values. Finally, the implementation of affirmative action strategies tends to be externally-driven and, therefore, they are viewed by many within organizations as policies being imposed upon the organization. A concern for full spectrum diversity, on the other hand, is generated from internal concerns about organizational and career success.

Figure 1   Differences Between Full Spectrum Diversity and Affirmative Action

Full Spectrum Diversity	Affirmative Action
• Proactive	• Reactive
• Concern about all groups in the community, including members of underutilized groups	• Concern for members of underutilized groups
• Recognition of diversity within the individual	• Simplification and stereotyping
• Value of merit and the value of diversity: competitive	• Value of merit and the value of diversity: noncompetitive
• Internally-driven factors	• Externally-driven factors

A Workplace Procedure for Implementing Full Spectrum Diversity

The shift in paradigm does not necessarily entail radical changes in the selection and promotion processes as found in many affirmative action policies. It does, however, assume much more clarity and rationality in the various stages of those processes in order to avoid the pitfalls commonly associated with many current affirmative action practices. The model, presented in Figure 2, illustrates how the shift to an internally-based paradigm might be implemented. It breaks the hiring (or promotion) process into five distinct steps: (1) creating the job description; (2) advertising the position; (3) creating a pool of applicants; (4) interviewing finalists; and, (5) the hiring decision.

The first step entails developing the job description. At this step, managers remain focused on the issue of technical merit. Duties are written strictly in terms of work-related skills. All discussions, even informal conversations, exclude the expression of hopes, concerns or expectations about hiring members of protected or non-protected groups. Doing so would only lead to some of the pitfalls of current affirmative action practices entailing confusion over the value of merit and the value of diversity, as well as permitting externally-based factors to take priority over the internal needs of the organization.

The second step entails advertising the position. As in the first step, the manager selfishly does what is in the best interest of the organization. This means that she now focuses on the diversity question, not because of existing and externally-driven affirmative action policies, but because it is in the best interest of the organization to have the largest possible pool of technically qualified candidates emerge from the search. It is in the best interest of the manager to search out for all technically competent people, whether they live in the gay community or in the Hispanic community.

Hence, managers now have an internally-based rationale to switch from a reactive routine of complying with affirmative action procedures to a more pro-

---

Figure 2   A Model For Full Spectrum Diversity Recruitment

Step 1:   *Job Description*
            Focus = Merit

Step 2:   *Job Advertisement*
            Focus = Aggressive action (AA)

Step 3:   *Job Pool Analysis*
            Focus = Merit

Step 4:   *Interviewing Top Candidates*
            Foci = Full spectrum diversity
                  Other job-related considerations

Step 5:   *Hiring one of Top Candidates*
            Result = Enhancement of the organization's table
                  Technical merit not in competition with full spectrum diversity

---

active mode of taking "aggressive action" to ensure that the widest net is used to capture a pool of applicants which adds to the organization's technical expertise. The position is advertised aggressively in general sources, where all qualified people might read it: local newspapers, postings in appropriate public buildings, job phone lines and the Internet, statewide job newsletters, and advertisements in *Public Administration Times*.

Since the manager is also cognizant of who is not present at the organization's table, she also takes aggressive action to ensure that technically qualified members of these groups are also aware of the position. Locally, this might entail advertising via non-English and special interest newspapers and radio stations, tapping the help of specific churches which tend to serve underutilized groups, contacting local chapters of professional societies, or using informal networks to "get the word out" to specific groups. Nationally, it might entail tapping the networks in a variety of specialized sections of the American Society for Public Administration, such as the Section on Women in Public Administration or the Conference of Minority Public Administrators.

The third step involves the review and narrowing of the pool of job applicants. As in each of the other steps, the manager has internally-based incentives to do what is best for the organization. At this point, however, attention returns strictly to matters of technical merit because workplace competency must be the primary goal of any organization. Discussions about diversity at the stage of reviewing resumes and job applications, therefore, encourage the seamy side of affirmative action politics—that is, the emergence of the artificial tension between merit and diversity, as well as allegations and innuendoes of tokenism.

Let us assume that this process results in selecting the top five applicants who are all technically qualified for the position. The manager invites the five individuals to interview with the organization, which is step four in the model. At this point, attention is directed to a wide array of job-related issues which extend beyond technical merit. Included here are concerns about effective oral communication skills, ability to work well in team settings, motivation, and personality traits which might help or hinder job performance. Verification of technical merit might also occur, but this is certainly not the focus of step four. Since the previous step established that each of the five finalists is technically qualified to perform the job tasks, merit is no longer a primary consideration.

It is at this step that full spectrum diversity becomes an issue. The manager looks at who is not at the organization's table and, more importantly, who needs to be at the table based on the demographics of the local community. The fulfillment of this assessment will, in all likelihood, result in compliance with current affirmative action guidelines because far too few members of protected groups have yet to gain a seat at any meaningful table in our society. Yet in certain communities, it also could mean that a Croatian American, or perhaps a Polish-speaking American, might offer intangible expertise needed in the organization. If European Americans or males are underrepresented at the organization's table, this process allows the manager to justify their hiring also on the basis of community demographics.

Step 5 entails the hiring of one applicant to fill the position. The selection of this person is based on a number of job-related factors. First, she or he is one of a handful of technically competent finalists and, therefore, the concern about merit is satisfied. Two, the successful applicant demonstrated competency in a number of other job-related areas during the interview. Third, he or she brings some intangible and underrepresented trait to the table.

Analysis

From the perspective of diversity, a shift to an internally-based paradigm does not guarantee desired results. For instance, five European American males might be finalists for the position of police chief in a community that is 75 percent African American. Or, five Latinos might be finalists for that position in a community that is overwhelmingly Italian American. There may be an absence of homosexuals who are police chief finalists in communities like San Francisco, California or Lakewood, Ohio which have significant concentrations of gay Americans.

While the results may not always reach our hopes, the process can certainly meet our expectations. Contrary to reactive affirmative action strategies, the approach described here prevents the value of merit from competing with the value of diversity. Hence, it also eliminates the chance of tokenism. Unlike current affirmative action policies, the model also reduces the chance of stereotyping by de-emphasizing the need to comply with federal regulations. The probability of achieving the original intent of affirmative action policies, however, is enhanced since managers will less likely think in terms of simply filling over-simplified boxes on annual Equal Employment Opportunity (EEO) reports. Embracing the concept of full spectrum diversity, moreover, limits the chance of adverse reactions toward personnel decisions throughout the entire work force.

The fact that this model relies on internally-based incentives means that management will investigate proactively to ensure that hopes and expectations are accomplished. The clarity and distinctiveness of each step helps in this search. If the person hired does not meet diversity expectations, then management may decide to invest more time and resources in Step 2 during the next round of hiring. If the pool does not produce a sufficient number of technically meritorious finalists, then management has an additional reason to make greater investments in Step 2. It might also want to revisit the job description process in Step 1 in order to assure that expectations of competency are reasonable and achievable.

Given the rapidly changing complexity of American society, it may be far easier for managers to determine expectations of competency and merit than it is for them to gauge diversity within the local community and among job applicants. Some individuals do not identify with specific groups, even though they may ostensibly "fit" into a particular category. Moreover, most individuals "fit" into several categories of diversity. Hence, one question arises: How should managers determine and assess the ethnic, religious, and linguistic attributes, as well as the sexual preference, of a job applicant and a community?

The answer may lie in the development of more elaborate EEO forms which encourage people to identify with a myriad of ethnic, religious and lifestyle categories. In terms of cultural stereotyping, however, over-specification on pre-employment documents could easily result in as much damage as the current practice of oversimplification. While people may identify with several categories, these categories are always evolving due to their unique life experiences. For instance, a Mexican American in Ohio or Minnesota may have a completely different self-identity than a Mexican American in California or Texas. A Prussian American may identify more with being a Christian than with any particular Junker quality. The sudden infliction of a physical disability, such as heart disease or arthritis, may alter drastically the self-identity and life priorities of a lesbian. In essence, the pre-determined categories are the product of a paradigm driven by external factors and, therefore, they do not necessarily reflect the evolving self-views of the specific job applicant, the changing nature of a particular community, or the special needs of each organization.

The nature of life itself necessitates more open-endedness to gauge the self-identity of the individual. From the point of view of what is best for the organization, what matters is not which pre-determined box on the pre-employment form is checked by the job applicant. The checked box merely represents a superficial snapshot of a complex, evolving human being. The task of the workplace manager in an increasingly diverse society is to rely less on the forced-choice response categories required by externally-driven considerations. Rather, the challenge for management is to assess holistically the additional perspectives and intangible skills, information, and expertise each meritorious job applicant can bring to the organization's table.

The shift in paradigms places a much greater burden on the organization. No longer willing to rely solely on predetermined forced-choice responses, workplace managers and selection committees must accept the responsibility of acquiring a better, holistic "feel" for the cultural dynamics of the communities in which they live and work. They may be assisted in this process with a variety of external devices, such as becoming involved in nonwork-related community and neighborhood groups, establishing community advisory boards to keep the organization informed about local concerns, and placing community members on selection and promotion committees. Modifications in internal processes will also be needed, such as devising a greater degree of open-endedness on pre-employment forms and integrating more subjectivity, perhaps in the form of essay-oriented material, into application practices. Certainly greater subjectivity is called for in Step 4 (see Figure 2) of the recruitment process. Managers must engage in cultural conversations in the interview stage in order to better gauge the potential contributions of each meritorious candidate. While fear of litigation currently prevents such conversations from occurring in earnest, the paradigmatic change will help place these conversations in the proper context and, thereby, reduce the chance of using responses for discriminatory purposes. Under the new paradigm, it is in the best interest of both the organization and job applicant to explore the unique and enhancing attributes which the meritorious job applicant can bring to the organization's table.

One final question remains: How can organizations get every manager, especially those who do not share an authentic appreciation for diversity, to embrace wholeheartedly the new paradigm?

A shift to an internally-based paradigm provides no inherent guarantee that past practices and current prejudices will not contaminate new procedures. Zealot advocates of protected groups might still find ways to insert diversity issues at inappropriate stages of the process. Bigoted members of hiring committees might still find ways of justifying the hiring of "same-type" people, or in spreading rumors about tokenism when the organization hires otherwise. Unfortunately, the motives of individuals can always bastardize the best intentions of organizations.

Yet leadership in any organization begins at the top, and leadership in every organization has the responsibility to monitor and evaluate the behavior of its staff, as well as the outcomes of its processes. Managers can be held accountable to the organization, and this is very much part of the shift to an internally-based ratio-nale. Internal incentives, perhaps in the form of raises or other organizational ben-efits, must be provided for managers who engage in the dual processes of acquiring a better "feel" for the cultural dynamics of the community and securing full spectrum diversity in the workplace. Penalties must be incurred by those who try to thwart those processes.

Public organizations are also accountable to the citizenry. It is ironic, there-fore, that a new set of external factors might be required to encourage the leader-ship of public organizations to accept and implement an internally-based paradigm. Citizens may have to be re-educated to understand the importance of having public organizations functioning effectively and responsively without regard to external preferences and politics and, consequently, striving to build a work force that truly represents the entire community. The history of our field reminds us that managers are not only responsible for leadership within the public organization, but they must also exert leadership among the public-at-large. Similar to what occurred toward the end of last century, therefore, another public service reform movement may be needed prior to the close of the present century.

Conclusion

Diversity has always represented America's greatest asset, in addition to being its most common attribute. Through the successive and incremental inclusion of many different groups over the past two centuries, diversity has helped shape and refine our democratic traditions and sociopolitical processes. This evolution will certainly continue well into the next millennium.

To the American workplace, the twenty-first century will present an increas-ingly complex layering of diversity that will demand much more thought and insight than is provided by the singular denotations of today. This will be demon-strated by the number of new groups which will be defined as "American" and, hence, will have the right to be seated at the organization's table. It will also be seen in how each individual—every "new" and "old" American—redefines him- or herself within the ever changing context of both macro and micro cultures.

As a result, the challenges placed before the public service will be greater than at any other time in our history. A shift away from the traditional view of affirmative action, to one more concerned with the full spectrum of diversity, will enable public servants to address more effectively and responsively the many, and as yet unknown, needs of a very new and different America. A shift in organizational paradigm, from one externally-driven to one that is internally-centered, will help the public service in preparing to meet these new challenges.

Notes

I wish to acknowledge the contributions made by my research assistant, Rhonda Castle, a graduate student in the Department of Public Policy and Administration at California State University-Bakersfield. I am also grateful for the support provided by James George, Associate Vice President for Academic Affairs, and Professor Beth Rienzi, Coordinator of the Mentor Program at California State University-Bakersfield. I also wish to thank the external referees and the symposium editor for providing very insightful comments on earlier drafts of this manuscript.

References

Chambers, T. & Riccucci, N. M. (1997). Models of excellence in workplace diversity. In C. Ban and N. M. Riccucci (Eds.), *Public personnel management: Current concerns, future challenges* (pp. 73–90). New York: Longman.

Guy, M. E. (1993). Three steps forward, two steps backward: The status of women's integration into public management. *Public Administration Review, 53* (4), 285–292.

Hale, M. M. (1996). Gender equality in organizations. *Review of Public Personnel Administration, 16* (1), 7–18.

Kellough, J. E. (1989). *Federal equal employment opportunity policy and numerical goals and time-tables: An impact assessment.* New York: Praeger.

Kelly, R. M., Guy, M. E. & Bayes, J. (1991). Public managers in the states: A comparison of career advancement by sex. *Public Administration Review, 51* (5), 402–412.

Mosher, F. C. (1982). *Democracy and the public service.* New York: Oxford University Press.

Murray, S. & Terry, L. D. (1994). The role demands and dilemmas of minority public administrators: The Herbert thesis revisited. *Public Administration Review, 54* (5), 409–417.

Naff, K. C. (1997). Colliding with a glass ceiling: Barriers to the advancement of women and minorities. In C. Ban and N. M. Riccucci (Eds.), *Public personnel management: Current concerns, future challenges* (pp. 91–108). New York: Longman.

Page, P. (1994). African Americans in executive branch agencies. *Review of Public Personnel Administration, 16* (1), 24–51.

Riccucci, N. M. (1997). Will affirmative action survive into the 21st century? In C. Ban and N. M. Riccucci (Eds.), *Public personnel management: Current concerns, future challenges* (pp. 57–72). New York: Longman.

L ike diversity, reform of the civil service and how staffing is done in government are an integral part of human resource management. And yet, much of it is hardly new. Arguably the most ambitious attempt to reform the federal civil service occurred during the Carter administration. Under the leadership of a distinguished public administration academic and practitioner, Alan K. Campbell, the Personnel Management Project in 1978 submitted numerous recommendations that were in some cases passed by Congress and in others promulgated by Executive Order. Among other things, these recommendations were designed to ease and decentralize the hiring and promotion process by shifting responsibility for examining job applicants from the civil service commission to the administrative agencies. They also allowed agencies to go beyond selecting from among the three candidates ranked highest by civil service—the so-called "rule of three"—and choose instead from the top seven job applicants. They sought to give managers greater power by easing removal of employees for cause by streamlining the appeals process. The report also proposed an Executive Service that eventually incorporated the three "supergrade" levels in the federal career civil service. Rewards would now be dependent on performance. Furthermore, these high-level officials no longer enjoyed full civil service protection—they could now be reassigned or in some cases removed by the president for inadequate performance of duties. And yet, when seeking to explain why these reforms were adopted in a surprisingly brief four month period and met with relatively little resistance, Peri Arnold, an expert on presidential reorganization, concluded that "it was the plan's virtue that its fundamental recommendations were not novel." In this respect Campbell and his colleagues "owed a debt to earlier proposals to reform the civil service. The Brownlow Commission (in 1936) and both Hoover Commissions (in 1947 and 1953) had called for major changes in that system."[a]

Yet Another Hopeful Beginning

We move now to 1997, and here are Steven Hays and Shawn Whitney writing about a "hope-filled beginning" at reinventing the personnel function by introducing many of these same recommendations in South Carolina. The authors are particularly interested in exploring these proposed changes, because they were part of Clinton's Reinventing Government (ReGo) initiative led by then-Vice President Al Gore, and at least some of these changes would be attempted by other states. Nor are Hays and Whitney and the Clinton-Gore team the only ones concerned with such changes. Other voices sounded similar themes and cast them largely in a human resource development context. Several Brookings Institution scholars mentioned such traditional concerns as redesigning the federal government's central personnel agency, promoting greater flexibility, performance-based compensation, and integrating the civil service with other management systems. In addition, they recommended the use of more privatization, heavier reliance on accountability for results, and developing a powerful core of career civil servants who would focus on policy, working with public, nonprofit, and private partners, information, and feedback in the form of performance measurement and program evaluation.[b] A group of leading public sector academics and practitioners issued a Wye River Conference Report that also reflected the HRD emphasis on "shifting from a traditional public-sector system to a system for the 21st century." Merit thus should no longer focus on protecting people and equating fairness with sameness; merit should lead to an outcome of encouraging better performance and allow for differentiation between different talents. Human resources should now be viewed as an asset and an investment rather than

---

[a]Peri E. Arnold, *Making the Managerial Presidency: Comprehensive Reorganization Planning, 1905–1996*, 2nd ed., rev. (Lawrence, KS: University Press of Kansas, 1998), pp. 332–335.

[b]Donald F. Kettl, Patricia W. Ingraham, Ronald P. Sanders, and Constance Horner, *Civil Service Reform: Building a Government That Works* (Washington, D.C.: Brookings Institution Press, 1996), pp. 61–86.

a cost, and performance appraisal should be based on demonstrated individual contributions to organizational goals.[c]

Hays and Whitney's appraisal of how comparable reforms fared in South Carolina underscores the remarkable staying power of the barriers to such change. It is noteworthy, though, how much of this resistance relates to organizational change generally rather than to something intrinsic to civil service reform. Hays and Whitney thus point to the burden that such changes place on middle managers and unions. For their part, veterans groups are no different from any other powerful interest seeking to perpetuate a competitive advantage—they simply are better at it.

Expending Political Capital and Civil Service Reform

Perhaps ultimately, what perpetuates the shortcomings of federal—and state and local—civil service systems is that the price that would have to be paid in political capital to uproot them is out of all proportion to the electoral benefits the chief executive would gain from the struggle.

Presidential candidate Al Gore in the 2000 election campaign tried to capitalize on his considerable work on reinventing government. The voters did not seem to know what he was talking about; while these efforts evoked enthusiasm in some federal and state political circles, they seemed to register approximately 1.5 on the electoral Richter scale. Presidents will sometimes rise above politics and take action in what they view as the public interest. But are they likely to do so for civil service reform? A Carter presidential aide, Sy Lazarus, put this in perspective when he told Peri Arnold that reorganization is "a nice second-level issue." Presidents in Arnold's view are more interested in *what* they want to do than *how* they want to do it.[d] President Clinton would support reinventing government but not at the price of alienating powerful public service unions or changing political arrangements that contribute to agency shortcomings.

Hays and Whitney's findings are consistent with this pattern. South Carolina's chief executive was supportive of reinventing government reform, but drew the line where it entailed spending more money on performance-based salary adjustments, group productivity incentives, or significant employee recognition cash awards that would have a larger electoral impact if spent elsewhere. For its part, the South Carolina legislature tried to introduce reform on the cheap. No special funding was provided to the agencies to subsidize the various incentive strategies.

Before we, as public administrators, dismiss these actions as just another example of "politics as usual," note that failure to implement civil service reform implicates us too. The South Carolina public managers in busy agencies also assigned a relatively low priority or shilly-shallied on implementing such reforms— they used the excuse of lack of time and resources to explain why they had not developed any form even of employee recognition. Furthermore, systematic and honest performance appraisal, a staple of proactive HRD plans, requires no political action— just managerial guts and willingness to look their employees in the eye and "tell it like it is." They also appear to have expended little effort in a number of agencies even to educate the affected workers as to civil service reform's intent. So Hays and Whitney wryly conclude that, in order to make managerialism and decentralization

---

[c]Patricia Wallace Ingraham, Sally Coleman Selden, and Donald P. Moynihan, "People and Performance: Challenges for the Future Public Service–the Report from the Wye River Conference," *Public Administration Review*, Vol. 60, No. 1, January/February 2000, p. 58.

[d]Peri E. Arnold, *Making the Managerial Presidency: Comprehensive Reorganization Planning, 1905–1996,* p. 380.

work, "central personnel offices may find themselves in the position of having to restore some of the monitoring and police functions that were surrendered in recent decades."

But this spotty reform response is hardly unique to South Carolina. A survey of 1200 agency heads in the 50 states by Brudney, Hebert, and Wright in 1999 concluded that while some agencies were selectively adopting such reforms as strategic planning and improved customer service, a concerted reinvention movement is not underway across state government.[e]

Reinventing the Personnel Function: Lessons Learned From a Hope-Filled Beginning in One State

Steven W. Hays and Shawn Benzinger Whitney

Although public institutions and administrative processes have been subjected to a virtually uninterrupted string of reform movements dating back to 1883, the staffing function in particular has always been regarded as "a work in progress" (Stevens, 1995, p. 2). Every president since Chester A. Arthur has tinkered with the civil service system, just as changes in staffing practices and/or career systems have been central fixtures in the final reports of every major reform commission (all 11) that met between 1905 and 1996 (Ingraham, 1992). Thus, it should come as no surprise that public personnel systems are prime targets of many of the salvos that have been fired by the recent reform armada.

Public administration's current preoccupation with the so-called reinventing government phenomenon (Carroll, 1996; Moe, 1993; Rosenbloom, 1993; Schachter, 1995) provides most of the backdrop for the current reform movement. Since the publication of Osborne and Gaebler's (1992) influential book, "reinvention" "revitalization," "reengineering," "redesign," and similar euphemisms have dominated the public management literature. Despite its clear vulnerability to the "old wine in new bottles" critique (Butler, 1991; Kamensky, 1996), the movement is notable in its own right for the enthusiasm that it has spawned among practitioners and politicians bent on reforming public management. The core ideas of reinvention— including emphasis on entrepreneurial solutions to public problems, decentralization of authority, deregulation, and a customer orientation—power the wave of reform efforts that is now sweeping across the management landscape. The federal government's national performance review, along with dozens of state and local initiatives (Egger & O'Leary, 1995), all incorporate one or more elements of the reinvention agenda.

Steven W. Hays and Shawn Benzinger Whitney. *American Review of Public Administration*, Vol. 27, No. 4, December 1997, 324–342. © 1997 Sage Publications, Inc.

[e] Jeffrey L. Brudney, F. Ted Hebert, and Deil S. Wright, "Reinventing Government in the American States: Measuring and Explaining Administrative Reform," *Public Administration Review*, Vol. 59, No. 1, January/February 1999, pp. 19–30.

This article examines one of the most ambitious efforts currently under way to reinvent a large public personnel system. Specifically, a 1993 revision of the State of South Carolina's merit system is assessed. The reforms initiated in July of 1993 by the state's General Assembly are borrowed directly from the national reinvention movement. They touch on almost all of the major personnel functions that are targeted in state and national reform programs. Thus, the progress that has been made and the detours that have been taken represent an interesting case study that may be useful in weighing the potential impacts of similar reform efforts in other jurisdictions.

Reinvention and Public Personnel Administration

The unremitting interest in reforming public personnel systems existed long before reinvention appeared on the scene and will undoubtedly persist long after it is supplanted by the next management fad. This desire to transform public sector personnel policies is largely attributable to two interrelated factors. First, civil service systems have a terrible reputation for inefficiency and unresponsiveness (Campbell, 1978; Savas & Ginsburg, 1973; Shafritz, 1975). Merit systems are blamed, rightly or wrongly, for impeding the performance of line managers by doing a poor job of recruiting, rewarding, evaluating, and disciplining civil servants. Thus, many reformers believe that attempts to "make government work better and cost less" (Executive Office of the President, 1993, p. 7) depend in large part, on the ability of public administrators to manage their human resources more effectively (Volcker, 1989).

The problems that are evident within public personnel administration are, in turn, byproducts of the role that civil service systems play in a democratic society. Ever since the Pendleton Act first introduced the notion of a professional public service, governments within the United States have wrestled with the tensions that exist between the seemingly incompatible values of merit and accountability (see Mosher, 1968). For most of our nation's history, the putative goal of almost all civil service laws was to ensure the political neutrality of public employees. It was (and is) believed that competent public administration could only be achieved by insulating civil servants from the corrupting influences of politicians. The inherent dilemma, of course, is that each additional measure designed to shield the civil service from political incursions further reduces the public employees' responsiveness to their elected leaders. Thus, the single-minded pursuit of a thoroughly neutral civil service is widely cited as a major cause of the field's ineffectiveness. The critics' basic complaint is simply that society has erred on the side of merit; too much emphasis is placed on neutralizing the civil service, thereby creating a personnel system that is much too rule encrusted, cumbersome, and unresponsive (Campbell, 1977; Sayre, 1948; Stevens, 1995).

Since the early 1950s, the public policy debate has been dominated by those who believe that the pendulum has swung too far in the direction of political neutrality (Ingraham & Rosenbloom, 1988-1989). The Hoover Commission (1949, 1955) advanced several ill-fated proposals that were aimed at making bureaucracy more responsive to political leadership. These included an increase in political appointments, the creation of a pool of senior civil servants who could be moved about according to their talents and abilities, the linkage of pay to performance, and program budgeting. Identical themes resurfaced during Jimmy Carter's successful campaign to modernize the federal merit system through passage of the Civil Service Reform Act of 1978. By placing a higher value on administrative responsiveness than on neutral competence, the act legitimized many of the proposals that would soon be included in later reform programs (Ingraham & Ban, 1984). Measures such as the abolition of the Civil Service Commission and the creation of a rank-in-person career system among high level federal executives (which represented the triumph of the initial Hoover Commission recommendation) were clearly intended to encourage political accountability at the expense of neutral competence (Rourke, 1992). Subsequent reform initiatives during the 1980s and 1990s extended this general trend. Measures aimed at strengthening the hands of public sector supervisors in the management of their subordinates are central features of both the Volcker (1989) and Winter Commission (National Commission on State and Local Public Service, 1993) reports.

When translated into specific reform proposals, the common themes that emerge are administrative flexibility and control in the management of human resources. At the federal level, the most coherent statement of a reinvention agenda is contained in Vice-President Gore's national performance review *From Red Tape to Results* (Executive Office of the President, 1993). Insofar as the personnel function is concerned, the national performance review urges that government staffing activities be reinvented through the following means (U.S. General Accounting Office, 1994).

- Enhance the flexibility of public managers in the hiring of civil servants by abolishing central job registers and application forms; decentralize hiring decisions to the operational level.
- Increase supervisory discretion in the management of human resources by eliminating many procedural restrictions on the assignment, reassignment, transfer, and appointment of civil servants.
- Improve public managers' ability to reward and motivate their employees by delegating salary-setting authority to operating agencies, introducing flexible pay and classification systems (especially broadbanding), and implementing assessment programs that set measurable performance objectives; supplement these steps with incentive award and bonus systems that stimulate productivity.
- Strengthen the ability of public managers to purge their organizations of under-performers by reducing the number of steps needed to terminate workers, improving the operation of progressive discipline procedures, and providing incentives (such as early retirement packages and outplacement assistance) for voluntary separations.

For the most part, these reform components reflect two interrelated facets of the reinvention agenda: decentralization and managerialism. The desire to decentralize the personnel function (and for that matter, all governmental authority) stems from the belief that centralized bureaucracies are unresponsive and wasteful. By decentralizing decisions to operating managers, government can move decisions closer to the problem and thereby diminish some of the inherent inefficiencies of concentrated bureaucracies.

The urge to decentralize public sector staffing gains additional momentum from the empowerment movement. Stated simply, worker empowerment focuses on granting employees the authority they need to perform their jobs with the least amount of interference. Decentralization of the personnel function is especially relevant to this objective because of the demoralizing effects that stodgy staffing practices putatively have on employee motivation and productivity (Ingraham & Eisenberg, 1995). According to reform proponents, today's civil service systems do an inadequate job of recognizing and rewarding outstanding performance and encouraging employees to assume greater responsibility for goal accomplishment. Seniority rather than merit is the chief measure of worth; performance is at best tangential and at worst irrelevant to many of the most significant staffing decisions.

Reform orthodoxy accepts the notion that these shortcomings can be ameliorated by a general loosening of staffing restrictions and the application of common sense. One manifestation of this so-called common sense is merit pay, along with other measures that are intended to reward accomplishment and punish incompetence. Incentive systems, employee recognition strategies, strengthened authority to discipline miscreants, and other market-based solutions to staffing dilemmas are common fixtures in reinvention programs.

These latter measures reflect reinvention's managerialism theme. Managerialism refers to the use of business ideology and practices in the handling of public workers. Because reinvention is essentially an attempt by governments to "regain control of their public sectors" (Halligan & Power, 1991, p. 96), private sector solutions are often viewed as the answer. These values are clearly reflected in proposals stressing productivity measures, supervisory flexibility in personnel matters, and streamlined procedures for disciplining workers. In many instances, they are supplemented with attempts to increase the number of political appointees while reducing the career protections of classified civil servants.

An implicit dilemma within this reform agenda is that decentralization and managerialism do not necessarily constitute a coherent theoretical or operational basis for managing a personnel system. Within a truly decentralized organization, managerialism's objectives would be very difficult to achieve. For the most part, managerialism emphasizes practices that work best in a centralized and control-oriented structure. The tendency to incorporate inconsistent and even contradictory goals is an oft-noted flaw in the reinvention catechism.

South Carolina's Experiment

Without much fanfare or debate, the South Carolina General Assembly passed the State Government Accountability Act in the summer of 1993. This legislation places the state at the forefront of the reinvention movement by reforming two major aspects of state government: procurement and personnel management. In both instances, the primary thrust of the legislation is to increase administrative flexibility through a decentralization of decision-making authority.

Although much of the state's reform agenda is entirely consistent with the conventional wisdom of reinvention, South Carolina's political culture is anything but typical. Legislative domination, a weak executive, and a strong antiunion bias make the lessons of this case study less transportable than they otherwise might be. Despite this fact, however, the underlying pressures that motivated the reform are similar to those that exist in most regions of the United States.

Although the exact genesis of the reform is difficult to pinpoint, two aspects of the state's recent political history are undoubtedly relevant. Like many states of the old confederacy, South Carolina's political establishment has become increasingly Republican in recent years. Republicans have held the governor's mansion for a decade and won control of the lower house of the General Assembly during the 1992 general elections. As the state's political leadership turned to the right, the vocabulary of reinvention gained currency. Privatization, cost cutting, and enhanced efficiency became watchwords of political campaigns. These sentiments ultimately found expression in a move toward the cabinet form of executive governance. After two centuries of highly fragmented, commission-based public administration, in the 1990s the state consolidated executive power by placing an ever expanding number of agencies directly under the governor's control.

In the context of a fundamental reconfiguration of both the political and structural components of state government, reinvention appears to have emerged as a logical complement. Once the governor's administrative authority over state agencies was established, he and his Republican colleagues had an interest in giving the newly appointed managers the requisite tools to implement their policies. Reinvention's emphasis on government efficiency and political accountability and its fixation on executive responsibility for public policy dovetail nicely with much of the emerging political agenda. The focus on personnel system reform, meanwhile, may be more attributable to this scenario than to any underlying dissatisfaction with the state's civil service. Thanks to a long tradition of antiunion sentiment, coupled with a spotty record in observing merit procedures (at least insofar as recruitment and selection are concerned), the civil service system is nowhere near as rule bound and restrictive as those that exist in many states (Argyle, 1982). Although the worst forms of crass political patronage are not common, who you know has long been more helpful in gaining state employment than what you know. Given this context, it appears as if the politicians' motives for supporting personnel reform were based more on achieving greater flexibility and efficiency in the management of human resources than on gaining expanded access to patronage appointments. Likewise, having established clear lines of responsibility to the governor's office, decentralization of staffing activities may have been viewed not only as less risky, but as a potentially fruitful means of expediting public policy initiatives within state government.

Consistent with these objectives, the personnel components of the Accountability Act authorize increased management flexibility in several critical areas. Reflecting changes proposed by the national performance review, they span such topics as merit pay, productivity incentives, employee recognition, quality of work-life considerations, and supervisory discretion over staffing decisions. Specific provisions include the following.

Performance-based salary adjustments. The act empowers agencies to develop procedures (and evaluation standards) to increase and decrease employees' salaries based on the results of the annual performance evaluation. This represents the first systematic attempt by the state to implement a true merit pay system applicable to all public employees. Previously, agencies commonly allocated merit raises in a (more or less) across-the-board manner, even when special monies were set aside for performance-based increases. The performance evaluation format, known as the Employee Performance Management System, combines some of the best characteristics of behaviorally anchored rating scales, critical incidents, and management-by-objectives evaluation strategies. As such, it provides—at least insofar as the conventional wisdom is concerned (Lovrich, 1995)—a reasonably accurate and relatively effective means of differentiating various levels of worker performance.

Group productivity incentives. The act encourages all state agencies to establish productivity standards and to devise procedures to reward work groups for their efforts. No special provisions were made for funding this incentive program, but most agencies possess wide latitude in the use of their appropriations (which, in many cases, are lump sums, not line items).

Employee recognition. In addition to merit pay and group incentives, the act empowers agencies to make cash awards to high performing workers and to devise other means of employee recognition. The use of plaques, certificates, monetary rewards, special parking places, and related measures is expressly encouraged. Again, no special funds were appropriated by the state legislature to underwrite the employee recognition program; agencies are expected to generate the needed revenue from their existing budgets.

Scheduling innovations. To improve the quality of work life and aid employees with young children, the act enables state agencies to implement flextime and job-sharing programs without acquiring centralized approval. Also, employees are permitted to work out of their homes in cases where such an arrangement is feasible. Prior to the passage of the act, flextime schedules were closely monitored by the State Department of Human Resources Management and were not very widespread.

Probationary period. The act extends the standard probationary period for all new workers from 6 months to 1 year. The implicit purpose of this change is that with additional time to monitor the performance of newly appointed workers, there is a greater likelihood that problem employees will be culled prior to the acquisition of full career protections. As is the case in almost all career systems, probationary employees do not enjoy any procedural protections from removal (except in the case of alleged discrimination).

Increased supervisory flexibility. Finally, the act contains authorizations that give public managers greatly expanded latitude over several staffing decisions.

They are now empowered to reassign, transfer, reclassify, and promote their subordinates, subject only to agency (but not higher level) approval. In the case of promotions, the maximum allowable upgrade is one organizational level. Before these changes were implemented, reassignment and transfer decisions were severely restricted by agency procedures and by the threat of grievances (e.g., reassignments and transfers involving a move of more than 15 miles from one's previous location were grievable actions). Likewise, promotion and reclassification decisions ordinarily required lengthy clearance processes that involved state-level approval.

In summary, the state's personnel reform agenda is fairly comprehensive. The newly adopted reforms resemble an executive summary of the personnel component of the national performance review report. Delegated authority over salary and promotion decisions, flexibility in reassignments and transfers, the aggressive use of employee incentive programs, emphasis on performance management strategies, and the empowerment of supervisors to deal more effectively with poor performers are all contained in both the federal and the South Carolina reinvention reforms. One function that did not need to be reformed was recruitment and selection. The state had long followed the practice of permitting agencies (at least those outside of the federally mandated merit system) to fill their own vacancies without reliance on a central job register. Once viewed as an invitation to abuse, this practice is now (ironically) perceived as progressive personnel management.

Method

In response to a request from the State Department of Human Resources Management, faculty and students affiliated with the University of South Carolina's MPA program conducted a mailed survey of the state's 78 agencies. The expressed purpose of the project was to determine the impact of the Government Accountability Act after 18 months of implementation. The surveys were addressed to the relevant agency directors; a cover letter cosigned by the personnel director endorsed the study and encouraged candid participation. Because much of the requested data was available only in the agencies' personnel departments, most of the individuals completing the questionnaires were human resource professionals. Many provided supporting documentation, including policies and procedures that were written to enforce the provisions of the act.

Readers should note the limitations of this particular research design. Although the survey yielded interesting aggregate data, it cannot tell us much about the texture of personnel actions that are occurring in response to reinvention reforms. A much more sophisticated design, including agency-specific inquiries and surveys of individual employees, would be required to provide a more complete picture of reform's impact on the public personnel system.

The initial mailing brought in responses from 35 agencies, with a follow-up mailing yielding an additional 28 responses. Thus, a total of 63 (81%) agencies complied with our request for information concerning the impact of the reform package. Of the 63 responses, 4 were not incorporated into the results. Two of these were submitted by agencies that, due to a recent restructuring, were enveloped into larger units. Another agency was so new—owing, again, to the just completed reorganization—that it was unable to provide a meaningful response. The fourth agency replied that it had not yet had an opportunity to fully digest the content of the legislation.

The approximate number of full-time employees per respondent agency ranges from 3 to 6,000. The 63 agencies represent more than 58,000 full-time state employees, which is about 90% of the entire state workforce.

The questionnaire consisted almost completely of open-ended and fill-in-the-blank items. The instrument was patterned after the enabling legislation, with separate sections devoted to each of the major legislative provisions (salary flexibility, group productivity incentives, employee recognition, flextime, extended probationary period, and supervisory discretion over promotions and reassignments).

Findings

As is summarized in Table 1, state agencies have made spotty progress at implementing the provisions of the Government Accountability Act. A cursory review of Table I shows that some progress has been achieved in the areas of merit pay, employee recognition, and scheduling. Relatively poor results are evident in regard

Table 1   Rates of Agency Compliance

	Agency Response				
	Yes	No	No answer	Not sure	Total
Pay for performance	43 (73%)	16 (27%)	0	0	59 (100%)
Salary decreases likely	6 (10%)	49 (83%)	2 (3%)	2 (3%)	59 (100%)
Group productivity incentives	2 (3%)	57 (97%)	0	0	59 (100%)
Employee recognition standards	33 (56%)	26 (44%)	0	0	59 (100%)
Plaque	24 (73%)	9 (27%)	0	0	33 (100%)
Certificate	20 (61%)	13 (39%)	0	0	33 (100%)
Money	7 (21%)	26 (79%)	0	0	33 (100%)
Recognition at staff meeting	4 (12%)	29 (88%)	0	0	33 (100%)
Parking space	3 (9%)	30 (91%)	0	0	33 (100%)
Pin	3 (9%)	30 (91%)	0	0	33 (100%)
Letter of commendation	3 (9%)	30 (91%)	0	0	33 (100%)
Newsletter mention	2 (6%)	31 (94%)	0	0	33 (100%)
Lunch	1 (3%)	32 (97%)	0	0	33 (100%)
Flextime	34 (58%)	25 (42%)	0	0	59 (100%)
Job sharing	11 (19%)	48 (81%)	0	0	59 (100%)
Promotions	17 (29%)	25 (42%)	15 (25%)	2 (3%)	59 (100%)
Reassignments	14 (24%)	28 (47%)	15 (25%)	2 (3%)	59 (100%)
Transfers	11 (19%)	29 (49%)	17 (29%)	2 (3%)	59 (100%)
Reclassifications	20 (34%)	29 (37%)	15 (25%)	2 (3%)	59 (100%)

Note: "Yes" responses signify that the agency has taken steps to implement reinvention reform. Rows may not add up to 100%, due to rounding.

to group productivity incentives and the various means of providing supervisors with increased staffing flexibility. The following sections assess developments in each substantive area.

Performance-Based Salary Adjustments

The installation of merit pay procedures was reported by 43 (73%) of the agencies. Since the implementation of the act, nearly 8,700 employees have had their salaries increased due to this provision.

On closer examination, however, it becomes apparent that these data are somewhat deceiving. Three large agencies admit that their merit increases—representing more than 3,700 of the reported cases—are administered "across-the-board" (thereby reducing the aggregate number of actual merit recipients to about 5,000). Another nine agencies gave increases to 50% or more of their employees, indicating that they are not quite as discriminating as one might expect in a rigorous merit pay system.

In context, however, these data are less damning. State employees had not enjoyed a meaningful pay increase for the 2 preceding years, so there may have been an understandable temptation to spread the money around. Moreover, the agencies that rewarded a majority of their workers did at least differentiate the amounts of raises, thereby indicating that merit-driven distinctions were being made. And, notably, 16 agencies (27%) provided salary increases to less than 10% of their total workforce and another 15 (25%) rewarded from 10% to 49% of their workers. Although the raise range is often fairly narrow (e.g., from 2% to 6%), this level of implementation is encouraging when one considers the voluminous literature documenting the impediments to merit pay in the public sector (Milkovich & Wigdor, 1991; Perry, 1986, 1995).

In response to a few attitudinal questions concerning merit pay, two general conclusions emerged. First, more than 90% of the respondents (54 agencies) enthusiastically endorse the idea of merit pay, even though many of the agencies have made no effort to follow through with their newly won salary authority. Most respondents also report that their employees are generally supportive of merit pay. Predictably, a majority of the agencies (five out of eight) that report employee unrest over merit pay have made no effort to install performance-based salary programs.

What factors explain the absence of merit pay initiatives in agencies expressing support for the concept? One possible explanation may be that some managers are reluctant to register opposition to merit pay. Like motherhood and voting, the concept carries a highly positive connotation. When placed in an organizational context, however, pay for performance does not look quite so enticing. Research findings point to any number of operational and attitudinal impediments, chief of which are employee mistrust of managerial motives, dissatisfaction with evaluation procedures, and the competition that merit pay engenders among workers (Perry, 1995). These factors are probably relevant to the South Carolina experience, especially in light of the fact that supervisors have long been accused of favoritism in the allocation of rewards (Hays & Tompkins, 1984). Likewise, the arrival of a new and more politically empowered leadership may have awakened the defensive instincts of many state workers.

Although at least some agencies are attempting to base salary increases on performance criteria, salary decreases are another matter. Only six agencies (10%) reported the likelihood that any employee salaries will be reduced due to performance-based inadequacies (no decreases had yet occurred). In contrast, 49 respondents (83%) feel that salary decreases are unlikely. Given the fact that employees retain the right to appeal a salary reduction to a grievance committee under some circumstances, this attitude is easily explained. Instead of running the grievance gauntlet merely to reduce a worker's salary, managers have probably concluded that progressive discipline leading to termination is a more effective means of handling workers with severe performance shortfalls.

Group Productivity Incentives

Bluntly speaking, almost no progress has occurred in the area of group incentives. Fifty-seven agencies (97%) have not established any program to provide productivity incentives to work groups. Only three agencies are considering the idea, whereas another two have actually implemented a group incentive plan. Of these two, one explained that productivity standards are handled at the department level and the other described its program as a "suggestion award" under which employee ideas are evaluated according to programmatic and productivity standards.

Interestingly, 19 respondents volunteered reasons why group incentive plans will be difficult to establish. Among the impediments that appear most frequently in their comments are concern over equity and fairness, the fear that unhealthy competition will erupt among the workers, the problems inherent in creating meaningful standards, a lack of time to devote to the administration of such programs, and the fact that some agency functions (e.g., corrections, law enforcement, regulation) are not conducive to group work. Another factor, the state government's failure to provide additional monies for the provision of group incentives, must also be cited as having a chilling effect on this particular reform component.

Employee Recognition

When asked whether they have established standards to recognize individual workers, 33 agencies (56%) responded affirmatively. To date, more than 3,200 workers have been recognized by these agencies for their contributions. For the most part, the forms of recognition are more symbolic than substantive. Plaques were the most prevalent form of award (24 agencies), followed by certificates of appreciation (20 agencies). Cash awards were provided in only 7 agencies (usually in the sum of about $50), and less than a handful use special parking spaces, employee pins, honorific lunches, and letters of commendation.

Eighteen of the 26 agencies that have not established employee recognition programs provided explanations. For the most part, their reasons center on a lack of time and/or resources to implement a meaningful recognition strategy. Several more note that their agencies are too small or too specialized for such programs to be relevant to their needs.

A number of respondents volunteered suggestions on how the recognition program might be made more effective. The failure of the state to provide special funds for the purpose is a major irritant to some, as is the fact that financial awards are not regarded as being sufficient (mentioned by 21 respondents). The legislation limits awards to $50 per person. Similarly, a few respondents are troubled by the 10% limit on the number of workers who can be recognized under the act in any given year. An apparent concern of this group is that some deserving workers will be left out under an arbitrary ceiling; to recognize some is to diminish others.

Scheduling Innovations

Thirty-four agencies (58%) permitted their workers to arrange flextime schedules, 11 (19%) allowed job sharing, and 9 (15%) enabled employees to work out of their homes. Although the Government Accountability Act contributed to some of these scheduling variations, many of the programs predate the reinvention movement.

Although the raw data show a promising trend in the acceptance rate of scheduling innovations, there is considerable reason to suspect that reform has actually exerted little impact on the working conditions of most employees. Typically, the flextime schedules that exist in South Carolina agencies are very restrictive. Most agencies require their employees to work during the core office hours, which are usually 9:00 a.m. to 4:00 p.m. Thus, employee flexibility is limited to a few options: 7:30 a.m. to 4:00 p.m., 8:00 a.m. to 4:30 p.m., or 9:00 a.m. to 5:00 p.m. Only two agencies provide workers with a wider range of choice, giving their workers the option of working 9 days in a 2-week schedule.

These data are, of course, consistent with the situation in much of the service sector. As service providers, the agencies' obligation to meet the needs of clients often precludes (or at least impedes) the aggressive use of flexible schedules.

Data concerning other scheduling variations are similar. Although 11 agencies reported the presence of job sharing, only 20 state employees participate. Similarly, although more than 400 employees are reported to be working out of their homes, the vast majority of these individuals are engaged in occupations that are not usually considered ripe for such an arrangement. The scheduling literature assumes that at-home workers will usually be engaged in intellectual and clerical activities; they complete their tasks inside their own homes, linked to the office through computer modems. Almost all of the South Carolina employees who work at home are departing from their homes to perform their jobs; they are primarily foresters, law enforcement officials, and inspectors.

Probationary Period

Support for the extended probationary period is very strong among the state's public managers. The respondents unanimously believe that the extension permits a more thorough and reliable evaluation of worker potential. Despite this ringing endorsement, the changed policy has not apparently exerted much of an impact on personnel outcomes. Only 10 agencies (17%) reported an increase in the average number of terminations under the extended probationary period. Surprisingly, 7 respondents terminated more employees under the 6-month probationary period than under the new 1-year policy. Possible explanations for this counterintuitive finding are (a) more hiring took place in fiscal year 1992–1993 under the 6-month probation, leading to a higher rate of probationary terminations; and/or (b) idiosyncrasies of the hiring process (particularly bad luck?) affected the termination rates. If either explanation is partially true, then the longer probationary period would logically result in more probationary departures over time.

Increased Supervisory Flexibility

Of all the changes fostered by the Government Accountability Act, those providing for the decentralization of staffing decisions are probably the most noteworthy. The reinvention and empowerment themes are both built on the idea that public administrators need more flexibility to manage their workers effectively. Localized control over promotion, reassignment, transfer, and reclassification decisions are major steps in that direction.

The survey results indicate that some agencies are taking their new powers seriously. Of the 59 agencies that provided usable responses, 20 (34%) report some level of activity. The most frequent use of supervisory flexibility is in employee reclassification; 20 agencies have reclassified almost 1,300 workers since the act took effect. The power to promote workers one organization level was the second most frequently occurring personnel action; 17 agencies have elevated 525 workers under the new authority. Similar trends occur in the areas of employee transfers and reassignments. Fourteen agencies reported reassigning 330 workers, whereas 11 agencies have transferred 340 employees.

Given the generalized perception that public managers are dissatisfied with their limited supervisory flexibility within traditional merit systems, this response pattern is somewhat surprising. About one third of the agencies appear to be making aggressive use of the new authority; yet the remaining agencies have been essentially unaffected. Thus, the act has exerted a deep but narrow effect. Possible explanations for this phenomenon and the other response patterns are offered in the next section.

Discussion and Conclusion

This case study indicates that the path to reform may be a bit more circuitous than might have initially been imagined by reinvention's proponents. The impact of the Government Accountability Act on many state agencies has been negligible. About 50% of the agencies report few if any alterations in their staffing practices. Almost all of the respondents applaud the content of reform, yet many of the act's provisions are not being implemented aggressively. Although an atypical state in many ways, South Carolina's experience does not bode well for the future of reform.

In attempting to explain the differences in agency compliance with the act, comparisons were made on the basis of organizational size, functional activity, employee type (professional, technical, labor intensive), and cabinet/noncabinet status. None of the relationships is sufficiently significant to explain much of the variability. However, a few interesting findings are evident. Generally speaking, smaller agencies are more likely to inaugurate a pay-for-performance plan; likewise, the smaller the agency, the higher the proportion of workers who have received a merit increase. This may be partly explained by the facts that (a) smaller agencies encounter fewer problems in devising performance standards, and/or (b) larger agencies possess a wider range of alternatives that can be used to recognize deserving employees without confronting the complexities of a merit pay plan. As is true throughout the public service (Baum, 1979; Staples, 1978), job reclassifications (grade creep) and promotions are commonly used in lieu of merit increases to reward valued workers. Logic dictates that large agencies have many more opportunities than smaller ones to use these measures as a way to circumvent the shortcomings of merit pay.

Relationships also exist between employee characteristics and the use of recognition programs and scheduling innovations. In both instances, such measures are most likely to be found in agencies that are staffed primarily by technical and professional workers. Agencies with large numbers of social workers, nurses, educators, and uniformed employees (e.g., highway patrol, corrections) may well have used special means of recognizing employee contributions long before 1993, thereby making compliance with the act especially easy. The uniformed services in particular are known for engineering various ways of acknowledging accomplishment. A similar situation exists with work schedules, because most of these groups are subject to highly variable job demands that require tailored (flextime) schedules.

One final area of noncorrelation deserves special note. On the basis of the political dimensions of reform discussed earlier, we expected to find significant differences between agencies inside and outside of the governor's cabinet. A logical hypothesis is that cabinet agencies are more compliant with the provisions of the act than are agencies that are shielded from the governor's direct influence. One would assume that this phenomenon would be especially apparent in regard to control-oriented reforms (reassignments, transfers, etc.). No such relationship was found to exist. In fact, it even appears as if cabinet agencies are slightly less likely to embrace reinvention than are their noncabinet cousins.

Without a more detailed examination of the conditions within each agency, we can only speculate as to the underlying reasons for the unenthusiastic response to personnel reform. Opposition from middle managers is one probable explanation (Colvard, 1994). In addition to being the group most affected by any proposed cutbacks that might occur, this group bears the brunt of interpreting and implementing the personnel reforms (Jasper & Alpern, 1994). The tendency of workers to resist change is legendary (see Argyris, 1992), as is their inclination to fear of being placed under an administrative microscope. Initiatives that involve the measurement of performance and the application of sanctions, even when counterbalanced by the promise of additional rewards, rarely receive a warm welcome in bureaucracy (Swiss, 1992; Walters, 1992). Although we received little direct feedback that this is a widespread problem, a few respondents expressed hostility to various reinvention themes. Merit pay attracted the lion's share of criticism, but even employee recognition and scheduling innovations were attacked by a handful of public managers. Clearly, the state's failure to adequately fund many of the reforms contributed to their poor reception. Moreover, the career civil service is probably intuitive enough to recognize the inherent contradictions (and risks) of reinvention. In the context of a reform agenda that seems to focus more on managerialism (centralization) than worker empowerment, public employees may perceive it as more of a threat than an opportunity.

Insofar as the cabinet agencies are concerned, latent employee hostility toward reform may have been exacerbated by the turbulent political environment. In the 5 years since the governor was granted extensive new powers, there have been several highly publicized housecleanings of top officials in newly configured cabinet agencies. As a result, there is reportedly a palpable sense of fear (and perhaps even paranoia) in some state offices. This hardly describes an environment that is conducive to reform (Wilson & Durant, 1994), especially when the planned changes strengthen the hands of politicians and their appointees against the career civil service (once again, the managerialism theme overrides the interest in decentralization). Perhaps the state's public managers are familiar with the experiences of their federal counterparts under the national performance review or perhaps their intuition alone dictates caution. Whatever the situation, foot-dragging on their part may simply represent a rational strategy of wait and see until the reform dust settles.

Obviously, these sentiments also reflect the inertia that typifies most large organizations. Flexibility and decentralized authority are appealing concepts, at least theoretically. But even if the workforce anxiously awaits the advent of reform (which, as noted, is seldom the case), time and initiative are required to create any benefit. Almost all of the reforms contained in the act necessitate follow-through on the part of state agencies. Performance measures need to be established, criteria for recognition and reward need to be devised, and policies and procedures need to be written. These are time-consuming and potentially controversial steps along the road to reinventing the personnel function. That some agencies are slow to adapt is not at all surprising, especially when one considers the natural tendency for routine work to drive out planning and innovation efforts. Stated simply, who has time to innovate?

Additional insight (however unscientific) into the languid pace of reform was gained during the survey. In interacting with various respondents by both mail and telephone, we encountered several public managers who were obviously unaware of many of the act's major provisions. A few asked us to refer them to the specific sections of the personnel code so that they could educate themselves. Although the central personnel office summarized the act's provisions in newsletters and other outlets, the message clearly was not conveyed in more than a few instances.

One obvious conclusion that is stimulated by this situation is that in the future, more attention needs to be paid to communicating the content of statutory changes. Additionally, states would probably be well served to provide training programs for personnel professionals on how the various changes might best be implemented. Little sharing of information or experiences between and among agencies is currently occurring in any overt sense. This situation is especially problematic because the enabling legislation left all of the details up to the individual agencies, many of which seem to be delaying a response until they can evaluate the effectiveness of actions taken by their sister agencies. In this cautious environment, an orchestrated program of information sharing would probably reap numerous benefits. Anything that can be done or taught to assuage public managers' concerns about the true objectives and implications of reform would be well worth the effort.

The secondary recommendation that springs from this conclusion is obvious. If a state wants rapid compliance from its agencies, more technical support will be essential. Otherwise, the implementation process will be uneven or erratic. Wealthy agencies or those with progressive leadership are likely to lead the pack. Those with burdensome workloads (the Departments of Corrections and Social Services are prime examples) cannot be expected to comply quickly. There are simply too many competing demands on the managers' time.

Another obvious lesson is that if the politicians truly desire quick action, the enabling statute should include legislative hammers. The law should specify implementation steps and timetables to channel the attention of the agencies. Instead of issuing a directive, the South Carolina legislature granted a permission slip. This approach to lawmaking, although quite common, probably invites delay among even the law's more enthusiastic supporters.

One final thought relates to the paucity of activity in the area of worker incentives. Merit pay, group incentives, and individual employee recognition programs all suffer from a lack of resources. Although the various reforms were written with the best of intentions, the state legislature tried to introduce reform on the cheap. No special funding was provided to the agencies to subsidize the various incentive strategies. This left the agencies, which were already strapped for funds, with few resources to devote to the task. The U.S. Congress has repeatedly followed a similar strategy with its merit raise and bonus programs, as have many other jurisdictions (Lewis, 1995).

Without adequate funding, many public managers are understandably reluctant to devote much energy to creating systems of recognition and reward. Underfunded programs of this nature can raise employee expectations, only to frustrate them when the promised rewards are not delivered. Thus, legislative bodies considering these types of reinvention strategies are confronted with the old dilemma of having to spend money to make money. In the current political environment, spending money—especially on public employees—is not on many legislators' minds.

In summary, this case study demonstrates that reinvention of the personnel function requires something more than legislative authorization (see Table 2). Some public servants may be eager to pursue a reinvention agenda, but others require education and assistance. Still others will demand assurances that reform will not be a step backward to a dark era of political manipulation and meddling.

Although there is no simple solution to this dilemma, a more assertive posture on the part of the state government is probably necessary to deepen and broaden the impact of personnel reform. Ironically, this suggests that the central personnel staff must play an integral role in cajoling some of the agencies to assume greater responsibility over their staffing systems. Even this, however, will probably yield few results if public managers interpret the reforms as assaults on the civil service.

Table 2   Lessons Learned in This Reinvention Experience

Inertia and defensiveness are likely to make initial progress slower and more variable than might otherwise be anticipated.

Reform will not be self-executing; successful implementation requires a considerable amount of groundwork, including the creation of policies and procedures within agencies, the establishment of evaluation criteria, and education of the affected workers.

Enabling legislation should include sufficient guidelines and standards ("hammers") to ensure agency compliance on a regularized schedule.

The central personnel office has an important role to play in the reform effort; diffusion of reform can be expedited by providing agencies with clear and concise explanations of specific reform initiatives and implementation guidelines.

Smaller agencies or those with unusually heavy workloads may require technical assistance or other special services to benefit from the reform program.

A systematic means of information sharing between and among agencies will foster experimentation and promote program acceptance.

Initiatives that require the direct expenditure of money must be funded by the legislature if they are to have their intended effect.

If so, the irony of the situation becomes even more pronounced, because central personnel offices may find themselves in the position of having to restore some of the monitoring and police functions that were surrendered in recent decades. Whether these seemingly contradictory objectives can be achieved simultaneously may well be one of the more engrossing personnel issues of the next decade.

References

Argyle, N. J. (1982). Civil service reform: The state and local response. *Public Personnel Management, 11*(1), 157–164.

Argyris, C. (1992). The next challenge for TQM: Overcoming organizational defenses. *Journal for Quality and Participation, 15*(1), 26–29.

Barzelay, M. (1992). *Breaking through bureaucracy: A new vision for managing in government.* Los Angeles: University of California Press.

Baum, B. H. (1979). The upward pressure on position classification. In F. Thompson (Ed.), *Classics of public personnel policy* (pp. 188–196). Oak Park, IL: Moore.

Butler, R. (1991). New challenges or familiar prescriptions? *Public Administration, 69*(4), 363–372.

Campbell, A. (1977). Is civil service reform possible? *Personnel Administration, 23*(6), 33–37, 73.

Campbell, A. (1978). Civil service reform: A new commitment. *Public Administration Review, 38*(2), 99–103.

Carroll, J. (1996). Introduction: Reinventing public administration. *Public Administration Review, 56*(3), 245–246.

Colvard, J. E. (1994). In defense of middle management. *Government Executive, 26*(5). 57–58.

Egger, W. D., & O'Leary, J. (1995). *Revolution at the roots: Making our government smaller, better, and closer to home.* New York: Free Press.

Executive Office of the President. (1993). *From red tape to results.* Washington, DC: U.S. Government Printing Office.

Halligan, J., & Power, J. (1991). A framework for the analysis of recent changes in the Australian executive branches. In A. Farazmand (Ed.), *Handbook of comparative and developmental administration* (pp. 91–99). New York: Marcel Dekker.

Hays, S. W., & Tompkins, M. E. (1984). *Employee attitudes in the South Carolina Department of Corrections.* Columbia, SC: Bureau of Government.

Hoover Commission. (1949). *The Hoover Commission reports: On organization of the executive branch of government.* New York: McGraw-Hill.

Hoover Commission. (1955). *The Hoover Commission reports: On organization of the executive branch of government.* New York: McGraw-Hill.

Ingraham, P. (1992). Commissions, cycles and changes: The role of blue ribbon commissions in executive branch change. In P. Ingraham & D. Kett (Eds.), *Agenda for excellence* (pp. 187–207). Chatham, NJ: Chatham House.

Ingraham, P., & Ban, C. (Eds.). (1984). *Legislating bureaucratic change: The Civil Service Reform Act of 1978.* Albany: State University of New York Press.

Ingraham, P., & Eisenberg, E. (1995). Comparative examination of national civil service and personnel reforms. In J. Rabin (Ed.), *Handbook of public personnel administration* (pp. 133–152). New York: Marcel Dekker.

Ingraham, P., & Rosenbloom, D. H. (1988-1989). Symposium on the Civil Service Reform Act of 1978 [Special issue]. *Policy Studies Journal, 17*(1).

Jasper, H., & Alpern, A. (1994). National performance review: The good, the bad, the indifferent. *Public Manager. 23*(1), 27–34.

Kamensky, J. M. (1996). Role of the "reinventing government" movement in federal management reform. *Public Administration Review, 56*(3), 247–255.

Lewis, G. (1995). Federal pay inside and outside the beltway. *Review of Public Personnel Administration, 15*(4), 37–57.

Lovrich, N. P. (1995). Performance appraisal: Seeking accountability and efficiency through individual effort, commitment, and accomplishment. In S. Hays & R. Kearney (Eds.), *Public personnel administration: Problems and prospects* (pp. 105–120). Englewood Cliffs, NJ: Prentice-Hall.

Milkovich, G. T., & Wigdor, A. K. (1991). *Pay for performance: Evaluating performance appraisal and merit pay.* Washington, DC: National Academy Press.

Moe, R. C. (1993). Let's rediscover government, not reinvent it. *Government Executive, 26*(6), pp. 46–48, 60.

Mosher, F. (1968). *Democracy and the public service.* New York: Oxford University Press.

National Commission on State and Local Public Service. (1993). *Hard truths/tough choices: An agenda for state and local reform.* Albany, NY: Rockefeller Institute of Government.

Osborne, D. (1993). Reinvention revisited. *Government Executive, 26*(7), 56.

Osborne, D., & Gaebler, T. (1992). *Reinventing government: How the entrepreneurial spirit is transforming the public sector from schoolhouse to statehouse, city hall to Pentagon.* Reading, MA: Addison-Wesley.

Perry, J. (1986). Merit pay in the public service: The case for a failure of theory. *Review of Public Personnel Administration, 7*(3), 57–69.

Perry, J. (1995). Compensation, merit pay, and motivation. In S. Hays & R. Kearney (Eds.). *Public personnel administration: Problems and prospects* (pp. 121–132). Englewood Cliffs, NJ: Prentice-Hall.

Rosenbloom, D. H. (1993). Have an administrative Rx? Don't forget the politics! [editorial]. *Public Administration Review, 53*(5), 503–507.

Rourke, F. (1992). Responsiveness and neutral competence in American bureaucracy. *Public Administration Review, 57*(6), 539–546.

Savas, E. S., & Ginsburg, S. G. (1973). The civil service: A meritless system. *Public Interest, 32*(3), 70–85.

Sayre, W. S. (1948). Triumph of technique over purpose. *Public Administration Review, 8*(2), 134–137.

Schachter, H. L. (1995). Reinventing government or reinventing ourselves: Two models for improving government performance. *Public Administration Review, 55*(6), 537.

Shafritz, J. (1975). *Public personnel management: The heritage of civil service reform.* New York: Praeger.

Staples, E. (1978). Short takes. *Civil Service Journal, 19*(3), 2–3.

Stevens, L. N. (1995). *Civil service reform: Changing times demand new approaches.* Washington, DC: U.S. General Accounting Office.

Swiss, J. (1992). Adapting TQM to government *Public Administration Review, 52*(4), 356–362.

U.S. General Accounting Office. (1994). *Management reform: Implementation of the NPR Recommendations.* Washington, DC: U.S. Government Printing Office.

Volcker, P. (1989). *Report and recommendations of the National Commission on the Public Service.* Washington, DC: National Commission on the Public Service.

Walters, J. (1992). The cult of TQM. *Governing, 5*, 38–44.

Wilson, L. A., & Durant, R. F. (1994). Evaluating TQM: The case for a theory driven approach. *Public Administration Review, 54*(2), 137–146.

VII

The Multiple Dimensions of Shaping Public Policy

The manager's role in the political environment sometimes involves participation in both the formulation and implementation of public policy. Although they play different roles, public managers, like politicians, must master every stage of the policy-making process—from policy formulation (starting with the emergence of an idea to its eventual legislative passage), through implementation (carrying out that policy), evaluation (determining what the policy has actually accomplished), and, finally, the policy's termination or modification as a result of going through all of the policy-making stages again. Public managers in some cases are the only actors involved in all of these stages—sometimes directly and sometimes in an advisory role to political officials.

Policy Formulation

In the next selection, Jeffrey Berry observes that, depending on the issue, gaining support during policy formulation entails the construction of coalitions, the cooperation of ongoing subgovernments, or the intervention of larger, more complex arrangements of *ad hoc* issue networks. Public managers cannot afford to remain on the sidelines during these bargaining processes. Such informal arrangements are necessary to bring together those actors inside and outside government who are most concerned with a particular issue area.

Politicians know that those who feel intensely on an issue are more likely to "remember in November" than those who disagree but feel less strongly, and cast their eventual electoral vote on the basis of other concerns. The electoral calculus of the politician must, then, take into account not only the *direction,* whether one is for or against an issue, but also the voters' *intensity* of feeling. Much of the rationale for democratic pluralism rests on the argument that it is important to accommodate intensely felt needs within the political system.

The issues in our political environment, almost without exception, have increased in complexity to the point where much (though by no means all) of the information, and consequently the expertise, necessary for decision making resides in companies, nonprofits, universities, and other organizations. Officials are thus to some extent dependent on these organizations and the interest groups they spawn. Without the stamp of approval of such groups, actors in formal positions of authority are sometimes unwilling to take a position. This is particularly true in the case of comparatively small and less visible issues.

The relationship, though, is hardly one way. These groups receive substantial numbers of grants and contracts—particularly from the federal government where these policy configurations are found in their most developed form. Environmental, consumer, affirmative action, health and safety, and other regulatory activities have also resulted from increased concern with governmental action—or inaction.

In a democracy, power comes largely through the accretion of people, money, and other resources, so it is not surprising that concerned individuals have either organized into groups or, more frequently, steered their already existing group activity to include the influencing of public policy to achieve common goals. That is all it takes to be an "interest group." These groups can then enter into trade associations or other institutional arrangements. They can choose to exercise their influence themselves, hire lobbyists to do it for them, or, increasingly, do both. Representation in the form of lawyers and other professionals is not difficult to hire. Berry found that the number of lawyers in Washington, D.C. alone rose from around 11,000 in 1972 to 63,000 in 1994.[a]

Electoral Mandates and Democratic Pluralism

Under these circumstances, having the support of a majority of the citizenry may not be sufficient to launch a policy. Much depends on how *intensely* the citizenry feels about an issue. Intense feelings by even a substantial minority of voters will certainly have an impact, if mobilized. For example, Presidential hopeful Ross Perot pursued this strategy in 1992 around the electoral issues of federal deficit reduction and congressional campaign reform. Electoral mandates are relatively rare, though they have led to action on environmental issues, health care, and, most frequently, changes in economic arrangements of one kind or another designed to "get the country moving again." Sometimes leaders will strive to increase the intensity of concern about an issue even as they struggle to build a

---

[a]Jeffrey M. Berry, *The Interest Group Society,* 3rd ed. (New York: Longman, 1997), p. 24.

movement separate and distinct from partisan politics. This occurred in the case of bipartisan public pressure to end the Vietnam war (which ended Lyndon B. Johnson's presidency) and to deal with the Watergate cover-up (which brought down President Richard M. Nixon).

A majority of concerned, informed citizens is difficult to mobilize. Eventually, however, television, fax machines, e-mail, national talk shows, and other, now widely used communication devices may lead to the development of more electoral mandates like these. In the absence of such a majority, the United States functions through "democratic pluralism." Political scientist Robert Dahl has succinctly explained how this works: "The 'normal' American political process," he observed, is "one in which there is a high probability that an active and legitimate group in the population can make itself heard effectively at some critical stage in the process of decision."[b] Then, as noted in Jeffrey Berry's summary of Dahl's argument in *The Interest Group Society*, "through bargaining and compromise between affected groups and political elites, democratic decisions are reached, with no group consistently dominating."[c]

The catch in the definition of the normal American political system is to be found, as Dahl well knew, not in the fine print, but in the adjectives.[d] The "normal" system would be one where the public at large was scarcely aware of the issue; admission of only "active" and "legitimate" groups would screen out the poor and numerous others by gender, race, ethnicity, religion, and the like whether or not they were organized. Perhaps the most critical problem for the underrepresented would be maintaining involvement through *all* stages of the policy process—a frequent necessity to achieve, and subsequently protect, political victories that often take years to accomplish.

The Public Manager as Political Stakeholder

Understanding democratic pluralism is of critical importance for public managers who are such an integral part of the process. One result of such a relatively decentralized political system was the emergence after World War II of what Dahl termed a "decentralized, bargaining bureaucracy" that became part of the normal American political system. This representation by bureaucrats over time has taken on several forms. *All* levels of government have lobbyists actively working on their behalf in Washington, D.C. Public managers themselves are represented through several employee union and management groups. But most significantly, federal leaders charged with the responsibility for implementing programs or enforcing regulations are active in the national political process in pursuit of their unit's or their administrative agency's overall policy goals.

[b] Robert A. Dahl, *A Preface to Democratic Theory* (Chicago: University of Chicago Press, 1956), p. 145.

[c] Jeffrey M. Berry, *The Interest Group Society*, 1997, p. 10.

[d] Robert A. Dahl, *Dilemmas of Pluralist Democracy: Autonomy vs. Control* (New Haven: Yale University Press, 1982), p. 208.

Public managers often have the task of formulating and implementing policies that may have support outside of, but not inside of, Washington, D.C. They must defend their statutory mission against the infighting of powerful groups that are well represented in the halls of Congress and the halls of the administrative agencies as well. In other cases, the public managers may be involved in one of the "safety net" programs that was passed during those fleeting moments in American history when sympathy for the poor or minorities was high.

Long after most supporters of these programs have moved on to other concerns, the public managers are left to defend their clients—hence the claim that "social equity" is such an important public administration value. There is no fire alarm that is automatically set off, however, when a proactive, public entrepreneur, in the role of serving such clients, is about to take a stance that the normal political system may view as beyond the pale. Public managers must struggle to decide politically, and to some extent ethically, how strong their advocacy should be on behalf of a less legitimate group or in support of an environmental issue that has attracted little popular support, but is deemed important by respected scientists.

Coalitions and Subgovernments

Public manager involvement is made all the more complicated because pluralistic politics can result in markedly different policy configurations depending on the political environment, the issues, and the actors involved. Berry examines here the roles of interest groups participating in coalitions, subgovernments, and issue networks. The public manager, also a participant in these policy configurations, must be able to gauge the power of these groups (which includes the organization of lobbying efforts by corporations, unions, and other formal organizations). This strength often depends on the group's ability to build *coalitions*. That capability, Berry shows, depends not only on money and information, but also on other considerations such as the group's internal strength, its ability to work with a wide variety of groups extending well beyond its normal allies, and its willingness to abandon ideology to achieve its immediate goal.

One way to avoid the hurly-burly, and the uncertainty, of politics is to convince other key actors to join in the formation of a *subgovernment*. Such an informal arrangement brings together those interest groups, legislative committee members, and public managers in a particular substantive area who have much to gain from forming a mutually beneficial alliance sometimes termed an "iron triangle." This *subgovernment* is one working level below the government as a whole in each of its three parts. The legislative committee is below the legislative leadership; the bureau chief is one level below the department secretary or agency director; and the interest group is one step below the political party (that would represent all the people if they were interested in and informed on the issue). The subgovernment relies on the relatively esoteric nature of its subject matter. Its political stock in trade is invisibility. When the losing side is able to bring enough pressure to place the issue on the top leaders' policy agenda, the subgovernment's days are, at least temporarily, numbered.

Issue Networks

To what extent the subgovernments still represent issue areas is in dispute, but it is certainly true that *issue networks* will result where large, competing interest groups and other actors have come into sharp conflict. Change is more likely to occur here because these large, sprawling conflicts spill over many issue boundaries and consequently disturb numerous other issue domains. The resulting conflict attracts media attention and raises the political stakes sufficiently to bring in numerous interest groups, corporations, unions, administrative agencies, a larger attentive public, and sometimes the public at large. The time of the president and congressional leadership is limited, but they are guided largely in setting their agendas by those issues that have achieved the level of visibility, conflict and public attention that Berry describes in his case study of the telecommunications issue network.

The characteristics of these issue networks differ markedly from those of subgovernments. The dynamic nature of these issue networks means that the cast of characters frequently changes. The network's boundaries are less set and thus, as Berry says, more permeable and "sloppy." No actors occupy the orchestra seats in such networks as are enjoyed by subgovernment actors. Rather, the issue center is a "hollow core" with a constant battle for possession waged by participants operating from different "issue niches." As in subgovernments, though, "the importance of being expert" matters in issue networks too.

The Rise of Issue Networks

Jeffrey M. Berry

Contemplating the frustrations that Republican presidential nominee General Dwight Eisenhower might find in the presidency, Harry Truman remarked, "He'll sit here and he'll say, 'Do this! Do that!' *And nothing will happen.*"[1] It's no wonder that a president can't simply snap his fingers and get the Congress, agencies, and interest groups to go along with him. When he wants to make a significant change in policy, he's likely to encounter many competing interests that prefer other policy options.

If someone as powerful as the president finds Washington politics frustrating, think of the task facing a single interest group. The Washington office may consist of only a handful of staffers. That office, in turn, represents just one interest group in a town that has thousands. The group's day-to-day activities are not newsworthy, and they rarely command much attention from the *Washington Post* or the *New York Times*.

How, then, does an interest group get things to happen? A basic strategy is to try to pyramid its resources. If it can find willing partners, a group will seek to form a *coalition* with other interest groups. Coalitions will usually reflect the immediate strategic interests of various lobbies who all want to influence the same policy in the same way. Over time, any one group is likely to coalesce with groups they have worked with in the past and who lobby in the same general issue area. The many interest groups who share expertise in a policy domain and who frequently interact constitute an *issue network*. In simpler times, when fewer lobbies worked the corridors of power in Washington, policymaking in an issue area was often consensual in nature and involved only a limited number of groups, legislators, and administrators in a *subgovernment*. In contrast, contemporary issue network politics tends to be highly complex and conflictual. The end result of the growth in groups, lobbying resources, and coalition formation is more pressure on the institutions of government to respond to demands for policy change.[2]

In this chapter we look at the basis of interest group cooperation and conflict. In particular, we are concerned with the rise of issue networks and the way in which interest group politics has been changed by the emergence of these dense policymaking communities. Moreover, we want to understand the relationship

---

Jeffrey M. Berry. *The Interest Group Society*, 3rd ed., NY: Longman, 1997, pp. 188–217.

[1] Richard Neustadt, *Presidential Power* (New York: John Wiley, 1980), p. 9.

[2] Frank R. Baumgartner and Jeffrey C. Talbert, "Interest Groups and Political Change," in Bryan D. Jones, ed., *The New American Politician* (Boulder, Colo.: Westview, 1995), pp. 92–108.

between issue networks and democratic policymaking. Do they enhance or inhibit a broad representation of interests before government? A first step, though, is to examine just why interest groups cooperate in the first place.

Coalitions: Everyday Politics

Coalitions are everywhere in Washington. Lobbyists form them instinctively out of practical necessity. One survey of lobbyists found that approximately 80 percent agreed with the statement that "Coalitions are the way to be effective in politics."[3] As one lobbyist put it, "If you're not a good coalition maker, you're not going to survive for long in D.C." Forming a coalition is always a step lobbyists consider in developing an advocacy campaign. Says another lobbyist, "The first thing we do when an issue comes up is sit down and contact people. We find out who our friends are and who our enemies are on the issue and then we form coalitions. I do it every day, on every issue."

Coalitions offer a number of advantages. Principally, they offer a means of expanding scarce resources. One interest group may have only two lobbyists; ten interest groups with the same number of lobbyists can provide 20 operatives for the coming battle. The Washington office of an interest group is often stretched thin with a number of issues to follow, so a coalition may enable it to take on a new issue without seriously diminishing its coverage of another. Coalition partners provide other types of resources besides lobbyists. The constituency of each group broadens the coalition's expertise on the issues and subissues before policymakers. When a bill affecting milk prices came before the Congress, "the Coalition to Reduce Inflated Milk Prices won considerable attention because different coalition members were able to address industrial production costs, noncompetitive U.S. prices, dairy surplus conditions, abuses in surplus distribution programs, and antitrust concerns related to the regulation of milk co-ops."[4]

Coalitions also extend the information net. A group added to a coalition is an extra set of eyes and ears and will expand the intelligence gathering that is crucial to any lobbying effort. Finally, a coalition adds to the credibility of an advocacy campaign. The formation of a coalition indicates that a group isn't an isolated maverick and that there is some breadth of support for its position. As the Washington representative for a pharmaceutical manufacturer noted, "Your chances for success are really much greater if you [form a coalition]. If you go in to see a congressman or staff member with other people who support your position, it's a lot easier to get their support."

Interest group coalitions are not inevitable, and it is not uncommon to uncover a group going it alone. On any given issue, a lobbying organization may

---

[3]Kevin Hula, *Links and Choices: Explaining Coalition Formation Among Organized Interests*, doctoral dissertation, Department of Government, Harvard University, 1995, p. 103.

[4]William P. Browne, *Private Interests, Public Policy, and American Agriculture* (Lawrence: University Press of Kansas, 1988), p. 185.

not find other groups that are highly concerned and in agreement with it. For some groups, few other organizations are natural allies. This is true of the National Cable Television Association, where "most of the time we go it alone. We rarely seek out a group." Interest groups are more likely to go it alone when they are lobbying an administrative agency rather than Congress.[5] Regulations are typically narrower in scope and may affect organizations in unique ways.

The most common pattern is that an issue will affect a number of groups, and natural allies will be clearly evident to the individual lobbyists. One corporate lobbyist said of advocacy in his industry, "I mostly work in coalitions. . . . In forest products, very seldom do you have an issue that only affects one corporation. An issue might affect just two or three, but not just one." As an issue begins to take shape, the search for coalition partners intensifies. A lobbyist for the National Coal Association describes how he put together a coalition to fight provisions in a bill governing fuel use that could hurt his industry:

> First, I met with gas consumers—they were industrial users—and got their support. If the bill passed, they would get cut off if there was a gas shortage. Second, I met with the railroads. Coal is the railroads' number one product—you can't move gas by rail. They have a direct interest in making sure that legislation isn't passed that favors gas over coal. . . . We also brought in labor unions. Gas isn't labor-intensive; coal is a very labor-intensive industry, so labor will support us. I called these meetings separately. There was no reason to include the consumer group with the railroads because their issues are different.

Most coalitions are ad hoc arrangements. They exist for the specific purpose of working on a single issue and dissolve when that issue reaches some resolution or when the coalition partners no longer feel the effort is worthwhile. When the Justice Department encouraged the Supreme Court to deny legal standing to associations that wish to file suits on behalf of individual members, eight interest groups coalesced to oppose the effort. The American Medical Association, the NAACP, the AFL-CIO, the Chamber of Commerce, the Sierra Club, the Alliance for Justice, the Chemical Manufacturers Association, and the National Association of Manufacturers filed a brief asking the Court not to accede to the Justice Department's request. This unusual partnership of groups was limited to this one issue of standing, and had no longer-term purpose.[6]

Ad hoc coalitions maximize flexibility. They are easy to enter and easy to leave. As will be discussed, organizations prefer not to commit financial support to a permanent coalition because they lose control of those scarce resources and cannot apply them to new and more pressing issues. Sometimes, however, advocates believe that an ad hoc alliance will not be sufficient and money must be committed to a permanent coalition. The Leadership Conference on Civil Rights is an unusually large and successful permanent coalition. It was founded in 1950 and has grown to over 185 member organizations. Throughout its history the Leadership Conference has played a key role in developing strategy over civil rights legislation.

[5] Hula, *Links and Choices*, pp. 139–144.

[6] Stuart Taylor, Jr., "Coalition Opposes Access Curb," *New York Times*, March 19, 1986.

Although the breadth of the coalition is a strength when the member organizations are in agreement, the diversity of the Leadership Conference has also led to considerable internal conflict. Over the years organizations representing blacks, Hispanics, Jews, labor, and women have quarreled over what issues the coalition ought to pursue.[7]

For an ad hoc coalition that primarily draws on the time and effort of lobbyists, bigger is not always better. Ten groups joined together on an ad hoc basis is much better than one group working on its own. Yet a hundred groups in an ad hoc coalition may not be much improvement over ten groups. The larger a coalition grows, the more peripheral members it attracts and the more effort is required to manage the coalition. Large coalitions also mean that each group is less accountable for its effort (or lack thereof). In a small coalition, an organization that does little work on that coalition's issues will be conspicuous.

Common Bedfellows, Strange Bedfellows

The old saw, politics makes strange bedfellows, aptly describes coalition politics among interest groups. Coalitions frequently encompass unlikely sets of partners. The American Civil Liberties Union, although often seen as liberal, has formed separate alliances with the tobacco industry, the American Bankers Association, and the National Conservative Political Action Committee. It joined with the ultraconservative National Rifle Association to stop the Justice Department from putting raw, unsubstantiated data into a national computer network. The ACLU regards such computerized databases as a violation of civil liberties, while the National Rifle Association regards this kind of national network as a step toward unlawfully denying its members the right to bear arms.[8]

For all the strange and even bizarre coalitions that form in Washington, the beginning point for any group seeking to form a coalition is still its usual allies. The American Podiatric Medical Association commonly allies with groups representing dentists and psychologists. Repeatedly these groups have found themselves fighting to be included in coverage by insurance plans. The services that podiatrists, dentists, and psychologists provide are not always seen as crucial parts of insurance coverage or worth a more costly premium. Because issues have so often touched upon the common interests of these groups, a pattern of frequent cooperation has developed.

A group's regular allies tend to come from the policy area that it primarily works in; this is where it is most in contact with other lobbies.[9] It is not only that common interests continue to bring the same groups into contact with each other but that trust and friendships develop over time among lobbyists. As they gain experience working with each other, their contact is likely to increase as they rely

---

[7] Dick Kirschten, "Not Black-and-White," *National Journal*, March 2, 1991, pp. 496–500.

[8] Robert Pear, "Tactical Alliances and the A.C.L.U.," *New York Times*, November 5, 1986; and Kirk Victor, "Strange Alliances," *National Journal*, August 15, 1987, pp. 2078–2079.

[9] John P. Heinz, Edward O. Laumann, Robert L. Nelson, and Robert H. Salisbury, *The Hollow Core* (Cambridge, Mass.: Harvard University Press, 1994), pp. 254–258.

on each other to gather information. The lobbyists, legislators, and administrators in a policy area who communicate with each other form an issue network. It is in these networks, which will be discussed more fully later in this chapter, that coalitions breed and multiply. A new coalition effort among frequently teamed partners can easily be initiated with a few phone calls. Thus the costs of forming a coalition, notably the lobbyists' time, are kept down.

But many coalitions extend beyond a small circle of friends. Issues can cut across a wide variety of groups, prompting alliances of lobbies from many different policy areas. It's understandable that groups that normally have little to do with each other, but do not work in contradictory ideological directions, can come together to work on an issue. What may be puzzling, however, is when groups that are usually in opposition to each other lay down their weapons and declare a truce while they join together on a particular issue. When the liberal ACLU and the conservative NRA put their differences aside and join together in a coalition, one may wonder if interest groups follow any principles in choosing their allies. Clearly, the norm among interest groups in Washington is that *no one is too evil to work with.* "We may be sworn enemies on one issue and work together on others," said one trade group lobbyist. Chrysler, for example, usually finds itself at odds with environmentalists. Yet when the Reagan administration proposed ending fuel economy standards after Chrysler had spent $450 million meeting those standards, the company chose to work with environmental groups to preserve them while other car companies fought them.

Why is it that interest groups have so little trouble working with their enemies when it suits their needs? Quite simply, it is because lobbying is a profession guided by pragmatism. "We're not fussy [about whom we work with]," a communications industry lobbyist noted bluntly. Short-term results, getting things done, are the day-to-day imperatives. There is not much credit to be gained with the corporate headquarters, member organizations, or rank-and-file members by staying pure in their choice of allies. To be sure, there are a few exceptions to the no-one-is-too-evil-to-work-with norm. Radical feminists and conservative Christian groups who are active in the fight against pornography could strengthen their efforts by coalescing, but they have generally worked separately on the issue rather than together.[10] This is an unusual case though, and few lobbies have moral qualms about whom they work with. Lobbies are generally much more interested in getting action out of Washington rather than in reserving a special place in heaven for the pure and righteous.

Sharing Resources

Coalitions flourish because they are a means of expanding and coordinating the resources needed for an advocacy effort. A member group enters a coalition with the knowledge that it will be expected to devote some resources to achieving the goals set by the partners. In practical terms, lobbyists must at least cooperate in splitting up the work. In some cases, financial contributions are also expected.

---

[10]Jean Bethke Elshtain, "The New Porn Wars," *New Republic*, June 25, 1984, pp. 15–20.

One resource that coalitions can share is their contacts and their constituency base. A corporate lobbyist says he and his allies divide the contacts this way: "We'll do it based on who knows which member better, who has a facility in his district, [and] the impact of the issue in his district." For large trade groups, the most effective coalition work is really internal. If a trade association can mobilize its member companies to participate in a lobbying campaign, it greatly improves its ability to gain access to the offices of many members of Congress. When the Chemical Manufacturers Association lobbies, it can draw on the 185 member companies that are involved in that industry. These companies are located all over the country and can play a critical role in a lobbying campaign by contacting their own representatives and senators.

Dividing up the lobbying is far easier than deciding to share the costs of a court suit or a research study. Groups do not want to spend money unless an issue is a high priority for them. When there is support for a financial assessment within an ad hoc coalition, the alliance must decide how to assign contributions. Since ad hoc coalitions are by nature voluntary, informally run groups, only peer pressure can force a group to contribute.[11] A lobbyist for a consumer products company noted that uneven contributions are common. "In terms of providing funding for studies, the biggest responsibility falls on the company with the highest stake in the outcome. Maybe one company will give $15,000 and another company will give nothing."

The scarcity of financial resources is not the only reason why groups do not do more to share costs or develop more permanent coalitions. Organizations have egos, and the more resources an interest group devotes to coalition activities, the less it has for doing things in its own name. Although interest group leaders can shamelessly claim credit for a policy victory that rightly belongs to a large coalition, few lobbying offices are satisfied with a constant diet of coalition politics. A group's organizational ego makes it want to shine on its own some of the time and to gain the reputation of being able to make things happen in Washington.

In sum, lobbying organizations commonly form coalitions in Washington but are likely to do so under well-defined circumstances. The chances of success increase when

1. The coalition is clearly intended to be of a temporary, ad hoc nature.
2. The coalition is limited to one specific issue.
3. The issue is of some immediacy with a good chance of government action.
4. The coalition is run informally and each group contributes lobbying by its own personnel rather than giving money to a separate coalition staff.
5. The coalition's members are part of an issue network in which the lobbyists have experience working with each other.
6. Participants believe there is "turn taking" in the leadership for the ad hoc coalitions that grow from their issue network.
7. The coalition itself is not likely to take on so much public visibility that any successes in lobbying will be entirely credited to it rather than being shared with the separate member organizations.

---

[11]See Marie Hojnacki, "Organized Interests as Coalition Members," paper delivered at the annual meeting of the American Political Science Association, Chicago, September, 1995.

From Subgovernments to Issue Networks

Coalitions operate within a broader pattern of interest group interaction. As noted above, interest groups commonly search for coalition partners among other members of their issue network. Issue networks, which are characterized by their dense environment of competing interest groups, bear little resemblance to an earlier model of interest group–government relations that was strongly embraced by political scientists. Indeed, few approaches for analyzing the American political system endured as long or as well as that of the policy subgovernment.

In simple terms a subgovernment consists primarily of interest group advocates, legislators and their aides, and key agency administrators who interact on an ongoing basis and control policymaking in a particular area. Its central belief seems indisputable: policymaking takes place across institutions. Thus government decision making can be best understood by looking at how key actors from different institutions and organizations interact with each other.

The subgovernment model can be traced back to Ernest Griffith's description of policy whirlpools in *Impasse of Democracy*.[12] The term *whirlpools* didn't have much staying power, but other terms that gained currency include *iron triangles, triple alliances, cozy little triangles,* and *subgovernments*. Whatever the label, the basic idea was the same: A small group of actors dominate the development of policy in a given field. Policymaking is consensual, with quiet bargaining producing agreements among affected parties. Partisan politics does little to disturb these relatively autonomous and stable arrangements. Douglass Cater's description of the sugar subgovernment is instructive:

> Political power within the sugar subgovernment is largely vested within the Chairman of the House Agriculture Committee who works out the schedule of quotas. It is shared by a veteran civil servant, the director of the Sugar Division in the U.S. Department of Agriculture, who provides the necessary "expert" advice for such a complex marketing arrangement. Further advice is provided by Washington representatives of the domestic beet and cane sugar growers, the sugar refineries, and the foreign producers.[13]

The subgovernment model proved popular with political scientists for a number of reasons. First, it provided an escape from the confines of institutional analysis. Research on the Congress or the bureaucracy could not capture the full nature of the policymaking process without going well beyond the boundaries of those institutions. Second, much scholarship in political science focuses on an individual policy domain. To those who wanted to study a particular issue area, the idea of subgovernments offered a conceptual framework to guide their research. Third, the subgovernment idea could be communicated easily to students and scholars alike. The model was based on straightforward, convincing case studies; those who read the relevant works were not required to make leaps of faith or to agree to any problematic assumptions. Fourth, the idea of subgovernments

---

[12] Ernest Griffith, *Impasse of Democracy* (New York: Harrison-Hilton Books, 1939). See John T. Tierney, "Subgovernments and Issue Networks," paper presented at the annual meeting of the American Political Science Association, New Orleans, August, 1985, p. 28.

[13] Douglass Cater, *Power in Washington* (New York: Vintage Books, 1964), p. 18

offered a critical perspective on the performance of American government. The closed nature of the policymaking system and the central role played by key interest groups in each area made subgovernments an inviting target for those who found fault with the direction of public policy. The public interest was not served because not all important interests were represented at the bargaining table.

Since the research on subgovernments was built around case studies, it is not clear how much government policymaking took place in these closed, consensual systems. By the late 1970s political scientists began to doubt that subgovernments characterized the policymaking process. However representative they once were, many subgovernments had crumbled, and a new model of interest group–government relations was needed. An alternative conception was offered by Hugh Heclo who argued that policymaking is best described as taking place within much larger issue networks. If we look "for the closed triangles of control," says Heclo, "we tend to miss the fairly open networks of people that increasingly impinge upon government."[14]

Heclo defines an issue network as "a shared-knowledge group" that ties together large numbers of participants with common technical expertise.[15] Unlike the simple and clearly defined nature of subgovernments, issue networks are difficult to visualize and rather ill defined. Participants move in and out easily, and it is "almost impossible to say where a network leaves off and its environment begins."[16] Networks are not radically different from subgovernments in their membership, since lobbyists, legislators, legislative aides, and agency administrators still make up the vast majority of participants. White House aides, consultants, and prominent, knowledgeable individuals can also be found in their midst, however. Rather, what is distinctive about issue networks is their size and accessibility to new participants. A large network can be made up of dozens and even hundreds of interest groups, a number of executive branch offices, and different congressional committees and subcommittees. Even a smaller network allows for broader and more open participation than a subgovernment.

A Pattern of Conflict

Despite some evocative imagery, Heclo's model was rather imprecise and did not offer strong empirical evidence on interest group behavior. His model was compelling, however, and as studies were completed, issue networks gained currency as an alternative to the increasingly discredited subgovernment model. Not all patterns of interest group government relations fit the issue network model, especially in policy areas that are relatively narrow in focus and involve a limited number of groups.[17] Still, the basic premise of the subgovernment model is now invalid. In

[14] Hugh Heclo, "Issue Networks and the Executive Establishment," in Anthony King, ed., *The New American Political System* (Washington, D.C.: American Enterprise Institute, 1978), p. 88.

[15] Heclo, "Issue Networks and the Executive Establishment," p. 103.

[16] Heclo, "Issue Networks and the Executive Establishment," p. 102.

[17] James A. Thurber, "Dynamics of Policy Subsystems in American Politics," in Allan J. Cigler and Burdett A. Loomis, eds., *Interest Group Politics*, 3rd ed. (Washington, D.C.: Congressional Quarterly, 1991), pp. 319–343.

other words, *the significant interest groups and key government officials in an issue area do not usually work in a consensual fashion to develop public policy.*

Instead, the research shows that interest groups are typically in open and protracted conflict with other lobbies working in their policy area. One study based on a survey of Washington lobbies found that over 70 percent of the citizen groups and for-profit groups (professional and trade associations) indicated that they face opposition by other lobbies. The figures were around 45 percent for nonprofit groups and 40 percent for organizations with mixed memberships from the profit and not-for-profit sectors.[18] Another study found pervasive conflict between business organizations and citizen groups. Seventy percent of corporations and 66 percent of trade associations said that the growing number of citizen groups had made their lobbying tasks harder. Less conflict was found among business groups themselves.[19]

A third large-scale study found that in four different policy domains, about 75 percent of interest group representatives cited lobbies that were adversaries.[20] The researchers analyzed agriculture, health, labor, and energy policymaking and in each area identified 20 "policy events," such as a committee vote on a bill or the issuance of new regulations by an agency. The typical pattern of interest group alignment for these events was a substantial division among the participating lobbies.[21]

Research also establishes that partisan change is a key factor in determining interest group access to policymakers. Subgovernments were said to be relatively autonomous from the electoral process. Presidents come and go, but subgovernments live on forever. This is not what Mark Peterson and Jack Walker found in their surveys of interest groups in 1980 and 1985:

> When Reagan replaced Carter in the White House, there was a virtual revolution in the access enjoyed by interest groups in Washington. In the past, many groups may have been able to maintain their contacts with the bureaucratic agencies of the federal government through politically isolated subgovernments or iron triangles, no matter what the outcome of the election, but it was difficult to build such safe enclaves around a group's favorite programs during the 1980s.[22]

Clearly the Reagan administration profoundly affected the Washington interest group community with its highly ideological agenda and its successful effort to cut budgetary sacred cows. Earlier, the election of Jimmy Carter in 1976 also had significant impact on interest group access to the executive branch. The large number of liberal citizen groups in Washington were a major beneficiary of his administration. Activists from these organizations filled important administrative positions and gave generous access to public interest lobbyists. These same

---

[18] Jack L. Walker, *Mobilizing Interest Groups in America* (Ann Arbor: University of Michigan Press, 1991), p. 129.

[19] Kay Lehman Schlozman and John T. Tierney, *Organized Interests and American Democracy* (New York: Harper & Row, 1986), pp. 283–287.

[20] Heinz et al., *The Hollow Core*, p. 252.

[21] Heinz et al., *The Hollow Core*, pp. 313–367.

[22] Mark A. Peterson and Jack L. Walker, "Interest Group Response to Partisan Change: The Impact of the Reagan Administration upon the National Interest Group System," in Allan J. Cigler and Burdett A. Loomis, eds., *Interest Group Politics*, 2nd ed. (Washington, D.C.: Congressional Quarterly, 1986), p. 172.

groups had found the doors to the Nixon administration's bureaucracies tightly shut. When Bill Clinton took office after 12 years of Republican control of the executive branch, lobbyists for liberal citizen groups rejoiced because a number of their colleagues were appointed to key agency positions. Environmentalists, for example, cheered the selection of Bruce Babbitt, who had headed the League of Conservation Voters, as Secretary of Interior. He was joined at Interior by George Frampton, former president of the Wilderness Society, who became the assistant secretary for Fish and Wildlife. Also at Interior, Brooks Yeager of the National Audubon Society became director of policy analysis, and John Leshy of the Natural Resources Defense Council became the department's solicitor. With friends in high places, environmental lobbyists had improved access and more sympathetic ears to listen to them.

In sum, the simple, stable structure of subgovernments gave way to a much different kind of policy community. Individual lobbying organizations constantly search for coalition partners in an effort to pyramid resources so that they can better contend with their interest group adversaries. A lobby's relations with government can be significantly affected by who is in the White House; this is especially true for citizen groups whose ideological character make them vulnerable to changes in administrations. These changes in interest group politics are considerable. Why did they happen?

Again, the Advocacy Explosion

The most important source of change affecting policymaking communities has been the proliferation of interest groups. The arguments . . . do not need repeating; our goal here is to explore how the growth in the number of lobbies and the increasing diversity of advocacy organizations affected the policymaking process.[23] In this respect the impact of the advocacy explosion was probably most profound in the way it altered the relations between groups and agencies. For example, the Department of Agriculture, long the bureaucratic center of many subgovernments, was transformed by a "proliferation of groups" that "destabilized the agricultural subsystem."[24] As new groups emerged and demanded to be heard, subgovernments weren't able to wall themselves off from those who wanted to be included in policymaking. Subgovernments flourished in the absence of competing interest groups, not in spite of them.

Most new groups approaching subgovernments had resources that made it difficult for the subgovernments to exclude them. Even if an administrative agency was antagonistic to a new group because of its ideological leanings, there were always legislators who held the same views and were willing to help. Particularly notable in this respect was the growth in the number of citizen groups. When these highly conservative or liberal groups found an administrative agency of the

---

[23] See Jeffrey M. Berry, "Citizen Groups and the Changing Nature of Interest Group Politics in America," *Annals of the American Academy of Political and Social Science* 528 (July 1993), pp. 30–41.

[24] William P. Browne, "Policy and Interests: Instability and Change in a Classic Issue Subsystem," in Cigler and Loomis, *Interest Group Politics*, 2nd ed., p. 187.

opposite persuasion, they worked with allies in Congress to attack agency decisions they disagreed with.[25] One study concluded, "Once these new groups of the Left and Right became permanent fixtures in Washington, the conditions that had nurtured the decentralized system of subgovernments were fundamentally altered."[26]

With the growing number of interest groups came a greater variety of interests. The new groups were not just carbon copies of those that already existed. A representative from the National Association of Realtors described the changes for his industry:

> If you go back a few years ago, you would have to say that if the National Association of Realtors and the [National Association of] Home Builders spoke, that was the whole industry speaking. Now there are more groups, such as low income housing groups, real estate developers, residential real estate developers, etc. . . . Members of Congress have to listen to all these groups.

Each new group brings with it a different set of priorities and will aggressively seek out policy makers on its own as well as frequently enter into coalitions with other groups. The expanding number of advocacy organizations heightens the competition between them because it is difficult for policymakers to find solutions for large numbers of client groups that make all of them winners.

Competition often shades into open conflict. This is most apparent between traditional adversaries, such as business versus labor or business versus liberal public interest groups. Conflict among businesses in the same industry also characterizes a number of policy domains. One important change that has fostered such conflict is the movement toward deregulation. Scholarly analyses of regulatory practices encouraged a view that much of the federal government's regulatory efforts led to inefficiency, unnecessary protection for privileged companies, stifling of competition, and a bad deal for consumers. The hold of industries such as trucking, airlines, and telecommunications over regulatory policy was shattered by the intellectual appeal of deregulation proposals, nurtured first in academe and in think tanks and then pushed by sympathizers in the legislative and executive branches.[27]

As regulatory barriers that parcel out markets to different types of business enterprises weaken, firms begin to push for further regulatory changes. This has happened in the broad area of financial services. As some regulatory practices have been changed to stimulate competition, various industry sectors have pressed for even more changes. Banks, insurance companies, and brokerage houses all want to encroach on each other's turf. Substantial conflict can exist even within one sector, as in banking. Large money center banks, small banks, and savings and loans do not see eye-to-eye on all issues.

New competition has come not only from traditional segments of the financial services community trying to steal business from each other but from entirely new

[25] Jeffrey M. Berry, *Feeding Hungry People: Rulemaking in the Food Stamp Program* (New Brunswick, N.J.: Rutgers University Press, 1984).

[26] Thomas L. Gais, Mark A. Peterson, and Jack L. Walker, "Interest Groups, Iron Triangles, and Representative Instiutions in American National Government," *British Journal of Political Science* 14 (April 1984), p. 166.

[27] Martha Derthick and Paul Quirk, *The Politics of Deregulation* (Washington, D.C.: Brookings Institution, 1985).

players entering the picture. When Microsoft announced its intention to purchase Intuit, producers of Quicken, a program for managing home finances on a personal computer, observers realized that Microsoft wanted more than just another popular piece of software. Rather, the software giant was trying to position itself to become a major player in financial services. In Microsoft's mind, why should banking be left to banks? (The federal government subsequently filed antitrust objections to the sale, and the deal was halted.[28]) In short, the expanding number of interest groups in conflict with each other has transformed policymaking in financial services.

Although the advocacy explosion was the primary reason for the collapse of subgovernments, change in the structure of government contributed to this transformation of interest group politics as well. The institutional arrangements within the Congress and the executive branch that helped to sustain subgovernments were altered by reforms and changing norms.[29] During the period when subgovernments were declining, the trend in Congress was toward decentralization of its structure of authority. An important part of this was a growth in the number of subcommittees, which in turn meant more overlapping jurisdictions. For example, 110 different committees and subcommittees claim some jurisdiction over programs of the Environmental Protection Agency.[30] As one observer pointed out, decentralization means that "the scope of conflict changes continually, usually expanding, as legislation passes from one stage to the next. Deals and accommodations devised at one stage cannot be adhered to later because negotiations must be reopened at each stage."[31]

More recently, there have been signs of recentralization in the House of Representatives. When Newt Gingrich took over as Speaker in 1995, he was able to instill more party discipline and reduce the autonomy of committee chairs. This may enhance the power of lobbies particularly valued by the leadership but will not lead to a reversal of issue network politics and the reemergence of subgovernments. It could mean, however, that the overlapping jurisdictions of committees that once enabled competing interest groups to play one committee against another will not be as significant a factor as they once were.

The growth of the executive branch also contributed to the fall of subgovernments. Policymaking became dispersed across more agencies and bureaus, and the authority of many such organizations was reduced as different units began working in the same broad policy area. The autonomy of individual bureaucracies was reduced further as the White House began trying to increase its control over the sprawling executive branch. Recent presidents have used the Office of Management and Budget or other parts of the Executive Office of the President to oversee

---

[28] G. Christian Hill, Don Clark, and Viveca Novak, "Microsoft Drops Bid for Intuit—A Victory for Antitrust Agency," *Wall Street Journal*, May 22, 1995.

[29] Jeffrey M. Berry, "Subgovernments, Issue Networks, and Political Conflict," in Richard A. Harris and Sidney Milkis, eds., *Remaking American Politics* (Boulder, Colo.: Westview, 1989), pp. 239–260.

[30] Robert F. Durant, "The Democratic Deficit in America," *Political Science Quarterly* 110 (Spring 1995), p. 37.

[31] Steven S. Smith, "New Patterns of Decisionmaking in Congress," in John E. Chubb and Paul E. Peterson, eds., *The New Direction in American Politics* (Washington, D.C.: Brookings Institution, 1985), p. 221.

regulatory policymaking. Over time, the structure of the executive branch and the growth of interest group politics has made agency policymaking more complex and conflictual.

The Qualities of Issue Networks

Issue networks are as complex as subgovernments were simple. To provide a concrete illustration of issue network politics, a case study of the telecommunications industry will be offered below. Before proceeding to this specific case, however, some of the general qualities of issue networks should be outlined.

A network can be defined as "a specific type of relation linking a defined set of persons, objects, or events."[32] In terms of interest groups and government, what does this mean? The "type of relation" is primarily one revolving around the exchange of information.[33] A fundamental axiom of Washington politics is that "information is power," and issue networks provide ways in which information may be gathered and disseminated quickly and inexpensively. As noted in the discussion of coalitions, no one interest group has the means of gathering or monitoring all the information it needs to operate at maximum effectiveness. It is always the case that other groups will have better relationships with some of the key policymakers, have superior knowledge of some aspect of the problem at hand, or will hear about new developments first.[34]

Interest groups develop relationships with other groups where they freely exchange information under a norm of reciprocity. That is, if one group gives information to a second, the second group is expected to give the first group information when the second acquires it. This does not apply when the groups find themselves on different sides of an issue, as commonly happens to even the best of friends. Information is exchanged in simple and straightforward ways through phone calls, chance meetings (like those at Capitol Hill receptions), and more formal meetings. Finding out what amendment the subcommittee chair is thinking of offering, or what transpired in a conversation between an agency head and a White House adviser, is information critical to a lobbyist.

The "set of persons, objects, or events" are those who exchange information in some recurring fashion in a particular policy area. They are individuals who speak for organizations, notably interest groups, congressional committees, and executive branch agencies. Not all of these individuals exchange information with all others in their network. Within a large network, there are likely to be clusters of lobbies grouped according to issue focus. People in government are eager to exchange information with lobbyists because it helps them to understand what policy alternatives are most politically acceptable and what kind of lobbying strategy is being

---

[32] David Knoke and James Kuklinski, *Network Analysis*, Sage Series on Quantitative Applications in the Social Sciences, no. 28 (Beverly Hills, Calif.: Sage, 1982), p. 12.

[33] Karen S. Cook, "Network Structures from an Exchange Perspective," in Peter V. Marsden and Nan Lin, eds., *Social Structure and Network Analysis* (Beverly Hills, Calif.: Sage, 1982), pp. 177–199.

[34] See, generally, Hula, *Links and Choices.*

planned to try to influence them. It is a form of intelligence gathering, and they may gain information that they can't otherwise acquire at a reasonable cost of time or money.[35] As issues develop, policymakers develop alliances with various groups and keep in touch with them on a regular basis to share information.

It is evident that issue networks are characterized by high degrees of conflict and cooperation. Political scientists have begun to explore the structure of issue networks to see what kinds of cleavages may divide these policymaking communities and to try to identify the different kinds of roles groups might play in network politics. Examining the structure of networks is important because it can offer insight into the distribution of power among interest groups.[36] Understanding how individual networks operate is the first step toward comparing networks and building models of the different kinds of issue networks that may exist.

Issue networks can be further defined by the following properties:

Hollow Cores. The research that has been done on issue networks shows some common patterns in their internal structure. In their study of four large policy domains, Heinz and his colleagues found that none of the four had a central lobbying group that acted as a broker among most of the other groups in the network. In the energy field, for example, there is no one trade association or large corporation that is at the center of all communication among energy groups. No one lobby coordinates all the major interest group activity, hence there is a "hollow core" in the middle of the network.[37] This is not only the case because policy differences and ideological divisions exist within a network, but because there are so many issues and organizations that no one group could provide such consistent leadership.

Multiple Niches. Another structural characteristic of networks is that most individual groups are narrowly focused. They generally operate within issue niches, interacting primarily with those groups representing similar interests.[38] For example, one agricultural lobbyist commented: "In agriculture it tends to be commodity groups working closely together. We have to. We're not all that different." These different groups representing dairy, soybean, peanut, wheat, cotton, cattle, and other such interests rely largely on each other.

The Importance of Being Expert. Much of the glamour and glitz of Washington lobbying is generated by the handful of lobbyists who have unusual access to those in power because of their high-powered reputations or political connections of some kind. For the foot soldiers of the lobbying profession, however, having extensive knowledge about one's issue area is critical to ongoing access to policymakers. It is not that being an expert in earlier times was not helpful.

---

[35] John Mark Hansen, *Gaining Access* (Chicago: University of Chicago Press, 1991).

[36] David Knoke, *Political Networks: The Structural Perspective* (New York: Cambridge University Press, 1990), pp. 1–27; and Barry Wellman, "Structural Analysis: From Method and Metaphor to Theory and Substance," in Barry Wellman and S. D. Berkowitz, eds., *Social Structures: A Network Approach* (New York: Cambridge University Press, 1988), pp. 19–61.

[37] Heinz et al., *The Hollow Core*, pp. 275–308.

[38] William P. Browne, "Organized Interests and Their Issue Niches: A Search for Pluralism in a Policy Domain," *Journal of Politics* 52 (May 1990), pp. 477–509.

Rather, as policymaking has become more complex and competition from other interest groups in the same area has increased, expertise has become a more significant means by which lobbyists qualify themselves as participants in the policymaking process.

Expertise is something more than familiarity with the issues. All lobbyists have a sound knowledge of the issues they work on. Expertise is a very high degree of knowledge about a policy area, including enough technical sophistication to gain the respect of those in government who are themselves specialists in the policy area. A lobbyist on issues such as toxic wastes, nuclear energy, or acid rain cannot get far without some working knowledge of the scientific issues at the root of the controversies.

Sloppy Boundaries. One criticism that can be made of the issue network model is that the lack of precisely defined boundaries can make a network seem like an amorphous blob. The membership and overall shape of networks are fluid; a new organization can enter a network by developing a relationship with just one other organization already in it. Becoming a critical player in a network may be difficult, but finding other organizations to exchange information with is not. Boundaries are sloppy because issue areas overlap considerably and because there is no central authority capable of excluding new participants.

Yet even within these broad generations, there is reason for caution. As the case study of telecommunications will demonstrate, networks do not always operate by the norms of well-defined niche politics. And although the research demonstrating that issue networks have hollow cores is very persuasive, the research was restricted to rather large policy domains. It's conceivable that in smaller networks, centrally located groups play more of a consistent leadership role.

The Telecommunications Network

At a hearing of the House Telecommunications Subcommittee in 1976, freshman Representative Tim Wirth (D-Colorado) was surprised at the large turnout for the session. He asked the witness from AT&T who was testifying to identify his colleagues sitting in the audience. After five minutes the AT&T executive had identified those in only one corner of the room. A reporter noted that a frustrated Wirth asked, "'Will everyone associated with AT&T just stand up?' Everyone in the audience stood up, all 150 of them."[39]

Today, a hearing on telecommunications would draw a crowd too, but they wouldn't all be from AT&T. The telecommunications industry has been radically transformed, and AT&T, which was once the world's largest corporation and monopolized the telephone industry, is a considerably smaller company facing competition in all aspects of its business. The days when policy was made quietly by AT&T lobbyists, the Federal Communications Commission (FCC), and the congressional subcommittees are as much a relic as party-line telephone service.

[39] Monica Langley, "AT&T Sends a Horde of Lobbyists to Fight a Phone-Bill Proposal," *Wall Street Journal,* November 4, 1983.

Policymaking in this area is now a free-for-all, and Washington is full of lobbyists and lawyers representing competing telecommunications companies. "Every day you see a new office popping up," says one telecommunications lobbyist.

Ma Bell Dies

How did all this happen? The history is complex, and only a thumbnail sketch can be offered here.[40] Our narrative focuses on how the breakup of the system led to the creation of an issue network organized around various commercial niches in the telecommunications industry and how that network then evolved into a different kind of structure.

The first major step toward the breakup of the Bell system monopoly came with the 1968 *Carterfone* decision. The FCC, which regulates the communications industry, ruled in *Carterfone* that "terminal equipment" could be sold by companies other than AT&T. As a result, individuals and businesses could buy a telephone from anyone and, presumably, enjoy the price and performance benefits of competition. A year later, Microwave Communications, Inc. (now known as MCI) won FCC approval to offer private long-distance lines between businesses in Chicago and St. Louis through microwave technology. Yet because the microwave transmissions still had to be connected to the local phone systems, AT&T would have to let MCI rent access to its lines. AT&T, outraged at the FCC's decision, was uncooperative, and negotiations with MCI dragged on. AT&T feared, correctly, that allowing MCI a foot in the door was an invitation to wholesale competition in long-distance services. MCI aggressively pushed forward, lobbying the FCC and eventually filing a complaint with the antitrust division of the Justice Department. Ma Bell was under siege.

The Justice Department began an investigation in 1973. In a decision that shocked the business community, it filed an antitrust suit against AT&T in 1974, charging it with monopolizing various parts of the telecommunications industry. Meanwhile, MCI had begun offering regular long-distance service rather than just its business-to-business private lines. AT&T counterattacked with an effort to get Congress to pass a law that would forbid competition in the long-distance business. Despite an extraordinary effort by AT&T, the bill didn't come close to passage. Although the Justice Department suit lay dormant during the mid-1970s, it was actively pursued toward the end of the decade. In January of 1981, the trial of *United States v. American Telephone and Telegraph* began in the courtroom of federal district judge Harold Greene.

As the trial proceeded, it became clear that AT&T stood a good chance of being handed a devastating decision by Judge Greene. Meanwhile, AT&T's lobbying of the White House to get the Justice Department to stop prosecuting the case had failed. Reading the handwriting on the wall, AT&T entered into negotiations with the Justice Department to break up the Bell system. It could at least

---

[40] For a full history of the AT&T breakup, see Steve Coll, *The Deal of the Century* (New York: Atheneum, 1986); and Peter Temin with Louis Galambos, *The Fall of the Bell System* (New York: Cambridge University Press, 1987). On the earlier history of AT&T's relations with government, see Alan Stone, *Public Service Liberalism* (Princeton: Princeton University Press, 1991).

horse-trade with Justice; there was no lobbying Judge Greene, who could deal them a much worse hand. In January of 1982, a basic agreement was reached, and the trial, which was still going on, was stopped.

In the out-of-court agreement, AT&T agreed to give up local telephone service. Seven new regional companies ("Baby Bells"), such as Pacific Telesis in the West and NYNEX in the Northeast, were created to take over local phone service. AT&T retained long-distance services, though it had to face competition from other companies. AT&T was also able to keep control of two of its prized possessions—Bell Labs, its research arm, and Western Electric, its manufacturing division. AT&T also won the right to enter the computer industry, an important goal of the company. It had long had the technological know-how, but as a regulated monopoly it had not been allowed to sell computers. This substantially sweetened the deal for AT&T, which was losing three-quarters of its assets in the settlement.

One of the political consequences of the AT&T breakup and the competition that had earlier come to the phone industry was a spectacular growth in telecommunications advocacy. Just about anybody with expertise on telecommunications could land a lucrative position with one of the newly established Washington offices of firms in the industry. All seven regionals set up lobbying offices to protect their interests against AT&T. The one part of AT&T that did not shrink was its political arm. After reorganizing its Washington operations in the wake of the breakup, it had 55 lobbyists on board.[41] For lawyers with the right experience, the AT&T breakup was a cause for celebration. "Washington D.C.'s 'telecommunications bar' boomed like a Nevada silver town."[42]

In the wake of the divestiture agreement there was substantial competition in many sectors of the industry, and both consumers and businesses enjoyed the benefits of expanded product choice and competitive pricing. Other sectors, notably basic local phone service, were not competitive markets. A large, fractious issue network developed as new companies freely entered some markets, and political alliances changed rapidly from issue to issue. Ad hoc coalitions quickly formed and then dissolved, often putting strange bedfellows together on one matter while they fought each other bitterly on another.

Telecommunications was not turned into an integrated market by the consent agreement. Federal district court Judge Harold Greene retained jurisdiction over questions left unclear by the out-of-court settlement and over petitions to expand competition by companies wanting to overturn parts of the initial agreement. As indicated by Figure 1, by 1988 the basic structure of the network was composed of distinctive industry niches. Most of the conflict within the network was generated by one industry niche wanting to gain Judge Greene's permission or congressional approval to move into a market it was prohibited from participating in. The businesses that held some regulatory advantage would vigorously defend their turf. For example, the consent decree forbid the seven Baby Bells from manufacturing telecommunications products. AT&T, concerned that the Baby Bells were going to

---

[41] Michael Wines, "Ma Bell and Her Newly Independent Children Revamp Lobbying Networks," *National Journal*, January 28, 1984, pp. 148–152.

[42] Coll, *The Deal of the Century*, p. 365.

get around this provision by designing products and then simply having another company manufacture them, pressed Judge Greene to rule that the consent decree's intent for the Baby Bells included a ban on design as well as manufacturing. Greene ruled in favor of AT&T and other manufacturers and against the regional phone companies.[43]

There is no agreed upon way to map out an issue network in Washington. In Figure 1 the two most important policymaking bodies, the Federal Communications Commission and Congress, are arbitrarily placed in the center. Other parts of government (such as the Office of the Special Trade Representative in the White House) are participants in the network as well. At the time, the various industry niches included long-distance carriers, regional phone companies, small telephone companies, computer and electronics firms, and domestic and foreign manufacturers. Labor unions, consumer groups, and various trade associations are also part of the telecommunications policy community.

In 1988 the telecommunications issue network was still primarily focused on telephone equipment and services. People in telecommunications certainly anticipated some integration of the telephone industry with the computer and cable TV industries, and many issues at the time concerned future opportunities that the large-scale integration of these fields would bring. Nevertheless, around this time the network was largely animated by conflict between different industries trying to encroach on each other's telephone service and equipment markets.

Market Integration

By 1994, in the space of only six years, the telecommunications issue network had been thoroughly transformed.[44] Although there is still conflict between different industries, it is no longer the defining characteristic of network politics. As Figure 2 illustrates, the political relationships among major companies in the network are not based on a primary manufacturing or service identity. Indeed, what is most conspicuous about the evolution of the telecommunications issue network are the large-scale integration of different companies into business alliances that provide a range of products and services to consumers. In some cases, this integration extends to foreign companies that have working agreements or cross-ownership ties with American firms.

The scope of some of these business alliances is staggering. For example, Time Warner, a publishing and entertainment colossus in its own right, has strategic alliances with many other key players in telecommunications. U.S. West, a Baby Bell, has a major ownership interest in Time Warner, which in turn has ownership interests in Turner Broadcasting (cable TV networks and a movie library), 3DO (a computer software company), and Teleport (a provider of phone lines). It has business agreements with Oracle and Microsoft (computer software companies) and

---

[43] Bob Davis, "AT&T Case Judge Berates Regulators, Reaffirms Manufacturing Ban on Bells," *Wall Street Journal*, December 4, 1987, p. 2.

[44] See Jeffrey M. Berry, "The Dynamic Qualities of Issue Networks," paper delivered at the annual meeting of the American Political Science Association, New York, September, 1994.

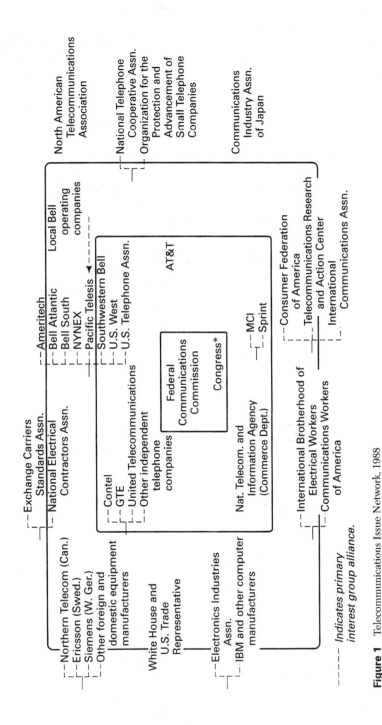

Figure 1 Telecommunications Issue Network, 1988

*The primary congressional actors in 1988 were the Subcommittee on Telecommunications and Finance, House Committee on Energy and Commerce, and the Subcommittee on Communications, Senate Committee on Commerce, Science, and Transportation.

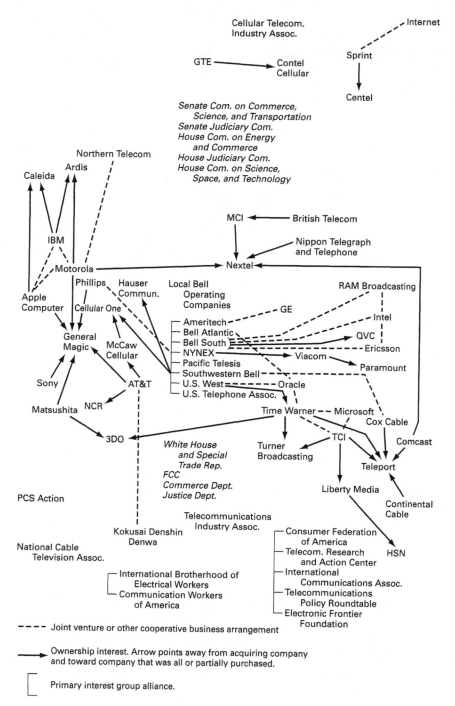

Figure 2 Telecommunications Issue Network, 1994

Note: Current as of March 1, 1994

Source: Jeffrey M. Berry, "The Dynamic Qualities of Issue Networks," paper delivered at the annual meeting of the American Political Science Association, New York, September 1994, p. 12a. Reprinted by permission.

TCI (the nation's largest owner of local cable TV companies). This set of alliances reflects the dominant strategy in the telecommunications industry: the future belongs to those companies who can provide all the key services of the information superhighway. And what are those key services? In simple terms, it is basic telephone service, cellular or wireless service, long distance, access to computerized databases, cable TV, electronic mail, an Internet gateway, and connections to a variety of consumer services (banking, travel reservations, shopping, and so on).

To position themselves to be a player in the telecommunications industry of the future, companies such as Time Warner are making sure they have all the pieces to compete. Despite the heavy competition today and the substantial diversity of interests within the network, telecommunications executives feel that the industry is moving toward a limited set of business alliances who are able to provide all the services that consumers want.

Whatever the future of telecommunications, the integration of companies pursuing this strategy has had profound political implications for participants in this issue network: predictable lobbying fault lines are disappearing, leadership within the network is changing, and there is extreme uncertainty because of the movement toward full deregulation of telecommunications.

Two Models

In examining telecommunications interest groups at two points in time, we see two very different models of an issue network. The 1988 model was characterized by well-defined industry niches, and interest group coalitions were built largely around these industry clusters. Competition existed within separate industry sectors, but many regulatory restrictions prevented certain companies (most notably AT&T and the Baby Bells) from freely entering particular markets. For shorthand purposes, we shall refer to the 1988 system as the industry *niche model*.

The 1994 model is characterized by business alliances that cross different markets. Mergers, joint working arrangements, and cross-ownership are common relationships connecting different kinds of telecommunications firms. By 1994 the regulatory framework for telecommunications was crumbling, and policy was moving rapidly toward open competition in most markets. Bell Atlantic, a Baby Bell, won permission to compete with cable television by offering programming through its phone lines. Time Warner gained regulatory approval in New York State to offer basic telephone service. All the Baby Bells formed partnerships with movie studios. We shall refer to the 1994 system as the *full market integration model*.

Since the time the research was done on the 1994 system, mergers, acquisitions, and new business alliances have continued at a dizzying pace. In February of 1996, new telecommunications legislation passed Congress and was signed into law by President Clinton. The law provides for sweeping deregulation of the long-distance, local telephone service, and cable-TV markets, allowing companies in any one of these industries to fully compete in the others. Below, we'll speculate on where this issue network might be headed in light of these changes. The question that must be first addressed is why did such a transformation take place? Why did an industry niche network evolve into a full market integration network?

There are a number of reasons. First, and foremost though, enormous technological change has occurred in the telecommunications field. When the consent agreement was signed, no one could have foreseen all the new technologies that would emerge. Everyone knew change was coming, but there was no adequate regulatory apparatus in place to continually redraw the boundaries to determine which companies could offer what services. Entrepreneurs came to conceive of this industry as one with limitless opportunities for combining markets. The shrewdness and imagination of business leaders like John Malone (TCI), Raymond Smith (Bell Atlantic), Gerald Levin (Time Warner), and others outran the capacity of the regulatory system to govern telecommunications.

Telecommunications is certainly not unique in being deeply affected by rapid technological change. Regulation of many industries has been affected by new inventions and changes in technology. What does seem unusual about telecommunications is the breadth of integration between so many important business sectors, most notably, telephones, television and movies, and computers.

There is not enough research to know how characteristic of Washington policymaking either of these models are. Moreover, there are surely other models of issue networks that can be found in Washington. There is certainly no reason to believe that all industries evolve into a full market integration network. Agriculture, for example, is an industry that has had its share of scientific breakthroughs and technological change; yet it remains an industry niche network.[45] The inference one would have to draw from the research that is available is that the industry niche model is more commonly found than the type of integration seen today in telecommunications.[46]

It is important to understand issue networks not only because it is helpful to have models to guide our thinking about complex policymaking environments, but because such analysis is useful for clarifying our thoughts about the role of interest groups in a democratic society. Is one of the models outlined here more conducive to democratic policymaking than the other? This is a complicated question, but at least a few considerations can be brought up here.[47]

One advantage of the contemporary telecommunications network is that the expanding breadth of the interest groups involved in policymaking enlarges the range of constituencies represented. A recent effort of the Baby Bells to enter some new markets generated conflict that involved over 300 corporations and other interest groups.[48] Everyone is affected by telecommunications policy, and an extensive array of interest groups involved in policymaking is surely desirable. In an industry niche network, the range of groups participating is more restricted. An added benefit of such broad interest group participation is that it increases the chances that policy problems will get reconceptualized in new and different ways.

---

[45] See Browne, "Organized Interests and Their Issue Niches."

[46] See Heinz et al., *The Hollow Core.*

[47] A more thorough discussion on networks and democratic policymaking can be found in Berry, "The Dynamic Qualities of Issue Networks."

[48] Kirk Victor, "Road Warriors," *National Journal,* March 20, 1993, p. 680.

Although this full market integration network has broadened participation in telecommunications policymaking, trends in the industry warrant some concern. As the regulatory barriers in telecommunications fall and corporate alliances position themselves in every part of the field, competition could give way to oligopoly. As consumers find advantages to purchasing all their telecommunications services through one vendor, those companies that are not part of the huge alliances that are developing will have a tougher time competing. The capital entry requirements of trying to build a new telecommunications alliance that serves all relevant markets are immense. A planned merger between Bell Atlantic and TCI, which eventually collapsed, was valued at as much as $32 billion.[49] Predicting the course of such a rapidly changing industry is hazardous at best, but it is certainly plausible that such corporate alliances could come to dominate the market. If so, it is equally plausible that government would step in and increase its regulatory control. If this occurs, a new type of issue network will evolve and present us with a different kind of policymaking model than the two discussed here.

Conclusion

In surveying the relationship of interest groups to other lobbies and government policymakers, both stability and change can be observed. Interest groups still coalesce with each other for the same reasons they always have. They need to share resources (staff, money, and contacts) because each group is limited in the amount of advocacy it can engage in and in its ability to influence the federal government. Coalitions also enhance the credibility of a group's position.

Change has come as well in the way lobbies interact with others in their political environment. For years political scientists argued that policymaking through subgovernments was characteristic of the way Washington works. This may have been true of an earlier time, but it is not accurate today. With the sharp increase in the numbers of interest groups, policymaking communities changed dramatically. One way to conceive of the interaction of large numbers of interest groups and government officials is to think of these organizations and people as a network. Issue networks facilitate communication between people working in the same policy area.

The decline of subgovernments and the rise of issue networks raise some important questions for political scientists and how they view interest group politics. When the subgovernment model was widely accepted, political scientists were highly critical of the relationships at the core of the policymaking process. To scholars, subgovernments suggested a privileged position for a small number of groups in each policy area. For those political scientists who thought that pluralist theory offered a far too generous assessment of American democracy, the subgovernment model offered a considerably different view of interest groups. At the heart of pluralist thinking is the belief that democratic ends are reached through

---

[49]The exact value of the merger was unclear because how much of TCI would be merged into Bell Atlantic was never finally determined. John Huey and Andrew Kupfer, "What That Merger Means for You," *Fortune*, November 15, 1993, pp. 82–94.

the bargaining and compromise of affected interests in an open political system. Subgovernments represented agency capture by clientele groups, highly restricted participation, stability that preserves the status quo, and centralized decision making. Subgovernments were evidence that a group-based policymaking system is deeply flawed and does not promote democratic government.

Issue networks suggest something else entirely. The policymaking process is seen as more open, more decentralized, more conflictual, more dynamic, and more broadly participatory. In short, issue networks come much closer to fulfilling the pluralist prescription for democratic politics. This is not to say that they are a perfect mechanism for promoting true pluralist democracy. Despite their expanded participation, issue networks do nothing to ensure that all affected interests are represented at the bargaining table. Lacking a centralized decision-making process, issue network politics may also favor the status quo by making compromise more difficult to achieve when there are sharply divergent views. In the last analysis, though, issue networks come closer to fitting our expectations of democratic policymaking than do subgovernments.

Policy Implementation

There is no more treacherous step in policy making for the public manager than implementation. Daniel Mazmanian and Paul Sabatier capture the scope of this challenge with the six conditions of effective implementation that they detail in *Implementation and Public Policy*. "A statute or other policy decision seeking a substantial departure from the status quo," they write, "will achieve its desired goals if:

1. The enabling legislation or other legal directive mandates policy objectives which are clear and consistent or at least provides substantive criteria for resolving goal conflicts.
2. The enabling legislation incorporates a sound theory identifying the principal factors and causal linkages affecting policy objectives and gives implementing officials sufficient jurisdiction over target groups and other points of leverage to attain, at least potentially, the desired goals.
3. The enabling legislation structures the implementation process so as to maximize the probability that implementing officials and target groups will perform as desired. This involves assignment to sympathetic agencies with adequate hierarchical integration, supportive decision rules, sufficient financial resources, and adequate access to supporters.
4. The leaders of the implementing agency possess substantial managerial and political skill and are committed to the statutory goals.
5. The program is actively supported by organized constituency groups and by a few key legislators (or a chief executive) throughout the implementation process, with the courts being neutral or supportive.
6. The relative priority of statutory objectives is not undermined over time by the emergence of conflicting public policies or by changes in relevant socioeconomic conditions which weaken the statute's causal theory or political support."[a]

---

[a]Daniel Mazmanian and Paul Sabatier, *Implementation and Public Policy* (Glenview, IL: Scott, Foresman, 1983), pp. 41–42.

It is worth noting how many of these conditions are dependent on what was done during the policy formulation stage and are political in nature. Where problems are unrecognized, skirted, or ignored, it is during the implementation stage that the chickens come home to roost. Coalitions are thus most easily constructed by "fudging" the varied, and sometimes conflicting, motives of their members—an ambiguity that too often finds its way into the legislation. Placement in an appropriate agency with resources and access to supporters also does not follow as logically as one would think. A subtle, but effective, way to kill a program is to place it in an agency where it cannot possibly succeed. President Franklin D. Roosevelt recognized this problem when he vetoed the Brownlow Commission's recommendation to place federal loan programs under the Treasury Department. "That won't work. If they put them in the Treasury, not one of them will ever make a loan to anybody for any purpose. There are too many glass-eyed bankers in the Treasury."[b]

Privatization

Over the last 25 years, the most significant policy implementation trend at every governmental level has been the growth in privatization. This implementation strategy has attracted numerous supporters both as a means of delivering local services and as an appropriate remedy for pruning overgrown state and federal bureaucracies. Privatization sometimes refers to a shift in the ownership of assets from the public to the private sector or to shrinking the size of government. American politicians and public managers have devoted more attention, however, to privatization as an alternative means of delivering goods and services. As Savas has written, privatization in this sense is concerned with *how* we should deliver goods and services and *who* should do it, rather than *whether* the good or service should be delivered at all.[c] A government agency may thus pay for a service while a corporation (or sometimes a nonprofit or other government agency) may deliver it.

The big payoff from privatization is clearly thought to be greater efficiency—more "bang for the buck." Privatization adherents are enthusiastic about public/private partnerships to which the private sector can bring its technical know-how, vigor and commitment to the bottom line.[d] The question then boils down to the conditions under which these advantages of privatization—usually achieved through "contracting out"—can be realized. Ideally, supply and demand in the marketplace, thanks to the discipline of competition, would provide the desired savings as well as goods and services of high quality.

There are, however, limitations to contracting out, particularly where imperfect competition and imperfect information lead to "market failures." The government then, as Kettl puts it, must be a "smart buyer" and not allow "market imperfections" to become "market failures."[e] Donahue points to other limitations to contracting out in the public sector. It is difficult to make privatization work when the government's goals are uncertain; the product is difficult to monitor; switching from one contractor to another in midstream is difficult; or the government agency itself knows more about the best means to accomplish the goal.[f]

[b] Harold Seidman and Robert Gilmour, *Politics, Position, and Power*, 4th ed. (New York: Oxford University Press, 1986), p. 168.

[c] E. S. Savas, *Privatization and Public-Private Partnerships* (New York: Seven Bridges Press, 2000), pp. 63–107.

[d] Peter Kobrak, "Privatization and Cozy Politics," *Public Integrity Annual*, Council of State Governments and American Society for Public Administration, Vol. 1, 1996, p. 14.

[e] Donald F. Kettl, *Sharing Power* (Washington, D.C.: Brookings Institution, 1993), pp. 20–30.

[f] John D. Donahue, *The Privatization Decision* (New York: Basic Books, 1989), p. 45.

Deciding What to Contract Out

George Avery in the next selection shows the numerous subtleties in deciding what to—and what not to—contract out even in the apparently straightforward case of outsourcing public health laboratory services. He observes that supporters of "efficiency" (the best alternative is that which provides the most output for a given level of resources) and "noncompetition" (the public sector should not compete with the private sector when both sectors are producing the same service) have gained momentum over the last decade. Avery observes that these two paradigms (or models that seek to explain a process) are not the same, but each or both may lead to the abandonment by a public agency of important functions or tasks.

Citing the work of James Q. Wilson, Avery explains that public agencies are judged on the basis of four criteria that overlap, but are different from, what drives the private sector. The public sector too must be concerned with efficiency, but in addition, it has to consider equity (or fairness to all citizens), accountability (responsiveness to citizens as to *how* it chooses to implement policy), and authority (those "indefeasible" functions that must be "done in the name of the people" since they reflect the society's "core values"). In the case of authority, Wilson explains that "anything so solemn as pronouncing on guilt or imposing a dreadful sentence should be done by the direct and sworn representatives of the people."[g] Equity, accountability, and authority are particularly important because they may go to the core values of an administrative agency.

But do these values really apply in the case of outsourcing state public health laboratory services? Avery argues that such state facilities are engaged in both clinical and public health activities; as a result, they must be concerned with all four values. The patient whose symptoms are active and whose disease is easily detected through routine testing is an excellent candidate for a private sector laboratory. An asymptomatic subject whose symptoms are latent requires further testing to identify the disease. Such out-of-the-ordinary and sometimes extensive testing to detect the infection, however, is not what the doctor ordered for an efficient private laboratory anxious to keep costs within the parameters of a managed care provider. Yet, the asymptomatic subject is sometimes the most important patient for a public health laboratory where responsibility revolves, as Avery explains, "around the activities of the detection, prevention, treatment, control, intervention, surveillance, and assessment of health threats to populations, a much more complex set of tasks than the diagnosis and treatment of the individual patient." Furthermore, efficiency is measured differently in these cases. When Wisconsin's public health laboratory was weakened, it proved unable to perform its core mission. The result was a 1994 cryptosporidiosis outbreak. Cryptosporidiosis is a gastrointestinal disorder particularly dangerous to people with weakened immune systems from an infectious disease such as AIDS. Avery concludes that because the laboratories failed to find the disease's cause *before* the disorder occurred, the result was a far greater loss in productivity and human misery than any gains that could have been made through outsourcing.

Furthermore, in the case of some diseases, the public sector becomes involved precisely because there is not a sufficient market to justify private sector provision of such specialized services. Tuberculosis is one such example of an "orphaned" service. But data on tuberculosis is critical to detecting a serious public health threat, and detecting this public health threat is, therefore, critical to the core mission of a public health laboratory.

---

[g]James Q. Wilson, *Bureaucracy: What Government Agencies Do and Why They Do It* (New York: Basic Books, 1989), pp. 346–349.

In addition, the state laboratories do not operate solely within their jurisdiction; the 50 state laboratories provide the public health data for the federal Centers of Disease Control (CDC). The CDC coordinates this integrated network and depends on uniform testing processes and standards for its national data system. If privatization weakens the capacity of a state's public health laboratory, that laboratory becomes the weakest link in the administrative chain.

Avery feels that there are appropriate roles for both private and public laboratory testing. Commercial laboratories too acknowledge the differences between their mission and that of the public health laboratories, and seek to avoid such specialized, labor-intensive testing. Avery argues that effective privatization requires monitoring by experts knowledgeable about the necessary practices thanks to their professional expertise and experience resulting from the retention of some in-house capability. He offers a Checklist for Evaluating Sources of Laboratory Services and a Checklist for Evaluating Lab Services. The reader may well be able to transpose this list into a series of questions relating to his or her own agency.

Outsourcing Public Health Laboratory Services: A Blueprint for Determining Whether to Privatize and How

George Avery

Introduction

The tasks addressed by public agencies have expanded, and the technical requirements for their operation have grown dramatically. Many tasks, such as public health, environmental and sanitation regulation, and forensics, were largely nonexistent prior to the turn of the century and require the collection of data through specialized scientific means. Other more traditional tasks, such as the construction and maintenance of transportation infrastructure, also require more specialized data than was available in the mid-nineteenth century. Governments have responded to these needs by creating laboratories to collect the data needed. Today, a typical state government has laboratories that test medical specimens for diseases such as AIDS or tuberculosis, water for pesticides, food for adulteration or contamination, conduct DNA matching to solve murders, or evaluate the weathering of paint used to lay down highway striping.

State laboratories typically play a variety of roles in government beyond the actual laboratory sample or specimen. A government that plays a role in specialized, technical areas requires access to expert advice and technical information sources not readily utilized by non-specialists. State laboratory scientists play this role in policy development. Even in cases of privatization, expert professionals assure that the contractors are fulfilling the needs of the contracting organization. In the field of public health, the laboratory plays a role in each of these tasks.

George Avery. *Public Administration Review*, Vol. 60, No. 4 (July/August 2000), pp. 330–337.

Public health, as opposed to the more familiar clinical practice, is concerned not with the care of individual patients, but the management of health in populations. Public health responsibilities are carried out by the assessment of threats to the health of the population, prevention and management of these threats, and the education of the public. The public health laboratories are crucial to the first two. The emphasis in the 1990s on cost containment in the area of clinical health, however, has spilled over into public health, threatening the laboratory network and the ability of the public health agency to manage potential threats to the health of the population.

In the 1990s, twin themes of fiscal restraint and management reform dominate the sphere of public management. Soaring federal deficits caused cuts in federal discretionary funds, cuts which have significant impact at the state level. Rising health care costs drive the health care system into the realm of managed care, where price-fixing by managed care organizations limit reimbursements in particular for clinical laboratory services. At the same time, public confidence in the ability of government agencies to accomplish credible goals and respond to public needs has been shaken.

Management reform in public agencies, spurred by the publication of Osborne and Gaebler's *Reinventing Government* (1992), and the subsequent volume *Banishing Bureaucracy* (1997), also drive the move towards privatization. *Reinventing Government* emphasizes the use of competition to improve the efficiency and effectiveness of service delivery. Osborne and Plastrik, in *Banishing Bureaucracy*, go further and suggest stripping agencies down to their core tasks and eliminating peripheral functions. The thrust of the two strategies is to force agencies to reexamine themselves and reduce inefficiencies in their operations. It forces them to scrutinize budget requests in the context of expectations about program performance (GAO 1997a, 10–14). Forcing agencies to compete in the area of service delivery causes the agencies to change their business practices and operational values to become more efficient, or lose the business that is their reason for existence. The focus is on bringing "market forces and market tests to bear—to increase efficiency, to reduce both costs and the drain on public budgets, and to improve the quality and effectiveness of services" (Yergin and Stanislaw 1998, 358).

Although *Reinventing Government* focuses on the act of competition as the mechanism for reform, the translation into practice often focuses on privatization. The two concepts can be complementary, as when public-private competition is used to seek the most cost-effective provider of services. In other cases, however, privatization is undertaken on the specific assumption that the public sector could not, or should not, compete with the private sector. This philosophy can lead to a drive to privatize, regardless of the cost effectiveness of the decision. When agencies make privatization decisions without reference to cost effectiveness, the decision is not so much to conserve resources, but to effectively subsidize the private service provider, disregarding the budget reform movement.

The two paradigms, efficiency and noncompetition, are not entirely compatible for privatization. Underlying both belief systems is a loss of faith in public institutions—a belief that the monopoly status of the public agency renders the agency unresponsive to public needs. Outsourcing based on the ideal of public non-competition assumes that the public sector should not or, in the extreme view, inherently cannot compete with the private sector. While a more efficient delivery of services may occur if the private sector provider is more efficient than the public sector, it is possible that the opposite is the result. Use of privatization based on the quest for efficiency, however, specifically requires competition, based on the view that competition from the private sector spurs improvements in the business practices of the public agency, and vice versa.

Ideally, the job of the administrative agency should not be to set public policy, but to administer it in the most efficient and effective manner consistent with the restraints put on policy implementers by those who have the policymaking responsibilities. Although these roles are, in practice, blurred, implicit in both roles is a responsibility to obtain the best value for the tax dollar. In order to do this, the public manager should not exclude consideration of the internal provision of support services when those services are best, and most efficiently, provided by the agency. The best value is often not the cheapest in dollar terms. As James Q. Wilson argued in *Bureaucracy* (1989, 346–64), four standards exist for evaluating alternatives for service delivery: efficiency, equity, accountability, and authority. All of these need to be considered in the planning process.

Public Health Laboratory Services

The expansion of government opened the door on policy issues that are more technical and specialized than ever before. Epidemics of cholera, typhoid fever, and yellow fever in the nineteenth century led to the creation of public health laws and attendant agencies. Exposes of poor sanitation as well as tainted or adulterated food and medical products led to the regulation of these and other products by government agencies such as the Food and Drug Administration. Concern over pollution led to environmental regulation.

The requirements of formulating and instituting policy in such areas resulted in a demand for specialized information, which in many cases requires the use of scientific information obtained by skilled specialists. These demands led to the creation of a loose national network of public health laboratories, spread across federal, state, and local jurisdictions. Among the first were the public health laboratories, created to improve sanitation through the detection of bacterial contamination (Institute of Medicine 1988).

The requirements of public health are quite different from those of clinical medicine. Public health revolves around the activities of the detection, prevention, treatment, control, intervention, surveillance, and assessment of health threats in populations, a much more complex set of tasks than the diagnosis and treatment of the individual patient. Unlike clinical medicine, the most important function of the public health practice is to find out what caused the disease or disorder, rather than treating the case. Ideally, the public health agency will find the causative factor and deal with it *before* the disorder occurs (Anderson et al. 1993, 9–12).

Often, the focus of a private sector laboratory is quite different from the core task of a public agency, and this can affect the ability of the public health agency to implement policy. For example, when private sector clinical laboratories are involved in the diagnosis of communicable disease, the focus is on the management of the disease in individual patients, while a public health agency concentrates on management and control in populations. The latter may require organization of patient results in a consistent manner for epidemiological studies and studies of vector organisms or pathways such as insects, food, or water. For example, the New Mexico Department of Health, Scientific Laboratory Division, conducts annual prevalence surveys of mosquitoes for equine encephalitis, a service not readily available in the private sector (Mills 1997, 2). Public sector state laboratories provide a degree of independence and impartiality that enhance the implementation of regulatory requirements. Finally, these laboratories maintain a reservoir of skilled professionals with the expertise to oversee the performance of private sector laboratories providing data to public agencies, so that reliable data of adequate quality, as well as other products and services, is assured. These scientists also provide a resource for policy development and assessment. For example, organic chemists at the Arkansas Department of Health, usually involved in the testing of drinking water supplies for chemical contaminants such as pesticides, also assist with emergency services personnel in the development of a response plan for potential disasters involving the destruction of chemical weapons at a military arsenal in the state.

Laboratories outside the public health system, such as "clinical" laboratories, and some environmental contract laboratories lack the focus and emphasis on the public health role. Their ties to the insurance, particularly the managed care system, limit their flexibility in providing public health services. For example, testing of asymptomatic subjects is likely to be anathema to the cost-containing paradigm of a managed care provider, yet is vital for disease assessment and epidemiology. Furthermore, the public health laboratories do not operate as individual entities, but are part of an integrated system. Data, to be meaningful, requires uniform testing processes and standards (Anderson et al. 1993, 13–19). The Centers of Disease Control, which coordinates the network, has found that serious weaknesses exist in the surveillance network, traceable to policy differences in the state health departments. A weakness at any point in the chain threatens to compromise the system (MMWR 1991, 173–5; Berkelman et al. 1994, 368–70). A recent report cites budget cuts and outsourcing of scientific capability as direct causes of this breakdown (Garrett 1994, 604–7).

All of the services currently provided by the public laboratories are not unique to these laboratories. Many, if not most, services are available on the market. The well-developed environmental testing market, for example, provides many similar services, although sufficient capacity does not exist for all needs (EPA 1994, 50–6). Basic clinical services often do not belong in the public health laboratory. Some needs, however, are solely, or primarily, met by public sector laboratories. For example, in Arkansas, two public sector laboratories, at the State Department of Health and the state-run medical school, are the only source for the diagnosis of tuberculosis and studies of the effectiveness of antibiotics in treating individual cases of tuberculosis. In many cases, the demand for the services is too small to generate a market, yet the need is real, as in the case of the diagnosis of the fungal disease histoplasmosis. A third case exists, where a partnership between the private and public sectors is appropriate or necessary, as in the case of a public health laboratory providing quality assurance oversight for a clinical diagnostic laboratory, or serving as a resource for non-standard diagnostic testing for clinical cases of rare or unknown etiology (McDade and Hausler 1998, 609–13; Skeels 1995, 592).

Many specialized services are orphaned in the private sector. Sufficient customer demand does not exist to generate enough business to justify the investment to offer the service. In such cases as tuberculosis or hantavirus, where the data is vital to controlling a serious public health threat, and hence to the core mission of the agency, the public sector may find that it has no alternative but to provide the service. In particular, a response to an emerging infectious disease requires a *public* health laboratory. The Institute of Medicine (1992) reports that the state public health laboratories have been the cornerstone of public health microbiology and disease assessment, a capability threatened by diminishing *state* capabilities. Without these assessments provided by state environmental and health laboratories, effective public policy cannot be developed (Valdiserri 1992, 645–46.)

Commercial laboratories have noted the differences between themselves and the public health laboratories. The Minnesota Department of Health interviewed commercial laboratory officials as part of a study of privatization. As one noted, "Private labs are geared toward making a profit. Public health labs are geared to identify and solve public health problems. The product is entirely different." Another commented, "no way a private laboratory could step in and do what state labs do. The state labs have a wealth of knowledge: the state will be disappointed [if it privatizes all public health testing]. It's up to the state labs to discover problems, to survey, investigate, and respond. If the state labs find a problem and want to monitor it, it makes sense to pass that responsibility to the private labs. Routine work is perfect for the private labs" (Minnesota Department of Health 1997, 16–18). Private sector laboratories increasingly do not want to handle specialized, labor intensive testing. As Cynthia Holland, the administrator of the relatively large and capable laboratory at the Arkansas Children's Hospital notes, the private sector lab has to ask "can we afford to be everything to everyone in the future?" (Holland 1998, 416) Where efficiency is the strongest determinant, the private laboratories can be effective. Where accountability and authority are required, the public laboratory may very well be the provider of choice. As Wilson (1989, 364) notes, "contracting works best for . . . bureaus with observable, often measurable outputs."

Confusion over the relative roles of public health, clinical, and environmental contract laboratories creates problems for the public health network. Restrictions arising from the Clinical Laboratory Improvement Act (CLIA), designed to regulate rote diagnostic testing and misapplied to the environment of public health, limit the ability of laboratories to do public health work. The existence of private diagnostic and environmental laboratories often leads to pressure to eliminate the public health laboratories, based on the mistaken assumption that they do the same type of work.

The public health laboratories are a critical resource in efforts to control disease within a population. This is the critical difference between the practice of public health and the practice of clinical medicine. Clinical medicine limits itself to the control of disease in the individual patient, rather than the population as a whole. This is reflected in differences in the practices of the public health laboratories and the private sector clinical laboratories that have developed to serve clinical practices. For example, where clinical diagnosis may require merely identifying the species of an infectious agent, epidemiological investigation is likely to demand the identification of a specific strain or genotype in order to trace the source of the disease. The data generated by these more advanced tests differ from that generated by the private diagnostic lab in that it creates a public good by aiding in the prevention of the transmission of disease in addition to the purely private good represented by the diagnosis and subsequent treatment. In the managed care environment, this public benefit is threatened through medical necessity requirements that often preclude any testing beyond the basic needs of the covered patient (McDade and Hausler 1998, 609–13). An excellent example is the surveillance and isolation of influenza strains, necessary to identify new strains and prepare vaccines. The 1919–20 influenza pandemic caused in excess of twenty million deaths, clearly demonstrating the potential disaster of abandoning or neglecting this type of capability (Snacken et al. 1999, 203). In addition to naturally occurring epidemics, the threat of biological terrorism is a very real concern, as witnessed by the activities of the Aum Shinrikyo group and the scare regarding the appearance of West Nile Fever in New York City. Dealing with these and naturally occurring epidemics requires not just the existing laboratory services but upgraded public health laboratory capabilities (McDade 1999, 593–4).

Elimination of the public laboratories, in the manner of the non-competition model, is potentially disastrous. In addition to a loss of flexibility, the timeliness, quality, and scope of laboratory data might be compromised. Cheaper, decentralized testing that compromises accuracy and reliability does not meet current or future health needs (Robinson et al. 1999, 883–9). The health department's ability to monitor performance weakens with regard to the loss of internal expertise, and costs rise with the loss of economies of scale. Costs and contracting requirements can adversely affect the decision to conduct testing for the purposes of assessment (Anderson et al. 1993, 19–22).

While some laboratory services are critical internal functions of the public health agency, others are not, and can be safely outsourced. Even for those that need to be internally maintained, or are orphaned, the evaluation tools appropriate for evaluating privatization can be productively applied to improve service delivery. These assessment tools improve the public manager's ability to identify present and future needs, excess or underutilized resources, and unnecessary inefficiencies in the business practices of the agency. Properly used, these tools improve the quality and value of the service delivered to the public by holding the laboratory functions to a standard of rigorous scrutiny. They protect the public interest by ensuring that the specialized services required for the surveillance and protection of the health of the population is preserved.

Government Purchasing Systems and Specialized Services

Friederich Hayek noted that "the function of competition is here to teach us who will serve us well, which . . . we can expect to provide the most satisfactory solution for whatever personal problem we may have to face . . . competition may be very intense, just because the services of the differing persons or firms will never be exactly alike, and it will be owing to this competition that we are in a position to be served as well as we are." (Hayek 1948, 97).

The typical government purchasing system, developed for the acquisition of bulk commodities and services such as office supplies and printing, originated in the reform measures of the Progressive Era of the early twentieth century. These measures were a response to the abuses of the political machines of the day, particularly in the use of printing contracts to reward friendly newspapers, as well as contractor abuses, such as the poor quality of rations and clothing provided to the military in the Civil and Spanish-American Wars. Furthermore, the procurement systems were designed in a manner intended to take advantage of economies of scale, which can be obtained for commodity purchases, but are less likely to be realized in the purchase of specialty goods. Weaknesses in the system hinder the acquisition of specialized goods and services.

Contracts are awarded through competitive bidding for major purchases of goods and services. Specifications for the purchase of these products are presented, and price solicitations are sought from vendors. The process strives to obtain the lowest price for products and reduce the possibility of kickbacks and other such corruption in the bidding process. On the other hand, tight expenditure controls restrict the freedom to operate, can induce significant opportunity costs to productivity, and often focus strictly on the nominal value of the bid, to the neglect of quality or performance considerations. In cases where personal or professional services are being procured, procurement may be difficult in a competitive context, due to the need to disqualify irresponsible or unreliable contractors (Lynch 1995, 331; Block 1993, 135–45).

The greatest success stories in privatization of services have occurred in the acquisition of administrative services such as advertising, printing, bookkeeping, telecommunications, and custodial services. Many of these services have long been provided by private vendors, and are of a nature that they are compatible with the commodity model around which public bidding rules are designed. Privatized medical services have worked, due to an existing network of providers in the private health care system, but there are cases of failures. New Jersey saw an effort to outsource public health responsibilities for tuberculosis and sexually transmitted diseases fail due to "critical infrastructure weaknesses [which] resulted in a complete deterioration of services." Pennsylvania, which outsourced much of its laboratory services, is reestablishing state capacity due to vendor instability (Minnesota Department of Health 1993, 3). Successful outsourcing requires a commitment to monitoring the performance of the contractor, competition to prevent exchanging a public monopoly for a private one, and safeguards against corruption, mismanagement, or service interruption by the private vendors (Chi

1993, 30–3). The traditional system, largely dependent on price for awarding contracts, often neglects less tangible, but equally real, issues of performance and quality. This is notably a problem when the services purchased are highly specialized and outside the expertise of the purchasing agent.

Successful privatization efforts have relied on obtaining reliable and complete cost information on internal activities in order to determine whether, in fact, a contractor can provide services at a lower cost. A recent Public Health Foundation study found that only one-fourth of privatization efforts studied yielded any real savings (Whitehand et al. 1997, 11). Absence of reliable cost data compromises reliable comparisons of the public and private costs (Stevens 1997, 10). Indianapolis and the states of Virginia and Michigan have been notably successful in developing this type of assessment tool (GAO 1997a, 34–41). Monitoring vendor performance and maintaining a fallback position have also proven useful, even in as prosaic an example as the privatization of garbage collection (Osborne and Gaebler 1992, 76–9).

Model Policy for Outsourcing Laboratory Services

Responsible management of agency laboratory services requires the careful use of a number of evaluation tools in order to obtain the most efficient use of public resources. Evaluation needs to be an ongoing project, considering short- and long-term needs. Competition, in terms of evaluating the needs of the organization and alternatives to service delivery, is a useful tool for managing these services but can be weakened when consideration of providers, public and private, is restricted. Competition forces full consideration of alternative means of acquiring services, internal and external, and gives a frame of reference for evaluation. It harnesses the network information-processing capabilities of markets to supplement the evaluation process.

The tools for evaluation are critical in making a system of competition work. In the acquisition of specialized laboratory services, where a full market structure does not exist, the criteria used to decide how to manage the services are vital to the success or failure, as well as the efficiency of the government efforts. Experimentation is underway in this area. Michigan has criteria in place for the evaluation of privatization services through the Michigan Commission on Total Quality Government. Joseph McDade and William J. Hausler (1998, 609–13), of the CDC and Iowa Hygienic Laboratory respectively, propose that states establish public-private partnerships for strategic planning in the area of public health. The following model is loosely based on the Michigan model, as outlined in Executive Order 1994–5 from the Governor of Michigan, and refined for use by the Arkansas Department of Health. The model also reflects lessons outlined by the General Accounting Office as a result of their study of state and local privatization efforts. (GAO 1997b, 2)

Agencies employing laboratory services should establish a review system and conduct annual reappraisals of their need for laboratory services. Programs

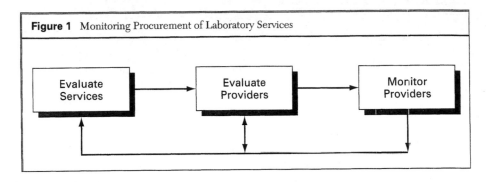

Figure 1 Monitoring Procurement of Laboratory Services

requiring laboratory services should submit projections of service needs (types of testing, numbers of samples, etc.) for both the near and projectable future (three to five years), updating these projections annually. The review system should evaluate testing activities based on cost, availability, stability of the provider, quality and reliability of the data generated by the provider, and impact upon the core missions of the agency. The purpose of the review process is to identify the most effective way to meet the policy goal of protecting public health. Without an ongoing review process, the agency lacks the basic tools to assess its programs, needs, and services.

An agency with significant service needs should establish a small staff to support the review process and should include people with expertise in the technical aspects of testing as well as procurement management. This staff will take service need projections, estimate the resources needed for in-house testing, as well as outside availability and the resources required for outsourcing, including costs associated with contract monitoring and bidding and conduct an on-going review of agency testing policies, and evaluate the effects of the projection on the baseline capacity of the department.

In order to evaluate the actual costs of testing activities, implementation of an activity-based accounting system is necessary in order to gain an accurate grasp on activity costs. Such a system should include a capital equipment depreciation fund to allow the laboratories to maintain the technical infrastructure necessary to support activities. An accurate assessment of internal activity costs is necessary to ensure that resources are properly allocated. In the absence of good data on internal resource use, it is very possible that an outsourced test could end up costing the agency more than if performed internally.

When considering agency needs for laboratory services, the evaluators need to consider critical issues regarding the services. First, the services in question should materially assist in forwarding the agency's core mission, and the agency should be the appropriate one to provide the service. Second, the agency must maintain a baseline laboratory capacity and infrastructure to respond to mission needs, and maintain the flexibility to meet unexpected demands. The capacity should be sufficient to provide a level of fault tolerance in the event of contractor default. Third, the testing must be consistent with the legal requirements placed on the agency. An agency involved in drinking water quality regulation, for example, must maintain sufficient laboratory testing capacity to maintain SDWA

Figure 2   Checklist for Evaluating Laboratory Services

1. What data is required by the agency?
2. How will the data be obtained? Does it require laboratory analysis?
3. Is this activity appropriate for the agency?
4. What volume of testing will be required?
5. How critical is the data to be generated to the agency's core mission?
6. What legal requirements arise from this activity?
7. Will this be a temporary or ongoing project?
8. What level of data quality and service is required?
9. Does the activity require specific testing protocols?

---

primacy requirements. The agency remains accountable for meeting mission requirements; therefore those requirements should be a priority (McDade and Hausler 1998, 611).

Internal business practices may require modification to ensure an accurate comparison of the costs of internal and external testing activities. The agency must account for all costs of the decision. It is not enough to compare the cost of a test done in-house to the amount charged by an external agent for the same service. The cost of privatization should include the costs of monitoring the performance of the outside agent and the cost of maintaining required capacity. A simple comparison of the cost of the test conducted within the public agency and the charge by a private sector service provider can ignore significant costs associated with the procurement and monitoring process for the outsourced test, or hidden subsidies to an internal laboratory.

In deciding to acquire laboratory services, the review body should ascertain whether an external provider exists, whether the capacity exists to handle the requirements, and whether the outside agents can credibly provide services of an adequate quality to meet public health goals. Outsourced services provide no return to the taxpayer if the outside contractor cannot reliably meet the needs of the program.

The agency should establish a system of performance monitoring and feedback from users and service providers. It is useless to seek provision of a service if the quality of that service is inadequate to meet public health goals. It is recommended that written performance goals be developed between the laboratory, public or private, and the internal clients, defining data quality and service objectives. For monitoring external providers, a team of contract monitors will need to be formed who have sufficient laboratory experience to audit data quality to ensure contract fulfillment. In some programs, such as drinking water quality regulation under the Safe Drinking Water Act, this is already a legal requirement. (40 CFR 142.10(b))

The effect of outsourcing on regulatory objectives needs to be considered before taking any action or proposing a new or existing test program. If the outsourcing action is liable to result in significant non-compliance with monitoring

---

Figure 3   Checklist for Evaluating Sources of Lab Services

1. What baseline capacity must the agency retain? Will privatization affect this capacity?
2. Does a private sector capacity exist? Is it adequate for agency requirements?
3. What are the total costs of internal testing versus outsourced testing?
4. Can the internal and external providers provide data of adequate quality for project need?
5. Can internal and external providers provide an adequate turnaround time on testing?
6. How do internal and external providers impact legal requirements and regulatory action? What are the impacts on chain-of-custody and record retention?
7. What are the relative costs of sample collection activities? Will the provision option aid or hinder collection activities?
8. Are the providers stable and reliable enough to fulfill contractual obligations?
9. How would privatization affect freedom of information and/or confidentiality concerns?
10. How will future testing requirements affect the cost and reliability of a provider?
11. What quality of data can the provider reliably generate?
12. Does the provider have the technical capacity to meet needs? Do they have the capability to meet needs using required protocols?
13. How do the providers assure the comparability of data they generate?
14. How will the agency handle testing in the event of the failure of a provider?

---

requirements, or risks the tainting of the integrity of data used for a regulatory enforcement action, then the test should be performed in-house to assure data integrity. The agency must implement safeguards to ensure that contractors provide acceptable chain-of-custody documentation, records confidentiality, and records retention to meet legal and ethical standards. Steps should be taken to ensure the viability of contractors to meet the contractual obligation to provide the service and should include the requiring of a performance bond when necessary.

A number of public sector business practices suggest themselves as loci for reform. Personnel policies oriented to clerical agencies, largely based on the civil service reforms of the nineteenth century, are serious handicaps to technical organizations based on professional expertise. Salary scales should reflect market conditions, so as not to hinder hiring or retention. Selection procedures, often with pre-screening by non-technically competent personnel employees, often hinder the hiring of the best candidates (Osborne and Gaebler 1992, 124–30). Relatively simple reforms can improve the quality and cost of services. For example, the replacement of requirements that excess leave be exhausted within a calendar year with cash buyouts of excess time would increase productivity, at no additional cost, by creating a more adequate level of staffing in the month of December.

Flexibility in managing budgets can also be used to reduce the costs of in-house services. Budgeting for capital depreciation would allow for an adequate capture of these costs and assure funds for modernization. Carryover of funds between fiscal years discourages the rush to spend that is typical of public agencies at the end of the fiscal year. Sole source purchasing for laboratory supplies, with justification, would reduce the administrative costs of purchasing because many supplies, parts, and services are vendor specific, particularly for scientific instrumentation (Osborne and Gaebler 1992, 117–24).

Conclusion

Outsourcing of public health lab services requires careful consideration of the implications of privatization. Rather than simply contracting out services, state health departments should establish a thorough, continuous process of evaluation based on cost, availability, and stability of vendors, and the policy implications of the provider. Any effort to outsource services must include adequate means to monitor laboratory performance and quality.

The implications of an on-going program to evaluate laboratory services extend far beyond short-term savings. It allows public health agencies the tools and opportunities to identify their strengths and weaknesses, manage their resources in an optimum manner, and improve the provision of service. Complete privatization does not allow this flexibility, risks weakening the existing system, and is not entirely supported even by the commercial laboratory community that would benefit the most from an outsourcing decision. At worst, privatization threatens the health of the wider population by eliminating specialized testing not necessary to treating the individual, but critical to identification of and intervention to end an epidemic.

The consequences of a weakened public health system are potentially dire. The 1994 cryptosporidiosis outbreak in Milwaukee, Wisconsin, as an example, affected over 100,000 people, hospitalizing over 1,000 and killing dozens. The potential consequences of an unarrested influenza epidemic are far greater. Even smaller outbreaks carry a heavy cost in lost productivity and human misery. A strong public interest exists in ensuring that the public health system maintains the proper set of tools to adequately protect public health. This is best done through careful assessment of needs and forethought in ensuring that they are met in the most suitable manner.

References

Anderson, George, Arthur DiSalvo, William J. Hausler, John Liddle, Joseph McDade, and Eric Sampson. 1993. Task Force Report on the Public Health Laboratory—A Critical National Resource. Washington, DC: Association of State and Territorial Public Health Laboratory Directors.

Berkelman, Ruth L., Ralph T. Bryan, Michael T. Osterholm, James W. LeDuc, and Jim M. Hughes. 1994. Infectious Disease Surveillance: A Crumbling Foundation. *Science* 254: 368–70.

Block, Peter. 1993. *Stewardship: Choosing Service Over Self-Interest*. San Francisco, CA: Berret-Koehler Publishers.

Chi, Keon S. 1993. Privatization in State Government: Options for the Future. *State Trends Forecasts* 2(2): 2–38.

Environmental Protection Agency. 1994. *Technical and Economic Capacity of States and Utilities to Meet Drinking Water Regulatory Requirements.* Washington, DC.

Garrett, Laurie. 1994. *The Coming Plague: Newly Emerging Diseases in a World Out of Balance.* New York: Farrar, Straus, and Giroux.

General Accounting Office. 1997a, *Privatization: Lessons Learned by State and Local Governments.* Washington, DC: General Accounting Office. GAO/GCD-97–148.

———— 1997b. *Privatization and Competition, Comments on H,R, 716, The Freedom from Government, Competition Act.* Washington, DC: General Accounting Office. GAO/T-GGD-97–185.

Hayek. Friederich A. 1948. *The Meaning of Competition. Individualism and Economic Order.* Chicago, IL: University of Chicago Press. 92–106.

Holland, Cynthia. 1998. Paving the Road to Maximum Productivity. *Clinical Laboratory Management Review* 12(6): 410–17.

Institute of Medicine. 1988. *The Future of Public Health.* Washington. DC: National Academy Press.

———— 1992. *Emerging Infections: Microbial Threats to Health in the United States.* Washington, DC: National Academy Press.

Lynch, Thomas D. 1995. *Public Budgeting in America.* Englewood Cliffs, NJ: Prentice-Hall.

McDade, Joseph E. 1999. Addressing the Potential Threat of Bioterrorism—Value Added to an Improved Public Health Infrastructure. *Emerging Infectious Diseases* 5(4): 591–2.

McDade, Joseph E., and William J. Hausler, 1998. Modernization of Public Health Laboratories in a Privatization Atmosphere. *Journal of Clinical Microbiology* 36(3): 609–13.

Mills, David E. 1997. *Managed Care: Considerations and Implications for the Scientific Laboratory Division.* Albuquerque, NM: New Mexico Scientific Laboratory Division.

Minnesota Department of Health. 1993. *The Role of the Public Health Laboratories.* St. Paul: Minnesota Department of Health.

Morbidity and Mortality Weekly Report. 1990. Update, Surveillance of Outbreaks—United States. 40(11): 173–5.

Osborne, David, and Ted Gaebler. 1992. *Reinventing Government: How the Entrepreneurial Spirit is Transforming the Public Sector.* Reading, MA: Addison-Wesley.

Osborne, David, and Peter Plastrik. 1997. *Banishing Bureaucracy: The Five Strategies for Reinventing Government.* Reading, MA: Addison-Wesley.

Robinson, Ann, Mario Marcon, Joel E. Mortensen, Yvette S. McCarter, Mark LaRocco, Lance R. Peterson, and Richard B. Thompson. Jr. 1999. Controversies Affecting the Future Practice of Clinical Microbiology. *Journal of Clinical Microbiology* 37(4): 883–9.

Skeels, Michael R. 1995. Public Health Laboratories Build Healthy Communities. *Laboratory Medicine* 26(9): 588–92.

Snacken, René, Alan P. Kendal, Lars R. Haaheim, and John M. Wood. 1999. The Next Influenza Pandemic: Lessons from Hong Kong, 1997. *Emerging Infectious Diseases* 5(2): 195–203.

Stevens, L. Nye. *Privatization and Competition: Comments on HR 716, The Freedom From Government Competition Act.* Washington, DC: General Accounting Office. GAO-T-GGD-97–185.

Valdiserri, Ronald O. 1993. *Temples of the Future: An Historical Overview of the Laboratory's Role in Public Health Practice.* Palo Alto, CA.: Annual Review of Public Health, Annual Reviews, Inc.

Whitehand, Lori, Michon Béchomps, and Ron Bialek. 1997. *Privatization and Public Health: A Study of Initiatives and Early Lessons Learned.* Washington, DC: Public Health Foundation.

Wilson, James Q. 1989. *Bureaucracy: What Government Agencies Do and Why They Do It.* New York: Basic Books.

Yergin, Daniel, and Joseph Stanislaw. 1998. *The Commanding Heights: The Battle Between Government and the Marketplace that is Changing the World.* New York: Simon and Schuster.

P A R T

VIII

Reform, Accountability, and the Public Entrepreneur

In Part I we identified the numerous value preferences of the internal and external stakeholders concerned with public bureaucracies (see Figure 1). Each of these value preferences—sensitivity to governmental institutions and the rule of law, flexibility, observance of strict standards of administrative behavior, fairness and impartiality, effectiveness, timeliness, efficiency, and reliability—involves a different kind of accountability. Some of the values pertain directly to implementing the agency mission. In other cases, however, the accountability is to other stakeholders who are less concerned with how efficiently or effectively the agency is meeting its goals than whether these goals are as legitimate and necessary in comparison with other local, state, or federal priorities. The public administrator then is engaged in the political task of managing expectations. Barbara Romzek and Melvin Dubnick thus argue that "public administration accountability involves the means by which public agencies and their workers manage the diverse expectations generated within and outside the organization."[a] The stakes of this balancing act among expectations are often of more than academic interest. Romzek and Dubnick analyzed the 1986 Challenger tragedy—where seven astronauts lost their lives when the space shuttle exploded in mid-flight—and concluded that the managers were at fault for considering political and bureaucratic accountability in a situation where they should have deferred to the technical expertise of engineers accountable for determining the

---

[a] Barbara S. Romzek and Melvin J. Dubnick, "Accountability in the Public Sector: Lessons from the Challenger Tragedy," *Public Administration Review*, Vol. 47, No. 3, May/June 1987, p. 228.

launch's safety. In recent years, performance measurement—particularly at the state and local levels—is "where the rubber meets the road,"[b] and performance measures certainly bolster an agency's case with its internal and external stakeholders, but numerous other expectations must be met as well. Quite apart from the Challenger tragedy, how does the political system come to play such a large part in managerial accountability?

The Public Manager and the Political System

The fragmented and decentralized nature of democratic pluralism has placed the public manager in a difficult position programmatically, constitutionally, and ethically. This is hardly surprising, since, as Richard Neustadt has emphasized, the founding fathers did not create a government of "separated powers"—rather, the constitutional convention created a government of separated institutions "*sharing* powers."[c] Congress and the president, for example, share power over the dispensing of authority and funds within the administrative process. Federalism similarly adds another layer of separated levels of government often at loggerheads over constitutional intent even while jointly implementing policy. The court system, in seeking to protect individual liberties and rights throughout the public policy-making process, functions as yet another overlay to the system.

No less than three additional "informal" institutions have also come to exercise power through democratic pluralism at every level of government. The language used in referring to their roles in the policy-making process reflects the legitimacy that they have acquired in performing their functions. Paul Appleby thus refers to interest groups as the seventh—"the agitational process"—of his eight political processes.[d] Douglass Cater in a similar vein speaks of the press (even before the full impact of television made itself felt) as a separate and quasi-official "fourth branch of government."[e] Meier encapsulates the entire bureaucracy as a "fourth branch of government."[f] A special form of bureaucracy, the independent regulatory commissions, has also been dubbed a "fourth branch of government" by lawyers as a result of the quasi-legal and quasi-judicial functions that they perform.

These formal and informal institutions participating in a democratic pluralism would not pose much of a problem for public managers if they were agreed on who was responsible for performing what function. However, in the

---

[b]Harry P. Hatry, "Where the Rubber Meets the Road: Performance Measurement for State and Local Agencies," *New Directions for Evaluation*, No. 75, Fall 1997, pp. 31–44.

[c]Richard E. Neustadt, *Presidential Power and the Modern Presidents* (New York: Free Press, 1990), p. 29.

[d]Paul Appleby, *Policy and Administration* (AL: University of Alabama Press, 1949).

[e]Douglass Cater, *Power in Washington* (New York: Vintage Books, 1964).

[f]Kenneth J. Meier, *Politics and the Bureaucracy*, 4th ed. (Forth Worth: Harcourt College Publishers, 2000).

case of the formal institutions, the founding fathers were more concerned with checking the potentially excessive exercise of power by any single institution than in constructing an elegant constellation of forces that could get things done. Far from aspiring to design a "rational" hierarchical system where each institution would focus on its carefully-defined role, they intentionally set institution against institution in performing the same function. The resulting "checks and balances" vested in constitutionally "separated institutions" then became intertwined through the policy-making process. Furthermore, the founding fathers could not have anticipated the extent of the proactive roles that the informal institutions would play. They did include in the initial ten constitutional amendments, though, rights that guaranteed seats at the bargaining table for all of these actors. Informal, as well as formal, institutions would come to be pitted against each other to prevent domination over time even, as it turned out, by an "imperial presidency."

Consensus is thus intentionally lacking on what the appropriate roles of public organizations are and to whom the public manager is accountable. The public organization is simultaneously a stakeholder active in policy formulation and a bureaucracy subordinate to the will of the three traditional branches of government during policy implementation. The bureaucracy's exercise of administrative discretion during the policy implementation stage is in every case drawn from legal authority granted to it by the executive branch, the legislative branch, or the judiciary.

The public agency is thus unique from the other formal and informal actors involved in democratic pluralism. It simultaneously functions as an equal in the policy-making process and as a subordinate, subject to control by the three formal branches of government.

Not only is it subject to control, but it is widely believed to be out of control. If so, it is not for lack of means to hold it accountable. Bernard Rosen is able to identify what he rightly terms "an awesome armada of policies, mechanisms, and processes to oversee bureaucracies and cause those that do not act in the public interest to change course."[g] To select just a few examples, the executive branch exercises oversight through the budgetary process or through organization and management, human resources, and legal work done by staff directly accountable to the mayor, governor, or president. Congress conducts oversight through the appropriations process, its standing committees, casework, and the General Accounting Office (an auditing staff unit that reports directly to the Congress).

"External" vs. "Internal" Controls

The means of holding bureaucracies accountable and of gaining influence over bureaucratic actions are generally discussed in terms of "external" and "internal" controls (or checks). "External controls" are designed to enable institutions outside of the bureaucracy to oversee its activities and compel it to act effectively

[g]Bernard Rosen, *Holding Government Bureaucracies Accountable*, 2nd ed. (New York: Praeger, 1989), p. 193.

(or competently), responsively, and constitutionally. The challenge is to wield these external controls vigorously without undercutting the capacity of the administrative agency to achieve its goals and without weakening the resolve of its public managers.

"Internal controls" advocates argue for devoting greater attention to the public manager's own professional and personal values and ethics. Concern with ethics was widespread in the public administration profession during its early years, but faded somewhat until the early 1980s, when American Society for Public Administration (ASPA) members became alarmed with the profession's declining public image in light of Vietnam, Watergate, and attacks on big government by both Democratic (Jimmy Carter) and Republican (Ronald Reagan) presidents. The professional association then pushed for "principles and moral standards that must guide the conduct of ASPA members not merely in preventing wrong, but also in pursuing right through timely and energetic execution of responsibilities."[h] The result was the passage of the ASPA *Code of Ethics* which appears on the back page of every *Public Administration Review* issue. It exhorts ASPA members to serve the public interest, respect the constitution and the law, demonstrate personal integrity, promote ethical organizations, and strive for professional excellence.

---

[h] Darrell L. Pugh, *Looking Back—Moving Forward: A Half-Century Celebration of Public Administration and the ASPA* (Washington, D.C.: American Society for Public Administration, 1988), p. 105.

In analyzing the effectiveness of external controls in state agencies, William T. Gormley argues that state administrative agencies, precisely because they have become so important, are now more subject to external controls and have lost some of the very discretion that public entrepreneurs need to implement policy. The resulting "proliferation of controls" is a result of new external controls that are simply piled on top of traditional ones. Little thought is given to how much control is enough.

Gormley points to numerous external controls exercised through state legislative oversight, judicial review, and executive management by the Office of the Governor and the political appointees in the agencies to whom the career executives report. One of the comparatively newer forms of control is "interest representation." Here, surrogates—either citizens and public interest groups or surrogates appointed by the governor or legislature—speak for broad, diffuse interests or for other interests underrepresented in democratic pluralism. While these surrogates are no substitute for groups possessing financial and grassroots political clout, the surrogates can sometimes challenge powerful interests, and, thereby, bring information into the open that might otherwise have been overlooked.

Regulatory Federalism

Another of the newer external controls discussed in Gormley's essay is *regulatory federalism*. This form of control normally involves the exercise of federal power over state administrative agencies, but sometimes pertains to a similar exercise of state control over local governments. In return for accepting federal funds, the "feds" can impose conditions. These conditions are imposed through one of four types of compulsory provisions. *Direct orders* mandate state or local actions to be obeyed under the threat of criminal or civil penalties in a particular issue area (such as environmental protection). *Crossover sanctions* stipulate that a recipient's failure to comply with regulations in one program can result in the termination or reduction of funds available in a separately authorized program (an example is the federal stipulation that if a state did not directly establish the age of 21 as the legal drinking age within two years, it would then lose five percent of its federal highway funds). *Crosscutting requirements* apply "horizontally" to many or all federal assistance programs—that is, the same provision, or obligation, is put into effect across-the-board in many pieces of legislation simultaneously (such as a requirement for affirmative action compliance or an environmental impact statement). *Partial preemptions* establish federal standards, but delegate administration to the states if they adopt standards equivalent to, or more stringent than, the national ones. An example is occupational health and safety statutes.[a] Gormley observes that in 1995, regulatory federalism finally gave way to a concerted effort to devolve—or transfer—power from the federal to the state level. But, he concludes, the history of intergovernmental relations is cyclical: "periodic grants of discretion to the states are usually followed by negative feedback and additional (federal) restrictions."

One can arrange external bureaucratic controls, Gormley observes, across a spectrum, ranging from *catalytic controls* (which stimulate change even while preserving administrative discretion), through *hortatory controls* (which strike more of

---

[a] Deil S. Wright, *Understanding Intergovernmental Relations*, 3rd ed. (Pacific Grove, CA: Brooks/Cole, 1988), pp. 367–373.

a balance between discretion and bureaucratic accountability), to *coercive controls.* In the case of coercive controls, discretion is largely eliminated, and the attempt to control compliance results in excessive emphasis on formal authority and the elimination of the informal understandings that are so critical to effectiveness in public and private organizations alike.

Particularly in the face of such complexity and such a potentially debilitating system of formal arrangements, a number of public managers have attempted to work more on the basis of intergovernmental relations (IGR), with its emphasis on cooperation between levels of government, and, through the use of informal means, to downplay some of the difficulties stemming from "competitive federalism." One should not exaggerate how much can be done informally, since, as we have seen, these competitive devices are built into the system. Nonetheless, administrators and some politicians at all levels are slowly coming to appreciate the limitations, spelled out by Gormley, to what coercion can accomplish.

Accountability Battles

Where peace has not broken out, the result of the proliferation of controls, the intensification of these controls, and the judicialization of controls, explains Gormley, is "accountability battles" in state government. As the number of controls increases, one result is the emergence of contradictory controls, with each separate control—and source of power—jealously defended by its group or institution. It is not new for state legislatures and governors to fight over who should control the bureaucracy, but the conflict has expanded to include the courts and informal actors more frequently. Each of these formal and informal actors can bring its weapons to bear on the agency which is caught between them.

Accountability Battles in State Administration

William T. Gormley, Jr.

State bureaucracies have paid a price for their growing importance, and that price is a loss of discretion. In recent years, state bureaucracies have become more permeable, more vulnerable, and more manipulable. They are subject to a growing number of controls, as governors, state legislators, state judges, presidents, members of Congress, federal bureaucrats, interest groups, and citizens all attempt to shape administrative rule making, rate making, and adjudication at the state level. Of equal significance, they are subject to tougher, more restrictive, and more coercive controls.

In other words, state bureaucracies have become more accountable for their actions. In a sense, this is both understandable and desirable. Even state bureaucrats concede the virtues of accountability, at least in theory. Yet accountability is a

William T. Gormley, Jr. In Carl E. Van Horn, ed., *The State of the States*, Washington, D.C.: CQ Press, 1996, pp. 161–78.

multidimensional concept. Increasingly, the question is not whether state bureaucracies shall be accountable but to whom. A related question is how accountability can best be structured to avoid damage to other important values, such as creativity and flexibility.

A variety of controls that limit the discretion of state bureaucracies recently has proliferated, primarily in the areas of legislative oversight, executive management, due process, and regulatory federalism. For example, "coercive controls" rely on coercion for bureaucratic performance, while "catalytic controls" may yield comparable progress with fewer adverse side-effects. The emergence of accountability battles pit competing claimants against one another, in bitter struggles over authority, with state bureaucracies as the ultimate prize. A key development in 1995 was strong pressure to shift control over shaping state programs and agencies from the federal government to the states' governors. As categorical grants and entitlements give way to block grants and discretionary spending, governors will acquire greater authority while the federal government cedes authority to the states.

The Proliferation of Controls

During the 1970s, 1980s, and into the 1990s, as state bureaucracies grew larger and more important, politicians, judges, and citizens strengthened their leverage over state bureaucracies by institutionalizing a wide variety of control techniques. Some of these techniques, such as sunset laws and ombudsmen, were new. Others, such as executive orders and conditions of aid, were old but not much utilized. Control techniques also differed in their directness, formality, durability, and coerciveness. However, they all shared a common purpose—to make state bureaucracies more accountable to other public officials or to the people.

Legislative Oversight

During the 1970s, state legislatures discovered oversight as a form of bureaucratic control. Legislative committees took an active interest in bureaucratic implementation or nonimplementation of state statutes and conducted hearings aimed at identifying and resolving problems. This became easier as the legislator's job became a full-time profession in most states and as legislative staffs became larger and more professional. More than their congressional counterparts, state legislators decided not to leave oversight to chance. Perhaps oversight needed an extra push at the state level. In any event, state legislatures established regular mechanisms for legislative review.

Following the lead of Colorado, approximately two-thirds of the state legislatures adopted sunset laws, which provide for the automatic expiration of agencies unless the state legislature acts affirmatively to renew them. Although the threat of extinction is far-fetched in the case of large agencies, the threat of review must be taken seriously by all agencies. The sunset review process is especially important for obscure agencies that might otherwise escape scrutiny by legislative committees.

In addition to sunset laws, many state legislatures substantially upgraded the quality of their legislative audit bureaus. Gradually, these organizations came to place greater emphasis on program evaluation and policy analysis, less emphasis on auditing and accounting. To ensure careful, well-crafted evaluations, state legislatures augmented the staffs assigned to these organizations.

Finally, the overwhelming majority of state legislatures provided for legislative review of administrative rules and regulations. In sixteen states, legislative vetoes enable the legislature to invalidate an administrative rule or regulation. Through the legislative veto process, state legislatures have exercised closer scrutiny of administrative rule making. The U.S. Supreme Court declared the legislative veto unconstitutional at the federal level,[1] and state courts have invalidated legislative vetoes in eight states.[2] Nevertheless, the legislative veto continues to be an important mechanism for legislative control in one-third of the states.

In thinking about legislative controls, a useful distinction can be made between inward-looking and outward-looking legislative changes. As political scientist Alan Rosenthal has observed, state legislatures have become more fragmented, more decentralized, and less cohesive in recent years. In some sense, this might be characterized as legislative decline. However, a fragmented legislature is not necessarily weaker in its dealings with other units of government, such as state bureaucracies. A highly fragmented legislature may provide more occasions for legislative oversight and more incentives for individual legislators to engage in oversight. Thus, as legislatures become weaker internally, they may become stronger externally. This is especially true of those forms of legislative control that do not require a legislative majority.

Executive Management

For years, governors have complained about the fragmented character of the executive branch. Many executive branch officials are elected or appointed to office for fixed terms that do not coincide with the governor's term. The number of state agencies, boards, and commissions can be overwhelming and disconcerting. Also, agencies have their own traditions and habits and may be reluctant to follow the priorities of a new governor. All of these factors have inhibited executive integration, coordination, and leadership.

During the 1970s, 1980s, and into the 1990s, many governors took steps to deal with these problems. Most governors spearheaded major reorganizations of the executive branch, striving for greater rationality and for a reduction in the number of boards and commissions. Minor reorganizations also were commonplace. In Minnesota, for example, five governors issued a total of 155 reorganization orders between 1970 and 1988.[3]

[1] *Immigration and Naturalization Service v. Chadha*, 462 U.S. 919 (1983).

[2] L. Harold Levinson, "The Decline of the Legislative Veto: Federal/State Comparisons and Interactions," *Publius* 17:1 (Winter 1987): 115–132.

[3] Thad L. Beyle, "The Executive Branch: Organization and Issues, 1988–1989," in *The Book of the States, 1990–1991* (Lexington, Ky.: Council of State Governments, 1990), 76.

Governors also institutionalized cabinet meetings, subcabinet meetings, or both to secure greater coordination and integration. During the 1970s, approximately fourteen governors established a cabinet for the first time and approximately twenty-five governors established subcabinets to advise and coordinate in broad policy domains.[4] The hope was that these meetings would ensure that key executive branch officials marched to the same drumbeat.

In addition, governors relied on new budget techniques, such as zero-based budgeting, to increase their control over agency budget submissions and, ultimately, agency budgets themselves. Under zero-based budgeting, the previous year's budget base is not taken for granted, although it may be incorporated into alternative budget submissions. During the 1970s, approximately twenty-five states adopted a modified form of zero-based budgeting.[5]

At the same time, governors fought successfully for shorter ballots to bring more top state officials under gubernatorial control. Between 1962 and 1978, the number of elected state executives declined by 10 percent.[6] As a result of these reforms, governors today are more likely to deal with state agencies headed more often by gubernatorial appointees in whom they can have confidence.

Finally, executive orders have become more popular in recent years. Many executive orders are aimed at controlling state bureaucracies, and some of them are both significant and controversial. For example, California governor Pete Wilson issued an executive order in June 1995 eliminating affirmative action preferences for state employees.[7] State hiring and promotion practices will change sharply as a result.

These gubernatorial control techniques have become even more important as a result of limitations on political patronage imposed by the U.S. Supreme Court in 1990. In *Rutan v. Illinois Republican Party,* the Court ruled that party affiliation could not be a factor in most state personnel decisions in Illinois.[8] That ruling, which has reverberated throughout the nation, has encouraged governors to control state agencies through other means.

Interest Representation

Unable or unwilling to control state agencies directly in every instance, politicians relied on surrogates to ensure better representation for favored points of view, such as consumers, environmentalists, and the elderly. Political scientists Matthew McCubbins and Thomas Schwartz referred to this phenomenon as "fire-alarm

---

[4] Lydia Bodman and Daniel Garry, "Innovations in State Cabinet Systems," *State Government* 55:3 (Summer 1982): 93–97.

[5] Thomas Lauth, "Zero-Base Budgeting in Georgia State Government: Myth and Reality," in *Perspectives on Budgeting,* ed. Allen Schick (Washington, D.C.: American Society for Public Administration, 1980), 114–132.

[6] Larry J. Sabato, *Goodbye to Good-time Charlie: The American Governorship Transformed* (Washington, D.C.: CQ Press, 1983).

[7] John Miller and Abigail Thernstrom, "Losing Race," *The New Republic,* June 26, 1995, 17–20.

[8] *Rutan v. Republican Party of Illinois,* 497 U.S. 62(1990).

oversight" because politicians in effect depend on citizens or other public officials to spot fires in the bureaucracy and help extinguish them.[9] During the 1970s, 1980s, and into the 1990s, states took a number of steps to improve representation for broad, diffuse interests or other underrepresented interests, especially before state regulatory agencies—a "representation revolution" occurred.[10]

For example, many states established "proxy advocacy" offices to represent consumer interests in state public utility commission proceedings, such as rate cases. In some instances, attorneys general served this function; in other instances, separate consumer advocacy offices were established. Wisconsin, meanwhile, established a Citizens Utilities Board, funded by citizens through voluntary contributions but authorized by the state legislature to include membership solicitations in utility bills.[11] State legislatures in Illinois, Oregon, and New York subsequently established similar organizations, though without provisions for inserts.[12]

Disappointed in the performance of occupational licensing boards, state legislatures mandated lay representation on the boards in the hope that fewer anticompetitive practices would result. Wisconsin law specifies that at least one public member shall serve on each of the state's occupational licensing boards. California goes even further. Since 1976, California has required that all occupational licensing boards have a majority of public members, except for ten "healing arts" boards and the Board of Accountancy.[13]

Many state legislatures require public hearings in various environmental policy decisions. Pursuant to the California Coastal Act of 1972, a coastal zoning commission must call for a public hearing whenever a developer submits a construction permit request for a project that might have an "adverse environmental impact" on coastal resources.

Some interest representation reforms that occurred on the state level were mandated by or encouraged by the federal government. For example, Congress required states to cooperate with the Environmental Protection Agency (EPA) in providing for public participation under the Federal Water Pollution Control Act; the Resource Conservation and Recovery Act; the Comprehensive Environmental Response, Compensation, and Liability Act; and other statutes. Through the Older Americans Act, Congress required states to establish long-term care ombudsman programs to investigate complaints by nursing home residents and to monitor the development and implementation of pertinent laws and regulations.

---

[9] Matthew McCubbins and Thomas Schwartz, "Congressional Oversight Overlooked: Police Patrols versus Fire Alarms," *American Journal of Political Science* 28:1 (February 1984): 180–202.

[10] William Gormley, Jr., "The Representation Revolution: Reforming State Regulation through Public Representation," *Administration and Society* 18:2 (August 1986): 179–196.

[11] Involuntary bill inserts later were ruled unconstitutional in a California case that effectively invalidated a key provision of the Wisconsin law. See *Pacific Gas and Electric v. Public Utilities Commission of California*, 106 S. Ct. 903 (1986).

[12] Beth Givens, *Citizens' Utility Boards: Because Utilities Bear Watching* (San Diego, Calif.: Center for Public Interest Law, University of San Diego Law School, 1991).

[13] Howard Schutz, "Effects of Increased Citizen Membership on Occupational Licensing Boards in California," *Policy Studies Journal* 2 (March 1983): 504–516.

Regulatory Federalism

The dynamics of regulatory federalism differ significantly from those of interest representation reforms. In both cases, politicians exercise indirect control over state bureaucracies, relying on surrogates to articulate their concerns. However, regulatory federalism is much more intrusive. If a consumer advocacy group recommends a new rule or regulation, a state agency may consider and reject it. If a federal agency instructs a state agency to adopt a rule or face a sharp cutback in federal funds, the state agency does not have much of a choice.

Regulatory federalism is a process whereby the federal government imposes conditions on state governments that accept federal funding.[14] Regulatory federalism arose as an adjunct to the new social regulations of the 1970s and as an antidote to the laissez-faire of general revenue sharing. Regulatory federalism includes a variety of techniques, such as direct orders (unequivocal mandates), crossover sanctions (threats in one program area if actions are not taken in another program), crosscutting requirements (obligations applicable to a wide range of programs), and partial preemptions (the establishment of minimal federal standards if states wish to run their own programs).[15] Some of these techniques apply to state legislatures; some apply to state agencies; many apply to both.

The number of federal statutes imposing significant new regulatory requirements increased dramatically during the 1970s. Given the Reagan administration's public support for federalism and deregulation, many observers expected regulatory federalism to decline during the 1980s. However, as political scientist Timothy Conlan has shown, the number of federal statutes with significant intergovernmental controls directed at the states increased even further.[16] Moreover, a disproportionate increase came about in the most coercive regulatory control techniques—namely, direct orders and crossover sanctions. In Conlan's words, "the 1980s rivaled the previous decade as a period of unparalleled intergovernmental regulatory activity.[17]

In 1995 regulatory federalism finally gave way to a concerted effort to devolve power to the states. Led by Republican governors and members of Congress, advocates of state discretion pushed for program consolidation, block grants, and the elimination of unfunded federal mandates. In some instances, these developments will allow state administrators to enjoy greater discretion than before. Certainly, they will have fewer federal auditing and paperwork requirements to meet. On the other hand, as the flow of federal dollars to the states diminishes, state administrators will find it difficult to extend funding and protection to previously uncovered

---

[14] Regulatory federalism also may be used to describe the relationship between state and local governments. For more on the growing burdens placed by state governments on local governments, see Catherine Lovell and Charles Tobin, "The Mandate Issue," *Public Administration Review* 41:3 (May/June 1981): 318–331. See also Joseph Zimmerman, "Developing State-Local Relations: 1987–1989," in *The Book of the States, 1990–1991,* 533–548.

[15] Advisory Commission on Intergovernmental Relations, *Regulatory Federalism: Policy, Process, Impact and Reform* (Washington, D.C.: Advisory Commission on Intergovernmental Relations, 1983).

[16] Timothy Conlan, "And the Beat Goes On: Intergovernmental Mandates and Preemption in an Era of Deregulation," *Publius* 21:3 (Summer 1991): 43–57.

[17] Ibid., 50.

target populations. For example, new federal child care legislation would allow state agencies to offer child care assistance to families who earn as much as 100 percent of their state's median family income, up from 75 percent in previous legislation.[18] Yet, an additional feature of the new legislation will eliminate a special child care program aimed at children at risk. Consequently, the states will probably be forced to ignore potential new beneficiaries to focus on these needier children whose program has been eliminated.

Due Process

In addition to serving as arbiters in intergovernmental disputes, federal judges have been active participants in efforts to control state bureaucracies. They have intervened vigorously in pursuit of such constitutional rights as "due process of law" and freedom from "cruel and unusual punishment." Dissatisfied with progress at the state level, they have gone so far as to seize, for example, state prisons and homes for the mentally ill or the mentally retarded, substituting their managerial judgment for that of state public administrators.

The 1971 case *Wyatt v. Stickney*[19] was the first in a long line of institutional reform cases in which federal judges decided to play a strong managerial role. Alabama's homes for the mentally ill and the mentally retarded were overcrowded, understaffed, dangerous, and unsanitary. In response to a class action suit, Judge Frank Johnson held that mentally disabled patients have a right to adequate and effective treatment in the least restrictive environment practicable. To secure that right, he issued extremely specific treatment standards and ordered rapid deinstitutionalization.

Shortly after the *Wyatt* decision, Judge Johnson found himself embroiled in an equally bitter controversy over Alabama's prisons. By most accounts, conditions in the state's prisons were deplorable. Rapes and stabbings were widespread, food was unwholesome, and physical facilities were dilapidated. In response to inmate complaints, Judge Johnson issued a decree calling for adequate medical care, regular fire inspections, and regular physical examinations.[20] When conditions barely improved, he issued detailed standards, including cell-space requirements, hiring requirements, and a mandatory classification system.[21]

The Alabama cases set the stage for a large number of similar cases throughout the country. In state after state, federal judges mandated massive changes in physical facilities, staffing ratios, health services, and amenities. They specified the size of prison cells, the credentials of new employees, and plumbing and hygiene standards. They shut down facilities and prohibited new admissions, even where alternative facilities were not available.

---

[18] For the details of this legislation, see S.850, a bill to amend the Child Care and Development Block Grant of 1990.

[19] *Wyatt v. Stickney*, 324 F. Supp. 781 (M.D. Ala. 1971).

[20] *Newman v. Alabama*, 349 F. Supp. 278 (M.D. Ala. 1972).

[21] *James v. Wallace*, 406 F. Supp. 318 (M.D. Ala. 1976); and *Pugh v. Locke*, 406 F. Supp. 318 (M.D. Ala. 1976).

The U.S. Supreme Court in 1982 finally applied the brakes on mental health orders in *Youngberg v. Romeo.*[22] In that decision, the Court ruled that mentally retarded clients are constitutionally entitled to minimally adequate treatment and habilitation but that professionals, including state administrators, should be free to decide what constitutes minimally adequate training for staff. Thus, the decision was viewed as a partial victory for state administrators.

More recently, the Court restricted other federal courts from correcting prison conditions in the absence of "deliberate indifference." In *Wilson v. Seiter,* the Court ruled that federal judges may address "cruel and unusual punishment" by state prison officials only if the plaintiff has demonstrated that prison officials exhibited a "culpable state of mind."[23] This imposes a higher hurdle for prison reform interventions than was previously the case.

Types of Controls

It is useful when thinking about recent efforts to control state bureaucracies to imagine a spectrum ranging from catalytic controls at one end to coercive controls at the other end, with hortatory controls falling in between. Catalytic controls stimulate change but preserve a great deal of bureaucratic discretion. Coercive controls require change and severely limit bureaucratic discretion. Hortatory controls involve more pressure than catalytic controls but more restraint than coercive controls.[24]

Moreover, different types of controls have different types of effects. In their public policy implications, catalytic controls have been surprisingly effective and coercive controls have been notably counterproductive.

Catalytic Controls

Catalytic controls require state bureaucracies to respond to a petition or plea but do not predetermine the nature of their response. As a result, such controls are action-forcing but not solution-forcing. While they alter bureaucratic behavior, they nevertheless permit a good deal of discretion and flexibility. Examples of catalytic controls include public hearings, ombudsmen, proxy advocacy, and lay representation.

Public hearings have enabled environmentalists to win important victories in their dealings with state bureaucracies. For example, citizens have used public hearings on state water quality planning in North Carolina to secure important modifications of state plans concerning waste water disposal, construction, and mining.[25] Similarly, citizens used public hearings before the California Coastal

---

[22] *Youngberg v. Romeo*, 102 S. Ct. 2452 (1982).

[23] 111 S. Ct. 2321 (1991).

[24] William Gormley, Jr., *Taming the Bureaucracy: Muscles, Prayers, and Other Strategies* (Princeton: Princeton University Press, 1989).

[25] David Godschalk and Bruce Stiftel, "Making Waves: Public Participation in State Water Planning," *Journal of Applied Behavioral Science* 17:4 (October–December 1981): 597–614.

Commission to block permits for development projects that would have an "adverse environmental impact" on coastal resources.[26]

Ombudsmen have been active in several areas but especially on nursing home issues. According to one report,[27] nursing home ombudsmen have been effective in resolving complaints on a wide variety of subjects, including Medicaid problems, guardianship, the power of attorney, inadequate hygiene, family problems, and the theft of personal possessions. Another study[28] found that nursing home ombudsmen provide useful information to legislators and planners.

Proxy advocates have effectively represented consumers in rate cases and other proceedings held by state public utility commissions. As a result of the interventions, utility companies have received rate hikes substantially lower than those originally requested. Proxy advocates also have been instrumental in securing policies on utility disconnections and payment penalties that help consumers who are struggling to pay their bills.[29] Even in complex telecommunications cases, proxy advocates have successfully promoted competition on behalf of consumers.[30]

Catalytic controls may be too weak in some instances. In several southern states, for example, public hearing requirements in utility regulatory proceedings have been pointless because consumer groups and environmental groups have not materialized to take advantage of such hearings.[31] Lay representation on occupational licensing boards also has been a disappointment. Lacking expertise, lay representatives typically have deferred to professionals on these boards .[32]

Overall, though, catalytic controls have been remarkably successful in making state bureaucracies more responsive to a vast array of formerly underrepresented interests. In effect, they have institutionalized what political scientist James Q. Wilson refers to as "entrepreneurial politics"[33] or the pursuit of policies that offer widely distributed benefits through widely distributed costs. Moreover, catalytic controls have achieved results without engendering bureaucratic hostility and resentment. Studies show that state administrators welcome citizen participation[34] and interest group interventions.[35] At their best, catalytic controls provide state bureaucrats with ammunition to justify policies that promote the public interest.

[26] Judy Rosener, "Making Bureaucrats Responsive: A Study of the Impact of Citizen Participation and Staff Recommendations on Regulatory Decision Making," *Public Administration Review* 42:4 (July/August 1982): 339–345.

[27] Administration on Aging, U.S. Department of Health and Human Services, *National Summary of State Ombudsman Reports for U.S. Fiscal Year 1982* (Washington, D.C.: U.S. Government Printing Office, 1983).

[28] Abraham Monk et al., *National Comparative Analysis of Long Term Care Programs for the Aged* (New York: Brookdale Institute on Aging and Adult Human Development and the Columbia University School of Social Work, 1982).

[29] William Gormley, Jr., *The Politics of Public Utility Regulation* (Pittsburgh: University of Pittsburgh Press, 1983).

[30] Paul Teske, *After Divestiture: The Political Economy of State Telecommunications Regulation* (Albany: SUNY Press, 1990), 63–85.

[31] Ibid.

[32] Gerald Thain and Kenneth Haydock, *A Working Paper: How Public and Other Members of Regulation and Licensing Boards Differ: The Results of a Wisconsin Survey* (Madison: Center for Public Representation, 1983).

[33] James Q. Wilson, ed., *The Politics of Regulation* (New York: Basic Books, 1980).

[34] Cheryl Miller, "State Administrator Perceptions of the Policy Influence of Other Actors: Is Less Better?" *Public Administration Review* 47:3 (May/June 1987): 239–245.

[35] Glenn Abney and Thomas Lauth, *The Politics of State and City Administration* (Albany: SUNY Press, 1986).

Hortatory Controls

Hortatory controls involve political pressure or "jawboning," usually by someone in a position of authority. They strike a balance between bureaucratic discretion and bureaucratic accountability. Some, such as sunset laws and administrative reorganizations, are relatively mild; others, such as partial preemptions and cross-over sanctions, are relatively strong.

The strength of hortatory controls depends primarily on two factors: their specificity (are the goals of the controllers clear?) and the credibility of the threat (how likely is it that penalties will be invoked?). Thus, sunset laws are relatively weak because the threat of termination is remote, except in the case of extremely small agencies.

To argue that some hortatory controls are mild is not to say that they are ineffective. A study of legislative audit bureau reports reveals that they do lead to changes in legislation, administrative practice, or both. Research by legislative audit bureaus is more likely to be utilized by state legislators than other types of research.[36] The literature on administrative reorganizations reveals that they do not reduce government spending but that they can promote coordination and integration if they are well-crafted and well-executed.[37] The key seems to be to put agencies with interrelated missions under the same roof.

Research on sunset laws roughly parallels the findings on administrative reorganizations. As a cost-containment device, sunset legislation has been a failure. However, as a mechanism for focusing legislative attention on agencies and issues low in visibility, sunset legislation has been a success. In a number of states, such as Connecticut and Florida, sunset laws have resulted in significant changes in statutes and agency rules.[38]

Stronger hortatory controls have been even more effective, though they also have been dysfunctional in some respects. In response to quality control systems in welfare, "errors of liberality" have declined, but "errors of stringency" have increased.[39] In effect, states have sacrificed accuracy for cost-containment. States also have enforced federal regulations that they know to be unreasonable, in response to partial preemptions in environmental policy. For example, the Minnesota Pollution Control Agency enforced a rigid EPA definition of hazardous waste, even though it meant that a lime sludge pile could not be removed from a highway site, could not be used for waste-water treatment, and could not be used to clean an electric utility company's smokestack emissions.[40]

---

[36] David Rafter, "Policy-Focused Evaluation: A Study of the Utilization of Evaluation Research by the Wisconsin Legislature," Ph.D. dissertation, University of Wisconsin, Madison, 1982.

[37] Kenneth Meier, "Executive Reorganization of Government: Impact on Employment and Expenditures," *American Journal of Political Science* 24:3 (August 1980): 396–412; and Karen Hult, *Agency Merger and Bureaucratic Redesign* (Pittsburgh: University of Pittsburgh Press, 1987).

[38] Doug Roederer and Patsy Palmer, *Sunset: Expectation and Experience* (Lexington, Ky.: Council of State Governments, June 1981).

[39] Evelyn Brodkin and Michael Lipsky, "Quality Control in AFDC as an Administrative Strategy," *Social Service Review* 57:1 (March 1983): 1–34.

[40] Eric Black, "Why Regulators Need a Don't-Do-It-If-It's-Stupid Clause," *Washington Monthly* 16:12 (January 1985): 23–26.

Strong hortatory controls place a premium on uniform standards and universal compliance with such standards. In some instances, such as civil rights, no practical alternative exists to strong controls, because local prejudices are too deeply ingrained to permit cooperation. In others, however, strong hortatory controls may impose premature closure, discouraging the innovation and experimentation that are necessary for the states to serve as "laboratories" for the nation and for other states.

Strong hortatory controls have been particularly prominent in intergovernmental relations. Indeed, conditions attached to federal grants-in-aid epitomize hortatory controls. Such conditions have remained formidable, despite periodic rhetoric in support of a new federalism. In 1995, however, Congress took steps to soften or eliminate certain restrictions that states found offensive. For example, Congress voted to eliminate federal speed limit requirements for automobiles on federally financed highways except for some rural freeways.[41]

Coercive Controls

Coercive controls rob state bureaucracies of their discretion. They compel a specific response, often within a specific time frame. Neither the solution nor the deadline may be reasonable, but the state bureaucracy does not have the luxury of responding reasonably. Immediate compliance becomes more important than rationality, and short-term "outputs" become more important than long-term "outcomes."

Coercive controls often trigger bureaucratic circumvention or resistance. In the former case, bureaucrats comply with the letter, but not the spirit, of a tough requirement. In the latter case, the bureaucracy goes to court. In both cases, an adversarial relationship develops that precludes cooperation, bargaining, and persuasion.

As a response to legislative vetoes, some state agencies have issued emergency rules, which are not subject to the usual legislative review process. In Wisconsin, for example, state agencies issued a total of fifty-four emergency rules during the 1985–1986 legislative session—a sharp increase over earlier years.[42] Reliance on emergency rules is especially unfortunate, because they do not involve public hearings. Thus, in escaping highly threatening legislative vetoes, agencies avoid less threatening public hearings as well.

Court orders have triggered some of the more dysfunctional bureaucratic responses. When Judge Frank Johnson required state prisons to reduce their overcrowding, Alabama prison officials simply released large numbers of prisoners, forcing county jails to take up the slack. Unfortunately, county jails were poorly equipped for the task; they lacked adequate space and personnel. Consequently, many prisoners, shipped to county jails, were forced to endure conditions even

---

[41] Don Phillips, "Federal Speed Limit, Set in 1974, Repealed," *Washington Post*, November 29, 1995, 1.

[42] Douglas Stencel, "Analysis of Joint Committee for Review of Administrative Rules Caseload 1085–1086," unpublished manuscript, Madison, Wis., April 1987.

worse than those they had experienced in the state prisons.[43] Yet the state agency was technically in compliance with the court decree.

A key problem with coercive controls is that they place far too much emphasis on formal authority. Many state agencies depend considerably on a series of informal understandings. This is especially true of prisons, where quick-thinking guards and cooperative inmates help to maintain a delicate balance between order and chaos. When that balance is disrupted, tragedy may result. This is precisely what happened in Texas, when Judge William Justice restricted the use of force by prison guards and ordered an end to the state's "building tender" system, in which inmates in effect guarded other inmates. The court's order dissolved the informal networks that enabled the prisons to function on a daily basis. As guards became more timid, direct challenges to authority rose sharply. Disciplinary reports reveal abrupt and dramatic increases in incidents where a guard was threatened or assaulted.[44] Inmates also turned on each other, with their fists or with makeshift weapons. By generating rising expectations and undermining bureaucratic morale, Judge Justice created a temporary power vacuum that prison gangs quickly filled. The tragic result was a series of riots and violent episodes that left fifty-two inmates dead within two years.[45]

Accountability Battles

Accountability battles have become more prominent in state politics for three principal reasons: (1) the proliferation of controls; (2) the intensification of controls; and (3) the judicialization of controls. As controls multiply, some are likely to be contradictory. Competing claimants emerge. As controls intensify, contradictory controls generate more friction. Competing claimants press their claims. As controls spill over into the courts, disputes are resolved according to legal criteria. Moreover, the courts themselves become active participants in these battles. Frustrated with both state politicians and state bureaucrats, judges have decided that they can do a better job and that they are entitled to do so under the U.S. Constitution, the state constitution, or both.

State Legislatures versus Governors

Accountability battles between state legislatures and governors have erupted in recent years. Although such disputes are not new, they seem to focus increasingly on directives to administrative agencies and on questions of legal authority instead of political preference. As a result, state judges have found themselves playing a key role in arbitrating disputes between governors and state legislatures.

---

[43] Tinsley Yarbrough, *Judge Frank Johnson and Human Rights in Alabama* (Tuscaloosa: University of Alabama Press, 1981).

[44] James Marquart and Ben Crouch, "Judicial Reform and Prisoner Control: The Impact of *Ruiz v. Estelle* on a Texas Penitentiary," *Law and Society Review* 19:4 (1985): 557–586.

[45] Aric Press, "Inside America's Toughest Prison," *Newsweek*, October 6, 1986, 46–61.

Legislative vetoes have aroused considerable conflict between state legislatures and governors, even when the same party controls both branches of government. In New Jersey, for example, the Democratic state legislature and Democratic governor Brendan T. Byrne clashed in court over a generic legislative veto and a more specific veto, whereby certain building authority proposals must be approved by both houses or the presiding offices of the legislature, depending on the nature of the proposal.[46] The New Jersey state supreme court upheld the specific legislative veto[47] but ruled the generic veto unconstitutional, citing violations of separation of powers and the presentment clauses of the state constitution.[48]

Executive orders also have triggered conflict between state legislatures and governors. In Pennsylvania, for example, Republican governor Dick Thornburgh issued an executive order "privatizing" the state's liquor control store system. The Democratic state legislature, which had just rejected such a plan, promptly took the governor to court. A Commonwealth Court judge ruled in favor of the legislature, noting that the governor's privatization plan was "without authority and contravenes the Sunset Act." He also accused both sides of playing an unseemly game of political football at the public's expense.[49]

Money, too, has fueled many disputes between state legislatures and governors. In Wisconsin, Republican governor Tommy Thompson refused to accept a decision by the Democratic state legislature to maintain welfare benefits at existing levels. Stretching the outer limits of his line-item veto authority, Thompson vetoed two digits and a decimal point from the state legislature's benefit formula, thereby effecting a 6 percent reduction in welfare benefits. The legislature promptly took the governor to court, but the Wisconsin supreme court upheld a generous interpretation of the governor's line-item power.[50] In 1990, the voters approved a constitutional amendment prohibiting "Vanna White" vetoes that build new words out of stray letters but allowed deletions of whole words, thus sustaining creative veto powers.[51]

Tensions between state legislatures and governors can be very stressful for administrative agencies, especially when the two branches of government are controlled by different political parties. During a bitter budget battle between Republican governor John Engler and Democrats in the Michigan State legislature in 1991, the child care licensing division was threatened with extinction and licensors received pink slips. A strong grass-roots lobbying campaign managed to save the division, but the experience was extremely unpleasant for state agency officials.[52]

[46] Levinson, "The Decline of the Legislative Veto," 121.

[47] *Enourato v. New Jersey Building Authority*, 448 A. 2d 449 (N.J. 1982).

[48] *General Assembly v. Byrne*, 448 A. 2d 438 (N.J. 1982).

[49] Gary Warner, "Despite Ruling, Future of Liquor Stores Up in Air," *Pittsburgh Press*, December 30, 1986, 1.

[50] Charles Friederich, "Lawmakers to sue Thompson over Budget Vetoes," *Milwaukee Journal*, September 2, 1987, B3: and Doug Mell, "Thompson Vetoes Win in Court," *Wisconsin State Journal*, June 15, 1988, 1.

[51] Charles Mahtesian, "The Captains of Conservatism," *Governing* (February 1995): 30–31.

[52] Personal interview with Ted DeWolf, Michigan Department of Social Services, July 13, 1993.

Federal Politicians versus State Politicians

State bureaucracies routinely are asked to implement federal statutes, such as environmental protection statutes. Often these federal statutes contradict state statutes or the policy preferences of the state's governor. Under such circumstances, a showdown is likely, with the federal government citing the "commerce clause" or the "take care clause" of the U.S. Constitution, while the state government cites the Tenth Amendment.

The U.S. Supreme Court and other federal courts have usually sided with the federal government in accountability battles where the allocation of federal funds is at issue. If states accept federal funding, they also must accept the conditions the federal government attaches to those funds. However, many intergovernmental disputes do not involve federal funding but a federal effort to preempt state activity in a particular policy domain. Here, also, the U.S. Supreme Court has sided with the federal government, though with occasional exceptions.

In *National League of Cities v. Usery*,[53] the Supreme Court surprised many observers by rejecting the federal government's attempt to extend minimum wage and maximum hour provisions to municipal employees. In doing so, the Court said that the Tenth Amendment prohibited any federal action that impaired "the State's freedom to structure integral operations in areas of traditional governmental functions." Thus, a key provision of the 1974 Fair Labor Standards Act Amendments was ruled unconstitutional. The decision was an important victory for both state and local governments.

In subsequent cases, the Supreme Court wrestled gamely with the "traditional governmental functions" criterion and offered further clarification. For example, in *Hodel v. Virginia Surface Mining and Reclamation Association*,[54] the Court articulated a three-fold test for determining when Tenth Amendment claims shall prevail. Specifically, the Court extended protection to the states if federal regulations: (1) regulate the states as states; (2) address matters that are indisputably attributes of state sovereignty; and (3) impair the states' ability to structure integral operations in areas of traditional function. In *Hodel*—a strip mining case involving a partial preemption statute—the Court concluded that Congress had acted properly and with restraint. Similarly, in *FERC v. Mississippi*,[55] the Court applauded Congress for imposing modest constraints on state public utility commissions, when it could have preempted the field entirely.

Finally, after years of painful efforts to distinguish between "traditional government functions" and other functions, the Supreme Court abandoned that doctrine outright in *Garcia v. San Antonio Metropolitan Transit Authority*.[56] Writing for the majority, Justice Harry A. Blackmun concluded that "State sovereign interests . . . are more properly protected by procedural safeguards inherent in the

---

[53]*National League of Cities v. Usery*, 426 U.S. 833 (1976).

[54]*Hodel v. Virginia Surface Mining and Reclamation Association*, 452 U.S. 264 (1981).

[55]*FERC v. Mississippi*, 456 U.S. 742 (1982).

[56]*Garcia v. San Antonio Metropolitan Transit Authority*, 105 S. Ct. 1005 (1985).

structure of the federal system than by judicially created limitations on federal power.[57] In effect, the states would have to protect themselves through vigorous lobbying on Capitol Hill. The Supreme Court no longer would invoke a rule that was "unsound in principle and unworkable in practice."[58]

If the *Garcia* decision left state and local governments discouraged about the future of intergovernmental relations, a more recent decision has left them jubilant. In *US. v. Lopez* (1995), the Supreme Court ruled that Congress had exceeded its constitutional authority in prohibiting the possession of a gun within 1,000 feet of a school.[59] In effect, the Court ruled that the commerce clause, which has justified numerous federal mandates in the past, cannot be equated with national supremacy. In writing an opinion for the majority, Chief Justice William Rehnquist said that in the future the Court will have to determine whether a regulated activity "substantially affects" interstate commerce.[60] This could make it difficult, though not impossible, for Congress to restrict activities, such as the possession of weapons or drugs, that do not necessarily involve interstate sales or transportation.

Federal Judges versus State Politicians

In accountability battles between federal politicians and state politicians, federal judges have served as arbiters. In other disputes, however, federal judges have served as both arbiters and combatants. In numerous institutional reform cases, federal district court judges have ordered sweeping changes that are attainable only if state legislatures allocate more money than they wish to spend in a particular policy domain. These decisions have had tangible effects on state budgets.[61] The decisions also have raised important questions concerning both federalism and the power of the purse.

A number of federal judges have acted with vigor, for example, Judge Johnson's efforts to overhaul the Alabama prison system and Judge Justice's response to Texas' prison program. In other institutional reform cases, federal judges have ordered sweeping changes in state treatment of the mentally ill and the mentally retarded. In New York, Judges Orrin Judd and John Bartels demanded more ward attendants, eighty-five more nurses, thirty physical therapists, and fifteen more physicians at the Willowbrook Developmental Center on Staten Island. They prohibited seclusion of patients and called for the immediate repair of broken toilets. They also ordered a sharp decrease in the Willowbrook population, stressing the advantages of deinstitutionalization. To implement these

---

[57] 105 S. Ct. 1018 (1985).

[58] 105 S. Ct. 1016 (1985).

[59] Ann Devroy and Al Kamen, "Clinton Says Gun Ruling is a Threat," *Washington Post*, April 30, 1995, 1.

[60] Jeffrey Rosen, "Fed Up," *The New Republic*, May 22, 1995, 13.

[61] Linda Harriman and Jeffrey Straussman, "Do Judges Determine Budget Decisions?" *Public Administration Review* 43:4 (July/August 1983): 343–351.

reforms, they appointed and preserved a Willowbrook Review Panel, which developed into a powerful agent of change.

In Pennsylvania, Judge Raymond Broderick went even further, after learning of unsanitary, inhumane, and dangerous conditions at the Pennhurst State School and Hospital for the mentally retarded. In a strongly worded opinion, Broderick ordered the eventual closing of the Pennhurst facilities, with residents being relocated in community facilities. In the meantime, he insisted on clean, odorless, and insect-free buildings, no new admissions, and less reliance on forcible restraint and unnecessary medication. To achieve these results, he appointed a special master and set deadlines for compliance.

More often than not, accountability battles between federal judges and state politicians have been won by federal judges. In reviewing lower court decisions, appeals court judges and the U.S. Supreme Court have agreed that "cruel and unusual punishment" is intolerable in state prisons and that the mentally ill have a constitutional right to "treatment" if admitted to a state facility. However, appeals courts also have raised questions about the extraordinarily detailed and specific remedies mandated by federal district court judges.

In *Newman v. Alabama*,[62] the U.S. Court of Appeals for the Fifth Circuit ruled that Judge Johnson went too far in specifying the size of new prison cells, in appointing human rights committees, and in insisting on rehabilitation opportunities for all prisoners. In the words of the court: "The Constitution does not require that prisoners, as individuals or as a group, be provided with any and every amenity which some person may think is needed to avoid mental, physical and emotional deterioration." In *Ruiz v. Estelle*,[63] the U.S. Court of Appeals for the Fifth Circuit ruled that Judge Justice went too far in outlawing double cells in Texas prisons (but supported his ban on triple and quadruple cells). In *New York State Association for Retarded Children v. Carey*,[64] the U.S. Court of Appeals for the Second Circuit concluded that Gov. Hugh Carey could not be held in contempt of court for failing to provide funding for the Willowbrook Review Panel. In *Pennhurst State School and Hospital v. Halderman*,[65] the U.S. Supreme Court ruled that a right to treatment exists only if a state accepts federal funds and if federal conditions of aid are clearly and unambiguously stated. In *Youngberg v. Romeo*,[66] the U.S. Supreme Court ruled that even when a right to treatment exists, it should be operationalized by qualified professionals, not judges.

Thus, accountability battles between federal district court judges and state politicians have given way to battles between federal district court judges and federal appeals court judges. On questions of constitutional rights, the appeals court judges generally have deferred to federal district courts, to the chagrin of the

---

[62]*Newman v. Alabama*, 559 F. 2d 283 (5th Cir. 1977).

[63]*Ruiz v. Estelle*, 679 F. 2d 1115 (1982).

[64]*New York State Association for Retarded Children v. Carey*, 631 F. 2d 162 (1980).

[65]*Pennhurst State School and Hospital v. Halderman*, 101 S. Ct., 1531 (1981).

[66]*Youngberg v. Romeo*, 102 S. Ct. 2452 (1982).

states. On questions of remedies, however, the appeals courts have cautioned lower courts against excessive specificity that stretches the limits of judicial expertise.

Conclusion

State administrative agencies once enjoyed considerable autonomy. Ignored by virtually everyone but clientele groups, they were "semi-sovereign" entities. In the early 1970s, that began to change. As state budgets grew and state bureaucracies increased in importance, this era came to a close. To make state agencies more accountable, politicians and judges institutionalized a wide variety of reforms. Through direct and indirect means, they attempted to bring state bureaucracies under control.

Ironically, this occurred at precisely the same time as the growing professionalization of state agencies. Thanks to civil service reforms, budget increases, rising education levels, and growing pressure for specialization, state bureaucracies acquired greater experience and expertise. Today, they are more adept at problem solving than ever before and arguably more deserving of discretion. Thus, they chafe at external pressure, particularly when it is highly coercive.

General agreement exists that state agencies ought to be accountable. Even state bureaucrats cheerfully concede that point. However, consensus on the need for bureaucratic accountability has given way to "dissensus" on lines of authority. If governors and state legislators both claim an electoral mandate, who is right? If federal and state politicians both cite constitutional prerogatives, who is correct? If judges and politicians disagree on spending priorities, who deserves the power of the purse?

In the 1990s, state agencies are more accountable to their sovereigns than they used to be. Yet accountability has become a murky concept. Principal-agent theories of politics[67] work only when the principal's identity is clear to the agent. In numerous policy areas, state bureaucratic agents face dual principals or even multiple principals.

Thus, accountability battles rage, as competing sovereigns press their claims. As one might expect in a federal system, different actors have won accountability battles in different settings and at different times. The 1994 congressional elections saw power shift from federal policy makers (both politicians and bureaucrats) to state policy makers (especially governors). If this trend continues, state administrative agencies will be more accountable to state politicians, less accountable to federal overseers. However, the history of intergovernmental relations suggests that periodic grants of discretion to the states are usually followed by negative feedback and additional restrictions. If this cycle repeats itself, state administrative agencies will once again find themselves subject to diverse, intense, and sometimes irreconcilable political pressures.

---

[67]Jonathan Bendor and Terry Moe, "An Adaptive Model of Bureaucratic Politics," *American Political Science Review* 79:3 (September 1985): 755–774.

G iven the numerous external checks on administrative agencies, one may well ask whether it is either feasible or desirable for public entrepreneurs to work for significant change in the public sector. Bellone and Goerl in their selection are dubious of public entrepreneurship as defined in the business model of leadership where the leader has greater latitude. We presented in Part II a less strident definition that emphasizes the need for leaders, middle managers, and street-level bureaucrats to act proactively but in accord with their agency's statutes and the constitution. Nonetheless, Osborne and Gaebler met a receptive audience in *Reinventing Government*[a] when they seemingly encouraged public entrepreneurs to act with the same freedom enjoyed by private entrepreneurs—external bureaucratic controls notwithstanding.

Bellone and Goerl feel the need to reconcile this business-inspired definition of public entrepreneurship with administrative responsibility. Would-be reformers in the public sector are not in business for themselves; they are accountable for their actions and those of their agencies in terms of how they proceed as well as what they accomplish. In a democracy, at least in peacetime conditions, the end does not justify the means. The authors begin by quoting other writers who have stressed the importance of evaluating the public entrepreneur in terms of "administrative responsibility," as well as competence and responsiveness, to determine whether their actions are "compatible with democratic values." In the hands of various writers, "responsibility" takes on somewhat different forms, but it is always normatively based, that is, it focuses on what "should be" rather than what "is." Usually it also pertains to how the public manager implements policy. Political scientist John Burke thus feels that where politicians have issued directives at variance with democratic principles, the public manager must act in a manner that is consistent with "an obligation to democratic government as a whole." Terry Cooper argues for public managers who, as "citizen-administrators," must be political educators for a citizenry that needs information in order to play important political and citizenship roles.

Bellone and Goerl are proponents of the principles of "democratic administration." They are aware, however, that in spite of this burgeoning literature on administrative ethics, a number of entrepreneurial initiatives by public managers reflect a preference for wide discretion at the expense of public accountability. The public entrepreneur sometimes seeks excessive autonomy, relies on secrecy, assumes unauthorized risks, and substitutes his or her own vision of what the agency should do for that of the public's.

The Civic-Regarding Entrepreneur—Hero or Villain?

There is thus often a tension between public entrepreneurship and democracy. The solution, in Bellone and Goerl's view, lies in more citizen participation. They therefore opt for a "civic-regarding entrepreneurship" that includes increased citizen education and involvement. Democracy's strength, after all, lies largely in participation by its citizens. One means of encouraging such involvement is for the public entrepreneur to provide citizens with more opportunities to participate in service design and delivery. This is far preferable, it is argued, than encouraging public entrepreneurs

---

[a]David Osborne and Ted Gaebler, *Reinventing Government* (Reading, MA: Addison-Wesley, 1992).

to seek ways to become "free of voter and taxpayer control." It is preferable to raise citizens to a level where they "themselves become more responsible agents of efforts to provide more public goods and services within the parameters of acceptable tax burdens." Democratic openness will then counter excessive bureaucratic secrecy, and citizens, rather than entrepreneurs, will become the stewards, or guardians, of their political and economic system.

There are those who are deeply suspicious of public entrepreneurship, and view the appropriate role of the public manager as a steward vested with responsibility for protecting the administrative agency's traditional core values that have survived often over several generations. They are the stewards of government and its time-honored tradition, and their authority stems from protecting those traditions. Bellone and Goerl are thus engaged in a misconceived quest in trying to reconcile public entrepreneurship with democracy. "The concept of civic-regarding entrepreneurship," contends Larry Terry, "seems to be a wolf in sheep's clothing."[b]

The rate of public agency change, however, seems more rapid than is suggested by Terry's analysis. Indeed, the challenge might be viewed as protecting an agency's core values even while confronting the necessity for rapid change. Furthermore, as Behn argued in Part II, given the limitations of the political system, the public administrator may have little choice but to lead. If so, the real question may then be how best to lead, and here Bellone and Goerl appear on sound ground. "A strong theory of public entrepreneurship," they conclude, "requires a strong theory of citizenship." This involvement depends on the motivation and concerns of the citizenry as well as the public entrepreneur. Citizens may prefer not to be involved, or to limit their participation to a level more in accord with "interest group mediation." Engaging citizens, however, is a challenge that administrators and politicians alike dare not avoid; there is no substitute for citizen participation in a strong democracy.

Reconciling Public Entrepreneurship and Democracy

Carl J. Bellone and George Frederick Goerl

The 1980s have been labeled the "age of the entrepreneur." Several commentators have given the Reagan administration credit for promoting the virtues of private enterprise, "leaner" governments, and entrepreneurial budgets (those that lower tax burdens). The rise of the public-sector entrepreneur is found in the advent of tax limitation movements, declining federal grants to state and local governments, and the growing fiscal crises faced by governments at all levels of the federal system. Public administrators as entrepreneurs and agents of entrepreneurial states seek to find new sources of revenue, besides the more traditional taxes, to increase tax bases through economic development projects and to augment the

Carl J. Bellone and George Frederick Goerl. *Public Administration Review*, Vol. 52, No. 2 (March/April, 1992), pp. 130–134.

[b] Larry D. Terry, "Why We Should Abandon the Misconceived Quest to Reconcile Public Entrepreneurship with Democracy: A Response to Bellone and Goerl's 'Reconciling Public Entrepreneurship and Democracy,'" *Public Administration Review*, Vol. 53, No. 4, July/August 1993, p. 395.

number of private-sector entrepreneurs within their boundaries. Current attention paid to public-private partnerships as solutions to the fiscal and social problems of government symbolizes the importance currently attached to both private and public entrepreneurship.

However, the characteristic behavior of public entrepreneurs (as well as traditional public administrators), must be evaluated in terms of administrative responsibility if their actions are to be compatible with democratic values. Administrative responsibility can be viewed as simply following policies and directions of hierarchical superiors. Because this approach can lead to the Eichmann phenomenon, some authors have argued that administrative responsibility must include certain democratic values when administrators are carrying out administrative directives. Other authors have even described responsibility as requiring the administrator to become an active agent of democratic education and reform. John Burke urges administrators to correct any departures from democratic principles by politicians, to feel an obligation to democratic government as a whole, and to act effectively to achieve policy ends.[1] Terry Cooper argues that public administrators, as "citizen-administrators," should be political educators for a citizenry that needs more information in order to play important political and citizenship roles.[2] In these two cases, theorists of administrative responsibility assume that the public administrator has a responsibility for furthering democratic values in the political process, in policy implementation, and for developing better opportunities for citizenship.

As entrepreneurs, public administrators have taken on the added responsibility of finding new and additional sources of revenue; but they have, at the same time, a vested political self-interest. The legitimacy of public entrepreneurs would seem to rest on their exercising administrative responsibility in the democratic manner described above so as to make public entrepreneurship compatible with democratic values and institutional roles. Four important characteristics of public entrepreneurs—autonomy, a personal vision of the future, secrecy, and risk-taking—need to be reconciled with the fundamental democratic values of accountability, citizen participation, open policymaking processes, and concern for the long-term public good (stewardship).

Entrepreneurial Autonomy Versus Democratic Accountability

First, a conflict exists between the autonomy/discretion desired by entrepreneurs and democratic accountability. With an increase in the complexity of revenue problems facing many governments, public administrators ask for greater discretion to carry out their entrepreneurial revenue searches.[3] Revenue crises have

---

[1] John Burke, *Bureaucratic Responsibility* (Baltimore: Johns Hopkins University Press, 1986) 42, 45, 50–54.

[2] Terry Cooper, "Public Adminstration in an Age of Scarcity: A Citizenship Role for Public Administration," in Jack Rabin and James S. Bowman, eds., *Politics and Administration* (New York: Marcel Dekker, 1984) 306–309.

[3] Eugene Lewis, *Public Enterpreneurship: Toward a Theory of Bureaucratic Power* (Bloomington, IN: Indiana University Press, 1980). George F. Goerl and Carl J. Bellone, "The Democratic Polity's Search for the Knowledgeable Public Administrator: An Argumentative Essay," *International Journal of Public Administration* 5:3 (1983) 217–266.

made public policy goals relatively less important in comparison to economic goals or revenue acquisition. In the name of revenue generation, programs and projects are set in motion that threaten to change drastically the character of a community and the authority relationships between professional public administrators and the citizenry. For example, user fees, redevelopment agencies, off-budget enterprises, investment revenues, tax-increment financing, and development fees can be seen as measures to avoid voter approval and, thereby, increase the autonomy of public officials and public administrators. Together with privatization, they contribute to the autonomy and discretion of public entrepreneurs while often making public accountability more difficult.

Because the public sector's bottom line is hard to measure, public accountability is most often attempted by measuring inputs or regulating administrative processes. Thus, through the budget process and administrative rules and regulation, legislative bodies have long sought to circumscribe the actions of public agencies in the belief that budgets and regulations ensure accountability.[4] A characteristic of public entrepreneurs, however, is their attempt to increase their influence over budget processes in order to be free from excessive rules and regulations. Public entrepreneurs ask for autonomy from line-item budget controls in order to be more effective and efficient. They want discretion to spend "their money" (public entrepreneurs are encouraged to see themselves as owners) for measures that they deem important and on items they, not others, choose. This means that, if public entrepreneurs are to be held accountable, measures of accountability must shift from an input or process focus to one based on an outcome analysis. Analysis of outcomes as a means to measure administrative accountability can be traced to the 1960s with program budgeting and evaluation.

A current example of outcome accountability for public entrepreneurs can be found in Fairfield, California, where the city council spends little time going over the city manager's budget or in holding budget hearings. Fairfield's budget is determined on a formula basis that includes cost of living, population growth, and available revenue indicies. Each department gets a predetermined percentage of the overall budget. Near the end of the year, however, each department head must come before the council and explain how the allocated money was spent to achieve the agreed-upon goals of the department. It should be noted, however, that because the goals of departments can be hard to measure, the open line of credit given department heads may not always result in effective public accountability.

Public Entrepreneurial Vision Versus Citizen Participation

A second conflict for a public entrepreneur who desires democratic legitimacy is between entrepreneurial vision and democracy's need for citizen input. Terence Mitchell and William G. Scott have suggested that entrepreneurs may be no more

---

[4]Judith Gruber, *Controlling Bureaucracies* (Berkeley: University of California Press, 1987).

prescient and knowledgeable than the rest of us.[5] Democratic politics and administration both demand that citizens be able to contribute views on issues of importance to them. However, if entrepreneurs are to be innovators, it means that they need to come with visions or ideas that are, by definition, uncommon. The Reagan administration's Iran-Contra arms entrepreneurial scheme, implemented by Oliver North and others, and the vision of the former Mayor of Oakland, California, and others to reacquire the Oakland Raiders by guaranteeing ticket sales, are examples of private visions which, by most standards, were not compatible with the tenets of democratic participation and approval.

The Los Angeles Olympic Organizing Committee's decision to have the 1984 Olympics privately financed and the decision of the City of Santa Clara, California, to buy a $100 million amusement park in order to save it from closing, although not widely held visions, gained acceptance by the public and public officials through open discussion. In the latter case, the citizenry of Santa Clara got to vote on the proposal.

Only by testing entrepreneurial vision through a meaningful public participation process can public administrators and others ensure that public entrepreneurship is compatible with the values of democratic participation.

Entrepreneurial Secrecy
Versus Democratic Openness

A third conflict is between the entrepreneur's need for secrecy and the democratic value of conducting the public's business in the open. Openness is defined as disclosure of information in policymaking stages that permits the public to be informed participants in the policymaking process. The Iran-Contra arms deal is a good example of an entrepreneurial activity requiring secrecy to be successful. Given the competitive nature of local governmental finance and land development, public-private entrepreneurial partnerships frequently require secrecy if they are to be successful. In the interest of the private developer, land-use decisions are often kept as secret as possible and, in the process, compromise the public's right to know.

Because many entrepreneurial deals are done in the face of competition from other cities, as in the case of auto malls in California and elsewhere, the pressure to help subsidize the private entrepreneur can yield large outputs of public money.[6] The wisdom of these, or, in the case of Oakland's fight to get "their" Raiders back, can produce major budgetary outlays, which may not prove to be very productive when open to public scrutiny and measured in terms of the overall public interest.

---

[5] Terence Mitchell and William G. Scott, "Leadership Failures, the Distrusting Public and Prospects of the Administrative State," *Public Administrative Review* 47 (November/December, 1987) 447–448.

[6] David Bellis, "Inner-City Competition Over Auto-Mall Development (or, How to Win Friends by Stealing Auto Dealers From Your Neighbors)." *Western Governmental Researcher* III (September, 1987) 15–29.

Entrepreneurial Risk Taking
Versus Democratic Stewardship

Fourth, entrepreneurial risk taking may conflict with the obligation to be a steward of the public good. Democratic stewardship is concerned with the prudent use of the public trust to achieve both long- and short-term goals compatible with a concept of the public interest. When directed by legislative or executive mandate, public administrators engage in risk-taking behavior (such as economic development projects) that are subject to changing business cycles. The administrator may face professional and ethical dilemmas if he or she believes that the risk taking demanded is unwise. When engaging in nonmandated risk taking, the responsibilities of the public administrator become even more a stewardship issue. High-risk investment schemes that have gone wrong and resulted in economic losses, failed arbitrage efforts in investing federal grant funds, and short-term borrowing to pay operating costs, as in the case of New York City's fiscal crises of the seventies, are all examples of entrepreneurial risk taking that ignored the prudent concern for the long-term public good.[7]

Entrepreneurial risk taking may be more congruent with democratic stewardship if it is preceded by public information, discussion, and formal acceptance by those who will have to bear the risks should they fail. Indianapolis found a professional football team to fill its stadium, but other cities have had a difficult time finding private developers to make their public entrepreneurial ventures profitable.

Toward a More "Public" Public Entrepreneurship:
The Case for a Civic-Regarding Entrepreneurship

The range of administrative and democratic responsibilities of public entrepreneurs helps describe the tension between such entrepreneurship and a democratic polity. Public administrators who seek to be entrepreneurial have added to their responsibilities by trying to generate new sources of revenue for financing public services and providing more services that pay for themselves. Given current fiscal crises, they have needed to be adept economic and political entrepreneurs. Although Mitchell and Scott raise questions as to how entrepreneurial public entrepreneurs or any entrepreneurs actually are, there is also the important question of how "public" are public entrepreneurs.[8] The answer to this is to be found in the earlier discussion of administrative responsibility. Public entrepreneurs need to take their political authority seriously and follow the principles of democratic theory in policy design and implementation as Burke and Cooper stated. We propose that, following Cooper's line of reasoning, they also need to be concerned with a more active approach to administrative responsibility which includes

---

[7]Martin Shefter, *Political Crises/Fiscal Crises* (New York: Basic Books, 1985).

[8]Mitchell and Scott, "Leadership Failures, the Distrusting Public and Prospects of the Administrative State," 1987, 445–452.

helping to facilitate increased citizen education and involvement. We call this a civic-regarding entrepreneurship.

Certainly, not all public administrators are concerned with citizenship and public participation, although many observers argue that they should be.[9] However, given the areas of conflict between public entrepreneurship and democracy listed above, it is important for a truly "public" entrepreneurship to be civic regarding.

To borrow from Benjamin Barber's distinction between thin and strong theories of democracy (strong theories being participatory), we maintain that only a thin theory of public entrepreneurship presently applies.[10] The thin theory, in accord with liberal democratic theory, is of a public entrepreneurship that effectively and responsively generates public revenue in order to provide public services. To do this, public entrepreneurs must have the autonomy and discretion to demonstrate their economic and political talents in the public interest. The citizenry's role is one of evaluation and trust in the entrepreneur's success and responsiveness. However, the evaluation and trust asked of the citizenry is problematic because public service delivery quality is difficult to measure, and entrepreneurs can often fail. Consequently, a citizen's continued passivity may only be a sign of political alienation.

A strong theory of public entrepreneurship (a civic-regarding entrepreneurship), following Barber's distinction, should be participatory or one where the citizenry have greater opportunities to participate in the design and delivery of their public goods and services. As a result of the more-services-less-revenue paradox handed the public administrator by the voter, citizens can be held accountable, in part, for current deficiencies in public services and financial resources. These deficiencies have led to the growth of a public entrepreneurship characterized by increased efforts by administrators to be free of voter and taxpayer control. It is the citizen's distrust of "big" government and the services that it provides that has led administrative theorists to call for greater citizen participation and an improved citizenship as a way of helping to regain the trust of the voter or citizen. Greater cooperation between administrator and citizen is the desired goal.

A civic-regarding entrepreneurship emphasizing public participation offers a remedy for over-zealous pursuits of self-interests. It offers a program of action that could make public entrepreneurship and democracy more compatible. Through developing citizens' opportunities to participate, the quality of citizenship could be raised to a level where citizens themselves become more responsible agents of efforts to provide more public goods and services within the parameters of acceptable tax burdens.

At the highest level of political aspiration, a civic-regarding entrepreneurship can be seen to be attempts, to use George Frederickson's words, to "recover civism," which embraces among other things, political community, self-aware citizens, and more adaptable and responsive government.[11] Expanding on

---

[9]H. George Frederickson, "The Recovery of Civism in Public Administration," *Public Administration Review* 42 (November/December, 1982) 501–508.

[10]Benjamin Barber, *Strong Democracy* (Berkeley: University of California Press, 1985).

[11]H. George Frederickson, "The Recovery of Civism in Public Administration," *Public Administration Review* 42 (November/December, 1982) 501–508.

Frederickson's call for our discipline to rediscover its own citizenship responsibilities, administrative theorists have stressed that public administrators should be held responsible for helping further "civic literacy,"[12] civility (as in forbearance),[13] and "civic capital." "Civic capital" can be defined as: "problem solving knowledge possessed by citizens, attitudes that guide civic action, and civic capacity for governance."[14] The goals of such efforts would be, to cite Charles Levine's list, the raising of citizen trust in government, the citizen's sense of efficacy, and, hopefully, a shared conception of the common good.[15]

A strong theory of public entrepreneurship requires a strong theory of citizenship. Better citizen participation, along with new sources of public revenue and better public policies and services, are high standards for public administrators to try to reach. These lofty aspirations, however, are abstract without clearer identification of the type of citizenship role one is talking about and specifications as to how opportunities for citizenship and a citizen's public education can be enhanced.

At a minimum, a civic-regarding entrepreneurship is no different from all other endeavors to increase citizen participation. However, as Dwight Waldo reminds us, not all citizen participation is of a public or collective character; it can simply be expressions of self-interest, interest group liberalism, or special pleading.[16] In addition, it can be more manipulative than facilitative and more symbolic than effective. It may also be more divisive than facilitative or benevolent. Lastly, it may require more concern for social-equity considerations than are found in liberal democracy.[17]

There are different degrees or levels of political participation.[18] In the case of administrative democracy, the same may be said. At a minimum, citizens can only take part in public service delivery systems if they receive public services. Not all do. Thus, considerable doubts exist as to fairness in such distributions of services. Equal access to high-quality public services should be a basic citizenship right that should not be jeopardized. However, fiscal limits threaten the provision of public goods and services. Thus, the entrepreneurial talents of public administrators are crucial to a civic-regarding entrepreneurship.

However, public administrators, as civic-regarding entrepreneurs, can go much further. They can increase the ability of citizens to complain about the quality of their public services and help to facilitate correcting efforts.[19] In similar fashion, New York City and other local governments that create uniform-service

---

[12] David Matthews, "The Public in Practice and Theory," *Public Administration Review* 44 (special issue, 1984) 124.

[13] David K. Hart, "The Virtuous Citizen, the Honorable Bureaucrat and 'Public' Administration," *Public Administration Review* 44 (special issue, 1984) 116.

[14] Eugene B. McGregor, "The Great Paradox of Democratic Citizenship and Public Personnel Administration," *Public Administration Review* 44 (special issue, 1984) 128.

[15] Charles Levine, "Citizenship and Service Delivery: The Promise of Coproduction," *Public Administration Review* 44 (special issue, 1984) 180.

[16] Dwight Waldo, "Response," *Public Administration Review* 44 (special issue, 1984) 107–109.

[17] Robert Bellah, et al., *Habits of the Heart* (Berkeley: University of California Press, 1985). H. George Frederickson and David K. Hart, "The Public Service and the Patriotism of Benevolence," *Public Administration Review* 45 (September/October, 1985) 547–554.

[18] Lester Milbrath, *Political Participation* (Chicago: Rand McNally, 1965) 5–38.

[19] Elaine B. Sharp, *Citizen Demand-Making in the Urban Context* (University, AL: University of Alabama Press, 1986).

districts that enable a citizen to use a single site for reaching the appropriate service providers are also increasing the opportunities for greater involvement in ensuring service systems that are responsive.[20]

When it comes to providing the rationale for spending public funds, a civic-regarding entrepreneurship would entail creating citizen budget committees to help set priorities before any formal budget approval is made by the executive and legislative branches. Portland, Oregon; Dayton, Ohio; and, in some respects, New York City all try to get citizens more involved earlier in the budgetary process.

Because public entrepreneurship often is manifested in the form of economic development projects, any effort at a civic-oriented entrepreneurship needs to increase the ability of citizens to see, comprehend, criticize, amend, and jointly design the projects so that their neighborhood or community is not disrupted or victimized by the development efforts of others. Where neighborhoods are well defined, neighborhood associations, citizen advisory boards, etc., may be in order if citizens are to defend and enhance their own community.[21] Although criticized for possibly raising the Not In My Back Yard problem, overall social equity concerns are better served by mutually agreeable zoning and development than when the citizenry and neighborhoods have no say.

Elevating citizen choice, as in the case of voucher systems, may still be the best way for enhancing citizen participation. Budget and land-use decisions are among the most important for all stakeholders. Being urged to become more responsible for one's public choices, with public sector staff providing needed information, may make citizen input far more informative for city staff and elected officials.

The use of citizen volunteers to help provide and produce public services has been suggested as another way of increasing opportunities for citizen participation. Volunteerism has increased in many fiscally troubled cities and counties out of self-defense. Neighborhood safety patrols and arson-prevention volunteers are cases in point. In upper-class suburbs, a highly educated citizenry often demands a high level of participation for themselves in the design and delivery of their public services. Such citizen volunteerism is a show of civic obligation and duty. It is a way of stretching scarce resources to enable citizens to provide more and better services than they would otherwise have received. It may also be a way of increasing the citizenship rights and especially the citizenship obligations of many people who would otherwise remain outside the service delivery systems of governments.

From an historical perspective, it has been entrepreneurial volunteers who have first provided most public services from the postal service, to the police, down to present-day neighborhood mediation services.[22] Volunteers, when aided by government offices of volunteerism, have been crucial to a delivery of many services, especially new and more innovative social services that facilitate compassion, benevolence, and the equal distribution of public goods.

---

[20] John Mudd, *Neighborhood Services* (New Haven: Yale University Press, 1984).

[21] Louise G. White, "A Hundred Flowers Blossoming, Citizen Advisory Boards and Local Administrators," *Journal of Urban Affairs* 5 (Summer, 1983) 221–230. Peter Marcuse, "New York City Community Boards: Neighborhood Policy as Results," in Naomi Carmon, ed., *Neighborhood Policy and Programmes* (New York: St. Martin's Press, 1990) 145–163.

[22] Susan J. Ellis and Katherine Noyes, *By the People* (Philadelphia: Energize Press, 1978).

Conclusion

De Tocqueville and John Stuart Mill saw the jury as a key to a citizen's public education. Today, there are more vehicles for increasing the opportunities for a citizen's participation and civic education.[23] Not all citizens may want to participate, and they should not be forced to do so under the tenets of liberal democratic theory.[24] However, as Morris Janowitz and Gerald Suttles have argued, there may not be enough opportunities for those who want to participate.[25] A civic-regarding entrepreneurship is about finding those opportunities. For those who find the opportunity to do so, a more deeply felt obligation to be better citizens may develop and perhaps a willingness to give more of themselves for the provision of needed public services. The willingness to pay is one important sign that civic-oriented entrepreneurship is present. A civic-regarding entrepreneurship is a reminder of our roles as both agents (participants) and members (with political obligations) to the polity.[26]

---

[23] Barber, *Strong Democracy*, 1985, 261–311.

[24] Diana Meyers, "Democratic Theory and the Democratic Agent," in John Chapman and Alan Westheimer, eds., *Majorities and Minorities* (New York: New York University Press, 1990) 126–150.

[25] Morris Janowitz and Gerald Suttles, "The Social Ecology of Citizenship," in Rosemary Saari and Yesheskel Hansenfield, eds., *The Management of Social Services* (New York: Columbia University Press, 1978).

[26] Joseph Tussman, *Obligation and the Body Politic* (New York: Oxford University Press, 1960).

PART

IX

Globalization and the Future of Public Management

Citizen Disillusionment

During the sixties and again for much of the nineties, America enjoyed remarkable prosperity. The resulting surge of national confidence in the sixties led, among other things, to expansion of Social Security and Medicare commitments, federal statutes that largely eliminated overt racism, and even a declaration of war on poverty. No such national confidence either in big government or in corporate America accompanied the "New Economy" of the nineties. Hence there was little hue and cry when the number of Americans without health insurance rose to 44 million, welfare reform tightened eligibility requirements, and Congress continued to struggle with federal deficits until additional tax revenue, like manna from heaven, appeared to balance the budget.

Why are Americans now fairly confident about their personal economic situation and yet so uncertain about what we can accomplish as a nation? Numerous explanations are offered. Some writers, as we saw in Part I, point to the rising power of conservative ideas with their emphasis on public sector shortcomings, shrinking government, and running government more like a business. Others argue that there is a breakdown nationally in a sense of community—the notion that we have some kind of social responsibility for one another—even though, as we saw in Part III, at the local level there is an increasing interest in citizen participation and commitment to "facilitating community and enabling democracy." Another explanation is that growing citizen disillusionment and lack of trust in the federal government has led citizens to opt for self-reliance and reject the value of social equity. John C. Rother, the director of legislation and public policy for the American Association of Retired Persons, thus identifies a broader cultural shift nationally: "It's part of the fragmentation of America, the breakdown in the idea of community, the ethic that we share some responsibility for each other."[a] Nonetheless, both presidential candidates in the 2000 election felt compelled to reassure voters of their intention to save Social Security and Medicare and supported a new federal program to provide prescription drugs for elderly Americans.

A more likely explanation of citizen disillusionment is that global competition has resulted in an economic and political transformation with profound and challenging implications. True, four-fifths of the American economy occurs within the 50 states, but a number of those businesses depend on the corporations comprising the remaining fifth, which often derive one-half or more of their revenues and profits from international trade. Furthermore, these global corporations are often politically as well as economically powerful and, like their European and Asian counterparts, they are widely acknowledged to represent the global economic future. The larger of these corporations have always possessed more power than other societal groups thanks to their privileged position in controlling jobs and the means of production.[b] That is increasingly the case now because the federal government—and increasingly its European and Japanese counterparts—has acknowledged that strategic trade policy (targeted subsidies for specific industries)—with a few striking exceptions such as Airbus—does not appear to work.

Letting the Genie Out of the Bottle

It is normal, economist Joseph A. Schumpeter has shown, for companies to disappear or triumph as a result of the "gale force of creative destruction" that rewards innovation and reallocates funds from sunset to sunrise industries. Nonetheless, as companies increasingly exploited computer hardware and software, the Internet and other telecommunications breakthroughs, and, most importantly, met their need for new profits from new markets, the result was somewhat akin to letting the genie out of the bottle. There was no turning back once global competition increased by such magnitude, and the plight of the losers was as dramatic as the growth of the winners. Even such apparently strong competitors as Lucent Technology and Xerox can rapidly encounter major problems. These global corporations—like WWII battleships—are not as impregnable as they appear.

Global corporations can make the decision to move from one community to another, and communities and cities are aware of their vulnerability to corporate mergers and bankruptcies. The demands of international competition, in turn have rendered these global corporations more dependent on government and the

---

[a]Julie Kosterlitz, "Do It Yourself," *National Journal,* November 23, 1996, p. 2532.

[b]Charles E. Lindblom, *Politics and Markets* (New York: Basic Books, 1977).

nonprofit sector for their growth and prosperity than in the old days. These firms must find communities, cities, or regions conducive to their "world class" needs, a play on words by Rosabeth Moss Kanter, "suggesting both the need to meet the highest standards anywhere in order to compete and the growth of a social class defined by its ability to command resources and operate beyond borders and across wide territories." This cosmopolitan elite is characterized by a mindset, she explains, and is rich in three intangible assets that translate into preeminence in a global economy: *concepts*—the best and latest knowledge and ideas; *competence*—the ability to operate at the highest standards of any place anywhere; and *connections*—the best relationships, which provide access to the resources of other people and organizations around the world."[c]

The needs of these small, medium-sized, and large global corporations are numerous and complex. Kanter thus speaks of three necessary community types. *Thinkers* are communities, such as Boston and San Francisco, that act as magnets for brain power to serve knowledge industries. *Makers*, such as Cleveland and Spartansburg, South Carolina, specialize in extraordinary competence in high-value, cost-effective production, and possess world-class blue-collar, rather than white-collar, work forces. *Traders*, like Miami, specialize in connections. But this is not connections in the good old boy sense of buying tires from a local distributor; Miami's connections extend throughout Latin America, and its airport handles more international cargo than any other U.S. airport.

Government as a Competitive Advantage

Neal Peirce too focuses on the local level, and speaks of the need for modern *citistates*. Like their earlier counterparts in antiquity and the Renaissance, these citistates too look beyond their borders and engage in global trade.[d] But Peirce's examples of citistates are sometimes regions. St. Paul, for example, is indissolubly linked with Minneapolis in a region. Indeed, these regions may sprawl across national boundaries. A civic activist group in Seattle thus visions its Pacific Northwest region as consisting of Oregon, Washington, British Columbia, and Alberta, and calls it "Cascadia."[e]

These cities and regions are also engaged in world competition with the counterpart communities around the world with which they compete and cooperate. That competition extends, as R. Scott Fosler has shown, to the restructuring of governance as well as economics, and involves developing and maintaining a capable and motivated work force, sound physical structure, knowledge and technology, enterprise development, quality of life, and fiscal soundness.[f] While

---

[c]Rosabeth Moss Kanter, *World Class: Thriving Locally in the Global Economy* (New York: Simon & Schuster, 1995, pp. 22–23.

[d]Neal Peirce, *Citistates* (Washington, D.C.: Seven Locks Press, 1993), p. 292.

[e]Rosabeth Moss Kanter, *World Class: Thriving Locally in the Global Economy,* p. 22.

[f]Cited in Neal Peirce, *Citistates,* p. 294.

numerous writers understandably emphasize the pivotal role of local and regional governments in this competition, Fosler's list makes clear that state and federal governments are also heavily engaged in this competition. Public and sometimes private universities, environmental quality, and social and public health services come under the purview of state government, while the national transportation system, national defense, community and regional economic development, and basic science research funding are administered by the federal government. Such basic science funding has played a major role in enabling the U.S. to lead the world in patents, copyrights, inventions, technology breakthroughs, and Nobel Prizes (just once, it would be nice to have a Nobel Prize winner "thank the federal government for its generous financial support without which this award would not have been possible"). Public managers at every governmental level will increasingly participate in—and be influenced by—the economic and political environment of globalization.

Uncentralization

Harlan Cleveland emphasizes that globalization will change how our organizations work. He anticipates the initial incredulous reaction of readers to the idea of *uncentralization*, and nudges them with the question: "If you think you can't, why think?" *Uncentralization* is an attractive answer to the question of just how corporations are going to govern themselves in the future. Cleveland gives the example of the uncentralized VISA International with its 22,000 financial institutions boasting $1.25 trillion in combined credit card sales.

Cleveland points to our political system of separation of powers and checks and balances as a precedent for a system in which no one is in charge (though uncentralization seems a strange way to describe a series of competing power centers). Global organization in his view lends itself better to "practical pluralism" than "unitary universalism." Global information systems have, indeed, permitted a rapid response time. Sometimes, though, uncentralization does not work where it seems applicable, as, for example, when most Americans defied international standards and refused to learn the metric system.

Uncentralization is an intriguing response to the new technologies of globalization, but Cleveland recognizes that there are also other forms of coordination that function without a pyramid. "Mutual adjustment" can occur either as an automatic response to generally accepted rules or as a result of successful bargaining among equals.[a] The discipline of price also supplies an information feedback system, as supply and demand—rather than a command and control hierarchy—set the ground rules for purchasing decisions. Frequently now, bureaucracies are operating with both hierarchies and uncentralized organizational arrangements when circumstances dictate. Cleveland points to marine platoons as an example of uncentralization, but neither he nor anyone who has ever served in the military would argue that the Pentagon lacks a hierarchy. The armed forces simply uncentralize under certain battlefield conditions.

The Donald C. Stone Lecture

Harlan Cleveland

The Future Is Uncentralized

I.

I am very grateful to Mary Hamilton and the others who arranged my "homecoming" to ASPA this week. I started my working life as a public administration intern 61 years ago; and though I've tried what looks like a variety of professions,

Harlan Cleveland. *Public Administration Review*, Vol. 60, No. 4 (July/August 2000), pp. 293–297.
[a]Robert A. Dahl and Charles E. Lindblom, *Politics, Economics, and Welfare* (New York: Harpers, 1953).

I always thought of myself as a public executive—and a writer of words designed to be useful to public executives.

That internship year was a bonanza: it led before long to a wedding. My not-yet wife Lois was really a pianist, but at Willamette University in Oregon she changed her major when her favorite piano teacher left. On the sound theory that in college you take professors, not courses, she selected an exciting new professor who was just starting a public administration major. She became his first graduate, and was selected for an internship in Washington, starting in the fall of 1939. I was at Oxford just then; but my Rhodes Scholarship was suspended that fall when Hitler's invasion of Poland started World War II. I was attracted by the dynamism of President Roosevelt's New Deal, and was accepted as a latecomer in Lois's intern program. That collection of accidents turned out pretty well: we're now in our 59th year of a very happy marriage.

That was also the year when we first came to know and admire Don Stone. He was already a "wheel" in President Roosevelt's New Deal bureaucracy, an assistant director in the Bureau of the Budget—which, the way FDR ran things, was more or less in charge of the whole Executive Branch. Don Stone quickly became, for us, a role model, a prime example of what it could mean to be a professional public administrator. Later I worked with him in the Marshall Plan; we shared a lively lifelong interest in international affairs, and kept in touch through ASPA and the National Academy. I'm delighted to be here to celebrate his life, his career, and thus the profession of public administration.

II.

I've undertaken to talk with you today about uncentralization. Let's start with a short but provocative question: *"If you think you can't, why think?"*

This can-do aphorism comes from the pioneer who helped invent, then brought to stunning success, the remarkably uncentralized enterprise called VISA International.

Philosopher-executive Dee Hock, a local banker in Seattle, had been brooding for years about why modern institutions seemed to depend so much on "compelled behavior," which he considered a "disguised form of tyranny." "The organization of the future," he had come to believe, "will be the embodiment of *community* based on *shared purpose* calling to the *higher aspirations of people*."

Most of us who ponder walking-in-the-woods thoughts like these don't get to try them on for size in the real world. But through a series of improbable accidents this small bank vice president got a chance to organize a deliberately uncentralized company that, three decades later, now handles the world's largest block of consumer purchasing power.

Owned by 22,000 financial institutions, accepted by 15 million merchants in more than 200 countries, the "products" of VISA International are used by three-quarters of a billion people to make 14 billion transactions a year worth $1.25 *trillion*. And during its first three decades, it has been growing by 20 to 50 percent a year.

Hock is now promoting a new vocabulary to help us talk about how to organize without centralizing. His keyword is "chaord," a fusion of *chaos* and *order*. His recent book, *Birth of the Chaordic World,* tells the dramatic story of VISA's origins. He doesn't claim VISA as a "model." But it stands as a very large and very successful example of some very practical ideas about human organization that will, I believe, come to characterize the twenty-first century.

III.

In the century we just said goodbye to, we learned again and again that complex social systems work badly if they are too centralized. In managing its agriculture, the Soviet Union put this proposition on public display for two-thirds of the twentieth century.

Yet for most twentieth century people, the image of "good organization" was a pyramid. In government, the pyramid's top was typically stuffed with political appointees, with serried ranks of civil servants—that is, servants expected to be civil to politicians—arranged in hierarchical fashion below. (When I became a Presidential appointee, I suggested dividing the noncareer officeholders into two categories: "merit" appointees, like me, and "political" appointees who could afford to make big contributions to an incumbent party willing to choose them. Somehow, that sensible trial balloon never flew.)

In corporations also, organization charts were drawn to look like pyramids, following Weber's model of bureaucracy. Nonprofit agencies usually did likewise; they assumed that organizations making a profit must be doing something right.

Organized religion had likewise developed hierarchical trappings—that's what the word "organized" was taken to mean. Holy men (and in some denominations, grudgingly, holy women) were up front in the pulpit; affluent laypersons served as middle managers; parishioners in the pews were expected to be religious but not necessarily "organized." Labor unions, despite a more egalitarian vocabulary, often had the look and feel of pyramids. And so did many social service agencies—though few went so far as the Salvation Army did in using military titles and uniforms.

In military organizations, of course, hierarchy had long been regarded as functional. It was symbolized, at the extreme, by the 1956 incident at Parris Island, South Carolina, where a Marine drill instructor barked an order to a platoon of recruits, who promptly marched into water over their heads. Some of them couldn't swim, and soon drowned. A few of the recruits must have reflected briefly on that probable outcome. But a later inquiry found that none of them had thought out loud about disobeying the order to march.

In every kind of organization, the people at the "top" were paid more, and had larger offices and expense accounts, than their "subordinates." (The exceptions, publicity heroes in professional athletics and the movies, were dramatic but few.) Even in hospitals and universities and movie studios and publishing houses, where physicians and professors and creative artists and writers instinctively resisted the notion that they were rank-ordered middle managers, the language used to differentiate functions often sounded more hierarchical than collegial.

IV.

Opting for pyramids as the "natural" form of organization might seem natural in some European, Japanese, and other cultures long submissive to monarchs or emperors governing by a mixture of divine rights and military readiness. But the founding fathers of the United States of America had something very different in mind. They were themselves undeniably upper class, some even slaveholders. But the rhetoric of their revolution had broken loose from hierarchies of right and might; it was full of inalienable rights and populist righteousness.

These leaders of an "underdeveloped" colony declared our eighteenth-century independence in human-rights language that much of the world caught up with only in the twentieth—under the leadership of that woman-of-the-century, Eleanor Roosevelt—and some parts of the world haven't yet understood.

Then they drafted a Constitution that departed dramatically from the oppressive pyramids the colonists had fled and learned to despise. Indeed, they created the basis for a nobody-in-charge society—quite literally a first-time experiment in uncentralized governance.

The "separation of powers" with its "checks and balances" was explicitly designed to deny any part of our federal government the chance to make too much yardage at the expense of the other parts—and of the people it was supposed to serve. The federal system itself was designed to create a continuous tussle between the states and the central government. That tussle was intended to be permanent; no part of the system was supposed to "win it all," not ever.

It is not just the durability of their extraordinary invention that testifies to the founders' wisdom. It is clear from the record they left that they—at least, the deepest thinkers among them, James Madison and Thomas Jefferson—knew just how unprecedented was the system they were proposing to build. The people were really *supposed* to be sovereign. Jefferson still believed this even after his eight years of trying to be their "servant leader."

"I know of no safe depository of the ultimate powers of the society but the people themselves," Thomas Jefferson wrote to a friend in 1820, "and if we think them not enlightened enough to exercise their control with a wholesome discretion, the remedy is not to take it from them, but to inform their discretion."

What's truly astonishing is that now, at the beginning of this new century, the practical prospect for a workable world seems to lie in reinventing their nobody-in-charge concept for *global* application.

The real-life management of peace worldwide seems bound to require a Madisonian world of bargains and accommodations among national and functional "factions," a world in which people are able to agree on what to do next together without feeling the need (or being dragooned by some global government) to agree on religious creeds, economic canons, or political credos. A practical pluralism, not a unitary universalism, is the likely destiny of the human race.

But let's not digress too far, into the future or the past. For our present purpose, my point is simply that pyramid building was always, and still is, essentially un-American. The real American tradition calls for the invention of systems in which nobody is in general charge—and, in consequence, each citizen is partly in charge.

V.

That authentic tradition began to take hold of our destiny in the second half of the twentieth century. Just below the surface in every kind of organization, something important was happening, something very different from the vertical practice—recommendations up, orders down—of both public administration and business management. The "bright future for complexity," foretold in a 1927 *New Yorker* story by E. B. White, was coming to pass in the U.S.A.—prodded and speeded by the modern miracles of information technology.

The sheer complexity of what had to get done—by governments and corporations, but also by their myriad contractors and subcontractors and their nonprofit critics and cheerleaders—required huge numbers of people to exercise independent judgment, think for themselves, and consult with each other, *not* just "do as you're told."

The marriage of computers and telecommunications multiplied the speed and extended to global range financial speculation, business transactions, military operations, political protests, and humanitarian activity. And the widening access to information about what's happening, and who is doing what, brought into financial markets and business decisions and military strategy and even humanitarian relief a host of kibitzers, lobbyists, and second-guessers who knew so much—or could readily discover it on the Internet—that they had to be taken into account.

There were still, to be sure, distinctions between organizations where the style of management is looser and more collegial and others where recommendations mostly go up and orders mostly come down. But by the end of the century, *every* kind of organization—from Marine platoons to urban hospitals—was moving away from vertical administration toward more consultative styles of operation.

The century just past thus opened a widening contrast between how organizations were described and how they really worked. So naturally, the search has been on for alternatives to *centralization* as an organizing concept. The first and seemingly obvious candidate was ***decentralization***.

But it turned out that most of the central administrators who opted to *decentralize* found, to their satisfaction, that this was a new way to preserve hierarchy. If things were becoming so complicated that grandpa could no longer understand it all, he could still subdivide and parcel out all the *work* to be done—while hanging onto central control with more and more creative accounting systems. Decentralization should therefore be considered an aspect, indeed a subhead, of centralization.

The real opposite of centralization is of course ***uncentralization***. Mao Tse-tung played with this idea for a time; he called it "many flowers blooming." Then he pulled back when it became clear that if China really permitted people's free exercise of opinion and initiative, the Communist Party's central control would be the first casualty.

Meanwhile, the underlying American bias favoring looser systems—featuring personal initiative, voluntary cooperation, joint ventures, committee work, and "networking"—was being reinforced by the dazzling progress of information technology and its impact on everything from elementary education to the understanding of our universe.

Very large systems, many of them global in scale, based on massive information outputs and widespread feedback, have been developed in the twentieth century. Global information systems unimaginable before the marriage of computers and telecommunications—currency and commodity markets, epidemic controls, automatic banking, worldwide credit cards, airline and hotel reservation systems, global navigation guidance, and the World Weather Watch come readily to mind—are now regarded as normal, almost routine. It is no accident of history that American leadership and imagination were the priceless ingredient in developing each of these systems.

In each of these cases, there are commonly agreed standards, plus a great deal of uncentralized discretion. The same is true, even more true, of the international foreign exchange market and the Internet, now the world's two most pervasive nobody-in-charge systems. In most cases, the standards so far are mostly technical. Ethical standards for global human behavior await the social inventors of the twenty-first century.

VI.

If all organizations are becoming "nobody-in-charge systems," how will anything get done? As I used to ask students in a management class: *How do you get everybody in on the act, and still get some action?*

We will do it, I think, by creating systems that manage to minimize, and clearly define, what "everybody" must agree on—common norms and standards—and in all other matters maximize each participant's opportunity and incentive to use his or her common sense, imagination, and suasive skills to advance the organization's common purpose.

This means, of course, that those who are going to pursue an organization's purpose together have to be openly consulted about the purpose, not only about the means of its pursuit.

Wisdom about uncentralized systems thus starts with a simple observation: most of what each of us does from day to day does *not* happen because someone told us to do it.

When you walk along a city street, you don't collide with other walkers; you, and they, instinctively avoid bumping into each other. To generalize: any human system that works is working because nearly all of the people involved in it cooperate to make sure that it works.

Political scientist Charles Lindblom called this *mutual adjustment:* in a generally understood environment of moral rules, norms, conventions, and mores, very large numbers of people watch each other, then modify their own behavior just enough to accommodate the differing purposes of others, but not so much that the mutual adjusters lose sight of where they themselves want to go.

Imagine (the image was suggested by Lindblom) a large clump of people on either side of a busy downtown intersection, waiting for the traffic light to change before crossing the street. There is *macro* discipline here. The convention of the red light means the same thing—danger—to all the participants in this complexity, even though there is no physical barrier to violating the norm at their own risk.

Then the light turns green. It would be theoretically possible, with the help of a sizable staff of computer analysts, to chart in a central *micro* plan the passageway for each pedestrian to enable him or her to get to the other sidewalk without bumping into any other pedestrian. But not even the most totalitarian systems have tried to plan in such detail. What works is mutual adjustment: somehow those two knots of people march toward each other and there are no collisions. Each person adjusts to the others, yet all reach their objective—a positive-sum game if there ever was one.

It is not only at street corners that mutual adjustment works. It works also in global markets. Even in markets dominated by cartels or monopolies, most decisions are not made by authorities giving orders; prices serve as an information feedback system that instructs people all over the world how to adjust their behaviors to take advantage of the system.

What enables mutual adjustment to work is the wide availability of relevant information, so each mutual adjuster can figure out what the others might do under varied conditions, and give forth useful signals about his or her own behavior.

Sometimes there are rules, developed by some rule-giving authority. That doesn't mean the rule-abiding citizens are serfs, doing some lord's bidding. If the rules work, it's because nearly all those who need to abide by them are motivated to abide by the rules because the rules make sense to them.

There may even be compulsion: In the United States, there are laws about driving on the right-hand side of the road. The laws are ultimately enforced by the state's police power. But if you don't agree with the law and try instead to drive to the left, you are quite likely to get killed well before the police arrive to enforce compliance. So, as a matter of common sense and common safety, you drive to the right. The effective "enforcement" is not the state's authority, it's the shared opinion of your neighbors with whom you share the public right-of-way.

VII.

The truth here comes, as truth usually does, in a small paradoxical package: The key to a genuinely *uncentralized* system is mutually agreed standards on whatever is *central* to the system and thus cannot be left to individual choices or market outcomes.

In some ways the most dramatic, and least remarked, nobody-in-charge system is illustrated by the way international standards are already set for many thousands of products and services.

It started in 1906, with engineers trying to make sure that "electrotechnical" gadgets would fit together and work the way they were supposed to work, anywhere in the world. Other engineers picked up the idea in some other fields. But it wasn't until after World War II, in 1947, that an International Organization for Standardization was formed.

The organization is called ISO. That's not an acronym, which wouldn't work for a multilingual club anyway. Derived from the Greek isos, meaning "equal," it's the root of the prefix "iso-" that occurs in many words such as "isometric" (of equal measure or dimensions), "isodynamic" (having the same strength or intensity), and "isonomy" (equality of political rights). As ISO's website puts it: "From 'equal' to 'standard,' the line of thinking that led to the choice of 'ISO' as the name of the organization is easy to follow."

The first ISO standard, a "standard reference temperature for industrial length measurement," was published in 1951. Less than half a century later, there are now more than 12,500 International Standards, contained in 356,427 pages. This standard-setting, coordinated by a nongovernment from a headquarters in Switzerland, costs only about $93,000,000 a year, but it engages the efforts of some 30,000 "experts on loan," working as equal partners in 2,867 committees and working groups, in a wide variety of technical fields. Their commonsense approach has been summed up this way: "Do it once, do it right, do it internationally."

ISO standards are *voluntary*—that is, enforced in the marketplace: if you produce something fastened by screws that aren't standard, the word will get around fast and customers will shun you. They are *industry-wide,* designed to provide global solutions to satisfy suppliers and consumers worldwide. And they are developed *by consensus.*

"Consensus" doesn't mean unanimous consent. An ISO standard can be adopted if it is approved by two-thirds of those actively involved and is blessed by three-quarters of the ISO members—national standard-setting bodies—that vote. That's a rough fit with a definition of "consensus" I found useful long ago while practicing multilateral diplomacy at the UN and in NATO: " . . . the acquiescence of those who care [about the particular decision], supported by the apathy of those who don't."

Once international standards are set (for metric screw threads, for bolts, for welding, for electronic data processing, for paper sizes, for automobile control symbols, for the safety of wire ropes, for film speed codes, for freight containers, and even for country names, currencies, and languages), a genuinely free market is possible. Competition within the rules of the game can be free and fair—and markets that are both free and fair are likely to grow faster than others.

The three VISA cards I carry in my wallet look very much alike—the magnetic code is in a predictable place on each card—because they adhere to an ISO standard. The three banks that issued them cooperated on that, but they happily compete for my custom—happily, because each is operating in a much larger market than any of them could reach if they hadn't first cooperated with each other.

VIII.

How human organizations can be conceived, organized, and led in ways that best release human ingenuity and maximize human choice is one of the great conundrums of the century now ahead of us.

The best public administrators of this new century will be those who learn, early and often, how to fuse chaos and order in uncentralized systems. They will help all of us, the sovereign "public," get used to the idea that no one can possibly be in general charge, so we're all partly in charge.

I don't know whether Dee Hock's intriguing word *chaordic* will make it into the next edition of my favorite dictionary. I hope it does. But what I'm sure about is this: the wave he is surfing has already rolled powerfully into this, the Global Century.

Global Reach—A Logical Next Step for Corporations and the Nation State

In thinking about globalization, Farazmand focuses on the increasing political and economic expansion of first world nations and global corporations and its implications for the developing world. Farazmand shares German philosopher George Friedrich Hegel's view of history as in constant flux with ideas and forces moving forward (thesis) and thereby eliciting contrary ideas and forces (antithesis). The result of the inevitable clash is a unity (or synthesis) whereupon the whole process begins again. For Farazmand, globalism is thus the logical next historical step after nationalism within this broader historical "framework of continuity." He provides a political economy analysis in which he argues that capitalism needs the nation-state to expand, and the nation-state needs capital to accomplish its goals. The resulting partnership between nation states and their global corporations serves the mutual interests of private and public sector elites.

Farazmand identifies several different analytical perspectives on globalization and "the new world order," but he stresses that most of these trends are characterized less by novelty than by significant expansion that benefits the first world at the expense of the developing world. While some see border openness stemming from global culture, the Internet, and information technology as a form of liberalization, Farazmand views such liberalization as beneficial mainly to global corporations operating in the third world. Similarly he is wary of globalization as ideology. TV images from CNN, a free press, computers, and satellite communication systems are a two-edged sword. They sometimes undercut political dictators and encourage business entrepreneurship, but the ideological force—and hence the propaganda value—of such key words as freedom, individualism, free enterprise, and plural democracy also project an image of an ideal political system, and thereby influence nations to adopt a form of democracy that may not be suitable under their socio-economic conditions.

Farazmand presumably would agree that the Internet and other technological innovations have resulted in some exciting global developments, but he views the fundamental causes of globalization less romantically. The drive for profits is not new; what did change dramatically in his view are the high rate of surplus accumulation and the transworld mobility of corporations—both facilitated by the political power of the nation-state. Global corporations were also assisted in their quest for "new markets, cheap labor, and unrestricted production sites" by such mechanisms as marketing simultaneously over the entire globe, merging or forming partnerships on a global scale, the utilization of unregulated global money, and the capture by the "trilaterals" (the U.S., Western Europe, and Japan) of such key international donor agencies as the World Bank and International Monetary Fund.

Among the numerous global consequences, Farazmand is particularly concerned about the global hegemony or dominance by one nation over others. That concern is not surprising, given the economic, military, political, and cultural global strength of the United States today. He sees potential consequences as the expansion of a corporate-dominated bureaucracy concerned more with coercion than preserving national and international safety nets, the triumph of corporate greed over equity and fairness, and the surrender of state sovereignty with its potential for promoting the public interest to centralized corporate and governmental elites bent on increasing the dependence of less-developed nations on the Trilateral countries.

The Role of Public Administrators in the Future Political Economy

While pessimistic, Farazmand believes that the forces pushing toward a dark global future can be countered by democratic forces that recognize the need to counterbalance the economic power of capitalism with the political power of democracy. He sees American public administrators as an elite that can contribute to such a balance if it shakes off its ethnocentrism and parochialism and comes to appreciate what administrative traditions in other first- and third-world countries have to offer. Note that this would include public administrators operating at the state and local—as well as the federal—level, since, as we saw earlier, citistates, states, and the national government are all engaged in diverse kinds of global activity.

Here Farazmand is in agreement with Harlan Cleveland who advocates in *Birth of a New World* that America must take the lead in building a club of democratic equals. Cleveland reaches this conclusion reluctantly, but is perhaps more optimistic than Farazmand because he views the American mindset as antithetical to assuming global leadership. He feels this is the first time that "imperial policy is being made by a whole people rather than a comparatively few leaders." His vision is of a nation that leads through "imagination, consultation, and persuasion, not just imagination backed by the power of the purse, Marshall Plan style."[a] Only time will tell whether such a global vision will take hold or the history of the 21st Century will merely record—this time writ large on a world stage—a saga of economic greed, political corruption, and unimaginative leadership.

Globalization and Public Administration

Ali Farazmand

Introduction

As the new millennium approaches, a new civilization is dawning. The qualitative changes of this civilization have been the subject of many studies. For example, Huntington (1996) speaks of the "clash of civilizations," Fukuyama (1992) predicts "the end of history and man," and Korbin (1996) indicates a "return back to medievalism." The hallmark of this change is the process of globalization, through which worldwide integration and transcendence take place, evoking at least two different intellectual responses. On one hand there are those who argue that the growth of transnational corporations, in particular because of their "state-indifferent" nature, and the spread of global capitalism have made state irrelevant or even obsolescent (Ball, 1967; Naisbitt, 1994; Ohmae, 1995). Some think of it as even the end of work (Rifkin, 1975) and of public administration (Stever, 1988). Others believe that global capitalism has led to the generation of suprastate

Ali Farazmand. *Public Administration Review*, Vol. 59, No. 6 (November/December 1999), pp. 509–522.

[a]Harlan Cleveland, *Birth of A New World* (San Francisco: Jossey-Bass, 1993), pp. 220–223.

governing agencies that are supplementing, if not supplanting, the territorial nation-states (Picciotto, 1989; Cox, 1993; Korten, 1995). Still others have suggested that this also has eroded the sense of community and urban power structure (Mele, 1996; Knox, 1997; Korten, 1995), causing the loss of urban jobs (Wilson, 1996). They also warn that the merging of the supranational governance agencies has deepened the dependency of less developed countries, exacerbated their fiscal crises, and created a serious problem of governability in those nations (Kregel, 1998).

On the other hand, some public administrators and public-policy analysts have predicted that global corporations will create a world order beyond nation-states (Reich, 1991), that is, a "global village" (Garcia-Zamor and Khator, 1994), a "world government" with "global management" (Wilson, 1994).

Some theorists have even attempted to develop a universal, global theory of public administration (Caiden, 1994). Others have vocally refuted the idea of the end of the state and have argued for the persistence of the nation-states with all the concomitant implications for public administration (Caiden, 1994; Heady, 1996; Scholte 1997).

Hirst and Thompson (1996), Zysman (1996), and Boyer and Drache (1996) have argued that globalization has been exaggerated and that states remain strong in the crucial functions of governance. Some realists in the international relations tradition have argued that "de facto [state] sovereignty has been strengthened rather than weakened" (Krasner 1993, 318). Similarly, sociologists and political scientists like Michael Mann (1993) and Theda Skocpol (1985), who "brought the state back in" to their disciplines during the 1980s, have maintained their skepticism about the disappearance of the state from history.

However, the latter group of thinkers recognizes that globalism has changed the nature of the administrative state worldwide. The globalized economic structure, with its many superstructural changes, including supraterritorial power structures, has led to profound implications for public administration (Mander and Goldsmith, 1996; Farazmand, 1994). Several social scientists have described the "retreating shifts" in the quality and quantity of state power and authority (Strange, 1996; Graycar, 1983; Lipsky, 1984). They also have explained the transitional nature of the state "from the welfare state to the competitions state," as governments attempt to "respond to, and shape and control, growing international political economic interpenetration" (Cerny, 1989), to "the hollow state" (Milward, 1994) or "the corporate state" (Farazmand, 1997a, b).

This article treats the concepts of globalism and globalization as phenomena produced by historical changes within the broader framework of continuity. These phenomena are expected historical, dialectical developments of late capitalism and are the products of the dynamic nature of rapid accumulation of surplus at the global level. The dynamic nature of the capitalist political economy in its latest development has shifted in favor of financial capital as opposed to the earlier production nature of capital. It has shifted from national to global capitalism. Change and continuity are dialectical characteristics of the development of socioeconomic systems. The qualitative and quantitative changes of the last few decades, which began after World War II and have accelerated since the 1970s, have altered the nature of capitalist economies and their respective structures and organizations of governance and administration.

I argue that globalization is the result of several factors, including surplus accumulation capital, the state, domestic constraints, information technology, international institutions, and ideology. In turn, globalization has had significant consequences for the capitalist state and for public administration. While the core of the state and public administration persists in the broader sense of continuity, major changes have occurred as a consequence of globalization that have altered the nature and character of the state and public administration from the traditional welfare administrative state to a corporate welfare state. Capitalism needs the state, and the state is not independent from capital; the elites of both work together in the globalization process because it serves both.

The discussion that follows is presented in four parts: Part one presents analytical perspectives on the concepts of globalism and the new world order. Part two examines the causes of globalization. Part three discusses the consequences of global capitalism for the state and for public administration, focusing on the changing character and role of the state in general and the administrative state in particular. In part four, a number of implications are outlined for public administration, with suggestions for public administrators worldwide.

Perspectives on Globalization and the New World Order

Although the concept of world order is not new, it became fashionable after World War II. With the emergence of the Soviet reformist leader Mikhail Gorbachev, who called for global restructuring, openness, a new way of global thinking, peace for all, superpower cooperation, and an end to the Cold War, the concept of a new world order reemerged (Sedghi, 1992). Following the Helsinki Summit in September 1990, U.S. President George Bush increasingly used the term. Today, the concepts of the new world order and globalism have become the subject of serious study. But what do they actually mean?

Meaning of the New World Order and Globalization

The new world order denotes a "system of collective world security where states and peoples can live in peace with each other, ideologies aside" (Farazmand, 1994, 65) and "observe each other's borders and maintain collective security interests" (Sedghi, 1992, 62). The Persian Gulf War was arguably fought in the service of the new world order, and President Bush announced that the war was waged to "stand up for what is right and condemn what is wrong" (Trudeau, 1992, 21). However, with the fall of the USSR, the concept of the new world order garnered a diverse meaning and consequently became vague.

Globalization means many things to many people. Economists consider globalization as a step toward a fully integrated world market. Some political scientists view it as a march away from the conventionally defined concept of the state, with territorial sovereignty and the emergence of nongovernmental power players in the world order (Falk, 1997). Business school academics and consultants apply globalization to a "borderless world" (Ohmae, 1990), and others view it as a phenomenon driven only by private-sector firms, not by governments (Strange, 1996; Julius, 1997). All discussions of globalization deal with the question of borders— "the territorial demarcations of state jurisdictions, and associated issues of governance, economy, identity, and community" (Scholte, 1997, 430). Five or possibly six meanings of globalization, as they relate to public administration, are briefly reviewed and assessed here.

Globalization as internationalization. This notion treats globalization in a narrow sense as an increase in cross-border relations among organizations, that is, identities and communities that extend beyond national jurisdictional boundaries. This is nothing new: international trade and other aspects of economic and political relations began to grow among nations centuries ago. The field of international relations is an outgrowth of such a development. The internationalization of public administration is not new either, though it gained momentum after World War II, when both the United States and the Soviet Union internationalized their satellite nations and, in turn, the ways in which public administration was thought about and practiced. The rise of the United Nations and its affiliate agencies also promoted internationalization. The birth and growth of the Comparative Administration Group (CAG) was the outcome of this development (Waldo, 1980; Riggs, 1998).

Globalization as border openness. This means large-scale openness of borders achieved by removing state regulatory barriers and protectionist measures, thus facilitating rapid financial transactions, communications, trade, and cultural relationships (Brown, 1992). Such a borderless world would be characterized by a unified global economy, global government, homogenous global culture, and, by implication, a global system of public administration (Scholte, 1997). The Internet and other means of information technology have contributed to this phenomenon beyond comprehension. Globalization of public administration has meant "thinking globally and acting locally." The concepts of the "new world" (Cleveland, 1993), the "global village" (Garcia-Zamor and Khator, 1994), and "global management" (Wilson, 1994) seem to characterize this notion of globalization and its implications for public administration.

This notion of globalization, however, is also limited and deficient in that it is synonymous with liberalization. The anticameralists raised it in favor of capitalist development, and the classical liberals raised it against statism in the nineteenth century. The liberal internationalists raised it against the doctrine of balance of power in the early twentieth century, and the transnationalists raised it against the "realist" view of nationalist and state sovereignty proclamations in international relations (Scholte, 1997), not to mention the internationalist mission and claims of socialists led by the USSR.

The concept is also redundant because the liberalization of borders for a new world has been around for many decades, especially among the satellite nations of the West led by the United States, such as the developing countries of Latin America, Asia, Africa, and the Middle East. Regulatory, labor, and administrative policies have always been concessionary toward multinational corporations operating profitable businesses in the Third World (Heeger, 1974; Bill and Springborg, 1990; LaFeber, 1984; Mandel, 1983; Halliday, 1989; Dos Santos, 1996; Frank, 1996; Farazmand, 1989, 1991; and Henderson, 1994). Again, CAG and other international public administration consulting groups have been active in less developed nations, and publications on comparative and development administration have produced voluminous literature attesting to this phenomenon.

Globalization as a process. Using a political economy view, this notion refers to globalization not as a phenomenon, but as a process—a continuing process of capital accumulation in modern capitalism that has been going on for centuries. Only recently has it intensified as a result of the availability of modern technology. Therefore, this view is also not new. The beginning of this globalization process goes back to the nineteenth and early twentieth centuries and was marked by the transition from early (competitive) capitalism to late (monopoly) capitalism, which was boosted by the two world wars and produced capitalism's "golden age" (1950–1970) at the height of the Cold War. Capitalism, this view contends, is "in its innermost essence an expanding system both internally and externally. Once rooted, it both grows and spreads" (Sweezy, 1997, 1). Beginning with the recession of 1974–1975, three trends have contributed to the accelerated rate of capital accumulation at the global level: a decreasing growth rate, the "worldwide proliferation of monopolistic (or oligopolistic) multinational corporation[s]," and the "financialization of the capital accumulation process" (Sweezy, 1997, 1–2). This view tells us little about the changing role of the state and public administration, especially under the new global order.

Globalization as ideology. The ideological underpinnings of Western capitalist democracy have acted as a driving force behind the globalization of American and Western European liberal democracy. The wealth of information—including propaganda—spread throughout the world by the media, the press, computers, and satellite communication systems offers an image of an ideal political system for other countries to emulate. The key words *freedom, individualism, free enterprise,* and *plural democracy* have characterized this ideological force of globalization (Lindblom, 1977, 1990). Important and effective as it may have been, this normative force of globalization says little about the political economy of the state and public administration.

Globalization as a phenomenon. As a cause-and-effect phenomenon in late capitalism, this perspective treats globalization as a cause of world capitalism's endless effort to reach global markets for accelerated accumulation of capital during the stagnant era of the 1970s. Globalization has produced significant consequences for the state and other institutions, whose territorial borders have "not so much crossed or opened as transcended. Here, 'global' phenomena are those that extend across widely dispersed locations simultaneously. Territorial distance and territorial borders hold limited significance in these circumstances; the globe becomes a single 'place' in its own right" (Scholte, 1997, 431). This view of globalization is useful for understanding global changes in the political economy of nations. It also considers the world as a global village and offers significant explanatory power. Yet, it gives limited weight to the role of the modern state and public administration in causing globalization. It also tells little about the future role of the state, institutional elites, and public administration in such a global "place." It tells nothing about the dialectical counterforces of change exerted from below.

Globalization as both a transcending phenomenon and a process. Sharing with and building upon the previous meanings, this perspective considers globalization to be a process of accumulation by global capitalism—a constant process of expansion into new frontiers and opportunities for increasing capital accumulation at the global level. It also views globalization as a phenomenon caused by the process of global capital accumulation—a phenomenon that has manifested its negative and positive effects almost everywhere. The impact has even been felt by the powerful nations of the West and Japan, where most, if not all, of the transcending organizations of capital accumulation have homebases and are backed by their globally dominant states. Unlike the Third World countries, which have been plagued by the devastating effects of globalization by multinational and transnational corporations for decades, the peoples, institutions, and communities of the advanced industrial countries of the North did not experience the impact of globalization until recently.

It is this qualitative change, spurred by the new globalization process, that has caused concerns and led to "new consequences" for the nation-states in the dominant West. Therefore, this perspective of globalization is rather novel and complementary to the views noted above, in that it adds an innovative dimension to the concept. It considers the state as an active institutional player in the process of globalization and in dealing with its consequences. Other factors, such as information technology, also have been effective. Here, in the new global community, the changing role of the administrative state and public administration is explored as both a cause and an effect.

Causes of Globalization

To avoid oversimplification, the process and phenomenon of globalization are not treated here solely in terms of advance capitalism, though that has been a major contributing factor. Indeed, several factors have contributed to the process of globalization, including surplus accumulation of corporate capital, the role of the dominant states and their bureaucracies, domestic constraints, rising human expectations, international institutions, and technological innovations.

Economic factors of surplus accumulation. The most important factor contributing to the globalization of capitalism has been the driving force of surplus accumulation that has crossed territorial borders and transcended national boundaries for decades. It accelerated after World War II and reached a high point after the 1970s, reaching its zenith in the 1990s. Surplus (or profit) accumulation is the lifeblood of capitalism, which needs constant expansion at any cost; hence the continuity of dynamic capitalism. Globalization has been a central feature of transnational corporations (also called multinationals), which have for many decades reached global markets and enjoyed cheap labor in less developed nations. What is *new* is the rapidity and high rate of surplus accumulation, made possible by a number of mechanisms, as well as the transworld mobility of corporations in a spaceless and timeless global place facilitated by the state. Borrowing from Scholte's (1997) list of factors, these mechanisms are briefly explained below.

Global marketing. In search of new markets, cheap labor, and unrestricted production sites, many multinationals and transnational corporations have decided to "go global." The movement out of the Snow Belt into the Sun Belt of the antiunion South, still in progress, has boosted surplus accumulation. But more American corporations found globalization a much faster and more profitable strategy. Global consumerism began to flourish, with monied consumers around the planet being able "to purchase the same goods at the same time," and coordinated corporate research and development activities produced new economies of scale beyond the reach of individual corporations (Modelski, 1979). These activities produced high profit rates and a significant upturn for globalizing firms and the home states supporting them. By 1989, the cost of corporate advertising reached $240 billion, in addition to the $380 billion spent on packaging, design, and promotion (During, 1992, 171–172). In 1992, almost all of the 40 largest advertising firms in Great Britain and the United States had specialized departments with global commercials (Sklair, 1995; Scholte, 1997, 433). By the 1990s, the corporate conviction that globalization "is not a luxury any more, it's a necessity" was expressed in the *Wall Street Journal* (September 26, R1).

Global production, with its reduced costs, also has begun to replace national production. Globalization of finance has facilitated this process and has produced "global sourcing," through which a production company can draw its components and materials from anywhere in the world. With the globalization of financial capital, it has become possible "to produce a product anywhere, using resources from anywhere, by a company located anywhere, to be sold anywhere" (Friedman, 1994; also cited in Naisbitt, 1994, 19; Scholte, 1997, 435). The result is a "global factory" in which different countries host different production activities, supply cheap labor and materials, and absorb all social and external costs associated with global production.

Global commodification of new items has transformed social as well as economic life worldwide. Traditional tangible trades and industries have shifted toward "intangibles" (Scholte, 1997, 436) which are considered new, unique, or different, and are appealing to global consumers, such as folk songs and cultural and ethnic features (Mele, 1996).

Reorganization of corporate structure. The rise and expansion of transworld corporations has resulted in vertical as well as horizontal organizational restructuring; this has led to a concentration of corporate power at the global level and the creation of a global ruling class (Korten, 1995; Brown, 1992; Brecher and Costello, 1994). The number of global corporations increased from 3,500 in 1960 to 40,000 in 1995, representing 40 percent of the world's total commerce (UNCTAD, 1996, ix). Vertically, the number of strategic alliances between globalizing enterprises have risen, and the global waves of successive mergers and acquisitions have produced a full-scale "fusion," reaching 6,000 in 1995, with an aggregate value of $229.4 billion (*Financial Times,* Jan. 20, 22). In fact, "mergermania" and "mega-merger" trends have produced a globally centralized organization and a concentrated power structure in which the largest 300 transnationals control 70 percent of all foreign direct investment and almost one third of the total assets of all corporations around the world (Dunning, 1993, 15; Harvey, 1995, 189).

This concentrated global corporate structure has also produced a globalizing cadre of "managerial elites," as well as a new level of "organizational elite" that tend to influence public policy and administrative decisions virtually anywhere on the planet. These global elites produce a global "organizational culture" (Pascale, 1984): they play governments against governments and stage coup d'ètats or counterinsurgencies against governments unsympathetic to them (Parenti, 1995; Korten, 1995).

Global money and financialization. Global money has no loyalty or attachment to any space, nation, or community of people. Unlike in the past, when money and its distribution were mainly territorial and promoted domestic communities—jobs, opportunities, commercial activities, community values—global money has now loosened its link to territorial finance, facilitated by the cyberspace of banking computers. In 1995, "over $9 trillion of the world's bank assets belonged to depositors non-resident in the country where the account was held and/or were denominated in a currency issued outside that country" (Scholte, 1997, 439–440). Global financialization has been accelerated (Sweezy, 1997) with the help of "cyberpolitiks," changing the "nature of power in the information age" (Rothkopf, 1998, 325).

Global state and administration. Ironically, capitalism needs a strong state and a stable environment to prosper. It demands order and social control (Weber, 1947; Offe, 1985). The globally dominant governments, particularly the United States and its European partners, have played an active role in promoting globalization of capital throughout this century. These governments have allocated large amounts of public expenditures to military and security systems to protect and promote corporate capital accumulation in less-developed nations, as well as in domestic marketplaces. They have intervened militarily in many countries, replaced legitimate governments, and installed and supported some of the most repressive and corrupt regimes in the world. Examples include Chile in the 1970s, Iran in the 1950s, and Indonesia in the 1960s (Parenti, 1995; Greenberg, 1986; LaFeber, 1984; Halliday, 1979).

Especially since World War II, Western governments have exported their ideologies, value systems, and systems of governance and administration as ideal models by using state-of-the-art communication systems. By conducting direct and proxy wars of intervention and invasions in Asia, Latin America, Africa, and the Middle East, American corporate interests were sought (Brown, 1992; Gill and Law, 1988; Korten, 1995; Bill and Springborg, 1990) and justified as protection of American global interests (Ball, 1967; Hamilton, 1989; Murphy, 1988).

The efficient functioning of the market depends on strong governments (Daly and Cobb, 1989). Capitalism needs a strong state and bureaucracy to flourish, and powerful business elites dominate the policy process and affect its outcomes (Jones, 1983; Lindblom, 1990). To protect the system from periodic collapse and to provide safety nets for promoting capitalist development, market failures demand government intervention in the economy (Burkhead and Miner, 1971; Parenti, 1995; Korten, 1995; Singer and Wildavsky, 1993). Thus, the modern state has, through public expenditures, played a pivotal role in the accelerated development of both capitalism and globalization for a new world order. However, in fairness to these systems, they also have spent significant portions of their budgets to finance the welfare state (Gilbert, 1983) to produce a balance of social and economic actions, a balance that was not acceptable to corporate elites (Henry, 1995).

Domestic decline. The 1970s were plagued by the domestic economic downturn marked by stagflation, energy crisis, budget deficits, political and presidential crises, a confidence-gap crisis in both corporate and governmental elite performance (Lipset, 1987; Rosenbloom, 1995; Henry, 1995), and general organizational decline and cutback management (Levine, 1978, 1980; Peters, 1991). These problems were accompanied by citizen tax revolts and the rising expectations of employee unions in corporate and public sectors. These domestic upsets were compounded by international challenges posed to the United States and other Western powers by revolutions in Iran and Nicaragua. The net result was that the state faced a legitimacy crisis of its own. It was unable to contribute to accelerated capital accumulation *and* to perform the increasingly costly social welfare function that was contributing to its "fiscal crisis" (O'Connor, 1973; Arrow, 1963; Heidenheimer et al., 1983, 330). These events, in turn, drove more corporations toward globalization.

Rising human expectations. The expectations of the general populace have been rising, particularly those of the employee unions; this has become evident by the unions' demands for "property rights" in jobs, greater participation in management of enterprises, the emerging role of women in the workforce, and so on. The corporate power structure has called many of these expectations of public- and private-sector employees unsuitable for their purpose of profit making. Moreover, the many lawsuits stemming from the Equal Employment Opportunity Act have encouraged more corporations to operate in outside global factories with cheap labor and little or no legal constraints. All of this has contributed to globalization.

Innovations. Innovations in information technology, communications and transportation systems, and the Internet have contributed significantly to the globalization phenomenon (Welch and Wong, 1998; Savitch, 1998). As Bill Gates (1995) of Microsoft promises, a future "shoppers' heaven" in cyberspace seems to provide a place where "all the goods for sale in the world will be available from home via Internet" (158).

United Nations agencies. The United Nations itself has been a major factor in globalization. Since the 1970s, its key affiliated organizations, such as the World Bank, the International Monetary Fund (IMF), and the World Trade Organization

(WTO), have been powerful instruments in this process, which has been dominated and controlled primarily by the Trilaterals (the United States, some West European governments, and the Japanese), the key donors of international aid. In the last two decades, these supranational organizations have played an effective role in globalization through "structural adjustment" requirements dictated to the poor and less-developed nations desperately seeking international aid (Chan, 1996).

A key feature of the structural adjustment program is the major reforms to the regulatory, financial, and administrative schemes imposed on those countries. These reforms have included massive privatization and promotion of the subsidiary private sector, removal of trade and other barriers, tax incentives for corporate operations, favorable labor laws allowing for unrestrained use of cheap labor, an emphasis on export-oriented production and economic growth versus development, and a reduction of government's role in the economy (Hancock, 1989; Korten, 1995; Gill and Law, 1991; Brown, 1992).

Consequences of Globalization

Globalization has facilitated connection and coordination among peoples, governments, and nongovernmental organizations. Global accessibility is a giant positive step toward human advancements. Yet, globalization is building the foundation of a new civilization characterized by many paradoxes. Not all states have been affected by or responded to globalization equally. This process has moved much faster in North America, East Asia, Western Europe, and Australia than in the rest of Asia and Europe, Africa, and Latin America. Nevertheless, the globalization of capital, politics, administration, and culture has affected virtually every nation; no country has been left untouched. For our purposes, the following discussion focuses only on the consequences of globalization for the state and for public administration. These consequences are discussed in the context of both developed and less-developed nations and their public administration.

Continuity and persistence of the state. Globalization has not brought about the end of the state and its bureaucracy; nor will it result in a decline of the state in the future. The territorial state as a sociopolitical identity will continue to exist, as it has for several millennia. The relationship between market and politics, capitalism and the state, the private- and public-sector management has been an intimate one. The relationship continues to exist because public administration and civilization, including capitalist civilization, have coexisted and promoted one another (Waldo, 1980/1992) with a bureaucracy that has also survived millennia of political and economic changes (Heady, 1996; Farazmand, 1998a, 1996b).

However, globalization has also caused major changes in the character of the modern state (Heady, 1998; Caiden, 1994; Esman, 1999; Scholte, 1997). At least five such major changes may be discerned. First is the reinforcement of supraterritorial governance organizations such as the IMF, the World Bank, and the WTO, whose decisions and codes of conduct are binding over the nation-states affecting their administrative systems. The second is the increasing degree of interdependence among modern states to handle territorial and supraterritorial issues and to seek cooperation for a host of matters of general interest, such as the alarming concern for the global environment and the viability of ecological sustainability. Here, the concepts of the global village, global environment, and global citizenship are among the emerging concerns that are pressed on all states and their public administration practices (Khator, 1994; Brown, 1992).

The third change is that all states have gained the information-age advantages to process information for almost all functions of governance and administration, both domestic and international, though less-developed nations will continue to trail behind for a while. More noteworthy is the increased military and technological capability of the dominant states, especially the United States, to globally dominate the world from both the earth and space—hence a global hegemony. The fourth change is the growing role of governments as partners with and promoters of the private sectors, often at the expense of public goods and services. Under forces of globalization, "the role of government is progressively shifting toward providing an appropriate enabling environment for private [corporate] enterprise" (UNCTAD, 1996, ICla22).

The fifth, and perhaps the most important change for public administrators, is the shift of the administrative state from a welfare state to a corporate state (Parenti, 1995; Korten, 1995) or "shadow state" (Wolch, 1990), "indifferent state," "contracting state" (Bowls and Wagman, 1997; Rathgeb and Lipsky, 1993), or "entrepreneurial state" (Eisinger, 1988). Corresponding changes in the nature of public administration and management have been characterized by such terms as "managerialism," "political management," "new public management," and the "hollow state" (Milward, 1994) or "the corporate administrative state" (Farazmand, 1997a, b).

Similarly, public administration will continue to persist as both a self-conscious enterprise and a professional field. Research and development in public administration may be negatively affected by globalization to some extent, but the continuity of the field of enquiry is intact; all states are needed for globalizing capitalism, and all states have public administration functions that cannot and will not be dismantled. The changing character of public administration as a field of enquiry, however, is manifest in its recent and current debate over the role of the state and the explorations into philosophical, institutional, organizational, and practical underpinnings in search of identity (Peters, 1997; Rockman, 1997). Correspondingly, the twin fields of comparative and developmental public administration have been filled with the shifting debate over the nature and size of the state and public administration in developing knowledge and building theoretical generalizations (Heady, 1998; Riggs, 1998). Similar changes have been observed in practical dimensions of the state and public administration.

The orientation and the role of the globalizing state have changed as a result of globalizing corporate capitalism. Unlike the welfare administrative state, which tended to balance corporate/market interests with social and political interests for several decades during the Cold War, the role of the new corporate welfare administrative state features several characteristics. These include the shrinking of the stabilizing welfare state as we know it; the expansion of the security and military or warfare state; and the expansion of the coercive bureaucracy—police, prisons, court systems, and their auxiliary functions such as social works, psychological networks, and counseling. Thus, the state and bureaucracy are actually alive and well (Korten, 1995; Lowi, 1995; Parenti, 1995; Farazmand, 1997a, b, c). However, equity and fairness may have been the casualties of corporate greed and globalization of capital (Farazmand, 1997a, b).

Negative consequences of globalization. The negative consequences of globalization are many: they include the diminished or lost sovereignty of states, constraints on democracy, loss of community, concentration of the global power structure, increased centralization of corporate and government organizational elites, and increased dependency among less-developed nations on globalizing powers.

Threat to state sovereignty. Sovereign statehood depends on territoriality, fixed locations, and supreme authority over land space, and sea (Helleiner, 1994; Scholte, 1997). But the pivotal role of the state in globalizing capitalism has, at the same time, threatened state identity by putting its "sovereignty at bay" (Vernon, 1971). Challenges to sovereignty mean a loss of unilateral ability by nation-states to exercise comprehensive macroeconomic policy. Many states have surrendered their national policy-making ability to regional or international organizations for collaborating with globalization efforts. Some governments have even revised their constitutions in the interest of regional collaboration (for example, Italy, Portugal, and Spain in the European Community, and Latin American countries are considering similar actions toward the Transamerican community). Since the 1970s, the IMF, the World Bank, and the WTO have enforced more authoritative measures on the monetary and fiscal policies of less-developed member countries. The structural adjustment programs mentioned above have forced these countries into reforms and changes that have deepened their dependency on globalizing corporations and their dominant governments.

By 1994, the World Bank had sought to "provide $200 billion to the Third World in the next decade to promote the private sector" (Milman and Lundstedt, 1994, 1667). Such international loans carry both cross-conditions and crossover conditions that deepen the financial, military, political, and economic dependency on Western powers and globalizing power elites, who can easily dictate policy choices to poor and less-developed nations. Such money usually enriches the host country's power elites at the expense of millions of people. It is also true that most foreign aid and international loans are returned to donor countries (Hudson, 1971). As Korten (1995) states, the "Bank-approved consultants often rewrite a country's trade policy, fiscal policy, civil service requirements, labor laws, health care arrangements, environmental regulations, energy policy, resettlement requirements, procurement rules, and budgetary policy" (165). Hancock (1989) calls the Bank leaders the "lords of poverty" leading global policy directions through "organizational elites" (Farazmand, 1997a, b) who execute the policy preferences of the "inner circle," global corporate elites (Useem, 1984; Domhoff, 1970).

Threat to democracy and community. The rise and expansion of globalizing capital pose a serious threat to democratic ideas around the globe. The very fact that global organizations such as the IMF, the World Bank, and the WTO, as well as a few transnational elites, prescribe and dictate fiscal, monetary, and other structural adjustment policies to poor and less-developed countries is, in a way, a negation of local democracy. People in these nations do not and cannot exercise their human and civil rights to determine their own policy preferences; their national and human interests are sacrificed to the interests of the dominant powers (Hancock, 1989). Globalization has resulted in deepening poverty, social disintegration, and environmental destruction. Globalization of corporations in these nations has resulted in the destruction of domestic production economics in favor of export-oriented, cash-crop activities and global interests. People in most of these nations have been struggling with repressive regimes and politico-administrative elites who are supported by global corporations and the Western democracies, including the United States (Cottam, 1979; LaFeber, 1984; Mander and Goldsmith, 1996).

Conversely, the threat to domestic Western democracy is also real when global corporations close factories overnight and take their business overseas without consulting local communities (Wilson, 1997), or when foreign investments in domestic enterprises are made without input from local communities. Local people have lost control of their communities (Mele, 1997; Korten, 1995, 22). Community displacement is a bitter pill that millions of farmers in many less-developed nations have been tasting for several decades. Self-sufficient farmers who contributed to their community and to the national economy have been forced out and dispossessed by globalizing agribusiness and agroindustry, which have had the full support of subservient governments and administrative elites. These farmers' migration to cities to seek undignified wage-earning jobs has only exacerbated existing urban problems (Chan, 1996; Helmut, 1975; Hoogland, 1970; McCoy, 1971; LaFeber, 1984; Farazmand, 1989, 1991b). However, such problems of displacement are justified by modernization theorists such as Huntington (1968). Similar charges of globalization focus attention on the "global pillage" (Brecher, 1993; Mander and Goldsmith, 1996) and "modern slavery" in "sweatshops behind the labels" (Udesky, 1994, 666–668), creating a "race to the bottom in which wages and social conditions tend to fall to the level of the most desperate" (Brescher, 1993, 685–688).

Globalizing managerial elites are making colonizing decisions that affect governments, communities, and peoples around the globe, and human beings are reduced to consumers of global markets. Contrary to some rational choice theorists (Buchanan and Tullock, 1962; Mueller, 1989), market and democracy are not synonymous; in fact, they are in serious conflict with each other (Lindblom, 1977; Macpherson, 1987). "Exporting democracy" has been a favorite slogan under the new world order and globalization (Lowenthal, 1991; Huntington, 1991). But the record shows that the great capitalist democracies of the West, including the United States, have supported "some of the most repressive and exploitative dictatorships" around the globe (Kitschell, 1992), forcing millions of people in less-developed nations to stage bloody revolutions (Magdoff, 1969; Schultz and Slater, 1990; Farazmand, 1989).

Equating democracy with market is both misleading and dangerous. It is misleading because their values clash in many ways. As Heilbroner (1990) notes, "it is of course foolish to suggest that capitalism is the *sine qua non* of democracy, or to claim that democracy, with its commitment to political equality, does not conflict in many ways with the inequalities built into capitalism" (105). Markets are inherently biased in favor of wealthy people, who may not necessarily realize the needs of a healthy society. With economic and political power concentrated in a few global corporations and government elites, policy choices are "impaired" (Lindblom, 1990), and it is increasingly difficult to exercise freedom of choice and to enjoy protected individual rights (Dugger, 1989). Global corporations are extremely difficult, if not impossible, to hold accountable. As Korten (1995) notes, "it is impossible to have healthy, equitable, and democratic societies when political and economic power is concentrated in a few gigantic corporations" (181).

Equating democracy with market is dangerous for two reasons. First, the equation is applied inconsistently around the world—friendly dictators are praised for promoting globalizing corporate enterprises and are considered democratic, whereas legitimate socialist and indigenously oriented capitalist governments that are not so friendly to global corporations are considered undemocratic (Gibbs, 1991; Hamilton, 1989). Second, it raises false expectations of democratic rights among people in less-developed nations who live under repressive regimes supported by Western democracies.

Corruption and elite empowerment. Globalization pushes privatization as a part of structural-adjustment programs, empowers the growing subsidiary elites (subservient comprador bourgeoisie) as agents of transworld corporations, and promotes corruption in less- as well as more-developed nations. Such corruption at the highest levels has already reached the point of national crisis. For example, Chile has been touted as a model of privatized economy, when in fact one-third of the population lives in miserable poverty, while the military-bureaucratic-business elites enjoy world-class lifestyles (Rehren, 1999; Gould, 1991). Similar problems are reported in the United States (see Henry, 1995; Thayer, 1984). Other studies refer to globalization- and privatization-induced corruption among elites at high levels around the world (Jreisat, 1997; Eisner, 1995; Farazmand, 1996a).

Elite empowerment leads to a new global organizational structure with the characteristics of a global "corporate empire" that requires flexibility in its giant transformation of the world power structure. It calls for concentration without centralization, similar to colonialism, with four elements: (1) downsizing to organizational core competencies; (2) computerization and automation; (3) mergers, acquisitions, and strategic alliances; and (4) headquarters teamwork and morale among core personnel (Harrison, 1993). This transformation draws a clear demarcation between the elites and the nonelites, the latter seen as expendable commodities (Dugger, 1989). Globalization empowers elite dominance under the new world order in which hegemonic theory prevails along with the globalization of capital (Korten, 1995). What, then, are the implications of globalization and the new world order for public administration?

Implications for Public Administration

The following paragraphs highlight the challenges facing public administration and offer suggestions for public administrators across the world.

1. There has been a major change in the configuration of public-private spheres in favor of the globalizing corporate sector. The leading economic role of the government and the public sector in the allocation of resources, the equitable distribution of wealth, the stabilization of economy, and economic growth has been overruled by the globalizing corporate elites. With the fall of the Soviet Union and increasing globalization, as well as the fiscal crisis of the state, the traditional administrative state has come under attack from all fronts, but especially from the corporate elites who no longer see a need for the welfare state. Therefore, the dismantling of the administrative welfare state has had negative consequences for public administration and citizens. The "public sphere" and the space for citizen involvement have been shrinking as a result of globalization and government restructuring (Rockman, 1997; Habermas, 1974; Offe, 1985). Public administrators should resist shrinking this realm of public service by engaging citizens in the administration of public affairs and by playing a proactive role in managing societal resources away from the dominant control of globalizing corporate elites. Their future legitimacy will be based on this action.

2. A bigger challenge lies in the change in the character and activities of the state and of public administration from "civil administration to non-civil administration" (Farazmand, 1997a, b). For several decades, the traditional administrative state balanced corporate elite interests with broad public interests, thus providing the social and political stability necessary for capital accumulation and system legitimacy. And it played a key role in system maintenance and regime enhancement. Now, the balanced administrative state has been replaced by the corporate-coercive state, which is characterized by a massively growing coercive bureaucracy in charge of incarcerating millions of citizens considered potential threats to social order. These citizen threats are created by market chaos under economic and social pressures caused by globalization and marketization (Schneider, 1993; Farazmand, 1997a, b, c). The criminalization of society is finding many victims among the most respected, hard-working citizens, who are trapped in unbearable socioeconomic conditions (Davey, 1995; Lowi, 1996). As a result, public administration is being transformed from traditional civil administration to noncivil administration of the "public"—not their affairs—for social control and facilitation of capital accumulation. This is a major change in the character of the state and should be resisted by all public administrators with a social conscience.

3. The globalizing state has forced public administration to do more with less. Indeed, public administrators must perform the impossible task of high output under severe psychological conditions of fear and downsized personnel, setting them up for failure only to prove the corporate claims of government inefficiency.

Public administrators can and should document their records of high performance as well as the failures of the corporate marketplace.

4. By extension, the professionalization of public administration is a response to the challenge of globalization. Professionalization brings both institutional and moral and ethical standards to public service at the global level, exposing the fallacies of globalizing transnational elites while learning from their organizational and technical skills. The excesses of globalization and market failure will invite more government intervention. A professionally sound public administration should be ready for future action.

5. Globalization pushes for increased privatization, which promotes greater opportunities for corruption (Gould, 1991). Corruption has turned societal resources into illegal, immoral, and unproductive activities. It also challenges the very foundations of societal health and destroys citizens' trust in leadership and system legitimacy. Privatization is based on the market-based, rational choice theory of self-interested individualism in search of maximizing self-interests at almost any cost to community and society. This behavioral and normative philosophy puts individual interests above the interests of the community and society (Bellah et al., 1991; Triandis, 1995); this is exactly what the globalizing transnational companies are trying to promote in order to build a global culture of consumerism that converges national cultures into a global culture (Schein, 1985). This global corporate culture is, in part, managed through human resources management practices, many of which are in sharp contrast with national and community cultures (Laurent, 1986). Public administrators must resist the market-based concepts of treating citizens as consumers and degrading them to market commodities.

6. Globalization tends to promote elitism and enriches elites—business, political, military, and managerial—most of whom operate as "subsidiaries" (Schneider, 1993) or agents of transnational corporations. The personal and career interests of these "global soldiers" generally override national and community interests; they actually become "corporate mercenaries" (Edstrom and Galbraith, 1977) and promote "cultural imperialism" (Said, 1993). People in less-developed nations are familiar with these subservient elites, who seem to rise to power and wealth overnight at the expense of millions. Because the globalizing governments are actively involved in corporate globalization through the implementation of public-private partnership programs with globalizing firms, public administrators and administrative consultants are challenged by the implications of this aspect of globalization. Many elites in less-developed nations run repressive regimes which violate the human rights of their own people. American advisors and consultants often enhance the domination of these bureaucratic elites—both military and civilian—over their own society in less-developed countries (Riggs, 1994, 36; Said, 1993; Parenti, 1995). Paradoxically, globalization has produced a massive concentration of corporate power and has centralized its organizational structure while at the same time governmental decentralization has been promoted across the world.

7. Globalization threatens communities (Korten, 1995) and "public spiritedness"—to borrow Frederickson's 1997 term—by removing local control and making irrelevant the participatory role of citizens and local public administrators

to make significant decisions that affect people's lives. Local governments' ability to forecast revenue bases will be undermined as global firms close operations overnight for more profitable locations (Eisner, 1995; Mander and Goldsmith, 1996). Public administrators should try to minimize such uncertainties by attaching long-term strings to dealings with global corporations. They should also build a sense of community, encourage citizen involvement in administration, and foster values of citizenship and community/public interest in balance against rugged self-interest. And they should treat citizens with respect and efficiency.

8. There is a growing knowledge explosion in public administration and related fields, including in its subfields of comparative and international administration (Savitch, 1998). I agree with Ferrel Heady's (1998) statement that these two subfields have been separately and disjointedly promoted in the past decades. There is a new subfield of globalization in town now, and there is a need to integrate the studies of public administration from the comparative, international, and global perspectives. ASPA members are challenged to undertake this new endeavor to produce materials that will help to generate generalizations across global spaces. Practitioners will be enlightened by the exposure to these needed studies and will likely be better administrators in the future global village.

9. Learning more about public administration from a comparative perspective broadens our world outlook. American students and scholars can broaden their personal and professional worldviews by appreciating the cultural, institutional, and religious underpinnings of the administrative cultures of less-developed nations, some of which have rich cultural and governance heritages. Globalization challenges the American parochial and ethnocentric tradition of public administration and shatters the politics-administration dichotomy while providing immense opportunities for consultancy and corporate-related public management practices in less-developed countries. Learning about other peoples, cultures, and public administration contributes to further "knowledge explosion." Already, rich administrative traditions exist around the world to which Americans have not been exposed. Examples include Scandinavian and Soviet systems of public administration (Caiden, 1994), as well as the systems of cooperatives in which democratic administration can be fostered. Similarly, Americans and other global citizens can learn about public administration under other indigenous systems. Comparative study of governance and public administration is not new and has a long tradition dating back to ancient times (Heady, 1996; Farazmand, 1996b); its focus for global studies of administration should be the agendas of the Section on International and Comparative Administration (SICA) of the American Society for Public Administration in the twenty-first century.

10. Globalization challenges the human conscience of the public administration community. Professional citizens of the global community have the opportunity—and the responsibility—to observe and examine what is happening around the corners of their global community. There are many issues that challenge their conscience, including the conditions and deprivations of the poor, wage slavery and sweatshops in global factories, environmental destruction, global warming, and inequity and injustice. Raising consciousness about global issues, both positive and negative, is both important and necessary, as public administrators can make a

difference when making decisions that affect their fellow citizens. They can question the sincerity of the elites, oppose exploitation, and resist being used for undemocratic, unjust, and inequitable purposes around the globe. In the 1980s, public administrators played an effective role in the globally successful campaign against South Africa's regime of apartheid. Raising such a global consciousness can challenge destructive forces of globalization and global elites on various grounds. The Internet and other communication systems can help administrators communicate globally with fellow professionals in outlying areas.

11. As guardians of "global community interests," public administrators in more- and less-developed nations have a global responsibility to act ethically and morally in a coordinated manner. They must expose and fight corruption at any level and at any time. Political appointees and politicians are temporal officials, many of whom have intimate financial and personal ties with global corporate elites; they are prone to corruption and abuse of authority, and their definition of public interest is narrow and aimed at the powerful constituencies.

12. Globalization does not end the state and public administration. There is a new global challenge that broadens public administration's scope of research, practice, and teaching. Public administration has just entered a new stage of human civilization, with a future that is both brightened and darkened by globalization and the hegemonic world order. We hope that prosperity for all will be the outcome.

References

Arrow, Kenneth (1963). *Social Choice and Individual Values.* New Haven: Yale University Press.

Ball, George (1967). "Cosmocorporations: The Importance of Being Stateless." *Columbia Journal of World Business* 2 (6).

Bellah, Robert, Richard Madsen, William Sullivan, Ann Swidler, and Steven Tipton (1985). *Habits of the Heart: Individualism and Commitment in American Life.* Berkeley, CA: University of California Press.

Bill, James, and Robert Springborg (1990). *Politics in the Middle East,* 3rd ed. New York: HarperCollins.

Boyer, Robert, and Daniel Drache, eds. (1996). *States Against Markets: The Limits of Globalization.* London: Routledge.

Brecher, Jeremy and Tim Costello (1994). *Global Village or Global Pillage: Economic Reconstruction From the Bottom Up.* Boston, MA: South End Press.

Brown, Seyom (1992). *International Relations in a Changing Global System: Toward a Theory of World Polity.* Boulder, CO: Westview Press.

Burkhead, Jesse, and Jerry Miner (1971). *Public Expenditures.* New York: Macmillan.

Caiden, Gerald (1994). "Globalizing the Theory and Practice of Public Administration." In Jean-Claude Garcia-Zamor and Renu Khator, eds. *Public Administration in the Global Village.* Westport, CT: Praeger, 45–59.

Cerny, Philip G. (1995). "Globalization and the Changing Logic of Collective Action." *International Organization* 49 (Aummn): 595–625.

Chan, Johnathan (1996). "Challenging the New Imperial Authority: The World Bank and the Democratization of Development." *Harvard Human Rights Journal,* 6.

Chilcote, R. and D. Johnson, eds. (1983). *Theories of Development.* Beverly Hills, CA: Sage.

Cleveland, Harlan (1993). *Birth of a New World: An Open Moment for International Leadership.* San Francisco, CA: Jossey-Bass Publishers.

Cottam, Richard (1979). "Goodbye to America's Shah." *Foreign Policy* (34): 3–14.

Cox, R. W. (1993). "Structural Issues of Global Governance." In S. Gill, Ed. *Gramci, Historical Materialism, and International Relations.* Cambridge: Cambridge University Press, 259–89.

Daly, Harman and John Cobb (1989). *For the Common Good: Redirecting the Economy Toward Commitment, the Environment, and the Sustainable Future.* Boston: Beacon Press.

Davey, Joseph (1995). *The New Social Contract: America's Journey from Welfare State to Police State.* Westport, CT: Praeger.

Domhoff, William (1970). *The Higher Circles.* New York: Random House.

Dugger, William (1989). *Corporate Hegemony.* New York: Greenwood Press.

Dunning, J. H. (1993). *The Globalization of Business: The Challenge of the 1990s.* London: Routledge.

During, Alan (1992). *How Much is Enough: The Consumer Society and the Future of the Earth.* New York: W. W. Norton.

Edstrom, A., and J. Galbraith (1977). "Transfer of Managers as Coordination of and Control Strategy in Multinational Organizations." *Administrative Science Quarterly* 22: 248–263.

Eisinger, Peter (1988). *The Rise of the Entrepreneurial State: State and Local Development Policy in the United States.* Madison, WI: University of Wisconsin Press.

Eisner, Mark (1995). *The State in the American Political Economy.* Englewood Cliffs, NJ: Prentice-Hall.

Esman, Milton (2000). "The State, Government Bureaucracies, and their Alternatives." In Ali Farazmand, ed., *Handbook of Comparative and Development Public Administration,* 2nd ed. New York: Marcel Dekker.

Falk, Richard (1997). "States of Siege: Will Globalization Win Out? *International Affairs* 73 (January).

Farazmand, Ali (1989). *The State, Bureaucracy, and Revolution in Modern Iran: Agrarian Reform and Regime Politics.* New York. Praeger.

———, ed. (1991a). *Handbook of Comparative and Development Public Administration.* New York: Marcel Dekker.

——— (1991b). "Globalization of Agrarian Reforms: The Role of Multinational Corporations." Paper presented at the World Congress of the International Political Science Association, Buenos Aires, Argentina, July 21–26.

——— (1994). "The New World Order and Global Public Administration: A Critical Essay." In Jean-Claude Garcia-Zamor and Renu Khator, eds., *Public Administration in the Global Village.* Westport, CT: Praeger, 62–81.

——— (1996a). "Introduction: The Comparative State of Public Enterprise Management." In Ali Farazmand, ed. *Public Enterprise Management: International Case Studies.* Westport, CT: Greenwood Press, 1–27.

——— (1996b). "Development and Comparative Public Administration: Past, Present, and Future." *Public Administration Quarterly* 20(3): 343–364.

——— (1997a). "From Civil to Non-Civil Administration: The Biggest Challenge to the State and Public Administration." Paper Presented at the 1997 ASPA Conference, Philadelphia, July.

——— (1997b). "Institutionalization of the New Administrative State/Role." Paper Presented at the 1997 Annual Conference of the American Political Science Association, Washington, DC, August 28–31.

——— (1997c). "Bureaucracy is Alive and Well: The Order that Supports Market Chaos." *Public Administration Times* 20(11): 5.

——— (1998a). "Contributions of the Ancient Civilizations to Modern Public Administration: A Symposium." *International Journal of Public Administration* 21 (1): 1–6.

——— (1998b). "Building a Community-Based Administrative State Under the New World Order." Paper presented at the 1998 Annual Conference of the American Political Science Association, September 2–6.

Frederickson, George (1997). *The Spirit of Public Administration.* San Francisco: Jossey-Bass.

Friedland, Roger, and A. F. Robertson, eds. *Beyond the Marketplace.* New York: Walter de Gruyter, Inc.

Fukuyama, Francis (1992). *The End of History and the Last Man.* New York: Free Press.

Garcia-Zamor, Jean-Claude, and Renu Khator (1994). *Public Administration in the Global Village.* Westport, CT: Praeger.

Gates, Bill (1995). *The Road Ahead.* London: Viking.

Gibbs, David (1991). "Private Interests and Foreign Intervention: Toward a Business Conflict Model." Paper presented at the 1991 Annual Conference of the American Political Science Association, Washington, DC, August.

Gill, Stephen, and David Law (1991). *The Global Political Economy.* Baltimore, MD: Johns Hopkins University Press.

Gilbert, Neil (1983). *Capitalism and the Welfare State.* New Haven: Yale University Press.

Gould, David (1991). "Administrative Corruption: Incidence, Causes, and Remedial Strategies." In Ali Farazmand, ed. *Handbook of Comparative and Development Public Administration.* New York. Marcel Dekker, 467–484.

Graycar, A. (1983). *Retreat From the Welfare State.* Sydney: Allen & Unwin.

Greenberg, E. S. (1986). *The American Political System,* 4th ed. Boston, MA: Little, Brown.

Habermas, Jurgen (1974). "The Public Sphere." *New Government Critique* 3: 49–55.

Halliday, Fred (1979). *Iran: Dictatorship and Development*, 2nd ed. New York: Penguin Books.

Hamilton, Edward (1989). *America's Global Interests: A New Agenda*. New York: W. W. Norton.

Hancock, Graham (1989). *Lords of Poverty*. New York: Atlantic Monthly Press.

Harvey, R. (1995). *The Return of the Strong: The Drift to Global Disorder.* London: Macmillan.

Heady, Ferrel (1996). *Public Administration: A Comparative Perspective*, 5th ed. New York: Marcel Dekker.

———— (1998). "Comparative and International Public Administration: Building Intellectual Bridges." *Public Administration Review* 58(1): 32–39.

Heeger, Gerald (1974). *The Politics of Underdevelopment*. New York: St. Martin's Press.

Heidenheimer, A. J., H. Heclo, and C.T. Adams (1983). *Comparative Public Policy: The Politics of Social Choice in Europe and America,*, 2nd ed. New York: St. Martin's Press.

Heilbroner, Robert (1991). *An Inquiry Into the Human Prospect*. New York: W. W. Norton.

Helleiner, E. (1994). *States and the Re-Emergence of Global Finance: From Breton Woods to the 1990s*. Ithaca, NY: Cornell University Press.

Helmut, Richard (1975). "Land Reform and Agribusiness in Iran." *MERIP Reports* 43 (Dec.)

Henderson, Keith (1994). "Rethinking the Comparative Experience: Indigenization versus Internationalization." In O.P. Dwivedi and Keith Henderson, eds., *Public Administration in World Perspective*. Ames, IA: Iowa State University Press.

Henry, Nicholas (1995). *Public Administration and Public Affairs*, 6th ed. Englewood Cliffs, N.J.: Prentice-Hall.

Hirst, P., and G. Thompson (1996).*Globalization in Question: The International Economy and the Possibilities of Governance*. Cambridge: Polity.

Hooglund, Mary (1970). *Lessons from India*. London: Oxford University Press.

Huntington, Samuel (1968). *Political Order in Changing Society*. New Haven, CT: Yale University Press.

———— (1996). *The Clash of Civilizations and the Remaking of World Order.* New York: Simon & Schuster.

Hudson, Michael (1971). "The Political Economy of Foreign Aid": In Dennis Goulet and Michael Hudson, eds. *The Myth of Aid*. New York: IDOC North America

Jones, Charles (1983). *An Introduction to the Study of Public Policy*, 3rd. ed. Monterey, CA: Brooks/Cole.

Jreisat, Jamil (1997). *Politics Without Process: Administering Development in the Arab World*. Boulder, CO: Lynne Reinner.

Khator, Renu (1994). "Managing the Environment in an Interdependent World." In Jean-Claude Garcia-Zamor and Renu Khator, eds., *Public Administration in the Global Village*. Westport, CT: Praeger, 83–98.

Kitschell, Herbert (1992). Political Regime Change: Structure and Process-Driven Explanations? *American Political Science Review* 86(4):1028–1034.

Knox, Paul (1997). "Globalization and Urban Economic Change." *The Annals of the American Academy of Political and Social Science* 551 (May): 17–27.

Korbin, Stephen (1996). "Back to the Future: Neomedievalism and the Postmodern Digital World Economy." *Journal of International Affairs* 51(2): 367–409.

Korten, Alicia (1993). "Cultivating Disaster. Structural Adjustment and Costa Rican Agriculture." *Multinational Monitor,* July/August: 20–23.

Korten, David (1995). *When Corporations Rule the World*. West Hartford, CT: Kumarian Press.

Krasner, Stephen (1993). "Economic Interdependence and Independent Statehood." In R. H. Jackson and A. James, eds., *States in A Changing World: A Contemporary Analysis*. Oxford: Clarendon.

Kregel, Jan (1998). "The Strong Arm of the IMF." *Report, of the Jerome Levy Economic Institute of Bard College* 8(1): 7–8.

LaFeber, W. (1984). *Inevitable Revolutions. The United States in Central America*. New York: W. W. Norton.

Laurent, A. (1986). A Cross Cultural Puzzle of International Human Resource Management. *Human Resource Management* 25(1): 91–102.

Lowenthal, Abraham, ed. (1991). *Exporting Democracy: The United States and Latin America*. Baltimore, MD: Johns Hopkins University Press.

Levine, Charles (1978). "Organizational Decline and Cutback Management." *Public Administration Review* 38 (4): 316–325.

———— (1980). *Managing Fiscal Stress: The Crisis in the Public Sector.* Chatham, NJ: Chatham House.

Lindblom, Charles (1977). *Politics and Markets: The World's Political-Economy Systems*. New York: Basic Books.

———— (1990). *Inquiry and Change*. New Haven: Yale University Press.

Lipset, Seymour (1987). "The Confidence Gap During the Reagan Years, 1981–1987." *Political Science Quarterly* (Spring): 1–23.

Lipsky, Michael (1984). "Bureaucratic Disentitlement in Social Welfare Programs." *Social Service Review* 58(1): 3–27.

Lowi, Theodore (1996). *The End of the Republican Era*. Norman, OK: University of Oklahoma Press.

Macpherson, C. B. (1987). *The Rise and Fall of Economic Justice*. New York: Oxford University Press.

Magdoff, Harry (1969). *The Age of Imperialism*. New York: Monthly Review.

Mandel, Ernest (1983). "Nation-States and Imperialism." In David Held et al., eds., *States & Societies*. New York: New York University Press, 526–539.

Mander, Jerry, and Edward Goldsmith, eds. (1996). *The Case Against the Global Economy and For a Return Toward Local*. San Francisco, CA: Sierra Club Books.

Mann, Michael (1980). *States, War and Capitalism*. Oxford, UK: Blackwell.

McCoy, Al (1971). "Land Reform as Counterrevolution." *Bulletin of Concerned Asian Scholars* 3(1): 14–49.

Mele, Christopher (1996). "Globalization, Culture, and Neighborhood Change: Reinventing the Lower East Side of New York." *Urban Affairs Review* 32(1): 3–22.

Milman, C. and S. Lundstedt (1994). "Privatizing State-Owned Enterprises in Latin America: A Research Agenda." *International Journal of Public Administration* 17(9): 1663–1677.

Milward, Brinton (1994). "Nonprofit Contracting and the Hollow State: A Book Review." *Public Administration Review* 54(1): 73–76.

Modelski, George, ed. (1979). *Transnational Corporations and World Order*. San Francisco, CA: W. H. Freeman and Company.

Mueller, Dennis (1989). *Public Choice II*. Cambridge, UK: Cambridge University Press.

Murphy, Richard (1988). *Protecting US Interests in the [Persian] Gulf*. Washington, DC: National Council on U.S.-Arab Relations.

Naisbitt, John (1994). *The Global Paradox: The Bigger the World Economy the More Powerful Its Smallest Players*. London: Brealey.

O'Connor, James (1973). *The Fiscal Crisis of the State*. New York: Harper & Row.

Offe, C. (1985). *Disorganized Capitalism*. Cambridge, MA: MIT Press.

Ohmae, Kenichi (1990). *The Borderless World*. London: Harper-Collins.

———— (1995). *The End of the Nation-State: The Rise of Regional Economies*. London: Harper-Collins.

Parentri, Michael (1995). *Democracy for the Few*. New York: St. Martin's Press.

Pascale, R. (1984). "The Paradox of 'Corporate Culture': Reconciling Ourselves to Socialization." *California Management Review* 27(2): 26–41.

Peters, Guy (1991). "Government Reform and Reorganization in an Era of Retrenchment and Conviction Politics." In Ali Farazmand, ed., *Handbook of Comparative and Development Public Administration*. New York: Marcel Dekker, 381–403.

———— (1997). "Bureaucrats and Political Appointees in European Democracies: Who's Who and Does it Make Any Difference?" In Ali Farazmand, ed., *Modern Systems of Government: Exploring the Role of Bureaucrats and Politicians*. Thousand Oaks, CA: Sage, 232–254.

Picciotto, S. (1991). "The Internationalization of the State." *Capital & Class* 43 (Spring): 43–63.

Rathgeb, Steven, and Michael Lipsky (1993). *Non-Profits for Hire: The Welfare State in the Age of Contracting*. Cambridge, MA: Harvard University Press.

Rehren, Alfredo (2000). "Management of Corruption in Chile." In Ali Farazmand, ed., *Handbook of Crisis and Emergency Management*. New York: Marcel Dekker.

Reich, R. B. (1991). *The Work of Nations: Preparing for 21st-Century Capitalism*. New York: Simon & Schuster.

Rifkin, Jeremy (1996). *The End of Work*. New York: G. P. Putnam's Sons.

Riggs, Frederick (1994). "Global Forces and the Discipline of Public Administration." In Jean-Claude Garcia-Zamor and Renu Khator, eds., *Public Administration in the Global Village*. Westport, CT: Praeger, 17–44.

———— (1998). "Public Administration in America: Why Our Uniqueness is Exceptional and Important." *Public Administration Review* 58(1): 22–31.

Rockman, Bert (1997). "Honey: I Shrunk the State." In Ali Farazmand, ed., *Modern Systems of Government: Exploring the Role of Bureaucrats and Politicians*. Thousand Oaks, CA: Sage, 275–294.

Rosenbloom, David (1993). *Public Administration: Understanding Management, Politics, and Law in the Public Sector*, 3rd ed. New York: McGraw-Hill.

Rothkopf, David (1998). "Cyberpolitik: The Changing Nature of Power in the Information Age." *Journal of International Affairs* 51 (2): 325–359.

Said, Edward (1993). *Culture and Imperialism*. New York: Alfred A. Knopf.

Savitch, H. V. (1998). "Global Challenge and Institutional Capacity: Or How We Can Refit Local Administration for the Next Century." *Administration & Society* 30 (3): 248–273.

Schein, Edgar (1985). *Organizational Culture and Leadership*. San Francisco, CA: Jossey-Bass.

Schneider, Susan (1992/1993). "National vs.Corporate Culture: Implications for Human Resources Management." In Vladimir Pucik, Noel Tichy, and Carole Barnett, eds., *Globalizing Management*. New York: John Wiley & Sons, Inc., 159–173.

Scholte, J. A. (1997). "Global Capitalism and the State." *International Affairs* 73 (3): 427–452.

Schultz, Barry, and Slater, Robert, eds. (1990). *Revolution and Political Change in the Third World*. Boulder, CO: Lynne Reinner.

Sedghi, Hamideh (1992). "The Persian Gulf War. The New International Order or Disorder?" *New Political Science* 21/22: 41–60.

Singer, Max, and Wildavsky, Aaron (1993). *The Real World Order*, Chatham, NJ: Chatham House.

Sklair, L. (1995). *Sociology of the Global System*. Hemel Hempstead: Harvester Wheatsheaf.

Skocpol, Theda (1985). "Bringing the State Back In: Strategies of Analysis in Current Research." In Peter B. Evans, Dietrich Rueschemeyer, and Theda Skocpol, eds. *Bringing the State Back In*. Cambridge, UK: Cambridge University Press.

Stever, James (1988). *The End of Public Administration*. New York: Transnational Publications.

Strange, Susan (1996). *The Retreat of the State: Diffusion of Power in the World Economy*. Cambridge, UK: Cambridge University Press.

Sweezy, Paul (1997). "More (or less) on Globalization." *Monthly Review* 49 (4): 1–2.

Thayer, Fred (1984). *Rebuilding America: The Case for Economic Regulation*. NY: Praeger.

Triandis, Harry (1995). *Individualism and Collectivism*. Boulder, CO: Westview Press.

Trudeau, Eric (1992). "The World Order Checklist." *New York Times*. 19 February, 2.

UNCTAD (1996a). *Globalization and Liberalization: Development in the Face of Two Powerful Currents. Report of the Secretary-General of UNCTAD to the Ninth Session of the Conference*. Geneva: United Nations Conference on Trade and Development.

——— (1996b). *Transnational Corporations and World Development*. London: International Thomson Business Press.

Useem, Michael (1984). *The Inner Circle*. New York: Oxford University Press.

Vernon, R. (1971). *Sovereignty at Bay*. New York: Basic Books.

Waldo, Dwight (1980/1990). *The Enterprise of Public Administration*. Novato, CA: Chandler & Sharp Publisher.

Weber, Max (1947). *The Theory of Social and Economic Organization*. In A. M. Henderson and Talcott Parsons, eds. and trans. New York: Oxford University Press.

Welch, Eric, and Wilson Wong (1998). "Public Administration in a Global Context: Bridging the Gaps of Theory and Practice Between Western and Non-Western Nations." *Public Administration Review* 58 (1): 40–49.

Wilson, David (1994). "Bureaucracy in International Organizations: Building Capacity and Credibility in a Newly Interdependent World." In Ali Farazmand, ed., *Handbook of Bureaucracy*. New York: Marcel Dekker, 305–318.

——— (1997). "Preface" [on globalization]. *The Annals of the American Academy of Political and Social Science* 551 (May): 8–16.

Wolch, Jennifer (1990). *The Shadow State: Government and the Voluntary Sector in Transition*. New York: The Foundation Center.

Zysman, J. "The Myth of a 'Global' Economy: Enduring National Foundations and Emerging Regional Realities.'" *New Political Economy* 1 (July): 157–184.

About the Authors

George Avery formerly worked as a chemist and quality assurance officer with the Division of Public Health Laboratories in the Arkansas Department of Public Health. He is now a doctoral student in public health policy at the University of Minnesota.

Robert D. Behn is professor of public policy at Duke University and director of its Governor's Center. Among his publications are *Leadership Counts: Lessons from Public Managers* and *Innovation in American Government* (with Alan A. Altshuler).

Carl J. Bellone is Dean of Graduate Programs at California State University, Hayward. His research interests include public entrepreneurship and the public service and the quality of working life. He has published articles in several personnel and management journals. **George Frederick Goerl** is an assocate professor of public administration at California State University, Hayward. He writes on the design and delivery of public services, citizen volunteerism, and other efforts in public entrepreneurship.

Jeffrey M. Berry is a professor in the Political Science Department at Tufts University. A specialist in citizen politics, his books include *The Rebirth of Urban Democracy* (with Kent E. Portney and Ken Thomson) and *New Liberalism: The Rising Power of Citizen Groups*.

Richard C. Box is an associate professor in the Department of Public Administration, University of Nebraska-Omaha. He is the author of *Citizen Governance: Leading American Communities into the 21st Century,* and previously worked in the field of local government.

Harlan Cleveland, political scientist and public executive, is a past president of the American Society for Public Administration and President Emeritus of the World Academy of Art and Science. He has served as Assistant Secretary of State and as U.S. Ambassador to NATO, and is the author of a dozen books on executive leadership and international affairs.

Sharon S. Dawes, Peter A. Bloniarz, David R. Connelly, Kristine L. Kelly, and **Theresa A. Pardo** are with the Center for Technology in Government, an applied research center devoted to improving government through technology, management, and policy innovation. Created by the State of New York in 1993, the Center is an Innovations in American Government Award winner. Dawes has written *The State of the Voluntary Sector: A Report of New York State Project 2000.*

Peter F. Drucker is professor of management at Claremont University. Thanks to his prolific publishing and extensive consulting over a six-decade career, he is often acknowledged as one of the leaders in the development of modern management. In 1990, he founded the Peter F. Drucker Foundation for Nonprofit Management.

Ali Farazmand is a professor in the School of Public Administration, Florida Atlantic University. He is the author of 14 books and handbooks, including *Privatization or Public Enterprise Reform?: International Case Studies with Implications for Public Management* and *Modern Systems of Government: Exploring the Role of Bureaucrats and Politicians.*

Myron D. Fottler is professor and director of the Ph.D. Program in Administration-Health Services in the Graduate School of Management and Department of Health Services Administration at the University of Alabama, Birmingham. He is the author of *Strategic Management of Human Resources in Health Services Organizations.*

William T. Gormley is professor of government and public policy in the Government Department at Georgetown University. His most recent books are *Organizational Report Cards* and *Everybody's Children: Child Care As a Public Problem.*

Steven W. Hays is a professor in the Department of Government and International Studies at the University of South Carolina. He is the author of numerous articles on public personnel administration and organizational theory as well as *Public Personnel Administration.* **Shawn Benzinger Whitney** received her MPA degree from the University of South Carolina. Her most recent job was as the project manager for South Carolina Kids Count, a program within the State Budget and Control Board.

Sally Helgesen is a journalist whose articles have appeared in the *New York Times* and *Harper's.* She is the author of *The Web of Inclusion: A New Architecture for Building Great Organizations* and *Everyday Revolutionaries: Working Women and the Transformation of American Life.*

John P. Kotter is the Konosuke Matsushita Professor of Leadership at the Harvard Business School and the author of several books, including *Leading Change* and *Corporate Culture and Performance* (with James L. Heskett).

Michael Lipsky is professor of political science at the Massachusetts Institute of Technology. He is the author, among other works, of *Street-Level Bureaucracy: Dilemmas of the Individual in Public Services* and *Nonprofits for Hire* (with Steven Rathgeb Smith).

Douglas Morgan is director and professor of public administration at Lewis and Clark College. His articles on administrative ethics and leadership have appeared in a variety of journals and edited collections. **Kelly G. Bacon** is the executive assistant to the district attorney of Multnomah County (Portland, Oregon). **Ron Bunch** is manager of the Long Range and Transportation Planning Division for the City of Lake Oswego, Oregon. **Charles D. Cameron** is county administrator of Washington County, Oregon. **Robert Deis** is director of the Support Services Department for Washington County, Oregon.

John Nalbandian is a professor of public administration at the University of Kansas. He is a member of the National Academy of Public Administration and the author of numerous articles on state and local government and *Public Personnel Administration* (with Donald E. Klingner).

Eric M. Patashnik is assistant professor of political science and lecturer of law at Yale University. He is the author of *Putting Trust in the U.S. Budget: Federal Trust Funds and the Politics of Commitment.*

Joseph A. Pegnato is director of contracts in the U.S. General Accounting Office. He received his doctorate from George Mason University. His research interest is in assessing federal procurement reform in the nineties.

Robert B. Reich served as secretary of labor during the Clinton administration, and is currently a professor at Brandeis University. Among his numerous books are *The Future of Success* and *The Work of Nations: Preparing Ourselves for 21st Century Capitalism.*

Kelly Rossman-McKinney is a partner in the Lansing-based PR firm of Rossman Martin & Associates. In 1996, RM&A was the only independent firm in the nation to win two Silver Anvil awards, the highest award in the public relations industry. In 1999, she was named to the *Lansing State Journal's* "100 People to Watch This Century." **R. Dee Woell** holds a doctorate in public administration from Western Michigan University, and has taught for a number of years as a WMU adjunct professor. She has served in several Michigan agencies as a public relations expert and is currently in the Michigan Department of State Executive Office, Special Projects. She is also a member of the Michigan Women's Commission.

Francis E. Rourke is emeritus professor in the Department of Political Science at Johns Hopkins University. Among his many books and articles on the politics of bureaucracy are *Bureaucracy, Politics, and Public Policy* and *Secrecy and Publicity: Dilemmas of Democracy.*

James D. Slack is professor and chair in the Department of Government and Public Service at the University of Alabama-Birmingham. His books include *HIV/AIDS and the Public Workplace: Local Government Preparedness in the 1990s* (with Chester A. Newland) and *U.S. Educational Policy Interest Groups* (with Gregory S. Butler).

Acknowledgments

Joseph A. Pegnato, Book Review of *The Death of Common Sense: How Law Is Suffocating America* by Philip K. Howard, *American Review of Public Administration*, Vol. 29, No. 4, December 1999, pp. 411–423. Reprinted by permission of Sage Publications, Inc.

Richard C. Box, "Running Government Like a Business," *American Review of Public Administration*, Vol. 29, No. 1, March 1999, pp. 19–43. Reprinted by permission of Sage Publications, Inc.

Robert D. Behn, "What Right Do Public Managers Have to Lead?" *Public Administration Review*, May/June 1998, Vol. 58, No. 3, pp. 209–224. Copyright © by the American Society for Public Administration (ASPA), 1120 G Street, NW, Suite 700, Washington, D.C. 20005-3885.

Michael Lipsky, "The Critical Role of Street-Level Bureaucrats" and "Street-Level Bureaucrats as Policy Makers," reprinted from his *Street-Level Bureaucracy: Dilemmas of the Individual in Public Services*, copyright © 1980 Russell Sage Foundation, New York, New York.

Douglas Morgan et al, "What Middle Managers Do in Local Government: Stewardship of the Public Trust and the Limits of Reinventing Government," *Public Administration Review*, July/August 1996, Vol. 56, No. 4, pp. 359–366. Copyright © by the American Society for Public Administration (ASPA), 1120 G Street, NW, Suite 700, Washington, D.C. 20005-3885.

Robert B. Reich, "Policy Making in a Democracy," in Robert B. Reich, ed., *The Power of Public Ideas* (Cambridge: Ballinger Publishing Co., 1988). Copyright © 1988 by Robert B. Reich. Reprinted by permission of HarperCollins Publishers, Inc.

John Nalbandian, "Facilitating Community, Enabling Democracy: New Roles for Local Government Managers," *Public Administration Review*, May/June 1999, Vol. 59, No. 3, pp. 187–197. Copyright © by the American Society for Public Administration (ASPA), 1120 G Street, NW, Suite 700, Washington, D.C. 20005-3885.

Reprinted by permission of Harvard Business Review. From John P. Kotter, "Power, Dependence, and Effective Management," *Harvard Business Review*, Vol. 55, No. 4 (July-August 1977). Copyright 1977 by the Harvard Business School Publishing Corporation; all rights reserved.

"The Web of Inclusion," from *The Female Advantage: Women's Ways of Leadership* by Sally Helgeson, copyright © 1990 by Sally Helgesen. Used by permission of Doubleday, a division of Random House, Inc.

Used with permission from "Assessing Key Stakeholders: Who Matters to Hospitals and Why?" *Hospital and Health Services Administration* by Myron Fottler, Vol. 34, No. 4, pp. 525–545 (Chicago: Health Administration Press, 1989).

Peter F. Drucker, "Really Reinventing Government," *The Atlantic Monthly*, February 1995, pp. 49–61. Used by permission of the Atlanta Monthly Group.

Frances E. Rourke, "Mobilizing Political Support" reprinted from *Bureaucracy, Politics and Public Policy*, 3rd ed. (Boston: Little, Brown and Company, 1984), Chapter 3. Copyright © 1984 by Frances E. Rourke. Reprinted by permission of Pearson Education, Inc.

Kelly Rossman-McKinney and R. Dee Woell, "Why Public Relations Is Important Even to Public Administrators." Written for this volume. Copyrighted © 2001 by the authors.

Reprinted with permission of the author from Eric M. Patashnik, "Budgeting More, Deciding Less," *The Public Interest*, No. 138, Winter 2000, pp. 65–78 © 2000 by National Affairs, Inc.

Sharon S. Dawes et al, "Four Realities of IT Innovation in Government," *The Public Manager*, Spring 1999, Vol. 28, No. 1, pp. 27–31. Reprinted with permission from The Public Manager.

James D. Slack, "From Affirmative Action to Full Spectrum Diversity in the American Workplace," *Review of Public Personnel Administration*, Fall 1997, pp. 75–87. Reprinted by permission of the author and the University of Georgia.

Steven W. Hays and Shawn Benzinger Whitney, "Reinventing the Personnel Function: Lessons Learned from a Hope-Filled Beginning in One State," *American Review of Public Administration*, Vol. 27, No. 4, December 1997, pp. 324–342. Reprinted by permission of Sage Publications, Inc.

"The Rise of Issue Networks" from The Interest Group Society, 3rd ed. by Jeffrey M. Berry. Copyright © 1997 by Jeffrey M. Berry. Reprinted by permission of Addison-Wesley Educational Publishers, Inc.

George Avery, "Outsourcing Public Health Laboratory Services: A Blueprint for Determining Whether to Privatize and How," *Public Administration Review*, July/August 2000, Vol. 60, No. 4, pp. 330–337. Copyright © by the American Society for Public Administration (ASPA), 1120 G Street, NW, Suite 700, Washington, D.C. 20005-3885.

William T. Gormley, "Accountability Battles in State Administration," reprinted from Carl E. Van Horn, ed., *The State of the States*, 3rd ed., Washington, D.C.: *Congressional Quarterly Press*, 1996, pp. 161–178. Reprinted by permission of Congressional Quarterly Press, Inc.

Carl J. Bellone and George Frederick Goerl, "Reconciling Public Entrepreneurship and Democracy," *Public Administration Review*, Vol. 52, No. 2 (March/April 1992), pp. 130–134. Copyright © by the American Society for Public Administration (ASPA), 1120 G Street, NW, Suite 700, Washington, D.C. 20005-3885.

Harlan Cleveland, Donald C. Stone Lecture: "The Future Is Uncentralized," *Public Administration Review*, July/August 2000, Vol. 60, No. 4, pp. 293–297. Copyright © by the American Society for Public Administration (ASPA), 1120 G Street, NW, Suite 700, Washington, D.C. 20005-3885.

Ali Farazmund, "Globalization and Public Administration," *Public Administration Review*, November/December 1999, Vol. 59, No. 6, pp. 509–522. Copyright © by the American Society for Public Administration (ASPA), 1120 G Street, NW, Suite 700, Washington, D.C. 20005-3885.

Index